Encyclopedia of
PRESIDENTIAL CAMPAIGNS,
SLOGANS, ISSUES, *and* PLATFORMS

Encyclopedia of
PRESIDENTIAL CAMPAIGNS, SLOGANS,
ISSUES, *and* PLATFORMS

Robert North Roberts and Scott John Hammond

GREENWOOD PRESS
Westport, Connecticut • London

Library of Congress Cataloging-in-Publication Data

Roberts, Robert North.
  Encyclopedia of presidential campaigns, slogans, issues, and platforms / Robert North
Roberts and Scott John Hammond.
    p. cm.
  Includes bibliographical references and index.
  ISBN 0–313–31973–1 (alk. paper)
  1. Presidents—United States—Election—History—Encyclopedias. 2. Presidential
candidates—United States—History—Encyclopedias. 3. Political campaigns—United
States—History—Encyclopedias. 4. Political parties—United
States—Platforms—History—Encyclopedias. 5. United States—Politics and
government—Encyclopedias. I. Hammond, Scott J. II. Title.
  E176.1.R6 2004
  324.973'003—dc22   2003059538

British Library Cataloguing in Publication Data is available.

Library of Congress Catalog Card Number: 2003059538
ISBN: 0–313–31973–1

First published in 2004

Greenwood Press, 88 Post Road West, Westport, CT 06881
An imprint of Greenwood Publishing Group, Inc.
www.greenwood.com

Printed in the United States of America

The paper used in this book complies with the
Permanent Paper Standard issued by the National
Information Standards Organization (Z39.48–1984).

10 9 8 7 6 5 4 3 2

To our wives Deborah and Cheree
and our children, William, Caitlin, Adriana, and Neil.

Contents

Preface

The *Encyclopedia of Presidential Campaigns, Slogans, Issues, and Platforms* is a comprehensive reference book for college undergraduates and high school students who are interested in the political history of presidential rhetoric and campaigns. Presidential politics is a rich, complex, and vitally important facet of American democracy. But knowledge of political history seems to be on the wane as fewer students appear on college campuses with a good grasp of the fundamental events, actors, episodes, issues, controversies, themes, principles, and ideas pertaining to the development of American political ideology and the story of American democracy. College students will gain from an accessible source that effectively addresses this lacuna; high school students will benefit from further instruction in the basics of political education. Such knowledge will support their future efforts in more advanced studies of political science and political history at higher institutions. While a new encyclopedia by itself cannot serve as the necessary corrective for the current state of political education, it can supply a mine of information that will stimulate the thinking student onward toward richer veins. This volume is designed with this purpose in mind. The *Encyclopedia* will support the initial stages of a student's inquiry and ensure the continued legacy of a particularly fascinating aspect of the American political past—presidential politics and its colorful history of persuasion, promotion, accusation, strategy, and campaign competition.

The *Encyclopedia* is divided into two parts. Part I contains chronologically arranged entries describing the course and nature of each presidential campaign since 1789. Each entry discusses the most important issues, slogans, and innovations in swaying voter support to come out of that particular campaign. Part II contains alphabetically arranged entries that discuss in detail important issues, programs, slogans, and platforms arising out of the history of American presidential election campaigns. Part II includes two types of entries: longer, general entries that discuss a campaign program or issue in broader terms (such as "Affirmative Action" or

"New Freedom"); and shorter, specific entries that focus on a single slogan, phrase, or discrete episode identified with a specific campaign or individual political actor (such as "Tippecanoe and Tyler Too," "Read My Lips," "Mulligan Letters," or "Donna Brazile").

Both within and across the two parts, entries are heavily cross-referenced to facilitate further exploration of a topic or theme. For example, the entry "In Your Heart You Know He's Right" in Part II is cross-referenced with the "Campaign of 1964" in Part I and with "A Choice, Not An Echo," the "Daisy" Ad, and "In Your Guts You Know He's Nuts," all in Part II. Cross-references appear both as boldface terms in the text of entries and in "*See also*" lines at the ends of entries. Through the use of these cross-references, a student can form connections between various entries, realize that political events and ideas are never isolated, and develop a fuller awareness of the political and historical context enveloping each entry. To strengthen this feature, a guide to related topics in both parts is included for a quick summary of thematic alternatives that are woven through the structure of the book. Readers will also find a basic timeline to augment the sense of historical context and political development.

Additionally, each entry in both parts is accompanied by a selected list of further references, encouraging the student to treat this encyclopedia as a first step toward more extensive and rigorous research. For each entry, this listing is not an exhaustive bibliography, but rather a list of recommended sources for the continuation of a student's investigation into a particular area of presidential campaigning. A selected bibliography of important general works is also included at the back of the book.

Finally, a chronological table of major party campaign platforms is provided as an appendix for a quick review of key issues, controversies, and policies pertinent to a particular campaign. Space limitations prevent the inclusion of a thorough reiteration or enumeration of every platform plank, but the key positions and developments are provided and categorized under basic platform concerns: economic policies, social and political principles, civil rights and liberties, foreign policies, and a general category for other noteworthy issues and controversies.

Political rhetoric is as old as politics itself, dating at least to the establishment of democracy in Athens and long preceding the high oratory of Pericles, Demosthenes, and Cicero. American presidential campaigning, by comparison, is still a new phenomenon within the long arc of the political history of the world, and in many ways continues to show the signs of the kind of rapid change that usually accompanies the early stages of development. While the thematic political phrase is at least as old as the Roman cry of *delenda est Carthago*, presidential campaign slogans remain an innovation in the grand scheme of things. While the eloquent and meaningful presidential oratory of Abraham Lincoln, Franklin Roosevelt, and John Kennedy are easily connected to the lineage of the ancients, we are hard pressed to confidently identify the ancestry of the slogans, sound bites, and rallying cries of the modern presidential campaign. Hence this encyclopedia discusses an aspect of politics that can at times still exhibit the unpredictable vigor characteristic of the new, and in so doing is itself influenced by the youthful energy of American democracy, and as such is directed at an audience of readers who approach new fields of the intellect with the openness and enthusiasm of the young everywhere.

Introduction

For more than 200 years the United States has engaged in a grand experiment of selecting individuals to serve as president of the United States. Over this period, the power of the presidency has increased with the size, population, and wealth of the nation. Today, the Republican and Democratic parties and their respective presidential campaigns spend hundreds of millions of dollars every four years to support their respective presidential candidates.

When a small number of electors, in 1789, selected George Washington as the first president, property requirements for voting were common throughout the states. By the **Campaign of 1828** adult white male citizens voted in all states with no property qualification attached. This increase in suffrage helped propel Andrew Jackson into the White House.

By the **Campaign of 1840**, the increase in the size of the electorate made it important for the Democratic and Whig parties to find new ways to reach voters. In the famous **"Log Cabin and Hard Cider"** campaign, the Whig Party remade the image of General William Henry Harrison into a candidate from humble origins. From the **Campaign of 1848** through the end of the Civil War, slavery divided the nation, destroying political coalitions. **"Free Soil, Free Speech, Free Labor, and Free Men"** served as a slogan for opponents of slavery's expansion. With the **Campaign of 1860**, the issue of slavery precipitated the Civil War. Across the Midwest and North, **Wide-Awake clubs** conducted candlelight parades to support Republican candidate Abraham Lincoln.

From the **Campaign of 1868** through the **Campaign of 1884**, supporters of Republican presidential candidates waved the **"bloody shirt,"** tagging Democrats as the party of insurrection. A Republican supporter of James G. Blaine, the 1884 Republican presidential candidate, inadvertently turned the tide of the 1884 election by attacking Democrats as the party of **"Rum, Romanism and Rebellion."** Indifferent to the Civil War amendments to the U.S. Constitution, Southern states enacted segregationist "Jim Crow" laws that burdened African Americans with a new kind of oppression.

By promising the American people a **"Full Dinner Pail"** and **sound money**, William McKinley, the 1896 Republican candidate, stifled a populist **free silver** movement led by Democrat William Jennings Bryan. Woodrow Wilson, during the campaign of 1912, proposed a **New Freedom** as an alternative to Theodore Roosevelt's **New Nationalism** and the conservative corporate philosophy of President William Howard Taft. Four years later, Wilson won reelection with the slogan **"He Kept Us Out of War."** Within months of his second inauguration, Wilson asked Congress to declare war on Germany.

Prohibition and a desire for a **"Return to Normalcy"** made the 1920s the decade of the Grand Old Party (GOP). Republicans Warren G. Harding, Calvin Coolidge, and Herbert Hoover soundly defeated Democratic challengers James Cox, John Davis, and Al Smith, respectively. Radio emerged as a new technology during the **Campaign of 1924**, permitting presidential candidates to directly reach millions of voters in their own homes. Significantly, the long struggle for women's suffrage concluded with the 1920 ratification of the Nineteenth Amendment, guaranteeing the voting rights of women.

From 1932 through his death in April 1945, Franklin D. Roosevelt dominated national politics. Roosevelt used his "Fireside Chats" to shed light during the darkness of the Great Depression. During the **Campaign of 1940**, Republicans believed that Roosevelt's decision to seek a third term provided Wendell Willkie a golden opportunity to recapture the White House. Despite concern over a third term, voters stuck with Roosevelt. After the end of World War II, **"Give 'em Hell, Harry"** Truman, the incumbent president, prevailed over conservative Thomas Dewey. The slogan **"I Like Ike"** helped General Dwight D. Eisenhower, the 1952 Republican nominee, win a landslide victory over Ambassador Adlai Stevenson. With the **Campaign of 1952**, television quickly emerged as the preferred medium of campaign advertising.

The **Campaign of 1960** introduced the televised **presidential debate** to the culture of presidential campaigning, benefiting Democrat John F. Kennedy at the expense of the more experienced Richard Nixon, who had been vice president for eight years under Dwight Eisenhower. Four years later, the campaign of President Lyndon Johnson unleashed a seemingly endless stream of **attack ads** depicting Senator Barry Goldwater, the Republican nominee, as too unstable to be entrusted with nuclear weapons. Driven by the desire to avoid a second presidential campaign defeat, the 1968 campaign of Richard Nixon perfected the **photo opportunity** and **media event**. Nixon defined himself as the law and order candidate, and won without providing a clear plan regarding the ongoing war in Vietnam.

In the **Campaign of 1976**, President Gerald Ford's election efforts were hampered both by his 1974 pardon of disgraced former president Nixon and an egregious gaffe committed during his debate with Democratic challenger Jimmy Carter, a former governor of Georgia. Carter promised to restore trust in government in the aftermath of the Watergate scandal. When former California governor Ronald Reagan asked Americans whether they were better off than they had been four years earlier, they responded by giving Reagan a landslide victory over Carter in 1980.

Twelve years later, Democrat Bill Clinton returned the White House to his party by reminding voters that **"It's the Economy, Stupid,"** thus successfully deflating criticism of his moral character. Eight years later, Vice President Albert Gore attempted to keep Democratic control of the White House by running on the Clinton/Gore economic record while distancing himself from Clinton's personal and ethical problems. Defining himself as a "compassionate conservative," Gore's Republican opponent, Texas governor George W. Bush lost the popular vote but managed an Electoral College majority following an election controversy in Florida.

Throughout American history, presidential campaigns have relied upon a panoply of strategies and methods to appeal to the hearts and minds of the American electorate. Today, presidential campaigns devote enormous funds and resources to sway a small percentage of unaligned, undecided voters. But despite the magnitude of these efforts, a steady decline in the percentage of voting age individuals who actually cast ballots in presidential elections has continued since the turbulent 1960s.

Guide to Related Topics

Campaign Management and the Tools of Political Persuasion

Advance Person
Advance Team
Ailes, Roger
Attack Ads
Atwater, Lee
Baker, James
Ballot Integrity Program
Battleground State
"Bloody Shirt" Politics
"Boston Harbor" Campaign Ad
Brazile, Donna
Bread-and-Butter Issues
Broadside
Buttons
Campaign Ads
Campaign Consultants
"Daisy" Campaign Ad
Deaver, Michael
Debates
Dial Groups

Tracking Poll
Truth Squad
Undecideds
Whistle-Stop Campaign
Wide-Awake Clubs
Willie Horton Ad

Defeat of Incumbent President

Campaign of 1800
Campaign of 1828
Campaign of 1840
Campaign of 1888
Campaign of 1912
Campaign of 1976
Campaign of 1980
Campaign of 1992

Disputed Presidential Elections

Campaign of 1800
Campaign of 1824
Campaign of 1876
Campaign of 2000

Economic Issues and Presidential Campaigns

"Advance Agent of Prosperity"
"Are You Better Off Than You Were Four Years Ago?"
Bread-and-Butter Issues
"Cross of Gold" Speech
Currency Issue
Economic Prosperity Issue
"Empty Market Basket"
Energy Issue
"Four More Years of the Full Dinner Pail"
Free Silver Movement
"Full Dinner Pail"

Gold Standard

"Happy Days Are Here Again"

"Harding and Prosperity"

"It's the Economy, Stupid"

"Jackson Forever: Go the Whole Hog"

"Let's Get America Moving Again"

National Bank Issue

"A New Deal, A New Day"

New Freedom

"Patriotism, Protection and Prosperity"

"Peace, Prosperity and the Public Trust"

Pocket-book Issue

Prosperity Issue

Protectionism Issue

"Read My Lips, No New Taxes"

"Rebuild with Roosevelt"

Social Security Issue

Sound Money

Square Deal

Tariff Issue

Tariff of Abominations

Third Rail of American Politics

Trust Busting Issue

"Vote Yourself a Farm"

"War on Poverty" Speech

"What This Country Needs Is a Good Five-Cent Cigar"

Whip Inflation Now (WIN)

Elections Decided by Electoral College Contrary to Popular Vote

Campaign of 1876
Campaign of 1888
Campaign of 2000

Elections Decided in the House of Representatives

Campaign of 1800
Campaign of 1824

International Affairs, Foreign Policy, and War and Peace

War and Peace Issue

"War in Europe, Peace in America"

"War in the East, Peace in the West, Thank God for Woodrow Wilson"

"We Are Going to Win This War and the Peace That Follows"

"We Want a Choice, Not an Echo"

"Win the War Quicker with Dewey and Bricker"

Landslide Presidential Elections (Winner received more than 55 percent of popular vote)

Campaign of 1828

Campaign of 1832

Campaign of 1864

Campaign of 1872

Campaign of 1904

Campaign of 1920

Campaign of 1928

Campaign of 1932

Campaign of 1936

Campaign of 1952

Campaign of 1956

Campaign of 1964

Campaign of 1972

Campaign of 1984

Leadership, Character, and Controversy

"All Hail Old Hickory"

Attack Ads

"A Better Man for a Better America"

"Blaine, Blaine, James G. Blaine, the Continental Liar from the State of Maine"

Bloody Chasm

"Bloody Shirt" Politics

Character Issue

Checkers Speech

Corruption Issue

Feeding Frenzy

"First in War, First in Peace"

"Fool, Hypocrite, Criminal, Tyrant"

"Four More Lucky Roosevelt Years"

"A Gallant Leader"

"Give 'em Hell, Harry"

"GOP Equals Gas, Oil and Petroleum"

"Grover, Grover, All Is Over"

"Grover the Good"

"He Kept Us Out of War"

Honest Abe

"I Like Ike"

"In Your Guts, You Know He's Nuts"

"In Your Heart, You Know He's Right"

"Jefferson, the Friend of the People"

"Leadership for the 60s"

"Ma, Ma, Where's My Pa?"

"Man from Appomattox"

"Mess in Washington"

Mulligan Letters

"No Third Term"

"Now More Than Ever"

"Old Fuss and Feathers"

"Old Hickory"

"Public Office Is a Public Trust"

"Return Integrity to the White House"

"Rum, Romanism and Rebellion"

"Shall America Elect a Cocktail President?"

"A Solid Man in a Sensitive Job"

"A Supreme Soldier—A Model President"

"Tilden and Reform"

"Turn the Rascals Out!"

"Van Is a Used Up Man"

"Who Is Polk?"

"Win One for the Gipper"

Media Coverage of Presidential Campaigns

Ad Watches

Boys on the Bus

Cable News Network (CNN)

Civic Journalism Movement
C-SPAN
Debates
Earned Media
Editorial Page Endorsement
Exit Polls
Feeding Frenzy
Free Media
Herblock
Horse-Race Campaign Coverage
Horse-Race Poll
Larry King Live
New Media
News Talk Coverage
Newspapers
Paid Media
Partisan Newspapers
Partisan Press
Photo Opportunity
Political Cartoons
Poll-Driven Campaign Coverage
Public Journalism Movement
Radio and Presidential Campaigns
Road to the White House
Sound Bite
Spin Doctor
Talk Radio
Tracking Poll
Truth Boxes

Presidential Campaign Ads

"Bear in the Woods" Campaign Ad
"Boston Harbor" Campaign Ad
"Daisy" Campaign Ad
"Eisenhower Answers America" Campaign Ad
"Revolving Door" Campaign Ad
"Tank" Campaign Ad

Presidential Candidates

Johnson, Lyndon
Kennedy, John F.
Kennedy, Robert
King, Rufus
Landon, Alfred F.
Lincoln, Abraham
Madison, James
McClellan, George B.
McGovern, George
McKinley, William J.
Parker, Alton B.
Pierce, Franklin
Pinckney, Charles Cotesworth
Polk, James K.
Reagan, Ronald
Roosevelt, Franklin D.
Roosevelt, Theodore
Scott, Winfield
Seymour, Horatio
Smith, Alfred E.
Stevenson, Adlai
Taft, William H.
Taylor, Zachary
Tilden, Samuel J.
Truman, Harry S.
Van Buren, Martin
Wallace, George
Willkie, Wendell
Wilson, Woodrow

Realigning Presidential Elections

Campaign of 1856
Campaign of 1860
Campaign of 1896
Campaign of 1932
Campaign of 1936
Campaign of 1980

Social Issues and Presidential Campaigns

Abortion Issue
Affirmative Action
Anti-Catholicism
Anti-Immigration Movements
Civil Rights Issue
"Compassionate Conservatism"
Crime Issue
Drys
Education Reform Issue
"Free Homes for Free Men"
"Free Soil, Free Labor, Free Speech, and Free Men"
Free State Issue
"Freedom, Freemen and Fremont"
Gay Rights Issue
"Great Society" Speech
Handgun Control Issue
Health Care Reform Issue
Immigration Issue
Law and Order Issue
"Millions for Freedom, Not One Cent for Slavery"
Nativism Issue
New Frontier
Poverty Issue
Prohibition Issue
Race Relations Issue
"Revolving Door" Campaign Ad
"Rum, Romanism and Rebellion"
"Safety, Solvency, Sobriety"
"Shall America Elect a Cocktail President?"
"Slavery Is a Moral, Social and Political Wrong"
Slavery Issue
Temperance Movement
"This Time Vote Like Your Whole World Depended On It"
Wets
Willie Horton Ad
Women's Suffrage Movement
"You Never Had It So Good"

Television and Presidential Campaigns

Ad Watches

Ailes, Roger

Attack Ads

"Bear In the Woods" Campaign Ad

"Boston Harbor" Campaign Ad

Campaign Ads

Campaign Consultants

Checkers Speech

C-SPAN

"Daisy" Campaign Ad

Earned Media

"Eisenhower Answers America" Campaign Ad

Flip-flop Campaign Ad

Free Media

"The Great Communicator"

Image-makers

Infomercial

Issue Ads

Larry King Live

"Laughing at Agnew" Campaign Ad

Media Advisor

Media Consultant

Media Event

New Media

News Talk Coverage

Paid Media

Photo Opportunity

Political Consultants

Reality Check

"Revolving Door" Campaign Ad

Road to the White House

Spin Doctor

Talking Head Campaign Ad

Television Campaign Spot Ads

Testimonial Campaign Spot Ads

Town Meeting Campaign Event

Twenty-Four-Hour News Cycle

Willie Horton Ad

Timeline of Presidential Campaigns

1789	George Washington unanimously selected as president by the Electoral College.
1800	Newspapers backing President John Adams, the Federalist candidate, and those supporting Vice President Thomas Jefferson, the Democratic-Republican candidate, engage in mudslinging; election is decided by the House of Representatives.
1804	Jefferson deflects personal attacks to easily win reelection.
1808 and 1812	James Madison, a Democratic-Republican, is elected and reelected president; the War Hawks emerge as dominant political faction; the Federalist Party is irrevocably weakened.
1816 and 1820	James Monroe's two election victories are virtually unopposed, establishing the so-called "Era of Good Feelings."
1824	Disputed election: Andrew Jackson wins the popular vote but fails to receive a majority of electoral votes; House of Representatives elects John Quincy Adams; caucus system for selecting presidential candidates begins to collapse.
1828	Populist upsurge sweeps Jackson into White House; expansion of suffrage forces adoption of new campaign methods to reach more voters; two-party system solidifies.
1831	Anti-Masons hold the first national political convention; as a method of selecting presidential candidates, "King Caucus" is officially dead.
1832	Whig Party portrays Jackson as a despot for his veto of a bill extending the charter of the Bank of the United States; Jackson

defeats Henry Clay after conducting a crusade against the Bank.

1836
Martin Van Buren continues the Democrats' domination of the White House, defeating a slate of Whig candidates; Van Buren's running mate, Richard M. Johnson, fails to obtain the same electoral vote and is elected vice president by the Senate.

1840
In the "Log Cabin and Hard Cider" campaign, the Whig Party portrays General William Henry Harrison as a national hero with humble beginnings; as Whigs make use of wide variety of campaign paraphernalia to take this message to voters, presidential campaigns take on many characteristics of religious revivals.

1844
Dark horse James K. Polk of Tennessee wins the Democratic presidential nomination as the "Manifest Destiny" candidate; possible war with Mexico over Texas is key campaign issue.

1848
Victory in the Mexican-American War opens vast tracks of southwestern land for settlement, rekindling sectional dispute over expansion of slavery; slavery quickly becomes the critical and defining national issue.

1850
By effectively revoking the Missouri Compromise of 1820, which had restricted the expansion of slavery, the Compromise of 1850 inflames rather than abates sectional tension.

1852
Whig Party weakens as pro-slavery Democrat Franklin Pierce is elected; Free Soil Party fails to expand its base.

1854
Kansas-Nebraska Act asserts the principle of "popular sovereignty" in the determination of the slavery question within territories and new states; in protest, the Republican Party is formed, and Abraham Lincoln, a former Whig, returns to politics after a long hiatus.

1856
Growing nativism movement gives birth to the American or Know-Nothing Party, which seeks tighter restrictions on immigration and citizenship; replacing the fading Whig Party as the main opposition to the Democrats, the new Republican Party assumes the role as the national anti-slavery party; Democrat James Buchanan defeats explorer John Fremont, the Republican nominee, but Fremont makes strong showing in northern states.

1860
Thanks to a split in the Democratic Party and his sweep of the northern states, Abraham Lincoln is elected president; the Republican victory prompts 11 southern states to secede from the Union, and civil war follows.

1864
Lincoln is reelected over Democrat George B. McClellan, the former commander of the Army of the Potomac, in the first democratic election conducted during wartime.

1865   President Lincoln is assassinated.

1868   In the first post–Civil War election, General Ulysses S. Grant successfully runs on the slogan "Let There Be Peace"; Radical Republican members of Congress use Grant's victory to push forward with Southern Reconstruction; waving the "bloody shirt" of Southern insurrection becomes a staple of Republican campaigns.

1870   Ratification of the Fifteenth Amendment protects the right to vote regardless of "race, color or previous condition of servitude."

1872   Objecting to the renomination of President Grant, Liberal Republicans leave the party and nominate Horace Greeley, who is also supported by the Democrats.

1876   Infamous disputed election ends in the Compromise of 1877: Disputed electoral votes are given to Republican Rutherford B. Hayes in exchange for his promise to end Reconstruction; termination of Reconstruction leads to the enactment of "Jim Crow" laws in Southern states, depriving freed slaves of their constitutional rights; Democratic Party regains control of Southern electoral votes and holds the solid South until the latter half of the twentieth century.

1880   Republican James Garfield defeats Democrat Winfield Scott Hancock, a former Civil War general.

1881   President Garfield is assassinated.

1884   Lacking major policy differences between Republicans and Democrats, the campaign between Democrat Grover Cleveland, the eventual winner, and Republican James G. Blaine decays into a mudslinging brawl, becoming one of the nastiest campaigns in American history.

1888   Tariffs return as a prominent issue and monetary policy emerges as an issue; Cleveland wins the popular vote over Republican challenger Benjamin Harrison, but loses in the Electoral College when he fails to win his home state of New York.

1892   Cleveland recaptures the White House for the Democrats in an unusually mild campaign.

1896   Populist William Jennings Bryan wins the Democratic nomination and leads a crusade for bimetallism; although the Democrats expand their political base, Republican William McKinley wins election.

1900   Spanish-American War makes the United States a colonial power; Republican Party places charismatic Theodore Roosevelt on the ticket to appeal to the growing number of progressive Republicans; while McKinley again remains at

	home, Roosevelt stumps the country and the Republican ticket is victorious.
1901	William McKinley is assassinated, making Theodore Roosevelt, at age forty-two, the youngest president in American history.
1904	Theodore Roosevelt throws his full support behind a progressive agenda; Roosevelt wins election in a landslide but promises not to seek another term.
1908	Democratic Party again nominates William Jennings Bryan, but a strong national economy makes it impossible for Bryan to defeat Republican William Howard Taft.
1912	Theodore Roosevelt's "Bull Moose" Progressives secure more votes than the Republication incumbent Taft, but Democrat Woodrow Wilson wins the election.
1916	Running a peace campaign, Wilson secures reelection; shortly after Wilson's second inauguration, the United States enters World War I.
1919	Ratification of the Eighteenth Amendment establishes federal prohibition.
1920	The Nineteenth Amendment is ratified, protecting the voting rights of women at the federal level; majority of Americans endorse a "Return to Normalcy" by electing Republican Warren G. Harding to the presidency; although Harding easily beats Democratic nominee James Cox, Cox's running mate, Franklin D. Roosevelt of New York, becomes a national political figure.
1924	President Calvin Coolidge easily wins election despite having to deal with a series of public corruption scandals disclosed after the August 1923 death of President Warren G. Harding; first presidential campaign to make extensive use of radio broadcasts.
1928	Democrat Al Smith becomes the first Roman Catholic presidential candidate nominated by a major party; Herbert Hoover convincingly defeats Smith in the general election.
1932	The Great Depression leads to political realignment: Franklin Roosevelt, promising a New Deal, reconfigures the Democratic Party along the lines of a new coalition, and wins reelection in a landslide over incumbent President Hoover; African Americans begin to leave the party of Lincoln for the party of Roosevelt.
1933	Franklin Roosevelt begins radio broadcasts known as "Fireside Chats."
1936	Franklin Roosevelt easily wins second term.

1940	Franklin Roosevelt breaks unwritten third term rule by winning third term as president.
1944	In the first wartime presidential election since 1864, Roosevelt wins fourth term with his new running mate, Senator Harry S. Truman of Missouri.
1948	Although the Dixiecrat defection splits the Democrats, Truman wins a surprise victory over the favored Republican, Thomas Dewey.
1952	First national television campaign ads are broadcast; Richard Nixon delivers his famous Checkers speech.
1956	Eisenhower wins reelection and carries several key southern states, clearing the path for subsequent Republican successes in this traditional Democratic bastion.
1960	First televised presidential debates between Senator John F. Kennedy of Massachusetts, the Democratic nominee, and Vice President Richard Nixon, the Republican nominee; Kennedy becomes the first and only Roman Catholic to be elected president.
1963	President Kennedy is assassinated.
1964	Conservatives capture the Republican nomination with the selection of their candidate, Senator Barry Goldwater of Arizona; incumbent President Lyndon Johnson responds with a negative campaign and wins in the biggest landslide in American history; Twenty-fourth Amendment abolishes the poll tax.
1965	Voting Rights Act of 1965 is enacted.
1968	In the most turbulent and traumatic election campaign since 1860, candidate Robert Kennedy is assassinated and the divided Democrats lose to a triumphant Richard Nixon.
1971	President Nixon signs into law the Campaign Finance Reform Act of 1971; Twenty-sixth Amendment lowers the age minimum for eligible voters to 18 years.
1972	Nixon forms Committee to Re-elect the President (CREEP) and goes on to soundly defeat Democratic challenger George McGovern; unknown at this time, CREEP undertakes numerous illicit activities to secure Nixon's reelection, including the infamous burglary of Democratic Headquarters at the Watergate Hotel in Washington, D.C.
1974	Resignation of President Richard Nixon.
1976	Democrat Jimmy Carter is elected president despite a strong late campaign recovery by incumbent President Gerald Ford.

1979	Federal Election Commission authorizes political parties to raise unlimited amounts of soft money for party-building activities.
1980	Former California Governor Ronald Reagan, the Republican nominee, defeats President Carter to become the fortieth president.
1984	Reagan wins landslide reelection.
1988	Vice President George H.W. Bush defeats Massachusetts Governor Michael Dukakis in a campaign dominated by attack ads; Bush takes full advantage of the growing role of Christian Conservatives in the Republican Party.
1992	Arkansas Governor Bill Clinton, running on the theme, "It's the Economy, Stupid," defeats President Bush and independent candidate H. Ross Perot.
1996	New media plays a larger and larger role in presidential campaigns; embarrassing personal scandals do not hamper reelection of President Clinton.
2000	In the most controversial election since 1876, George W. Bush, son of former President George H.W. Bush, is elected even though Al Gore received the highest popular vote total in American history; Bush describes his ideology as "compassionate conservatism."

Part I
Presidential Campaigns, 1789–2000

On the first Wednesday in January 1789, state legislatures selected the first members of the new Electoral College, in accordance with the requirements of the Constitution. Due to a delay in assembling a congressional quorum to count the ballots, the votes of the electors remained unopened until early April. North Carolina and Rhode Island did not select electors because of their continued unwillingness to ratify the Constitution. Because of an impasse between factions within its state legislature, New York also missed an opportunity to select electors for the 1789 presidential election.

The campaign of 1789 involved little suspense. Despite serious divisions between various factions, almost all major factions considered George Washington the inevitable choice for president. Through the summer and fall of 1788, community leaders and the press sang the praises of George Washington. Supporters of Washington frequently referred to him as the "New Cincinattus," the "Great Washington," and "the Savior of America."

Unlike future presidential candidates, Washington hesitated at the prospect of serving as president. After having served arduously throughout the revolution as the commander of the Continental Army, and later as presiding officer of the Constitutional Convention of 1789, Washington preferred to remain a private citizen, at home on his farm in Mt. Vernon, Virginia.

The campaign for vice president turned out to be more of a contest. Prior to the ratification of the Twelfth Amendment, the Constitution required that the candidate with the second highest vote total in the Electoral College be designated as the vice president. Confidence in Washington's universal appeal was vindicated as he received a unanimous 69 electoral votes. In contrast, fellow Federalist John Adams received votes from just under half of the electors. Other prominent national figures receiving votes included John Jay, John Rutledge, John Hancock, and George Clinton.

Neither Washington nor Adams put forward a platform as we know it nor identified key concerns or favorite issues. The electors voted for Washington and Adams as the result of their reputations and their public support for the Constitution and the new national government. Despite the absence of a full-blown presidential campaign, the election of 1789 sowed the seeds for the future growth of national political parties. Supporters and opponents of the Constitution held markedly different views regarding the structure of the new government and the respective powers of the federal and state governments. Additionally, major regional differences continued to have a major impact upon political views in different regions of the new nation. Efforts to fashion a North-South ticket (Washington, a Virginian, represented the South while Adams from New England represented the North) became an important and recurring feature of the presidential contest. The electors of 1789 understood the prudence of including both regions in the selection of the nation's highest offices.

Suggested Readings: Paul F. Boller, *Presidential Campaigns* (New York: Oxford University Press, 1984); Arthur M. Schlesinger, Fred Israel, and William P. Hansen, eds., *History of American Presidential Elections, 1789–1968* Vol. 1 (New York: Chelsea House, 1985).

Campaign of 1792

In spite of abundant criticism over Alexander Hamilton's mercantilist domestic policies and a rapidly widening schism within the administration between "Federalists" (led by Hamilton) and "Republicans" (led by Jefferson and not to be confused with the modern party), a hesitant George Washington agreed to serve a second term as president of the young republic. While opposition to the activities of Washington's administration grew in both quantity and intensity, Washington himself remained comparatively removed from public attack. Once again, by virtue of his character alone, Washington easily rode into a second term without a challenger to oppose him. The contest for the executive in 1792 was thus again shifted to the vice presidency.

Incumbent Vice President John Adams continued to draw criticism. Openly decried by his political enemies as a monarchist, only vaguely supported by the influential leaders of rival factions Hamilton and Jefferson (but supported nonetheless), and distrusted by electors in the South, Adams was pushed along with Hamilton's mercantilism into the center of conflict in the 1792 campaign.

As with the previous election, the standard features of the modern campaign were entirely absent. However, factional vitriol was freely exchanged in the press, Philadelphia's *National Gazette*, a pro-Jeffersonian publication, was particularly aggressive in its criticism of the Federalists in general. *The Gazette of the United States* led the Federalist charge, publishing letters written by Adams summarizing his political philosophy. No slogans or **sound bites** were available then, but there was an abundance of insult—with the Federalist press accusing the Jefferson faction of Jacobinism and the Republicans countering with aspersions against the alleged monarchism of Adams and his long-wigged royalist cronies.

There was also considerable gaming behind the scenes, especially among the Republican leaders. Benjamin Rush and John Beckley in Pennsylvania, and James Madison and James Monroe in Virginia, for example, emerged as important players in the Republican decision to challenge Adams. From the start, New York Governor George Clinton, an old enemy of Hamilton, served as the logical choice to lead the Republican charge for the second spot. Strenuously opposed to Clinton, visible horror was stirred in Hamilton at the prospect of a challenge from his fateful nemesis, New York's flamboyant junior senator, Aaron Burr. With the young Burr's name sent into currency along with Clinton's, a tri-state axis involving leading politicians in New York, Pennsylvania, and Virginia briefly formed around the issue of displacing the incumbent vice president. For his part, Adams withdrew to his home in Quincy to ride out the storm, and even though Hamilton nervously took the Burr challenge seriously, Clinton soon emerged as the strongest candidate on behalf of the Republican faction.

Adams was victorious in the end. And for the second and final time in American presidential elections, Washington garnered unequivocal and unanimous support within the Electoral College—which amounted to 132 votes across fourteen states, all of them now fully participating. Even though he faced more opposition than in 1789, Adams was able to actually gain a larger percentage of "second" votes—receiving 77, or just over 58 percent. Fifty votes went to Clinton, which represented a far more respectable third place showing, in absolute numbers, compared to the previous election.

An important development unfolded in Virginia, the Electoral College giant of the day, through its support of Clinton. New York and North Carolina, two other comparatively significant electoral states, also fell in behind the Republican faction, to be joined by Georgia as the fourth state in support of the governor.

The real significance of the election of 1792 is in what it portends. The factional divisions and growing rancor between the major figures that characterize the contest for vice president in 1792 serve as a foretaste of both 1796 and, even more importantly, 1800. The battle lines were clear and the trenches were rapidly deepening, and the landscape of American presidential politics was being prepared for the full combat of two American titans.

Suggested Readings: Paul F. Boller, *Presidential Campaigns* (New York: Oxford University Press, 1984); John F. Hoadley, *Origins of American Political Parties, 1789–1803* (Lexington: University Press of Kentucky, 1986); Arthur M. Schlesinger, Fred Israel, and William P. Hansen, eds., *History of American Presidential Elections, 1789–1968*, Vol. 1 (New York: Chelsea House, 1985); James Roger Sharp, *American Politics in the Early Republic: The New Nation in Crisis* (New Haven: Yale University Press, 1993).

Campaign of 1796

After eight years of service, a wearied George Washington, now embattled where once he was embraced, offered his conclusions about partisan politics: "It [the spirit of party] serves always to distract the Public Councils and enfeeble the Public administration. It agitates the Community with ill-founded jealousies and false alarms, kindles the animosity of one part against another, foments occasionally riot and insurrection. It opens the door to foreign influence and corruption, which find a facilitated access to the government itself through the channels of party passions." These reflections, looking back on the fragmentation within his own administration along partisan lines, testify to the sense of discouragement that descended upon Washington in the latter years of his administration. They also look forward as an augury of things to come—of two presidential elections that would feature the republic's two most prominent statesmen, John Adams and Thomas Jefferson, and further drive the wedge between the leading parties, the Federalists of Alexander Hamilton and the Jeffersonian Republicans.

The divisive issues were of both a domestic and foreign nature. Washington himself was no longer above the fray, as increasingly harsher criticism came at him from Republicans over allegations of not doing enough to end British impressments of American sailors and for favoring the policies and programs of Alexander Hamilton. The heroic general, once universally acclaimed as above reproach, was now being scolded from some quarters as a deceitful "debaucher" of the nation. Had Washington decided to stand for a third term, and even if he had managed another victory, his base of unanimity had vanished.

In domestic politics, the first lines of an ongoing debate in American political philosophy were clearly and dramatically drawn. Generally, the ruling Federalist Party followed Hamilton in favoring active central government; nationalism; a mercantilist view toward commerce, finance and industry; a national bank; and a strong executive. Jefferson's Republicans advocated local and state power, minimal government and free trade, an economy rooted in the agrarian ideal, and opposition to the national bank or any institution of its like.

Moreover, interparty divisions were evident over issues of foreign allegiance. The Federalists were anglophiles, deeply sensitive to the common heritage shared by the United States and Britain as well as appreciative of the economic advantages of close ties with the industrial power of London and Manchester. Ever the ardent Republicans, the Jeffersonian faction found spiritual kinship in the egalitarian principles of the French Revolution. As France and Britain were mortal enemies in the eighteenth century, there was no moderate compromise between these two positions other than complete neutrality, a narrow line that Washington desired to draw but one that his subordinates could not trace.

Adams and Jefferson had both previously served as ambassadors to these enemy nations: Adams in Britain, Jefferson in France. As such, they both held personal affection for their respective favorites in addition to any intellectual kinships formed around political principle and cultural affinity. Seen as a Jacobin "Franco-maniac" by the Federalists, Jefferson was heartened by the spread of democratic ideals under the French tricolor. Perceived as a thinly veiled pro-British autocrat by the Republicans, Adams saw in English government and law the deposit of centuries of political and juristic wisdom. Both men had been ardent champions of liberty in the 1770s, but now one was cast by his enemies into the role of despotic reactionary, the other by his enemies into the role of dangerous leveler. Neither was the case.

Both leading candidates exhibited "disinterest" in the office, leaving it to others to press their respective cases. While there were as yet no formal party mechanisms in the modern sense, both candidates received "campaign" support from networks of supporters. Most of this support came from prominent citizens, newspapers, and nascent political "clubs." Benjamin Franklin Bache, grandson of the elder Franklin and editor of the pro-Republican paper *Aurora*, referred to Jefferson as "the good patriot, statesman, and philosopher." At a pro–Jay's Treaty rally in Ipswich, John Adams was toasted as a "[man of] virtues, genius, and knowledge . . . the first planet of our political sun."

Significantly, the North-South ticket strategy continued. The Federalists supported Thomas Pinckney of South Carolina, whose distinction as a diplomat might also have been deployed as a counter to the Jay controversy. Jefferson's side looked northward toward Aaron Burr as their second man to complement the southerner from Virginia. With the pre–Twelfth Amendment process still in place, the possibility of a divided outcome was high—one that Adams and other Federalists anticipated with a sense of dread. And this was in fact the result. Adams narrowly won with 71 votes, only 3 more than Jefferson who would now sit as his rival's vice president. Pinckney finished with a respectable 59, but Burr, the only candidate to actively and openly campaign on his own behalf, managed only 30 votes. The remaining 48 votes were scattered among nine additional names, almost a third of those going to Burr's ally, Samuel Adams.

The intensification of party politics, rising rhetorical animosity, and the outcome of divided government are the main legacies of 1796, serving as a prelude for an even more rancorous and historically momentous election to be held four years later. But the most remarkable characteristic of 1796 is the way in which party enmity subsided once the election was resolved. Jefferson and the Republicans gestured supportively to Adams, and for his part, Adams attempted to moderate his anti-French tone. This renewed amity would establish a model for post-election conduct throughout the many elections to come.

Suggested Readings: Paul F. Boller, *Presidential Campaigns* (New York: Oxford University Press, 1984); Arthur M. Schlesinger, Fred Israel, and William P. Hansen, eds., *History of American Presidential Elections, 1789–1968*, Vol. 1 (New York: Chelsea House, 1985); James Roger Sharp, *American Politics in the Early Republic: The New Nation in Crisis* (New Haven: Yale University Press, 1993).

Campaign of 1800

Students of politics and American history frequently point to the pivotal election of 1800 as the most important in the story of American campaigns.

Jefferson, the challenger and sitting vice president, and John Adams the incumbent, had been comrades throughout the American Revolution. Then they were in full agreement on their objectives, sat as allies on the same revolutionary committees, took the same risks, and collaborated together on the Declaration of Independence. But 1800 was not a year of political concord for these erstwhile allies. Their philosophical differences sounded during the Washington administration, becoming further amplified during the **Campaign of 1796**. However, that election did end amicably, with Jefferson offering his loyal support to his victorious rival and old friend.

This support dissipated as Jefferson assumed the office of vice president under the old rules of Article II, section one. The disagreements of the 1790s were still there: England versus France, centralized versus localized government, Hamilton's economic activism versus free markets and governmental minimalism, modernizing commerce and industry versus agrarian tradition. Soon, the rift was widened as the Jeffersonian Republicans excoriated Adams for the Alien and Sedition Acts, enacted by Congress with Adams's endorsement to quell anti-administration criticism and punish "Jacobin" newspapers. Naval hostilities between the United States and France drew still further recriminations from Francophile Republicans, and the confusion surrounding the XYZ Affair drew questions about the administration's diplomacy skills.

During the campaign, Republicans distributed their positions on policy in what could be called a forerunner to the party platform, with particular use of the press in Virginia and Pennsylvania. In the *Examiner* of Richmond, several policy points formally adopted by state activists were published in the form of negative resolutions opposing current Federalist programs. Included among these resolutions were the Republican opposition to a standing military, affirmation of the need for neutrality in foreign affairs, criticism of national debt, and the denouncing of Alien and Sedition Acts. In Philadelphia, the pro-Republican *Aurora* published a catalog of eleven antinomies punctuating the differences between "things as they have been" under the Federalists and "things as they will be" under Republicans. Under this catalog, Republicans were for the principles of the Revolution, peaceful neutrality in the world and domestic unity at home, fair and tolerant government separated from church hierarchy, elimination of public debt, reduction of taxes, a free press, and freedom of religion. By implication, the Federalists were depicted as opponents of these unassailable principles.

The Federalists stood their ground, choosing to claim their achievements rather than respond directly to Republican charges. They emphasized their experience in statesmanship, the overall prosperity enjoyed under Federalist policies, and the need for continuity and stability in the face of international tumult. One pro-Federalist address in Rhode Island pointedly asked why the nation should follow the lead of aristocratic Virginia, a state proud of its undemocratic class structure and institutionalized slavery. Through newspapers, **pamphlets, posters,** and **handbills,** both sides addressed the issues. But the question of character was also broached, creating a particularly tense mood throughout the campaign.

Despite their genteel posture of civility, the Federalists were not above vituperation, describing Jefferson, in addition to the old charge of Jacobin heresy, as cowardly, mean, a son of a "half-breed," a phony southern rube who fed on course cornmeal and "fricasseed bullfrog," a robber of widows, and a profane threat to Christian civilization whose administration would foster fearsome crime and wretched malfeasance. In what nearly amounts to the coining and circulation of an early political slogan, Philadelphia's *Gazette of the United States* boldly and repeatedly framed the choice as between "God—and a religious president; or impiously declare for Jefferson—and no God!!!"

Returning such verbal fire, personal insult was also heaped upon Adams by Republicans. Tyrant, fool, intemperate whirlwind of "malignant passions," were epithets now added to old charges of monarchism and aristocratic ambition. To further the old charge of Adams's pro-British and royalist sympathies, rumor mongers disseminated a madcap fiction that Adams was hatching a scandalous plan to reunite Britain and America through an arranged marriage between a scion of his household and a daughter of George III. According to this canard, it was Washington himself who saved the country from the clutches of such cynical treason. With brandished sword, the story went, he was to have forced Adams to abandon his royalist ambitions. Preposterous as this all seems today, the story was for a while taken seriously by the more gullible enemies of the Federalists.

Alexander Hamilton's continued ambivalence toward Adams degenerated into unequivocal dislike. Hamilton, the true leader of the early Federalists and a stalwart to their principles, saw Adams as far too moderate in his attitudes toward the rabble-rousing Republicans and their French sympathies. Hamilton supported Charles Pinckney of South Carolina, whom he saw as truer to the party's principles. In a private letter addressed to South Carolina Federalists, Hamilton vilified Adams's record and character. A copy of this letter mysteriously fell into the hands of Aaron Burr, and soon "Hamilton's Thunderbolt" decrying the meanness, incompetence, and petty egotism of Adams was circulated. Adams fueled intra-party vitriol by denouncing Hamilton as an unscrupulous "bastard" greatly schooled in cunning intrigue.

Because the Constitution did not originally separate the election of the president from that of the vice president, Burr was also in the center of more controversy. Clearly the Republicans' choice for vice president, Burr managed to match Jefferson's total electoral vote—each candidate winning 73 votes, with 65 and 64 going to Adams and Pinckney, respectively, and a lone Rhode Island vote cast for John Jay. Under the Constitutional provision, failure to win a majority in the Electoral College directs the decision to the House of Representatives, which was still controlled by outgoing Federalists. Many Federalists despised Jefferson enough to support Burr, providing Burr with enough votes to extend the deadlock. Burr neither affirmed nor rejected his claim to the presidency, allowing the balloting to run through several tense and wearisome mid-February days. Eventually, it was Hamilton, who in loathing Burr more than disliking Jefferson, reluctantly threw his influential weight behind the Virginian. On the 36th ballot, Jefferson was elected president.

The election of 1800 prompted the Twelfth Amendment, finally separating the selection of the vice president. This was in direct response not only to problems in the Electoral College, but more importantly to the reality of what Washington feared, the "spirit of party." While still informal and rudimentary compared to the modern party apparatus, political parties had become a durable feature in American society. James Madison's observation in "Federalist 10" proved again brilliantly insightful; faction is indeed "sown in the nature of man." *See also* Reign of Terror.

Suggested Readings: Paul F. Boller, *Presidential Campaigns* (New York: Oxford University Press, 1984); Arthur M. Schlesinger, Fred Israel, and William P. Hansen, eds., *History of American Presidential Elections, 1789–1968*, Vol. 1 (New York: Chelsea House, 1985); Frank Van der Linden, *The Turning Point: Jefferson's Battle for the Presidency* (Washington, D.C.: R.B. Luce, 1962); Bernard A. Weisberger, *America Afire: Jefferson, Adams, and the Revolutionary Election of 1800* (New York: William Morrow, 2000).

Campaign of 1804

King Caucus, first employed by congressional Jeffersonian Republicans in the summer of 1804, soon became the sole method of nominating candidates for president on into the mid-1820s. Thomas Jefferson received this first endorsement from a formal party caucus and proceeded to win the general election in a landslide, a record 162 electoral votes to only 14 for the distinguished Federalist stalwart Charles Pinckney of South Carolina.

The Republican caucus unanimously rejected the renomination of Vice President Aaron Burr, choosing to replace him with his fellow New Yorker, Governor George Clinton. Clinton received 67 caucus votes, with 41 votes distributed across five remaining candidates. Aaron Burr did not receive a single vote. Burr retreated to New York to run for governor but was soundly defeated, due in large part to Alexander Hamilton's vehement public opposition. The collapse of Burr's once promising political career was accelerated later that year when he repaid Hamilton with fatal pistol fire. Burr, who in 1800 tied Jefferson for Electoral College votes for the presidency, had become a pariah.

The Federalists did adopt the congressional caucus. In late winter/early spring of 1804 pro-Federalist newspapers offered Pinckney's name. Rufus King of New York, a loyal Hamilton ally as well as friend of Governor Clinton, received Federalist press support for the vice presidency. Pinckney was uncontroversial, already established as a national leader, holding firm support among both Southern and Northern Federalists. His succinct rebuke, "No! No! Not a sixpence" to French minister Talleyrand's expectation that American envoys bribe French officials in the infamous XYZ Affair strengthened his reputation at home. Pinckney's adamant refusal was soon embellished into the still more famous slogan, "**Millions for Defense, But Not One Cent for Tribute.**" It was the strongest ammunition the Federalists could muster.

Organized campaigning was more evident on the Republican side. The pro-Republican press was more successful in conveying democratic sentiments. Whereas moneyed families, professionals, and international merchants generally read the Federalist press, the Republican press, written in a more accessible style, was addressed to a far more popular audience. Republicans also organized more political events. While both parties observed Independence Day, the Republicans added elaborate public celebrations of Jefferson's inauguration (March 4) and the Louisiana Purchase (May 11). In some parts of the nation, local militia units were in allegiance to a particular party, and the Republicans took advantage of this by involving the "Republican militia" in the patriotic pomp and display of these celebrations. The purpose of these events was twofold: to promote the cause of democratic principles as understood by the Republican faction, and to lionize Jefferson. Federalists turned to Washington's Birthday as their principal civic observance.

Such adulation of Jefferson came easy after a four-year term filled with remarkable success. In addition to the purchase of the vast Louisiana territory, Jefferson benefited from an economic boom largely caused by growth in agriculture, successfully deployed Stephen Decatur and his warships against the Barbary Pirates in North Africa, diffused the tension with England and France (although much credit for this must be given to his predecessor, President Adams), produced a budgetary surplus while cutting taxes, and oversaw the expiration of the hated Alien and Sedition Acts. Additionally, by leaving untouched many of Hamilton's economic programs, most notably the national bank, the opposition was denied much of its own ammunition. The Federalists were reduced to falling back on old charges of Jefferson's demagoguery, alleged atheism, and to deriding Jefferson for the inland beaching of a gunboat in a Georgia cornfield in the aftermath of a hurricane—an act of God that had nothing to do with the president and everything to do with Federalists clutching at straws.

Party platforms were still a thing of the future, but both parties did advertise their principles. The Republicans stood on Jefferson's record. The *Raleigh Register* came the closest to promoting a Republican manifesto by publishing a formal list of twenty tenets that consisted mostly of a repetition of such Jeffersonian articles of faith as "We believe that God created all men free and equal" and "We believe that virtue and knowledge is the basis of a Republic." The Federalists reiterated the Hamiltonian vision.

By and large, the Federalists were a party in trouble. In some states the party was completely inactive. Uncomfortable with their status as a party out of power, a minority cabal of Federalists in New England, calling themselves the "Essex Junto," joined by allies in New York, entertained the idea of abandoning the republic, advocating withdrawal from the union and the creation of a new northeastern confederacy. By shifting their focus to an unrealistic secession scheme, the northern Federalists further estranged the average citizen—already alienated by the elitist and undemocratic rhetoric of some of the more aristocratic Federalists. Such grand designs distracted Federalist leaders from the campaign, and from support of Pinckney and King. By the time the general election occurred, they could only muster the full allegiance of two states: Connecticut, contributing 9 electors, and Delaware, 3.

In sharp contrast to the election of 1800, Jefferson's victory was both overwhelming and national, securing unanimous support in the "big" electoral states of Virginia (24), Pennsylvania (20), New York (19), Massachusetts (19), and North Carolina (14), cutting across north and south, as well as reaching into the western frontier with a clean sweep through Kentucky, Tennessee, and the newly added state of Ohio.

At this point in his presidency, Jefferson's record was invulnerable, the Federalists criticisms thin and untenable. Such achievement would not mark the second half of Jefferson's administration.

Suggested Readings: Paul F. Boller, *Presidential Campaigns* (New York: Oxford University Press, 1984); Kevin Gannon, "Escaping 'Mr. Jefferson's Plan of Destruction': New England Federalists and the Idea of a Northern Confederacy, 1803–1804," *Journal of the Early Republic* 21 (Fall 2001), pp. 413–441; Arthur M. Schlesinger, Fred Israel, and William P. Hansen, eds., *History of American Presidential Elections, 1789–1968*, Vol. 1 (New York: Chelsea House, 1985).

Campaign of 1808

The campaign of 1808 began with the backdrop of a fading Federalist Party and the Republican Party assuming the position as the dominant national political party. Jefferson had easily won reelection in 1804. As a result, when President Jefferson took the oath of office for his second term, the Jeffersonian Republicans held a commanding political advantage so strong that the young republic appeared to be growing toward a one-party system. Except in New England, the Federalists were a fading minority party discordant to public attitudes. However, by the start of the campaign of 1808, international disputes had seriously weakened Republican support and provided an opportunity for the weakened Federalist Party to make a comeback.

The central controversy in Jefferson's second term revolved around the administration's response to renewed conflict with Britain and France (seizure of American merchant shipping by both countries, resumed British impressment of American sailors, and the attack of the British ship-of-the-line, *Leopard*, on the American frigate *Chesapeake*). Determined to prevent entanglement in the Napoleonic Wars, Jefferson rejected military options and resorted to an embargo of all exports to France and Britain. The Great Embargo of 1807, however, led to considerable economic discomfort at home and embarrassment for the young country's image abroad. New England merchants and grain farmers north and south suffered. Consequently the minority Federalists solidified their New England base, and perturbed by the perception that aristocratic Virginians were the cause of their entrepreneurial crisis, the engine of Federalist indignation was duly stoked. Jefferson's popularity plummeted, leaving his successor on the defensive.

Saddled with defending the recent Republican record, James Madison, currently Jefferson's secretary of state, was the party favorite. Despite admirable political experience and unsurpassed ability, Madison's anointing was forcefully challenged within the party. His campaign, directed by senators William Giles and Wilson Nicholas, forerunners of the modern **campaign manager**, encountered serious intra-party resistance in all three Electoral College powerhouses: his home state of Virginia, Pennsylvania, and New York.

In New York the Republicans splintered into three factions: followers of Morgan Lewis, De Witt Clinton (Vice President George Clinton's nephew), and Aaron Burr. Only the Lewis faction supported Madison for president. Burr and his followers were vociferous anti-Jeffersonians. Spurred by New York publisher James Cheetham, the "Clintonians" sought national office for either Clinton. In Pennsylvania, the influential Congressman James Sloan, an erstwhile Madison supporter, moved his weighty support to George Clinton, thus for a time raising the possibility of Madison losing support in the Keystone State.

In Virginia, John Randolph of Roanoke contemptuously attacked Madison, pressing for an alternative in another favorite son, James Monroe. Randolph's campaign against Madison deteriorated into invective, thus diminishing his credibility within the party leadership. However, through unkind and manipulative correspondence Randolph succeeded in infecting Monroe with an unfair distrust of Madison and Jefferson, leading to his decision to stand for the nomination. George H. May, father of Monroe's fiancée, organized the Monroeites, serving as the manager of the campaign. Randolph also worked through the press to further divide the state party between Madison and Monroe factions. Alert to this, the Cheetham Press in New York dwelled on the split in Madison's home state and seized the opportunity to promote their favorite son, the incumbent vice president.

As the party splintered in critical states, a new term, "Quid" appeared in vogue.

From the Latin for "what," Quids were divisive factions who were accused of caring more for personal power than advancing the common political values and interests of their party. Thus the question was raised as to "what" their principles were, and "what" they really stood for. Party Quids ultimately failed to secure the nomination for either Monroe or Clinton, as key Republican newspapers came around to supporting Madison. Madison's supporters in the press defeated the quiddism of intra-party insurgents by carefully detailing the administration's record. In particular, they effectively compared the diplomatic records of Madison and Monroe with a favorable result for the secretary of state.

Dissenting Republicans joined the Federalists in blaming Madison for his visible role in the embargo—called the "Dambargo" by Federalist critics—and the resultant economic and diplomatic problems. Added to this was the allegation of anti-English "Bonapartism," raised by spurious stories of Madison's fictional capitulation to Napoleon's ominous insistence that America was already at war with Britain and thus was expected to support France. Federalists also delighted in pointing out that the blood-soaked French revolutionary government had granted, *in absentia*, French citizenship to Madison in 1793, thus making him a fellow traveler with "bloody Robespierre" as well as the "Beast" Napoleon. Cheeky Republicans deflected this broadside by pointing out that Citizen Washington and Citizen Hamilton had also been so honored, but not Thomas Jefferson!

The Federalists were firm in their support of the familiar tandem of Charles Pinckney and Rufus King. There was a brief flirtation with the idea of combining forces with renegade Republican George Clinton, but the idea failed to inspire interest outside of New York. The Federalist press continued to attack citizen Madison as a toady of France and a slavish Bonapartist, but Madison's reputation, having emerged unscathed in the aftermath of intra-party grappling, remained largely unaffected by these tactics.

In the general election the Federalists managed to improve over their 1804 showing, but Madison still carried the day with 122 votes to Pinckney's 47. The vice president received 6 New York electoral votes for president, and 113 for vice president, having remained on the ticket with Madison despite their recent differences. No enduring slogans or phrases were spun out of the 1808 campaign, but the influence of foreign events, the power of the press, campaign managers, and political songs are all evident. Above all, this campaign illustrates that even a party with a dominating majority is vulnerable to the ambitions and enmities that can squander a comfortable advantage.

Suggested Readings: Paul F. Boller, *Presidential Campaigns* (New York: Oxford University Press, 1984); Eugene H. Roseboom, *A History of Presidential Elections* (New York: Macmillan 1964); Arthur M. Schlesinger, Fred Israel, and William P. Hansen, eds., *History of American Presidential Elections, 1789–1968*, Vol. 1 (New York: Chelsea House, 1985).

Campaign of 1812

"Mr. Madison's War," "Virginia Dynasty," "No More Virginia," "Mr. Madison and War! Mr. Clinton and Peace," "Peace and Commerce," the "Peace Party," and "[Madison,] the Little Man in the Palace" were the catch phrases and slogans employed by the Federalists in their last credible challenge to regain the presidency. The campaign and election of 1812 is the first in American history to occur during wartime. Five months before Election Day, Congress declared war against the old nemesis, Britain—a war that was not universally approved. "War hawks" and "peace doves" represented the polarized division throughout the country at the time, with incumbent President Madison caught in the middle. Federalist merchants and export farmers, most of whom were located in the northeast with some interlaced as a minority faction in parts of the South, vocally opposed the war with Britain, their largest foreign market. In some regions where anti-war opinion was high, the Federalists employed the appellation of Peace Party, while referring to their opponents as the War Party.

In 1812, only New England retained a broad Federalist base and identity—with Republican pockets in Vermont and upper Massachusetts (Maine). New Jersey, New York, and Pennsylvania—the mid-Atlantic states—remained divided between the parties. Support for the Federalists in the northwestern state of Ohio had attenuated. The South was rapidly evolving into a Republican one-party region, with pockets of minority support in scattered areas. The southern Federalists were strongest in the Potomac-Shenandoah watersheds of western Virginia, the eastern shore area of Virginia, Maryland, Delaware, and the Cape Fear Valley of North Carolina. The southernmost states were decidedly Republican and the most enthusiastic for the war, particularly in South Carolina.

In addition to the continuing evolution of early parties, politically charged fraternal organizations such as the Tammany Society (or "Sons of Tammany") and the Washington Benevolent Societies were formed, particularly in New York, where they originated, as well as in parts of New England and Ohio. Claiming historical roots antecedent to the Revolution, the Tammany group was folded into the Republican faction due largely to the efforts of the notorious Aaron Burr. In 1812, the Sons of Tammany held considerable power in New York City, and were emulated by other local groups throughout the northeast and Ohio. In reluctant response, the Federalists formed the Washington Benevolent Societies, first brought into existence in New York City on the occasion of Washington's Birthday, 1809. These organizations acted as a bridge between political elites and the general public, developing a broader base of support through club activities, fundraising events, public celebrations, political canvassing, and even secretive ritual. The later emergence of "machine politics" could be traced to the formation of these para-political, fraternalistic organizations in the early nineteenth century.

Within the formal parties themselves, the Republican Party congressional caucus unanimously supported Madison. However, the old congressional caucus institution no longer held a monopoly on the nominating process, as several state legislatures introduced nominating procedures of their own, independent of the congressional practice. For the most part, Madison's support was obtained throughout state legislatures, but it was from a particularly nettlesome exception, the old De Witt Clinton faction in New York, that Madison was to meet notable resistance.

New York governor Daniel Tompkins, along with many prominent New York Republicans and the leadership of the Tammany faction supported Madison, but the New York legislature, exercised by resentment of the "Virginia Dynasty" and the perception that southern policies undermined northern interests, broke ranks and with near unanimity endorsed the candidacy of Clinton, the state's incumbent lieutenant governor.

With the legislature of the country's most populous state behind him, the younger Clinton was propelled on to the national scene as a potential contender to Madison's office. Clinton's strategy was to cynically play to both the Hawks and the Doves: advocating peace to the latter audience while criticizing Madison's lack of martial resolve to the former. Clinton could not break Madison's national hold on the Republicans, but this strategy of "being all things to all people" as the situation demanded caught the attention of the northern peace Federalists, who saw the war as the central issue of the campaign.

Meanwhile, the Federalist Party was finding it difficult to forward a reasonable challenger on their behalf. Chief Justice John Marshall was frequently mentioned as the only person of stature equal to the task, but his role on the Supreme Court was considered indispensable and too dear to the Federalists to risk a potentially losing campaign for chief executive. Drawn by Clinton's protean appearance as a Dove and cognizant of his growing political base, the Federalists began to recruit the New York Republican to their side. In September, the Federalists held a convention involving delegates from eleven states—a forerunner to the national nominating conventions of the late 1820s—but the results were inconclusive. Along with the names of Marshall and John Jay, Clinton's was offered as a possible "fusion" candidate capable of mustering support against the war across party lines. Due to uncertainties about Clinton and hesitation regarding Marshall, a deadlocked convention was unable to produce a nominee, but Clinton emerged as the most visible choice and only viable challenger.

Some Federalists took exception to the turncoat Republican. A Virginia state convention meeting shortly after the national meeting in the Shenandoah Valley town of Staunton, a Federalist stronghold in the South, combated the Clintonian faction by endorsing Federalist stalwart Rufus King. But the Federalists in Virginia were a disaffected minority party within the incumbent's home state. In every other state, it was Clinton and not King who was able to cross party lines and capture the Federalist nomination to run against Madison in the general election.

Following the model of Washington, Madison preferred to remain aloof in the campaign, relying on the advocacy of friendly newspapers and local politicians. His primary concern was the war, campaigning was viewed as unseemly for a Virginia gentleman attending to his duty. However, he was required to become involved in settling the question of his running mate. The incumbent vice president, George Clinton, erstwhile political rival to the president and uncle of the current Federalist nominee, died in April, leaving vacant both the vice presidency as well as the leadership of the party in New York. Madison turned to Elbridge Gerry, signer of the Declaration of Independence, one of the three diplomats in the XYZ trio, former governor of Massachusetts, and the namesake for the unfortunate practice of "gerrymandering." In turning to Gerry, Madison sustained the north-south strategy while drawing upon the prominence of Virginia and Massachusetts, the only states to produce presidents to this point.

Clinton's campaign, in contrast, was energetic. It was also chameleon. Here he was against the war, there he was all for it. For his running mate, he turned to Pennsylvania attorney general and signer of the Constitution, Jared Ingersoll.

After 1812, the declining Federalist Party would rapidly diminish and ultimately vanish as an identifiable faction. Even by 1812, many Federalists were frequently referring to themselves as "federal republicans," while using the term "Democrats" for their Republican opposition. This was designed to remind constituents of the Federalists' own republican pedigree rooted in the Constitution and its defense during the ratification debates, and to implicitly emphasize the more radical democratic and egalitarian (or "Jacobin") elements among the party of Jefferson. Nonetheless, in spite of the decline of Federalist political strength nationwide, the election of 1812 was the closest and most divisive since 1800. It was also sectionally polarized. Madison received only 6 electoral votes in the North (Vermont's), while Clinton found support only in the 9 Southern electoral votes in the border states of Maryland and Delaware. Only the elections of 1860 and 1964 would surpass the election of 1812 in commanding sectional loyalties. Madison's victory numbered 128 total electoral votes to Clinton's 89. Twelve years would pass before a presidential election would involve another serious contest between the contenders. *See also* War and Peace Issue.

Suggested Readings: Paul F. Boller, *Presidential Campaigns* (New York: Oxford University Press, 1984); Roger Hamilton Brown, *The Republic in Peril: 1812* (New York: Columbia University Press, 1964); Eugene H. Roseboom, *A History of Presidential Elections* (New York: Macmillan, 1964); Arthur M. Schlesinger, Fred Israel, and William P. Hansen, eds., *History of American Presidential Elections, 1789–1968*, Vol. 1 (New York: Chelsea House, 1985).

Campaign of 1816

Between 1815 and the campaign of 1824, the Jeffersonian Republican Party reached the zenith of its national preeminence, and thus set the political tone for what would become known as the Era of Good Feeling. Even though the war against Britain was inconclusive, the War Hawk Republican Party enjoyed considerable political capital after General Andrew Jackson's astonishing, albeit irrelevant, victory at New Orleans.

Ironically, when it mattered, the administration's war effort was ineffective. With the exception of a few surprising naval victories against the world's greatest maritime fleet, the execution of the war was checkered with blunder and stalemate. Washington, D.C., was captured and burned in 1814, and the war's unpopularity led to a brief but rapid resurgence of public support for the dissenting Federalists. Federalists were in the majority in Massachusetts, Delaware, and Maryland, while in New York, Pennsylvania, New Jersey, and even in the southern Republican strongholds of Virginia and North Carolina, the strength of the Federalist minority waxed significantly. With renewed confidence, anti-war New England Federalists convened the secret Hartford Convention, the issue of a secessionist movement that threatened to split the union almost five decades before the Civil War.

All this was inverted after the big naval victory of McDonough on Lake Champlain and especially with the extraordinarily lopsided victory over the British army at New Orleans. The latter had absolutely no bearing on the outcome of the war or the treaty it had already produced, but it made all the difference for the political fortunes of the Republicans. Jackson's triumph reconfigured national attitudes regarding the war, now seen as a "second war for independence," with the result that the anti-war Federalists were now widely regarded as treasonous separatists. After their sudden ascent in 1814, the Federalist Party abruptly dipped into a tailspin from which there was no escape.

Additionally, President Madison's post-war programs implemented traditional Federalist principles such as the creation of a second national bank, the imposition of a protective tariff aimed at fortifying domestic industry and agriculture, and federally funded construction for turnpikes and canals. Hamilton's party had been absorbed in Jefferson's; there appeared little reason to seek alternatives. In the summer and autumn of 1814, the Federalists had been rapidly rebuilding their political base, but by the election of 1816, the party of Jefferson became the party of the nation.

James Monroe, an experienced public servant and close friend of Thomas Jefferson, was the obvious heir. Monroe, who in spite of a former association with renegade Senator John Randolph that prompted his Quidite challenge to Madison for the nomination in 1808, had been appointed by the president to serve as secretary of state in 1811, a position that, having already been held by Jefferson and Madison, was the apparent preparation for future chief executives. Monroe had only one problem: he was from Virginia, and there was a growing discomfort in several quarters with the quasi-dynastic practice of relying on Virginia for presidential leadership. Popular New York governor Daniel Tompkins and the recently appointed secretary of war William H. Crawford of Georgia both challenged Monroe's claim. Tompkins's popularity did not cross state lines and his hopes quickly faded, but for a brief moment Crawford's candidacy mounted a serious challenge.

Monroe enjoyed a wider base of support, but his position was still vulnerable; hence his supporters lobbied Crawford to withdraw, implicitly suggesting the possible reward of future support. Crawford responded favorably to these overtures and graciously yielded to Monroe's claim. Shortly thereafter, Republicans convened their official congressional nominating caucus. Crawford's home state delegation was instructed to attend the caucus and, on Crawford's behalf, formally defer to Monroe. But inexplicably the eleven Georgian delegates chose not to attend. Monroe won the nomination by a surprisingly narrow margin of 9 votes. Had the absent Georgian contingent attended, and had they rejected their commission in light of circumstances, William Crawford might well have become the nation's fifth president.

The waning Federalist Party did not formally nominate a candidate. There was no consensus on a party champion among Federalist newspapers, and there seems to have been no effort on the part of congressional Federalists to forward an official nominee. Senator Rufus King of New York, the former Federalist candidate for vice president (1808), somehow managed to receive 34 electoral votes from Massachusetts (22), Connecticut (9), and Delaware (3), but by some accounts King might not have even been aware that he was a candidate until after the Electoral College had cast their votes. Resigned to defeat, the Federalist Party did not actively challenge Monroe's candidacy in Vermont, Ohio, New Jersey, or throughout the entire South. With no formal campaign, Rufus King would be the last Federalist to receive votes for president.

Monroe won 183 electoral votes in 1816—a new Electoral College record. New York governor Tompkins stood as Monroe's running mate, duplicating the now customary north-south strategy that had marked every successful candidacy since Washington. The Virginia Dynasty was to persist another eight years, marking a period of comparative political unity anomalous to the American experience.

Suggested Readings: Paul F. Boller, *Presidential Campaigns* (New York: Oxford University Press, 1984); Arthur M. Schlesinger, Fred Israel, and William P. Hansen, eds., *History of American Presidential Elections, 1789–1968*, Vol. 1 (New York: Chelsea House, 1985).

Campaign of 1820

President James Monroe, running unopposed for a second term, fell just one vote short of a unanimous election—an accomplishment that would have placed him in the company of George Washington as one of two presidents elected without explicit opposition. The *Columbian Sentinel*, a Massachusetts newspaper fiercely loyal to the Federalists, is credited with first describing Monroe's administration as the Era of Good Feelings. For eight years, the United States was without party competition, and after two decades of heated inter-party animosity, a one-party system appeared to have fallen into place.

However, the Era of Good Feelings was not without problems. In 1819, the country faced a serious economic depression. Banks closed, the production of manufactured goods dropped sharply, and the government went into deficit. On the foreign policy front, negotiations with Spain over Florida stalled. Without congressional permission, Andrew Jackson brazenly led an occupation force into Florida. In the West, the proposed admission of Missouri raised the ugly issue of slavery. "Good Feelings" was not sufficient to eliminate potentially volatile antipathies.

Abolition sentiments waxed and southern Republicans had reason to be concerned. Early in 1820, New York senator Rufus King delivered a speech calling for the exclusion of slavery as a condition for the admission of the new state of Missouri. King's speech helped fuel rumors of a possible new abolitionist party. In Pennsylvania, influential and provocative Republican publisher William Duane, denouncing Monroe's administration as pro-slavery sponsored a movement to draft New York's De Witt Clinton and persuaded one-third of the participating voters to choose electors pledged against Monroe. Despite the minor revolt, Monroe still controlled two-thirds of Pennsylvania's electors and subsequently received Pennsylvania's 25 electoral votes.

Monroe remained essentially unchallenged. Roanoke's John Randolph described Monroe's acclamation as "unanimity of indifference, and not of approbation." Even so, regardless of the dangerous political currents beginning to stir below the surface, James Monroe enjoyed what would become and remain the biggest Electoral College landslide in the history of American elections.

Suggested Readings: Harry Ammon, *James Monroe: The Quest for National Identity* (New York: McGraw-Hill, 1971); Noble E. Cunningham, *The Presidency of James Monroe* (Lawrence: University Press of Kansas, 1996); Arthur M. Schlesinger, Fred Israel, and William P. Hansen, eds., *History of American Presidential Elections, 1789–1968*, Vol. 1 (New York: Chelsea House, 1985).

Campaign of 1824

James Monroe, in following the now customary two-term pattern set by Washington, chose not to run for a third term, leaving the most open and competitive field of candidates to date. By 1822 the names of over a dozen potential candidates were in circulation, and by the election year of 1824 five names were still under serious consideration: John Quincy Adams of Massachusetts, who was serving as Monroe's secretary of state; William H. Crawford of Georgia, Monroe's (and formerly Madison's) secretary of the treasury and a Virginian by birth; Henry Clay of Kentucky, a former War Hawk and Speaker of the House; John C. Calhoun of South Carolina, another former War Hawk and Monroe's secretary of war; and Senator Andrew Jackson of Tennessee, the hero of the Battle of New Orleans. Crawford was the early favorite, Jackson the winner of pluralities in both the Electoral College and the popular vote, and Adams the eventual president-elect.

Monroe, as well as Madison and Jefferson, preferred Crawford. Two events deflated Crawford's chances: a debilitating stroke suffered in September 1824, and his nomination by the Republican congressional caucus. By the early 1820s, King Caucus had grown politically unpopular. The general public perceived the old nominating system as antiquated and undemocratic. Crawford held the support of those sixty-six members of Congress who chose to participate in the caucus, nominating him with near unanimity and naming Pennsylvania's Albert Gallatin as the nominee for vice president. But the endorsement actually undermined Crawford and Gallatin. The other candidates were nominated by their respective home state legislatures or in state conventions. Crawford did receive the endorsement of the Virginia legislature, but was not able to inspire other state assemblies to follow in kind. The field was well populated, and even included marginal candidates such as New York's De Witt Clinton, nominated by a convention in Steubenville, Ohio. Even the savvy of the politically astute Martin Van Buren, working behind the scenes on Crawford's behalf, was unable to exploit his initial advantage. With Crawford's candidacy hobbled by the caucus and his health broken, Adams and Jackson soon established themselves as the front-runners.

All the candidates identified themselves as Republicans, the one-party system that was the consequence of the War of 1812 and the legacy of Monroe's Era of Good Feelings prevailed. With no opposition party, the Republicans were not compelled to produce an official platform. Consequently, no dramatic slogan or persuasive phrase spun out of the issues or the candidates' positions. However, policy differences did set the principal candidates apart. Clay's "American System" was a repackaging of Hamilton's Federalism, favoring the national bank, federal funding of infrastructure development, and the imposition of protective tariffs. Adams and Calhoun joined Clay in these preferences. Crawford had been a long-term supporter of the national bank and had on separate occasions both opposed and supported the notorious embargo of 1808. Jackson despised the national bank and was favorably disposed to the free market. Among the issues, slavery continued as a disturbing and latently volatile source of conflict. There was also visible disagreement over economic issues in the wake of the depression of 1819. But the issues were overshadowed by personality. Candidate loyalties were primarily based on personal reputation, friendship, or regional allegiance.

As with the campaign of 1800, discussion over the qualifications of the candidates grew increasingly personal. Scandal mongering and character assassination replaced dialogue over issues, and no real slogans were circulated on behalf of any one candidate or policy. Adams was unjustly accused of caving in to the British at Ghent over navigation rights on the Mississippi River. It was noted that he had an English wife; he was also ridiculed as slovenly and undignified. Crawford was unfairly rumored to have mismanaged public funds. Clay was inaccurately rumored to be a gambler, drunkard, and too ill to run. Jackson's more exercised critics labeled him a murderer for having summarily executed six mutinous deserters during the Creek War of 1813.

Nonetheless, Adams and Jackson established themselves as the front-runners. Adams enjoyed unchallenged support in the Northeast. At one point Adams, having emerged as the new favorite, entertained the idea of naming Jackson as his running mate, producing the closest thing to a slogan or catch phrase from the 1824 campaign: **"Do You Want John Quincy Adams Who Can Write, or Andrew Jackson Who Can Fight?"** But Jackson was not geared for second-best; his whole life was defined by his peerless ability to lead.

Initially confined to the West, the movement for Jackson soon gained momentum in the critical mid-Atlantic swing states. Pennsylvania propelled Jackson's effort outside the West. Calhoun had anticipated winning the support of Pennsylvania, and saw the Keystone State as the key state in his campaign. But Calhoun's campaign fizzled when a sudden grass-roots movement supporting Jackson began in the western portion of the state. Quickly spreading eastward to Philadelphia, the movement gained credibility when a local group of Jackson supporters, simply calling themselves "democrats," voted to endorse Old Hickory. This event is notable for two reasons: it could be regarded as a precursor of the Democratic Party, and in the resolution we find one of the earliest projections of the Jackson myth. The resolution endorsing Jackson described him as a virtuous patriot, "consistent democrat," "statesman and warrior," and a "friend to the rights of man and universal suffrage." From here, the pro-Jackson momentum carried into the state convention in Harrisburg, where Jackson received a critical nomination outside his own state. The "democratic" tenor of Jackson's campaign spread elsewhere. In New Jersey, which initially favored Adams, Jackson's supporters endorsed what they called the "People's Ticket," and successfully turned the state in their direction.

The actual election was full of uncertainty and fragmentation. Jackson won a plurality of 99 votes in the Electoral College carrying twelve states: Pennsylvania, most of the South, and portions of the West. Adams won all of New England and New York, gaining 84 votes in eleven states. Crawford won 41 votes from five states, including 24 from Virginia. Clay held his home state of Kentucky as well as Ohio, Missouri, and four renegade votes from New York for a total of 31. Officially preserved on record for the first time, the national popular vote also went to Jackson, who managed a plurality of just over 150,000 to Adams's 114,000. Clay and Crawford each earned approximately 47,000 votes. Failing a majority in the Electoral College, the election was decided in the House of Representatives as stipulated in the Constitution. By contrast, Calhoun was the vice president–elect, earning over two-thirds of the Electoral College vote.

On February 9, 1825, Adams won thirteen states in the House, the minimum required to capture a majority. Jackson managed seven states, four stood by Crawford. New York nearly went to Crawford, but Adams's majority was ensured when Representative Van Rensselaer, leaving it in God's hands, opened his eyes from prayer to the sight of a fateful Adams ballot, taken as a sign from above.

Stung by gaining more votes all around than Adams and still losing the election, Jackson brooded darkly, bristling when Clay received a plum position as Adams's secretary of state after marshaling his influence in the House behind Adams. Clay wondered aloud if killing 2,500 British soldiers qualified Jackson for the presidency. Incensed, Jackson described Clay's appointment as the fruit of a "corrupt bargain."

Jackson was capable, confident, shrewd, and charismatic, but Adams was far more qualified as a statesman. A prominent diplomat since the Washington administration, former member of Congress, accomplished secretary of state, and coauthor of the highly regarded Monroe Doctrine, Adams was the ablest American statesman of his time. Jackson had experience as a member of Congress, but his reputation as a warrior generated his popular appeal. To punctuate his war hero credentials, Jackson projected an image of himself as a man of the people in spite of the fact that he enjoyed the affluence of a wealthy slaveholding planter. Jackson was lionized as Old Hickory, formidable war chief and archetypal man of the people. Adams, while respected among his peers, was perceived by the general public as an aloof aristocrat and vintage Federalist in republican clothing. And yet Adams was a champion of republican values, while Jackson's personality was autocratic. More than most, this and the following campaign of 1828 revolved around the inversion of image and fact, serving as examples of the power of propaganda even in the earliest democratic elections.

Suggested Readings: Robert V. Remini, *Andrew Jackson and the Course of American Freedom, 1822–1832* (New York: Harper & Row, 1981); Robert V. Remini, *The Election of Andrew Jackson* (Philadelphia: Lippincott, 1963); Arthur M. Schlesinger, Fred Israel, and William P. Hansen, eds., *History of American Presidential Elections, 1789–1968*, Vol. 1 (New York, Chelsea House, 1985).

Campaign of 1828

"Expired at Washington on the 9th of February," a pro-Jackson editor groused, "of poison administered by the assassin John Quincy Adams, the usurper, and Henry Clay, the virtue, liberty and independence of the United States." Losing the election of 1828 was one of the significant consequences of Adams's pyrrhic victory in the election of 1824. Andrew Jackson, embittered by Adams's apparent maneuver involving Clay—the "corrupt bargain" of American political lore—stormed back with a vengeance, this time to win clear margins in both the Electoral College and within the burgeoning popular vote. The notable election of 1828 was likely decided four years earlier.

Acrimony intensified before and during the election of 1828. The Adams-Clay alliance stirred enemies even before the inauguration. Clay found himself dueling with Virginia senator John Randolph over a particularly cutting insult publicly

PROTECTOR & DEFENDER OF BEAUTY & BOOTY.

ORLEANS

This campaign portrait of Andrew Jackson, issued during the presidential election of 1828, refers to Jackson's victory at New Orleans during the War of 1812. Courtesy of Library of Congress.

cast by Randolph in the Senate against the integrity of the administration. Vice President John Calhoun, still harboring designs on the presidency, abandoned the Adams ship almost immediately for the Jacksonians. The phrase "corrupt bargain" dominated rhetorical currency for four years. Against this backdrop, the first enduring and extant modern American political party was formed—the party of Jackson, eventually to be called the Democrats.

The Era of Good Feeling, long dead since the controversy of the previous election, and King Caucus were both extinct relics of the early republic. Evolving in their stead was a distinctly bipartisan dynamic that was no longer attached to the congressional caucus. Thoroughly polarized around both personal allegiance and political vision, the new factions carried further the policy debate ongoing since Alexander Hamilton and Thomas Jefferson fixed the initial parameters. Adams was associated with Henry Clay's "American System," a vision of governmental activity that included federally funded public works, protective tariffs, a strong central government, and a national bank; in a word, the latest edition of the Hamiltonian vision. Jackson was not a committed ideologue; rather, he sought moderate positions on many of the pressing issues of the time, his zealous contempt for the national bank an important exception. While not a Jeffersonian purist, Jackson nonetheless gravitated toward the agrarian, strict constructionist, and states-rights ideals of the Old Republicans.

The Old Republicans, or "Radicals," represented the remnant of the party's Jeffersonian origins. In 1824 their champion had been Crawford in spite of his support of a national bank and his vacillation on the embargo controversy. Crawford had retired to Georgia in 1825, leaving leadership of the Radicals to his erstwhile supporter Martin Van Buren. As one of the keenest politicians of his age, Van Buren avoided zealotry—winning campaigns was his principal concern.

Courting the popular Jackson thus became his priority, and it was through the efforts of Van Buren, exerting influence behind the scenes, that Jackson's renewed challenge was given coherence and direction. Van Buren guaranteed his home state of New York, held influence in Virginia, and could muster support from among Crawford's base. Van Buren was committed to the old north-south alliance, and in spite of his opportunism, adhered to a genuine desire to reanimate Jeffersonian principles against the Hamiltonian turn that had characterized public policy since the war. With Jefferson as their philosophical touchstone, Van Buren, Jackson, and Calhoun formed the leadership of what would come to be known as the "Democratic Republicans," commonly referred to as the "Jackson Party" in deference to its dominant figure. By 1832 this party accepted the name of Democrats. Adams and Clay were referred to as "National Republicans," (also "Coalitionists"), the closest heirs to Hamilton and forerunners of the Whigs. Additionally, two minor parties appeared, the Anti-Masonic Party suddenly materialized in response to an inflammatory wave of anti-masonry that began with scandal and murder in New York. The Workingman's Party organized in 1828 as an advocate for the cause of labor. But it was the Jeffersonian Democratic Republicans and the Hamiltonian National Republicans standing as the dominant combatants.

Jackson's 1828 campaign ran throughout the duration of the Adams administration. As early as October of 1825, only seven months after Adams's inauguration, the Tennessee state legislature nominated Jackson for president. Jackson supporters began working on his election soon after. Jackson partisans in Congress caucused regularly throughout Adams's term, and worked as a coherent political faction. Jackson's cohort successfully accumulated an unprecedented campaign fund. Liberal use of the franking privilege for political purposes among Jackson's Congressional supporters amplified the influence of the monies raised. The role of money had expanded in proportion to the increase of eligible voters. With all states now having lifted property requirements, and all but two states (Delaware and South Carolina) employing direct election of the Electoral College, democratization of American politics was well under way. Winning votes within such a large pool of new voters required money and organization, and the Jackson Party quickly mastered the necessary methods of obtaining funds and building a network of allied committees and clubs. "Hickory Clubs" sprouted throughout the various states, working diligently at the local level to stage events, recruit supporters and promote the cause. Hickory poles were raised in towns nationwide, reminders of Jackson's heroic stature, the political *axes mundi* of grassroots democracy. Rallies and barbecues, accompanied by songs of Jackson's exploits, became commonplace events. The "new Washington" had succeeded in stirring fervent support across the vast spaces of the new republic.

The president's own efforts at reelection were quite another matter. The American System was continually emphasized—Adams and Clay choosing to focus on policy more than promotion. Adams, who lacked the personal warmth and social graces needed for the hustings, refused to engage in vulgar politicking, leaving the task largely to Clay, Pennsylvania's Richard Rush, and other notables such as the young Daniel Webster. The National Republicans also held rallies and campaign events, but with less frequency. The Nationals banked on Adams's reputation as a statesman and self-confidence in their policies, counting on the Electoral College to affirm its function as buffer between good government and popular passions. But after the election of 1826 wherein the Jackson Party captured both chambers of Congress, the momentum for the general was too strong to effectively resist.

More than ever, newspapers provided a visible and ubiquitous service to political partisans. The Jacksonians enjoyed the support of an impressive network of newspapers throughout the country. This network successfully defined the campaign as a decisive and historic contest pitting popular, egalitarian democracy against aloof and reactionary aristocracy. Unfortunately, this was accomplished through a combination of Jackson hagiography and *ad hominem* mudslinging aimed at Adams. General Jackson was the self-made hero of the people, Adams the effete scion of New England aristocrats. Adams was depicted in the pro-Jackson press as undemocratic, misanthropic, anti-immigrant, and anti-Catholic — a "Unitarian," no less, an affiliation that was often perceived by the general public as atheistic. Jackson was depicted as a true American democrat, friend of the common man, and devout Presbyterian (even though he deliberately chose not to attend services until he was out of politics). The "corrupt bargain" was repeatedly raised as proof of Adams's contempt for the masses. Jackson's wartime heroics were touted as reminders of his steadfast courage and impeccable patriotism. Jackson was referred to as the "People's Candidate," the "Hero of New Orleans," and the simple "Farmer from Tennessee." Causing scandal, the Jacksonian press accused Adams of vicious acts such as procuring young American women for the czar of Russia, using the White House as a gaming den, and practicing loose habits regarding his relations with women. Above all, the theme of Adams's elitism was drummed throughout the campaign — the haughty "King John the Second" was no friend of the people, no choice for democracy, and the "corrupt bargain" was the one note that sounded throughout the attack on the administration.

Partisan newspapers for Adams fueled this frenzy of invective. Dragging the campaign further into the gutter, pro-Adams newspapers accused Jackson of murder, gambling, conspiracy with Aaron Burr to commit treason, adultery, and bigamy — the latter charge fracturing the health of his wife Rachel. The old canard alleging Jackson's bloodthirsty murder of wrongly accused deserters in the 1813 Indian War was recycled. Philadelphia's *Democratic Press* published a morbid oblong flyer, known as the Coffin Hand Bill, to expose the bloody affair. Nothing seemed beyond the pale. Even Jackson's mother was defamed.

Additionally, congressional Jacksonians adroitly manipulated the tariff issue to boost their advantage. Passing the Tariff of 1828, also known as the **Tariff of Abominations**, the Jackson Party managed to punish an already isolated New England, garner support in the West, and while alienating the South to the extent that Calhoun, the old nationalist, turned toward regional and states rights — even to the point of possible secession — nonetheless held the South in their camp knowing all the while that Adams was not an alternative for the southern electorate.

Given the storm and stress of the campaign, the actual election was anticlimactic. Jackson won impressively in the popular vote: 647,292 to 507,730. Jackson's margin of victory among the popular vote would stand as the highest in the nineteenth century. This time the Electoral College gave Jackson a decisive majority: 178 to 83. John Quincy Adams left the executive branch under unfavorable conditions, but would return to serve with distinction in Congress. Andrew Jackson's legend survived the mudslinging barrage of 1828 and continued to wax larger than life through the duration of his presidency.

Suggested Readings: Robert V. Remini, *The Election of Andrew Jackson* (Philadelphia: Lippincott, 1963); Arthur M. Schlesinger, Fred Israel, and William P. Hansen eds., *History of American Presidential Elections, 1789–1968*, Vol. 1 (New York: Chelsea House, 1985).

Campaign of 1832

Lacking the drama and intensity of previous elections such as 1800, 1824, and 1828, the campaign of 1832 played a crucial role in making organized political parties a fixture of the American political system.

In 1831, the anti-Masonic party held the first national nominating convention in Baltimore, Maryland. The anti-Masonic movement had its roots in the 1826 abduction and disappearance of William Morgan of Batavia, New York. Morgan allegedly disappeared as a direct result of his plans to publish a book claiming to detail the allegedly sinister side of Masonic clubs. In the aftermath of Morgan's disappearance, anti-Masonic candidates began to run for office in New York and other states. For president, the anti-Masonic party nominated Maryland's William Wirt, himself a former Mason, and Amos Ellmaker as Wirt's running mate. Intent on denying Jackson a second term, the National Republicans, who were also meeting in Baltimore, named Kentucky's Henry Clay, champion of the Hamiltonian "American System," as their presidential candidate and John Sergeant of Pennsylvania to fill the bottom of the ticket.

In late May 1832, the Democrats held their first nominating convention in Baltimore as well, but it merely endorsed nominations that President Andrew Jackson had previously secured in state conventions. However, the Democratic convention refused to renominate John C. Calhoun as vice president. Many Democrats opposed Calhoun as the result of Calhoun's tariff policy, his defense of the doctrine of nullification, bad blood over General Jackson's seizure of Florida in 1819, and an embarrassing feud between Calhoun's wife, Floride, and Peggy O'Neil Timberlake Eaton, the wife of secretary of war John Eaton.

The nullification controversy foreshadowed the slavery controversy that would become the most divisive national political issue in American history. Calhoun's home state of South Carolina had ignited a secession crisis over the **Tariff of Abominations**. South Carolina, with Calhoun's full support, espoused the nullification doctrine that claimed that a state had a right to nullify federal laws within its own borders. To replace Calhoun, Jackson and the Democrats plucked Jackson's political mastermind and erstwhile secretary of state, Martin Van Buren of New York. With the selection of Van Buren, Jackson attempted to restore the north-south strategy.

The strategy of the National Republicans and Henry Clay hinged on persuading the electorate that Jackson had become despotic, intent upon destroying the nation's democratic institutions. Clay and his supporters decided to make Jackson's opposition to the renewal of the charter of the National Bank as the vehicle to discredit Jackson. Clay, attempting to force the issue, persuaded Nicholas Biddle, the powerful president of the National Bank, to petition for an early renewal of the bank's charter, thus provoking Jackson's wrath.

Jackson's hatred of the bank stemmed from losses incurred through unpaid promissory notes connected to land speculation in Tennessee before Jackson became a national political figure. Because of the loss and the similar experiences of other Tennessee residents, Jackson despised banks and their "rag money," flimsy notes, and easy credit. Jackson zealously adhered to "hard" currency, or specie (gold and silver coin) as the only true currency.

Despite being strongly opposed by Jackson, the National Bank had many friends in Congress. After a protracted congressional debate, both chambers of Congress approved a renewal of the National Bank's charter. Determined to rebuff this challenge, Jackson did not hesitate to veto the legislation renewing the charter of the National Bank. In seeking the confrontation with Jackson, Clay badly underestimated Jackson's popular support. Jackson seized the opportunity to frame the entire campaign around the bank issue, thereby challenging the American people to choose between disparate political and monetary visions.

Throughout the campaign of 1832, the opposing camps resorted to a mutual exchange of vicious tactics. Supporters of Jackson and Clay made effective use of **political cartoons** and caricatures lampooning Jackson and Clay. To the dismay of Clay supporters, the National Bank issue failed to catch on with the majority of voters. Jackson went on to win the popular vote by 157,000 votes and the Electoral College by a 219 to 49 margin. Flirting with nullification and secession, South Carolina cast its 11 votes for sympathetic Governor John Floyd of Virginia. With only 7 votes from Vermont, the anti-Masonic party failed to become a major factor in the outcome of the 1832 presidential election.

Suggested Readings: Samuel Rhea Gammon, *The Presidential Campaign of 1832* (Baltimore: Johns Hopkins Press, 1922), Arthur M. Schlesinger, Fred Israel, and William P. Hansen, eds., *History of American Presidential Elections, 1789–1968*, Vol. 1 (New York: Chelsea House, 1985).

Campaign of 1836

Eighteen thirty-six brought an election far closer than the Jackson landslides of recent history. In defeat, the Whigs had proven to be a viable political force, but their 124 electoral votes were distributed among four different candidates, General William Henry Harrison of Ohio, Tennessee senator Hugh L. White, Senator Daniel Webster of Massachusetts, and Willie P. Mangum of North Carolina. The Democrats fielded one candidate, the incumbent Vice President Martin Van Buren of New York, and gathered 58 percent of the electoral votes. But despite the outcome in the Electoral College the Whigs' electoral muscle had been duly and noticeably flexed in the popular vote.

This state of affairs had been foreshadowed by Whig gains in congressional and state elections in 1834 and 1835. The Whigs actually managed to win majorities in state assemblies in Virginia as well as President Andrew Jackson's home state of Tennessee. In Congress, the Whigs remained a minority but had closed the gap, most significantly through electoral gains in Jackson's southern base. Jackson had made enemies inside his own party; the Force Bill estranged South Carolina and other southern supporters. Additionally, his stand against the bank exacerbated disagreements with the old National Republicans. Jackson's personality and legend would likely have given him a third term had he chosen to pursue it, but it would have been at the cost of a weakened electoral mandate and a diminished legacy. The mood of the country had clearly polarized, leaving Van Buren and the Democrats less dominant, their victory less decisive.

By and large party positions remained static; the Democrats reaffirmed the states rights doctrine of Jefferson and Jackson, continued their recalcitrant opposition to the national bank, and sustained their rejection of Clay's "American System." The Whigs held fast to high tariffs, public works, the national bank, and related activism championed by Clay and inherited from Hamiltonian Federalism. Nonetheless, there were visible fissures within both major parties. In New York, the party split into conservative and radical wings, the former being Tammany loyalists willing to modify their anti-bank position to permit banks chartered by party loyalists, the latter, the "Equal Rights" wing labeled the **Locofocos** by their estranged party brethren, adhered to a purer Jacksonian ideology. Originally an insult, Locofoco soon became a moniker adopted nationally by the party populists. Where advantageous, Whigs were willing to sing the tune of the other side; Illinois Whigs supporting White avowed the principles of Jefferson and Jackson, choosing instead to personally attack Van Buren and the Democrats' monopoly of power. For their part, the Democrats were more cohesive on party platform but just as likely to adjust their rhetoric to secure a regional advantage. Northern Democrats, aware of anti–Van Buren sentiment in the South, attacked abolition to mollify southern voters. The parties were sincere in their principles, but neither party was without division nor blind to the necessity of political stratagem.

Both parties played to the people; the Jacksonians made much of the Whigs alleged aristocratic pretensions, defined the Whigs as simply repackaged Federalist blue bloods, and continued to portray Jackson and Van Buren as the true men of the people. By way of counterattack Whigs delighted in promoting the image of King Andrew the First with Van Buren as his autocratically aloof and imperious sycophant and successor. The Whigs reached a low point when, in an appeal to anti-Catholic prejudices, they attempted to portray Van Buren as a "papist" based upon his record of correspondence with the Vatican during his service as secretary of state. Democrats countered with charges that Whigs held a secret agenda to establish a national church.

Ironically, the Whigs, who advocated centralized government, loudly criticized centralized political organization. The Democrats, proclaiming states rights and local government, benefited from a sophisticated national, centralized party network. The Whig Party chose not to hold a national convention in 1836 as they had four years earlier and relied instead on state nominating conventions, a strategy that fragmented allegiance.

Van Buren, the "Little Magician," was a master politician, but it was Jackson who choreographed the Democratic Convention. Van Buren was Jackson's chosen heir. Following Jackson's example, martial heroism remained a strong attractor in electoral politics. On the Whig side, former general William Henry Harrison, renowned for the Battle of Tippecanoe, emerged as the more popular and sustainable candidate. Jackson responded by promoting for vice president Kentucky's Richard M. Johnson, whom some claimed was the true slayer of Tecumseh. Although many distrusted Van Buren, especially in the South, his coronation was not resisted. It was Johnson who was drawn into controversy; his personal life, marked by a mixed-race relationship, drew public condemnation.

In the election Van Buren won the Electoral College easily, but his controversial running mate, having alienated the southern bloc, did not carry Alabama and thus failed to secure a majority for his half of the ticket. Unique in American political history, Johnson's election to the vice presidency was thrown to the Senate where he was elected by a vote of 33 to 16.

The racial controversy over Johnson and the Democrats self-serving eagerness to denounce and prohibit abolition indicate the menace that slavery and race posed in antebellum politics. The bank war and Clay's "American System" remained the more visible issues, but with each election the "peculiar institution" would become a steadily polarizing and increasingly vitriolic concern.

Suggested Reading: Arthur M. Schlesinger, Fred Israel, and William P. Hansen, eds., *History of American Presidential Elections, 1789–1968*, Vol. 1 (New York: Chelsea House, 1985).

Campaign of 1840

Political historians credit the campaign of 1840 with ushering a new era in presidential campaigns heavily dependent upon the ability of campaigns to reach a rapidly expanding electorate. Desperate to recapture the White House, the Whig Party searched far and wide for a candidate to appeal to voters who had cast their lot with former president Andrew Jackson and Jackson's heir apparent incumbent President Martin Van Buren. The Whig Party found their savior in General William Henry Harrison. By carefully putting forward aristocratic Harrison as a man of the people, the Whig Party drew on still fond memories of President Andrew Jackson.

With one of the more famous political slogans in American history, **"Tippecanoe and Tyler Too"** William Henry Harrison was guaranteed a permanent place in the presidential campaign hall of fame. Drawing hard on his warrior reputation as the leader who had defeated the Indian leader Tecumseh years earlier, the Whig Party sought to establish Harrison as another Andrew Jackson. The Whig Party made use of a combination of hagiographical promotion, festive atmosphere, exaggerated personal attack against the opposition, superficial treatment of the real issues, and an uninhibited appeal to the ever-multiplying, variegating voters to propel Harrison to victory.

Metaphorically the campaign of 1840 was the rhetorical return of General Jackson, or Old Hickory, the Hero of New Orleans now repackaged as the Whig's own General Harrison, or "Old Buckeye," brave hero of Tippecanoe, commonly nicknamed "Old Tip." Harrison, who in truth came from a background of affluence and privilege, was deliberately and falsely depicted as the humble frontiersman, the small farmer's candidate—for this was the famous **"Log Cabin and Hard Cider"** campaign. Van Buren, whose credentials as a democrat were sound, was successfully redefined by Whig campaigners as an Eastern aristocrat with no connection to common Americans. It was brilliant deployment of creative imagery and unabashed sloganeering.

As for the issues, both parties hewed the same line as 1836. States rights, decreased federal activity, frugality, anti-abolitionism, opposition to a national bank, and the "cardinal principles" of Jeffersonian philosophy continued to be numbered among the planks of the Democrats' official platform. Whigs criticized the administration for the Panic of 1837, and Whig policy continued to be well summarized through Henry Clay's Hamiltonian ideal of the "American System." Clay himself was still regarded as a possible Whig candidate for the highest office, as was Winfield Scott. But Harrison was still riding the momentum of his promising popular reception four years earlier, and his supporters deftly perpetuated the drama Tippecanoe. The issues were still there; especially the growing controversy over slavery, but what became palpably significant about 1840 was the growing importance of presentation and image management, popular entertainment and populist appeal. Never mind that Harrison was to the manor born, and the closest he came to living in a log cabin was a brief residence in a five-room log house as a newlywed. Even the young Abraham Lincoln contributed to the mythmaking, abandoning his political mentor, Henry Clay, for Old Tip who was "first rate."

The Democrats groused at having their populist thunder stolen by the phony Federalist-Whig usurpers. Van Buren's supporters attempted to resuscitate the issues, particularly the battle over the bank, while dismissing the log cabin story as the superficial trumpeting of mere celebrity. The Whigs intentionally steered from the issues. Harrison was not known for political acuity or philosophical clarity. His manner of speaking was often fragmented and confusing—incoherent to some, and he could appear both uninformed about and indifferent to important questions. Harrison's more influential supporters, particularly Nicholas Biddle, were understandably nervous when he actively campaigned. A committee of campaign managers was formed with the specific charge of monitoring and coaching Harrison's public statements. But for the most part Whig packaging overwhelmed discussion with festivals, parades, barbecues, and a glut of mock log cabins filled with both hard and soft cider free for the taking—once again borrowing heavily from the Hickory Pole and public event tactics used to great effect by Jackson in 1828 and 1832.

Merchandising was a signal mark of the Whig promotion. Bobbles such as promotional handkerchiefs and campaign buttons were common. Boisterous Whig campaign songs were abundant and widely circulated through sheet music and songbooks. Familiar melodies such as "The Star Spangled Banner," "La Marseillaise," and "Yankee Doodle" now accompanied pro-Whig or anti–Van Buren lyrics. Political cartoons continued their new role as effective statements for quick and entertaining contrasts between the candidates. The western frontiersman/ordinary fellow/log cabin builder/hard cider consumer/no-nonsense ploughman/Indian fighting, Red Coat stomping war hero/humble friend of the people imagery played out well in the cartoons and songs, and Van Buren's New York refinements and eastern manners served as easy foils for exaggerated comparisons. Van Buren, pinned with the pejorative "Sweet Sandy Whiskers" and denounced as "King Mat," was accused by Whig politicians of indulging in opulent hedonism at the expense of the taxpayers, imbibing in fine wines and clothed in delicate laces while

This campaign broadside for William Henry Harrison, the 1840 Whig nominee for president, recounts Harrison's military exploits. Courtesy of Library of Congress.

General Harrison's simpler taste ran toward buckskins and the ubiquitous cider. In truth, Van Buren's White House was comparatively frugal and Harrison was not above extravagance, but the fiction was nonetheless politically devastating to the Democratic ticket.

The Democrats countered with attempts to humanize Van Buren, assigned the endearment of "Old Kinderhook" after his hometown, and pointed to his record as a seasoned Jacksonian. Typically, aspersions were exchanged in kind. Aware that Harrison's "war hero" legend was built on the thin foundations of a minor player in the War of 1812, the Democrats attacked the General's authenticity, competence, and manhood. "Granny Harrison, the Petticoat General" was the insult that Democrats hurled at the aging challenger. Working hard to demolish the General's war record, the Democrats accused Harrison of lacking political sensibility and moral spine, more the ignorant and effeminate coward than self-made rugged warrior. To the Democrats Old Tippecanoe was in reality a dainty "General Mum." The Democrats eagerly referred to Harrison's speech coaches as a "Conscience-Keeping Committee," and pointed out that the doddering general was really guided by the "leading strings" of his managers. Defamation and opprobrium were greedily pitched to and fro between the major parties. But the

Wood engraving of President
Martin Van Buren, the 1840
Democratic nominee for presi-
dent. Courtesy of Library of
Congress.

Democrats were unable to mar Harrison's well-polished image, while Whig slan-
ders against Van Buren were more difficult to deflect. Reputation was what mattered in this campaign, and the party that erected the sturdiest and shiniest façade
would claim victory.

Harrison carried all the large states except Virginia—including the 42 electoral
votes from the colossus of the Electoral College, Van Buren's New York. Van
Buren became the third incumbent to be turned out by the voters (John Adams
and John Quincy Adams were the other two). He had also been the third vice
president to succeed the previous incumbent by election (1836) and the last incumbent vice president to be elected until the elder George Bush 152 years later.
Harrison would be the third general to ascend to the presidency (following Washington and Jackson), the oldest candidate to win election until President Reagan
in 1984, and the first president to die in office, leaving the balance of his term
under the leadership of Tyler.

The election of 1840 is notable for several reasons: diminished sectionalism as
support for both parties spread throughout the union, campaign tactics, image
building and rhetorical devices remarkably modern in their approach, the introduction of enterprise in the merchandising of candidates (especially Harrison), the
high-pitched populist appeal in the wake of an expanding electorate, the introduction of a campaign special committee specifically designed for candidate management (Harrison's), and the coining of slogans and expressions either still in
use or well-known to this day. "Old Kinderhook's" abbreviated nickname "O.K."
is claimed by some students of language to be the origin of the common expression—"okay." "Tippecanoe and Tyler Too" and "Log Cabin and Hard Cider" still

resonate as archetypal sloganeering. The slang term "booze" was invented due to the widespread consumption of whisky sold in log-cabin shaped packages and distributed by the E.G. Booz Distillery of Philadelphia. Even the term, "keep the ball rolling" can be traced to the Whig stunt of rolling a large ball around Whig campaign rallies throughout 1840.

> What has caused the great commotion, motion, motion
> Our country through?
> It is the ball a-rolling on,
> For Tippecanoe and Tyler too, Tippecanoe and Tyler too.
> And with them we'll beat the little Van, Van, Van;
> Van is a used-up man,
> And with them we'll beat little Van!

Suggested Readings: Robert Gray Gunderson, *The Log-Cabin Campaign* (Lexington: University of Kentucky Press, 1957); Arthur M. Schlesinger, Fred Israel, and William P. Hansen, eds., *History of American Presidential Elections, 1789–1968*, Vol. 1 (New York: Chelsea House, 1985).

Campaign of 1844

John Tyler ascended to the presidency upon the death of President William Henry Harrison one month into his term. From the beginning of his presidency, Tyler's states rights philosophy clashed with the Whig Party's support for a strong federal government. Tyler soon found himself in a series of veto battles over Whig legislation that conflicted with Tyler's views. With Tyler alienated from members of his own party, Henry Clay reassumed the mantle of the head of the Whig Party.

Animosity between Tyler and Whig members of Congress reached such a fevered pitch that a House Committee drafted articles of impeachment for the first time in American history. The split between Tyler and the Whig leadership motivated the Whigs to look elsewhere for a candidate capable of holding on to the White House. Whig Party leaders briefly considered General Winfield Scott and firebrand Senator Daniel Webster for the presidential nomination. However, they ultimately threw their support behind Henry Clay, the "Great Embodiment" of Whig principles.

While Clay easily took the Whig nomination, the Democrats required nine ballots at their convention before choosing Tennessee's James K. Polk. Early in the campaign, former president Martin Van Buren, mustering forces for a comeback, seemed in a strong position. Like Clay, Van Buren sought to evade the divisive issues of slavery and expansion. Both Clay and Van Buren understood that the admission of new states into the Union would raise controversy over whether to allow slaves in the newly admitted states. The southern states feared that in the long run a ban on new slave states would lead to the eventual abolition of slavery in all states. As a result, Van Buren's southern support vanished.

The supporters of the westward expansion movement used the theory of **Manifest Destiny** to provide moral justification for expansionism. Ironically, the Dem-

This Whig campaign badge from 1844 portrays the party's presidential and vice presidential nominees, Henry Clay and Theodore Frelinghuysen. Courtesy of Library of Congress.

ocrats, reputed defenders of a states rights and limited government promoted the acquisition of new territories reaching to the Pacific while their Whig counterparts, to add symmetry to the irony, adhered to their standard nationalist and governmental activist principles but cautiously demurred from continental ambitions.

In contrast to the cautious Whig position on territorial expansion, Democrats demanded that the United States pursue its territorial claims in the Oregon territory. Democrats also demanded that the United States proceed with the friendly annexation of Texas even though such a step might result in a war against Mexico. Northern abolitionists and their sympathizers bristled at the possibility of the annexation of Texas. Southern slave owners and champions of the South coveted Texas. The fact that Oregon would enter the Union as a free state did not placate abolitionist opposition to Texas annexation.

Older issues lingered. The Whigs held to their pro-bank, soft currency position. For example, the Whig platform advocated a protective tariff to protect domestic labor from competition. The Democrats, for the most part, maintained opposition to a national bank and stood firmly behind their hard money policy. Accordingly, the Democratic platform reaffirmed support for limited government, laissez-faire economic policies, governmental frugality, restrictions on abolitionism, protection of presidential veto power, and further resistance to the chartering of national banks.

To the dismay of the Whig Party and Henry Clay, the Democratic Party and James K. Polk turned the election of 1844 into a referendum on expansionism and the annexation of Texas. Clay's ambivalence and well-publicized vacillation on Texas annexation and general expansionism seriously undercut his support in both key southern and northern states. In sharp contrast, Polk was unequivocal in his views toward expansion and annexation. Throughout the campaign, Polk preached Manifest Destiny and the annexation of Texas and Oregon even if such a course of action might lead to war with Mexico and Britain. Efforts by the Whig Party to belittle Polk's qualifications for President led to the widespread use of the **"Who Is Polk?"** slogan by supporters of Clay. Polk supporters countered with **"Polk and Texas, Clay and No Texas."** In the end, Polk pulled out a narrow victory based largely on widespread support for expanding the boundaries of the United States northward and southward.

The Liberty Party, now into its second general election, affirming the "cardinal doctrine of true Democracy [and] pure Christianity," resolutely stood for the abolition of slavery. The party nominated James G. Birney as standbearer.

The election of 1844 turned out to be the closest since 1824. Polk and his running mate, Ambassador George M. Dallas of Pennsylvania, won 49.5 percent of the popular vote and carried fifteen states with 170 electoral votes. Henry Clay received 48.1 percent of the popular vote and 105 electoral votes. The Liberty Party received 62,300 votes, a significant number since Polk only won the popular vote by 38,000 votes.

In the aftermath of the campaign of 1844, war fever with Great Britain intensified. The slogan **"Fifty-four Forty or Fight"** became the most frequent chant for Americans opposed to any concessions to end the dispute over the boundary between the Oregon Territory and Canada. In the end, negotiations between Great Britain and the United States set the northern boundary of the United States at the 48th parallel. But before Polk left office in 1849, the United States had annexed Texas and had defeated Mexico in a war that stripped Mexico of all of its territory above the Rio Grande.

Suggested Readings: Sam W. Haynes, Oscar Handlin, eds., *James K. Polk and the Expansionist Impulse* (New York: Longman, 1997); Arthur M. Schlesinger, Fred Israel, and William P. Hansen, eds., *History of American Presidential Elections, 1789–1968*, Vol. 1 (New York: Chelsea House, 1985).

Campaign of 1848

Hunkers, Barnburners, Free Soilers, and "Old Rough and Ready" all entered America's political lexicon in the campaign of 1848. With the establishment of the Free Soil Party, the specter of slavery continued to haunt presidential politics.

Again the Whig Party turned to a war hero in an effort to recapture the White House. Mexican War hero Zachary Taylor seemed the perfect candidate to take advantage of expansionist longing that had constituted such a key factor during

This banner from the 1848 campaign portrays the Democratic presidential and vice presidential nominees, Lewis Cass and William O. Butler. Courtesy of Library of Congress.

the **Campaign of 1844**. William O. Butler of Kentucky was tapped for the party's vice presidential candidate. General Butler had distinguished himself as a volunteer during the Mexican-American War. Similarly, the Democratic Party turned to War of 1812 veteran Lewis Cass of Michigan. Although Cass came from a free state, he had recently expressed his support for the doctrine of "squatter's sovereignty," a principle which argued that the issue of slavery be independently resolved by the citizens in the states and territories, absent from any intervention by the federal government. The Free Soil Party nominated former president and New York politico Martin Van Buren as their presidential candidate and Charles Francis Adams, famous son of John Quincy Adams (a former rival of Van Buren), of Massachusetts as the Free Soil Party's vice presidential nominee.

Ironically, Whig nominee Zachary Taylor, plantation owner and a reputedly cruel master of over 100 slaves, quietly favored the policy of limiting slavery to those states that presently allowed slavery. He saw no reason to allow slavery into areas where sugar and cotton were not major crops. Yet, during the campaign, most southerners believed that Taylor fully supported slavery and its expansion into the new western territories.

Because of Taylor's long and distinguished military record, the Whig Party hoped that the public would ignore the fact that Taylor refused to take public position on a wide range of controversial issues. By focusing the entire campaign on Taylor's distinguished war record, the Whig Party helped to repeat the successful **Campaign of 1840**, in which General William Henry Harrison defeated the incumbent President Van Buren. Prior to winning the 1848 Whig presidential nomination, Taylor fought with distinction in the northwestern theater of the War of 1812, the Black Hawk War, and the Second Seminole War in Florida and finally played a key role in the Mexican-American War battles of Palo Alto and Buena Vista. Taylor's lack of political experience had not stood in the way of Taylor defeating such Whig luminaries as Daniel Webster and the venerable Henry Clay and fellow Mexican-American War hero, General Winfield Scott, for the Whig Party's presidential nomination.

In the Democratic Party, division over slavery created serious fissures that weakened the party's ability to attract both northern and southern voters. Controversy over the Wilmot Proviso (1846), a failed attempt to ban slavery from the new territories, seriously polarized the party along lines similar to factions within the New York delegation: the conservative Hunkers who evaded the slavery issue and the reformist Barnburners who vehemently attacked it.

Following the anti-slavery precedent set by the Liberty Party during the **Campaign of 1844**, the new Free Soil Party combined elements of Democratic Barnburners and New England abolitionists. By nominating Van Buren, the Free Soil Party helped to provide a political voice to prevent the further expansion of slavery into any new states. Coining the slogan, **"Free Soil, Free Labor, Free Speech, and Free Men,"** the Free Soil Party embarked on a crusade directed at limiting the further spread of the "Peculiar Institution."

Taylor and Fillmore polled 163 electoral votes to 127 for Cass and Butler. The 36 electoral votes received from New York proved the difference in the contest. Had the defecting Barnburner Democrats remained in the fold, Cass might very well have won the election. Equally significant, Van Buren took 120,510 popular votes with him to the Free Soil cause, leaving 114,318 for the remaining Democrats. Taylor received 218,603 popular votes in New York, 16,225 less than the combined vote of Cass and Van Buren.

Sadly, Taylor would serve as president from March 5, 1849 until his sudden death on July 9, 1850.

Suggested Readings: Paul F. Boller, *Presidential Campaigns* (New York: Oxford University Press, 1984); Arthur M. Schlesinger, Fred Israel, and William P. Hansen, eds., *History of American Presidential Elections, 1789–1968*, Vol. 1 (New York: Chelsea House, 1985).

Campaign of 1852

During the late 1840s, the growing dispute over the future status of slavery in new states and territories eroded the Union. To prevent further decay, congressional leaders crafted the Compromise of 1850. Under the compromise, Congress agreed to admit California as a free state and end the slave trade, but not slavery itself, in the District of Columbia. In return, Congress enacted legislation requiring citizens of free states to return escaped slaves to their Southern masters. Finally, the compromise left it up to the citizens of new territories and states to resolve the free state–slave state issue. Typically, instead of resolving the dispute, the compromise only intensified animosity between the issue's opposing camps.

A competitive slate of candidates sought the 1852 Whig Party nomination. The list included President Millard Fillmore, Daniel Webster of Massachusetts and

Mexican-American hero General Winfield Scott. On the 53rd ballot, Scott defeated Fillmore and Webster. During the fight over the nomination, Scott had guarded his position on the enforcement of the Fugitive Slave Law. Almost immediately upon receiving word of the nomination, Scott finally expressed his support for the controversial law. Scott's campaign was consequently hobbled among New York's many Free Soil partisans, and a number of New York Whigs defected to the Free Soil Party.

Similarly, the Democratic Party, like Caesar's Gaul, was divided into three major factions: cross-regional Unionists led by James Buchanan of Pennsylvania, young Stephen A. Douglas of Illinois and previous nominee Lewis Cass of Michigan; northern Free Soil radicals allied with Martin Van Buren's Albany Regency; and southern Fire Eaters identified with the indomitable John Calhoun's extreme sectionalism. Young Douglas, "the Little Giant," enjoyed celebrity in the West but had yet to build a national following. Buchanan, the most conservative candidate, vigorously pursued the nomination, but fell short of a majority at the convention.

New England politicians, hoping to revive their national influence, threw their early support behind New Hampshire's Justice Levi Woodbury, an old school Jacksonian who was neutral on the slavery issue. When Woodbury died in 1851, many New England Whigs committed support to New Hampshire's Franklin Pierce. It was to Pierce that the Democrats turned on the 49th ballot, breaking a convention deadlock. The convention selected Alabama's Senator William King for the second spot on the ticket in an effort to provide the ticket sectional balance.

Spinning the new slogan, "We Polked 'em in '44, we'll Pierce 'em in '52," the Democratic Party reached back to the days of Andrew Jackson for campaign strategies designed to overcome sectional differences. Pierce supporters lauded him as a patriot and war hero cut from the same bolt as Old Hickory himself. "Granite Clubs" sprouted across the nation celebrating his Granite State solidity, raising "Hickory Poles to the honor of the Young Hickory of the Granite Hills." Democrats targeted Scott, describing him as **"Old Fuss and Feathers,"** a vain, conceited, and arrogant fop. Whig supporters of Scott countered with the slogan **"First in War, First in Peace."**

In the end, Pierce received 50.8 percent of the popular vote and 252 electoral votes. Although Scott received 43.9 percent of the popular, he only managed to win 42 electoral votes. John P. Hale, the Free Soil Party's presidential candidate, received only 4.9 percent of the popular vote. However, the Free Soil Party made a strong showing in the states of Ohio, Massachusetts, New York, Vermont, Wisconsin, and New Hampshire. In a cautious mood, tentative voters admittedly saw in Pierce the safer choice.

Suggested Readings: Paul F. Boller, *Presidential Campaigns* (New York: Oxford University Press, 1984); Arthur M. Schlesinger, Fred Israel, and William P. Hansen, eds., *History of American Presidential Elections, 1789–1968*, Vol. 1 (New York: Chelsea House, 1985).

Campaign of 1856

In the off-year campaign of 1854, opponents of the extension of slavery into new territories and states met in Ripon, Wisconsin, followed by a larger meeting in

Jackson, Michigan. Those attending these two meetings sought to establish a new political party in response to passage of the Kansas-Nebraska Act of 1854. The Act opened the way for the citizens of the Kansas and Nebraska territories to independently decide the issue of slavery for themselves. From these meetings the new Republican Party was established, quickly emerging as a significant political force throughout the North and West, and even within pockets inside the Border States.

In June of 1856, the Republicans held their first national presidential nominating convention in Philadelphia, Pennsylvania. Their platform strongly opposed the further expansion of slavery, expressed its support for the legitimacy of the free-state Topeka Constitution of the Kansas Territory while calling for the immediate admission of Kansas as a free state, opposed the unilateral annexation of Cuba as a slave state, lent government support for a transcontinental railroad, and, in a direct attack against the new Mormon religion, recommended prohibiting polygamy in the United States. Famed explorer and adventurer John C. Fremont was selected as their first presidential nominee. Fremont supporters quickly spliced Fremont's name into a new party slogan, **"Freedom, Freemen and Fremont!"** The convention selected New Jersey's W. L. Dayton for the bottom of the Republican ticket.

Adding to political complexities, the country had recently experienced a growing xenophobic and religiously intolerant **nativism issue.** Characterized as anti-immigrant and anti-Catholic, the nativist movement drew supporters from reactionary elements of both the Whig and Democratic parties. Initially interested in quietly controlling elections behind the scenes from within the major parties, the secretive "Know-Nothings," grew into the American Party. When Papal Emissary Cardinal Bedini visited the United States in 1853, widespread anti-Catholic sentiment became manifest, providing a significant boost to the "Know-Nothing" movement. The "Know-Nothings" supported the strict regulation of immigration and further limitations on citizenship eligibility. In an effort to bring legitimacy

Col. JOHN C. FREMONT,
REPUBLICAN CANDIDATE FOR PRESIDENT OF THE UNITED STATES.

Banner for John C. Fremont, 1856 Republican candidate for president. Courtesy of Library of Congress.

to the movement, the American Party nominated former Whig President Millard Fillmore as their presidential candidate. Any hope that the American Party would become a major factor in the 1856 campaign ended when the party splintered over the slavery issue. The Free State faction of the American Party threw their support behind Fremont and the Republicans, while the southern wing of the party held firm behind Fillmore.

Challenged by the emerging Northern Republican Party and the insurgent "Know-Nothings," the Democratic Party held their National Convention in Cincinnati, Ohio. Surprisingly, President Franklin Pierce did not actively seek the Democratic presidential nomination. James Buchanan of Pennsylvania and Stephen Douglas of Illinois arrived at the Democratic Convention as the leading contenders for the Democratic presidential nomination. On the 16th ballot, Douglas withdrew and the party settled on the less controversial James Buchanan, popularly known as "Old Buck." The convention then selected John C. Breckinridge of Kentucky as Buchanan's running mate. With "Buck and Breck!" as their rallying slogan, the Democrats advanced a platform supporting "popular sovereignty" and the Kansas-Nebraska Act, and condemning Know-Nothing intolerance as contrary to "the spirit of toleration and enlarged freedom which peculiarly distinguishes the American system of popular government."

Faced with the growing possibility of a Republican victory, the Democratic Party desperately resorted to mudslinging tactics to defeat Fremont instead of standing on the issues. In an effort to build a wedge between more tolerant Northern Republicans and anti-Catholic "Know-Nothings," Buchanan supporters cynically alleged that Fremont, an Episcopalian, was really a Catholic. Democrats also smeared Fremont as a drunkard and a cruel tyrant.

Additionally, the Democrats referred to the upstart party as "Black Republicans," which shamefully sought to inflame anxieties potentially held by many white voters that a Republican victory would lead to equal rights for African Americans. Buchanan supporters also prophetically argued that a Republican victory would

JAMES BUCHANAN,
DEMOCRATIC CANDIDATE FOR PRESIDENT OF THE UNITED STATES.

Banner for James Buchanan, 1856 Democratic candidate for president. Courtesy of Library of Congress.

lead to secession of southern slave states and a possible armed confrontation between the North and South. "No Sectionalism" became one of the key slogans of the Buchanan campaign.

The Republican Party embraced the underdog role against the establishment candidacies of Buchanan and Fillmore. To mobilize their supporters, Republicans adopted many traditional Democratic and Whig campaign tactics such as parades and barbecue rallies. Capitalizing on Fremont's role in the Bear Flag Revolt, Republicans formed "Bear Clubs" in California with counterpart **Wide-Awake clubs** in the East. Quite oddly, partisans at some rallies even wore black face paint and called themselves "White Negroes" as a tasteless visual response to the racial aspect of the slavery issue.

Buchanan won in November with 500,000 more popular votes than Fremont, nearly a million more than Fillmore. Buchanan received 174 electoral votes from nineteen states. On the other hand, the Republican Party did surprisingly well for a new party. Fremont won 114 electoral votes from eleven states, including the electoral votes of New York, Ohio, and Massachusetts. Although the Democratic Party prevailed once again, the Republican Party demonstrated immediate political clout at the national level.

Suggested Readings: Paul F. Boller, *Presidential Campaigns* (New York: Oxford University Press, 1984); Arthur M. Schlesinger, Fred Israel, and William P. Hansen, eds., *History of American Presidential Elections, 1789–1968*, Vol. 1 (New York: Chelsea House, 1985).

Campaign of 1860

During the **Campaign of 1856**, the Democratic Party had ominously warned that the election of a Republican president would provoke "secession and revolution." Between the end of the 1856 election campaign and the beginning of the campaign of 1860, sectional polarization over the slavery issue exponentially intensified. *Scott v. Sanford*, the infamous "Dred Scott Case" of 1857, irrevocably demarcated political allegiance. In the decision, the high court effectively nullified the Missouri Compromise by holding that as "articles of merchandise" slaves could be taken as property anywhere in the United States, thus even free states were forced to recognize ownership of slaves as legally legitimate. The decision split the Democratic Party over regional lines. Northern Democrats disagreed with the decision because it destroyed the party doctrine of popular sovereignty. Southern Democrats regarded the decision as a vindication of the rights of individuals to own slaves anywhere within the boundaries of the entire United States.

Unable to close the breach, the Democrats broke into two conventions. Northern Democrats held their convention in Baltimore while the Southern Democrats held their convention in Charleston, South Carolina. The Baltimore convention nominated Stephen Douglas of Illinois as the presidential candidate of the Northern wing of the Democratic Party and the Charleston convention nominated John C. Breckinridge of Kentucky as their champion. Breckenridge received the endorsement of incumbent lame-duck President Buchanan and former presidents Tyler and Pierce.

Campaign poster for Abraham Lincoln, 1860 Republican candidate for president. Courtesy of Library of Congress.

ABRAHAM LINCOLN

Much like the 1856 Democratic platform, the platform of the Northern Democrats reasserted the defense of popular sovereignty, support of the Fugitive Slave Laws, annexation of Cuba, and the westward expansion of the railroad. The platform of the Southern Democrats included similar planks on issues such as Cuba and the railroads, but added the more insistent demand for the protection of slavery, declaring that ". . . all citizens of the United States have an equal right to settle with their property in [a] Territory, without their rights, either of person or property, being destroyed or impaired by Congressional or Territorial legislation."

Republicans, who numbered both moderates who conceded tolerating slavery only where it existed in the hopes of its gradual extinction and "radicals" who demanded immediate and direct abolition, were universally incensed over the Dred Scott decision. Moderate Republicans feared that the decision would allow the spread of slavery to new territories and even to current free states. Radical Republicans saw the decision as vindication of their view that complete and rapid abolition constituted the only viable salvation of the union. The moderate wing of the Republican Party prevailed and nominated Abraham Lincoln of Illinois, recently famous through his remarkable performance in the 1858 senatorial campaign debates against Douglas, as their presidential candidate.

Those few remaining Whigs who had folded into the Republican Party gathered in Baltimore to form the Constitutional Union Party and nominate John Bell for president. Their brief platform consisted of one resolution to the effect of pledging patriotic devotion to the defense of the Constitution, the Union, and the law. Bell offered nothing on the issue of slavery, but he was on record as having earlier supported John Quincy Adams's denunciation of the congressional gag order blocking petitions against slavery. Bell's silence on slavery in the 1860 campaign caused critics to lampoon him as a "Do Nothing" candidate with no allegiance, "no North, no South, no East, no West—no Anything."

The Republican Party conducted a vigorous campaign that made use of every available method to get out the vote for Lincoln. Republican slogans included, **"Free Homes for Free Men"**; **"Millions for Freedom, Not One Cent for Slavery"**; **"The Constitution and the Union, Now and Forever"**; **"Slavery Is a Moral, Social, and Political Wrong"**; **"Vote Yourself a Farm"**; and with a reference to a famous biblical line cited by Lincoln in his debates against Douglas, **"A House Divided Against Itself Cannot Stand."** With the help of **Wide-Awake clubs**, the Republican Party conducted numerous rallies and marches replete with songs celebrating Lincoln. To his supporters Lincoln was "Honest Abe," the "Rail Splitter," the "People's Nominee," slogans drawing upon his bona fide humble origins. Lincoln cagily remained distant from the campaigning, leaving it to the Wide-Awakes and other political allies such as New York's William Seward and Kentucky's Cassius Clay to mount the campaign stage.

Lincoln carefully dealt with the slavery issue during his campaign. Throughout his political career, Lincoln had openly criticized slavery on four counts: as patently immoral, illogical, contrary to the political creed of the nation as affirmed in the Declaration of Independence, and in violation of the economic principles of free labor. As a moderate, Lincoln had favored gradual abolition, arguing that the containment of slavery would eventually lead to its natural extinction. Lincoln had opposed the Mexican War because the acquisition of vast new western lands would stimulate a counterforce to this natural extinction. In line with Lincoln's views, the Republican platform denounced the pro-slavery Lecompton Constitution of Kansas; scolded the Supreme Court for perversely, inhumanely, and criminally restoring the "slave trade, under cover of [the] national flag . . ."; asserted that the "normal condition of all the territory of the United States is that of freedom . . ."; and denied "the authority of Congress, of a territorial legislature, or of any individuals, to give legal existence to slavery in any territory of the United States."

With a badly split Democratic Party, Stephen Douglas invested tremendous energy into the campaign. The Little Giant traveled extensively, addressing large crowds throughout all sections. Douglas refused to abandon his support for the doctrine of popular sovereignty or to comment either way on the moral considerations of slavery.

Shamefully, the campaign of 1860 grew ugly. Hostile political prints presented cruel and racist images of a simian Lincoln fraternizing with slaves and favoring interracial "free love."

Largely as the result of strong support in electoral rich northern states, Lincoln won the election with only 39.9 percent of the popular vote but gained 180 electoral votes, securing the needed majority. Lincoln's percentage of the 1860 popular vote would become and remain the lowest in American history for a winning candidate. Although Douglas received 29.5 percent of the popular vote, he only managed to win 12 electoral votes from the states of Missouri and New Jersey. Southern Democratic candidate, John C. Breckinridge, received 18 percent of the popular vote and 72 electoral votes, all from southern slave states. Interestingly, Constitutional Union candidate John Bell only received 12.6 percent of the popular vote but won 39 electoral votes from the states of Virginia, Kentucky, and Tennessee.

True to their word, Southern leaders began the movement to break from the Union. South Carolina, historically at the center of Fire Eater agitation, moved first to secede from the Union. Other slave states soon joined South Carolina to form the rebellious Confederate States of America.

Suggested Readings: Paul F. Boller, *Presidential Campaigns* (New York: Oxford University Press, 1984); David Emerson Fite, *The Presidential Campaign of 1860* (Port Washington, NY: Kennikat Press, 1967); George Harmon Knoles, *The Crisis of the Union, 1860–1861* (Baton Rouge: Louisiana State University Press, 1965); Arthur M. Schlesinger, Fred Israel, and William P. Hansen, eds., *History of American Presidential Elections, 1789–1968*, Vol. 1 (New York: Chelsea House, 1985).

Campaign of 1864

In early 1864, even with Union victories at Gettysburg and Vicksburg, Lincoln faced defeat in the upcoming presidential election. Many Northerners blamed Lincoln for numerous military blunders by Union forces. The dismal state of affairs led some of Lincoln's advisors to recommend that Lincoln might use his wartime powers to delay the presidential election until the end of the crisis. "We cannot have a free government without elections," Lincoln mused, "and if the rebellion could force us to forego, or postpone a national election, it might fairly claim to have already conquered and ruined us." Thus the campaign of 1864 became the first democratic election held during a time of civil war.

Concern over the ability of Lincoln to win the 1864 presidential election caused some Republican factions to quietly consider possible alternatives. The list included Salmon Chase, Lincoln's secretary of the treasury, war hero Benjamin Butler, 1856 Republican presidential nominee John C. Fremont and even General Ulysses S. Grant. Hopes of a draft Grant movement died when Grant made clear he had absolutely no interest in running for president.

On the other hand, the fact that the Northern Democratic Party had broken into war and peace factions, made it much more difficult for the Democratic Party to mount a strong challenge to any Republican candidate. "War Democrats," "Peace Democrats," and "Copperheads," fought for control of the Democratic Party. Many Northerners regarded Copperhead Democrats as treasonous because of their open sympathies to the Confederate cause. Owing to Lincoln's overtures, "War Democrats," joined with pro-Lincoln Republicans to form the Union Party. In May 1864, the Republican Party convened its nominating convention in Chicago. By this time, Senator William H. Seward of New York became Lincoln's principal challenger. Although Seward led the first and second ballots, Lincoln won the nomination on the third ballot. In a move to broaden support for the Lincoln candidacy, the party dumped Radical Republican and incumbent Vice President Hannibal Hamlin from the ticket. Lincoln strategically replaced Hamlin with "War Democrat" Andrew Johnson of Tennessee.

Led by the Radicals, the Republican platform broke from the gradualist/containment position regarding slavery affirmed in the platforms of 1856 and 1860 and now adopted a direct abolitionist position. The party officially stated that the cause of the war was slavery, and demanded its "utter and complete extirpation from the soil of the Republic. . . ." The Republican platform also demanded "un-

Campaign banner for the 1864 campaign of Democratic presidential candidate George B. McClellan and vice presidential candidate George H. Pendleton. Courtesy of Library of Congress.

conditional surrender" of all rebel forces, rejecting all suggestions of compromise with Confederate rebels. Equally important, the platform endorsed Lincoln's Emancipation Proclamation by guaranteeing the "full protection of the laws" to freed slaves serving in the Union Army. Rejecting the pre–Civil War nativism movement, the platform encouraged foreign immigration, particularly as a means of asylum for those fleeing from old-world oppression.

Even though the party as a whole now supported immediate rather than gradual abolition, Radical Republicans wanted more drastic social reform at the end of the war, including punitive measures targeted at the old Southern slaveocracy. When Lincoln pocket vetoed the Wade-Davis Manifesto outlining reconstruction measures more extreme than Lincoln's moderate plan, Radical Republicans attempted a break from the party with the intent of nominating John Fremont as an alternative candidate. Encouraging news from the war front led Fremont to abandon his plan.

The Democrats, divided and estranged from their southern base by rebellion, turned to General George B. McClellan, Lincoln's ineffective, former commander of the Army of the Potomac. Conservative in his views, McClellan openly preferred slavery to emancipation. While commanding the army, he refused to protect escaped slaves and obeyed the old Fugitive Slave Law. However, unlike Copperheads, McClellan believed fervently in preserving the Union. The platform of the Northern Democratic Party reaffirmed its commitment to the Constitution and the Union, and drew upon fidelity to both in demanding the "immediate cessation of hostilities [with the South]." The Democratic platform accused Lincoln and his administration of violating the Constitution by suspending basic civil liberties. The platform remained silent on slavery, but Democrats in general opposed abolition.

Lincoln and his supporters made use of the same campaign tactics that had proven effective during 1860. **Wide-Awake clubs** conducted torchlight parades through major northern cities. Lincoln supporters rallied around three prominent slogans: **"Don't Change Horses in Mid-Stream,"** "The Constitution and the Union, Now and Forever," and "Slavery Is a Moral, Social, and Political Wrong." Lincoln partisans insulted McClellan's lackluster war record, and made much of the tension between the two men during the early months of the war.

Taking the low road, McClellan's campaign relied on attacks on Lincoln's character. Democrats called Lincoln a corrupt and incompetent tyrant, a buffoon, a fanatic, a third-rate lawyer, a filthy storyteller, a ridiculous joke incarnate, a liar, an ignoramus, a butcher, and a baboon. In the end, McClellan's campaign fizzled when General Sherman victoriously led Union forces through the South in his relentless march to the sea. Lincoln amassed a record 2,213,655 popular votes, or 55 percent, without a single vote cast for him in the South. In the process, Lincoln received 212 electoral votes. McClellan won only 21 votes from three states. Lincoln became the first president since Andrew Jackson in 1832 to win a second term.

Sadly, less than one month after delivering a compassionate inaugural address "with malice toward none, with charity for all," calling for the rapid and complete reunification of the republic, Lincoln tragically became the first president slain by an assassin.

Suggested Readings: Paul F. Boller, *Presidential Campaigns* (New York: Oxford University Press, 1984); Arthur M. Schlesinger, Fred Israel, and William P. Hansen, eds., *History of American Presidential Elections, 1789–1968*, Vol. 1 (New York: Chelsea House, 1985).

Campaign of 1868

The 1865 assassination of President Abraham Lincoln thrust Vice President Andrew Johnson into the White House. As a border state Democrat, Johnson had nothing in common with the Radical Republican wing of the Republican Party. Almost immediately upon assuming the presidency, Johnson found himself at war with the Radical Republicans over how to reconcile with the South. Johnson wished to follow Lincoln's plans for establishing lenient conditions hastening the South's return to the Union. In sharp contrast, Radical Republicans, for various reasons, sought to impose numerous requirements on reentry. Ultimately, the dispute between Johnson and Radical Republican members of Congress led the House of Representatives to impeach Johnson. One vote in the Senate saved Johnson from removal. Hobbled as a lame duck, the Republican Party began a search for a candidate who would not stand in the way of Radical Republican leadership in Reconstruction.

The Republicans, now formally under the name of the National Union Republican Party, naturally turned to General Ulysses S. Grant, the hero "who saved the

Campaign banner for the 1868 Republican ticket of Ulysses S. Grant and Schuyler Colfax. Courtesy of Library of Congress.

Union," to carry the banner into the election of 1868. Young and politically inexperienced at age 46, Grant had an inexhaustible supply of political capital. The party supported his ascent with unanimity. For the first time in the history of political conventions, a small number of black delegates, all from the South, participated. For vice president the convention nominated Indiana's Schuyler Colfax, Radical and former Speaker of the House, further demonstrating the power of the party's Radical wing.

Operating under the slogan, "Let us have peace" from Grant's letter of acceptance, the Republican platform affirmed Congressional control over Reconstruction, demanding equal political rights for all. Foreshadowing the emergence of the **currency issue** as one of the most contested issues during the post–Civil War period, the Republican Party adopted a **hard money** currency position that opposed the printing of large numbers of greenbacks (paper money) to permit debtors to pay back their debts with cheaper money. The Republican platform also called for the restoration of citizenship rights to those former rebels fully cooperating with Reconstruction efforts.

The Democrats held their convention in New York City's Tammany Hall. Interestingly, the convention welcomed the participation of a number of southern political leaders. Choosing a candidate proved difficult. Early in the year rumors circulated that Chief Justice Salmon Chase might make a run at the nomination. Chase had the support of northeastern business Democrats as well as the endorsement of New York power broker Horatio Seymour, who would preside at the convention. Chase had also been considered as a possible Republican presidential candidate.

Southern Democrats would not support a Chase candidacy. Ohio's George Pendleton, the party's candidate for vice president during the **Campaign of 1864**, led early but lost the support needed to secure the two-thirds majority needed to carry the nomination. Although supporters of General Winfield S. Hancock of

Campaign banner for 1868 Democratic presidential candidate Horatio Seymour and his vice presidential running mate Francis Preston Blair. Courtesy of Library of Congress.

Pennsylvania managed to build considerable support for his candidacy, Hancock also failed to obtain sufficient support. In the end, the Democratic convention turned to Seymour to break the deadlock. The convention then selected General Francis Blair of Missouri for the bottom of the ticket.

The Democratic platform called for the "Immediate restoration of all the States rights in the Union . . . ," rapid payment of the public war debt, frugality in government, political reform in the executive branch, and sympathy for and protection of the rights of labor. Interestingly, the Democratic platform adopted a **soft money** currency platform plank that supported the printing of paper money to serve as legal tender for all debts. The platform saved its harshest criticism for the Reconstruction policies pursued by the Radical Republicans. The platform attacked the Radicals, accusing them of subjecting "ten States, in time of profound peace, to military despotism and Negro supremacy." Included among anti-Reconstruction invective was an accusation by Democrats claiming that the Republicans were attempting to "Africanize" the South at the expense of white citizens.

Throughout the campaign Democrats persistently demanded the end of Reconstruction and the restoration of rights to former rebels who had been stripped of their voting and officeholding rights. Democrats accused Grant of being a drunken, opportunistic butcher. Colfax was accused of having once been an anti-Catholic Know-Nothing. Republicans returned the volley by associating the Democratic Party with treason and rebellion, "Scratch a Democrat and you will find a rebel." Massachusetts Radical Benjamin Butler intensified the drama of the campaign by waving the blood-stained garment of a victim of the Ku Klux Klan. Waving the **Bloody Shirt** would remain a recurring anti-Southern image in subsequent nineteenth-century campaigns. To his credit, Grant remained above the fray throughout the campaign.

Faced with Republican control of the electoral machinery of the Southern states and the continued inability of the voters of Texas, Mississippi, and Virginia to cast a presidential vote, the Democratic Party and Seymour faced a nearly impossible task of defeating popular Northern war hero, Ulysses S. Grant. In November, Grant received a record 3,012,833 popular and 214 electoral votes. Freed slaves cast nearly a half million votes for Grant. Although Seymour received 2,703,249 popular, he only managed to win 80 electoral votes. The black vote, however whittled down by post-Reconstruction tactics of disenfranchisement, would subsequently remain Republican for six decades.

Suggested Readings: Charles H. Coleman, *The Election of 1868: the Democratic Effort to Regain Control* (New York: Columbia University Press, 1933); Arthur M. Schlesinger, Fred Israel, and William P. Hansen, eds., *History of American Presidential Elections, 1789–1968*, Vol. 1 (New York: Chelsea House, 1985); Brooks D. Simpson, *Let Us Have Peace: Ulysses S. Grant and the Politics of War and Reconstruction 1861–1868* (Chapel Hill: University of North Carolina Press, 1991).

Campaign of 1872

Civilian leadership and military command are of different breeds. Corruption, incompetence, nepotism, and dissent against the course of Reconstruction fragmented the Republican Party during the first term of President Ulysses S. Grant's administration. Grant himself, former Union general and war hero, was capable and essentially honest, but poor decisions regarding appointments, based more on loyalty and sentiment than administrative considerations, hurt his personal integrity. Grant produced the most corrupt administration to date by filling offices with favorites and relatives, many of whom were either unfit for their appointments or devoid of moral sense. Scandal gripped the presidency.

Additionally, the Radical Republican goals of Reconstruction began to lose their luster among more moderate partisans. Democrats had decried the Federal military occupation of the South in the campaign of 1868, and as early as 1870, some Republicans were also suggesting the withdrawal of troops, a move that would surely end Reconstruction. New issues now attracted the party's attention.

By the beginning of the 1872 campaign, a faction emerged with the Republican Party that demanded **civil service reform** as a way to control the corruption resulting from the expansion of the "spoils system." Members of the faction included some of the party's more capable and influential leaders, including famed journalist Horace Greeley, Charles Francis Adams (son and grandson of presidents), Justice Salmon P. Chase, Supreme Court Justice David Davis, Senator Lyman Trumbull (author of the Thirteenth Amendment and the Civil Rights Act of 1866), and Missouri Senator Carl Schurz.

Campaign banner for the 1872 campaign of Republican President Ulysses S. Grant and his running mate
Henry Wilson. Courtesy of Library of
Congress.

Led by Schurz, the Liberals split from the main party and convened in Cincinnati to nominate their own presidential candidate. On the 7th ballot, Horace
Greeley won the nomination with Missouri's B. Gratz Brown tapped as his running mate. The Liberal Republican platform included three central planks: civil
service reform, phasing out Reconstruction, and the lowering of high tariffs.

In a unique twist in American political history, the 1872 Democratic Party
Convention gave Greeley the endorsement of the Democratic Party, hoping that
the action would help to weaken the Republicans. Although the Democrats endorsed the candidacy of Greeley, their convention produced a separate platform
that expressed support for the Civil War Amendments, called for **amnesty** for all
former rebels, asserted the supremacy of civilian over military authority, and insisted on extensive civil service reform.

A month after the Liberal Republicans met in Cincinnati, Grant supporters held
their convention in Philadelphia. As before, Grant was nominated without opposition. The convention dropped incumbent Vice President Schuyler Colfax from
the ticket and replaced him with Senator Henry Wilson of Massachusetts. In an
effort to defuse the crisis over the integrity of the Grant administration, the convention adopted a number of progressive planks. The platform reaffirmed statutory
support for the Civil War Amendments, begrudgingly endorsed civil service reform, and continued support for protective tariffs. Significantly the party added a
plank recognizing obligations to women, proposing their "admission to wider

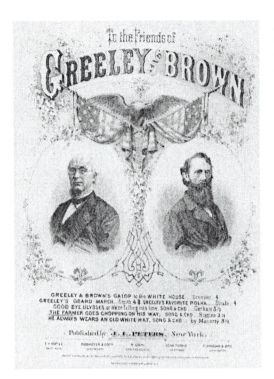

A facsimile of an ornate cloth banner for the 1872 Liberal Republican candidates Horace Greeley (for president) and Benjamin Gratz Brown (for vice president). Courtesy of Library of Congress.

Campaign banner of the 1872 Republican national ticket of Ulysses S. Grant and his vice presidential running mate Henry Wilson. Below the two portraits is a shield inscribed with the words "Let Us Have Peace. The Nation's Choice. Novr. 1872." Courtesy of Library of Congress.

fields of usefulness," and suggesting the "respectful consideration" of "additional rights" for their sex. This constituted the first women's rights plank in American politics and its inclusion won the endorsement of suffragette Susan B. Anthony.

The Liberal Republicans and Democrats overestimated the effectiveness of the civil service reform and amnesty issues and underestimated Grant's personal popularity. Equally important, Greeley proved a weak candidate unable to deal with relentless Republican attacks. Republican-aligned newspapers depicted Greeley as an eccentric troublemaker espousing weird ideas. For instance, political cartoonist **Thomas Nast** incessantly mocked Greeley with caricatures of a pumpkin-headed, mole-eyed know-it-all, easily corrupted and foolishly arrogant. Nast's cartoons also impugned Greeley's loyalty and patriotism through images of the candidate congratulating rebel soldiers, aiding and abetting murderous Klansmen, and scandalously joining hands with the notorious assassin John Wilkes Booth gloating over Abraham Lincoln's grave. Once again, waving the **bloody shirt** worked to great effect against Republican opponents.

Mudslinging was a tactic also employed by the Liberal Republican-Democratic coalition. Greeley supporters trotted out tired accusations of drunkenness and military butchery, and attempted to tie Grant to scandals that had implicated his friends and associates. Matt Morgan, an editorial cartoonist stridently critical of Grant, drew the president as a cretinous cigar-chomping crook, a crowned petty thief swilling mass amounts of liquor, palm opened for bosses to grease. But in the end, Grant was again victorious, soundly defeating the politically naïve Greeley in spite of the scandals of his administration and the insults launched against him.

Suggested Reading: Arthur M. Schlesinger, Fred Israel, and William P. Hansen, eds., *History of American Presidential Elections, 1789–1968* (New York: Chelsea House, 1985).

Campaign of 1876

Coming a full century after the signing of the Declaration of Independence, the campaign of 1876 evinces the ongoing tension between the egalitarian ideal of 1776 and its limited application throughout the social and political life of the republic. Reconstruction had been under way for a decade, but the attempt to restructure politics in America along lines more congruent with the principles of liberty and equality continued to encounter sustained resistance. The continuing dispute, often vituperative, over Reconstruction was further darkened by the shadow of "Grantism" (i.e., the public's reaction to years of misadministration under President Grant, an honest and sincere leader undermined by unscrupulous self-servers). Reconstruction and corruption are the axes defining the rhetorical grid of 1876. A depressed economy served to aggravate the situation and enervate Republican dominance.

Within this context the centennial election was nearly calamitous, even to the point of precipitating civil war. The campaign prior to the election was pocked with bitter invective, prevarication, and scandal mongering. The election itself was an undemocratic fraud. The only self-evident truth marking the centennial of the

Declaration of Independence was that life, liberty, and the pursuit of happiness are ever-mocked and occasionally trumped by callous partisan ambition.

Deep sectional animosity, the legacy of the Civil War, and the bane of Reconstruction reverberated throughout the campaign of 1876. Republican politicians on the hustings forthrightly reminded the electorate that it was the Democratic Party that supported slavery, betrayed the Union, and killed Northern sons—culminating in the assassination of the Great Emancipator himself. Campaigning in late September for the Republican candidate, firebrand Robert G. Ingersoll, invoking the spirit of the **bloody shirt**, reiterated Democratic perfidy:

> "Every State that seceded from the Union was a Democratic State," he declaimed, "Every man that tried to destroy the nation was a Democrat. Every man that shot Union soldiers was a Democrat. . . . Every man that loved slavery better than liberty was a Democrat. The man that assassinated Abraham Lincoln was a Democrat. . . . Every man that wanted the privilege of whipping another man . . . was a Democrat. Every man that raised bloodhounds to pursue human beings was a Democrat. . . . Soldiers, every scar you have . . . was given you by a

Banner portraying the 1876 Democratic ticket of Samuel J. Tilden (for president) and Thomas A. Hendricks (for vice president). Courtesy of Library of Congress.

Democrat. . . . every arm that is lacking, every limb that is gone, is a souvenir of a Democrat. I want you to recollect."

From the perspective of the South, the Republican Party represented an oppressive occupation force, depriving Southern civilization of the dignities of self-government. Even though Reconstruction was losing momentum, Southerners still bristled at the presence of Federal troops in three states (South Carolina, Louisiana, and Florida), and the state governments—described in the pejorative as "carpetbag" regimes—that had been installed in the South after the war were deemed fraudulent, Jacobin, and opportunistic. As the parties were identified with sections, residual *post-bellum* enmities between North and South were the same enmities shared between Republicans and Democrats.

James G. Blaine of Maine and governor and war hero Rutherford B. Hayes of Ohio were the main contenders to succeed Grant as the Republicans' champion. Blaine appeared to have early momentum, and he received a famous endorsement from Ingersoll at the convention. But Blaine's reputation had suffered owing to public scandal involving unscrupulous railroad deals. To Ingersoll, Blaine was a heroic **Plumed Knight** on a crusade to reform the government, but to cartoonist Thomas Nast, Blaine was sketched as a "Tattooed Man," displaying in ink the wages of shady deals, graft, and corruption. Thus a deftly managed opposition steered the party toward Hayes, who had built a reputation as a civil service reformer. With William Wheeler of New York as his running mate, Hayes attacked the spoils system, advocated "rigid responsibility" in civil service through reform, and embraced a more conservative Republican platform that now jettisoned its commitment to Reconstruction. "Hurrah! For Hayes and Honest Ways" was the

President Rutherford B. Hayes, the 1876 Republican presidential nominee. Courtesy of Library of Congress.

slogan leading the GOP onward, affirming distance from government scandal, and abandoning the egalitarian commission of the party's radicals.

The Democrats nominated New York Governor Samuel Tilden, a proven reformer and enemy of corruption, on the first ballot of their convention. Tilden and Hayes were nearly identical in their approach. "Tilden and Reform" was the Democrats' primary slogan. Tilden also favored rolling back Reconstruction and, with Hayes, advancing the policy of hard currency. With two candidates nearly identical in attitude and policy, the parties resorted to the familiar and reliable *ad hominem* rhetoric of the gutter.

Republicans referred to Tilden as a pro-slavery, pro-Confederate friend of the rich, accusing him of tax evasion and swindling. Democrats charged Hayes with murder—alleging the shooting of his own mother—and theft. The facts were not important to either side: the opposition candidate was diabolical.

In spite of the scandal mongering, lighter moments did occur. Mark Twain, who publicly tilted his pointed wit toward an incompetent and corrupt system, endorsed Hayes. A Hayes-Wheeler songbook was released into wide circulation, political campaign music now enjoying a revival after decades of melodic drought in American politics. Greenback and Prohibitionist parties offered alternative diversions. But for the most part the campaign was burdened with mean-spirited aspersions from both directions. Nastiness was the rule, wit and innovation the exception.

The absurdity of the actual election eclipsed the malice of the campaign. Ballot boxes were stuffed, polling was woefully inaccurate, and African American voters suffered widespread intimidation and deprivation of their constitutional rights. When the polls did close, Tilden apparently became the first Democrat in twenty years to win the popular vote with 4.3 million polled, nearly a quarter of a million more than his opponent. But he managed only 184 electoral votes, one short of the needed majority, to Hayes's 165. Twenty electoral votes, however, were disputed: Louisiana (8 votes), South Carolina (7 votes), Florida (4 votes)—all three states still under military occupation—and one rogue vote in Oregon. The two minor parties gathered over 90,000 votes between them—most of them going to the Greenbacks. They did not influence the outcome.

From November 8 until March 2 of the following year, just two days before the scheduled inauguration of the still unnamed new president, the battle for the disputed votes lingered. A divided Congress, unable to fairly resolve the issue, appointed a fifteen-member electoral commission charged with the proper assignment of electoral votes. In the end, the focus of the group was on an electoral quagmire in Florida, and by a partisan vote of 8 to 7, Hayes was awarded all 20 disputed electoral votes and thus the presidency; a decision that nearly sparked armed resistance in some parts of the South. But Hayes was not far removed from Tilden, and a compromise was reached that in effect delivered the *coup de grace* to Reconstruction. Already threatened with reactionary white backlash and Klan terror, the right of the franchise protected under the Fifteenth Amendment was henceforth in practice denied the freed slaves and their descendents. The Hayes-Tilden Compromise, the consequence of partisan self-indulgence, unethical and incompetent election management, and racism in the republic's centennial year insured that the African American vote would be chronically underrepresented, and in some parts of the country persistently absent, for another century. *See also* Tilden and Reform.

Suggested Readings: Robert G. Ingersoll, "Speech at Indianapolis," in *The Works of Robert G. Ingersoll*, Dresden edition, Vol. 9 (New York: C. P. Farrell, 1900), pp. 157–187; Roy Morris, *Fraud of the Century: Rutherford B. Hayes, Samuel Tilden, and the Stolen Election of 1876* (New York: Simon & Schuster, 2003); Keith Ian Polakoff, *The Politics of Inertia: The Election of 1876 and the End of Reconstruction* (Baton Rouge: Louisiana State University Press, 1973); Robert North Roberts, *Ethics in U.S. Government: An Encyclopedia of Investigations, Scandals, Reforms and Legislation* (Westport, CT: Greenwood Press, 2001).

Campaign of 1880

After the tempestuous campaign and election of 1876–1877, the election of 1880 blandly calmed the churning waters of electoral disaffection. The leading candidates, James A. Garfield and Winfield Scott Hancock, were ideologically indistinguishable; their only disagreement amounting to a minor difference on tariff policy.

Both parties produced platforms celebrating their respective past achievements and denouncing the sins of the opposition; the Democrats scolding Republicans for the "great fraud of 1876–1877," the Republicans countering with the **"bloody shirt"** ever-waved in impugning the patriotism and integrity of Democrats. But behind the self-congratulations and invective, party policies blended together. Both parties favored hard currency and restrictions on immigration, specifically targeted against Chinese laborers in the far West. Both parties advocated civil service reform, and neither party lamented the untimely demise of Reconstruction. The Republican Party attached a plank in their platform blaming Southern Democrats for "[obstructing] all efforts to promote the purity and to conserve the freedom of the suffrage," but this reference to the disenfranchisement of black voters did not find its way into the rhetoric of the campaign. Republican songsters did lampoon the Southern practice of bullying black voters away from the polls, but the tenor of the lyric was hardly an example of racial understanding. By and large, the pressing political issues and social currents of the day—disenfranchisement, racism, industrialism, monopolies, revolutions in transportation and communication, and increasing urbanization—were ignored. Only the Greenback-Labor Party addressed aspects of the larger picture, but the party remained decidedly minor, pushed to the fringe by the inertia of the two-party system. The Prohibition Reform Party remained essentially a one-trick pony.

The Republican Party split into two factions: Stalwarts, identified with opposing political and governmental reform, and Half-Breeds, defined not so much by identifiable positions as by their apparent indifference. New York Senator Roscoe Conkling was the Stalwart boss; Maine's James G. Blaine led the Half-Breeds. Together, Conkling and Blaine commanded over 80 percent of the convention delegates, and both agreed that Hayes, whose record for moderate nonpartisanship alienated the party faithful, was correct in his earlier decision not to seek a second term.

Potentially the most interesting event of the campaign of 1880 involved an attempt by a Republican faction, directed by Conkling and the Stalwarts, to nom-

Banner for the 1880 campaign of Republican presidential nominee James A. Garfield and his running mate Chester A. Arthur. Courtesy of Library of Congress.

inate former President Grant for a third term. Grant had been out of the country on a world tour for over two years, and was constantly met with enthusiasm by world leaders, a phenomenon that helped scour away the tarnish of his presidency. Grant's popularity was never higher, for a time his name eclipsed Lincoln as the foremost hero of the Union. But Grant returned from abroad to his hero's welcome too early; by the time of the convention in the summer of 1880, six months after docking in San Francisco, party enthusiasm for Grant had waned. Only Stalwart leaders remained behind the former president. A strong anti-Grant movement called for "Anyone to Beat Grant," and two candidates emerged, Blaine and Ohio's John Sherman. But Blaine still carried the odor of scandal; and Sherman was regarded as suspiciously sympathetic to Catholics, anti-Catholicism still a prejudice harbored by elements in both parties. Throughout most of the convention, Grant remained the front-runner.

Grant was able to sustain a leading plurality of support through 33 ballots but was unable to find the needed majority. On the 34th ballot, Garfield, whose impressive nominating speech on behalf of Sherman had drawn the attention of many delegates, received 17 votes from Wisconsin. Garfield's support quickly accelerated, and in spite of his insistence that he was not a candidate, two ballots later he received 399 votes to Grant's 306, giving him the majority denied the former president.

Garfield's meteoric ascent surprised and humiliated the Stalwarts. It became

Portraits of the 1880 Democratic presidential nominee
Winfield Scott Hancock and his
running mate William H. English. Courtesy of Library of
Congress.

clear to some that Garfield was a faux Dark Horse, and that a degree of machi-
nation beginning before the convention actually positioned Garfield into the advantage at a well-timed moment. Garfield, now the acknowledged spokesman of
the Half-Breed faction, realized that a split party would be vulnerable in the general election. Thus he successfully approached Stalwart Chester A. Arthur of New
York to serve as his running mate.

Democrats initially favored Samuel Tilden, the sentiment being that Tilden had
been unjustly deprived of the presidency by the scandalous usurpation of "Ruth-
erfraud" Hayes. But Tilden suffered declining health and the acrimony of Tammany Hall, and was unable to pursue the nomination. Several potential candidates
were reviewed, but few leading personalities held wide appeal. The Democrats
turned to Pennsylvania's Winfield Scott Hancock, supported in the North for his
heroism at Gettysburg and in the South for the compassionate nature of his service
as occupation governor in Texas and Louisiana. William English of Indiana,
known for his conservative management of state finances, was plucked for the
bottom half of the ticket.

With little difference between Garfield and Hancock, both parties once again
trotted out the tactic of personal smear, albeit lacking the zeal of previous campaign attacks. Republicans delighted in Hancock's thin record, and depicted him
as a political lightweight. The contrast to Garfield, who claimed substantial experience and achievement in public life, was amplified. Democrats responded by
finding dirt in Garfield's past, linking him to the Credit Mobilier Scandal, thus
evoking uncomfortable memories of the Grant years. Democrats circulated a
phony Garfield letter supporting Chinese immigration, a move that probably cost

California. Garfield polled only 10,000 more popular votes than Hancock but was able to amass a significant majority, 214 to 155, in the Electoral College. His presidency was brief; he was soon mortally wounded by a bullet from a gun ignobly fired by an assassin, who upon completing his murderous act, unabashedly confessed the pettiness of his motivation, "I am a Stalwart, and now Arthur is president!"

Suggested Reading: Herbert John Clancy, *The Presidential Election of 1880* (Chicago: Loyola University Press, 1958).

Campaign of 1884

President Chester A. Arthur entered the campaign of 1884 lacking Republican support for a second term. After being sworn in as president following President Garfield's death, Arthur, a reformist, was an able administrator and honest executive but could not sustain broad support within the party. Instead, the Grand Old Party, an alternative name for the Republicans now gaining popular use, tapped James G. Blaine to lead the party to victory but only after favorite candidate General William Tecumseh Sherman made clear that he would not accept a draft. Sherman demurred that "If nominated, I will not run. If elected, I will not serve," leaving the nomination open to the **Plumed Knight**.

Eight years earlier, during the **Campaign of 1876**, Blaine lost the Republican nomination as the result of the Mulligan Letters scandal that had implicated Blaine in railroad influence peddling. The Blaine nomination did not sit well with all Republicans. An influential and vocal minority faction, soon to be known as the Mugwumps, vehemently opposed the Blaine nomination.

Still nursing wounds from the 1876 debacle, the Democratic Party looked for a candidate capable of winning key northeastern states. The leadership of the Dem-

President Chester A. Arthur, who failed to generate sufficient support among Republicans to win the party's nomination in 1884. Courtesy of Library of Congress.

Banner portraying the 1884 Democratic presidential candidate Grover Cleveland and his running mate Thomas A. Hendricks. Courtesy of Library of Congress.

ocratic Party understood that even though it could count on the Solid South, it needed to make inroads into the Republican Midwest and North by appealing to reform-minded Republicans. Democrats believed they found the perfect candidate in Grover Cleveland, the honest governor of New York. Because of Cleveland's impeccable public reputation as a man of integrity, many Republican Mugwumps joined the cause on behalf of **"Grover the Good."**

With partisan allegiance now evenly split between, both parties again resorted to attacking the character of their respective opponents. Blaine supporters uncovered an allegation that Cleveland had fathered a child out of wedlock. To the surprise of many observers Cleveland admitted paternity and hid nothing of his relationship with the mother and child, which included providing financial support and the placement of the child in a respectable home upon the collapse of the mother's health. Nonetheless, Blaine's supporters vilified Cleveland as a debauched libertine, cad, "gross and licentious man," and "moral leper," pounding Cleveland with the chant **"Ma, Ma, Where's My Pa?"**

Cleveland's supporters retaliated, chanting **"Blaine, Blaine, James G. Blaine, the Continental Liar from the State of Maine."** They also referred to Blaine as "Old Mulligan Letters" and "Slippery Jim." As in 1876, Blaine continued to deny any wrongdoing in the railroad scandal despite the fact that newly found evidence raised serious questions about the veracity of Blaine's denials. Typically, all the personal attacks made against Blaine and Cleveland did little to shake partisan allegiance to the two candidates.

Both parties realized that the electoral votes of New York could determine the outcome of the election. Pursuing New York votes nigh to the election, Blaine attended a campaign event for pro-Republican Protestant ministers in New York City. During his introduction of Blaine, the Reverend Samuel D. Burchard launched a stinging indictment of the Democratic Party and Grover Cleveland. Using a phrase that was actually introduced eight years earlier, Burchard referred to the Democratic Party as the party of "Rum, Romanism and Rebellion." Blaine did nothing to repudiate the comments of Burchard. News of the gaffe spread rapidly. By the following day, a few anti-Catholic Republicans embraced the slogan, catching Blaine off guard when he saw the "three R's" prominently displayed in a Republican handbill. On November 1, Blaine issued a weak and convoluted rejection of the sentiment. His apology came too late; the damage was already done as New York's Irish Catholic vote was now amassed against the Republicans.

On Election Day, Cleveland dominated the South and Border States. Blaine carried the Republican strongholds of the Northeast and Midwest with the important exception of New York. With New York's 36 prized electoral votes, Cleveland won the Electoral College by the margin of 219 to 182. Grover the Good became the first Democrat to win a presidential election since James Buchanan. The Republican chant of "Ma, Ma, Where's My Pa?" could now be answered by delighted Democrats, "Gone to the White House, ha, ha, ha!" *See also* "Blaine, Blaine, James G. Blaine, the Continental Liar from the State of Maine"; "Ma, Ma, Where's My Pa?"; "Rum, Romanism and Rebellion."

Suggested Reading: Mark Wahlgren Summers, *Rum, Romanism & Rebellion: The Making of a President, 1884* (Chapel Hill: University of North Carolina Press, 2000).

Campaign of 1888

Grover Cleveland's 1884 victory over James G. Blaine shocked the once-dominant Republican Party. Even though Congress had passed the Civil Service Reform Act of 1883 that reduced the abuses of political patronage, the loss of the White House still meant that the Republican Party lost thousands of patronage appointments. As a result, the Republican Party revived an old issue that they hoped would lead them back to the White House. Tariffs once again emerged as the dominant issue of a presidential campaign.

Cleveland, the incumbent president and the first Democrat to occupy the White House since before the Civil War, held fast to the traditional Democratic position. Since the days of Andrew Jackson, the Democratic Party, by and large, had stood for laissez-faire economic policies, which included low tariffs strongly favored in the South because of the region's historic reliance upon exports. Western states now joined the South in opposing protective tariffs. The Democratic Party's tariff policy, supported by Cleveland, helped to strengthen their Southern base of support. But this eroded Cleveland's tenuous support in the Northeast, which included New York.

At the St. Louis Democratic National Convention, Cleveland easily won renomination. However, growing divisions between conservative and populist wings of the Democratic Party threatened to split the Democratic coalition. The Bourbons of the Northeast and the Redeemers of the South represented the conservative faction of the party, which sought to place states rights at the top of the Democratic Party's agenda. In contrast, the populist wing of the party placed bimetallism or the free coinage of silver at the center of its agenda. Cleveland and conservative

Benjamin Harrison, the 1888 Republican presidential nominee. Courtesy
of Library of Congress.

Democrats supported the gold standard, as did the Republicans. To this end,
Cleveland recommended the suspension of the circulation of silver coins, alienating
Democratic populists. Additionally, Cleveland's sincere efforts to expand civil service reform angered many partisans who believed Cleveland should make full use
of his patronage powers to reward his Democratic supporters.

The Republican National Convention nominated Civil War hero General Benjamin Harrison of Indiana, grandson of William Henry Harrison. Harrison had
the support of James G. Blaine, whose declining health and continued bitterness
over his 1884 loss to Cleveland kept him from entering the race. Harrison won
the nomination on the 8th ballot after beating back a challenge from party veteran
John Sherman.

Significantly, the convention produced a new generation of party leaders, characterized by their close ties to northern banking, commerce, and industry. Ohio
industrialist **Mark Hanna** backed Sherman. Wharton Baker, a prominent finan-
cier, and Stephen B. Elkins, a Blaine loyalist who made his fortune through mining
and land speculation, joined other wealthy industrialists and financiers in support
of Harrison.

Both Harrison and Cleveland chose to conduct **front porch campaigns** by
remaining at home, periodically meeting with supporters and issuing brief statements for distribution by their supporters. Making use of their greater financial
resources, the Republican Party put together a much more effective campaign
organization.

In comparison to the scandal mongering of the **Campaign of 1884**, the 1888 campaign involved little **mudslinging**. One unscrupulous **dirty trick** did damage Cleveland's chances to carry New York. Under the alias of Charles Murchison, George Osgoodby, a Republican fruit-grower from California, wrote a phony letter to Britain's Washington minister. Osgoodby pretended to be a newly nationalized American from Britain requesting advice on which candidate to support in the upcoming election. When the minister, duped by the ruse, responded favorably for Cleveland, Osgoodby shared the British endorsement with the press. The Murchison letter angered New York's Irish Catholic voters who were decidedly anti-British.

Cleveland won the popular vote by a little more than 90,000 votes. However, Harrison won the electoral vote. Again, New York's 34 votes determined the outcome, helping Harrison win 233 electoral votes to Cleveland's 168. A Cleveland victory in New York would have given him 202 electoral votes and Harrison 199. For the fourth time in presidential election history, the candidate with the most popular support failed to take the White House. *See also* "Grover, Grover, All Is Over."

Suggested Reading: Edward Homer Socolofsky, *The Presidency of Benjamin Harrison* (Lawrence: University of Kansas Press, 1987).

Campaign of 1892

In 1892 Grover Cleveland became the first of only two people to formally, nationally, and exclusively win three nominations of a major party for president of the United States. Franklin Roosevelt is the only candidate to match, and eventually surpass, Cleveland's campaign achievement.

Cleveland's nomination set him against the incumbent Benjamin Harrison, his rival in 1888. In spite of sharing the ease of first ballot nomination, both candidates enjoyed only lukewarm support from their parties. Cleveland had earned a reputation for obstinacy, an independent agent not willing to curry the favor of either the party elites or the general voters. Harrison was viewed as dispassionate and aloof, and, like Cleveland, an independent thinker unbound by party discipline. Furthermore, his Calvinist piety alienated even his close supporters.

Prior to the Republican convention, dissatisfied Republicans floated the idea of replacing Harrison with the more popular James G. Blaine. Before the start of the convention, Blaine made clear that his health did not permit him to run. The rumor of a possible Blaine challenge for the nomination opened a rift between Blaine and Harrison, compelling Blaine to resign as Harrison's secretary of state.

Similar to the previous two elections, both parties understood that victory hinged upon a handful of midwestern and northeastern states. To increase his chances in the Midwest, Cleveland, a New Yorker, chose Adlai E. Stevenson of Illinois as his running mate. To balance his ticket, Harrison dropped incumbent Vice President Levi Morton from the ticket to make room for New York publisher Whitelow Reid on his ticket.

Compared to the majority of prior presidential campaigns, the campaign of 1892 lacked intensity. Harrison supporters attempted to resurrect the **bloody shirt** by trying to associate Cleveland and the Democrats with the Confederacy, to little effect. Tariff policy remained the definitive issue. Cleveland refused to compromise his steadfast low-tariff principles that hampered Cleveland's previous campaign. Additionally, despite pressure from the growing populist wing of the Democratic Party, Cleveland refused to support bimetallism and the **free silver** movement.

In 1890, the emerging Populist Party won nine congressional seats in the off-year election. The Populists appealed to farmers, miners, ranchers, and rural Americans who blamed their economic problems on eastern industrialists, bankers, financiers, speculators and railroad magnates. Appealing to the "common man," Populists advocated government action to control the power of corporate trusts and monopolies. Bolstered by its mid-term election victories, the Populist Party nominated former Greenback candidate James Weaver of Ohio for president and James Field of Virginia for vice president. The Populist platform supported free silver, labor reform, universal adult suffrage, and amending the Constitution to provide for the popular election of senators.

Effectively stirring recruits to the people's cause, Mary Lease of Kansas stumped with Weaver throughout the West and South. Exhorting her audience to "raise less corn and more hell," Lease quickly became a central figure in the campaign. Her attacks against the empires of finance epitomized the Populist attitude. "Wall Street owns the country," she declared, and, through parody of a mythic sentiment, declaimed the American state as a "government of Wall Street, by Wall Street, and for Wall Street." Because both parties found themselves vulnerable to charges of plutocracy and elitism, the Populists drew votes away from both parties. However, labor unrest and Harrison's support for high tariffs created more serious problems for the Republicans.

Supporters of high tariffs argued they would protect American jobs by limiting foreign competition. To labor, high tariffs seemed to have the opposite effect. When Andrew Carnegie ordered a significant reduction in the wages of Pennsylvania steel workers, the workers went out on strike. The Homestead strike led to intense violence between the strikers and Carnegie's armed Pinkerton security agents. Many industrial workers blamed Republicans for the anti-labor practices of Carnegie and other industrialists. But instead of throwing their support behind Populist Weaver, many industrial workers threw their support behind Cleveland.

Interestingly, neither Cleveland nor Harrison campaigned aggressively. Burdened by his wife's terminal illness, Harrison had no heart for the campaign. She died a few days before the election. Cleveland appeared more interested in fishing than winning reelection.

In the end, Harrison's lifeless campaign and Cleveland's ability to attract angry industrial workers in midwestern and northeastern states cost Harrison a second term. Cleveland received 46.1 percent of the popular vote against the 43 percent of the popular vote received by Harrison. More important, Cleveland received 277 electoral votes against the 145 electoral votes received by Harrison. To the dismay of the leadership of the Republican Party, Harrison failed to carry the Republican strongholds of Illinois, Indiana, New York, and Wisconsin.

Populist Weaver attracted over a million votes to win four states (Colorado, Idaho, Kansas, and Nevada, with one vote each from Oregon and North Dakota) and 22 electoral votes. While unable to break the stranglehold of the Republican and Democratic parties on the presidency, the success of the Populist signaled the beginning of a major realignment in American politics. *See also* "Grover, Grover, Four More Years of Grover, In He Comes, Out They Go, Then We'll Be in Clover."

Suggested Readings: George Harmon Knoles, *The Presidential Campaign and Election of 1892* (New York: AMS Press, 1971); William R. Hal, *Years of Decision: American Politics in the 1890s* (New York: Wiley, 1978); Homer Edward Socolofsky, *The Presidency of Benjamin Harrison* (Lawrence: University Press of Kansas, 1987).

Campaign of 1896

"You shall not press down upon the brow of labor this crown of thorns, you shall not crucify mankind upon a cross of gold!" Candidate William Jennings Bryan's famous speech illustrates the overheated passion of the election of 1896, which realigned the parties primarily around the issue of bimetallism combined with increasing populism, with sectional allegiance remaining solid in the South with significant gains in the West for the Democrats, while the Northeast and Midwest remained predominantly Republican. Amidst the excitement are found two distinctly disparate candidates: the subdued conservative Republican William McKinley, last of the Civil War veterans, governor of Ohio, protégé of industrialist–king maker **Mark Hanna** and former straddlebug now turned Goldbug; and for the Democrats the young, tempestuous populist Bryan—"the Great Commoner," "the Peerless One," the "Silver Knight of the West."

Sixteen to One was the proposed ratio between the two precious metals, 16 ounces of silver being the equivalent of 1 ounce of gold. Thus proceeded the great campaign over the state of the dollar, a mundane concern that would quickly become the most volatile political question since slavery. Owing to the Panic of 1893, which precipitated an economic catastrophe that nearly ruined American farmers, populist elements within the Democratic Party suddenly waxed in strength. Contrary to the conservative policies of the incumbent Democratic president, Grover Cleveland, who favored the gold standard and economic conservatism, the party's populist wing radicalized, committing partisan energies to a denunciation of the gold standard and steering their platform in a direction that aligned them with the Populist Party. Attempting to shake, once and for all, the **bloody shirt**, Democrats now saw their future in returning to the mythos of Jacksonian democracy. The common man wanted bimetallism and economic reform, and the newly aligned Democrats would deliver.

Supporters of free silver were also numbered among the Republican ranks, but they were drawn primarily from the newly formed western states and thus remained in the minority. At the 1896 convention in St. Louis a small faction of Silverite western Republicans objected to a plank in the platform that opposed free silver. Led by Colorado Senator Henry Teller, the Silverites stalked out of the convention, established the National Silver Party, and eventually threw their support behind the Democrats. With the more populist-oriented Silverites abandoning the GOP, conservative elements in the party met little resistance in the nomination of McKinley. Since the end of Reconstruction, the party of Abraham Lincoln, Frederick Douglass and Thaddeus Stevens had been increasingly ignoring

Campaign portraits of Democratic presidential candidate William Jennings Bryan and his running mate Arthur Sewall. Courtesy of Library of Congress.

its progressive roots while drawing closer to the interest of the industrial and commercial elite. With McKinley's nomination, the turn toward plutocracy seemed complete.

While the Republicans were now seen as the party of wealth, the Democrats, the party that once defended slavery and promoted Southern aristocracy, were emerging as the new champion of the people, ordinary citizen and underprivileged alike. The Democrats nailed planks into their platform supporting populist reforms such as a graduated federal income tax, low tariffs, regulation of industries, and support for the cause of labor. And yet not all Democrats identified with their populist and bimetallist factions. After Bryan's oratorical triumph at the convention roiled the delegates into a revolutionary frenzy, Gold Democrats separated from the party to form the National Democratic Party, nominating John M. Palmer to challenge Bryan. The National Democrats hewed more closely to the older values embodied by Cleveland. But their efforts were against the current; the Democratic Party was moving rapidly to incorporate the populist agenda, and in so doing, absorbing the Populist Party within their ranks. Behind Bryan but objecting to the more conservative nominee for vice president, Arthur Sewall, the Populists insisted on a separate ticket nominating Bryan and Thomas Watson, the latter selected from their own ranks.

The Great Commoner campaigned with unprecedented abandon. McKinley tactically stayed home. Bryan's campaign events resembled charismatic tent revivals; McKinley's effectively combined the proven front porch strategy of Benjamin Harrison with the inexhaustible fund-raising abilities of Hanna and the GOP elite. Bryan traveled thousands of miles to reach the people. The people traveled thousands of miles to reach McKinley. Bryan spoke for hours on end at innumerable venues at an impassioned and febrile pitch; McKinley's speeches were subdued, succinct, and short—and all delivered from the same place. Both sides perceived the campaign as a battle between cosmic forces of good and evil: the bimetallist cause of silver was cast as a sacred battle against the iniquities of gold

William McKinley, the 1896 Republican presidential nominee. Courtesy of Library of Congress.

standard plutocracy, the cause of monometallism explained as the only hope against the demonic forces of rabble-rousing anarchists. Republicans openly charged the Democrats for moving so far to the left that they precipitated socialism, communism, and anarchy. Democrats accused Republicans and Gold Democrats of being duped pawns of the robber barons.

The "Cross of Gold" remained the Democrats' central slogan. The Republicans defiantly maintained that the dollar was "good as gold." The most famous Republican slogan punctuated the promise of economic stability and future prosperity with the phrase a **"Full Dinner Pail,"** which emphasized the traditional reliability of monometallism and conservative policies.

The propaganda mill churned out disinformation from both sides: workers collecting their wages would find their pay envelopes accompanied by Republican flyers admonishing them against the dangers of Democratic irresponsibility, alerting workers to the threat that a vote for Bryan would precede immediate unemployment. Democrats depicted McKinley as a mindless puppet of Hanna, a diminutive figure moved only by the commands of his party boss. Republicans returned the volley with shrill denunciations of Bryan as an ignorant, irreligious madman, seducing the uneducated masses with silken speeches wrought from the spirit of impiety. The "Cross of Gold" speech, widely acclaimed by Bryan's supporters, was criticized by pro-Republican clergy as thoroughly sacrilegious.

McKinley and his running mate, Garret Hobart of New Jersey, held the

Northeast-Midwest axis reflected in their ticket, collecting 271 Electoral College votes and over 7 million popular votes. Winning the entire South and most of the West was not enough for Bryan. With impeccable timing the Republicans regained the White House; an economic recovery had begun toward the end of the campaign year, which, in the exchange of American politics, translates into political capital of inestimable value. *See also* "Advance Agent of Prosperity"; "Cross of Gold" Speech; Free Silver Movement; "Patriotism, Protection and Prosperity"; Sound Money.

Suggested Readings: Paul W. Glad, *McKinley, Bryan, and the People* (Philadelphia: Lippincott, 1964); Stanley Llewellyn Jones, *The Presidential Election of 1896* (Madison: University of Wisconsin Press, 1964); George Frisbe Whicher, *William Jennings Bryan and the Campaign of 1896* (Boston: Heath, 1953).

Campaign of 1900

"Four More Years of the Full Dinner Pail" was the slogan that served the incumbent Republican message. Gold, empire, and trusts were the plutocratic demons attacked by the Democrats. The campaign of 1900 was among the more unremarkable in American political history, save for one source of excitement: the nomination for vice president of Rough Rider Theodore R. Roosevelt, recent hero of the Spanish-American War and current New York governor, to replace the recently deceased incumbent, Garret Hobart. Aside from Roosevelt's charisma, the only element that separates the campaign of 1900 from the more dramatic election of 1896 was the experience, new to the American political psyche, of now numbering among the world's imperial powers. Having shattered Spain in the brief war, the United States now possessed an empire that reached far beyond the North American continent. A new, decidedly modernist America was laboring to be born.

McKinley's opponent, William Jennings Bryan, also won renomination as his party's standard-bearer on the first ballot of an uninspired convention. Bryan initially campaigned by beginning exactly where he ended four years earlier—relaunching jeremiads against the wickedness of gold and reaffirming his enthusiasm for the **free silver movement**, reiterated as "the paramount issue" in anticipation of a strategy in imitation of the 1896 effort. Bryan's recalcitrant reliance on the main issue of 1896 hardened before the convention, his dedication to silver more ardent than ever. However, with the dramatic revival and sustained expansion of the economy—boosted by a bountiful gold strike in the Klondike—bimetallism was an issue that could no longer spark the zealous and pseudo-religious allegiance of the previous campaign. Eventually Bryan's campaign realized that free silver's political capital had been significantly devalued with the onset of prosperity, forcing other issues into the crosshairs. As the campaign aged, the attack was retargeted, for the most part, on trusts and imperialism.

Manifest Destiny had always been understood as a continental ambition. Now that the United States had projected its power not only into the Caribbean but deep into the Philippine Islands, some concern grew over possible conflict between republican principles and imperial aspirations. Anti-imperialist leagues formed op-

Political cartoon indicating the willingness of Democrat William Jennings Bryan to make a second run at the presidency in 1900. © National Archives.

posed to the annexation of the Philippines and the Hawaiian Islands, drawing mostly Democrats into their ranks. Both Bryan and former president Cleveland vocally expressed concern over the fate of a republic that sought empire abroad, and once free silver was de-emphasized, Bryan aimed his rhetorical saber at the bloated and grasping: trusts and empire.

This was a miscalculation. Save for the South, which was a firm Democratic base, the annexation of Pacific territories was a popular course of action. McKinley knew this after touring extensively throughout the West and Midwest, and thus threw his support behind annexation. Bryan turned his oratory toward sympathy for "our brown brothers" in Mindanao, but with little effect. The popularity of the war and its outcome served the Republicans, and placed the Democrats in the risky position of appearing unpatriotic. Bryan alienated former allies such as Silverite and Mugwump Republicans who supported him in 1896, and was uncomfortably backed into the position of criticizing an administration that had overseen both unprecedented economic growth as well as astonishingly one-sided military victory. Events in China helped McKinley's cause. Able to move a large force of U.S. Marines from new bases in the Philippines in response to threats on diplomats during the Boxer Rebellion, McKinley deftly demonstrated the advantages of projected military power. With Roosevelt equipped with martial bravado on board and the Boxer's faced down, anti-imperialism soon withered in the breach.

Bryan turned to the trusts. The Great Commoner appealed to the working class against the excesses of the robber barons, and the Democratic Party disseminated literature denouncing the exorbitant wealth of America's captains of industry and finance. Bryan set his sites on the "Full Dinner Pail," explaining that the use of such a metaphor was in truth demeaning to "the laboring man," who was implicitly and condescendingly portrayed by Republicans as "[being] all stomach [with] neither head nor heart. The Republican party assumes that a laboring man is like the hog that squeals when it is hungry and sleeps when it is full."

Bryan's appeal to labor resulted in a reanimation of his campaign, and gained him needed support in New York, until, in the latter weeks leading up to the election, his judgment began to slip. In mid-October, Bryan inexplicably praised Tammany Hall and its associates, blindly ignoring Tammany's own ties to trusts and allegations of corruption. In late October, Bryan then suddenly shelved his working-class appeal and returned to a reaffirmation of the 1896 platform, and by implication, free silver. He also began to revive the anti-imperialist rhetoric once thought ineffective. By going back to imperialism and free silver, Bryan squandered his temporary momentum.

McKinley never left home, quietly and confidently holding forth from his "front porch" in a fashion even more subdued than the 1896 version of this tactic. Roosevelt, a reluctant candidate for an office he despised, nonetheless proved an asset. Charismatically a match for Bryan and at the height of his popularity, he forged on as a self-described "bull moose," traveling across the country captivating audiences with the force of his personality. **Mark Hanna** disliked McKinley's running mate, but soon appreciated the political capital that he brought to the Republican cause. McKinley's victory was thorough, capturing nearly 900,000 more votes than Bryan, accompanied by a substantial majority in the Electoral College. Regarding Roosevelt askance, Hanna famously admonished McKinley to remain alive for his full term as a guarantee against T.R.'s continued ascent, the vice presidency then being perceived as a political dead end. But the Fates are capricious, and within six months of the inauguration, an obscure anarchist in Buffalo gunned down McKinley, and the Rough Rider was now behind the "bully pulpit."

Suggested Readings: Louis L. Gould, *The Presidency of William McKinley* (Lawrence: Regents Press of Kansas, 1980); Margaret Leech, *In the Days of McKinley* (New York: Harper, 1959).

Campaign of 1904

Teddy Roosevelt, propelled into the White House by an accident of history, became the most popular president in recent memory. A vigorous and visionary leader, Roosevelt began the process of building a national reputation as a progressive. To control the excesses of corporate America, Roosevelt supported the aggressive enforcement of antitrust laws. To safeguard the natural resources of the country, Roosevelt pressured Congress to place millions of acres of forests under federal protection and sought to use these forests as wildlife preserves. He also tightened management of federally owned public land.

Reflecting the roots of the Republican Party, Roosevelt adopted a comparatively sympathetic attitude toward African Americans, reaching out to Booker T. Washington and other black leaders. He punished a postal district in Mississippi for resisting the appointment of an African American postmistress by shutting down all postal services to that area. Roosevelt also supported black participation in the

Republican convention and excoriated Americans for tolerating the lawless brutality of lynching.

In moving the Republican Party back toward the party of Lincoln and taking on the abuses of big business, Roosevelt estranged the new generation of corporate conservatives in the GOP. Although some Republicans circulated the name of Mark Hanna as a potential challenger to Roosevelt, support for this quickly deflated in the light of Roosevelt's overwhelming popularity. To the chagrin of monied interests, Roosevelt forced Hanna out as national party chair, replacing him with a less notable personality, his own secretary of commerce and labor, George B. Cortelyou.

Reflecting his progressive philosophy, Roosevelt stated that "We must treat each man on his worth and merits as a man. We must see that each is given a square deal, because he is entitled to no more and should receive no less." When large trusts and monopolies fixed prices and established artificially low wage rates, government had a moral obligation to intervene to guarantee workers a **"Square Deal."** Roosevelt's promise of a Square Deal became the central principle of his campaign.

The Democrats turned away from William Jennings Bryan in an effort to find a more conservative candidate able to draw more votes. Steering the party away from the Great Commoner, the anti-Bryan wing of the Democratic Party initially courted Maryland's Arthur Gorman. However, Gorman was against the popular Panama Canal project. After Grover Cleveland then made it clear that he was not interested in a third term, the Democratic Party nominated New York judge Alton B. Parker. The convention then selected Henry Gassaway Davis, born during the administration of President James Monroe, as Parker's running mate. In a victory for old Gold Bug Democrats, Parker came out in favor of the gold standard.

With Roosevelt immensely popular with the public, Parker did not have a realistic chance. However, the Democrats fought on, resorting to smear tactics to tarnish T.R.'s reputation. Democrats alleged that Republicans had obtained large campaign contributions from corporations and trusts in return for a "silent understanding" regarding the enforcement of antitrust laws. Roosevelt refuted the charges, indignantly dismissing all allegations as "an atrocious falsehood," and defended Cortelyou's activities as party leader. When Parker failed to produce any hard evidence the public quickly lost interest in the allegations.

Roosevelt enjoyed a landslide victory, 336 electoral votes to Parker's 140. Eugene Debs and the Socialist Party enjoyed a surge in support, quadrupling their popular tally with over 400,000 votes.

In the aftermath of the campaign of 1904, Roosevelt threw his support behind **campaign finance reform** legislation. *See also* Square Deal.

Suggested Readings: Paul F. Boller, *Presidential Campaigns* (New York: Oxford University Press, 1984); Arthur M. Schlesinger, Fred Israel, and William P. Hansen, eds., *History of American Presidential Elections, 1789–1968*, Vol. 1 (New York: Chelsea House 1985).

Campaign of 1908

Despite a level of popularity reminiscent of George Washington and Andrew Jackson, Theodore Roosevelt decided to respect the two-term tradition by not seeking the 1908 Republican presidential nomination. With the full support of Roosevelt, the Republican Party turned to William Howard Taft of Ohio. Much like former Republican president William McKinley, Taft had strong ties to the leaders of major American corporations. Unlike Roosevelt, Taft lacked connections to the progressive movement. However, Taft went out of the way during the campaign of 1908 to underplay his corporate ties and to highlight his strong support for the progressive policies of the Roosevelt years.

After the miserable 1904 campaign of conservative Democrat Judge Alan Parker, the Democratic Party turned for the third time to William Jennings Bryan. Learning a lesson from his stubborn free silver fixation eight years earlier, Bryan now advocated a more balanced and varied set of reforms reflecting the prevailing progressive mood. In addition to the abolition of trusts, Bryan drew on his dedication to the social gospel, which insisted that material prosperity should be pursued and gained but accompanied by charitable programs for the poor. Bryan insisted on only "necessary" taxation, advocated nationalization of the railroads, and denounced the imperialism of the past decade by championing independence for the Philippines.

But Bryan lost confidence when facing Taft on policy, and thus resorted to personal attacks. He criticized the religious beliefs of Taft, a Unitarian, arguing that rejection of the Trinity disqualified a man from holding the White House. Bryan also battled conservative elements of the party who preferred the cautious policies of Cleveland. Above all else, conservative southern Democrats

Campaign handbill for 1908 Republican presidential nominee William Howard Taft. Courtesy of Library of Congress.

pushed Bryan and the Democratic Party to again reassert the doctrine of "states rights."

Taft could not match Bryan's charisma, but Roosevelt was more than equal to the task. After T.R.'s coaching failed to cure Taft of his dry style, the Bull Moose personally took the reigns and charged forward, energetically campaigning on behalf of his friend and chosen heir. Bryan could beat Taft one-on-one but he was thoroughly overshadowed by the progressive achievement and inexhaustible personal power of Taft's ally, the heroic Rough Rider. Frustrated again, the Great Commoner led his party in defeat. *See also* "Let the People Rule."

Suggested Reading: Donald F. Anderson, *William Howard Taft: A Conservative's Conception of the Presidency* (Ithaca, NY: Cornell University Press, 1973). .

Campaign of 1912

The campaign of 1912, one of the most theatric in American history, generated a host of ear-snagging and mind-catching phrases, including **New Freedom, New Nationalism,** Bull Moose Party, Covenant with the People, "Bryanized," "Regulated Competition versus Regulated Monopoly," "My Hat Is in the Ring and I'm Stripped to the Buff!," "Have Another Cup of Coffee?," "I'll Do the Best I Can but There Is a Bullet in My Body," and **"What This Country Needs Is a Good Five-Cent Cigar."** When the dust cleared, an academic named Woodrow Wilson would mount the national stage to signal a new direction for the development of the federal government in the United States.

Four years out of office, an African safari and European tour behind him, and again "feeling like a Bull Moose"—Teddy Roosevelt charged back into the thicket of presidential politics like a force of nature determined to reclaim the Republican

Political cartoon depicting candidates Theodore Roosevelt, Woodrow Wilson, and William Howard Taft before the 1912 presidential election. © National Archives.

Party for the progressive cause. Friend and political benefactor to William Howard Taft four years earlier, T.R. felt betrayed by what he perceived to be Taft's rejection of progressive policies, and set himself to run for an unprecedented third term. Roosevelt's spleen hurled epithets at the "fathead" Taft, opening an irreconcilable breach between the former friends. Between an animated Roosevelt and emerging midwestern progressive star Robert Lafollette, Taft's position in the party was undermined and his very presidency, which had in fact continued elements of Roosevelt's progressive agenda, drifted nearly dead in the water at the launching of the campaign.

Political parties traditionally favor incumbents, and this was no different in 1912. Taft enjoyed the full support of party leaders and the institutional party's full endorsement. But Roosevelt remained universally beloved among the party regulars, and with the introduction of nonbinding presidential primary elections in ten states, Taft's weakness was soon evident as he lost nine states to Roosevelt. But the primaries did not choose the nominee in 1912, the convention did, and at the convention it was Taft who held the cards. Undeterred, Roosevelt blithely broke from the party, declared his candidacy as an independent, and promptly formed the Progressive Party, which naturally assumed the Bull Moose nickname. This broke the Republican Party in two: Taft, representing the conservative element friendlier to business—in spite of his having dismantled more monopolies than Roosevelt before him, and Roosevelt, last champion of progressive reform within the GOP. Lincoln's party was battling over its future and its soul, and in so doing, opened the way for the first Democratic victory since 1888.

William Jennings Bryan, finally realizing his weakened appeal, concentrated his energies on helping to reshape the mentality of the Democrats. Progressivism infused both parties; each battling their conservative wings, and Bryan was at the center of the movement. Even Roosevelt acknowledged Bryan's influence on his own proposals, admitting, "So I have [taken ideas from Bryan]. That is quite true," but adding the disclaimer, "I have taken every one of them except those suited for the inmates of lunatic asylums." More importantly, Bryan's trebled failure to gain the presidency obscured his success at changing the ideological framework in his own party. The older states rights, laissez-faire strain was still present, but it was fast becoming a minority voice representing the thinking of the past. Led forward by Bryan, the party was embracing the full scope of progressivism. The Democrats favored electoral and governmental reform that went beyond trust-busting and envisioned the remaking of American politics into a far more partic-ipatory form of democracy. Conservatives in both parties recoiled, but the tide was in favor of the reformers. The party was "Bryanized," but the Great Com-moner would not lead it into victory, that task would fall upon a new Democratic hero, the erudite professor from Princeton.

Wilson possessed a different kind of charisma in contrast to Roosevelt's inex-haustible ebullience and bravado. Wilson lacked Roosevelt's colorful persona, but he possessed charms of his own that were more than capable of moving public audiences. Articulate, confident, astute, possessing a quick wit, and brimming with intelligence, Wilson knew how to communicate effectively. Recognizing the sim-ilarities shared by the progressive wings of both parties, Wilson redefined the respective positions on his own terms. Roosevelt's New Nationalism, which held much in common with the Democratic agenda, was reinterpreted by Wilson as a series of ideas and policies that worked to preserve monopoly power rather than eliminate it. Roosevelt, in Wilson's view, merely wanted to regulate but not abolish the trust. Wilson claimed to be the true trustbuster, and his New Freedom was advanced as a way to restore competition and opportunity to the American dream through the abolition of a monopolists system. Wilson's message was effective in drawing out the contrasts within the progressive movement. In a sense, the "Bryanized" Wilson had succeeded in "Wilsonizing" Bryan, and in so doing, regained the thunder for the Democrats that Bryan had accused Roosevelt of stealing for the Republicans.

Even though the 1912 campaign was ideologically deeper than any campaign since 1860 and rhetorically more interesting than any campaign since 1896, the outcome of the election had more to do with the numbers game than with high ideas or provocative slogans. A divided Republican Party could not defeat the Democrats, particularly given the political muscle that Roosevelt took with him into a third party. Roosevelt succeeded in gaining more votes than any third-party candidate in history, the only third-party candidate to outpace an incumbent president. Had Roosevelt allied with Taft they would have outpolled Wilson by 1.3 million votes and the GOP could have maintained their dominance of the White House. While Eugene Debs and the Socialists Party rode the progressive wave to their highest point to date, gathering more than 900,000 votes with increasing support in all states, if all the minor party votes went to the Democrats—and they would have not—the Republicans, with forces combined, would have won the day.

Wilson was elected with 435 electoral votes, a new record in spite of winning only a plurality of 42 percent at the polls, the lowest for a winning candidate since Lincoln in 1860. The discrepancy between those figures in itself speaks volumes on the nature and structure of democracy in the American Republic. *See also* "Empty Market Basket"; New Freedom; New Nationalism.

Suggested Readings: Francis L. Broderick, *Progressivism at Risk: Electing a President in 1912* (New York: Greenwood Press, 1989); Frank K. Kelly, *The Fight for the White House: The Story of 1912* (New York: Crowell, 1961); Norman M. Wilensky, *Conservatives in the Progressive Era: The Taft Republicans of 1912* (Gainesville: University of Florida Press, 1965).

Campaign of 1916

The slogan **"He Kept Us Out of War,"** a reminder of Woodrow Wilson's commitment to peace, was first uttered at the Democratic convention in St. Louis, and quickly became the defining phrase of the election of 1916. Wilson's domestic agenda introduced as part of his New Freedom ideology had turned into Roosevelt's New Nationalism. Both were progressive, but in moving back toward Roosevelt, Wilson exhibited the similarities between the two parties that had been wrought by the progressivist climate in the early decades of the century. So it was in foreign policy—and thus in successfully steering the United States away from the carnage now under way in Europe—where Wilson had made a visible difference. Wilson was the peace candidate, and his record had proved his ability to maintain neutrality.

The Republican candidate, Supreme Court Associate Justice Charles Evans Hughes, was not a hawk on the war issue, but partisan attitudes led to equivocation. Theodore Roosevelt, who was zealously hawkish and committed to immediate war against Germany, remained the Great Man of the party, and held pervasive influence within the GOP base. Hughes was thus caught in the hot box between a neutral **America First** position and the more pro-Anglo critique of Wilson for not protecting American maritime interests against U-Boat attacks in the North Atlantic. When speaking to audiences with a high Germanic mix, Hughes took a softer line. Such waffling on the war spurred the candidate's critics to label him with a new nickname—Charles *Evasive* Hughes.

Roosevelt hated Wilson and thereby reluctantly supported Hughes. He had desired the nomination, but since his renunciation of the party in 1912, the Republican leadership, which already considered Roosevelt politically too progressive and personally too unpredictable, was determined to look elsewhere. Roosevelt could have run as the Progressive nominee a second time, but in a concession to the wisdom of the two-party system, refused to continue supporting a third faction and reconciled himself with his old party. As to Hughes, Roosevelt held little regard for him, noting that only a good shave separated the bearded Hughes from the clean-shaven Wilson. But as lukewarm as he was regarding Hughes, he despised Wilson, whom he referred to as a hypocrite and "Byzantine logothete." Thus Roosevelt campaigned for the Republican cause, and for entering the war.

Initially, peace was not the primary issue for the Democrats. Americanism was the theme of the convention—intended to develop Wilson's Big America approach to the future role of the United States as a new power in the world. But the delegates received this theme blandly, and it was not until keynote speaker Martin Glynn, the current governor of New York, spontaneously and dramatically shifted the focus to neutrality and peace, that the party stirred with authentic purpose. Glynn extemporaneously thundered against the war and in praise of Wilson's restraint. Poignantly, Glynn mentioned those mothers and wives who had been able to keep their sons and husbands near the heart and out of "the moldering dissolution of the grave." In a call and response cadence, the delegates would answer Glynn's encomiums of Wilson with the chant, "We didn't go to war, we didn't go to war." By the second day of the convention, Wilson's persistent neutrality was *the* theme of the convention, and the slogan, "He kept us out of the war" generated spontaneously.

With the Progressive Party moribund in the wake of Roosevelt's refusal to carry their banner, the Republicans now enjoyed the possibility of a united party against Wilson, a situation that would have guaranteed them victory four years earlier. Wilson, whose first administration was well received both for domestic as well as foreign policy, was a formidable incumbent, but Hughes was able—not as electrifying as Roosevelt or as canny as McKinley, but capable and commanding in his own right. However Hughes carried three liabilities to the polls in November: the perception by many of a cold personality, Theodore Roosevelt's martial alarums, and California. To address the former, Hughes made a point of portraying himself as an ordinary chap: meeting crowds to shake hands and kiss babies, attending ball games and seeking out the players, and acting like a tourist at points of interest along the campaign trail. Hughes did enjoy some success in this, as he was perceived as more appealing than his speeches, which, owing to his considerable learning and juristic proclivities, could be long, dry, and dull.

Eluding Roosevelt's shadow proved more difficult. Additionally, Roosevelt's militarism tagged the Republicans with the war party label, further muddying Hughes's real sentiments. The Democrats could claim that "The less is plain: if you want WAR, vote for Hughes! If you want Peace with Honor VOTE FOR WILSON!"

California is what, in the end, made the difference. An inadvertent snub by Hughes of California's Progressive Republican governor Hiram Johnson while visiting the Long Beach hotel where Johnson was also staying alienated the party faithful. Hughes lost the state by fewer than 4,000 votes, allowing Wilson a clean sweep in the West, and victory in what would become the closest election since the 1880s. The early returns from the East favored Hughes in a possible landslide. At midnight Hughes had claimed 254 Electoral College votes, and major newspapers announced the election of a new president. By morning, with California's returns reported, Wilson led by 600,000 popular votes, winning by 277 to 254 in the Electoral College. California, which Hughes squandered, was the difference.

History's many ironies mock great women and men. Wilson, the candidate of peace, would within a few months of his electoral triumph commit Americans to join a bloody battle. Big America joined the Great War, and Wilson's health would shatter in pursuit of the lasting peace that his party had so ardently affirmed.

Suggested Reading: S.D. Lovell, *The Presidential Election of 1916* (Carbondale: Southern Illinois University Press, 1980).

Campaign of 1920

"**Back to Normalcy**" stands as the defining phrase of the 1920 campaign. Large issues and large men were a thing of the recent past. Woodrow Wilson, Theodore Roosevelt, William Jennings Bryan, Charles Evans Hughes were for various reasons no longer available as candidates to the American public. Hughes's prominence in GOP politics quickly faded in spite of nearly defeating Wilson four years earlier. Bryan had been stigmatized by three embarrassing losses. Had Wilson's health been sound, he would not have broken Washington's precedent for a third term, and Theodore Roosevelt, who had already established his position on that tradition, had unexpectedly passed away in 1919. Had Roosevelt lived he would probably have been the Republican candidate, but with his death, and the inexplicable political decline of Hughes, the GOP was left without a major personality.

Republicans turned to Warren G. Harding, an amiable senator from Ohio, who admitted his own lack of qualifications but nonetheless accepted the party nomination. Massachusetts governor Calvin Coolidge joined him on a ticket that appeared uncharacteristically ordinary.

The Democrats promoted a candidate equally overshadowed by his predecessors, James M. Cox, governor of Ohio. However, Cox's running mate did bring to the ticket a name of immediate recognition—Roosevelt. Franklin Delano Roo-

Warren G. Harding, the 1920 Republican presidential nominee. Courtesy of Library of Congress.

James Cox (left), the 1920 Democratic presidential nominee, and his running mate Franklin D. Roosevelt (right) in Dayton, Ohio. © Franklin D. Roosevelt Library/National Archives.

sevelt, assistant secretary of the Navy under Wilson, entered the national political arena with great promise as a future star within the Democratic Party. But 1920 was not Roosevelt's hour, it belonged to politicians of lesser stature, perhaps in response to a general need among the electorate for issues and men more manageable than the great controversies and charismatic personalities of the preceding two decades.

The large issues—progressive social reform and the Great War—had exhausted the parties and the public in general. For the most part, progressivism had won the day, and it was only a matter of adjusting to the new shape the republic was now assuming. No candidate could run against the legacy of both Teddy Roosevelt and Woodrow Wilson. The progressive movement had irrevocably transformed the American polity. The Great War had left the American public suspicious of what Washington referred to as "foreign entanglements," Wilson's grand vision for an international League of Nations now soundly rejected. Added to this was confusion and doubt over events in Russia, producing a Red Scare against Bolshevism and any type of foreign-born ideology. Internal divisions over the war and the revolution undermined even the Socialist Party, which had become a thriving third party in the early decades of the century. A return to normality is what Americans sought, and Harding's phrase effectively reflected that sentiment, and conveyed a message of sympathy with the new proclivities of the public.

Among the issues under discussion during the campaign of 1920 were the enforcement of Prohibition under the Volstead Act, continuation of progressive reforms on behalf of labor, government regulation of industry and transportation, rising cost of living, conservation and reclamation of natural resources, the state of American farming, immigration, campaign funding, and the League of Nations. The debate over joining the League of Nations stood out as the principal single issue of 1920. Led by Cox and Roosevelt, the Democrats regarded the League as the paramount issue, and placed it as the central plank of their platform. For the most part, Democrats were behind endorsing the League, but Republicans remained divided. Harding felt pressure from both supporters and opponents of the League, and awkwardly tried to steer a middle course. Cox attempted to make it his defining principle, and he attacked Harding for equivocating on the issue. Pro-League Republicans backed Harding in spite of his confused stance, but the party reiterated in its platform its position against the Treaty of Versailles, and praised the Senate for its opposition. Harding's support of some type of organization was included, but the League itself was implicitly rejected in the Republican platform.

In November the Republican Party returned to the White House by winning with a landslide. Harding won 60 percent of the popular vote, setting a new record, and he captured 404 Electoral College votes to Cox's 127—the second-highest total in history behind Wilson's 435 in 1912. The Socialist Party, with its leader in prison and a high number of its members abandoning it for more radical organizations, managed over 900,000 votes, half a million more than the previous election. The Farmer-Labor Party won over a quarter of a million votes. Oddly enough, the Prohibition Party, having completed its mission with the ratification of the Eighteenth Amendment the previous year, still ran candidates for office, and managed to win almost 200,000 votes. *See also* "America First."

Suggested Readings: Wesley Bagby, *The Road to Normalcy: the Presidential Campaign and Election of 1920* (Baltimore: Johns Hopkins Press, 1962); James E. Cebula, *James M. Cox: Journalist and Politician* (New York: Garland, 1985); John A. Morello, *Selling the President, 1920: Albert D. Lasker, Advertising, and the Election of Warren G. Harding* (Westport, CT: Praeger, 2001).

Campaign of 1924

The party conventions of 1924 could not have been more disparate. Republicans were universally behind incumbent Calvin Coolidge who, in succeeding President Harding after the latter succumbed to a sudden heart attack, had acquitted himself admirably as the new chief executive. The Democrats took three weeks and a record 103 ballots to nominate John W. Davis, ambassador to Great Britain and former solicitor-general under Wilson.

Coolidge helped to prosecute corrupt officials of the Harding administration who had been involved in the infamous **Teapot Dome Scandal**, and had managed to win over the American public with his dry, laconic, and dignified manner. Coolidge had restored a sense of unity rare to the GOP, thus producing a convention that was purposeful if lacking in drama. Prior to the convention a challenge from liberal Republican California Governor Hiram Johnson seemed likely, and Republican progressives were preparing to split again from the party and back Wisconsin progressive Robert LaFollette, but by the time of the convention Coolidge was well in command, the party well settled behind a platform calling for government frugality through a reduced national debt, restrictive immigration policies, and the sustained enforcement of Prohibition.

Early in the convention, an ascending Herbert Hoover was mentioned as a

Calvin Coolidge, the 1924 Republican presidential nominee. Courtesy of Library of Congress.

possible running mate, but concern over his possibly eclipsing Coolidge led the party to consider alternatives. Coolidge neither endorsed nor opposed Hoover or any other potential candidates, and left the nomination of his running mate to the delegates, who chose the dramatic and provocative orator and former budget director Charles G. Dawes, stylistically the "anti-Coolidge," to balance the ticket. The delegates saw Dawes as a partisan lance wielder, on the attack while the ever-taciturn Coolidge would coolly remain aloof and above it all. This tactic was a forerunner of a similar approach in later campaigns, choosing a hard-nosed hatchet man, such as Dawes, Richard Nixon (1952 and 1956), or Bob Dole (1976) for the bottom of the ticket to deflect political heat away from the more mellow top half—Coolidge, Dwight Eisenhower, and Gerald Ford. **"Keep Cool with Coolidge"** was the Republicans' defining slogan, Silent Cal himself their prominent image.

In contrast to Republican homogeneity, the Democrats were a party divided along numerous lines: conservative versus progressive, pro-Prohibition (**wet**) versus anti-Prohibition (**dry**), and pro-Catholic/anti–Ku Klux Klan versus anti-Catholic/ pro-Klan. The issue of Prohibition was largely divided along sectional lines, with the Northeastern Democrats, the wets, favoring repeal of Prohibition; Southern and Western Democrats tending to be dry. Similarly, Northeastern Democrats tended to be liberal, pro-Catholic, and anti-Klan, while the Klan held strong support in the South and parts of the West, where there were also found strong elements of anti-Catholicism and anti-Semitism along with the traditional prejudices against African Americans and other ethnicities.

The Republicans remained, as the party of Lincoln, the party of preference for African American voters, but there was a growing movement among progressive Democrats to reach out to the black vote. As the Democratic convention opened, two names were prominent as likely nominees: New York governor Al Smith, a Roman Catholic popular with the liberal wing and supported by party heavyweights such as Franklin Roosevelt, and California's William G. McAdoo, son-in-law of and former secretary of the treasury under Woodrow Wilson. The Klan, representative of the more reactionary element of the Democratic Party, supported McAdoo. It should be noted that McAdoo did receive some support from anti-Klan newspapers, and that two prominent anti-Klan leaders—Bernard Baruch, a Jew, and Senator Thomas Walsh, a Catholic, atypically endorsed McAdoo.

A curious and critical debate at the Democratic Convention revolved around a proposal to censure the Klan in the official party platform. Pro-Klan elements backing McAdoo were incensed at the suggestion, anti-Klan forces favoring Smith insisted upon it. William Jennings Bryan, the old firebrand and titular leader of the party, opposed the Klan in principle, but argued against specifically censuring the Klan by name. Bryan's reasoning was driven by two concerns: a fear of giving the Klan too much publicity and too much importance by the need to mention them by name, and a concern over driving a further wedge between the reformist and reactionary wings of the party. In the end the party settled on compromise language safely affirming that "[Democrats] insist at all times upon obedience to the orderly processes of the law and deplore and condemn any effort to arouse religious or racial dissension."

On the 103rd ballot the Democrats turned to John W. Davis of West Virginia as the nominee, with Charles Bryan, governor of Nebraska and brother of the

Great Commoner, as his running mate. The divided Democrats not only faced a unified Republican campaign, they were further weakened by the presence of a coalition third party led by LaFollette and uniting socialist and progressive forces that would draw away more reformists from the Democrats than Republicans. Without a unifying theme or defining slogan, the Democrats were unable to sustain a credible challenge against the solid Coolidge. LaFollette only added to their troubles, showing better than the Democrats on election day in twelve states, all in the West or Midwest, and including Wisconsin, where LaFollette beat both candidates for 13 electoral votes, and California, where he outpolled Davis by over 3 votes to 1. But Coolidge's numbers were the most impressive, winning 15.7 million votes, more than Davis and LaFollette combined, with 382 Electoral College votes to 136 (all Southern) for Davis and the 13 for LaFollette. Coolidge ran an effortless campaign, keeping his cool while Democrats undermined their campaign internally. Silent Cal would continue on as the leading political figure of the roaring 20s. *See also* "Coolidge or Chaos"; "GOP Equals Gas, Oil and Petroleum."

Suggested Reading: Burl Noggle, *Teapot Dome: Oil and Politics in the 1920s* (Baton Rouge: Louisiana State University Press, 1962).

Campaign of 1928

In 1928 Governor Al Smith of New York became the first Roman Catholic in American history nominated by a major political party to run for president of the United States. Smith was a progressive Democrat, advocating reformist social policies, economic programs favorable to labor, federal control of the power industry, and the repeal of Prohibition. Smith's progressivist bent was both alike and dissimilar to the legacy of Williams Jennings Bryan. Smith, who lacked a college education and who spoke with the accent of a New York working man in the street was representative of common folk, much like Bryan, the archetypal prairie politician. But in an important contrast to Bryan, Smith's reforms spoke to the immigrant and Catholic citizens of the industrial and urban Northeast whereas Bryan's populism was spun from the more traditional rural, agrarian Protestant attitudes of the South and West. But Bryan's influence had been fading, and Smith, as other New York governors before and since, had emerged as the principal leader in the party after the disastrous campaign of 1924.

Herbert Hoover, engineer, humanitarian, expert administrator for Democrats (Wilson) and Republicans (Harding and Coolidge) alike, and one of the most capable men of his time, easily won the endorsement of the GOP. Hoover was a marked contrast to Smith: a Quaker from rural Iowa, educated as an engineer at Stanford, a supporter of Prohibition and government frugality, Hoover was a thoroughly self-made man who had combined real talent with discipline to rise to the top of his calling: public service. But Hoover and Smith also held much in common: both men were genuinely dedicated to principles of honest service, and had earned their reputations as solid and trustworthy statesmen. Furthermore, the two men also held in common the angularity of their religious beliefs. Quakers and Catholics were a rare breed of cat at the highest level of national politics.

Herbert Hoover, the 1928 Republican presidential candidate, surveys a crowd from the back of his train during a campaign trip. Courtesy of Library of Congress.

(Curiously, the only other time a Roman Catholic Democrat, John Kennedy, would run for president, would be against another politician from a Quaker background, Richard Nixon—32 years after the Hoover-Smith campaign). Together the two candidates embodied the meaning of the First Amendment's protection of religious liberty.

Anti-Catholicism was again on the rise in American society and politics. Having already experienced waves of know-nothing anti-Catholic sentiment in the nineteenth century, a new wave was swelling through American political culture in the 1920s. Set into motion by disenchantment with "foreign" influences owing to the rise of immigration and the social aftershocks of the Great War, and fueled by the reemergence of the Ku Klux Klan and other militant nativist groups, anti-Catholic prejudice climaxed as Smith accepted his party's standard for president. The party sought balance in nominating Senator Joseph Robinson, a southern Protestant dry for vice president. But Smith's critics were not placated by such moves. Extremist groups like the Klan warned that a "vote for Al Smith [was] a vote for the Pope," and, given Smith's support of the repeal of Prohibition, the old chestnut of **Rum, Romanism and Rebellion** was repackaged as "Rum, Romanism, and Ruin," and critics asked **"Shall America Elect a Cocktail President?"** "Al-coholic" Smith, according to his less restrained enemies, secretly planned to move the Pope to Washington and annul Protestant marriages once in office. Such was the hysteria of the times.

Additionally, connections to the politics of Tammany Hall damaged Smith's national image. Typical of New York political culture, Smith owed his initial success to the support of Tammany, and now the chickens were coming home to roost. The corrupt image of the urban political machine was, understandably, an easy target for critics of big city politics, and many voters saw Smith as the product of the Boss and the iniquitous culture of graft. These machine connections hurt

A small dog sits in a derby and looks at an Alfred E. Smith poster from the 1928 Democratic presidential campaign. Courtesy of Library of Congress.

Smith's case as much as his religious differences. By contrast, Hoover was genuinely independent who, having made his mark through skillful performance and enduring achievement, owed nothing to power brokers or patrons. Hoover thus projected a safer image of independence and competence that appealed to the heartland, Smith seeming far too atypical in his beliefs and undesirable in his background.

Hoover also held the advantage of a strong economy. The economic turbulence encountered in the early 1920s had subsided, and prosperity was the apparent trend. While Smith was distracted by the controversies regarding his religion, Tammany Hall, and his stand on Prohibition, Hoover was able to emulate Coolidge by "keeping cool," staying close to Washington, and quietly relying on the proven Republican record. "A Chicken in Every Pot" became the defining Republican slogan, as the voters would be asked, "Is your bread buttered?" and then reminded to "Remember hard times when we had a Democratic president. You can't eat promises. Play safe! Vote a straight Republican ticket!" Smith could not dismantle the claims of his opponents, Hoover benefited from the good times, high spirits, and general optimism of the Roaring Twenties.

Hoover won the election decisively. Hoover took 444 electoral votes to Smith's 87, the latter unable to hold even his home state of New York. With another electoral landslide behind them, the Republicans were at the height of their power, and prepared to meet the promise of the oncoming decade, confident that the voters had made the intelligent choice in answer to a question posed by one of their more ironic campaign boilerplates, "Prosperity didn't just happen. Hoover and happiness or Smith and soup houses? Which shall it be?" *See also* "Safety, Solvency, Sobriety."

Suggested Readings: Alan Lichtman, *Prejudice and the Old Politics: The Presidential Election of 1928* (Chapel Hill: University of North Carolina Press, 1979); Ruth Silva, *Rum, Religion, and Votes: 1928 Re-examined* (University Park: Penn State University Press, 1962); Robert Slayton, *Empire Statesman: The Rise and Redemption of Al Smith* (New York: Free Press, 2001).

Campaign of 1932

Nineteen thirty-two is remarkable for four principal reasons. First, the outcome of the election of 1932 would signal the end of the Republican Presidential dynasty that had reigned since 1860 with only three interruptions—the non-consecutive terms of Grover Cleveland and the presidency of Woodrow Wilson, which had been handed to the Democrats owing to the Republicans' internal divisions. This would initiate the era of Democratic dominance in both the White House and Congress that would remain, with one brief exception, the shape of American politics until the 1980s. Second, with 1932, and beginning with trends four years earlier, African Americans abandoned the Party of Lincoln, the Great Emancipator, and formed a new allegiance with the Democratic Party. Throughout the balance of the twentieth century, the majority of African Americans would support the Democrats after having been loyal to the Republicans from Reconstruction to the Depression. Third, the Democratic Party would establish a new coalition of widely disparate groups and interests, and thus would evolve as the more heterogeneous of the two parties throughout the remainder of the century. The most liberal northern Democrats would become allies of southern conservatives; workers and intellectuals would find common cause in the party's platform; Catholics and Jews as well as southern Baptists would each represent important voting blocs for the Democrats; and a variety of racial and ethnic groups would give the Democratic Party a pluralistic flavor seldom seen in democratic politics of any kind.

Finally, and most importantly for American politics as it would unfold over the next five decades, the campaign and election reflected a deep shift within American political culture on ideological grounds. Beginning with the progressive and populist movements of the late nineteenth and early twentieth centuries, American political consciousness had been drawing a new vision of the relationship between government and social responsibility. Throughout the first two decades of the twentieth century, both parties included progressive elements that insisted upon various degrees of governmental activism in the social and economic life of Americans. But in the 1920s the progressive wing of the GOP waned significantly, and by 1928, the contrast between Herbert Hoover's "rugged individualism" and Al Smith's activist policies had further clarified the growing distinction between the two parties. In 1932, with the Great Depression smothering all vestiges of the prosperity that helped elect Hoover four years earlier, these differences were sharply polarized. While some pundits and wags complained of little real difference

President Herbert Hoover, the 1932 Republican candidate for president. Courtesy of Library of Congress.

between the candidates, attention to their speeches and statements regarding the crisis reveal the outlines of the ideological shift. The Republicans had abandoned their progressivist and liberal roots, and had fallen back on the mythos of self-reliance and restrained government. The Democrats were no longer the laissez-faire party of Andrew Jackson and Martin Van Buren, nor the gold standard party of Grover Cleveland, but were developing along lines that would lead them to champion the imminent emergence of a welfare state.

Franklin Delano Roosevelt, cousin of Theodore Roosevelt, had been the Democrat's rising star since his campaign for the vice presidency twelve years earlier. A crippling battle against polio only temporarily impeded his political ambitions. Roosevelt was a major influence in the nomination of Al Smith, and in 1930 had successfully campaigned for the governorship of New York, winning the election in a landslide. FDR was able to secure the nomination on the 4th ballot, with John Nance Garner agreeing to run as Roosevelt's vice presidential nominee.

With a victory in hand, Roosevelt went on the stump, campaigning so energetically that the frail state of his health was completely overlooked. Assisted by his "brain trust"—an informal circle of campaign managers and academics, Roosevelt mapped a campaign strategy and executed it with aplomb, surprising even those critics who had always regarded him to be something of a political lightweight. Roosevelt's vigor and optimism were infectious. "**Happy Days Are Here Again**," Roosevelt's campaign theme song, typified the campaign's mood more effectively than any speech or slogan, with the possible exception of one phrase, coined in the following promise: "I pledge you, I pledge myself, to a **New Deal** for the American people." By the next day the New Deal was the most important slogan for the Roosevelt campaign and throughout his presidency.

Herbert Hoover, unfairly blamed for a depression that no one could foresee or forestall, attempted to reassure the American people that, with his policies and administrative style, the country would pull itself out of the catastrophe. But he seemed defeated from the outset; he did little to campaign throughout the summer, and it was only in October that he really entered the fray, and then primarily as a defense against his critics. Hoover attempted to inform the public of the measures that he had taken to address the crisis, insisting that had it not been for his administration, the Depression would have been "infinitely worse." He pointedly contrasted his rugged individualism with Roosevelt's "alien" ideas, insinuating that with FDR and the Democrats the very ideals that underpin American society would be replaced by "sinister," foreign doctrines similar to Bolshevism. Hoover warned that if the electorate turned to the radicalism of Roosevelt, ". . . the same philosophy of government which has poisoned all Europe" would infect the values of American society as well. Roosevelt blithely dismissed Hoover, describing the latter's administration in apocalyptic and alliterative terms as led by "the Horsemen of Destruction, Delay, Deceit, Despair."

The election was a landslide for Roosevelt and Garner. Roosevelt reshaped the political landscape. Thus would begin the central presidency of the twentieth century, and the ascent of one of America's greatest statesmen, and the first American politician to achieve lasting prominence as a world leader. *See also* "A New Deal, A New Day"; "Rebuild with Roosevelt."

Suggested Readings: Elliot Rosen, *Hoover, Roosevelt, and the Brains Trust: From Depression to the New Deal* (New York: Columbia University Press, 1977); Rexford Tugwell, *The Brains Trust* (New York: Viking Press, 1968).

Campaign of 1936

By 1936, Roosevelt's **New Deal** had succeeded in improving conditions for most Americans but had failed to restore prosperity. The Depression still weighed heavily on the American economy, and the future remained uncertain. Nonetheless, the social and economic policies promoted by the administration and enacted by Congress had altered the way Americans perceived the uses of government. The Republican Platform of 1936, while generally critical of the Democrats' reckless deficit spending and intrusive federal interference with free enterprise, included endorsements of social security for the elderly, collective bargaining for labor, and relief programs for the unemployed. Differences were not as sharp as in 1932, but even so, the Democratic Party represented the New Deal while Republicans, as the allies of business, advocated minimal federal government.

In addition to embracing a portion of the progressive agenda forwarded by Roosevelt, Republicans, in turning to former Bull Moose progressive, Alfred Landon of Kansas as their nominee in 1936, recognized the wisdom of avoiding the ideological polarities of 1932. The Republican Party was more conservative and homogeneous than it had been in the first two decades of the century, but it still contained moderate elements that accepted elements of the New Deal. For the most part Landon himself avoided the red baiting of more conservative Republicans.

Roosevelt was demonized by his harshest critics, even to the point of portraying him as a puppet of Moscow, but the American public in general embraced Roo-

President Franklin D. Roosevelt accepting the 1936 Democratic nomination. © AP/ Wide World Photos.

sevelt, many with uncommon enthusiasm. No president could inspire such a mix of devoted adoration and intemperate condemnation as Franklin Roosevelt. Polls of the day, although often inaccurate, indicated that the general population loved Roosevelt more than the New Deal. Meanwhile, Roosevelt's name became anathema among the powerful in America—tycoon households were known to have forbidden the use of his name. To some, Roosevelt was a savior, to others— especially among the high social strata—he was scornfully and abruptly referred to as "that man."

Strategically, Landon was an intelligent choice to challenge Roosevelt. He was a proven ally of business and an advocate of free enterprise, and yet his Bull Moose credentials appealed to the progressive mood of the times. As governor of Kansas he had openly supported many of Roosevelt's New Deal reforms, and yet he forthrightly championed fiscal frugality, the gold standard, and the implementation of policies favorable to business and industry. In Kansas he expanded state government for the sake of regulation while at the same time reducing taxes. And as a governor who was sympathetic to civil rights reform Landon reemphasized the Republican Party's historic origins.

Above all, Landon had the support of several powerful newspaper publishers such as William Randolph Hearst, who was particularly aggressive in deploying reporters to convey Landon's common man attributes to his readers. Reporters working for Hearst described Landon as the "Lincoln of Kansas," a "liberal Coolidge," and the "Horse and Buggy Governor," a man of simple tastes, self-reliance, and prairie common sense.

In a particularly curious and embarrassing act of self-deception, the media participated in spinning the illusion of Landon's imminent victory. The *Literary Digest*, which through a quadrennial straw poll had predicted with accuracy the outcome of the four previous elections, confidently predicted an imminent Landon landslide. Roosevelt and his brain trust were not intimidated by the *Digest's* previous record; they went into November with full confidence in spite of the appearance of uncertainty, generated by the media, on the eve of the election.

When the election came, the results were stunning. Roosevelt shattered every electoral record, winning 28.7 million votes, amounting to 60.8 percent of the popular vote, and taking 523 electoral votes, leaving Landon with just 8 from Vermont and Maine. The Roosevelt coalition that was forged in the election of 1932 and foreshadowed in 1928, had not only held its base, but also expanded its reach.

Landon was an able governor and adept politician, but Franklin Roosevelt was a political genius. Charismatic, vigorous, forthright, confident, graceful, articulate, quick-witted, warm, and genuinely friendly in crowds, Roosevelt was *the* political colossus of his times. Given to opening his remarks with the simple and reassuring phrase, "my friends," Roosevelt exuded trust and ability. He was a master of the uses of radio, and in personal appearances he emitted the raw presence of naturally great leadership. Rhetorically he was without peer in his day. In his dazzling performance in his acceptance of renomination at the convention in Philadelphia, Roosevelt coined, with the help of his brain trust, a new phrase that would help to define his entire presidency when he affirmed that his generation of Americans had a "rendezvous with destiny." Not knowing what world events awaited the United States over the next ten years; Roosevelt had spoken with uncanny prescience. *See also* "Four More Lucky Roosevelt Years."

Suggested Readings: Michael J. Webber, *New Deal Fat Cats: Business, Labor, and Campaign Finance in the 1936 Presidential Election* (New York: Fordham University Press, 2000); Clyde P. Weed, *The Nemesis of Reform: The Republican Party During the New Deal* (New York: Columbia University Press, 1994).

Campaign of 1940

When Americans turned to the presidential campaign of 1940, world war had once again gripped the community of nations. The crisis of the Depression gave way to the cataclysm of war, and the burning issue in the American heartland revolved around the nature of America's response. Hawks and Doves again flocked to their respective corners of the political arena, and the country confronted the choice between internationalism and war on the one hand and peace, neutrality, and even isolation on the other. The crisis was such that, for the first time in American political history, an incumbent president broke the tradition of the venerable Washington, and stood for a third consecutive term.

As late as 1939, Roosevelt had indicated ambivalence regarding a third term, and even encouraged other party members to seek the nomination. But with war exploding in Europe in September of 1939 and expanding through the first half of 1940, Roosevelt decided to break tradition. Officially, Roosevelt demurred, but unofficially he expected to be drafted by the convention, an expectation that was realized on the first ballot. Initially there was some minority grousing in both parties about Roosevelt's alleged dictatorial ambitions, but the broken tradition seemed insignificant given the magnitude of the decisions at stake.

By and large the critics of Roosevelt's third run were Roosevelt bashers to begin with. The only real controversy at the 1940 Democratic convention involved the choice of a running mate. Roosevelt wanted zealous New Dealer Henry A. Wallace, current secretary of agriculture. Delegates wanted to open the nomination for vice president to other candidates, there being a large groundswell against Wallace and his more radical approach to the New Deal. Roosevelt bristled upon hearing of resistance to Wallace, threatening to withdraw his name from consideration. This was prevented by the efforts of Harry Hopkins, First Lady Eleanor Roosevelt, and others from the brain trust working arduously at the convention to successfully generate support for Wallace. Aside from this brief crisis, the path was clear for Roosevelt to receive his third nomination.

The Republican convention was more dramatic. The leading candidates at the beginning of the convention were Thomas Dewey of New York and Robert Taft, son of William Howard Taft, of Ohio. But the delegates were deadlocked, and a third candidate, Indiana's Wendell Willkie, a personable political tenderfoot new to the party, having been a Democrat as recently as the previous year. For this reason, Willkie was distasteful to the party leadership, but he was an effective and personable if not naïve campaigner who commanded a loyal and energetic following among the party's more youthful cohort. Willkie skillfully concealed his complete absence of governmental experience through a brash confidence that belied his late arrival to the hard world of political campaigning.

Willkie deployed a two-pronged attack. The first prong depicted the Republicans as the party of peace and implied that Roosevelt desperately wanted to get into another foreign war. The second prong attempted to associate the New Deal with European totalitarianism. "[If] you return this Administration to office," he declaimed in California, "you will be serving under an American totalitarian government before the long third term is up." Willkie made claims that Roosevelt was an enemy of liberty, and punctuated claims of his opponent's authoritarian ambition by referring to Roosevelt as "the third term candidate." Understandably, **"No Third Term"** became one of the key Republican slogans of the campaign.

Most voters were not persuaded by this line of reasoning, but Willkie's first-prong, the promise of peace, did draw some attention, and support, to his campaign. Lend-Lease, Roosevelt's plan to supply Great Britain with fifty destroyers in exchange for the use of British naval bases, helped to provoke the issue. Initially, FDR had requested Willkie's public endorsement of the plan. Willkie declined the invitation, and initially issued a lukewarm rebuke of the president for not allowing enough time for public debate over the issue of military aid to Britain. However, Willkie soon changed his tone when political allies urged him to assume a more severe criticism. "[T]he most arbitrary and dictatorial action ever taken by a President in the history of the United States" was Willkie's second response to Lend-Lease, and from this point Willkie increased the volume of his anti-war rhetoric. Willkie, who began the campaign from a position supportive of Britain, transformed himself into an isolationist. In the process, Willkie became increasingly more shrill, alarming his audience with "wooden crosses for sons and brothers and sweethearts" if Roosevelt returned for a third term. The Republican's rhetoric intensified even to the point of acrimony directed against Roosevelt, with whom he had actually enjoyed an amicable relationship.

Typically, Roosevelt remained "above the fray," choosing to ignore Willkie's isolationist rhetoric. But when polls indicated Willkie had gained support, Roosevelt reassured the American public that he did not intend to lead America into another foreign war. Toward the end of the campaign, Roosevelt placated nervous handlers with a bold reminder, "I have said this before, but I shall say it again and again and again: Your boys are not going to be sent into any foreign war." Roosevelt quietly instructed his more nervous advisors and handlers that a direct attack on the United States was not a "foreign" war, remarking, "of course we'll fight if we're attacked."

November 5th brought the reelection of Franklin Roosevelt to an unprecedented and unique third term. Even though he received half a million fewer votes than in 1936 Roosevelt still won convincingly in the popular vote with 27.2 million (54.8 percent) to 22.3 million for Willkie. Willkie's total amounted to the highest popular vote for a Republican candidate in history. With the election decided, Willkie graciously restored his friendship with Roosevelt, who admitted to sincerely liking his opponent, and as the nation approached war, Willkie supported the president in the spirit of political nonpartisanship and national unity.

Suggested Readings: Warren Moscow, *Roosevelt and Willkie* (Englewood Cliffs, NJ: Prentice-Hall, 1968); Herbert S. Parmet and Marie B. Hecht, *Never Again: A President Runs for a Third Term* (New York: Macmillan, 1968).

Campaign of 1944

"The Republican Party accepts the purposes of the National Labor Relations Act, the Wage and Hour Act, the Social Security Act and all other Federal statutes designed to promote and protect the welfare of American working men and women, and we promise a fair and just administration of these laws." Inserting this plank into their 1944 campaign platform, the GOP pledged to sustain these as well as many other programs that were generated by the Democrats under Franklin Roosevelt's New Deal. Even though the platform abstractly vilified the New Deal, when it came to specifics, much of Roosevelt's social vision was accepted.

Between Pearl Harbor and the presidential campaign of 1944, the United States had entered the most destructive and horrific war in history. The full force and might of American resources were brought to bear in that conflict, resulting in the creation of astonishing military and economic power. Franklin Roosevelt was at the helm of this Herculean effort, and while some grumbled about his disorganized style of management and his odd proclivity to stimulate conflict among his subordinates, he was widely lionized as a statesman of world caliber. Even though Republicans were tempted to publicize rumors that Roosevelt may have known about the imminent Pearl Harbor attack in time to intercept it, in the end they suppressed the temptation, partly for national security reasons, and partly because of Roosevelt's formidable stature. The Republicans would not base their strategy against Roosevelt around either the New Deal or the war.

Three options remained for the Republicans: first, they could amplify Roosevelt's administrative inefficiency and claim that the administration had become enervated, and even slightly corrupt, with age; second, they could draw attention to what they perceived to be dangerous connections to communism and communist sympathizers, in the same spirit that would produce the McCarthy hearings of the next decade; and third, they could dwell at length on the health of the president, who at only sixty-two years of age, was showing visible signs of fatigue and physical decline. All three approaches were attempted.

That Roosevelt was a purportedly incompetent and manipulative administrator was unconvincing. After twelve years of dealing with social, economic, and foreign crises of previously unknown magnitude, the public was unmoved by such claims. The red baiting that was employed played well in parts of the country, but again, only in those parts that were already anti-Roosevelt and thus looking for more reasons to hate "that man."

Health concerns served more effectively. An aging, fatigued president should retire. However critics could only suggest, imply, or insinuate; no one wanted to publicly embarrass Roosevelt over the issue of his physical condition. It would also play too well in Berlin or Tokyo, thus the health issue, their strongest weapon, could only be hinted at obliquely.

Against Roosevelt, the Republicans nominated the youthful, energetic, and serious New York governor Thomas Dewey. Sharply contrasted to the friendly contest of 1940, a tangible animosity existed between the two New Yorkers. Dewey had an abrasive, humorless, and somewhat aloof personality that had alienated most of the members of the press working the campaign trail. He deliberately presented himself as the epitome of efficiency, formality, planning, and organization, but it left those around him cold.

Republicans had made substantial gains during the congressional and state elections of 1942, stoking Dewey's momentum. Dewey assaulted the administration, describing it as an inefficient, backbiting, quasi-socialistic, geriatric empire in decay. In retrospect, Roosevelt referred to the Dewey contest as "the meanest campaign in my life."

Roosevelt himself maintained his preferred tactic of remaining above the fray, not mentioning his opponent by name, running on his record, and reminding the voters of the troubles brought to the country by the former dominance of the Grand Old Party. His lieutenants, however, would target Dewey personally. Harold Ickes had already mocked Dewey's youth. When the Republican unsuccessfully ran for his party's nomination in 1940, Ickes commented that Dewey had "thrown his diaper in the ring." Again in 1944, when candidate Dewey adopted positions consonant with New Deal accomplishments, Ickes remarked that the Republican nominee had "thrown a sponge into the ring."

But Roosevelt remained the master of rhetorical wit. When Roosevelt finally joined the battle, the press was eager to experience the relaxed warmth and spontaneous wit of the century's master politician. On September 23rd Roosevelt delivered a nationally broadcast speech addressed to the International Brotherhood of Teamsters. With well-timed humor Roosevelt dissected the Republican platform. In Lincolnesque fashion he deflated the GOP charge that the country had still been in a depression as it entered the war in 1941. Instructing his audience, Roosevelt quipped "Now there is an old and somewhat lugubrious adage which says: 'Never speak of a rope in the house of a man who's been hanged.' In the same way, if I were a Republican leader speaking to a mixed audience, the last word in the whole dictionary that I would be using is that word 'depression.' "

But the high point of the speech was reached with reference to Republican allegations that Roosevelt had cavalierly squandered naval resources to retrieve his lost dog Fala who, as the story goes, had been inadvertently abandoned in the Aleutians. Roosevelt chided the Republicans, "You know, you know, Fala is Scotch, and being a Scottie, as soon as he learned that the Republican fiction writers . . . had concocted the story that I had left him behind on an Aleutian island and had sent a destroyer back to find him—at a cost to the taxpayers of two or three or eight or twenty million dollars—his Scotch soul was furious. He has not been the same dog since."

With what would become known as the Fala speech, Roosevelt deftly and comically demolished the Dewey campaign. Pining for some campaign excitement after weeks of suffering Dewey's arid and officious campaign, the press was completely won over by FDR's inexhaustible good nature. Reporting on the Fala speech, *Time* magazine declared that "[Roosevelt] was like a veteran virtuoso playing a piece he has loved for years, who fingers his way through it with a delicate fire, a perfection of tuning and tone, and an assurance that no young player, no matter how gifted, can equal. The President was playing what he loves to play—politics."

With his new (and last) running mate, Senator Harry Truman of Missouri, Roosevelt won the election by 4.5 million popular votes, receiving 432 electoral votes to Dewey's 99. Roosevelt would not serve out his full fourth term—in less than six months the great man would pass away, leaving the White House to the indomitable vice president from the Show Me state. *See also* "Never Swap Horses in Mid-Stream; "We Are Going to Win This War and the Peace That Follows;" "Win the War Quicker with Dewey and Bricker."

Suggested Readings: Robert E. Divine, *Foreign Policy and the U.S. Presidential Elections, 1940–1948* (New York: New Viewpoints, 1974); Hugh Evans, *The Hidden Campaign: FDR's Health and the 1944 Election* (Armonk, NY: M.E. Sharpe, 2002).

Campaign of 1948

On April 12, 1945, President Franklin Roosevelt died in office. Vice President Harry Truman, in office for less than two months, immediately assumed the presidency. With Truman's momentous decision to use atomic weapons against Japan, the horrors of World War II finally came to an end.

The transition from a wartime to peacetime economy created a multitude of problems for the young Truman administration. With the end to wartime wage and price controls, inflation soared as Americans bid up the prices for scarce consumer goods. Seeking to protect the wages, labor unions called a record number of strikes. In response to labor unrest, Congress passed the Taft Hartley Act of 1947, which prohibited labor unions from making campaign contributions to candidates for federal office and authorized states to pass "right to work" laws.

Truman also faced pressure from a growing civil rights movement to end seg-

Thomas E. Dewey (center), the 1948 Republican presidential candidate, returns to New York City from a campaign tour. Courtesy of Library of Congress.

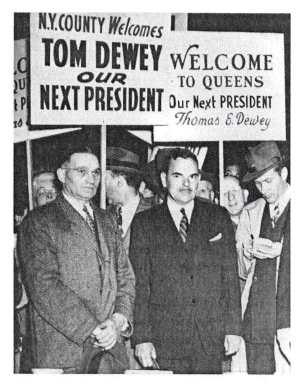

regation in the United States. The liberal wing of the Democratic Party demanded that Congress take more aggressive steps to guarantee all Americans, regardless of race, an equal opportunity to participate in the political process and the right to compete for a job. In sharp contrast, the southern wing of the Democratic Party, controlled by supporters of segregation, used a states rights argument to defend their culture of separation. A split between liberal and southern Democrats threatened to destroy Franklin Roosevelt's New Deal coalition. Many southern whites began to look for an alternative to the Democratic Party.

Equally important, by the beginning of the 1948 campaign, the euphoria associated with the end of World War II and the establishment of the United Nations gave way to a cold war between the United States, the Soviet Union, and Communist China. Concern increased over the activities of communist subversives inside the United States. The Republican Party strongly supported new loyalty security programs; liberal Democrats expressed reservations about the potential impact of such programs on the civil liberties of Americans.

In late June 1948, the Republican National Convention without controversy again nominated New York Governor Thomas E. Dewey, previously defeated by Roosevelt, as their presidential candidate. Unlike the calm that prevailed at the Republican convention, a fierce battle over a civil rights plank broke out at the Democratic National Convention. Although Truman was easily nominated, the adoption of a strong civil rights plank led a number of angry southern Democrats to bolt the Democratic Party, establishing the States' Rights Party, or Dixiecrats. The convention chose Governor Strom Thurmond of South Carolina as its pres-

Political cartoon showing President Harry Truman running behind Thomas Dewey in presidential preference polls prior to the 1948 election. © National Archives.

idential candidate and Governor Fielding L. Wright of Mississippi as his running mate. Strongly defending segregation, the Dixiecrat platform warned that increased federal power put the nation on course toward a totalitarian police state.

Early in the campaign of 1948, political experts gave Truman little chance of defeating Dewey. Besides having the backing of a united Republican Party, Dewey had a large campaign war chest. Equally important, the Dewey campaign expected Strom Thurmond to deprive Truman of many votes from southern states.

Undaunted, Truman embarked on a nationwide "whistle-stop" campaign to mobilize support and warn the nation about the "do-nothing" Congress. Truman traveled some 31,000 miles bashing congressional Republicans. Much in the style of William Jennings Bryan, Truman positioned himself as the friend of working

President Harry Truman sights a shotgun during a 1948 campaign trip to Sun Valley, Idaho. © Harry S. Truman Library/National Archives.

men and women. At every stop, Truman supporters would yell, **"Give 'em Hell, Harry!"**

To counter Dewey's money advantage, the Truman campaign depended upon organized labor to get out the Democratic vote. Angered by the enactment of Taft-Hartley, passed by Republicans over Truman's veto, unions resolved to thwart Dewey. The right-to-work provisions of the law allowed states to seriously threaten union power, especially in the largely anti-union South. Truman called for the repeal of Taft-Hartley to protect the rights of workers.

Throughout the campaign Truman argued that a Republican victory would threaten the survival of important New Deal programs. He pledged to continue the New Deal system of farm price supports and urged the passage of new civil rights laws.

The media prematurely and inaccurately reported Dewey's "victory" before all the votes were counted. In the end, Truman stunned the Republicans with convincing results in both electoral and popular counts. Instead of finding himself on the way to retirement, the indefatigable Truman extended his influential presidency another four years.

Suggested Readings: Gary Donaldson, *Truman Defeats Dewey* (Lexington: University Press of Kentucky, 1999); Zackery Karabell, *The Last Campaign: How Harry Truman Won the 1948 Election* (New York: Knopf, 2000); Irwin Ross, *The Loneliest Campaign: The Truman Victory of 1948* (New York: New American Library, 1968); Truman Presidential Museum & Library, Project Whistlestop, http://www.trumanlibrary.org/whistlestop.

Campaign of 1952

After being courted by both parties, General Dwight David Eisenhower was nominated for president by the Republican Party in 1952. With the selection of Eisenhower, Republicans hoped to end twenty years of Democratic control of the White House. During World War II, Eisenhower had served as supreme commander of the Allied Expeditionary Force in Europe. In 1950, President Truman appointed Eisenhower supreme commander of the North Atlantic Treaty Organization (NATO) forces. He entered the campaign a resilient and proven leader.

A number of individuals announced their interest in the Democratic nomination after President Truman declined to seek a second full term as president. Senator Estes Kefauver of Tennessee arrived at the July Democratic Convention with the most votes in Democratic primaries. Despite Kefauver's primary strength, Kefauver lacked sufficient support to win the nomination. Reluctantly, Illinois Governor Adlai Stevenson allowed his name to be placed into nomination. Although Kefauver won the first two ballots, Stevenson won the nomination on the third ballot. Before his 1948 election as Illinois governor, Stevenson had served in various high-level federal government positions and had become widely known as a foreign policy expert and a strong supporter of New Deal policies and programs.

Eisenhower was one of the most celebrated and respected figures of his day, but he had never run for or held public office. Taking full advantage of the new medium of television, the Eisenhower campaign put together a sophisticated ad campaign emphasizing his credentials as a leader. In a series of spot ads called

General Dwight D. Eisenhower, the 1952 Republican candidate for president, arrives at Washington National Airport. © Harry S. Truman Library/National Archives.

"Eisenhower Answers America," Eisenhower fielded questions from American citizens. This approach was not without its critics. Stevenson viewed such ads as demeaning, as he preferred formats, established in radio, which allowed extended discussions of complex issues. Despite criticism, the use of television spot ads successfully positioned Eisenhower as an individual who understood the problems of average Americans.

Besides facing a national hero, a number of other problems plagued the Stevenson campaign. Stevenson and his fellow Democrats were forced to defend themselves against allegations that they were "soft on communism." Despite the

Governor Adlai E. Stevenson of Illinois, the 1952 Democratic presidential nominee, meets with President Harry Truman in the Oval Office. © Harry S. Truman Library/National Archives.

fact that the Truman administration had forcefully resisted Communist threats in Berlin, Greece, and Korea, many Americans blamed Truman for the loss of China. Late in the campaign, Senator Joseph R. McCarthy, Republican of Wisconsin, accused Stevenson of associating with leftist fellow travelers.

Stevenson was also confronted by a series of influence peddling scandals that had tainted the reputation of the Truman Administration. **"Korea, Communism, Corruption"** joined **"I Like Ike"** as effective Republican campaign slogans.

An ethics controversy involving California's Richard M. Nixon, the Republican vice presidential nominee, provided the only glimmer of hope for Democrats. On September 18, 1952, the *New York Post* reported that a group of wealthy California businessmen had provided Nixon with gifts and money upon Nixon's election to the Senate in 1950. Nixon allegedly used this "slush fund" to cover personal expenses. Owing to this, Nixon was under pressure to withdraw from the Republican ticket. In a high stakes effort to save his political career, Nixon delivered a nationally televised address denying allegations of impropriety. Referring to his wife's "Republican cloth coat," and refusing to return the family's cocker spaniel, "Checkers," a gift from an admiring Texan, Nixon persuasively restored public support and his running mate's confidence. The Checkers speech remains a defining moment in the evolution of political television.

General Eisenhower and his youthful vice president defeated Stevenson in a landslide. *See also* "All The Way With Adlai"; Checkers Speech; "First In War, First In Peace"; "Madly for Adlai."

Suggested Readings: John Robert Greene, *The Crusade: The Presidential Election of 1952* (Lanham, MD: University Press of America, 1985); Kathleen Hall Jamieson, *Packaging the Presidency: A History and Criticism of Presidential Campaign Advertising* (New York: Oxford University Press, 1984); Darrell West, *Air Wars: Television Advertising in Election Campaigns, 1952–1992* (Washington, DC: Congressional Quarterly, 1993).

Campaign of 1956

Despite being soundly defeated by Dwight Eisenhower four years earlier, Adlai Stevenson received strong support from the liberal wing of the Democratic Party for his loyalty to the New Deal policies of Franklin Roosevelt, leading to his renomination in 1956. Equally important, Stevenson, a foreign policy expert, openly supported efforts to slow the arms race between the United States and the Soviet Union, including a ban on atmospheric testing of nuclear weapons, especially the city-busting hydrogen bomb. As expected, Republicans renominated their incumbents, President Dwight David Eisenhower and Vice President Richard Nixon.

Throughout the campaign, Stevenson attempted to start a national debate over the direction of the nation's foreign policy. Although Stevenson did not openly reject the need to contain the spread of communism, Stevenson argued that efforts to contain communism must include more than building and testing increasingly more powerful nuclear weapons. The United States needed to understand what made communism attractive to the residents of developing countries around the world.

Stevenson's primary interest was in the future of American foreign policy, but fellow Democrats urged him to add criticism of Eisenhower's domestic policies, particularly regarding labor. The Democratic platform promised the immediate repeal of the Taft-Hartley Act. Besides prohibiting unions from making political contributions to federal campaigns, the "right-to-work" provisions of the law permitted state legislatures to prohibit labor agreements, which required the dismissal of employees who refused to join a union. Equally important, many Democratic loyalists wanted Stevenson to attack the close ties between big business and the Eisenhower administration in an effort to mobilize working class men and women to support the Stevenson candidacy. However, because of his privileged upbringing and academic demeanor, Stevenson did not make a credible populist. The slogans "Get the Country Moving Again" and "Give 'em Hell, Adlai" failed to ignite the passion that led to Harry Truman's come-from-behind victory in 1948.

The Eisenhower campaign experienced little difficulty countering Stevenson. Despite allegations that Eisenhower policies harmed labor, Eisenhower's personal popularity remained high. A strong economy also greatly reduced the effectiveness of populist messages. Much like the campaigns of 1896, 1924, and 1928, good economic times permitted Eisenhower to run on the slogans of "Peace, Progress, Prosperity" and "Keep America Strong with Ike." As important, the Eisenhower campaign effectively portrayed Stevenson's support of a nuclear test ban as naive. Taking everything into consideration, Stevenson had little hope of defeating Eisenhower. By and large Americans trusted Eisenhower to keep the peace.

The 1954 Supreme Court decision in *Brown v. Board of Education* also had a direct impact on the Stevenson campaign. In an effort to calm white voters in southern states, the Democratic platform rejected the use of force to integrate segregated schools. Despite this fact, a larger and larger number of southern white voters abandoned the Democratic Party to vote for Eisenhower in the 1956 presidential election. Stevenson only won 73 electoral votes from southern states. The Eisenhower/Nixon ticket again won a decisive victory in both the electoral and popular votes.

Suggested Readings: Charles Thompson, *The 1956 Presidential Campaign* (Washington, DC: Brookings Institution, 1960); Theodore White, *America in Search of Itself: The Making of the President, 1956–1980* (New York: Harper & Row, 1982).

Campaign of 1960

Vice President Richard Nixon easily won the Republican nomination for president in 1960. Over his eight years as vice president, Nixon had worked to establish himself as a foreign policy expert capable of standing up to the dual threats of the Soviet Union and Communist China. United Nations Ambassador Henry Cabot Lodge was tapped as his running mate. Republicans believed that the Nixon/Lodge ticket offered voters the mature and experienced leadership requisite to the challenges and crises of the nuclear age.

After a competitive primary contest between Massachusetts senator John F. Kennedy, Senate majority leader Lyndon Johnson of Texas, and Minnesota senator Hubert Humphrey, Kennedy arrived at the July Democratic Convention in Los

John F. Kennedy, the 1960 Democratic nominee, campaigns in New York City in October with his wife Jacqueline. © AP/Wide World Photos.

Angeles with sufficient delegate support to win nomination on the first ballot. To win the general election, Kennedy realized that he needed to attract white southern voters suspicious of Kennedy's strong civil rights record. By selecting Lyndon Johnson, a southerner, as his running mate, Kennedy hoped to shore up his weak support among southern whites.

Both candidates were moderates on the issues; hence the campaign of 1960 quickly evolved into a debate over the leadership abilities of Kennedy and Nixon. Republicans argued that Kennedy lacked the foreign policy experience to deal with global communism. To counter the charges, Kennedy supporters pointed to Kennedy's wartime record. During World War II, a Japanese destroyer had rammed and cut in half Kennedy's PT-109. Kennedy's leadership and heroic actions led to the rescue of the surviving crew.

Equally effective, the Kennedy campaign raised doubts about the Eisenhower/Nixon team by claiming the existence of a "Missile Gap" in favor of the Soviet military. The administration denied the gap, and the facts were on their side, but in the wake of *Sputnik* the tactic was persuasive.

The Kennedy campaign had its own problems. The **Campaign of 1928** had seen **anti-Catholic** forces play a major role in the defeat of Al Smith, the Democratic presidential candidate. Although the Nixon/Lodge campaign did not raise the Catholic issue, other critics of the Kennedy candidacy argued that a Kennedy victory would give the Pope far too much influence over an American president. Kennedy responded by stating that there was absolutely no conflict between being a Roman Catholic and president of the United States. Kennedy assured the public that the Pope would not dictate White House policy.

Historians regard televised debates as the turning point in the campaign of 1960. On October 7, Nixon and Kennedy met in the Washington, D.C., television studios of WRC-TV, an NBC affiliate. Prior to the debate, Nixon had exhausted himself in a whirlwind tour of all fifty states. Kennedy rested and prepared. On the air, Kennedy's youthful and healthy appearance contrasted dramatically against Nixon's pasty, bedraggled visage, punctuated by a slightly disheveled five-o'clock shadow. Both candidates debated well, but the tanned, charismatic Democrat impressed television viewers. Radio listeners were more divided.

By Election Day, polls indicated a dead heat between Nixon and Kennedy. In one of the closest presidential elections in American history, John Kennedy received 49.7 percent and Richard Nixon received 49.5 percent of the popular vote. Kennedy won the Electoral College vote, 303 to 219. Rumors of rigged precincts favoring Kennedy in Illinois and Texas circulated, but Nixon chose not to press an investigation. On November 22, 1963, the country was wounded by the brutal assassination of President Kennedy while campaigning for reelection in Dallas. *See also* "All the Way With JFK"; "Leadership for the 60s"; "Peace without Surrender."

Suggested Readings: Theodore White, *The Making of the President, 1960* (New York: Atheneum Publishers, 1961); Commission on Presidential Debates, http://www.debates. org.

Campaign of 1964

Less than a year after succeeding the slain John Kennedy, President Lyndon Baines Johnson announced his intention to seek the Democratic presidential nomination. Republicans selected conservative Arizona senator Barry Goldwater as their presidential candidate to challenge LBJ. Republican national chairman, William E. Miller of New York, was selected to serve as Goldwater's running mate.

The Goldwater selection symbolized a revolution within the Republican Party. Goldwater represented the growing conservative wing of the Republican Party angered by the expansion of federal power over state governments and the rapid expansion of federal social and welfare programs since the New Deal. Stridently anti-Communist, the Goldwater wing strongly opposed the nuclear test ban treaty and any further negotiations with the Soviet Union. The Republican platform also promised to "move decisively to assure victory in South Vietnam." With respect to social issues, Goldwater Republicans supported a constitutional amendment to permit **school prayer** and the passage of legislation to curb the distribution of obscene materials through the mail.

In sharp contrast, Johnson and his running mate, Senator Hubert H. Humphrey of Minnesota, promised a **Great Society** expanding the federal government's efforts in guaranteeing the civil rights of all Americans and dedicating billions of dollars of new federal programs designed to address poverty and other social ills. In the wake of the Cuban Missile Crisis of 1962 Johnson strongly supported the nuclear test ban treaty and the continuation of negotiations between the United States and the Soviet Union to ease tensions abroad.

Not surprisingly, the Johnson campaign took full advantage of Goldwater's his-

Campaign advertisement for
Barry Goldwater, the 1964
Republican nominee. Cour-
tesy of Library of Congress.

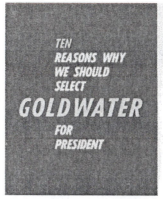

WHY WE NEED SEN. BARRY GOLDWATER

1. Barry Goldwater is the unifying force for the GOP—the single most popular man in all sections of the country, north, south, east and west.

2. Barry Goldwater is an experienced lawmaker with 11 years service in the United States Senate, our Nation's most important legislative body.

3. Barry Goldwater has traveled widely and is a widely acclaimed expert in foreign affairs who will lead the Free World to greater unity and resolution in the Cold War.

4. Barry Goldwater is a fiscal conservative who believes in a balanced budget and a tax structure which will promote economic growth and individual initiative.

5. Barry Goldwater is a staunch defender of personal freedom and the rights of every American, regardless of race, creed or color.

6. Barry Goldwater is a practical businessman who successfully managed a business and met a payroll even during the Depression.

7. Barry Goldwater is a World War II veteran and jet pilot—presently a major general in the U.S. Air Reserve—who knows we must remain militarily strong.

8. Barry Goldwater is a man devoted to his family, with a lovely wife and four children.

9. Barry Goldwater is an extraordinary all-American man—author, explorer, linguist, historian, pilot, photographer, "ham" radio operator, and athlete.

10. Barry Goldwater is a dedicated Party man who will actively support every Republican running for office on the local, state and Federal levels.

BARRY GOLDWATER IS THE REPUBLICAN OPPORTUNITY TO WIN IN 1964!

tory of making controversial statements. For instance, Goldwater had speculated that nuclear weapons might help to end the Vietnam War. Goldwater had also speculated about making participation in the Social Security system voluntary. Hiring the nationally known agency of Doyle, Dane, Bernbach, the Johnson campaign was determined to take advantage of Goldwater's prickly provocations. Goldwater was effectively depicted as bellicose, trigger happy, and politically immature, a loose cannon who had no business controlling the nation's nuclear arsenal. Although only broadcast one time, the now famous **"Daisy" campaign ad** depicted a little girl playing in a bed of flowers whose childhood is obliterated a moment later by the explosion of a nuclear bomb.

Besides raising public fears over a Goldwater presidency, the Johnson campaign also highlighted Johnson's key role in the passage of the Medicare program and other programs directed at helping the less fortunate members of society.

On the defensive, the Goldwater campaign found itself forced to devote a great deal of time attempting to rebut the charges leveled by the Johnson campaign. In the end, Goldwater found little support for his brand of conservatism. On election day, voters handed Lyndon Johnson a mandate to go forward with his plans for a "Great Society." Johnson carried every state but Goldwater's home state of Arizona. *See also* "All the Way With LBJ"; "Extremism in the Defense of Liberty Is No Vice"; Great Society Speech; "In Your Guts You Know He's Nuts"; "In Your Heart You Known He's Right"; "War on Poverty."

Lady Bird Johnson, wife of President Lyndon B. Johnson, traveling on the Lady Bird Special during the 1964 campaign. © Lyndon B. Johnson Library/ National Archives.

Suggested Readings: Harold Faber, *The Road to the White House: The Story of the Election of 1964* (New York: McGraw-Hill, 1965); Rick Perlstein, *Before the Storm: Barry Goldwater and the Unmaking of the American Consensus* (New York: Hill and Wang, 2001); Theodore White, *The Making of the President, 1964* (New York: Atheneum Publishers, 1965).

Campaign of 1968

By the beginning of 1968, the American people were deeply divided by the Vietnam War, racial tension, urban violence, youth counterculture, rising crime, and the social and economic reforms of Lyndon Johnson's Great Society. Thus the presidential campaign of that year stands as the most critical since 1932 and the most dangerously divisive since 1860.

On January 31, 1968, North Vietnam and their Viet Cong allies launched the "Tet" offensive. Although American and South Vietnamese forces successfully repelled the offensive, press and public perceived only an indomitable enemy. The leadership of the department of defense had assured the public that victory was at hand in Vietnam while influential television anchorman Walter Cronkite announced that the war in Vietnam was now "unwinnable." Johnson's progressive presidency was thrown into crisis over the war.

Challenging a vulnerable incumbent, Minnesota senator Eugene McCarthy, the poet-warrior of the 1960s youth movement, undertook an insurgent primary campaign to deny Johnson the 1968 Democratic presidential nomination. McCarthy's campaign fit the tenor of the times; geared toward youth (supported by young volunteers nationwide known as the "McCarthy Million"), intellectually oriented, and fundamentally iconoclastic. To the surprise of almost every political observer, McCarthy won 42 percent of the vote in the New Hampshire primary in mid-March with Johnson receiving 49 percent. More importantly, McCarthy walked away with twenty of twenty-four delegates committed to his nomination. McCarthy's strong showing exposed the incumbent's vulnerability and opened the door for New York senator Robert Kennedy and South Dakota senator George McGovern to enter the race for the Democratic presidential nomination.

On March 31, 1968, Johnson addressed the American people announcing a number of steps to attempt to bring the Vietnam War to an end. Wearily, Johnson concluded his remarks with a surprise announcement to the effect that he would not seek renomination or reelection, committing all energy to ending the war. Shortly thereafter, Vice President Hubert Humphrey announced his intention to seek the nomination. McCarthy had intellectual appeal and the loyalty of America's youth, Kennedy had family mystique and charisma, and Humphrey had the advantage of incumbency and an unparalleled record of liberal service.

Then on April 4, 1968, an assassin killed beloved civil rights leader Martin Luther King, Jr., at a Memphis hotel. Rioting erupted in several major cities, leading to loss of life and costly property damage. Robert Kennedy, who had helped prevent a riot in Indianapolis in the wake of King's death, was himself cut down by an assassin two months later at a Los Angeles hotel while leaving a celebration of his fresh victory in the California primary. California had given RFK the momentum needed to win at the convention, but it was all lost in a few violent, insane, and hopelessly bitter seconds.

The following events at the Democratic National Convention in Chicago were unprecedented and remain singular. Rioting roiled the streets as Democrats battled in the convention hall. With Kennedy slain, Johnson out, and McCarthy's momentum spent, the vice president snagged the nomination without a single victory in the primaries. Distinguished Maine senator Edmund Muskie was tapped as his running mate. But Humphrey was saddled by his association with LBJ and thus the unpopular war, which continued to divide the Democrats throughout the remainder of the campaign. At the convention, youthful delegates chanted, "Dump the Hump," emphasizing their distaste for Humphrey who they now saw as the establishment candidate and Johnson's boy—a man who could not be trusted. The party also suffered from the third-party candidacy of Alabama governor and famed segregationist George C. Wallace, depriving Democrats of their southern base. This divisive state among Democrats and the loss of the South worked to the advantage of the other side.

Dramatically different from the Democrats, the Republicans demonstrated remarkable unity. Former vice president Richard Nixon easily defeated New York governor Nelson Rockefeller and California governor Ronald Reagan for the nomination.

Remembering the disaster of the 1960 television debates, the Nixon campaign worked diligently to remake his public image. After his narrow 1960 defeat to John F. Kennedy, and his 1962 failure to win governorship of California, Nixon worked tirelessly for five years to rebuild his political career by traveling thousands of miles to attend Republican events from coast to coast. After the 1964 Goldwater debacle, Republicans looked for an established, comparatively moderate fig-

Vice President Hubert Humphrey, the 1968 Democratic nominee. © Lyndon B. Johnson Library/National Archives.

ure who could attract a cross-section of American votes. Rockefeller was too liberal for many Republicans, and Reagan too close to Goldwater; Nixon was the only major Republican who seemed to strike the middle ground.

Nixon promoted himself as a conciliator, capable of bridging the nation's many divisions. The old Cold Warrior and Kitchen Debater was shelved, the unifier was brought forward. Strategically, Nixon emphasized leadership and reconciliation; Nixon was "the one" who could bring the nation together. His running mate, Maryland's Spiro Agnew served as hatchet man, vehemently attacking Humphrey and his liberal supporters, with particular criticism aimed at the loud and unruly protestors who represented in Agnew's eyes the deterioration of American values. Both Agnew and Nixon frequently stressed that they would represent the **silent majority** in their administration.

Equally important, the Nixon campaign successfully made law and order a key issue. Nixon argued that the liberal policies of recent Democratic administrations combined with the rulings of the liberal Warren court had crippled law enforcement officers and the prosecution criminals. Nixon promised to nominate law and order judges to the federal bench and to devote millions of dollars in federal funds to state and local government law enforcement. Adding to these campaign elements a promise to end the Vietnam War with honor, Nixon began the presidential campaign with a huge lead in the polls.

Unlike the unified Republican Party, the Humphrey campaign faced the problem of reassembling the apparently fractured Democratic coalition. Although Humphrey succeeded in mobilizing African American and progressive white voters, he failed to persuade conservative Southerners to support his candidacy. Moreover, Wallace received 46 electoral votes from Deep South states, undermining the Democrats. In the end, Nixon received 43.4 percent, Humphrey 42.7 percent, and Wallace 13.5 percent of the popular vote. Despite the fact that Humphrey came within 500,000 votes of Nixon, Humphrey only received 191 electoral votes to the 301 electoral votes for Nixon. *See also* "Let the People Rule"; "Nixon's the One"; "Stand Up for America"; This Time Vote Like Your Whole World Depended On It"; "Who but Hubert?"

Suggested Readings: Lewis L. Gould, *1968: The Election that Changed America* (Chicago: Ivan R. Dee, 1993); Joe McGinniss, *The Selling of the President, 1968* (New York: Trident Press, 1969); Theodore White, *The Making of the President, 1968* (New York: Atheneum Publishers, 1969).

Campaign of 1972

In 1972 the Republican Party overwhelmingly renominated President Richard Nixon for a second term. By the time of the August Republican National Convention, presidential preference polls showed President Nixon with a large lead over Senator George McGovern of South Dakota, the Democratic presidential nominee. McGovern had defeated a dozen other Democrats for the presidential nomination including early front-runner Senator Edmund Muskie, who had been damaged by media reports that he shed public tears over defamatory rumors regarding his wife.

Other personal issues damaged the Democrats. The McGovern campaign suffered from the withdrawal of Missouri senator Thomas Eagleton from the Democratic ticket after disclosing having once voluntarily hospitalized himself for "nervous exhaustion and fatigue." McGovern then selected R. Sargent Shriver of Maryland, a member of the Kennedy family by marriage, to replace Eagleton.

Despite the continuing Vietnam War, Nixon had succeeded in reducing the number of U.S. soldiers in Vietnam and had sustained ongoing negotiations aimed at ending the war. Equally important, Nixon's stunning trip to China and arms reduction negotiations with the Soviet Union had eased tensions with these two countries.

Nixon's 1972 campaign was confident, steady, and flawless. Nixon was convincingly depicted as a respected world leader who would use his vast experience,

Senator George McGovern of South Dakota accepts the 1972 Democratic presidential nomination on July 14 at Miami Beach, Florida. © AP/Wide World Photos.

President Richard M. Nixon, the 1972 Republican candidate, departs for the Republican National Convention. © Nixon Presidential Materials Staff/National Archives.

wisdom and skill to bring the Vietnam War to an honorable end and promote peace with all rival powers. Making effective use of the "Peace With Honor" slogan, the president emphasized his tough, realistic approach to negotiated peace in sharp contrast to McGovern's "peacenik" proposal for unilateral withdrawal. With ongoing peace negotiations in Paris, Nixon effectively argued that his re-election would force North Vietnam to negotiate. The slogan "President Nixon, Now More Than Ever" emphasized the importance of leaving Nixon and his foreign policy team in office.

While the McGovern campaign called for a series of presidential debates, Nixon remained aloof and presidential, appearing only at carefully staged campaign events designed to produce only positive media coverage. Determined to deny McGovern a nationwide television audience, the Nixon campaign refused to agree to any presidential debates. Nixon worked hard and remained on the high road, leaving the low road to Agnew.

While the public saw a confident White House, the Nixon reelection campaign led by the Committee to Re-elect the President (CREEP), nervously sought to leave nothing to chance. Unknown to the public and ignoring provisions of the Federal Election Campaign Act of 1971 (FECA), the Nixon White House and CREEP solicited millions of dollars in illegal campaign contributions. With full knowledge of the White House, CREEP set up a "dirty tricks" operation to disrupt the primary campaigns of contenders for the Democratic presidential nomination, including Muskie, for it was the dirty tricksters behind the defamation of the candidate's wife that provoked his public display of emotion. Late in 1971 and early in 1972, CREEP hired former FBI special agent G. Gordon Liddy and former CIA operatives E. Howard Hunt and James McCord to operate a political intelligence unit. On June 23, 1972, District of Columbia police arrested McCord and four Cuban exiles caught burglarizing the offices of the Democratic National Committee at Washington's Watergate Hotel. A short time later, police arrested G. Gordon Liddy and E. Howard Hunt for planning the burglary. The White House immediately denied any knowledge or involvement with the burglary, and managed to cover up the scandal until well after the election was decided in Nixon's favor.

Nixon received 60.7 percent of the popular vote and 520 electoral votes. In 1973 the Watergate cover-up began to unravel. On August 9, 1974, Nixon became the first president to resign the presidency. *See also* Dirty Tricks.

Suggested Readings: Robert North Roberts, *Ethics in U.S. Government: An Encyclopedia of Investigations, Scandals, Reforms, and Legislation* (Westport, CT: Greenwood Press, 2001); Gordon Weil, *The Long Shot: George McGovern Runs for President* (New York: Norton, 1973); Theodore White, *The Making of the President, 1972* (New York: Atheneum Publishers, 1973).

Campaign of 1976

Two years after the Watergate scandal prompted the resignation of President Richard Nixon, the new Republican president Gerald R. Ford, found himself in a close contest for the Republican nomination against a determined challenge by former California governor, Ronald Reagan. Influential conservative forces within the Republican Party preferred Reagan to the moderate Ford, drawing much of the president's energy away from the Democrats throughout much of the summer to deflect the Reagan charge. Additionally, Ford's preemptive pardon of former president Nixon raised suspicion within the electorate.

Unlike the difficult primary battle fought by Ford, Democratic nominee Jimmy Carter surprised seasoned political observers with the ease of his political victory. Carter had keenly positioned himself as a moderate, liberal on social issues such as abortion, affirmative action, and gun control but conservative on fiscal policy. Instead of calling for higher taxes to pay for the expansion of federal programs, Carter pledged spending discipline and frugality, touting "zero-based budgeting" as a method to enhance federal investment. Furthermore, Carter effectively pledged to restore honesty in government in the aftermath of the Watergate scandal.

For the first time in presidential campaign history the Presidential Election

Republican President Gerald Ford (right) and his Democratic challenger Jimmy Carter debate in Philadelphia on September 23, 1976. © Gerald R. Ford Library/ National Archives.

Campaign Fund Act made available federal funds to presidential campaigns in compliance with spending limitations, a new post-Watergate measure designed to prevent campaign abuses.

Equally important, Carter and Ford agreed to a series of televised presidential debates that would also involve their running mates in a separate venue. The debates were the first at the presidential level since Kennedy and Nixon held theirs sixteen years earlier.

After the end of the Republican convention in mid-August, presidential preference polls showed Carter enjoying a double-digit lead over Ford. Deciding to adopt a cautious strategy, the Carter campaign continued to stress his impeccable reputation by emphasizing the theme of integrity in government. **"Return Integrity to the White House"** became the main slogan of Carter's fall campaign.

Nonetheless and to the dismay of the Carter campaign, by late September the initial gap had closed significantly. Carter faced strong criticism from inside his party and from the Ford campaign for giving an interview to *Playboy* magazine. In the interview, Carter, a devout Southern Baptist, confessed that he had been scrupulously faithful to his wife throughout his marriage but had "lusted in his heart." Besides granting the interview, many political observers wondered why Carter would volunteer such information.

Despite the Carter misstep, a major Ford gaffe during the second presidential debate seriously wounded the president's campaign. In response to a question regarding the relationship of the United States with the Soviet Union and its satellite dependents, Ford responded by stating that he did not believe that Eastern Europe remained under Soviet hegemony.

> I don't believe, uh—Mr. Frankel that uh—the Yugoslavians consider themselves dominated by the Soviet Union. I don't believe the Poles consider themselves dominated by the Soviet Union. Each of those

Betty Ford holds an impromptu press conference in the press car during President Gerald Ford's whistle-stop campaign trip through Michigan in 1976. © Gerald R. Ford Library/National Archives.

countries is independent, autonomous: it has its own territorial integrity and the United States does not concede that those countries are under the domination of the United States.

Much like Carter's *Playboy* interview gaffe, Ford's Eastern Europe goof forced the Ford campaign to devote badly needed time to diffuse the controversy and focus the attention of voters on **"The Man Who Made Us Proud Again,"** and **"Peace, Prosperity and the Public Trust."**

On Election Day, Carter received 50.1 percent of the popular vote against 48 percent of the popular vote for Ford. Carter's electoral vote margin proved much narrower. Carter received 297 electoral votes against the 240 received by Ford. Historians credit Carter's victory to his ability to recapture a number of southern states previously lost to Richard Nixon. Even more importantly, African Americans voted for Carter as a block, demonstrating the expanding influence of the minority vote in presidential politics. *See also* "Whip Inflation Now (WIN)."

Suggested Readings: Patrick Anderson, *Electing Jimmy Carter: The Campaign of 1976* (Baton Rouge: Louisiana State University Press, 1994); Sidney Kraus, *The Great Debates: Carter v. Ford, 1976* (Bloomington: Indiana University Press, 1979); Martin Schram, *Running for President, 1976: The Carter Campaign* (New York: Stein and Day, 1977); Jules Witcover, *Marathon: The Pursuit of the Presidency, 1972–1976* (New York: Viking Press, 1977).

Campaign of 1980

Economic problems and foreign policy crises dominated the campaign of 1980. To combat runaway inflation, the Federal Reserve Board had raised interest rates to historic levels, significantly slowing economic growth. The frustrating Iran hostage standoff, the Soviet Union's invasion of Afghanistan, and incumbent President Carter's boycott of the Moscow Olympic games made it difficult for the administration to devote its full attention to its domestic agenda. Meanwhile, Carter found himself facing a serious challenge from Massachusetts senator Edward M. Kennedy. Even so, Carter exuded confidence that he could "whip" Ted Kennedy.

The 1976 defeat of President Gerald Ford by Carter immediately made former California governor, Ronald Reagan, the front-runner for the 1980 Republican presidential nomination. Reagan ultimately went on to win the Republican nomination. In an effort to soothe the moderate wing of the Republican Party, Reagan offered Ford the vice presidential nomination. Ford turned him down, and Reagan extended the offer to his moderate rival, George Bush, who accepted.

Through the winter and early spring of 1980, Jimmy Carter allowed **surrogates** to conduct his campaign for the Democratic presidential nomination. In defending his decision not to campaign, Carter explained that he needed to devote full time to freeing the hostages being held by Iranian militants and to resuscitating the nation's economy. Reminiscent of the nineteenth century "front porch" campaign, Carter conducted his campaign from the White House Rose Garden. The strategy helped against Kennedy, but a disastrous failure to rescue the hostages further eroded public confidence in the Carter presidency.

Ronald Reagan delivers his acceptance speech to the Republican National Convention in Detroit, Michigan, on July 17, 1980. © Ronald Reagan Library/National Archives.

Coincidentally, on the day the mission failed, Representative John B. Anderson, a moderate House Republican, announced his intention to run for president as an independent. In announcing his decision to run, Anderson argued that neither the Democratic or Republican parties had the political will to take on the serious problems facing the nation. Anderson put forward a fiscally conservative and socially liberal platform, including a call for a 50-cents-a-gallon tax on gasoline to slow consumption to reduce the dependence of the United States on foreign sources of oil.

Despite the economic problems of the nation and the Carter administration's foreign policy mistakes, presidential preference polls predicted a close race. Although the polls indicated widespread blame assigned to the Carter administration for the nation's problems, both foreign and domestic, many of the same voters held serious doubts about Reagan's presidential qualifications. The public also harbored serious reservations regarding the governor's conservative positions on a wide range of issues.

To persuade voters to give the Carter administration a second chance, the Carter campaign emphasized reputation for integrity and hard work. Slogans such as "Stand by the President," "Leadership and Strength," and **"A Solid Man in a Sensitive Job"** reflected this strategy. Simultaneously the Carter campaign criticized Reagan for simplistic solutions to foreign policy problems that excessively focused on exorbitant defense spending.

Making a case for denying President Carter a second term, the Reagan campaign stressed that the nation needed new leadership to get the country moving again and to restore international respect for the United States. Slogans such as "Make America Great Again" and "Together—A New Beginning" reflected this strategy.

Many observers believed that television debates between Reagan and Carter might determine the outcome of the election. Through much of the fall election campaign, the Carter campaign refused to debate Reagan because the Reagan campaign team insisted on the inclusion of Anderson. Carter balked, and Reagan and Anderson debated without him. Carter finally acceded to a debate but remained insistent on leaving Anderson out. Reagan accepted, and on October 28, only a week before Election Day, Carter and Reagan faced off in their first and only debate.

Despite the fact that Carter demonstrated a superior mastery of complex facts and governmental expertise, a disarming, telegenic Reagan weakened Carter by repeatedly illustrating Carter's failure to control inflation, revitalize the sluggish economy, and rebuild confidence in the nation's foreign policy. Reagan promised that a sharp cut in taxes and a reduction in unnecessary government expenditures would revive the economy. In one of the most effective sound bites in political campaign history, Reagan charmed the American people by asking **"Are You Better Off Than You Were Four Years Ago?"** As if in response, the electorate handed Reagan a landslide victory one week later.

Suggested Readings: Mark Bisnow, *Diary of a Dark Horse: The 1980 Anderson Presidential Campaign* (Carbondale: Southern Illinois University Press, 1983); David S. Broder and Richard Harwood, *The Pursuit of the Presidency of 1980* (New York: Berkley Books, 1980); Elizabeth Drew, *Portrait of an Election: The 1980 Presidential Campaign* (New York: Simon & Schuster, 1981); Jack Germond and Jules Witcover, *Blue Smoke and Mirrors: How Reagan Won and Why Carter Lost the Election of 1980* (New York: Viking, 1981).

Campaign of 1984

To challenge President Ronald Reagan, a popular incumbent, in the 1984 campaign the Democratic Party selected Walter Mondale, vice president under President Carter, and Representative Geraldine Ferraro, the first woman to receive a vice presidential nomination from a major political party. Mondale won the nomination after surviving a tough primary battle against Colorado senator Gary Hart

President Ronald Reagan (right), Nancy Reagan, Barbara Bush, and Vice President George H.W. Bush at the 1984 Republican National Convention in Dallas, Texas. © Ronald Reagan Library/National Archives.

and civil rights activist Jesse Jackson. In selecting Ferraro as his running mate, Mondale hoped to demonstrate that women's concerns would receive high priority within his administration.

A short time after the selection of Ferraro, controversy involving the financial affairs of Ferraro's husband emerged. The controversy was eventually dismissed, but only after weeks of costly media distraction.

While the Mondale campaign appeared disorganized, the Reagan reelection campaign ran like a fine watch. Seeking to take advantage of a booming economy, the Reagan campaign adopted a "Morning in America" theme for the campaign. Throughout the campaign, Reagan touted the nation's economic recovery from one of the deepest recessions in decades. Equally important, the Reagan campaign reminded voters that his administration had rebuilt the nation's military, restoring America's global superpower reputation. The campaign slogan **"America Is Back, Standing Tall"** captured this theme.

Finally, the Reagan campaign continually asked the American people whether they wanted to return to the days of high unemployment and inflation; a direct reference to the Carter/Mondale administration.

The Mondale/Ferraro campaign attempted to turn the election into a referendum on controversial Reagan administration policies. Mondale sharply criticized the administration for allegedly refusing to enforce environmental laws, reducing funding for vital social programs, and wasteful defense spending. In a controversial decision, Mondale promised the American people that if they elected him president he would raise taxes to fund important programs and to prevent an exploding federal debt and interminable deficit spending from bankrupting the nation.

In the end, nothing seemed to work for the Mondale/Ferraro campaign. Although Reagan visibly faltered in the first television debate with Mondale, he came back strong two weeks later in a second debate that put to rest speculation and doubt about Reagan's age. In a moment worthy of FDR, Reagan deftly turned the tables on Mondale, promising not to hold his opponent's youth and inexperience against him.

President Ronald Reagan on a whistle-stop tour through Ohio during the 1984 presidential campaign. © Ronald Reagan Library/National Archives.

On Election Day, Reagan crushed Mondale by winning 58.8 percent of the popular vote and taking 525 out of 538 electoral votes. The Mondale/Ferraro ticket only won the 13 electoral votes of Minnesota, Mondale's home state.

Suggested Readings: Elizabeth Drew, *Campaign Journal: The Political Events of 1983–1984* (New York: Macmillan, 1985); Jack Germond and Jules Witcover, *Wake Us When It's Over: Presidential Politics of 1984* (New York: Macmillan, 1985); Jane Seaberry, "From Prosperity to Problems: Camp Seeks to Shift Campaign's Focus to the Future," *Washington Post*, October 14, 1984, p. H1.

Campaign of 1988

The Democratic Party entered the campaign of 1988 with high hopes of taking back the White House. The Iran-Contra scandal had seriously damaged public support for the policies of the Reagan administration. A budget stalemate between congressional Democrats and the Reagan White House had caused ever-expanding federal deficits, adding red ink to the exploding federal debt. Partisan differences over **abortion, affirmative action**, and gun control sharply divided the Democratic and Republican parties.

After a primary campaign marked by the withdrawal of former Colorado senator Gary Hart over an infidelity controversy and civil rights leader Jesse Jackson's decline, the July Democratic convention selected Massachusetts governor Michael Dukakis. The distinguished Texas senator Lloyd Bentsen was picked for the bottom of the ticket. Many Democrats saw the Dukakis/Bentsen alliance as a parallel to another Massachusetts/Texas ticket, the victorious Kennedy/Johnson **Campaign of 1960**. Post-convention presidential preference polls showed Dukakis with a double-digit lead over likely Republican presidential nominee Vice President George H. W. Bush.

Recognizing that Dukakis had positioned himself as a moderate Democrat, Bush's media team planned a **negative ad** campaign to define Dukakis as a standard "tax and spend" Democrat, typically soft on crime and disinterested in national defense. In one of the most effective ad campaigns in election history, the Bush campaign blamed Dukakis for polluting **Boston Harbor**, attacked the governor for vetoing a bill requiring all students in Massachusetts schools to recite the pledge of allegiance, and for supporting the dreaded tax increases.

Dukakis also found himself under fierce attack for approving a prison furlough program. In at least one instance, a convicted murderer on furlough terrorized and raped a Maryland woman. The independent **Willie Horton** ad, using controversial imagery to convey this message, skirted the edge of propriety.

By early October 1988, Dukakis found himself significantly behind Bush in presidential preference polls. Efforts by Dukakis to turn the 1988 election into a referendum on the Iran-Contra scandal failed, the vice president insisting that he was "out of the loop." Slogans such as "Good jobs at good pay in the old U.S.A." failed to catch on. Bush went on to soundly defeat Dukakis in the popular and electoral votes.

In the aftermath of the election of 1988, media observers sharply criticized electronic journalists for allowing both Bush and Dukakis campaigns to avoid addressing issues such as the exploding national debt and providing health care for millions of uninsured Americans. *See also* "Next Frontier;" "Read My Lips, No New Taxes."

Suggested Readings: Richard Cramer, *What It Takes: The Way to the White House* (New York: Random House, 1992); Jack Germond, *Whose Broad Stripes and Bright Stars? The Trivial Pursuit of the Presidency, 1988* (New York: Warner Books, 1989); Peter Goldman, Tom Mathews, and the *Newsweek* Special Election Team, *The Quest for the Presidency, 1988* (New York: Simon & Schuster, 1989).

Campaign of 1992

After twelve years of Republicans in the White House, the Democratic Party found itself desperately searching for a candidate who might reverse their presidential fortunes. With President George Bush riding high in the public opinion polls after victory in the Persian Gulf War, many Democratic contenders, perceiving the presidency to be beyond reach, decided against running in 1992.

But by the close of 1991, the nation's political landscape had undergone a dramatic transformation. An economic recession and an exploding federal deficit had led to a sharp plunge in President Bush's approval ratings. Besides facing these problems, Bush drew increasing criticism from his party for having betrayed the legacy of Ronald Reagan by reneging on his "No New Taxes" pledge. When Bush accepted the 1988 Republican presidential nomination, he had brought the delegates at the convention to their feet by stating **"Read My Lips, No New Taxes."** This unexpected decline in the political fortunes of President Bush opened the way for Democratic challengers.

Nearly a decade earlier, a number of moderate Democrats had established the Democrat Leadership Council (DLC) in an effort to move the Democratic Party from the left to the middle of the political spectrum. Arkansas governor Bill Clinton had played a major role in building the DLC into a major force in Democratic politics. When Clinton announced his intention to seek the Democratic presiden-

President George H.W. Bush, the 1992 Republican nominee, waves from the back of a train outside Bowling Green, Ohio. © George Bush Library/National Archives.

Governor Bill Clinton of Arkansas, the 1992 Democratic nominee, waves as he boards a bus with running mate Al Gore. © AP/Wide World Photos.

tial nomination in August of 1991, he immediately became one of the party's leading candidates.

Based in Little Rock, Arkansas, the Clinton campaign adopted a simple strategy for winning the nomination and for defeating Bush in the November general election. **"It's the Economy, Stupid"** became the overriding issue for the Clinton campaign. Furthermore, the Clinton campaign refused to allow others to characterize their candidate as a classic "soft on crime" Democratic liberal. But Clinton also held to some traditional Democratic principles, promising millions of jobs if elected.

Within a short time of announcing his campaign, Clinton found himself embroiled in a number of serious ethics controversies. The first involved allegations of Clinton's habitual marital infidelity. An appearance by Bill Clinton and his wife, Hillary Rodham Clinton, on the CBS news magazine *60 Minutes* helped to diffuse the controversy. Additionally, a dispute arose over allegations of Clinton's draft dodging during the Vietnam War.

In the end, these controversies did not prevent Clinton from easily securing the nomination. Clinton selected Tennessee senator Albert Gore as his vice presidential running mate.

Through the 1992 primary season, President Bush faced the problem of unifying a badly split Republican Party. Angered by Bush's alleged repudiation of Republican principles, conservative commentator and former Nixon aide Pat Buchanan decided to challenge Bush for the Republican nomination. Buchanan blamed the recession on too much taxation and burdensome federal regulation of American business. Furthermore, Buchanan declared his strong support for prayer in schools, education vouchers, and prohibiting abortions except when a mother's life is endangered. Although Buchanan made a strong showing in the New Hampshire primary, Bush went on to win nomination, but the Buchanan challenge left the president damaged.

By early spring of 1992, both Bill Clinton and George Bush had won enough delegates to assure their respective nominations. Intensely dissatisfied with the choice awaiting the American people, charismatic Texas billionaire populist H.

Ross Perot announced his intention to conduct an independent bid for the presidency. Through the early months of 1992, Perot appeared on CNN's *Larry King Live* indicating disapproval with both Bill Clinton and George Bush. However, Perot reserved his sharpest criticism for President Bush for supporting free trade legislation and for failing to stem the exploding federal deficit. Finally, Perot entered the race as the leader of a new Reform Party.

Presidential preference polls indicated that Perot had widespread support among angry and alienated voters. Then suddenly, during the middle of July 1992, Perot announced his intention to withdraw from the presidential race because he lacked a realistic chance of winning the presidency. But Perot again threw the presidential race into turmoil when he changed his mind and announced his intention to reenter the contest in late September.

A few weeks later Perot received a major boost when the Commission on Presidential Debates voted to allow Perot to participate in all televised debates. In an unorthodox move, Perot opted not to purchase spot ads. Instead, Perot opted to broadcast thirty-minute **infomercials** in which Perot used graphs and charts to graphically dramatize the dangers of the growing federal debt.

To the surprise of many political observers, presidential preference polls showed little movement between Bill Clinton and George Bush from late August through Election Day. Clinton maintained a small but comfortable lead, particularly among women and African Americans. In contrast, George Bush experienced persistent difficulty mobilizing the Republican base and rebuilding support among independent voters crucial to Bush winning the election. Throughout the fall campaign, support for Ross Perot fluctuated in direct proportion to fluctuations in Perot's commitment. But as November drew near, Perot's popularity surged. Perot did not manage to win the election, but his presence drew votes away from both Bush and Clinton. On Election Day, Clinton received a little more than 42 percent of the vote, the lowest percentage of the popular vote enjoyed by a winning candidate since Abraham Lincoln. Against Bush's 36 percent, the worst for an incumbent since President Taft was damaged by another bully third candidate, it was all that was needed.

Suggested Readings: Jack Germond and Jules Witcover, *Mad as Hell: Revolt at the Ballot Box, 1992* (New York: Warner Books, 1993); Peter Goldman et al., *Quest for the Presidency, 1992* (College Station: Texas A & M University Press, 1994); Mary Matalin and James Carville, *All's Fair: Love, War, and Running for President* (New York: Random House, Simon & Schuster, 1994).

Campaign of 1996

Two years before the election of 1996, many political **pundits** declared that incumbent President Bill Clinton had little chance of winning reelection. In the November 1994 midterm congressional elections the Republican Party took control of the House of Representatives for the first time since 1952. With both the House and Senate under Republican control, a hostile Congress blocked Clinton's legislative agenda, and instead passed key provisions of Speaker of the House Newt Gingrich's Contract with America. Besides having to deal with a Republican-controlled Congress, Bill Clinton and Hillary Rodham Clinton faced an ongoing criminal investigation by independent counsel Kenneth Starr.

As part of the Clinton strategy to reintroduce himself to the American public as a moderate, the Clinton White House and the Democratic National Committee embarked on a program to raise tens of millions of dollars in **soft money** contributions to pay for the broadcast of **issue ads** during the early months of 1996 recounting the administration's achievements. Unprecedented and sustained economic growth was their most convincing argument for election.

During the second week of August the Republican Party nominated former Senate majority leader, Bob Dole, as their standard bearer. In an effort to appeal to moderates Dole selected former New York representative Jack Kemp as his running mate. Recognizing that Republicans needed to do much better with women voters to win the upcoming election, Dole's supporters attempted to remove the anti-abortion plank from the Republican platform. Since 1976 the platform had included an anti-abortion plank. While the anti-abortion position of the Republican Party had played a major role in recruiting the support of conservative religious fundamentalists, Republican candidates alienated millions of women voters. Thus the Dole campaign recognized that it needed to narrow the **gender gap** if they had any hope of regaining the White House.

Months before the August Democratic National Convention, the Democratic National Committee began broadcasting expensive issue ads celebrating the successes of the Clinton administration, emphasizing millions of new jobs, reduced crime, and significant welfare reform. Facing Clinton's decisive lead in the polls, Dole tried various strategies in an attempt to close the gap. The most controversial strategy targeted Clinton's real vulnerability, his character. Making use of the **"A Better Man for a Better America"** slogan, Republicans contrasted Dole's record as a war hero to Clinton's history of infidelity. In desperation, the Dole campaign adopted the slogan "Wake Up, America" in an attempt to sound the moral alarm.

Clinton countered by running on a booming economy and shrinking deficits. Correctly reasoning that a decisive plurality of independent voters would see the economy as the key issue and suspend their concern over character, Clinton managed to sustain his lead.

Emboldened by his strong showing in the 1992 presidential campaign, Reform Party candidate Ross Perot returned hoping to use the 1996 presidential campaign to transform the Reform Party into a viable third party. But Perot also found that the strong economy significantly reduced the impact of his anti-deficit message. Frustrated and peevish, Perot furiously joined the attack on Clinton's character, to no avail.

Written off as dead in the water by pundits two years earlier, Bill Clinton became the first Democratic President since Franklin Roosevelt to win a second term. *See also* Soccer Mom.

Suggested Readings: Elizabeth Drew, *Whatever It Takes: The Real Struggle for Political Power in America* (New York: Viking Press, 1997); Dick Morris, *Behind the Oval Office: Winning the Presidency in the Nineties* (New York: Random House, 1997); Roger Simon, *Show Time: The American Political Circus and the Race for the White House* (New York: Times Books, 1998).

Campaign of 2000

The campaign of 2000 opened with the Republican National Convention nominating Texas governor George W. Bush, son of former president George H.W. Bush, as their candidate. The Democratic Party nominated incumbent Vice President Albert Gore as their standard bearer. Both Bush and Gore overcame challengers during the 2000 primary season. Gore easily defeated Bill Bradley while Bush faced a more difficult task repelling the challenge of Arizona senator John McCain. Running on a government reform platform, McCain had used his primary campaign to lobby heavily for campaign finance reform and a ban on **soft money** contributions to national political parties.

Prior to the beginning of the general election campaign, both the Republican and Democratic parties had raised tens of millions of soft money contributions to set up sophisticated voter identification and get-out-the-vote operations. Also by the beginning of the fall general election campaign, the Gore and Bush campaigns determined that the outcome of the election hinged on a small minority of **battleground states**, including Arkansas, Florida, Iowa, Kentucky, Michigan, Missouri, New Hampshire, New Mexico, Ohio, Oregon, Pennsylvania, Tennessee, Washington, West Virginia, and Wisconsin.

Throughout the general election campaign, presidential preference polls fluctuated. After the July Republican National Convention, Bush held a substantial lead in the polls. After the August Democratic National Convention, Gore pulled even with Bush. In an effort to appeal to moderate suburban voters, Bush defined himself as a **"Compassionate Conservative"** committed to education reform. Taking a page out of Ronald Reagan's successful 1980 presidential campaign, Bush proposed a significant tax cut to return part of the nation's growing budget surplus to American taxpayers. A proposal to allow workers to invest part of their social

With his wife Laura, Texas governor George W. Bush, the 2000 Republican candidate, acknowledges the crowd at the Joliet, Illinois, train station. © AP/Wide World Photos.

security contributions in the stock market and other private investments constituted the most controversial element of the Bush campaign.

The Gore campaign relied upon traditional Democratic messages to hold together the coalition that proved crucial in Bill Clinton's 1992 and 1996 victories. Besides sharply criticizing Bush's social security proposal, the Gore campaign emphasized the need to expand Medicare to cover prescription drugs. Because of the cost associated with expanding Medicare coverage and guaranteeing future Social Security benefits, the Gore campaign argued that Bush's proposed tax cuts would result in the return to large deficits or force Congress to tap the Social Security trust fund.

Equally important, the Gore campaign stressed that during the eight years of Democratic control of the White House, the United States had experienced an unprecedented period of economic prosperity. Gore also reiterated the party's pro-choice stance on abortion.

The tightness of the race led to intense interest in the three scheduled presidential debates. However, the debates did little to shake the race loose. Neither Bush nor Gore made major mistakes. On the other hand, Gore did make a number of minor misstatements that seemed self-congratulatory and drew attention to Gore's exaggeration of his own importance regarding certain events and developments. Additionally, Gore experienced considerable difficulty distancing himself from Clinton's ethics problems.

Throughout the campaign of 2000, the Bush and Gore campaigns targeted particular voting blocks. The Gore campaign targeted African American voters, single, college-educated women, union members, and urban voters. On the other hand, the Bush campaign targeted religious conservatives, white males, and rural voters. Both campaigns heavily targeted suburban voters in the key battleground states.

When the dust settled the morning after Election Day, the election was hung on problems with the tally in Florida. Massive confusion had surrounded media coverage of election returns. After first declaring Gore the president-elect, late Florida election returns forced a number of news operations to withdraw their call. Many of the same news operations then subsequently declared George Bush president-elect. Albert Gore won the national popular vote by approximately 543,000 votes, but the states, not the people, elect presidents, and without Florida he fell one vote short of the 270 electoral votes needed to win the presidency. The morning following the election, Bush held a tenuous, paper-thin lead in Florida. Then an explosive controversy over alleged voting irregularities in certain Florida counties erupted. Irregularities also appeared to have occurred in New Mexico and Wisconsin.

For thirty-six days the United States was embroiled in a raging controversy over the true outcome in Florida. The Bush and Gore campaigns fought over whether election officials should attempt to determine voter intent by examining ballots to detect "over votes" and "under votes." After a series of partial recounts left Bush with a lead amounting to a few hundred votes, Florida's secretary of state certified the election of Bush. Ultimately the Florida Supreme Court ordered local election officials to recount ballots where under-voting was suspected. Instead of establishing a statewide standard, the Florida Supreme Court allowed local election officials to assess voter intent. Shortly after the action by the Florida Supreme Court, the United States Supreme Court issued a stay suspending the Florida recount. On December 12, 2000, by a vote of 5 to 4, the Supreme Court imposed a midnight December 12 deadline on the Florida recount. The majority opinion argued that the recount procedures adopted by the Florida Supreme Court violated the equal protection and due process rights of Florida voters. Since the high court issued its opinion at 9:00 P.M., the decision effectively ended the Florida recount with the younger George Bush still holding a slim lead in the popular tally, but with this lead Bush won Florida's electoral votes, and thus the election. A comparison of the election controversy of 2000 eerily resembles the historic dispute of the election of 1876.

Suggested Readings: James W. Ceaser and Andrew Busch, *The Perfect Tie: The True Story of the 2000 Presidential Election* (Lanham, MD: Rowman & Littlefield, 2001); Richard A. Posner, *Breaking the Deadlock: The 2000 Election, the Constitution, and the Courts* (Princeton, NJ: Princeton University Press, 2001).

Part II
Presidential Campaign Slogans, Issues, Platforms, and Programs

The 1973 landmark decision of the Supreme Court in *Roe v. Wade* forced both major parties to express public positions on the abortion issue. Prior to the decision, each state exercised authority to regulate abortions. Relying on a preceding constitutional interpretation by the Supreme Court of an inherent right to privacy (*Griswold v. Connecticut, 1965*), the high court struck down all state laws imposing any absolute ban on abortion. Although many women's groups applauded the decision, other groups regarded the decision as an assault on the sanctity of life and an abuse of the Supreme Court's interpretive authority. However, both major parties hesitated to immediately embrace the young "right to life" movement.

By the campaign of 1976, the situation had changed dramatically. Leaders of the conservative wing of the Republican Party embraced the "right to life" movement as part of a much larger emphasis on family values. Although President Gerald Ford held on to defeat former California governor Ronald Reagan for the Republican nomination, conservative delegates made clear their intention to push for a platform plank calling for a constitutional amendment banning abortion.

Beginning with the 1980 Republican National Convention and extending throughout all GOP conventions through 2000, Republican platforms included planks calling for the reversal of the *Roe* decision. In sharp contrast, every Democratic Convention since 1976 has included a plank reaffirming support for *Roe*. Equally important, conservative Republicans began to apply a "right to life" litmus test for Republican presidential candidates and liberal Democrats began demanding that Democratic presidential nominees hold a "pro-choice" position. The debate has since been defined by the terms "Pro-Life" versus "Pro-Choice."

Ronald Reagan's 1980 and 1984 presidential victories provided support for the claim that a majority of Americans would vote for a "right to life" president. On the other hand, public opinion polls continued to show that the majority of Americans supported *Roe v. Wade* and opposed a constitutional amendment banning abortion. Pro-Choice groups would play a major role in lobbying the Senate to reject President Reagan's 1987 Supreme Court nominee Robert Bork, who was openly opposed to the judicial interpretation claiming the implicit generation of the right to privacy by the Constitution and known for his critical posture toward *Roe.*

In the **Campaign of 1988,** Vice President George Bush warmly embraced the Pro-Life movement despite the fact that during the 1970s he had supported *Roe.* Although the elder Bush went on to defeat Democratic Presidential nominee Michael Dukakis, the abortion issue did not recede as a **wedge** or **hot button** issue. Both the "Pro-Life," and "Pro-Choice" movements turned the presidential power to nominate individuals to the Supreme Court into an important and recurring campaign issue defined by a candidate's stance regarding *Roe.*

Bill Clinton and the Democratic Party used the abortion issue to take advantage of the growing gender gap between men and women voters during the **Campaigns of 1992** and **1996.** Clinton did well with Pro-Choice women in both campaigns, emphatically warning Pro-Choice voters that a Republican president would have the power to nominate Supreme Court justices who would act to overturn the *Roe* decision.

Bent on closing the gender gap, 2000 Republican candidate George W. Bush attempted to downplay the significance of the Republican Party's Pro-Life plank. On the other hand, the Democratic Party and the campaign of Vice President Albert Gore spent millions of dollars highlighting the Pro-Choice position of the Gore campaign. Exit polls indicated that the gender gap was a factor in Gore's popular vote majority, further demonstrating the enduring influence of the issue of legal abortions on presidential politics. *See also* Campaign of 1980; Campaign of 1992; Campaign of 1996; Campaign of 2000; Hot Button Issue; Gender Gap; Wedge Issue.

Suggested Readings: John Herbers, "Abortion Issue Threatens to Become Profoundly Divisive; Debate Is Central to Campaign and Is Unlikely to Disappear Afterward," *New York Times,* October 14, 1984, p. E3; Larry Hugick, "Women Voters Key to Democratic Ticket's Chances," *The Gallup Poll Monthly,* August 1992, pp. 2–6; Dave McNeely, "The Democratic Convention: Abortion Highlighted as Issue to Show Differences with GOP," *Atlanta Journal and Constitution,* August 18, 2000, p. 4B; Frank Rich, "Dole's Women Trouble," *New York Times,* August 10, 1996, p. A23; Robin Toner, "Dukakis Renews Support of Abortion Choice," *New York Times,* November 1, 1988, p. A27.

Absentee Ballots

See Get-Out-the-Vote programs.

Ad Watches

Ad watches have become a fixture of the coverage of presidential campaigns by print and electronic news operations. News operations use "ad watches" to report on the veracity of statements made by campaigns in their spot ads.

During the 1992 presidential campaign, a number of major newspapers and networks began ad watches. After the 1988 presidential campaign, media operations faced intense criticism for allowing deceptive and misleading presidential campaign ads to go unchallenged. Throughout the 1992 campaign, major newspapers and networks ran features or spots that reviewed the accuracy of campaign ads. The perceived success of 1992 ad watches, led many print and electronic news operations to make ad watches a regular feature of campaign coverage.

Televised ads were introduced in 1952, becoming a crucial part of presidential campaigns by the end of the 1960s. During the sixties the **negative** or **attack ad** became a common feature of presidential campaigning. The most dramatic example of this remains to this day the infamous **"Daisy"** commercial, a television spot run by the campaign to elect incumbent Democrat Lyndon Johnson. At the height of the Cold War the ad juxtaposed the carefree innocence of childhood with the terrifying imagery of nuclear apocalypse, implying that Republican candidate Barry Goldwater was a hawkish loose cannon who would, if elected, lead the nation into nuclear war. Broadcast only once in 1964, the **"Daisy" Campaign Ad** became the archetype for the modern attack ad.

The periodic sprinkling of negative ads in presidential campaigns broke into an attack ad torrent during the presidential **Campaign of 1988**. The campaign of Republican candidate George Bush scorched Democratic candidate Michael Dukakis with a series of effective commercials criticizing Dukakis's record as governor of Massachusetts. The television ads also cleverly manipulated imagery to depict the governor as a political lightweight. The campaign of Michael Dukakis responded with ads of their own attacking Bush's selection of Indiana senator Dan Quayle, also accused of being a political lightweight, as his running mate.

Considerable doubt surrounds the effectiveness of ad watches as a method for holding campaigns accountable for untruthful or deceptive campaign ads. Critics of ad watches argue that they do not prevent campaigns from running deceptive, false, or negative ads because far more potential voters view campaign ads than consult ad watch reviews. Supporters of ad watches argue that they deter campaigns from running deceptive attacks. *See also* Campaign of 1964; Campaign of 1992; Public Journalism Movement.

Suggested Readings: Howard Kurtz, "Media Alter Approach to Campaign Coverage; ABC to Play Down Staged Events, Sound Bites," *Washington Post*, September 11, 1992, p. A10; Howard Kurtz, "Negative Ads Appear to Lose Potency," *Washington Post*, October 26, 1992, p. A1.

Adams, John

See Campaign of 1792; Campaign of 1796; Campaign of 1800.

Adams, John Quincy

See Campaign of 1824; Campaign of 1828.

"Advance Agent of Prosperity"

"Advance Agent of Prosperity" was a slogan used by the 1896 presidential campaign of Republican candidate William McKinley dramatizing the different approaches to economic policy represented by **free silver** Democrats and his party's adherence to gold standard monometallism.

At the direction of **Mark Hanna**, McKinley's unofficial campaign manager, the Republican Party launched an expensive campaign to educate the voters and discredit the free silver movement and its leader, Democratic candidate William Jennings Bryan. Depicting McKinley as the true guardian of American economic success, Hanna groomed the image of his candidate as the "advance agent of prosperity," dismissing the fulminations of Bryan and the claims of the free silverites as half-baked ranting. This slogan joined the more colorful **"Full Dinner Pail"** in the successful promotion of McKinley as the clear-headed champion of sound business and free trade. *See also* Campaign of 1896; Free Silver; "Full Dinner Pail"; 16 to 1.

Suggested Readings: Paul W. Glad, *McKinley, Bryan, and the People* (Philadelphia: Lippincott, 1964); Stanley Llewellyn Jones, *The Presidential Election of 1896* (Madison: University of Wisconsin Press, 1964).

Advance Person

Advance person is a term used to describe an individual responsible for the preliminary preparation of personal campaign appearances of presidential candidates. Advance persons help to assure media coverage of campaign events and the careful screening of supporters recruited for such events.

Through the 1880s presidential candidates rarely campaigned by touring the country, exceptions can be cited, but by and large the **front porch** strategy served as the norm. Departing from expectations, 1896 Democratic candidate William Jennings Bryan traveled over 18,000 miles delivering over 600 speeches. This continued as a trend into the first half of the twentieth century as pressure increased for candidates to make personal appearances around the country. **Whistle-stop campaigns** soon became a common feature of presidential campaigns in the century's first half. After 1950 the growing availability and practice of air travel made it possible for a presidential candidate to make campaign appearances hundreds of miles apart within the same day.

The proliferation of campaign appearances forced candidates to devote more time and energy to the logistics of these events. By 1960 campaigns routinely employed individuals to prepare personal appearances in advance. "Advance men" worked with state and local party officials to ensure the presence of large numbers of supporters eager to warmly welcome the candidate at all campaign appearances.

By the 1980s campaign stops had evolved into carefully staged media events designed to produce maximum local and national television coverage. Due to the growing sophistication of these events, advance "teams" evolved to replace the single advance person. Such teams have become an increasingly vital element of any well-executed political campaign of national import. *See also* Campaign Management; Photo Opportunity.

Suggested Readings: Joel Achenbach, "Fast Forward: For Dole Advance Man, Success and Disaster Are in the Details," *Washington Post*, October 21, 1996, p. D1; Ronald Brownstein, "Public Seeing Campaign Through Eye of TV Cameras," *National Journal*, September 22, 1984, p. 1752; Jennifer Warren, "Clinton Advance Man a Well-Kept Secret," *Los Angeles Times*, September 29, 1992, p. A5.

Advance Team

See Advance Person.

Affirmative Action

Affirmative action is a policy designed to actively correct the consequences of past discrimination and prejudice by promoting the employment and education of racial minorities, women, the disabled, and other groups who have been traditionally blocked from economic opportunities and social advancement. Affirmative action, as its name implies, differs from other correctives of social prejudice in that it actively and *affirmatively* redresses discrimination by encouraging the hiring of women and minorities as well as their admission into the institutions of higher education. Most programs and policies designed to remedy discrimination are prohibitive in nature; anti-discrimination laws and equal opportunity laws prohibit discrimination, whereas affirmative action promotes integration.

The concept and policy of affirmative action is a legacy of Title VII of the 1964 Civil Rights Act. In September of 1965 President Lyndon Johnson issued Executive Order #11246, which required federal contractors to "take affirmative action to ensure that applicants are employed, and that employees are treated during employment without regard to their race, creed, color, or national origin." Two years later Johnson amended this language to include women.

In the early 1970s, President Nixon issued a series of orders that strengthened affirmative action requirements for federal contractors and the recipients of federal grants. Throughout his administration, President Jimmy Carter strongly supported the expansion of affirmative action programs. In October 1978, President Carter signed into law the Civil Service Reform Act that required all federal agencies to take affirmative steps to increase the representation of minority groups within their respective organizations.

Through the 1970s, the major parties did not attempt to make affirmative action a campaign issue. To the contrary, bipartisan congressional support led to the 1977 passage of the Public Works Employment Act (PWEA) that included a 10 percent minority set aside. Other minority set-aside programs made their way through Congress prior to the presidential election of 1980.

Despite congressional support, affirmative action drew controversy leading to grassroots opposition in the late 1970s, with critics charging that it is a form of "reverse discrimination," giving preferential treatment to a group based on race or sex, and thus violating the constitutional requirement of "equal protection under the laws." Proponents of affirmative action maintained the necessity of some preferential treatment, especially in higher education and certain occupations traditionally dominated by white men, to effectively eliminate the lingering effects of slavery, segregation, and the pervasive social and economic exclusion of women. Negative prohibitions against discrimination, the argument maintains, are not enough to produce an integrated and fair society. For supporters of affirmative action, the policy protects the qualified minority and ensures fairness for those seeking a better job or advanced education. Critics claim that affirmative action forces companies and schools to hire and admit the lesser qualified in preference to those who are more qualified.

In 1978, the Supreme Court ruled in *Baake v. University of California* that, while affirmative action is an acceptable method of redressing past social injustice, institutions cannot use quota systems as a means to force the right end. With the Baake case, affirmative action entered the stage of national politics, and thus influenced debates at the level of the presidential campaign.

Democrats generally side with the supporters of affirmative action and view the Baake decision as regressive; Republicans openly embrace the anti-quota doctrine of the court. Frustrated conservatives charge that public debate over affirmative action is discouraged by a climate of "political correctness"; frustrated liberals argue that opposition to affirmative action has impeded real progress in the improvement of the quality of life for minorities still suffering from decades, and even centuries, of social bigotry and politically and legally sanctioned oppression.

These divisions were polarized in the campaigns of the 1980s and 1990s, with Republican candidates (Reagan, the elder Bush, Dole, and the younger Bush) all vocally critical of "quota systems," the implication being that quotas, while unconstitutional, are still imposed, and Democratic candidates (Mondale, Dukakis, Clinton, and Gore) pledging themselves to the steadfast support of the spirit of affirmative action, modified in such a way as to prevent the unfair imposition of quotas. The **Campaign of 1980** became the first presidential campaign in which the Republican and Democratic candidates appeared to differ on the affirmative action issue. Republican candidate and former California governor Ronald Reagan pledged to enforce civil rights laws and continue affirmative action programs, but the Reagan campaign made clear that the governor did not support a "quota system" for minority hiring.

In the **Campaign of 1984** the Democratic platform continued its support for "the use of affirmative action goals [and] timetables" to repair the legacy of discrimination in American society. Conversely, the Republican platform described "quotas" as reverse discrimination. Although the recovery of the nation's economy played the most important role in persuading voters to give President Reagan a second term, the Reagan campaign used affirmative action and a number of other issues to characterize the Democratic ticket of former vice president Walter Mondale and Geraldine A. Ferraro as too liberal for most Americans. Between 1985 and the **Campaign of 1988**, the Supreme Court would issue a number of high-profile decisions narrowly construing the scope of key civil rights laws.

Faced with two consecutive losses to Ronald Reagan, the Democratic campaign of 1988 attempted to moderate its position on numerous issues that had driven **swing voters** into the Republican camp. Unlike the 1984 Democratic platform, the 1988 Democratic platform did not include a specific platform plank defending affirmative action. Like its 1988 platform, the Republican platform included a plank sharply critical of the use of quotas as part of affirmative action programs. Interestingly, affirmative action did not grow into a decisive campaign issue during the presidential campaign of 1988.

In 1990 the elder Bush vetoed legislation that he argued contained language supporting quotas, which set the stage for a long battle over the drafting and passage of the Civil Rights Act of 1991. By the beginning the **Campaign of 1992**, a serious economic recession overshadowed social issues such as affirmative action and abortion. The 1992 Clinton campaign sought to focus public attention on high unemployment and the nation's weak economy.

In the 2000 presidential campaign, the younger Bush adamantly opposed any kind of quota system based on preference for a minority, Vice President Gore affirmed the Clinton administration's policy of "mend it, but don't end it." Both Clinton and Gore argued that discrimination has not been sufficiently addressed in American society, and that affirmative action, though flawed, remains a valid corrective to social injustice. However, while clear policy differences between the parties remain, the issue of affirmative action did not have a major impact on the outcome of the presidential elections of 1996 and 2000. *See also* Campaign of 1996; Campaign of 2000; Hot Button Issue; Wedge Issue.

Suggested Reading: Judy Keen, "Affirmative Action Takes New Turn for '96," *USA Today*, June 13, 1995, p. 5A.

Ailes, Roger (1940–)

Roger Ailes played a key role in the development of the media strategy for Vice President George Bush's 1988 successful campaign against Democrat Michael Dukakis.

Ailes began his television career during the mid-1960s as a prop boy on "The Mike Douglas Show." Within a few years, Ailes became the executive producer of the show. In 1968 Ailes entered politics when Republican presidential nominee Richard Nixon hired Ailes as a political media consultant. Political media historians credit Ailes with helping to craft the "New Nixon." Nixon subsequently defeated Democratic candidate Vice President Hubert Humphrey.

From 1969 through 1970, Ailes served as a White House media consultant. Through much of the 1970s and early 1980s, Ailes produced entertainment and news programs. During 1984, Ronald Reagan's reelection campaign hired Ailes as a media consultant. Ailes played a major role in crafting the Reagan campaign's "Morning in America" campaign theme.

In 1988, Ailes served as the chief media advisor for the presidential campaign of Republican Vice President George Bush. Far behind in the August 1988 polls, political historians give Ailes credit for planning and directing a media campaign that ruthlessly and effectively attacked Democratic candidate Michael Dukakis's performance as Massachusetts's governor. From 1989 to 1993, Ailes ran Ailes Communications. From 1992 through 1996, Ailes produced the Rush Limbaugh syndicated television show. From 1993 through 1994, Ailes served as president of CNBC. In 1996, Ailes accepted the position as chair and CEO of Fox News. Between 1996 and 2002, Ailes built the Fox Cable News operation into a major competitor to Time Warner's Cable News Network (CNN) and MSN-NBC. *See also* Campaign of 1988, Negative Campaigning.

Suggested Readings: Peter Johnson, "Fox News Surges Past CNN in Total Ratings," *USA Today*, January 30, 2002, p. 3D; Howard Kurtz, "Crazy Like a Fox: Question His News Judgment, Perhaps, But Never Underestimate Roger Ailes," *Washington Post*, March 26, 1999, p. C1; Joan Vennochi, "The Brains of the Bush Offensive; Strategist Roger Ailes Remade the Candidate," *Boston Globe*, October, 26, 1988, Living, p. 67.

"All Hail Old Hickory"

See Old Hickory.

"All the Way with Adlai"

"All the Way with Adlai" was one of the standard campaign slogans used by the Democratic presidential nominee, Adlai Stevenson, during the **Campaign of 1952**. Faced with a formidable opponent in Republican nominee and war hero General Dwight D. Eisenhower, the Stevenson campaign needed an ear-catching slogan capable of motivating supporters while countering the memorable Republican shibboleth, **"I like Ike."**

President Harry Truman (left) confers in the Oval Office with Governor Adlai E. Stevenson of Illinois (right), the 1952 Democratic nominee for president, and Senator John J. Sparkman of Alabama (standing), the Democratic vice presidential nominee. © National Park Service Photography/ Harry S. Truman Library.

In 1952 the Democratic National Convention drafted Illinois governor Adlai Stevenson as their presidential nominee. Prior to being elected Illinois governor in 1948, Stevenson had practiced law and had devoted himself to the fight for civil rights and foreign affairs. From 1941 to 1944, Stevenson served as assistant to the U.S. Secretary of the Navy. Between 1945 and 1947, Stevenson held a number of positions related to the establishment of the United Nations.

The Stevenson campaign made use of the slogan "All the Way With Adlai" as part of a campaign strategy to broaden Stevenson's appeal to a cross-section of the American people. By using Stevenson's first name in the slogan, the Stevenson campaign wanted voters to view Stevenson as a friend or neighbor. Although exceptionally popular with party regulars, critics questioned whether Stevenson's scholarly demeanor would appeal to millions of **swing voters**. Although Stevenson succeeded in shedding his aloof image, he faced the unenviable and insurmountable task of competing against one of the most respected figures in American history.

Suggested Readings: Jeff Broadwater, *Adlai Stevenson and American Politics: The Odyssey of a Cold War Liberal* (New York: Twayne, 1994); Rodney M. Sievers, *The Last Puritan? Adlai Stevenson in American Politics* (Port Washington, NY: Associated Faculty Press, 1983).

"All the Way with JFK"

Strikingly similar to the 1952 campaign slogan **"All the Way with Adlai,"** "All the Way With JFK" was a campaign slogan used during the Democratic nominee John F. Kennedy's **Campaign of 1960** in an attempt at boosting confidence in the young senator by echoing the folksy slogan of the cerebral Stevenson and thereby emulating the beloved elder statesman in the process.

Suggested Reading: Theodore White, *The Making of the President, 1960* (New York: Atheneum Publishers, 1961).

"All the Way with LBJ"

"All the Way with LBJ" was a 1964 variation of the 1952 **"All the Way with Adlai"** and the 1960 **"All the Way with JFK"** Democratic presidential campaign slogans. The slogan attempted to convey confidence and optimism in contrast to the more defensive mood set by Republican Barry Goldwater's slogan, "In Your Heart You Know He's Right." But sloganeering was not the strength of LBJ's campaign; rather, the legacy of a slain president and uncertainty about an apparently extremist candidate sealed a landslide for the incumbent. *See also* Campaign of 1964.

Suggested Reading: Theodore White, *The Making of the President, 1964* (New York: Atheneum Publishers, 1965).

President Lyndon B. Johnson, the 1964 Democratic presidential nominee, reaches out to greet a crowd of supporters. Note the "All the Way with LBJ" sign in the background. Courtesy of Library of Congress.

"America First"

"America First" was a familiar slogan of Republican candidate Warren G. Harding's 1920 election campaign. The Republican Party made effective use of the slogan as part of its strategy to position Harding as the candidate who would restore economic prosperity and focus on the domestic concerns of the American people.

With the nation tired of war and lingering economic uncertainty and weary of foreign entanglements, "America First" became the most important slogan of the Harding campaign. According to historian David Muzzey, the Harding campaign found the "America First" slogan in a dinner speech given by Harding to the Ohio Society shortly before Harding received the Republican nomination. In the speech, Senator Harding said, "Stabilize America first, prosper America first, think of America first, exalt America first." The phrase thus became shorthand for the sentiments of the Harding campaign. Along with the **"Back to Normalcy"** slogan, the "America First" slogan permitted Warren Harding and the Republican Party to push home the argument that the country needed to devote its energy to solving its problem at home rather then squandering scarce resources and the blood of American youth on wars abroad.

Harding's election ushered in an era of isolationism, rejecting the Wilsonian vision of a League of Nations, and fostering an attitude toward foreign conflict that delayed American action against fascism and imperialism abroad. Only with the bombing at Pearl Harbor was the tide of public opinion irrevocably turned away from "America First" insularity.

More recently, Republican Pat Buchanan, conservative pundit and politico, recycled the "America First" slogan in his 1992 effort to deny incumbent President George Bush the Republican presidential nomination. Buchanan blamed the loss of high-paying manufacturing jobs on free trade laws that made it economically profitable for American corporations to ship manufacturing jobs overseas, and on illegal immigration that permitted American employers to hire illegal immigrants for substandard wages.

Although Buchanan failed to deny President Bush the Republican presidential nomination, his insurgent campaign forced the Bush effort to divert resources and energy to party primary contests rather than to the upcoming battle against Bill Clinton, the Democratic nominee and the independent candidate Ross Perot in the campaign for the general election. *See also* Campaign of 1920; Campaign of 1992; Isolationism.

Suggested Readings: E.J. Dionne Jr., "Buchanan Challenges Bush with 'America First' Call; Conservative Opens GOP Presidential Bid," *Washington Post*, December 11, 1991, p. A1; David Muzzey, *The United States of America: From the Civil War*, Vol. II, Boston (New York: Ginn and Company, 1922) p. 767.

"America for the Americans"

"America for the Americans" was the slogan used by the American Party (Know-Nothings) during the **Campaign of 1856** in an effort to mobilize popular support against immigration and immigrants. Know-Nothings believed that immigration threatened what they perceived to be the homogeneous fabric of American society.

The Know-Nothings held their first and only national convention in February 1856 in Philadelphia. They sought to sharply restrict immigration into the United States and to make it much more difficult for immigrants to obtain citizenship and the associated right to vote and the ability to run for public office. Former president Millard Fillmore was nominated to run for president by the convention's delegates.

Four years before the outbreak of the Civil War, sharp differences over slavery led to a split within the party along sectional lines. Northern members of the Know-Nothings strongly opposed allowing slavery in new territories or states, while southern members remained loyal to their sectional position.

After the 1856 presidential election, the Know-Nothings ceased being an effective political force in the United States, but "nativist" anti-immigration attitudes would occasionally reemerge throughout American political history, particularly within minor parties or through the campaigns of fringe candidates. *See also* Anti-Catholicism; Campaign of 1856.

Suggested Reading: Tyler Anbinder, *Nativism and Slavery: The Northern Know Nothings and the Politics of the 1850s* (New York: Oxford University Press, 1992).

"America Is Back, Standing Tall"

"America Is Back, Standing Tall" was one of a number of effective slogans used by President Ronald Reagan's 1984 reelection campaign to stress the successes of Reagan's first term. By implicitly drawing a contrast between the current administration and that of former President Jimmy Carter, the slogan attempted to

On September 3, 1984, President Ronald Reagan and his wife Nancy hit the campaign trail in Fountain Valley, California, with California senator Pete Wilson (left) and California governor George Deukmejian (right). © Ronald Reagan Library/National Archives.

remind voters of the condition that the country was in when Reagan assumed the presidency after defeating Carter in 1980.

Early in his presidency Reagan's approval rating fell below 40 percent in the polls as the result of a serious economic recession, foreign policy controversies and public concern over conservative policy initiatives. To the great relief of Republicans, the economy rebounded in late 1983. Equally important, large increases in defense expenditures improved military readiness and the morale within the armed services.

The 1984 presidential election recalled the contest of 1980 as Reagan faced Democratic nominee Walter Mondale who had served as vice president during Carter's administration. Making the most of improved economic conditions and the increased strength of the military and taking advantage of the Mondale-Carter connection, the Reagan campaign sought to remind voters of the economic and international turmoil that characterized the Carter years, all of which was amplified by vivid, painful, and recent memories of the Iranian hostage crisis that defined the last year of the Carter presidency. Mondale thus faced the problem of guilt by association, which is usually impossible to shake in the political arena.

Critics argued then and still argue now that all of Reagan's slogans glossed over the fact that the Reagan years were marked by exploding deficits and unabashed attempts by the administration at reducing or eliminating funding for social programs designed to help the less fortunate. However, the focus of the Reagan campaign was to position their man as a strong leader who had succeeded in pulling the nation out of the "crisis of confidence" experienced under the previous administration. *See also* Campaign of 1984.

Suggested Readings: Peter Goldman, Tony Fuller, and Thomas DeFrank, *The Quest for the Presidency 1984* (Toronto, New York: Bantam Books, 1985); Hedrick Smith, "One Campaign Issue Dominates: The Leadership of Ronald Reagan," *New York Times*, January 30, 1984, p. A1.

"America Needs a Change"

"America Needs a Change" was a slogan used by the 1984 presidential ticket of Democratic candidates Walter Mondale, former vice president under President Carter, and Congresswoman Geraldine Ferraro. The Mondale/Ferraro campaign argued that a change was needed in response to the policies of President Reagan, who was accused by the Democrats of favoring the wealthy and privileged at the expense of the vast majority of Americans.

The 1982 mid-term congressional election had raised Democratic hopes for a presidential victory. A serious economic recession had led to a sharp rise in the unemployment rate. As a result, Reagan's standing in public opinion polls had dropped dramatically and the Democratic Party picked up a number of seats in both congressional chambers.

However, by the start of the 1984 campaign, Reagan had experienced a dramatic reversal in his political fortunes. Late in 1983 the economy began to recover. In the early months of 1984, unemployment and interest rates dropped sharply. The improvement in the nation's economy quickly overshadowed issues that Democrats had hoped to take advantage of during the fall 1984 presidential campaign. Large tax cuts enacted at the beginning of the Reagan administration and increased spending for Social Security, Medicare, and national defense had led to large annual deficits and a much larger national debt. Critics accused the Reagan administration of attempting to dismantle the nation's environmental laws and spending billions on an escalating arms race with the Soviet Union that might bring the two superpowers closer to nuclear war. And critics attacked President Reagan for a series of ethics controversies involving high-level Reagan administration officials.

Throughout the fall 1984 campaign, Mondale and Ferraro sought to convince voters that the country was headed in the wrong direction. The slogan "America Needs a Change" reflected the central strategy of the Mondale/Ferraro campaign. Nonetheless, the incumbent president's campaign was not seriously threatened by such efforts, the voters ultimately rejecting any change at the White House. *See also* Campaign of 1984.

Suggested Reading: Jonathan Moore, ed., *Campaign for President: The Campaign Managers Look at '84.* (Dover, MA: Auburn House, 1986).

American Party

See Anti-Catholic Issue; Campaign of 1856.

Amnesty Issue

Since George Washington, presidents have exercised the power to issue pardons and general amnesties. Throughout American history, presidents have issued large numbers of pardons but only a small number of general amnesties.

On July 10, 1795, President Washington granted a general amnesty to participants in the Whiskey Rebellion who had agreed to sign "an oath of allegiance to the laws of the United States." Although Washington's Whiskey Rebellion amnesty did not become a major political controversy, the Civil War amnesties of Abraham Lincoln and Andrew Johnson became entangled in a broader power struggle with Congress. On December 25, 1868, Johnson issued a broad amnesty for those who had supported the Confederate cause. With the ratification of the Fourteenth Amendment, Congress barred some 150,000 Southerners from voting. During May of 1872, a presidential election year, a congressional amnesty restored the voting rights to all but a few thousand Southerners.

Over two thousand individuals were jailed under the Espionage Act of 1917 and the Sedition Act of 1918. Among those arrested, the government jailed hundreds of Socialists who had openly opposed the war. Despite strong pressure from civil liberties groups after the end of World War I, President Woodrow Wilson refused to issue a general amnesty for individuals arrested as the result of alleged subversive activities. After World War II, President Truman refused to grant a general amnesty for military deserters or draft evaders although he did issue a number of pardons on a case-by-case basis.

During the **Campaign of 1976**, Democratic nominee Jimmy Carter expressed his support for a pardon for Vietnam era draft evaders who did not commit violent acts. President Gerald Ford, the Republican nominee, opposed a blanket pardon. On January 21, 1977, President Carter, fresh from his inauguration, issued a pardon to Vietnam era draft evaders who did not commit violent acts. Public opinion polls taken after the Carter pardon indicated that the majority of the American public opposed Carter's action. Although the campaign of Republican Ronald Reagan did not make the Carter pardon a major issue during the **Campaign of 1980**, the pardon weakened Carter's support among conservative and moderate rural and southern voters. *See also* Campaign of 1872.

Suggested Readings: Allan L. Damon, "Amnesty," *American Heritage*, October 1973, pp. 8–9; 78–79; David Schichor and Donald R. Ranish, "President Carter's Vietnam Amnesty: An Analysis of a Public Policy Decision," *Presidential Studies Quarterly*, Vol. 10, 1980, pp. 443–450; "The Vietnam Pardon," *Washington Post*, January 24, 1977, p. A22.

Anti-Catholicism

Throughout the nineteenth century and during a significant part of the twentieth century anti-Catholicism played a major role in American presidential politics. Historians trace anti-Catholicism in the United States to the Protestant Reformation that began with Martin Luther and allied German princes in sixteenth-century Europe, but antecedents can be found earlier in movements led by John Wycliffe in England and John Hus in Moravia. The Reformation generated a number of Protestant churches that rejected papal authority and opposed significant beliefs, teachings, and liturgical practices of the Catholic Church. As religious wars between Catholics and Protestants bled Europe, rancorous and uncharitable accusations from both sides promoted an enduring climate of suspicion and ignorance that exacerbated the division of Western Christendom. Sadly, these newly fixed animosities were imported into the colonies.

Although seventeenth and eighteenth century colonial history included the migration of Catholics to the new colonies, particularly into Maryland, the vast majority of colonists belonged to Anglican, Calvinist, Baptist, or other Protestant sects. However, while distrust of other faiths remained within American culture, from the Revolutionary War through the early decades of the nineteenth century anti-Catholicism was not a visible factor in national politics. By the 1840s, the combination of a surge of Catholic immigrants, expanded suffrage and the rise of urban political machines heavily dependent on immigrant voters amplified anti-Catholic sentiment. Equally important, the Second Great Awakening of the early nineteenth century stimulated an intensity of devotion within Protestant congregations, producing new ground for religious polarization.

Anti-Catholic concern focused on the fear, held by some (certainly not all) Protestants, that the Pope and the Roman Catholic Church might attempt to control the political behavior of American Catholics and elected Catholic public officials. By the 1850s, the anti-immigrant movement had spurred the appearance of nativist Know-Nothings. Growing out of a loosely knit collection of secret societies, the Know-Nothings sought to sharply curtail immigration into the United States and to make it much more difficult for immigrants to become citizens. Irish-Catholics were particularly bothersome to nativists, thus coupling the issue of immigration with anti-Catholic sentiment. In 1856, the Know-Nothing party led by candidate Millard Fillmore won 21 percent of the popular vote, thereby carrying 8 electoral votes. Fillmore's electoral showing remains among the highest for a third-party candidate in American history. There is no doubt that a combination of anti-immigrant hostility and anti-Catholic prejudice contributed to Fillmore's political support.

After the Civil War, many Americans continued to harbor anti-immigrant and anti-Catholic views. The Ku Klux Klan not only attacked African Americans, but also targeted Jews and Catholics and even less conventional Protestants for persecution. By the 1880s, with national party allegiance almost evenly split between the major parties, Protestant affiliation remained a characteristic of the majority of voters in both parties. However, with Catholic and Jewish urban immigrants both inclined to support Democrats while rural and small town Protestants outside of the South tended to favor Republicans, the two parties began to display different religious configurations.

Anti-Catholic sentiment played a major role in the final outcome of the 1884 race between Republican James G. Blaine and Democrat Grover Cleveland. Both Blaine and Cleveland badly needed the electoral votes of New York to win the election. And New York had a large Catholic vote. On October 29, 1884, Blaine attended a meeting of pro-Blaine Protestant clergy in New York City. In his introduction of Blaine, Reverend Samuel D. Burchard commented that "we are Republicans, and don't propose to leave our party and identify ourselves with the party whose antecedents have been **"Rum, Romanism and Rebellion"**." The Cleveland campaign made effective use of Burchard's comments against Blaine. Democrats were able to mobilize support among New York Catholics in response to Burchard's impolitic remarks. Cleveland ended up winning New York and the 1884 presidential election.

In 1928, the first Roman Catholic to be nominated for president, Alfred E. Smith, entered the race as the Democratic standard-bearer. The Republican National Convention nominated a Quaker, Herbert C. Hoover. Even though Hoover was not anti-Catholic, Smith was met with renewed anti-Catholic attacks throughout the campaign. Critics trotted out the old canard that, if elected president, Smith would have to follow directives issued from the Vatican. Besides having to deal with anti-Catholic sentiment, Smith faced strong criticism for supporting the repeal of prohibition; "rum and Romanism" was once again attached to a presidential campaign.

From 1928 until 1960, major party candidates remained Protestant. In 1960, the Democratic National Convention nominated John F. Kennedy, a Roman Catholic, as their presidential candidate. Throughout the campaign, Kennedy faced media questions regarding the influence that the Catholic Church would exert over a Kennedy administration. Kennedy repeatedly assured the public that his Catholicism would not influence the policies adopted by his administration. Political historians generally agree that Kennedy's ability to defuse the Catholic issue played a major role in his narrow defeat of Vice President Richard Nixon (who, like Hoover, came from a Quaker background) for the presidency. The Kennedy victory is significant in proving that the American public will support a viable Catholic candidate.

Anti-Catholicism as a political sentiment has faded considerably since the Kennedy administration. However, during the 2000 Republican Party primary battle between Texas governor George Bush and Arizona U.S. Senator John McCain, President Bush became embroiled in a controversy over his visit to Bob Jones University, on record as a decidedly anti-Catholic institution, prior to the Republican South Carolina primary. Although Bush went on to defeat McCain in the South Carolina primary, the fallout from the visit threatened Bush support with Catholic voters. In a February 27 letter to Cardinal John O'Connor, the Roman Catholic archbishop of New York, Bush expressed regret for missing the opportunity to disassociate himself from anti-Catholic statements associated with the founder of the college.

The apology did not end the controversy. Bush sharply criticized GOP rival John McCain for allegedly allowing his supporters in Michigan to use phone calls to create the impression among Michigan voters that Bush was anti-Catholic. McCain subsequently denied that **push polling** portrayed Bush as anti-Catholic. However, McCain expressed few reservations about pointing out to primary voters that Bush had visited an institution that was known for its anti-Catholic attitudes.

For the most part, anti-Catholic attitudes are not enough to prevent a practicing Catholic from gaining high office, but such a candidate might meet with political difficulties over social and moral issues such as abortion and capital punishment. That aside, it would be easier for another Catholic to reach the White House in the twenty-first century than it would be for an adherent from some of our other faith traditions. We will now likely see another Catholic win the presidency before we see an Evangelical Fundamentalist, Mormon, Muslim, or Buddhist ascend to that political height. *See also* Campaign of 1884; Campaign of 1928; Campaign of 1960; "Rum, Romanism and Rebellion."

Suggested Readings: Frank Bruni, "The 2000 Campaign: The Texas Governor Bush Rues Failure to Attack Bigotry in Visit to College," *New York Times*, February 28, 2000,

p. A1; Benton Dulce and Edward J. Richter, *Religion and the Presidency: A Recurring American Problem* (New York: MacMillan, 1962).

Anti-Immigration Movements

See Campaign of 1856; Campaign of 1876; Campaign of 1880; Campaign of 1884; Nativism.

"Are You Better Off Than You Were Four Years Ago?"

"Are You Better Off Than You Were Four Years Ago?" was a **sound bite** used by Republican nominee Ronald Reagan in his bid to defeat Democratic incumbent President Jimmy Carter. The Reagan campaign used the sound bite to focus the attention of voters on the nation's tenuous economic condition.

Throughout the **Campaign of 1980** Reagan excoriated Carter for the poor state of the nation's economy. Continuing high rates of inflation and associated high interest rates had seriously eroded the buying power of American households. The Reagan campaign aggressively blamed the situation and the sluggish economy it produced on the policies of the Carter administration.

Going into the final weeks of the election, presidential preference polls showed Reagan holding a small lead over Carter. Up through the middle of October 1980, the Carter campaign had resisted a proposed televised debate between Carter and Reagan. To deflect criticism of his refusal to debate, Carter argued that he needed to devote his full attention to the affairs of the nation, including the resolution of the Iranian hostage crisis.

On October 28, 1980, Carter finally met Reagan in Cleveland for the one and only presidential debate of the campaign of 1980. Reagan had earlier debated

Republican nominee Ronald Reagan and his wife Nancy during the 1980 campaign, during which Reagan successfully used the sound bite "Are You Better Off Than You Were Four Years Ago?" against the Democratic incumbent, Jimmy Carter. © Ronald Reagan Library/National Archives.

independent presidential candidate John Anderson. In his summation, Reagan stressed the importance of the election. "Next Tuesday," Reagan explained, "all of you will go to the polls, will stand there in the polling place and make a decision." Reagan emphatically continued, "I think when you make that decision, it might be well if you would ask yourself, are you better off than you were four years ago?" The question effectively encapsulated public dissatisfaction with President Carter, and boosted Reagan's image in the media and the public eye. A week later Reagan won a landslide popular and electoral vote. *See also* Campaign of 1980; Presidential Debates.

Suggested Readings: David S. Broder, "Carter on Points, but No KO.:Carter Took the Bout on Points but Failed to KO Challenger Reagan," *Washington Post*, October 29, 1980, p. A1; Debate History, Commission on Presidential Debates, http://www.debates.org/pages/debhis.html.

Attack Ads

See "Boston Harbor" Campaign Ad; Campaign of 1964; Campaign of 1988; "Daisy" Campaign Ad; Negative Campaigning; Opposition Research; Willie Horton Ad.

Atwater, Lee (1951–1991)

Political consultant best known for directing the 1988 rise-from-behind victory of Vice President George Bush against Democratic presidential candidate Michael S. Dukakis. Born in Atlanta, Georgia, Atwater lived in Columbia, South Carolina, from the age of nine before attending nearby Newberry College. While attending Newberry, Atwater worked his way up to become state chairman of South Carolina's College Republicans and a delegate to the 1972 Republican National Convention, which nominated Richard Nixon for a second term as president. After graduating from college in 1974 and serving a brief time as executive director of the College Republicans' national office, Atwater returned to Columbia to establish a political consulting firm. Atwater soon established a reputation for a campaign management style making heavy use of **attack ads** and **negative campaigning**.

During the 1980s, Atwater served in key roles in Ronald Reagan's 1980 and 1984 campaigns and the 1988 presidential campaign of Vice President George Bush. Atwater served as southern regional director of the Reagan-Bush campaign in 1980, and in 1984 he worked as director for the Reagan-Bush reelection campaign. In 1988, Atwater directed the Bush-Quayle ticket in victory over the Democratic ticket of Dukakis and Geraldine Ferraro. The campaign spent millions of dollars on negative campaign ads attacking Dukakis's record as governor of Massachusetts. The polluted **"Boston Harbor"** ad and the vetoing a bill requiring public school teachers to lead students in the Pledge of Allegiance were deployed by Atwater against candidate Dukakis.

Even though Atwater faced strong criticism for using **wedge issues** to divide the electorate, late in 1988 President Bush named Atwater Chairman of the Republican National Committee.

In March 1990 Atwater collapsed while giving a speech. Examined by doctors, a diagnosis of inoperable cancer was given as the cause. During his illness, Atwater publicly apologized for the campaign tactics he used against Michael Dukakis in 1988. Atwater died on March 29, 1991 at the untimely age of 40. *See also* Campaign of 1980; Campaign of 1984; Campaign of 1988.

Suggested Readings: John Brady, *Bad Boy: The Life & Politics of Lee Atwater* (Reading, MA.: Addison Wesley, 1991); *Current Biography Yearbook, 1989*, pp. 25–29; *Current Biography Yearbook, 1991*, p. 631 (New York: H.W. Wilson Company).

"Back to Normalcy"

"Back to Normalcy" was the defining phrase of Republican candidate Warren Harding's 1920 campaign. It originated as a mistake based on the candidate's misreading of a passage in one of his own speeches delivered in May of that year. Responding to a public now growing weary of war and reform, Harding observed that "America's present need is not heroics but healing, not nostrums but normalcy; not revolution but restoration . . ." Harding's manuscript reveals that he originally intended to use the word "normality," but in the spoken text he inadvertently slipped in "normalcy." The error became the slogan, and the slogan captured the mood of a nation ready to slow down and think within smaller issues.

The slogan captured the Harding campaign's ultimately successful strategy of promising a calmer political climate. "Back to Normalcy," along with "**America First**," tapped into public fatigue over the war and internationalist ambitions of ailing incumbent President Woodrow Wilson. Early in the **Campaign of 1920**, the Republican Party and the Harding campaign adopted a strategy of promising the American people recovery from the turmoil of World War I and its aftermath.

Seeking a return to simpler times, voters gave Harding an overwhelming victory over James C. Cox.

Suggested Readings: Wesley Marvin, *The Road to Normalcy: The Presidential Campaign and Election of 1920* (Baltimore: Johns Hopkins Press, 1962); John A. Morello, *Selling the President, 1920: Albert D. Lasker, Advertising, and the Election of Warren G. Harding* (Westport, CT: Praeger, 2001).

Baker, James (1930–)

In the 1970s James A. Baker III of Houston, a lawyer by training, quickly established a national reputation as an exceptional political strategist and, subsequently, as an expert in international diplomacy. A self-described Republican moderate, Baker served from 1975–1976 as commerce secretary during the administration of Republican President Gerald Ford. When the elder George Bush decided to run for the 1980 Republican nomination, Bush tapped Baker to serve as his campaign chairman. After Ronald Reagan defeated Bush for the nomination, Baker

Former secretary of state James Baker during the 2000 presidential election recount battle in Florida. © AP/Wide World Photos.

joined the Reagan campaign and served as a key political advisor throughout the campaign. Baker's status was boosted after Reagan selected Bush as his running mate. Baker was rewarded with an appointment to serve as Reagan's White House Chief of Staff, a post he held from 1981–1985. Political observers credited Baker with playing a key role in obtaining legislative approval for much of Reagan's political agenda of tax cuts, reductions in the growth of domestic expenditures, and a large military buildup.

After Reagan's 1984 reelection victory he surprisingly nominated Baker as secretary of the treasury. Baker served as treasury secretary until he resigned in August 1988 to become the campaign chairman of the presidential campaign of Vice President George Bush. Along with **Lee Atwater**, political historians credit Baker with turning around Bush's floundering campaign. President Bush then nominated and the Senate confirmed Baker to the office of secretary of state. As secretary of state, Baker assumed a prominent position in assembling the 1991 Gulf War coalition that succeeded in expelling Iraqi troops from Kuwait.

After Bill Clinton defeated George Bush in the 1992 campaign, Baker returned to Houston to practice law. Through the eight years of the Clinton presidency, Baker stayed out of the political spotlight. However, the 2000 contest between Texas governor George W. Bush, the Republican nominee and Democratic incumbent Vice President Albert Gore again pressed Baker into service. In the dispute over Florida's mishandled votes, the younger Bush enlisted Baker's help in overseeing the legal and political battle over the recount. By a vote of 5 to 4 the Supreme Court ordered the end to the Florida recount, a decision that guaranteed the election to the governor. Political observers gave Baker high marks for calmly pursuing an effective political and legal strategy during the recount dispute. *See also* Campaign of 1980; Campaign of 1988; Campaign of 2000.

Suggested Readings: James A. Baker III and Thomas M. DeFrank, *The Politics of Diplomacy: Revolution, War, and Peace, 1989–1992* (New York: Putnam, 1995); Ronald Brownstein and Nina Easton, *Reagan's Ruling Class: Portraits of the President's Top Hundred Officials* (New York: Pantheon, 1983); Peter B. Levy, *Encyclopedia of the Reagan-Bush Years* (Westport, CT: Greenwood Press, 1996).

Ballot Integrity Program

See Poll Watcher.

Banners, Political

Through the 1820s, presidential candidates relied heavily on partisan newspapers and political **pamphlets** to get their message to the small portion of the population eligible to vote. By the **Campaign of 1828**, many states had significantly increased the number of individuals eligible to vote. To reach the growing electorate, partisans found it necessary to find new methods to mobilize supporters and reach newly enfranchised voters. Major improvements in the quality and the cost of printing technology made it financially viable for political parties to print and distribute large numbers of political banners supporting their respective presidential and vice presidential candidates. For instance, the Whig Party distributed numerous "Log Cabin and Hard Cider" banners during the 1840 campaign.

From the campaign of 1840 through the end of the nineteenth century, campaigns routinely used banners. Prior to the Civil War, campaigns typically posted paintings of their various candidates. After the Civil War, photographs became more common.

Suggested Readings: Roger A. Fisher, *Tippecanoe and Trinkets Too: The Material Culture of American Presidential Campaigns, 1828–1984* (Urbana: University of Illinois Press, 1988); Keith Melder, *Hail to the Candidate: Presidential Campaigns from Banners to Broadcasts* (Washington, DC: Smithsonian Institution Press, 1992).

Battleground State

The term battleground state refers to those states political experts regard as winnable by either major candidate. With the adoption of the electoral vote system for selecting the president, the Constitutional Convention sought to assure the states a dominant place in the selection of the president. Under the Constitution, each state decides how to distribute electoral votes among presidential candidates. Unless a candidate receives a majority of electoral votes (currently 270), the House elects the president.

Hence the Electoral College has forced presidential candidates to campaign on a state-by-state basis. For instance, the 2000 presidential election between Republican candidate George Bush and Democratic candidate Albert Gore was marked by a large number of battleground states. The Bush and Gore campaigns both spent a large percentage of their campaign budgets attempting to sway voters in the states of Ohio, Michigan, Wisconsin, Oregon, Washington, West Virginia,

Arkansas, Iowa, Missouri, Tennessee, New Hampshire, Pennsylvania, New Mexico, and Florida. After an unprecedented dispute over the electoral votes of Florida, George Bush won 271 Electoral College votes.

Some critics argue that the battleground state strategy forces campaigns to devote a disproportionate percentage of expenditures and candidate visits to a relatively small number of competitive states. As a result, many voters never have the opportunity to see a candidate in the flesh. Reformers suggest that states adopt a proportional system for allocating electoral votes based on the percentage of the vote received by each candidate. *See also* Campaign of 2000.

Suggested Readings: William J. Crotty, *America's Choice 2000* (Boulder, CO: Westview Press, 2001); Hedrick Smith, "Reagan Given an Edge in 'Big 9' Battleground States," *New York Times*, September 14, 1980, Section 1, p. 32.

"Bear in the Woods" Campaign Ad

The "Bear in the Woods" was a spot ad used by the 1984 reelection campaign of President Ronald Reagan rebutting charges by Walter Mondale, the Democratic challenger, that the Reagan administration threatened world peace by conducting one of the largest military buildups in American history. Reagan's military budget was justified on the grounds that the Soviet Union remained an imminent threat to national security and world peace. The strength and vigilance of the American eagle was necessary to protect the free world from the menace of the Russian bear. As the viewers watch a shadowy, large black bear amble through the woods, the announcer states "There is a bear in the woods. For some people the bear is easy to see. Others don't see it at all. Some people say the bear is tame. Others say it is vicious and dangerous. If no one can really be sure who is right, isn't it smart to be as strong as the bear, if there is a bear?" *See also* Campaign of 1984.

Suggested Reading: Jack Germond and Jules Witcover, *Wake Us When It's Over: Presidential Politics of 1984* (New York: Macmillan, 1985).

"A Better Man for a Better America"

"A Better Man for a Better America" was a slogan used by the campaign of Republican presidential nominee Bob Dole during the election of 1996. The slogan reflected an effort by the Dole campaign to turn the election into a referendum on Bill Clinton's character. Republican strategists believed that the majority of voters seriously doubted Clinton's moral fiber. To take advantage of this perception the Dole campaign sought to focus the attention of voters on Dole's distinguished service during World War II.

Through the fall 1996 campaign, the Dole camp impugned Clinton's character with little effect. The Clinton campaign succeeded in neutralizing the charges by focusing on the accomplishments of the Clinton administration; particularly the millions of jobs created by the robust economy. *See also* Campaign of 1996.

Suggested Reading: Ann Oldenburg and Patricia Edmonds, "Election '96 a Battle of 'Family Values': Republicans Attempt to Make Issue Their Own," *USA Today*, August 7, 1996, p. 4A.

"Blaine, Blaine, James G. Blaine, the Continental Liar from the State of Maine"

"Blaine, Blaine, James G. Blaine, the Continental Liar from the State of Maine" became one of many slogans used by supporters of Democratic candidate, Grover Cleveland, in his hotly contested battle with Republican James G. Blaine during the election of 1884.

Historians regard the **Campaign of 1884** as one of the most vicious in American history. Blaine's troubles can be traced to 1876, when Blaine lost the Republican nomination to Rutherford B. Hayes largely as the result of a scandal involving questionable financial dealings between Blaine and a number of powerful railroads while serving in the House of Representatives. Although Blaine survived the scandal, there was sufficient evidence to prove that Blaine had received significant financial favors as the result of his position in Congress.

Eight years later, Blaine found himself locked in a tight race against a reinvigorated Democratic Party. Blaine and the Republicans found that waving the **bloody shirt** had lost much of its impact. With relatively few major issues dividing the Democratic and Republican parties, the campaign quickly degenerated into a series of personal attacks against Cleveland and Blaine. Cleveland supporters resurrected the railroad influence peddling scandal, popularly known as the "Mulligan Letters" scandal. Evidence gathered by Cleveland supporters provided proof that Blaine had lied about his involvement in the scheme, even to the point of advising in his own handwriting to burn a particular incriminating letter in the Mulligan batch. And so went the Democratic campaign song,

> Burn this letter!
> Burn this letter!
> Burn, burn, oh burn this letter!
>
> Blaine! Blaine!
> The Continental liar
> From the State of Maine!
> Burn this letter!

See also Campaign of 1884; Mulligan Letters.

Suggested Reading: Mark Wahlgren Summers, *Rum, Romanism & Rebellion: The Making of a President, 1884* (Chapel Hill: University of North Carolina Press, 2000).

Bleeding Kansas

"Bleeding Kansas" became the rallying cry for opponents of the extension of slavery to free states during the election of 1856. The Kansas-Nebraska Act of 1854, which allowed the new territories to resolve the issue of slavery by popular vote, had deeply polarized the nation and stimulated the establishment of the anti-slavery Republican Party. The Republican Party sought to prohibit any further expansion of slavery while Democrats, in supporting the Kansas-Nebraska Act, argued for "popular sovereignty," claiming that the citizens of each territory or state must have the final say with respect to the slavery issue.

The 1856 presidential election pitted Democrat James Buchanan against Republican John C. Fremont and Know-Nothing Millard Fillmore. To counter the major threat from the young Republican Party, Democrats argued that Fremont's election would lead to the dissolution of the nation.

The phrase "Bleeding Kansas" came to symbolize the conflict between opposing forces in Kansas over the slavery issue. Throughout 1855–1856, violence raged across Kansas between forces opposed to slavery and pro-slavery forces. A fraudulent election led to the creation of a pro-slavery territorial legislature at Lecompton. Rejecting the results, anti-slavery elements set up their own government in Topeka. Democratic President Franklin Pierce then recognized the pro-slavery Lecompton Constitution. Pierce's decision outraged Republicans and abolitionists. "Bleeding Kansas" thus became a rallying cry directed at turning out the abolitionist vote. Although Buchanan won the presidency with 174 electoral votes, Fremont earned 114 and thus put the new Republican Party in position to challenge the Democrats in 1860. *See also* Campaign of 1856.

Suggested Reading: James A. Rawley, *Race & Politics: "Bleeding Kansas" and the Coming of the Civil War* (Philadelphia: Lippincott, 1969).

Bloody Chasm

"Bloody chasm" was a phrase used after the Civil War to symbolize the wide gulf between the Democratic and Republican parties over the legacy of the Civil War. Radical Republicans in particular were interested in characterizing the Democratic Party as the party of treason and rebellion. In the South, the Republican Party, the party of Lincoln and the Union, was anathema to voters still bristling over Reconstruction policies.

Unhappy with the policies of President Ulysses S. Grant, Liberal Republicans broke from the party to form their own wing during the summer of 1872, nominating newspaper publisher Horace Greeley as their candidate. In a May 20, 1872 acceptance speech, Greeley expressed the view that Americans north and south were "eager to clasp hands across the bloody chasm which has too long divided them." Instead of furthering Greeley's candidacy, Greeley's "bloody chasm" speech provided fuel for critics who sought to characterize Greeley as a turncoat. Political cartoonist, **Thomas Nast**, used the "bloody chasm" to ridicule Greeley's attitude of forgiveness toward the defeated Confederacy. *See also* Bloody Shirt Politics; Campaign of 1872.

Suggested Reading: Hans Sperber and Travis Trittschuh, *American Political Terms* (Detroit: Wayne State University Press, 1962).

Bloody Shirt Politics

The term "bloody shirt" traces its origins to an actual incident involving torture inflicted upon a federal officer by the Ku Klux Klan in post–Civil War Mississippi. Under cover of night, Klan Nightriders intimidated and then severely whipped A.P. Huggin, a tax collector and superintendent of schools. Wounded and with bloody nightshirt in hand, he sought assistance from federal troops quartered nearby. The commanding officer thereupon passed the shirt along to Radical Republicans who took it to Washington as a vivid symbol of Klan terrorism. Radical congressman Benjamin Butler, while proposing legislation empowering stricter enforcement of federal law by the army in the South, waved the bloody shirt on the House floor for graphic and dramatic emphasis.

Through guilt by association with their southern base as well as the resistance by some of their number to Lincoln's war policies, Democrats were subsequently associated with the defeated South, suffering the stigma of rebellion and slavery. Even though Republican President Abraham Lincoln had mercifully favored leniency toward the South and rapid reunification of the nation, the Radical Republicans insisting on punitive measures against the South were not above reminding voters of Southern—and Democratic—treason.

In the elections of 1868, 1872 and 1876 Radical Republicans waved the "bloody shirt" to fortify waning support for Reconstruction policies among Northern voters and to secure allegiance of newly enfranchised voters—the former slaves. Radical Republicans used the "bloody shirt" to remind Union veterans and other Northern voters of the sacrifices of those who fought, died, and were wounded to preserve the Union. The "bloody shirt" image proved particularly effective during the presidential **Campaign of 1868** and the **Campaign of 1872**. Bloody shirt imagery proved much less effective during the **Campaign of 1876**. *See also* Campaign of 1880; Campaign of 1884.

Suggested Readings: Stanley Hirshson, *Farewell to the Bloody Shirt* (Bloomington: Indiana University Press, 1962); Hans Sperber and Travis Trittschuh, *American Political Terms* (Detroit: Wayne State University Press, 1962).

"Boston Harbor" Campaign Ad

The **"Boston Harbor"** spot ad was used by the campaign of President George Bush during the election of 1988 to discredit the environmental record of Massachusetts governor Michael Dukakis, the Democratic presidential nominee.

Public opinion polls taken after the August 1988 Democratic National Convention gave the Democratic ticket of Dukakis and Lloyd Bentsen a lead of twenty points over the Republican ticket of Bush and Dan Quayle. Political observers criticized the Bush campaign for a state of disarray. To save the day, **James Baker** resigned his position as President Reagan's secretary of the treasury to become chairman of the Bush campaign. Baker joined **Lee Atwater**, Bush's campaign manager and Bush media advisor **Roger Ailes**.

Within a short time of the Democratic National Convention, the Bush campaign launched an aggressive media blitz to raise questions regarding Dukakis's record as governor of Massachusetts. Turning the tables on Dukakis, the Bush campaign attacked the governor for the polluted condition of Boston Harbor. After detailing the dismal condition of the harbor, the narrator warned viewers "Michael Dukakis promises to do for America what he did for Massachusetts." Along with other ads critical of the Dukakis record in Massachusetts, the "Boston Harbor" ad placed the Dukakis campaign on the defensive, resorting to implicating the vice president in the Iran-Contra scandal.

In the aftermath of their decisive victory, the Bush campaign faced strong criticism for resorting to attack ads to discredit the Dukakis record. *See also* Roger Ailes; Lee Atwater; Campaign of 1988; Negative Campaigning.

Suggested Readings: T.R. Reid, "Dukakis Renews Attack, Is Soon Back on Defensive, on Eve of Bush Visit, Boston Harbor Pollution Overshadows Iran-Contra as Issue," *Washington Post*, August 31, 1988, p. A16.

"Boys on the Bus"

The phrase "Boys on the Bus," referred to the practice of a predominantly male press corps accompanying presidential candidates on various campaign stops. Timothy Crouse's 1972 book, *The Boys on the Bus*, presented a somewhat unflattering picture of the press corps that covered the presidential campaigns of Democratic presidential candidate George McGovern and the reelection campaign of President Richard Nixon. Crouse chronicled a convivial, party-addled press corps that often had inappropriately close relationships with campaign staffers.

With the rise of television as the primary medium for presidential candidates during the 1950s and 1960s, the press corps found itself increasingly the subject of attempted manipulation by presidential campaigns. The value of carefully staging campaign events to magnify positive local and national media coverage was quickly learned. Because Richard Nixon largely blamed his 1960 loss to John F. Kennedy on the infatuation of the liberal press with Kennedy's telegenic, movie star image, the 1968 Nixon campaign carefully staged every event and sharply limited press access to their candidate.

President Nixon's 1972 reelection campaign repeated this successful strategy, while the McGovern campaign was, by contrast, fairly ineffective in managing the media. But in the aftermath of the Watergate scandal, the media came under considerable criticism for allowing Nixon's Committee to Re-elect the President to successfully manipulate coverage of the 1972 campaign.

By the 1990s, significant changes had taken place with respect to media coverage of presidential campaigns. First, with the proliferation of print, electronic, cable, and Internet news outlets, far more reporters now cover primary and general election contests. Second, news outlets now assign many more women to cover politics in general and presidential campaigns in particular. Third, reporters now assigned to cover presidential campaigns tend to be much more adversarial than their earlier counterparts. Whether or not this is an improved situation compared to the decades of the 1960s and 1970s remains a matter of continued debate. *See also* Horse-Race Campaign Coverage; Poll-Driven Campaign.

Suggested Readings: Clara Bingham, "The Girls On the Bus," *Vogue* (August 1992), p. 158; Timothy Crouse, *The Boys On the Bus* (New York: Ballantine Books, 1974); Edwin Diamond and Wendy Martens, "With Girls and Boys on the Bus Has Campaign Coverage Changed?" *National Journal* 24 (October 10, 1992), pp. 23–26.

Brazile, Donna (1959–)

Donna Brazile, a seasoned grassroots activist and prominent leader within the Democratic Party, is the first African American woman in history to have managed the presidential campaign of a major party candidate, Vice President Al Gore, the party's nominee for the 2000 election. Known for her proclivity to "shoot from the hip," Brazile's vibrant and colorful personality presented a marked contrast to Gore's more reserved, measured persona. It was her brashness that both attracted her to the arid Gore campaign in 1999 and caused her removal from the campaign team of Governor Michael Dukakis eleven years earlier over an untoward remark impugning the marital relationship of the elder Bush and his wife Barbara. Her removal from the Dukakis campaign was a temporary snag in an otherwise meteoric rise to prominence as a leading mover and shaker within the Democratic Party.

Born and raised in New Orleans, she first made her mark as National Student Coordinator for the Martin Luther King, Jr., Holiday Committee, thus allowing Brazile the opportunity to play a leading role in the successful inclusion of the martyred reverend's birthday among nationally designated holidays. Continuing her efforts to sustain Dr. King's memory, she served as the National Mobilization Director commemorating the 20th anniversary of Dr. King's famous March on Washington in August of 1963. She remained active in various social causes throughout the 1980s, culminating in her critical role in founding the National Political Congress of Black Women.

She is currently a Senior Fellow at the James MacGregor Burns Academy of Leadership at the University of Maryland, as well as continuing her service as a member of the Democratic National Committee. As a result of the numerous errors in casting and tabulating the popular vote for president in the state of Florida during the 2000 election, Brazile accepted the position of national chair on the newly formed Voting Rights Institute, replacing the short-tenured Maynard Jackson, the former mayor of Atlanta. Additionally, Brazile is familiar to radio talk show audiences as the host and producer of "A View from the Hill" broadcast via Radio One News throughout the District of Columbia and surrounding areas. *See also* Campaign of 2000; Campaign Manager.

Suggested Readings: "Brazile on the Move." *Washington Post*, August 30, 2001; "The Woman Behind Al Gore." *Staten Island Advance*, November 28, 1999.

Bread-and-Butter Issues

"Bread-and-butter" is a commonly used political metaphor used to describe the use of a political issue by a candidate to both maintain support of the party faithful and to attract swing or undecided voters.

Since the end of World War II, Democratic candidates have made effective use of the Social Security issue by accusing Republican presidential and congressional candidates of supporting the elimination of or significant changes in the Social Security program. To Republican candidates the Social Security issue constitutes the **Third Rail of American Politics**. "Touch it and politically you're dead." During the presidential **Campaign of 2000**, Texas governor George Bush proposed partial privatization of Social Security as part of a plan to protect the long-term solvency of the program. Although Bush ultimately won a majority of electoral votes, Bush lost the popular vote.

On the other hand, tax cuts have become the most important bread-and-butter issue for Republican presidential and congressional candidates. During the 1980 campaign, Republican Ronald Reagan argued that a large tax cut would provide the nation the economic boost necessary to get the country out of a serious economic recession. In 1984, Democratic nominee Walter Mondale's campaign misfired when he promised to raise, not lower, taxes. And Texas governor George Bush made tax relief the centerpiece of his reform agenda during the campaign of 2000. Despite strong Democratic opposition, both Reagan and Bush obtained congressional approval of their large tax cuts.

From the late 1960s through the end of the early 1990s, Republican presidential and congressional candidates successfully used the **law and order issue** to attract by categorizing Democrats as being soft on crime. This tactic was particularly effective in Richard Nixon's campaign against then-incumbent Vice President Hubert Humphrey in 1968. In 1988, Republican presidential candidate and Vice President George Bush used a rape committed by a furloughed inmate to discredit the law and order record of Massachusetts governor and Democratic candidate Michael Dukakis. In the **Campaign of 1992**, by contrast, Democrat Bill Clinton diffused the law and order issue by atypically taking a strong stand in favor of the death penalty. *See also* Pocket-book Issue; Wedge Issue.

Suggested Readings: Ann Scott Tyson, "Tax Cuts: Hype Now, Money Later: Republicans and Democrats Squabble Over the Size of a Cut and Who Gets It, But Some Relief Is Likely—Eventually," *Christian Science Monitor*, July 15, 1999, p. 1; Jules Witcover, "Social Security Reform Means Danger for Bush," *Baltimore Sun*, July 27, 2001, p. 23A.

Broadside

Single-page notices, announcements, advertisements, brief declarations, statements of protest, and promotional posters all intended to draw attention to an event, issue, candidate, or celebrity, broadsides were once a familiar feature within the landscape of American political imagery, a genre of political ephemera intended to catch the eye and deliver easily digested messages, information, proclamations, or remonstration. Broadsides were designed to provoke rather than persuade. Broadsides often contained a compelling word, phrase, drawing, caricature, or photograph printed in large type, naturally drawing the attention of the eye to the rest of the text. The text itself was often printed with a degree of aesthetic style, particularly in the nineteenth century, attempting to convey in one page just enough information to promote an event, rally the party faithful, or evoke an emotion about an issue, candidate, or party. The broadside could range from a single slogan to extensive text typeset in very fine print and running into thousands of words. It could be a political cartoon or a lengthy, miniaturized discourse the length of a small pamphlet, all printed in two or three columns on a single page. Through the Civil War, broadsides typically included paintings of presidential and vice presidential candidates. With the invention and increased use of photography, daguerreotype images of the candidates replaced paintings.

The history of the broadside is traced back to the early days of movable type. In Britain they became common vehicles for royal proclamations, news, warnings, and other official announcements. With the growth of democracy and the emergence of party politics, broadsides became a frequent tool for political activism and opposition to official policies. Broadsides were also commonly used to announce political and religious events, or to disseminate brief statements regarding religious principles. Theater, poetry, advertising, music compositions or lyrics, wanted posters, sermons, and numerous other activities appeared as broadsides to convey or promote messages, events, programs, performances, revivals, political rallies, party positions, and social causes.

Perhaps the most famous broadside in the history of political ephemera does not involve a presidential campaign. In protest over the cynical manipulation of voting districts in Massachusetts in 1812, pro-Federalist broadsides were printed and posted depicting the image of the oddly salamander-shaped redistricting courtesy of the Republican governor Eldridge Gerry. The now infamous Gerrymander, "a new species of monster," remains to this day an important term in the lexicon of American politics.

While presidential campaign broadsides can be found well into the mid-twentieth century, with the advent of television and more recently the news sound bite, the posting of broadsides has become increasingly infrequent. At the height of their use in the nineteenth and first half of the twentieth century, the broadside would often convey through accessible language and attractive style an amount of information exceeding the most finely honed sound bite of today's campaigner. *See also* Banners, Political.

Suggested Readings: Roger A. Fisher, *Tippecanoe and Trinkets Too: The Material Culture of American Presidential Campaigns, 1828–1984* (Urbana: University of Illinois Press, 1988); Keith Melder, *Hail to the Candidate: Presidential Campaigns from Banners to Broadcasts* (Washington, DC: Smithsonian Institution Press, 1992).

Bryan, William Jennings

See Campaign of 1896; Campaign of 1900; Campaign of 1908.

Buchanan, James

See Campaign of 1856; Campaign of 1860.

Buchanan, Pat

See "America First"; Campaign of 1992; Campaign of 1996.

"Building the Bridge"

The 1996 presidential reelection campaign of Bill Clinton and Albert Gore adopted the REO Speedwagon song "Building the Bridge," as their campaign song. The Clinton campaign used the song in relation to the campaign slogan "Building the Bridge to the 21st Century." *See also* Campaign of 1996.

Suggested Reading: Bill Nichols, "Clinton Team Building the Bridge and Battling Over-confidence along the Way," *USA Today*, September 13, 1996, p. 10A.

"Building the Bridge to the 21st Century"

After the 1994 congressional midterm election led to a Republican takeover of the House of Representatives, political **pundits** wrote Bill Clinton off as a viable presidential candidate for the 1996 presidential election. With the help of political consultant Dick Morris, Clinton crafted a political comeback by positioning himself in the middle of the political spectrum while the Republican-controlled Congress pushed their conservative agenda. As in the campaign of 1992, Clinton depicted himself as the candidate of moderate change in 1996.

In his 1996 acceptance speech at the Democratic National Convention, Clinton pledged to build a bridge to the 21st century. "Building the Bridge to the 21st Century" became a central theme of the Democrat's 1996 campaign to retain the White House. *See also* Campaign of 1996.

Suggested Reading: Dan Balz, "Clinton Sounds Education, Security Themes; President Proclaims 'Hope Is Back' in Accepting Party's Renomination," *Washington Post*, August 30, 1996, p. A01.

Bull Moose

Bull Moose, the nickname given to Teddy Roosevelt's 1912 Progressive Party, is a term that originated during his campaign for the vice presidency in 1900. Responding to concerns from Mark Hanna, President McKinley's political manager, who had expressed doubts about Roosevelt's qualifications as a credible politician, TR boasted, "I am as strong as a bull moose and you can use me to the limit, taking heed of but one thing and that is my throat."

Harboring serious doubts about TR, even to the point of referring to him as a "madman," Hanna reputedly advised McKinley. "Your duty is to live for four years from next March (Inauguration Day)." A murderous bullet kept McKinley from his post, and the Bull Moose ascended to become the most important statesman of his era. *See also* Campaign of 1900; Campaign of 1912.

Suggested Reading: Edmund Morris, *Theodore Rex* (New York: Random House, 2001).

Bush, George Herbert Walker

See Campaign of 1980; Campaign of 1984; Campaign of 1988; Campaign of 1992.

Bush, George W.

See Campaign of 2000.

Buttons

See Political Buttons.

Cable News Network (CNN)

From the late 1940s through the 1970s, the ABC, NBC, and CBS networks shared unchallenged dominance of all political coverage broadcast by television and radio. NBC's John Cameron Swayze, the first television news anchor, set a precedent with live on-site broadcasts from the national conventions of both major parties in 1948. CBS's Walter Cronkite, NBC's Chet Huntley and David Brinkley, and ABC's Howard K. Smith became fixtures at national political conventions and during election night coverage, sustaining the established dominance of the three national networks.

But in 1980, billionaire Ted Turner, owner of an Atlanta "super station" that had the capability of drawing a national audience, took the risky step of establishing a 24-hour news channel, the Cable News Network. Initially, many media observers doubted the ability of CNN to match network news coverage and to attract wealthy advertisers. But CNN gradually established itself as a competitive news operation and an appealing alternative to the formulaic network broadcasts. By the end of the 1980s, CNN had evolved into a major force in national and international news coverage.

During the 1992 presidential election, CNN overshadowed all of the major network news operations. Texas billionaire Ross Perot turned to CNN's *Larry King Live* to reach the American people. Allowing interviews with the major networks, Perot used the opportunity to sharply criticize incumbent President George Bush, building public support for a third-party presidential run. Perot captured enough air coverage to elbow his way into the campaign as a credible alternative to the major party candidates, becoming the first third-party candidate to participate in nationally televised presidential debates.

In 1996 and 2000 presidential campaign coverage by cable news outlets continued to increase. CNN and still newer cable news operations such as MSNBC and Fox News significantly expanded coverage of the **Campaign of 2000**. Spurred by the close, competitive nature of the race, cable news coverage increased its appeal as the first source of political news for informed voters. *See also* New Media.

Suggested Readings: Edwin Diamond, Martha McKay, and Robert Silverman, "Pop Goes Politics: New Media, Interactive Formats, and the 1992 Presidential Campaign," *American Behavioral Scientist* 37 (November–December 1993), pp. 257–262; Peter Marks, "The 2000 Campaign: The Media: Networks Cede Political Coverage to Cable," *New York Times*, April 7, 2000, p. 18; Dan Trigoboff, "Cable Steps Up," *Broadcasting & Cable*, June 26, 2000, p. 4.

Calhoun, John C.

See Campaign of 1824; Campaign of 1828; Campaign of 1832.

Campaign Ads

See Presidential Campaign Ads.

Campaign Consultants

See Political Consultants.

Campaign Finance Reform

See Hard Money; Soft Money.

Campaign Manager

The political campaign manager was created to coordinate and direct the increasingly more complex campaign organizations needed to achieve success within the ever-broadening landscape of presidential politics. Campaign managers are masters of strategy and tactics; playing a key role in working with the candidate to set campaign goals as well as attending to the specific details of life on the stump. The campaign manager must help develop and clarify a candidate's ideological principles and policy goals; design rhetorical strategies; refine and promote a candidate's personal image; cultivate relationships with key reporters working in the media; assess information from pollsters, researchers, and analysts; develop issue strategies in response to the hard data provided by these services; review a candidate's position on various issues given this information; direct spin; deploy effective sound bites; advise a candidate on potential running mates and possible cabinet appointees; coordinate media events; manage candidate travel and ensure the effectiveness of live appearances through proper choice of location and venue; cultivate alliances with important local politicos; and seek, identify, and exploit the vulnerabilities of the opposition. The campaign manager is often as important as the candidate in winning the presidency.

A successful manager of presidential campaigns exerts great influence in American politics. Ohio industrialist **Mark Hanna**, who directed the 1896 campaign of Republican William McKinley, is the archetypal campaign manager. Hanna reorganized the Republican Party on a national scale, and raised an unprecedented amount of money on behalf of McKinley. His energy and fund-raising acumen enabled McKinley to remain home in Ohio, holding court from his front porch while Hanna directed a sophisticated campaign against populist William Jennings Bryan's. Hanna regarded Bryan as a formidable opponent. Bryan, the greatest orator of the era, had turned the "free silver" issue into a national crusade. To counter Bryan's populist appeal, Hanna raised some $3.5 million to pay for a nationwide education campaign to promote McKinley's **"sound money"** platform and McKinley's promise to workers the **"Full Dinner Pail."** To accomplish this task, Hanna hired hundreds of speakers to explain the Republican platform from the east coast to the west coast. Hanna's strategy succeeded in gaining the White House for the Republicans.

Hanna's precedent provided a model that was emulated by several kingmakers throughout the twentieth century. James Farley played a leading role in the ascent of Franklin Roosevelt, conducting FDR's first two campaigns. **James Baker** is one of the more prominent campaign managers, directing five campaigns in less than two decades: Gerald Ford in 1976, Ronald Reagan in 1984, and the Elder Bush in 1980, 1988, and 1992. Baker's efforts in 1984 and 1988 helped secure the reelection of President Reagan and the election to the presidency of Vice President Bush.

Victorious campaign managers are frequently rewarded with plum appointments in the high echelons of the new administration. Robert Kennedy, who managed the successful campaign of his brother John in 1960, was appointed, not without some controversy, to the office of Attorney General. In 1968, a victorious Richard Nixon followed the Kennedy example by naming his friend and campaign manager, John Mitchell. Hamilton Jordan served as Jimmy Carter's campaign manager before being selected by the president-elect for the position of White House chief of staff. William Casey, who managed Ronald Reagan's first campaign in 1980, was given the directorship of the Central Intelligence Agency. Farley served as postmaster general, and Baker as both chief of staff and later secretary of the department of the treasury under Reagan, and as secretary of state for the elder Bush.

Other notable individuals who have managed recent presidential campaigns are: Gary Hart, manager of George McGovern's failed 1972 campaign, who later went on to the U.S. Senate; Susan Estrich, the first woman to run a national presidential campaign (Dukakis, 1988); James Carville, Bill Clinton's savvy campaign manager whose experience and achievement are reminiscent of Farley and Baker; Donna Brazile, the first African American to serve as a presidential campaign manager (Al Gore, 2000); and Karl Rove, campaign manager and current special advisor for the younger Bush. *See also* Lee Atwater; James Baker; Donna Brazile; James Carville; Mark Hanna.

Suggested Readings: R.W. Apple Jr. "Bush's Friend in Need," *New York Times*, August 14, 1992, p. A1; Gerald M. Boyd, "Atwater, Playing Hardball Politics, Is Mapping a Fall Strategy for Bush," *New York Times*, May 30, 1988, p. 11, Katharine Q. Seelye, "Dole Campaign Chief Relying on Determination, and Luck," *New York Times*, June 3, 1996, p. A1.

Cass, Lewis

See Campaign of 1848.

Character Issue

Through much of presidential election history, major policy differences between candidates and their parties have often overshadowed issues surrounding personal character. The Watergate scandal and the subsequent August 1974 resignation of President Richard Nixon ushered in a new era of close scrutiny over private lives and public integrity of political candidates.

Long before the Watergate scandal, a number of character controversies influenced presidential contests. Bitter blood resulting from the **Campaign of 1824** led supporters of Andrew Jackson and incumbent President John Quincy Adams to unleash acrimonious personal attacks. Jackson supporters accused Adams of patronage abuse and of entering into a "corrupt bargain" with Henry Clay that helped Adams rob Jackson of the presidency. Friends of Adams also revived a mean-spirited attack on Jackson and his wife, Rachel, falsely accusing them of a bigamous marriage.

During the **Campaign of 1872**, President Ulysses S. Grant also suffered from accusations that he was an inept drunkard, unable to manage a corrupt administration. Grant's enemies badly misjudged popular concern over corruption in the Grant administration. Grant was a war hero, and in the end, his more ardent supporters once again waved the **bloody shirt**. Grant went on to a popular and electoral vote landslide.

Four years later, Maine Congressman James C. Blaine's campaign was derailed by the "Mulligan Letters" influence, peddling scandal and ruining his chances of winning his party's nomination.

Without question, the 1884 presidential campaign ranks as one of the nastiest in American history. Both Republican presidential candidate James C. Blaine and Democratic candidate Grover Cleveland entered the election campaign with personal baggage. Throughout the campaign, Blaine and Cleveland faced sharp attacks for alleged misdeeds in private and public life. Democratic critics dredged up the 1876 Mulligan Letters controversy.

In July 1884, the Buffalo *Evening Telegraph* published a story that Cleveland had sired an illegitimate child. To the amazement of Cleveland supporters, Cleveland took full responsibility for his indiscretions, diffusing the controversy. Blaine also hurt his chances by allowing himself to appear anti-Catholic in the waning days of the campaign. This cost him the election, as New York's powerful Irish-Catholic vote made the difference.

From 1884 through the 1940s, character attacks in presidential campaigns diminished. Political historians credit this to the fact that the print media preferred not to report on the private lives of politicians. Historians also credit the lack of character controversies on the fact that presidential candidates did an exceptional job of being more discrete in their more questionable activities. Elected president in 1920, Warren Harding's marital infidelity did not become known until after his death in 1923. But Harding had been damaged by public scandal. After

Harding's death, Democrats had hoped to ride the Harding scandals into the White House. Specifically, many Democrats believed that the Teapot Dome and "Ohio Gang" scandals would turn the American public against Republican rule, but they badly misjudged the impact of the scandals and the persuasive power of a healthy economy on the American people.

Prior to John F. Kennedy's 1960 presidential victory, rumors circulated around the Washington press corps that Kennedy had a strong appetite for women other than his wife. The rumors were not printed until long after Kennedy's death.

A turning point in the coverage of the private lives of presidential candidates took place during the 1988 Democratic primary campaign of Democratic front-runner, the former senator from Colorado, Gary Hart. Attempting to deflect rumors of his marital infidelity, Hart challenged reporters to "follow him around," guaranteeing a boring time for all. But after a reporter spied a young woman enter his Washington, D.C., townhouse, followed by photographic exposure of Hart cavorting with model Donna Rice while in Florida partying on a yacht aptly named *Monkey Business*, a media **feeding frenzy** drove Hart out of the race. Even though Hart subsequently reentered the race, the scandal hampered his efforts to regain his early lead.

During the campaign of 1992, Gennifer Flowers alleged in a tabloid story that she had a lengthy affair with the Arkansas governor and candidate Bill Clinton. Appearing with his wife Hillary on *60 Minutes* following the Super Bowl, Clinton admitted to having had problems in his marriage but denied any affair with Flowers. Besides the infidelity allegation, allegations that Clinton used improper influence to avoid the draft during the Vietnam War also dogged his campaign. But Clinton was able to dodge scandal, and with his economic message and personal charisma, he managed to defeat the incumbent president.

Clinton went on to win reelection in the 1996 presidential election despite the best efforts of Republican challenger Bob Dole to turn the 1996 election into a referendum on the Whitewater scandal and other Clinton administration ethics controversies. To the surprise of many political observers, who regarded him as politically finished in the wake of the GOP's off-year triumph in 1994, Clinton easily won reelection.

In the **Campaign of 2000**, Republican candidate George W. Bush (the younger) admitted that during his youth he partied excessively. However, Bush assured voters he no longer had any substance abuse problems. Late in the campaign, a Maine Democratic operative leaked to a number of news sources that during the 1970s, the younger Bush had been cited for driving under the influence. Public opinion polls indicated that few potential voters intended to change their vote as the result of the Bush disclosure. *See also* Campaign of 1824; Campaign of 1872; Campaign of 1884; Campaign of 1988; Campaign of 1992; Campaign of 1996; Campaign of 2000.

Suggested Readings: Thomas Bailey, *Presidential Saints and Sinners* (New York: Free Press, 1981); Robert North Roberts, *Ethics in Government: An Encyclopedia of Investigations, Scandals, Reforms, and Legislation* (Westport, CT: Greenwood Press, 2001); Eugene H. Rosenbloom, *A History of Presidential Elections* (New York Macmillan, 1957); Jeffrey D. Schultz, *Presidential Scandals* (Washington, DC: CQ Press, 2000).

Checkers Speech

In early July 1952, the Republican National Convention nominated General Dwight D. Eisenhower as president. General Eisenhower then selected 39-year-old Senator Richard M. Nixon as his running mate. On September 18, 1952, the *New York Post* published the headline "Secret Rich Men's Trust Fund Keeps Nixon in Style Far Beyond His Salary." The story proved extremely embarrassing for the Eisenhower-Nixon ticket, and for Republicans who had previously accused the Truman administration of corrupt practices. As a result, pressure quickly built for Nixon to drop off of the ticket.

Instead, Nixon went over the heads of the media directly to the American people. On September 23, 1992, Nixon defended himself on national television, denying any impropriety. After insisting upon his honesty and emphasizing his modest lifestyle, including a reference to his wife's "Republican cloth coat," Nixon disarmed his critics with a sentimental story about Checkers, the dog given to his family as a gift from an admirer.

> A man down in Texas heard Pat on the radio mention that our two youngsters would like to have a dog, and, believe it or not, the day before this campaign trip we got a message from Union Station in Baltimore, saying that they had a package for us. We went down to get it. You know what it was? It was a cocker spaniel dog, in a crate that he had sent all the way from Texas, black and white, spotted, and our little girl Tricia, the six-year-old, named it Checkers. And you know, the kids, loved the dog, and I just want to say this right now, that regardless of what they say about it, we are going to keep it.

Nixon's gamble worked. The Eisenhower campaign received thousands of telegrams supporting Nixon's place on the ticket. On Election Day the Republicans enjoyed a landslide victory. Nixon's Checkers speech foreshadowed the importance of television for the political fortunes of national political candidates. Ironically, political historians blame Nixon's loss to John F. Kennedy, in the 1960 presidential election, to Nixon's poor performance in the first televised **presidential debates**. *See also* Campaign of 1952.

Suggested Reading: "Richard M. Nixon 'Checkers Speech,' " The History Place, http://www.historyplace.com/speeches/nixon-checkers.htm.

Civic Journalism Movement

See Public Journalism Movement.

Civil Rights Issue

Upon emancipation, the freed slaves confronted a multitude of political, legal, social, and cultural obstacles to the full enjoyment of their inherent, natural rights as guaranteed under the Civil War Amendments. From the very beginnings of Reconstruction, civil rights emerged as a singularly critical issue in the political culture of America, and one that has endured with a gravity surpassing all other issues in the political debate of campaigns and elections at all levels.

To protect and enforce the constitutional rights and liberties of minorities, and especially (historically) African Americans, Congress has enacted civil rights legislation in 1866, 1870, 1871, 1875 (all of which are considered to have failed), 1957 (the first act since the end of Reconstruction in 1877), 1960, 1964 (the most significant, comprehensive and successful of all the civil rights acts), 1968, and 1991. Additionally, the Supreme Court, beginning with the Brown case in 1954, generated a series of court decisions affirming the equal protection of the civil rights of all citizens. Presidential politics, owing to the electoral muscle of the solid, segregationist South that emerged after Reconstruction and maintained its resistance to civil rights into the 1960s, has been late in joining the civil rights efforts of the other branches.

Nonetheless, the issue of civil rights has concerned both major parties and remained an ongoing feature of party platforms. In the second half of the nineteenth century and early elections of the twentieth century, the Republican Party was the party of civil rights, including platform planks endorsing equal rights for all, while Democratic platforms included planks more concerned with states rights and even critical of federal interference with state policies. With the creation of the Roosevelt coalition in the 1932 and 1936 elections that led to the shifting of the allegiance of the African American vote to the Democratic Party in the 1930s, both parties advocated civil rights protections for all citizens. As the Democratic Party became more dedicated to the cause of civil rights, southern conservative elements grew increasingly alienated. In the 1948 Democratic convention, southern delegates defected in protest over a liberal pro–civil rights plank drafted by the young Hubert Humphrey. Assuming the nickname Dixiecrat, the southern Dem-

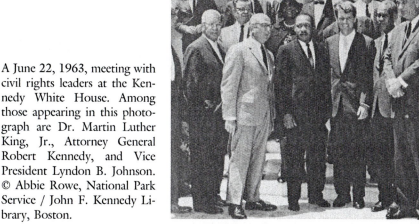

A June 22, 1963, meeting with civil rights leaders at the Kennedy White House. Among those appearing in this photograph are Dr. Martin Luther King, Jr., Attorney General Robert Kennedy, and Vice President Lyndon B. Johnson. © Abbie Rowe, National Park Service / John F. Kennedy Library, Boston.

ocrats ran their own candidate, Strom Thurmond, advocating a strict states rights position. Throughout the 1950s, the major parties both continued to include civil rights planks, but were plagued by continued resistance from their respective conservative wings.

Nineteen sixty-four produced a presidential election that drew a sharp contrast between the moderate and liberal pro–civil rights position and the conservative reaction to civil rights legislation. Conservative Republicans also sympathetic to states rights and thus opposed to federal civil rights legislation, led by firebrand Arizona governor Barry Goldwater, managed to capture the nomination and thus polarize the debate over the civil rights policies of the Kennedy and Johnson administrations. Goldwater received support from the pro-segregation factions of the Dixiecrat South, but was thoroughly humiliated by Johnson, a major force in the successful advancement of civil rights legislation both as a senator in 1957 and 1960 and as president in 1964, throughout the rest of the country.

Goldwater's embarrassing defeat signaled the Republican Party to avoid further polarization on civil rights, and future GOP candidates with more moderate views became the preferred choice within the party. Nonetheless, Democrats continued to receive support from racial minorities, especially African Americans, in large numbers. The close 1976 election of southern Democrat Jimmy Carter, governor of Georgia, may have been decided on the power of the black vote, even though both candidates were political moderates, and the GOP candidate, incumbent President Gerald Ford, had a record of support for civil rights legislation while a member of the House of Representatives.

Civil rights reemerged as a visible issue in the 1992 campaign in reaction to the policies of the incumbent president, the elder George Bush. Bush's opposition to civil rights legislation drew hostile fire from Democrats and further alienated minority voters to the benefit of the Clinton campaign, which was regarded as particularly sensitive to issues of race, sex, sexual orientation, and minority rights in general. Throughout the 1990s, the major parties appeared more polarized on civil rights issues, the image of Republican candidates appearing less moderate than the campaigns of previous Republicans such as Richard Nixon, Gerald Ford, and even the more conservative Ronald Reagan. This was reflected in the 2000 election, with the urbanized minority vote, especially that of the African American population, throwing its electoral weight wholly behind the Democrat Al Gore. Thus, while both parties continue to champion civil rights in their platforms and official campaign positions, the American public, and especially the public of voting minorities, regard the Democratic Party as the current and, somewhat ironically, historic party of civil rights. *See also* Campaign of 1948; Campaign of 1964; Campaign of 1980; Campaign of 1984; Race Relations Issue.

Suggested Reading: Jeremy D. Mayer, *Running on Race: Racial Politics in Presidential Campaigns, 1960–2000* (New York: Random House, 2002).

Civil Service Reform

During the decades between 1828 and 1880 the political patronage, or "spoils system," grew rapidly. By the 1870s, growing concern that the "spoils system"

Harper's Weekly political cartoon attacking the spoils system. Courtesy of Library of Congress.

CIVIL SERVICE REFORM.

OFFICE-SEEKER. "St. Jackson, can't you save us? Can't *you* give us something?"

contributed to a dramatic increase in political corruption stimulated proposals regarding civil service reform. Supporters of reform argued that government agencies should select public employees on the basis of merit rather than political affiliation.

Through the early 1870s, the vast majority of federal and elected state officials viewed the civil service reform movement as a direct threat to their political survival. Early in 1872, controversy over reform contributed to a major split in the Republican Party. Liberal Republicans left the Republican Party in protest over the lack of support for reform and in objection to corruption in the Grant administration. Republican refusal to end federal oversight of Reconstruction was also an issue.

Grant won the election, but the reformers gained more support. *Harper's* magazine helped fuel the movement, publishing the work of political cartoonist **Thomas Nast**, an enemy of patronage. But throughout the 1870s and early 1880s, Congress continued to resist civil service reform.

In 1872, the Republican Party nominated James Garfield as president and Chester A. Arthur as vice president. This dismayed many as President Rutherford B. Hayes, a reformist, had earlier removed Arthur from his post as customs collector for the port of New York in an effort to control patronage abuses. The Garfield/Arthur ticket won the election, but the Fates played an unexpected hand.

Charles J. Guiteau, forever known as the "disappointed office-seeker," shot President Garfield in July of 1881. Garfield's assassination thrust Arthur into the presidency. Responding to the tragedy, Congress passed and Arthur signed into law the Civil Service Reform Act of 1883, more commonly known as the Pendleton

Act. The law established an independent Civil Service Commission to conduct competitive examinations to fill a small number of federal positions and to enforce a new prohibition on political assessments of federal employees. Finally, the law gave the president the authority to extend merit system protection to jobs not covered by the Pendleton Act.

After the passage of the Pendleton Act, civil service reform was no longer a national political issue. Gradually, a series of presidential administrations would extend merit system protection to a majority of federal employees. *See also* Campaign of 1872; Campaign of 1876; Campaign of 1880.

Suggested Reading: Frederick C. Mosher, *Democracy and the Public Service* (New York: Oxford University Press, 1982).

Clay, Henry

See Campaign of 1824; Campaign of 1832; Campaign of 1844.

"Clean for Gene"

Eugene McCarthy's idealistic run in 1968 was driven by the "McCarthy Million," a cohort of the young, educated, middle-class, and politically committed who, against the fashion of many of their peers, cut their hair, shaved, and went "clean for Gene" so as to lend credibility to their efforts.

Suggested Reading: George Rising, *Clean for Gene: Eugene McCarthy's 1968 Presidential Campaign* (Westport, CT: Praeger, 1997).

Cleveland, Grover

See Campaign of 1884; Campaign of 1888; Campaign of 1892.

Clinton, De Witt

See Campaign of 1812.

Clinton, William Jefferson

See Campaign of 1992; Campaign of 1996.

"Compassionate Conservatism"

Adopting the "compassionate conservatism" slogan, Republican candidate George W. Bush hoped to attract the support of those independent and moderate Republican voters, and particularly nonaffiliated women voters who had helped Bill Clinton win the presidency in 1992 and 1996. Four years earlier, Jack Kemp, the

Republican nominee for vice president, had angered Republican conservatives by arguing that the Republican Party needed to moderate their positions on a number of issues if they wished to recapture the White House and close the **gender gap**.

After losing both the 1992 and 1996 presidential elections to Bill Clinton, the Republican Party looked for a candidate that had the ability to piece together a winning electoral vote coalition for the 2000 election. After a bitter primary fight with Arizona senator John McCain, Bush secured the Republican nomination. Bush faced the extremely difficult task of defeating the Democratic nominee, Vice President Albert Gore.

Reflecting the "compassionate conservatism" theme, the Bush campaign made education reform a priority. The Bush education plan called for the establishment of national standards to evaluate the effectiveness of public schools from coast to coast. Also reflecting the "compassionate conservatism" theme, Bush argued that government should work closely with charity and faith-based organizations to help the less fortunate in American society. Bush campaign strategists hoped a moderate Republican agenda would convince women voters in key **battleground states**.

Democratic critics attacked the "compassionate conservatism" theme as a cynical attempt to hide the true nature of the Republican agenda. In an effort to appeal to women, the Gore campaign stressed that "compassionate conservatism" did not include protecting a woman's choice regarding abortion. The Gore campaign also sharply criticized the Bush campaign for refusing to support the expansion of the Medicare program to include prescription drug coverage for the elderly.

In the end, the "compassionate conservatism" theme failed to close the gender gap in the key states. Bush won the election due to his Electoral College majority, but Gore won more popular votes, protecting the Democrat's gender gap advantage. *See also* Battleground State, Campaign of 2000; Gender Gap.

Suggested Readings: Adam Nagourney, "Ideas & Trends; Republicans Stalk a Slogan, Hunting for Themselves," *New York Times*, June 20, 1999, Section 4, p. 1; Terry M. Neal, "Bush Outlines Charity-Based Social Policies," *Washington Post*, July 23, 1999, p. A02.

Conservation Issue

No president has played a more seminal role in lending credibility and momentum to the conservation movement than Theodore Roosevelt. His administration undertook unprecedented efforts to establish a policy of conserving the vast resources and natural beauty of an increasingly industrial, urbanized nation.

The nineteenth century Industrial Revolution and the westward expansion of the United States stimulated a demand for natural resources. Massive coal mining operations sprang up in a number of eastern states. Mining and other extraction operations dramatically multiplied throughout the West. Congress thus established the Department of the Interior to manage vast tracks of federal land.

Congress also granted private individuals and corporations development and resource extraction rights within the boundaries of federal lands. In response, the conservationist movement of the late nineteenth century took root with the goal of preserving the natural condition of these areas. Political and corporate interests adamantly opposed any effort to limit access to any deposit of natural resources.

In 1904 Roosevelt easily won the election, running on a platform that included support for the conservationist programs, giving the conservationist movement a strong friend in the White House. Roosevelt appointed well-known conservationist Gifford Pinchot as the Interior Department's "chief forester." When Republicans nominated William Howard Taft to succeed Roosevelt, the party renewed its pledge to continue conservationist policies. After Taft's successful election in 1908, conservationists soon grew disillusioned by the emergence of his conservative and pro-development business instincts.

Conservationists were angered when Taft nominated Richard A. Ballinger, a friend of Western business interests heavily invested in development and extraction of natural resources. When Ballinger supported opening a tract of Alaskan land rich in natural resources to private developers, conservationists' fears were confirmed. In 1910, Ballinger dismissed Louis Glavis, an Interior Department employee opposed to the action, prompting Chief Forester Pinchot to send an open letter to a senator supporting Glavis and sharply criticizing Ballinger. President Taft responded by dismissing Pinchot for gross insubordination.

As Taft's relationship with Theodore Roosevelt soured, the former friends engaged in bitter battle for the 1912 Republican nomination. Taft prevailed against Roosevelt, who subsequently accepted the nomination of the newly formed Progressive Party, but the divided Republicans drained support from both candidates, allowing Woodrow Wilson to win for the Democrats.

From the election of 1912 through the **Campaign of 1972**, both the Republican and Democratic parties threw their support behind various conservation initiatives. The administration of President Franklin D. Roosevelt made conservation a major element of the New Deal during the 1930s. Roosevelt's Civilian Conservation Corps helped to substantially rebuild the national park system. As industrial pollution poisoned air, land, and water at exponential rates, and as rivers burned and smog choked the larger cities; the conservation movement gave way to a new environmental protection movement during the 1960s and early 1970s. Rachel Carson's *Silent Spring* sold widely, Lady Bird Johnson, first lady from 1963 to 1969, promoted a program to "Keep America Beautiful," and television viewers were introduced to the poignant image of a wandering Indian warrior quietly weeping over a scarred and raped landscape. Today environmental policy issues revolve around toxic cleanup, preservation of the remaining pristine areas of Alaska, and addressing concerns over suburban sprawl encroaching on former farmland and undeveloped areas. *See also* Campaign of 1912.

Suggested Reading: Doug Stewart, Lisa Drew, and Mark Wexler, "How Conservation Grew From a Whisper to a Roar," *National Wildlife* (December/January 1999), p. 22.

"The Constitution and the Union, Now and Forever"

In 1860, four presidential candidates appeared on the ballot, representing different viewpoints regarding the preeminent issue of the day—slavery. The Republican Party nominated the eventual winner, Abraham Lincoln, opposing the expansion of slavery with the radical wing urging its complete abolition. The northern faction of the Democratic Party nominated Illinois U.S. Senator Stephen Douglas, who reiterated his adoption of the policy of "popular sovereignty." The southern faction, nominating John C. Breckinridge, defended the claims of slave owners, and the newly formed Constitutional Union Party, led by John Bell, took a decidedly neutral stance toward the volatile issue.

Instead of taking a position on any issue, the platform of the Constitutional Union Party denounced sectionalism and called for national unity. For their slogans the party adopted the words of the great Whig orator, Daniel Webster, "The Constitution and the Union, Now and Forever," and "Liberty & Union, Now & Forever, One and Inseparable," boldly summarized the only position of Bell's campaign. On Election Day Bell finished fourth in the final tally. *See also* Campaign of 1860.

Suggested Readings: David Emerson Fite, *The Presidential Campaign of 1860* (Port Washington, NY: Kennikat Press, 1967); George Harmon Knoles, *The Crisis of the Union, 1860–1861* (Baton Rouge: Louisiana State University Press, 1965); "The Presidential Elections 1860–1912," HarpWeek, http://elections.harpweek.com.

Coolidge, Calvin

See Campaign of 1924.

"Coolidge or Chaos"

During the **Campaign of 1924** the Republican Party successfully characterized the Democratic ticket of John W. Davis and Charles W. Bryan as a threat to the nation's booming economic recovery. Typically, the Democratic Party advocated their traditional policy of low tariffs. To the contrary, Republicans affirmed strong support for high, protective tariffs. The slogan "Coolidge or Chaos" reflected the Republican strategy.

Republicans used the slogans "Coolidge or Chaos" and "**Keep Cool with Coolidge**" as a way to raise doubts about the radical economic policies of Progressive candidate Robert La Follette as well as the Democratic nominee John W. Davis. The slogans insinuated the notion that voting for the Democrats or Progressives would lead to social and economic turmoil. Coolidge's record and the advantage of prosperity worked in his favor as he convincingly won the election. *See also* Campaign of 1924; "Keep Cool with Coolidge."

Suggested Readings: Leonard J. Bates, "The Teapot Dome Scandal and the Election of 1924," *American Historical Review* 60 (1955) pp. 303–322; Burl Noggle, *Teapot Dome: Oil and Politics in the 1920s* (Baton Rouge: Louisiana State University Press, 1962).

Corruption Issue

See Character Issue.

Cox, James

See Campaign of 1920.

Crawford, William

See Campaign of 1824.

Crime Issue

See Law and Order Issue.

"Cross of Gold" Speech

Historians regard William Jennings Bryan's 1896 "Cross of Gold" speech delivered at the Democratic Convention as a landmark of political oratory. When the Democratic convention opened in Chicago, a platform battle immediately broke out between two factions: one faction, the bimetallist, advocated the coinage of **free silver** at a ratio of **16 to 1** as a function of the value of gold, and a second, the monometallists, favored strict adherence to the gold standard, warning that free silver would severely undermine the monetary system and thus weaken the economy. But free silver delegates hoped to find a quick fix to the mounting debt of farmers. Silver meant more and cheaper money, and farmers could then use the inflated money to clear their debts. Free silver supporters also argued that the free

A poster reprinting the famous "Cross of Gold" Speech of 1896 Democratic nominee William Jennings Bryan. Courtesy of Library of Congress.

coinage of silver would force American corporations to raise the salaries of workers. Additionally, mining companies in western states eagerly supported bimetallism.

Bryan saw the free silver issue as part of a much larger populist crusade designed to reduce the power of monopolies and eastern corporations. In a dizzying whirl of rhetorical flourish, Bryan brought his speech to an impassioned conclusion by uttering the now famous phrase, "You shall not press down upon the brow of labor this crown of thorns, you shall not crucify mankind upon a cross of gold." Whipped to a frenzy, free silver delegates carried the day, and handed the nomination to their champion.

Seen by some as an inspiring oratorical masterpiece, and by others as nothing short of sacrilege, the "Cross of Gold" speech became and remained Bryan's defining political moment. But his fiery persona and populist affinities did not win the confidence of the electorate. The less flamboyant William McKinley took the White House for the more staid Republicans and the gold standard. *See also* Campaign of 1896; Currency Issue; Free Silver.

Suggested Readings: Stanley Llewellyn Jones, *The Presidential Election of 1896* (Madison; University of Wisconsin Press, 1964); George Frisbe Whicher, *William Jennings Bryan and the Campaign of 1896* (Boston: Heath, 1953).

C-SPAN

The cable television industry established C-SPAN in 1979 to provide public access to the political process. The C-SPAN networks comprise C-SPAN, C-SPAN 2, C-SPAN 3, C-SPAN Radio, and C-SPAN.org. The C-SPAN networks provide gavel-to-gavel coverage of the proceedings of the House of Representatives and United States Senate. C-SPAN coverage of Congress deeply affected the way Congress operates.

During presidential election years, the C-SPAN networks provide extensive coverage of presidential primary battles, the party conventions of major political parties and the general election campaign. The weekly *Road to the White House* broadcasts provide viewers the opportunity to follow presidential primary and general election campaigns including campaign spot ads. As major networks sharply cut back the number of prime time hours devoted to covering national political conventions, C-SPAN became the only network providing gavel-to-gavel convention coverage. *See also* Media Event.

Suggested Readings: Glen Dickson, "C-SPAN Branches Out" (Covering Campaign 1996), *Broadcasting & Cable*, January 1, 1996, p. 48; Juliana Gruenwald, "C-SPAN from Novelty to Institution," *Congressional Quarterly Weekly Report*, November 29, 1997, pp. 29–48; Lou Prato, "Politics in the Raw," *Washington Journalism Review*, September 1992, p. 35.

Currency Issue

A major policy concern of the latter nineteenth century, the currency debates dominated American political rhetoric until the turn of the century.

By the mid-1870s, growing panic provoked the wrath of farming interests, with particular anger focused on railroads for imposing excessive cargo rates and the operators of grain elevators for demanding exorbitant storage charges. Meanwhile, the period was marked by a general and growing interest in the circulation of federal paper currency, which would help farmers by inflating the prices of farm produce. By the late 1870s, farm groups joined with labor groups to create the Greenback Party. In the **Campaign of 1876**, Peter Cooper of New York ran for president on the Greenback ticket, followed in 1880 by James Baird Weaver. Cooper had little impact on the 1876 election, but Weaver, whose campaign was fueled by increased agricultural stress, drew 305,997 votes in a race won by Republican James A. Garfield by scarcely more than 2,000 votes. In 1884, however, the Greenback Party only managed 175,000 votes.

By the early 1890s, the **"free silver" movement** had replaced the Greenback movement as the solution for debt ridden rural America. Progressive Democrats, backed by mining interests in the West and allied to the agrarian block of southern voters who distrusted northern money and power, stood behind the position of bimetallism, or the coinage of "free silver" at a ratio of **16 to 1** measured against the value of gold.

Republicans and conservative Democrats, influenced by the interest of industrialist and financiers in the Northeast and Midwest, attached their economic policies to the inviolate principle of the gold standard as the only viable medium of currency. The debate over currency became so heated as to assume a religious tone, reminiscent of the more rhetorically ardent expressions during the controversy over slavery.

Currency policy, while a critical issue in the latter nineteenth century, and remaining a dear concern of elements on the political fringe well into the twentieth century, quickly faded from the arena of electoral politics as the American economy diversified and grew deeper connections to the complexities of the international system. Shortly after taking office, President Franklin Roosevelt took the nation off of the gold standard. Currency no longer inspires debate in the mainstream parties, but in historical terms, the monetary question is remembered as a defining issue in the evolution of the two-party system. *See also* Campaign of 1896; "Cross of Gold" Speech; 16 to 1.

Suggested Reading: Gretchen Ritter, *Goldbugs and Greenbacks: The Antimonopoly Tradition and the Politics of Finance in America* (Cambridge: Cambridge University Press, 1997).

"Daisy" Campaign Ad

During the **Campaign of 1964**, incumbent President Lyndon Johnson openly criticized Republican challenger Barry Goldwater's hawkish rhetoric. Goldwater was outside the political mainstream, but the Johnson campaign took the Goldwater threat seriously. Making sophisticated use of the media, the Democrats stressed the successes of the Johnson administration while depicting Goldwater as dangerously volatile. Johnson's campaign sponsored numerous TV ads painting Goldwater as an extremist willing to engage in atomic brinkmanship. Johnson's rhetoric reached its highest pitch with the television broadcast of one of the more controversial political commercials in history, the "Daisy" ad.

The ad began with a small girl at play in a flowered field, pulling petals from daisies, innocently counting as they fall. Her voice fades and another, disembodied electronic voice rises in the ominous cadence of a launch countdown. Suddenly the senses are shocked by the nightmarish mushroom cloud of an exploding atomic bomb, a horrific image juxtaposed to the sweet idyll among nature's flowers. As the atomic death cloud billows, the grave voice of Lyndon Johnson darkly warns that "these are the stakes: to make a world in which all of God's children can live or to go into the dark. We must either love each other or we must die." Concluding the ad, an announcer urges the audience to "Vote for President Johnson on November 3. **The Stakes Are Too High For You to Stay Home.**"

Shown only once, the ad was unforgettable. The Johnson campaign became the subject of intense criticism for using apocalyptic scare tactics against Goldwater, but despite the negative reaction, media coverage of the ad played into the hands of the Johnson campaign by drawing the public's attention to Goldwater's more bellicose posture regarding the permissible use of nuclear weapons. With the October 1962 Cuban missile crisis still fresh in the minds of the American public, the Johnson campaign bet the majority of voters would not pull the lever for a presidential candidate effectively depicted as a trigger-happy warmonger. *See also* Campaign of 1964; Negative Campaigning.

Suggested Readings: Harold Faber, *The Road to the White House: The Story of the 1964 Election* (New York: McGraw Hill, 1965); Kathleen Hall Jamieson, *Packaging the Presidency: A History and Criticism of Presidential Campaign Advertising* (New York: Oxford University Press, 1984); Theodore White, *The Making of the President, 1964* (New York: Atheneum Publishers, 1965).

Davis, John W.

See Campaign of 1924.

Deaver, Michael (1938–)

As deputy chief of staff to President Reagan from 1981 to 1985, Michael Deaver played a key role in Ronald Reagan's election victories in 1980 and 1984. Deaver had become close friends with Reagan while Reagan served as governor of California from 1966 to 1974, serving as Reagan's cabinet secretary and assistant. He served as an important fundraiser and helped develop strategies for Reagan's presidential run in 1980. Upon victory, Deaver served as Reagan's deputy chief of staff from 1981 to 1985.

Early in 1985, Deaver left the White House to establish his own Washington public relations and lobbying firm. In April 1986, Deaver found himself the subject of a criminal investigation for allegedly violating a provision of the Ethics in Government Act of 1978 prohibiting former high-level federal officials from lobbying for one year after leaving federal service. In September of 1987, a U.S. District Court jury convicted Deaver of lying about his lobbying activities. Deaver received probation, 1,500 hours of community service, and a $100,000 fine. *See also* Campaign of 1980.

Suggested Readings: Michael Deaver, *Behind the Scenes* (New York: Morrow, 1987); Peter B. Levy, *Encyclopedia Of the Reagan-Bush Years* (Westport, CT: Greenwood Press, 1996).

Debates

See Presidential Debates.

Dewey, Thomas E.

See Campaign of 1948.

Dial Groups

Through the 1980s and 1990s, presidential campaigns significantly increased the use of opinion research in an effort to evaluate the impact of various campaign strategies on prospective voters. By the **Campaign of 1988** it became common practice for presidential campaigns to use **focus groups** to test the impact of spot ads and issues on voters. In an effort to reduce the influence of focus group dynamics on individual responses, opinion research experts developed dial group technology allowing focus groups participants to anonymously respond by simply turning a dial. News organizations also began using dial groups during the campaigns of 1996 and 2000 to measure responses to speeches at national conventions and statements made by candidates during presidential debates.

Critics of focus and dial groups argue that they contribute to a growing trend of presidential campaigns to carefully and cynically craft campaign messages in an effort to appeal to the widest possible cross-section of voters and thus preventing substantive discussions of policies and issues. *See also* Campaign Manager.

Suggested Reading: Mike Allen, "The Applause-O-Meter Still Thrives in Politics," *New York Times*, August 26, 1965, p. D5.

Direct Mail

Modern presidential election campaigns make use of a wide variety of methods to convey messages throughout the electorate, partisan, and undecided alike. Besides **campaign ads** and phone banks, presidential campaigns routinely make use of direct mail to deliver messages to likely voters. Compared to the expense of broadcasting campaign ads, campaigners regard direct mail costs as reasonable. Equally important, direct mail effectively targets particular groups of voters while allowing for personalization of campaign literature. *See also* Get-Out-the-Vote Programs.

Suggested Reading: Jeff Leeds, "Parties Bankroll Get-Out-the-Vote Efforts; Strategy: the GOP Plans an Unprecedented $100 Million Campaign, While Democrats Will Enlist Help from Unions and Other Groups," *Los Angeles Times*, August 9, 2000, p. A1.

Dirty Tricks

In late 1971, President Nixon's attorney general John Mitchell resigned to take the position as Chairman of the Committee to Re-elect the President (CREEP). In addition to conducting a traditional presidential campaign, the White House and CREEP authorized various and illicit activities directed at creating turmoil with the Democratic Party. Within the White House, Nixon's chief of staff, H.R. Haldeman, supervised a series of "dirty tricks" operations conducted by special assistant to the president Dwight Chapin. Within CREEP, G. Gordon Liddy and E. Howard Hunt supervised a political intelligence unit.

Burglary, wiretapping, phony letters, invasion of confidential psychiatry files, rumormongering, and other tactics constituted CREEP's dirty tricks. With the capture of the Watergate burglars in the summer of 1972 and the subsequent revelation of their association with the White House, CREEP's dirty tricks were exposed, imperiling the Nixon presidency. *See also* Campaign of 1972; Negative Campaigning; Push Polling.

Suggested Readings: Jack Mitchell, *How to Get Elected: An Anecdotal History of Mudslinging, Redbaiting, Vote Stealing and Dirty Tricks in American Politics* (New York: St. Martin's Press, 1992); Shelly Ross, *Fall from Grace: Sex, Scandal, and Corruption in American Politics from 1702 to the Present* (New York: Ballantine Books, 1988).

"Do You Want John Quincy Adams Who Can Write, or Andrew Jackson Who Can Fight?"

Having established a reputation as a scholarly statesman and man for all seasons, John Quincy Adams emulated the venerable, sober leadership of the founding era. By contrast, Andrew Jackson, irascible, swaggering, pugilistic, and an experienced duelist, was criticized by more refined elites as an uncouth, unlettered choice for the chief executive. Initially coined as "Adams who can write, Jackson who can fight" by those who proposed a joint effort, the phrase evolved into a slogan promoting the erudite Adams over the ruffian Jackson: "Better Adams, who can write, than the pugnacious brawler." *See also* Campaign of 1828.

Suggested Reading: Robert V. Remini, *The Election of Andrew Jackson* (Philadelphia: Lippincott, 1963).

Dole, Bob

See "A Better Man For a Better America"; Campaign of 1976; Campaign of 1996.

"Don't Change Horses in Mid-Stream"

"Don't change horses in mid-stream" is a campaign adage that was probably coined by Abraham Lincoln in his 1864 reelection bid. In the same way that one does not change horses in crossing a river, one does not change leaders during a time of crisis. Franklin Roosevelt reiterated the adage in his 1940 bid for a third term during an equally grave crisis.

Facing a potentially extremist candidate in Republican nominee Barry Goldwater, Lyndon Johnson's 1964 campaign quoted the phrase again to emphasize two points: first, that it would be unwise to switch to a less steady horse during a cold war, marked by dangerous hot spots abroad, particularly in Vietnam, and second, Johnson's significant achievements on a wide variety of social and domestic programs would likely be damaged by a new and reactionary leader. *See also* Campaign of 1864, Campaign of 1940; Campaign of 1964.

Suggested Readings: Harold Faber, *The Road to the White House: The Story of the 1964 Election* (New York: McGraw-Hill, 1965); Theodore White, *The Making of the President, 1964* (New York: Atheneum Publishers, 1965).

"Don't Stop Thinking About Tomorrow"

"Don't Stop," written by Christine McVie and recorded by her band, Fleetwood Mac in the mid-1970s, became the theme song of the 1992 campaign of Bill Clinton and Al Gore. Unveiled at the convention, the song's optimistic lyric and ebullient melody conveyed a youthful, energetic, forward-looking image that the Clinton handlers hoped would contrast effectively with the more conservative image of the incumbent president, the elder George Bush. Bush's admitted inability to grasp the "vision thing," played well into this contrast.

The song appealed to Clinton's baby boom supporters, and quickly became the most familiar and popular campaign song since Franklin Roosevelt's **"Happy Days Are Here Again."** *See also* Campaign of 1992.

Suggested Readings: "Democrats Redefine Party Music," *Los Angeles Times*, July 18, 1992, p. A19; Tom Shales, "The Windup and the Pitch," *Washington Post*, July 17, 1992, p. C1.

"Don't Worry, Be Happy"

Composer and famed vocal stylist Bobby McFerrin's signature song became a campaign theme for Republican candidate and incumbent Vice President George H.W. Bush during his 1988 run for the White House.

The song's easy, carefree advice helped to allay concern over allegations linking Bush to the **Iran Hostage Crisis** as well as the Reagan administration's mounting deficit spending. While Democratic candidate Michael Dukakis enjoyed a post-convention surge in the polls, McFerrin's light-hearted lyric helped deflect anxiety produced by the recent turn in fortunes. Additionally, the Bush campaign needed to reassure the public that a crisis did not exist and a return to the Democrats was not justified.

In the end, the "Don't Worry, Be Happy" campaign slogan was not the decisive message for the Republicans. A series of Dukakis missteps and an extremely effective negative media campaign succeeded in demolishing the Democrats. However, the popular song did help to reinforce the Bush campaign message that the country needed to stay the course, not worry, and not elect Democrats. *See also* Campaign of 1988.

Suggested Readings: Jack Germond and Jules Witcover, *Whose Broad Stripes and Bright Stars? The Trivial Pursuit of the Presidency, 1988* (New York: Warner Books, 1989); Peter Goldman, Tom Mathews, and the Newsweek Special Election Team, *The Quest for the Presidency, 1988* (New York: Simon & Schuster, 1989).

Douglas, Stephen

See Campaign of 1860.

"Douglas and Johnson: The Union Now and Forever"

Stephen Douglas and his running mate, Herschel Johnson employed a reference to Daniel Webster's famous phrase, "Liberty and Union, now and forever, one and inseparable," to promote their belief in preserving the Union in response to secessionist threats from the South. One of four candidates in the campaign of 1860, Douglas famously advocated the policy of popular sovereignty regarding the question of slavery in the territories and new states. Even so, Douglas was a defender of the Union, and reemphasized this throughout his failed campaign.

Suggested Readings: James L. Abrahamson, *The Men of Secession and Civil War, 1859–1961* (Wilmington: Scholarly Resources, 2000); George Harmon Knoles, *The Crisis of the Union, 1860–1861* (Baton Rouge: Louisiana State University Press, 1965); "The Presidential Elections 1860–1912," HarpWeek, http://elections.harpweek.com.

"Down with King Caucus"

Supporters of Andrew Jackson's 1824 presidential campaign used the slogan "Down with King Caucus" to mobilize the common man on their behalf. For over two decades the congressional party caucus selected presidential candidates. Defenders of the caucus system argued that it assured strong party support for credible candidates. Critics attacked the caucus system for investing all nominating power to a small circle of party elite at the expense of the general populous.

Following the Era of Good Feelings, the dominant Republican Party (not to be confused with the modern Republican Party, or GOP), fragmented. At the beginning of the 1824 campaign, Georgia's William H. Crawford was the clear favorite. Crawford, who had served as President Monroe's secretary of the treasury, enjoyed strong southern support but faced serious opposition from a number of other strong regional candidates: John Quincy Adams from New England, Andrew Jackson of Tennessee who enjoyed a strong western base, and South Carolina's rising star, John C. Calhoun.

In an effort to gain the upper hand in the presidential race, Crawford supporters convened a congressional caucus in an effort to ensure his early nomination. The action backfired as only Crawford supporters attended the caucus, while others did not participate. When a stacked caucus nominated Crawford without real opposition, supporters behind other contenders bristled. Jackson, Adams, Calhoun, and Henry Clay were subsequently nominated by their respective state legislatures in defiance of the caucus system, setting a precedent for alternative methods of selection that would eventually lead to national nominating conventions in the early 1830s. *See also* Campaign of 1824.

Suggested Readings: Robert V. Remini, *Andrew Jackson and the Cause of American Freedom, 1822–1832*, Vol. II (New York: Harper & Row, 1981); Arthur M. Schlesinger, Fred Israel, and William P. Hansen, eds., *History of American Presidential Elections 1789–1968*, Vol. I (New York: Chelsea House, 1985).

Drys

A term used to describe supporters of prohibition. During the late nineteenth century and early twentieth century, the temperance and **prohibition** movements lobbied to end the production and consumption of alcoholic beverages. Their lobbying campaign culminated with the 1919 ratification of the Eighteenth Amendment. Both major parties supported the passage and ratification of the Eighteenth Amendment, but by the **Campaign of 1928** many Democrats representing urban areas campaigned to end prohibition.

In 1920, the Democratic nominee, James Cox, an anti-prohibitionist, suffered criticism from temperance advocates, equating the Democrats with "Cox and Cocktails." Although the 1928 Democratic platform did not call for the repeal of the Eighteenth Amendment, Al Smith, the party's nominee, openly expressed support for such a repeal. Smith badly underestimated the ability of the Republican Party to define Smith as the "Cocktail Candidate."

In 1932 the Democrats did include a plank in their platform promising the repeal of the Eighteenth Amendment. Following Democrat Franklin Roosevelt's victory, Congress set an amendment speed record by almost immediately sending the Twenty-first Amendment, repealing the Eighteenth, to the states for ratification. After passage of the Twenty-first Amendment, "Drys" turned their attention to prohibition laws at the state and county level. Today a few "dry" counties remain in some regions of the country. *See also* Campaign of 1928; Campaign of 1932; Prohibition; Temperance Movement.

Suggested Readings: Thomas Coffey, *The Long Thirst: Prohibition In America, 1920–1933* (New York: Norton, 1975); Thomas R. Pegram, *Battling Demon Rum: The Struggle for a Dry America, 1800–1933* (Chicago: Ivan R. Dee, 1998).

Dukakis, Michael

See Campaign of 1988.

Earned Media

See Free Media.

E-Campaign

See Internet Campaigning.

Economic Prosperity Issue

See Prosperity Issue.

Editorial Page Endorsement

Through much of the nineteenth century, newspapers played an active role in presidential election campaigns. For ideological reasons, newspapers commonly aligned themselves with major political parties and candidates. Newspapers also had important financial ties to political parties. A number of urban newspapers depended on government printing contracts for revenue. Up through the beginning of the Civil War, few newspapers attempted to separate the editorial policy of the paper from the coverage of news events, including presidential election campaigns.

From the end of the Civil War to the turn of the century, newspapers gradually separated editorial policy from news coverage. Manufacturers, enjoying the low cost of production during the industrial boom of the nineteenth century began relying on newspaper advertising to boost sales, increasing newspaper circulation and generating revenue for publishers. More space in newsprint followed higher profits, enabling the separation of news and opinion. Through the 1920s, editorial page endorsements continued to carry weight with voters, but the growing use of radio by candidates decreased the impact of endorsements in the 1930s.

Republican candidates picked up the majority of major newspaper endorsements during the campaigns of 1932, 1936, 1940, and 1944, however, Franklin Roosevelt easily won four consecutive presidential elections. Roosevelt made masterful use of radio, instantly transmitting his message into millions of American homes. Newspapers continued to support GOP candidates through the 1940s, while Democrats were more effective on radio.

With the rise of television spot ads and sound bites, the power of the editorial appears to have reached the ebb of its influence. *See also* Partisan Newspapers.

Suggested Reading: Howard Kurtz, "Newspaper Endorsements in Full Swing," *Washington Post*, October 25, 2000, A18.

Education Reform Issue

Through the 1950s, the federal government played a minor role in public education. After the Civil War, Congress passed the Morrill Act to help finance the construction of land grant colleges. Similarly, after World War II, Congress passed the G.I. Bill to finance the college education of millions of soldiers returning from war.

The 1957 launch of Sputnik by the Soviet Union raised national alarm over a perceived science education gap between the United States and the Soviet Union. Simultaneously the post-war "baby boom" placed tremendous resource pressure on local school systems. The combination of the Sputnik "threat" and booming enrollment turned education into a national issue by the early 1960s. With bipartisan support, Congress significantly increased funding for elementary and secondary education.

After President Lyndon Johnson easily defeated Barry Goldwater in the 1964 presidential election, Congress moved to enact Johnson's **Great Society** program, which earmarked new federal funds for various antipoverty programs; including spending for elementary and secondary education. The federal School Lunch and Head Start programs began during this era.

To correct the ill effects of school segregation, the federal courts of the early 1970s ordered forced busing to racially integrate public schools. Controversy swelled over the busing issue, particularly in large urban centers such as Boston. Throughout the 1970s and 1980s, Democrats supported forced busing while Republicans opposed it.

By the **Campaign of 1976**, a split had developed between the major parties over a range of public education issues. Strongly supported by teachers unions, Democratic nominee, Jimmy Carter, heavily endorsed the establishment of a new Department of Education to coordinate the federal education programs. On the other hand, incumbent President Gerald Ford, the Republican nominee, opposed the plan on the grounds that the federal government should avoid increased bureaucracy. In 1980, President Carter signed legislation establishing the Department of Education. Although the education issue did not dominate the **Campaign of 1980**, Ronald Reagan, the Republican presidential candidate, did promise to eliminate the Department of Education if elected. President Carter promised to protect it.

The Reagan administration continued opposition to busing, supported school prayer, abolition of the Department of Education, and the implementation of public school voucher programs. The Reagan administration argued that parents should not be forced to send their children to failing schools. Despite lobbying for these reforms, the Reagan administration failed to obtain congressional action on the majority of their education reform proposals. The Republican campaign of the elder Bush in 1988 continued supporting Reagan's agenda.

By contrast, the 1988 Democratic platform expressed strong support for the Department of Education, increased federal aid to public education, and opposed any type of school voucher program. But these differences between the parties did not prove decisive in the eventual Republican victory.

Following the pattern of the 1970s and 1980s, the presidential elections of 1992 and 1996 were marked by major differences in educational policies of the major parties. Twelve years later, during the **Campaign of 2000**, Texas governor George W. Bush made education reform the cornerstone of his **"compassionate conservatism"** agenda. Instead of focusing on the divisive issue of school vouchers, the Bush campaign put forward a proposal to require each state to install a system of student performance standards tied directly to rigorous standardized tests. Bush made effective use of the slogan "No Child Left Behind" to emphasize education reform that would not cost the federal treasury vast amounts. Conversely, the Gore campaign proposed to funnel billions of new federal dollars to local schools to pay for new construction and building renovation and to retrain teachers and to provide additional teacher pay. *See also* Campaign of 1988.

Suggested Readings: M.J. Marshall and R.J. McKee, "From Campaign Promises to Presidential Policy: Education Reform in the 2000 Election," *Educational Policy* 16 (March 2002); pp. 96–118; Susan Besze Wallace, "Learning Division: Bush, Gore Offer Different Ideas on Reform for Nation's Schools," *Denver Post*, October 22, 2000, A1.

Eisenhower, Dwight David

See Campaign of 1952; Campaign of 1956.

"Eisenhower Answers America" Campaign Ad

Television advertising as a presidential campaign tactic first appeared in the 1952 election year. The campaigns of Republican nominee General Dwight D. Eisenhower and the Democratic nominee Adlai Stevenson ran a number of television ads. Besides the simple "I Like Ike" spots, the Eisenhower campaign ran the very effective "Eisenhower Answers America" event.

"Eisenhower Answers America" grew out of concern that some voters might regard Eisenhower as aloof given his military background. Eisenhower had served as Supreme Commander of all allied forces in Europe during World War II. To make the general more accessible, Eisenhower's campaign broadcast their candidate responding to questions about a wide variety of issues raised by "average Americans." Eisenhower provided common sense solutions to the questions raised. *See also* Campaign of 1952.

Suggested Readings: John Robert Greene, *The Crusade: The Presidential Election of 1952* (Lanham, MD: University Press of America, 1985); William B. Picket, *Eisenhower Decides to Run: Presidential Politics and Cold War Strategy* (Chicago: Ivan R. Dee, 2000).

"Empty Market Basket"

In a deliberate parody of the **"Full Dinner Pail"** slogan of previous Republican campaigns, the "Empty Market Basket" was a slogan used by the Democratic Party during the campaign of 1912. The slogan was designed to attack President William Howard Taft for failing the needs of American workers and for supporting high tariffs on imported goods, thus driving up the price of consumer goods and making it difficult for working Americans to fill their weekly market baskets. The majority of Americans understood empty baskets more easily than the **New Freedom** slogan of Democratic nominee Woodrow Wilson. *See also* Campaign of 1912.

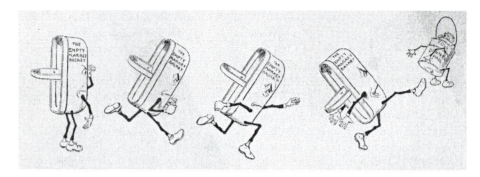

The "Empty Market Basket" was a slogan used by Democrats in the campaign of 1912 to attack Republican President William Howard Taft's support for high tariffs. Courtesy of Library of Congress.

Suggested Readings: Francis L. Broderick, *Progressivism at Risk: Electing a President in 1912* (New York: Greenwood, 1989), Frank K. Kelly, *The Fight For the White House: the Story of 1912* (New York: Crowell, 1961).

Energy Issue

Through the nineteenth century, few Americans gave a second thought to the possibility of energy shortages. Vast deposits of coal powered the Industrial Revolution. But with the emergence of oil as the fuel powering the Navy's modern fleet in the early twentieth century, sufficient petroleum reserves became an important national security concern. To assure a steady supply of oil for the growing number of U.S. warships, Congress put aside a number of oil fields located on federal lands at Elk Hills, California, and Teapot Dome, California.

By the end of the 1920s, the discovery of vast new western oil fields created a surplus. But the October 1929 stock market crash brought to a halt the boom times of the 1920s and deflation ravaged the world economy, reducing the value of surplus resources. However with the unprecedented production of oil-burning military vehicles during World War II and the booming automobile industry of the 1950s, oil became a major force in the American economy.

During the 1940s and 1950s, conservation issues faded from political campaigns, but in the late 1960s a number of trends coalesced to restore the importance of conservation, environmental, and energy issues. The environmental movement drew national attention to the damage caused by water, air, and land pollution.

As American companies relied more on foreign sources in the late 1960s and 1970s, continued Middle East tension involving Israel threatened the flow of oil imports from petroleum fields in Arabia, Persia, and other Middle Eastern and Northern African regions. In 1973, the Yom Kippur War threw the world's oil supply into crisis. Organization of Petroleum Exporting Countries (OPEC) increased prices by limiting supply. The shortage was compounded by a series of terrible winters that taxed low supplies. From 1976 through 1980, the Carter

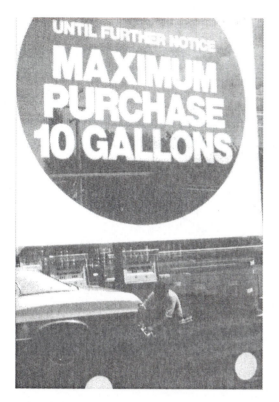

Taken in May 1973, these photographs illustrate the energy crisis of the 1970s. © National Archives.

administration pressed for the expansion of energy conservation and for the development of alternative energy sources.

But the American people repudiated the energy policies of the Carter administration. During the 1980 campaign, Republican presidential candidate Ronald Reagan promised the nation that his administration would free the hands of energy companies to discover and develop new sources of oil and natural gas.

With the Three Mile Island crisis of the late 1970s, the nuclear power industry faced close scrutiny from groups that doubted the safety of nuclear power plants and the ability of the nuclear power industry to safely dispose of large quantities of spent nuclear fuel.

In 1970, Congress established the Environmental Protection Administration (EPA) to oversee the enforcement of new environmental laws directed at cleaning the air and water, and assuring the safe disposal of solid and hazardous waste.

From 1980 until the early 1990s Gulf War, the energy crisis receded in importance as a national political issue. The victory of the Gulf War coalition over Iraq guaranteed the steady supply of Middle Eastern oil. Instead of continuing the trend, set in the mid-1970s, of producing smaller, fuel-efficient cars, the auto manufacturers returned to the production of larger, gas-guzzling vehicles in the mid-1990s. Classified as light trucks for purposes of federal fuel efficiency standards, the sport-utility vehicle, or SUV, became widely loved by American consumers. Higher fuel consumption again strained oil supplies, and increased dependency on foreign oil.

Neither major party pursued fuel efficiency and alternative energy as agenda items in the presidential campaigns of the late 1980s and 1990s. Suburban "soccer moms" grew dependent on the SUV. For decades national politicians had regarded Social Security as the **"Third Rail of American Politics."** Touching the rail constituted political suicide. Asking the American people to give up their minivans and SUVs evolved into the fourth rail of American politics.

Equally important, the American people continued to express strong reservations about resuming the construction of nuclear power plants, and promotion of alternative fuels stalled.

With energy crises in California, renewed controversy over drilling in Alaska and off the coast of California, and ever-persistent problems in the Middle East and Central Asia, energy policy promises to return as a major focus in future presidential campaigns.

Suggested Readings: James Dao, "The 2000 Campaign: The Vice President; Gore to Unveil a Plan to Foster Cleaner Energy," *New York Times*, June 26, 2000; E.J. Dionne Jr., "A Shifting Wind Alters Energy and Environment as Political Issues in Presidential Race," *New York Times*, October 28, 1980, A25.

Exit Polls

Exit polls are employed on Election Day to anticipate election outcomes and to evaluate voting patterns and voter motivations. Major electronic news operations in particular use exit polls to call elections prior to the final tabulation of votes. Intense competition among major news organizations has led to increasingly early projections of final election results. Critics of media use of exit polls argue that calling the election early deters many voters from visiting the polls in Western states where the polls close later.

On election night of the **Campaign of 2000**, exit polls indicated that Democratic presidential candidate, Vice President Al Gore, would secure the needed electoral victory in Florida that would ensure his election. However, later indicators showed Republican candidate George W. Bush leading in the Florida vote. Network television received considerable criticism for calling Gore the winner, then retracting that call in favor of Bush, and then declaring the election "too close to call" in light of the tight nature of the Florida vote and the uncertainty of the final tally.

Suggested Reading: Neil A. Lewis, "The 2000 Elections: The Polling Organization, Data of Little-Known Service Led to Wrong Call in Florida," *New York Times*, November 9, 2000, B. p. 2.

"Extremism in the Defense of Liberty Is No Vice"

Accepting the Republican nomination at the national convention in July of 1964, controversial conservative Barry Goldwater remarked, "Extremism in the defense of liberty is no vice, moderation in the pursuit of justice is no virtue." Inclusion of the phrase is generally attributed to the advice of eminent Professor Harry Jaffa, a major scholar steeped in the classical tradition of political philosophy. The phrase is originally attributed to the Roman statesman and Stoic philosopher Cicero.

Goldwater's opponents drew inferences from such language to the effect of further proving the dangerous extremism of the Republican choice. President Johnson rejoined by arguing, "Extremism is an unpardonable vice. Moderation in the affairs of the nation is the highest virtue." *See also* Campaign of 1964.

Suggested Reading: Theodore White, *The Making of the President, 1964* (New York: Atheneum Publishers, 1965).

Farley, Jim (1888–1973)

Born to a family of first generation Irish-Catholics, and known for his dedication to public service, love of political battle, and a photographic memory, Jim Farley first broke into politics through his election to the position of town clerk in Stony Point, New York. From there, Farley quickly made his name as a leader in the Democratic Party through his management of Al Smith's successful 1918 campaign for governor of New York. Farley served as chairman of the Rockland County (New York) Democratic Party throughout the 1920s, and managed to get elected to the New York state assembly for one term. In 1930, Farley was named chair of the New York State Democratic committee, and from this important position he began an early campaign to promote the political credentials of fellow New Yorker Franklin Roosevelt for the party nomination for president in 1932.

Among the more influential politicians of the first half of the twentieth century, Farley was instrumental in securing Roosevelt's eventual nomination, leading to his being tapped to run Roosevelt's campaign against Hoover, and then moving on to serve as national chairman of the Democratic Party. Roosevelt rewarded Farley by naming him to the position of Postmaster General shortly after completion of the 1932 campaign, and he continued his success as Roosevelt's campaign manager during the stunningly successful reelection of 1936.

In 1940 the once loyal Farley broke ranks with the administration in protest over the president's decision to run for a third term. Farley resigned from his position as postmaster, and ran his own brief and unsuccessful campaign for the party nomination for president. Farley then returned to New York where he again assumed the mantle of state party chair until 1944. After leaving politics in the mid-1940s, Farley devoted his energies to the private sector as an employer of Coca Cola. *See also* Campaign of 1932; Campaign of 1936.

Suggested Reading: James Aloysisus Farley, *Jim Farley's Story: The Roosevelt Years* (Westport, CT: Greenwood Press, 1984).

Feeding Frenzy

The early 1970s Watergate scandal ushered in an era of heightened scrutiny of the personal lives and public integrity of public officials. By the close of the 1980s, the media faced severe criticism for profiting from the reporting of scandal. In 1991, University of Virginia political scientist Larry Sabato analyzed this phenomenon in his book, *Feeding Frenzy*. Published less than two years after Gary Hart's "monkey business" affair, Sabato sharply criticized print and electronic journalists for devoting excessive coverage to the personal vices of politicians.

The publication of *Feeding Frenzy* prompted a period of soul searching within the media. But despite the temporary mood of self-criticism, intense media coverage of the private lives of public officials continued, and even rose in intensity. During the 1992 Democratic presidential primary campaign, Arkansas governor Bill Clinton faced media scrutiny of his alleged infidelities. In 1998 Clinton, now a second term president, again found himself in the midst of a media firestorm over his sexual indiscretions with a White House intern.

Media feeding frenzies tend to be bipartisan in their appetites. During the campaign of 2000 and less than two weeks before Election Day, an anonymous tipster leaked to the press an episode involving Republican candidate George W. Bush's 1976 drunk driving record. Inured to such accounts of youthful indiscretions, the electorate was unaffected. *See also* Negative Campaigning; Politics of Personal Destruction.

Suggested Readings: Anne E. Kornblut, "Campaign 2000/Arrest Record; Bush Charged in '76 with DUI in Maine," *Boston Globe*, November 3, 2000, A 25; Larry Sabato, *Feeding Frenzy: How Attack Journalism Transformed American Politics* (New York: Free Press, 1991).

"Fifty-four Forty or Fight"

A slogan referring to an ongoing dispute with Great Britain over the Northwestern boundary between the United States and Canada, "Fifty-four Forty or Fight" was used by the 1844 campaign of Democrat James K. Polk to support expansionist policies.

Polk and the Democrats, following the popular principle of **Manifest Destiny**, argued the northwestern border should be drawn at the latitude of 54 degrees and 40 minutes. That Polk also favored annexation of Texas further strengthened his campaign.

The Whig Party was more cautious. Henry Clay, the Whig Party nominee, opposed Texas annexation and pressed the northern border issue. Clay's primary fear stemmed from the possible expansion of slavery and the power of slave states into the West, particularly Texas.

After Polk's election in 1844, a boundary commission negotiated a more southerly boundary between Oregon territory and the British territory at 49th degree latitude. More interested in Texas, Polk and the Democratic Congress agreed to the compromise. *See also* Campaign of 1844.

Suggested Reading: Sam W. Haynes and Oscar Handlin, eds. *James K. Polk and the Expansionist Impulse* (New York: Longman, 1997).

Fireside Chat

On March 12, 1933, President Franklin D. Roosevelt gave his first fireside chat speech to the American people. Broadcast on major national radio networks, tens

President Franklin D. Roosevelt having a fireside chat via radio with the American people in 1935. © Franklin D. Roosevelt Library/National Archives.

of millions of Americans sat in front of their radios waiting to hear their new president. Given the economic tribulations of the times, the public needed to hear the voice of calm reassurance and confident hope. Roosevelt was more than capable of supplying this need.

In his speech, Roosevelt announced his administration's plans for dealing with the banking crisis including a nationwide banking holiday. After Roosevelt reassured the public that his administration would take immediate steps to guarantee the solvency of the banks, the panic ended and many Americans redeposited their funds when the banks reopened.

Because of the warm public response to the speech, Roosevelt frequently used

President Jimmy Carter in the White House Library during a televised fireside chat on energy in 1977. © Jimmy Carter Library/National Archives.

"fireside chats" to reach the American public regarding numerous matters, delivering thirty chats between March 1933 and June 1944. *See also* Campaign of 1936; Radio and Presidential Campaigns.

Suggested Reading: "Fireside Chats of Franklin Roosevelt," Mid-Hudson Regional Information Center, http://www.mhrcc.org/fdr.html.

"First In War, First In Peace"

A phrase originally used to describe the preeminence of George Washington, "First in War, First in Peace," was a political slogan used by the 1852 campaign of General Winfield Scott, the Whig Party's presidential nominee, highlighting Scott's exploits in the Mexican American War, and attempting to draw a contrast between Scott and Democratic candidate Franklin Pierce's image. *See also* Campaign of 1852.

Suggested Readings: John S.D. Eisenhower, *Agent of Destiny: The Life and Times of General Winfield Scott* (New York: Free Press, 1997); Charles Elliott Winslow, *Winfield Scott, The Soldier and The Man* (New York: Macmillan, 1937).

Flip-flop Campaign Ad

Flip-flop ads are one of the most common promotional tools in modern campaigning. Flip-flops highlight contradictory statements made by opposition candidates. Modern **opposition research** programs permit adversaries to collect vast amounts of information detailing an opponent's public record on political issues throughout careers.

During the **Campaign of 1988**, for instance, the campaign of Michael Dukakis sharply criticized his opponent Vice President George Bush for waffling on offshore drilling and extending the Clean Air Act. During the spring, Bush publicly supported a moratorium on the sale of offshore oil leases in northern California. Later, during a campaign swing through East Texas, Bush announced his support for offshore oil leases. Bush's flip-flop did not prevent him from easily defeating Dukakis in November.

During the primary and general election **Campaign of 1992**, President George Bush faced intense criticism from fellow Republicans for turning his back on his 1988 no-new-taxes pledge. Faced with an exploding federal deficit Bush agreed to levying a number of taxes as part of a deal to reduce annual deficit spending. Two years later, when Pat Buchanan challenged Bush for the Republican presidential nomination, Bush attempted to diffuse the controversy by telling reporters that he had simply made a mistake in agreeing to renege on his pledge. Bush deflected Buchanan, but could not win reelection.

During the campaign of 2000, Vice President Albert Gore, the Democratic nominee, faced criticism for changing his positions on several key issues. As a member of Congress from Tennessee, Gore opposed gun control and federal funding of abortions. During the same period, Gore supported tobacco price supports and opposed a ban on tobacco advertising. Between Gore's 1992 election as vice president and his 2000 run for president, Gore changed his positions on these issues. Gore went on to win the 2000 popular vote but lost the electoral vote largely because of his failure to carry Arkansas, Missouri, Tennessee, Kentucky, and West Virginia; states in which the Bush campaign made effective use of Gore's flip-flop on the gun control issue.

Critics of flip-flop ads argue they unfairly punish candidates for changing their views on important issues. Supporters of the ads argue that the public has a right to know how the views of presidential candidates have changed over time. *See also* Attack Ads; Negative Campaigning; Opposition Research.

Suggested Readings: Terry Cooper, "Negative Image Challenging Your Competitor's Weakness," *Campaign & Elections* (September 1991); Maria L. La Ganga, "Campaign 2000, Change, Credibility Underlie Campaign; Politics: In an Era of 'Gotcha Politics' and Increasingly Skeptical Electorate, Candidates Don't Have the Luxury of Being Able to Flip-Flop," *Los Angeles Times*, November 1, 2000, p. A18.

Focus Groups

Presidential campaigns and the news operations covering them routinely make use of focus groups to gather insights regarding campaign issues from small groups of potential voters.

The 1988 presidential campaign of George Bush, for example, used a focus group to evaluate effectiveness of using the Massachusetts furlough program as an issue against Democratic nominee Michael Dukakis, the state's governor. On furlough from a Massachusetts prison, **Willie Horton** raped a woman and attacked her fiancé. Bush focus groups indicated that the furlough issue would play very well with a cross-section of voters. Subsequently, the Bush campaign made extremely effective use of the furlough issue to depict Dukakis as soft on crime.

Electronic news operations made use of focus groups to evaluate the effectiveness of candidates during and after presidential debates of the 2000 campaign. Some news operations made use of **dial group** technology that permitted focus group participants to indicate their moment-to-moment reaction throughout the debate.

By the late 1990s, critics alleged that presidential campaigns had grown overly dependent on focus groups for developing campaign strategy, and news operations received criticism for relying too much on polls and focus groups to measure public reaction to presidential debates and other events. *See also* Presidential Campaign Management.

Suggested Reading: Pamela Hunter, "Using Focus Groups in Campaigns: A Caution," *Campaign & Elections* (August 2000), p. 38.

"Fool, Hypocrite, Criminal, Tyrant"

Should anyone accuse modern political campaigns of being more defamatory than those conducted by our august Founding Fathers, awareness of this mean-spirited broadside hurled at John Adams by Jefferson partisans during the election of 1800 will quickly disabuse them of that error. *See also* Campaign of 1800; Negative Ads.

Suggested Reading: Bernard A. Weisberger, *America Afire: Jefferson, Adams, and the Revolutionary Election of 1800* (New York: William Morrow, 2000).

Ford, Gerald R.

See Campaign of 1976.

"Four More Lucky Roosevelt Years"

An upbeat slogan used Franklin Roosevelt's 1936 presidential campaign designed to draw attention to the achievements of Roosevelt's **New Deal**. The Roosevelt campaign used the slogan to counter Republican criticism that the New Deal had done little to reduce high levels of unemployment along with the charge that the expanded federal bureaucracy was now overshadowing state governments and routinely trampling on the individual liberties.

Throughout the campaign the Republican Party and its nominee, Alfred Landon, tried to persuade the American people that New Deal policies and programs threatened the Constitution and endangered American democracy. Roosevelt and the Democratic Party responded by illustrating renewed confidence in government held by the majority of Americans even when confronting great economic turbulence.

On November 3, 1936, the American people rewarded Roosevelt with one of the greatest landslides in American election history, receiving 523 electoral votes, losing only Maine and Vermont. *See also* Campaign of 1936.

Suggested Reading: Clyde P. Weed, *The Nemesis of Reform: the Republican Party during the New Deal* (New York: Columbia University Press, 1994).

"Four More Years of the Full Dinner Pail"

See "Full Dinner Pail."

"Free Homes for Free Men"

"Free homes for Free Men" was a slogan used by the Republicans during the **Campaign of 1860** to emphasize its free soil sentiments and their party's strong opposition to the expansion of slavery. It was not a call for immediate abolition.

Abraham Lincoln, the Republican candidate in 1860, while a lifelong opponent of slavery, withheld support for immediate abolition, instead endorsing slavery's containment hoping that in preventing its spread it would eventually become extinct. This was the prevailing sentiment within the Republican Party; demands for immediate abolition were expressed in its more radical wing. And yet many Southern Democrats considered the Republican position on slavery, including a denunciation of the Dred Scott decision in their platform, as a direct threat to their traditions. The growing secessionist movement argued that any ban on slavery imposed on the new territories would inevitably lead to abolition by ensuring that free states would always outnumber, and outvote, slave states. *See also* Campaign of 1860.

Suggested Readings: Eric Foner, *Free Soil, Free Labor, Free Men: The Ideology of the Republican Party before the Civil War* (New York: Oxford University Press, 1970); William Freehling, *The Road to Disunion* (New York: Oxford University Press, 1990); Stephen B. Oates, *The Approaching Fury: Voices of the Storm, 1820–1861* (New York: HarperCollins, 1997).

Free Media

The terms free media, or **earned media**, refer to the ability of a campaign to obtain media coverage of their candidate without paying for it. Because of the high cost of **paid media**, modern campaigns depend heavily on free media to convey their message to voters.

Presidential campaigns use various strategies to acquire free media. **Photo opportunities** are commonly used for such exposure. For instance, a candidate may visit an elementary school to convey interest in **education reform issues**, or frequently appear at public ceremonies to accept the endorsement of an influential interest group. Campaigns make available to electronic news operations spokespersons or **surrogates** who present a candidate's views on a wide range of issues. After every major campaign event, such as a presidential **debate**, campaigns deploy numerous **talking heads** and **spin doctors** in a highly calculated effort to shape media coverage.

Under federal law the Federal Election Commission (FEC) requires campaigns to spend **hard money** to purchase television and radio ads that promote or oppose a candidate. Until March of 2002, FEC regulations have permitted national political parties and **independent advocacy groups** to use **soft money** to broadcast **issue ads**. Unlike hard money ads, regulations prohibit issue ads from promoting or opposing a candidate for federal office. Federal campaign finance legislation enacted in March 2002 banned soft money contributions to national political parties and election committees. *See also* Electioneering; Media Event.

Suggested Readings: James A. Barnes, "For Bush, Paid Media Isn't Enough," *National Journal*, September 23, 2000; Dan Patlak, "How to Get on the Radio: A Big Earned Media Campaign Opportunity," *Campaign & Elections*, June 2001, p. 62.

Free Silver Movement

The free silver movement arose in the 1880s and 1890s as a solution to a perceived inadequate supply of currency. The movement sought to move the United States from a strict gold standard toward a bimetallic standard by increasing the coinage of silver as legal tender.

Article I Section 8 of the Constitution grants Congress the authority "[to] coin

Money, regulate the Value thereof, and of foreign Coin, and fix the Standard of Weights and Measures." Not until the 1863 passage of the National Bank Act, however, did Congress move to deter private state banks from issuing their own bank notes by heavily taxing any notes that they independently issued. Simultaneously, the government temporarily moved from the gold standard during the Civil War by issuing paper "greenbacks" as legal tender. Then, in January 1875, Congress passed the Resumption Act that mandated the United States to restore the gold standard at the beginning of 1879.

The decision by Congress to put the United States back on the gold standard had the greatest impact on farmers who often needed to borrow money to finance their crops. With a sharp reduction in the money supply, the cost of borrowing increased.

In response, the Greenback Party was formed by a coalition of farmers and Western interests during the campaign of 1880. The party's platform "called for the unlimited coinage of silver and gold and the issuance of currency by the federal government and not private banks."

A late 1880s agricultural depression, led to renewed interest in the free silver movement. Because many farmers found themselves with massive debts, they saw the free coinage of silver as a way to increase the supply of currency. In 1892 both major parties supported bimetallism, but the Democratic Party went further by endorsing federal greenbacks. The People's Party, commonly known as the Populist Party, demanded "free and unlimited coinage of silver and gold at the present legal ratio of 16 to 1." The platform of the People's Party also insisted "that the amount of circulating medium be speedily increased to not less than $50 per capita."

The major parties sharply divided over the free silver issue in the campaign of 1896. William Jennings Bryan, the Democratic nominee, strongly endorsed the party's platform plank promising free coinage of silver at 16 to 1, international concerns notwithstanding. By contrast, Republican nominee William McKinley adopted a "sound money" policy that opposed the free coinage of silver without an international agreement.

Four years later, McKinley again ran on a "sound money" platform while Bryan continued to advocate the free coinage of silver, but the Alaskan Gold Rush and more pressing foreign issues deflated the political value of monetary policy. *See also* Campaign of 1896; Currency Issue; 16 to 1.

Suggested Readings: Jeffrey Frieden, "Monetary Populism in Nineteenth-Century America: An Open Economy Interpretation," *Journal of Economic History* 57 (June 1997) pp. 367–395; Milton Friedman and Anna Jacobson, *A Monetary History of the United States, 1867–1960* (Princeton, NJ: Princeton University Press, 1963).

"Free Soil, Free Labor, Free Speech, and Free Men"

"Free Soil, Free Labor, Free Speech, And Free Men," was a slogan used by the Free Soil Party during the **Campaign of 1848** to demonstrate its strong opposition to allowing admission of any more slave states into the Union.

In August of 1848, dissatisfied Whigs, Democrats, and some abolitionists from

Banner portraying 1848 Free Soil Party candidate Martin Van Buren and his vice presidential running mate Charles F. Adams. Courtesy of Library of Congress.

eighteen states met in Buffalo, New York to organize the Free Soil Party, adopting the slogan at their nominating convention. Former President Martin Van Buren received the presidential nomination of the Free Soil Party. Significantly, the party platform did not demand the abolition of slavery where it existed.

Although Whig Party candidate Zachary Taylor defeated both Van Buren and Democrat Lewis Cass, the Free Soil Party received 10.1 percent of the popular vote, demonstrating the power of slavery as a national political issue.

Suggested Readings: Frederick Blue, *The Free Soilers: Third Party Politics 1848–54* (Urbana: University of Illinois Press, 1973); John Mayfield, *Rehearsal for Republicanism: Free Soil and the Politics of Antislavery* (Port Washington, NY: Kennikat Press, 1980).

Free State Issue

With the continuing expansion of the Union during the first half of the nineteenth century, conflicts arose over the issue of slavery in the new territories and potential states. The Missouri Compromise of 1820 had been weakened by the conquest of a vast territory taken in the military victory over Mexico, renewing debates over the issue of slavery in the West, with most of the controversy revolving around the California territory. Lewis Cass, the Democratic candidate for president in

1848 first forwarded the concept of "popular sovereignty," holding that the decision regarding slavery in new territories should be determined through popular territorial elections rather than leaving such matters in the hands of Congress.

Passage of the Kansas-Nebraska Act of 1854 irrevocably disrupted the shape of American national politics. The act allowed for inhabitants of a new territory to decide by popular elections whether to forbid or permit slavery (i.e., whether to become a "free state" or a slave state"). Far from resolving the issue, a brutal civil war between pro- and anti-slave factions immediately erupted in Kansas, leading to the ascent of both the prairie avenger John Brown and a reinvigorated politician from Illinois named Abraham Lincoln, and the beginnings of what some historians understand to be a series of episodes culminating in the outbreak of the American Civil War seven years after the passage of the act.

The impact on presidential politics was immediate, spurring the formation of a new major party, the Republican Party, and accelerating the decline and termination of the older Whig Party. Minor parties such as the Free Soil Party and Liberty Party also appeared, helping to define the perimeters of public debate on the issue of slavery in the decade just before the war. Matters were further clouded and aggravated by the actions of James Buchanan through his support of the Lecompton Constitution proposed by the pro-slavery faction in Kansas and the *Dred Scott* decision of 1857, which sounded the death knell of the Missouri Compromise, forcing the federal government to support the property claims of slave owners. Stephen Douglas of Illinois championed Cass's principle of popular sovereignty, and Lincoln forthrightly denounced it while also criticizing slavery in general. Lincoln's position as a candidate for Senate and later president was deemed moderate, advocating the prevention of the spread of slavery into the new territories, the restriction of slavery to those states wherein it already existed, and anticipating its gradual extinction. More radical factions settled for nothing less than immediate abolition. However, Lincoln's hatred of slavery and his insistence on the admission of only "free" new states to the Union was enough to cause panic among southern politicians, eventually provoking the secession of the South and the onset of the war. It was only then that the free state issue was resolved, not by electoral politics, but through bloody, bitter war. *See also* Campaign of 1848; Campaign of 1852; Campaign of 1856; Campaign of 1860; Campaign of 1864; Civil Rights Issue; "Free Soil, Free Labor, Free Speech, and Free Men"; "Freedom, Freemen and Fremont"; Race Relations Issue.

Suggested Readings: Frederick J. Blue, *The Free Soilers: Third Party Politics, 1848–54* (Urbana: University of Illinois Press, 1973); John Mayfield, *Rehearsal for Republicanism: Free Soil and the Politics of Antislavery* (Port Washington, NY: Kennikat Press, 1980).

"Freedom, Freemen and Fremont"

In June 1856, John C. Fremont received the presidential nomination of the new Republican Party. As a western explorer, Fremont had become a national hero. The Republican platform focused on the free state issue, promising a ban on the admission of any new slave states into the Union and admission of Kansas as a free state. As with the Free Soil Party of 1848, direct abolition of slavery where it existed was not endorsed at this time. "Freedom, Freemen and Fremont" was an effective alliteration summarizing the central position of the young party. *See also* Campaign of 1856.

Suggested Reading: William E. Gienapp, *The Origins of the Republican Party 1852–1856* (New York: Oxford University Press, 1987).

"Freedom and Clay"

During the **Campaign of 1832**, National Republicans and their candidate, Henry Clay, attempted to depict President Andrew Jackson as a despot. The slogan "Freedom and Clay" reflected this strategy.

In 1829, Jackson entered the White House openly hostile to the political establishment. Soon after moving into the White House, Jackson became particularly distrustful of the National Bank headed by Nicholas Biddle. The bank operated under a federal charter but was legally a private bank. Yet, the Philadelphia-based bank served as the depository for federal funds. Early in 1832, at the urging of Clay and other Jackson enemies, Biddle asked Congress to extend the bank's charter. Jackson promptly vetoed the ensuing legislation. Clay's campaign responded by attacking Jackson's "despotic" use of the veto throughout the 1832 campaign.

Jackson and his supporters did not sit quietly during the 1832 election, depicting the National Bank as a monster capable of using its financial power to control the country. To the surprise of Clay and his supporters, the National Bank issue helped Jackson instead of harming him. Democrats successfully rallied to victory around Jackson's crusade against the "monster."

Suggested Readings: Samuel Rhea Gammon, *The Presidential Campaign of 1832* (Baltimore: The Johns Hopkins Press, 1922), Bernard A. Weisberger, "The Bank War," *American Heritage* 48 (July/August 1997), pp. 10–12; "On President Jackson's Veto of the Bank Bill," Furman University, http://www.furman.edu/%7Ebenson/docs/clay.htm.

Fremont, John C.

See Campaign of 1856; "Freedom, Freemen and Fremont."

Front Porch Campaign

While both Benjamin Harrison and Grover Cleveland employed the strategy of remaining home and campaigning from the "front porch" during the contest of 1888, the phrase "front porch campaign" is more commonly used to describe Republican William McKinley's 1896 strategy against William Jennings Bryan.

In Bryan, McKinley faced one of the most gifted speakers in American history, and while McKinley was widely regarded as a good speaker, **Mark Hanna**, McKinley's chief political advisor, believed that McKinley lacked Bryan's extraordinary ability to stir the crowd. Instead of having McKinley travel the country, Hanna kept McKinley home while thousands of McKinley supporters made a pilgrimage to McKinley's flag-draped Canton, Ohio house to meet the Republican standard bearer and hear McKinley present carefully scripted remarks. To ensure the distribution of McKinley's message, Hanna used hundreds of **surrogates** to deliver his candidate's remarks. In sharp contrast, Bryan traveled from coast to coast delivering hundreds of speeches.

McKinley's front porch campaign proved remarkably successful. The majority of potential voters saw McKinley to be more presidential. Bryan appeared somewhat frantic in his quest for the presidency. In 1920, Republican presidential nominee Warren G. Harding borrowed from McKinley's playbook and conducted his presidential campaign from the front porch of his Ohio home. Both McKinley and Harding won their respective contests.

Through the twentieth century a number of incumbent presidents adopted a similar strategy, known as Rose Garden campaigns, referring to the famous White House garden. Largely because of his fragile health, President Franklin Roosevelt made relatively few campaign appearances during his three campaigns for reelection. Roosevelt extensively used radio and intimate meetings with small groups of reporters to convey his message.

In 1972, incumbent President Richard Nixon left much of the campaigning to surrogates while he remained in Washington or traveled around the world acting presidential. In 1984, incumbent President Ronald Reagan made relatively few campaign appearances around the country. Reagan, however, appeared at numerous White House and Washington area **photo opportunities** and made exceptionally effective use of radio and television to highlight the successes of the first four years of the Reagan administration. Reagan's predecessor, Jimmy Carter, employed a failed Rose Garden strategy. *See also* Campaign of 1896; Campaign of 1920; Campaign of 1984.

Suggested Readings: Lewis L. Gould, *The Presidency of William McKinley* (Lawrence: Regents of the Press of Kansas, 1981); Margaret Leech, *Days of McKinley* (New York: Harper, 1959).

"Full Dinner Pail"

Evoking the promise of material abundance, the most popular slogan of William McKinley's 1896 campaign for president was "McKinley and the Full Dinner Pail." The "Full Dinner Pail" slogan was deployed by McKinley's campaign manager, Mark Hanna, as an attempt to blunt populist Democratic candidate William Jennings Bryan's appeal with labor in key midwestern states and northeastern cities, thereby stealing some of Bryan's populist thunder. Laborers of the period were purported to have carried their lunch or dinner to work in metal lunch pails or buckets. The McKinley campaign successfully used slogans such as the "Full Dinner Pail," "Sound Money," and **"Advance Agent of Prosperity"** to persuade voters that voting for Bryan was simply too risky. Fearful that the election of Bryan would result in large layoffs by major industries, many midwestern and northeastern industrial workers were convinced and supported McKinley.

The slogan was recirculated in 1900 as **"Four More Years of the Full Dinner Pail,"** taking advantage of the prosperity enjoyed by the country as it moved into the next century. A successful and popular image, the dinner pail reemerged in subsequent campaigns, most notably coupled with the "Big Stick" during Teddy Roosevelt's run in 1904. In the 1900 election, the dinner pail found its way into the paraphernalia market, with thousands of mock pails with candidate's names punched into the tin sold to the party faithful as lanterns.

By and large, the dinner pail symbolized the ongoing appreciation by political candidates of the power of material interests and the need to promise comfort and financial security. Similar to the mythological cornucopia, the full dinner pail is the political assurance that American's bounty is best preserved, replenished, and even expanded in the hands of a specifically designated party or candidate. In broader historical terms, the "full dinner pail" is another variant of the first half of the ancient Roman formula, usually offered with a cynical sense of resignation to the vulgar preferences of the crowd, of *panem et circenses*—bread and circuses. *See also* Campaign of 1896; Campaign of 1900; Mark Hanna.

Suggested Readings: Lewis L. Gould, *The Presidency of William McKinley* (Lawrence: Regents Press of Kansas, 1981). Margaret Leech, *The Days of McKinley* (New York: Harper & Brothers, 1959).

"A Gallant Leader"

"A Gallant Leader" was a slogan used by Franklin Roosevelt's 1936 reelection campaign to emphasize his leadership during the Great Depression. Both Roosevelt and his Republican challenger, Alf Landon, saw the election as a referendum on Roosevelt's New Deal.

Democrats believed that if Americans compared the condition of the country in 1936 to 1933, Roosevelt would easily defeat Landon. Despite the fact that unemployment remained high, the Roosevelt campaign highlighted New Deal achievements, particularly those steps committed to economic recovery.

Blaming the Republican Party for the Great Depression, the Roosevelt campaign focused on depicting Roosevelt as an exceptional leader. The strategy worked. Roosevelt defeated Landon in a landslide. *See also* Campaign of 1936.

Suggested Readings: Michael J. Webber, *New Deal Fat Cats: Business, Labor, and Campaign Finance in 1936* (New York: Fordham University Press, 2000); Clyde Weed, *The Nemesis of Reform: The Republican Party During the New Deal* (New York: Columbia University Press, 1994).

Garfield, James A.

See Campaign of 1880.

Gay Rights Issue

The issue of gay rights is new to American political discourse. Civil rights for homosexuals was not a political issue until the 1969 Stonewall riot in Greenwich Village brought the disaffection and alienation of New York City's homosexual population to the attention of the general public. In 1972 the Democratic National Convention adopted the first gay rights platform in American history. Delegates to the convention viewed the gay rights issue as consistent with the commitment of the modern Democratic Party to civil rights.

Even though the Gay Rights movement began to gain momentum in the 1970s and 1980s, it was not an issue that major presidential candidates agreed to address until the 1990s. During the 1992 campaign Democratic nominee Governor Bill Clinton promised to correct the problem of discrimination against gays in the military. The gay community pinned considerable hope on the prospect of a ban against anti-homosexual discrimination in the armed forces, anticipating a Trumanesque executive order reminiscent of the 1948 official presidential action against discrimination against blacks in the military. When the new Clinton administration, bowing to pressure from conservative factions in both parties, issued the diffident "don't ask, don't tell" policy, the gay community was universally disappointed by the decision not to decide, experiencing renewed disenchantment with the Clinton administration, which was no longer perceived as a reliable ally in the cause of gay rights.

While the Republican Party has repeatedly condemned all forms of bigotry and discrimination, it has yet to openly condemn discrimination based on sexual orientation. In its 1996 platform, the party explicitly denounced the defense of "sexual preference" as a distortion of traditional civil rights guarantees against discrimination on grounds of race, sex, religion, creed, and national origin. In the 2000 platform, the GOP removed this language, but included additional language that carries the implication of resistance to the legal rights of gays.

During the 2000 campaign, the Democratic Party added to its platform a proposal for legislation that would include within the definition of hate crimes violence deliberately targeted against gays. The Republican Party's implicit opposition to gay rights was sustained through its resolve to protect traditional marriage, defend the Boy Scouts' First Amendment right of "freedom of association," (thus supporting attempts by the Boy Scouts to discriminate against gay troop leaders), and reject the administration's position on gays in the military. Democratic candidate Vice President Al Gore forthrightly condemned all discrimination against homosexuals, and notably criticized the "don't ask, don't tell" policy for its lack of compassion and tolerance. Gore claimed acceptance of the idea that same-sex unions should be recognized as legitimate under civil law. However, an ambivalent Gore averred support of the Defense of Marriage Act, passed by a Republican majority in Congress and signed by Democratic President Bill Clinton. The legislation defines traditional marriage as heterosexual, and Gore asserted his belief that a fundamental difference separates the institution of marriage from the same-sex union shared by homosexual couples. Republican candidate George W. Bush did not equivocate, rejecting the legitimacy of any legal recognition of same-sex unions.

Gay rights remains an issue of national scope, particularly in the wake of a series of violent gay bashing episodes that have led to the death of the targeted victims. Additionally, with the revelation that family members, such as the daughter of 2000 GOP Vice Presidential candidate Dick Cheney, are homosexual, the issue of civil rights for gays will likely remain fixed in the topography of presidential campaigning into the 21st century.

Suggested Readings: Thomas B. Edall, "Bush Abandons 'Southern Strategy': Campaign Avoids Use of Polarizing Issues Employed by GOP Since Nixon's Time," *Washington Post*, August 6, 2000, A19; Michael Isikoff, "Gay Mobilizing for Clinton as Rights Become an issue," *Washington Post*, September 28, 1992, A1; Thomas Morgan, "Pro-Reagan TV Spots Depict President as Gay Rights Advocate," *Washington Post*, October 31, 1980, A5.

Gender Gap

The gender gap refers to the tendency of female voters to support Democrats at a higher percentage than Republicans. Through the latter half of the nineteenth century and the early decades of the twentieth century, the **women's suffrage movement** fought to secure women's voting rights at all levels of government. After securing voting rights in western states such as Wyoming and Colorado in the 1880s, women finally won their rights at the federal level and throughout all of the states with the 1920 ratification of the Nineteenth Amendment.

To the surprise of many political observers, female voters did not immediately become a major voting bloc. Factors other than gender played a much more important role in predicting voting behavior. Through the 1970s, women evenly supported both parties. However, as a result of the abortion controversy of the 1970s and early 1980s combined with the Republicans' 1980 decision to abandon support, held since 1940, of the proposed Equal Rights Amendment (ERA), women voters began to gravitate toward Democratic candidates.

In 1976 delegates to the Republican National Convention voted for a plank that supported a constitutional amendment outlawing abortions. In contrast, Democrats voted for a platform supportive of *Roe v. Wade*.

Republican critics of the ERA argued that ratification could subject women to the possibility of future military conscription. In contrast, delegates to the 1980 Democratic National Convention reaffirmed strong support for the ratification of the ERA.

Through the 1980s, the opposing positions of the major parties hardened on the abortion rights and ERA ratification issues. By the 1988 presidential election, pollsters found evidence of a growing gender gap at all levels of American politics. Although Republican candidates sustained support from middle-class married women and homemakers, **exit polls** indicated that single working women increasingly voted at higher rates for Democrats.

Through the 1990s the gender gap widened still further. Presidential historians credit Bill Clinton for his ability to put together a new Democratic coalition heavily dependent on the votes of working women, African Americans, labor, and moderate white males. The gender gap also played a major role in helping Al Gore win the popular vote in 2000.

Badly burned by the gender gap in the 1990s, 2000 Republican nominee George Bush attempted to narrow the gap by adopting **compassionate conservatism** as a campaign theme in part directed at working women voters. In a number of key western, midwestern, and eastern **battleground states**, the strategy failed. Exit polls indicated that Gore did substantially better than Bush with unmarried working women. *See also* Campaign of 1992; Campaign of 1996; Campaign of 2000.

Suggested Reading: Carol Mueller, "The gender gap and women's political influence," *The Annals of the American Academy of Political and Social Science* 515, May 1991, pp. 23–38.

Get-Out-the Vote (GOTV) Programs

With the emergence of national political parties during the late 1820s and early 1830s, the effectiveness of party organization became requisite to successful presidential campaigns. Through the remainder of the century, the political party remained a vital factor in mobilizing millions of new voters. In large cities, partisan ward or precinct workers helped immigrants find a place to live and work and to obtain their citizenship. These new citizens usually demonstrated their appreciation with loyal party affiliation and voting straight tickets. This accelerated the growth and strengthened the power of urban political machines.

After World War II, television, phone banks, and the use of direct mailing gradually reduced the dependence of presidential campaigns on party workers. Professional political consultants also replaced volunteer activists in campaign operations. These trends continued through the 1960s and 1970s.

The Federal Election Campaign Act of 1971 and subsequent amendments (1974, 1976) made raising money for **party-building activities** including get-out-the-vote programs more difficult. To help restore the role of political parties in presidential campaigns, the Federal Election Commission (FEC) in 1979 authorized political parties to raise unlimited amounts of "soft money" for party-building activities. During the 1980s and 1990s, the increased availability of soft money provided national political parties with the opportunity to increase spending on party-building activities.

Today presidential campaigns make use of a number of get-out-the-vote tools. Campaigns make extensive use of automated phone banks to contact millions of potential voters. Direct mail programs typically spend millions of dollars. Paid and volunteer campaign workers often canvass neighborhoods to encourage likely voters to get to the polls. Campaigns typically provide transportation to the polls on Election Day.

For the 2000 campaign both parties heavily emphasized early voting programs that involve absentee balloting. Arkansas, Colorado, Kansas, New Mexico, North Carolina, Tennessee, and Texas currently permit early voting. On the cutting edge, Oregon conducted the entire 2000 election by mail. *See also* Campaign of 2000; Soft Money.

Suggested Readings: Cathy Allen, "Get Out Your Vote," *Campaigns & Elections* 21, October 2000, p. 20; Joyce Howard Price, "Eight States Start Voting Early to Stave off Poor Turnout," *Washington Times*, October 27, 2000, p. A13, Edward Walsh and Ben White, "Early Voting Changes Face of Elections; Increases in Absentee, Mail Balloting May Be Key," *Washington Post*, November 7, 2000, p. A16.

"Give 'em Hell, Harry"

A phrase used by supporters of President Harry S. Truman during his 1948 come-from-behind victory over Thomas E. Dewey, the Republican challenger. Truman

President Harry S. Truman (left) and Vice President–elect Alben W. Barkley arrive at the Washington, D.C., train station after their victory in the 1948 presidential election. © Harry S. Truman Library/National Archives.

had previously assumed the presidency in 1945 upon the death of Franklin Roosevelt.

Despite the fact that Truman occupied the White House, he portrayed himself as a Washington outsider and a common man who understood the problems of hard-working Americans. In so doing he earned the reputation of a straight-talking political fighter known for using colorful, defiant language in response to critics. Attacked by Thomas Dewey and "do-nothing" Congressional Republicans, rebellious states rights Dixiecrats, and sanctimonious progressive Democrats complaining that his Fair Deal diluted the New Deal, Truman was lauded by supporters for his singularly blunt ability of "giving 'em hell."

With the polls showing Dewey in the lead, Truman conducted a nationwide **whistle-stop campaign** by train and plane from June of 1948 through the end of the campaign. At each stop, Truman excoriated the "do nothing" Congress for rejecting his legislative priorities. As the campaign progressed, supporters frequently chanted, "Give 'em Hell, Harry" energizing their man. *See also* Campaign of 1948.

Suggested Readings: Irwin Ross, *The Loneliest Campaign* (New York: New American Library, 1968); Linda DeCota, "1948 Whistle Stop Tour," Truman Presidential Museum and Library, http://www.trumanlibrary.org/whistlestop/TruWhisTour/coverpge.htm.

Gold Standard

See Campaign of 1896; Campaign of 1900; "Cross of Gold" Speech; Currency Issue.

Goldwater, Barry

See Campaign of 1964.

"GOP Equals Gas, Oil and Petroleum"

"GOP Equals Gas, Oil and Petroleum" was a slogan exploiting the Grand Old Party's acronym and used by Democrats during the campaign of 1924 decrying the Teapot Dome Scandal involving the Republican administration of Warren Harding and insinuating a connection to Harding's vice president, the incumbent President Calvin Coolidge.

Between Harding's death in August of 1923 and the beginning of the 1924 presidential campaign, investigations uncovered a number of public corruption scandals involving former high-level Harding administration officials. When Coolidge assumed the presidency, he took immediate steps to investigate and remove those officials accused of misconduct.

Of the Harding administration scandals, Teapot Dome received the most notoriety. In a complex series of transactions, President Harding's secretary of the interior, Albert Fall, leased United States Navy oil fields in Wyoming and California to oilmen Harry S. Sinclair and Edward L. Doheny. Fall had earlier convinced President Harding and Secretary of the Navy Edwin Denby to shift the management of naval oil fields to the Department of the Interior. After a protracted investigation and trial, the federal court found Sinclair and Doheny not guilty of bribing Fall. However, another federal court found Fall guilty of accepting a bribe from Sinclair and Doheny. Fall became the first cabinet member in American history to serve time in prison.

Because Coolidge had taken immediate steps to clean house, few Americans blamed him for Harding's scandals. To the dismay of Democrats, voters ignored Teapot Dome and turned to Coolidge on Election Day. The health of a booming economy also worked to Coolidge's advantage. *See also* Campaign of 1924; "Keep Cool with Coolidge."

Naval oil fields at Teapot Dome, Wyoming. © National Archives.

Suggested Readings: Burl Noggle, *Teapot Dome: Oil and Politics in the 1920s* (Baton Rouge: Louisiana State University Press, 1962); Robert North Roberts, *Ethics in Government: An Encyclopedia of Scandals, Reforms, and Legislation* (Westport, CT: Greenwood Press, 2001).

Gore, Albert

See Campaign of 1992; Campaign of 1996; Campaign of 2000.

Grant, Ulysses S.

See Campaign of 1868; Campaign of 1872.

Grass Roots Campaigning

See Campaign Manager.

"The Great Communicator"

Ronald Reagan's gift for persuasion, keen understanding of public sentiment, amiable personality, and media skill inspired his followers and critics alike to assign him the title of "The Great Communicator." His years as an actor in both film and television prior to his successful 1966 California gubernatorial campaign helped Reagan to develop exceptional media acumen and television presence. Reagan also effectively used radio, having sustained a radio presence in the late 1970s prior to his 1980 run for the White House. Throughout his two terms, Reagan consistently lived up to his image as a Great Communicator. *See also* Campaign of 1984.

President Ronald Reagan, who was known as "The Great Communicator," delivers a speech in Texas during the 1984 presidential campaign. © Ronald Reagan Library/National Archives.

Suggested Reading: Wilber Edel, *The Reagan Presidency: An Actor's Finest Performance* (New York: Hippocrene Books, 1992).

Great Society Speech

On May 22, 1964, President Lyndon Johnson delivered a major domestic policy speech at Michigan State University in which he expressed his vision for a "Great Society." "The Great Society," emphasized Johnson, "rests on abundance and liberty for all. It demands an end to poverty and racial injustice, to which we are totally committed in our time. But that is just the beginning." Johnson committed the nation to rebuilding urban America, to protect the beauty of the nation's countryside and to revive the public schools.

Throughout the 1964 presidential campaign, Johnson highlighted the accomplishments of the Kennedy-Johnson administration. This served as a dramatic contrast to the Republican candidate, Barry Goldwater, who advocated less government while also drawing criticism for his hawkish position on Vietnam and the possible use of nuclear weapons. Following Goldwater's leadership, the Republican platform held conservative positions on a wide range of issues, from accusations that Johnson was soft on communism and pledged to substantially reduce federal spending.

Instead of calling on the federal government to do less, Johnson's "Great Society" speech and the Democratic platform called on the federal government to assist states in dealing with a wide range of social and economic problems. The Johnson campaign was more effective in gauging the mood of the people, defusing anxiety over Indochina, and promoting the "Great Society." LBJ won the 1964 election with the greatest popular vote landslide in history. Democrats also added to their majority in Congress, which enabled Johnson to successfully push most of his "Great Society" agenda. *See also* Campaign of 1964.

Suggested Readings: Milton Cummings and Paul Tillett, *The National Election of 1964* (Washington, DC: Brookings Institution, 1966); Theodore White, *The Making of the President, 1964* (New York: Atheneum Publishers, 1964); "Lyndon B. Johnson's Great Society Speech," Family Education Network, http://www.teachervision.com/lesson-plans/lesson-4319.html.

Greeley, Horace

See Campaign of 1872.

"Greeley & Brown—Amnesty"

A slogan used by the insurgent 1872 campaign of presidential candidate Horace Greeley in his battle to deny President Ulysses S. Grant a second term. Greeley enjoyed the support of both the Democratic Party and Liberal Republicans, a faction recently splintered from the GOP. Along with accusations of corruption against Grant, Greeley sought to accelerate the restoration of political liberties to the South and to withdraw the remaining federal troops installed to enforce Re-

"Honesry in Government."
"Equal Rights to all Men."
THE CHAPPAQUA FARMER.
"No gifts received for Office."
"No place reserved for poor relations."

Campaign banner for Horace Greeley, the candidate of both the Democrats and the Liberal Republicans in 1872. Courtesy of Library of Congress.

construction reforms. Amnesty for Confederate veterans thus became one of the major themes of his campaign. Once Greeley secured the Liberal nomination, the Democrats fell behind with their endorsement.

Greeley proved to be an extremely weak presidential candidate. Grant supporters depicted Greeley as an insolent traitor, accusing him of providing aid and comfort to enemies of the Union. Editorial cartoonist, **Thomas Nast**, reserved some of his harshest cartoons for Greeley. By waving the **bloody shirt** and depicting Greeley as a comic figure, the Republican Party succeeded in destroying the Greeley candidacy and putting down the Liberal Republican rebellion. *See also* Amnesty Issue; Campaign of 1872.

Suggested Reading: Suzanne Schulze, *Horace Greeley: A Bio-bibliography* (Westport, CT: Greenwood Press, 1992).

Ground War

The phrase "ground war" refers to **"get-out-the-vote"** activities during the final weeks of a presidential campaign to animate supporters and sway undecided voters. During the 1970s and 1980s, presidential campaigns spent relatively little on get-out-the-vote efforts. By the 1990s, the influx of **soft money** contributions into Democratic and Republican coffers permitted both parties to significantly increase the funding of traditional get-out-the-vote activities. Republicans and Democrats spent an unprecedented amount of money on get-out-the-vote activities in **battleground states** during the **Campaign of 2000**. With an increasingly smaller percentage of voting age individuals casting ballots in presidential elections, campaigns must devote more resources to turn out supporters in hotly contested states.

Besides making millions of automated or personal phone calls to **targeted** voters, volunteers and paid campaign workers canvass neighborhoods making **literature drops** at the residences of targeted voters. Volunteers assist those voters who need transportation to the polls. *See also* Campaign Manager; Pollster; Robocalls.

Suggested Readings: Eric Bailey, "Campaign 2000; Foot Soldiers Fight to Boost Turnout." *Los Angeles Times*, October 29, 2000, p. A1; Thomas B. Edsall, "Parties Use 'Ground War' as Close Race Nears End; Old Tactics Seen as Key to Rousing Core Voters," *Washington Post*, October 20, 2000, p. A1.

"Grover, Grover, All Is Over"

A slogan used by the Republican Party to ridicule President Grover Cleveland during his 1888 reelection campaign. Cleveland faced Indiana Senator Benjamin Harrison, the Republican nominee and grandson of former President William Henry Harrison.

In sharp contrast to the **Campaign of 1884**, the **Campaign of 1888** focused on issues rather than the character of the presidential candidates. Cleveland and the Democrats maintained their traditional opposition to high tariffs; Republicans typically supported high protective tariffs. Cleveland also ran on his record of strong support for civil service reform.

Suggested Reading: Edward Homer Socolofsky, *The Presidency of Benjamin Harrison* (Lawrence: University of Kansas, 1987).

"Grover, Grover, Four More Years of Grover, In He Comes, Out They Go, Then We'll Be in Clover"

A slogan used by the 1892 campaign of Grover Cleveland to rally support for Cleveland's efforts to return to the White House. Four years earlier Republican Benjamin Harrison defeated Cleveland in his 1888 reelection bid. Now it was Cleveland's turn to challenge the incumbent Harrison. This time Cleveland was boosted by a resurgent Democratic Party, unfortunately strengthened by the disenfranchisement of pro-Republican African Americans throughout the South. Added to this was the unpopularity of Republican economic policy, particularly the high tariff that Democrats traditionally oppose. Voters were more easily persuaded that a vote for Cleveland would put them back "in the clover," an expression for a nice place to be in slang and popular song. *See also* Campaign of 1892.

Suggested Reading: Eugene H. Roseboom, *A History of Presidential Elections* (New York: Macmillan, 1964).

"Grover the Good"

Against the backdrop of a particularly ugly campaign, Democrats advertised their candidate, Grover Cleveland, as "Grover the Good," a man of public integrity and personal honesty. Prior to winning the 1884 nomination, Cleveland established an impeccable reputation as the reform governor of New York.

Cleveland faced Republican James G. Blaine, whose reputation was sullied by railroad corruption. Prior to winning the Republican nomination, Blaine survived a series of highly publicized ethics scandals. The Mulligan Letters scandal cost Blaine the 1876 presidential nomination. Democrats hoped that Cleveland's reputation would appeal to voters tired of a series of scandal-plagued Republican administrations.

Halfway through the 1884 campaign, Blaine supporters caused scandal by reporting Cleveland's paternity of a child born out of wedlock. But when the story broke Cleveland disarmed his accusers by taking full responsibility for his conduct. To the surprise of Blaine supporters, Cleveland's admission did not derail his campaign. Cleveland supporters retaliated with increased attacks on Blaine for alleged ethical indiscretions during his years of public service.

Cleveland's approach worked, and Grover the Good maintained both his reputation and won the election of 1884. *See also* Campaign of 1884; "Ma, Ma, Where's My Pa?"; "Rum, Romanism and Rebellion."

Suggested Reading: Mark Summers, *Rum, Romanism & Rebellion: The Making of a President, 1884* (Chapel Hill: University of North Carolina Press, 2000).

President Grover Cleveland. Courtesy of Library of Congress.

Gut Issue

See Wedge Issue.

Haldeman, H.R.

See Campaign of 1968; Campaign of 1972.

Hancock, Winfield S.

See Campaign of 1880.

Handbill

Similar to broadsides but usually intended for distribution by hand to individual readers rather than for public posting or display, a handbill, or circular, is a popular, inexpensive, assertive, and at times controversial expression of political speech. Handbills have been distributed by hand in public places, sent through the mail, left on automobile windshields and even slipped into employee paychecks (a common practice in the nineteenth century at the height of tensions between labor unions and private companies). Unlike posters and broadsides, handbills have been found at the center of First Amendment controversies (e.g., *Schenck v. United States* which involved the mailing of pro-Socialist and pacifist literature in the form of circulars), and are often regarded as a more aggressive campaigning tactic compared to other types of political ephemera. Additionally, handbills differ from posters, broadsides, buttons, bumper stickers, novelties, and other types of political ephemera in that they are in most cases truly ephemeral, and not as popular with collectors of campaign media. *See also* Pamphlet.

Suggested Readings: Roger A. Fisher, *Tippecanoe and Trinkets Too: The Material Culture of American Presidential Campaigns, 1828–1984* (Urbana: University of Illinois Press, 1988); Keith E. Melder, *Hail to the Candidate: Presidential Campaigns from Banners to Broadcasts* (Washington, DC: Smithsonian Institution Press, 1992).

Handgun Control Issue

During the 1920s and early 1930s, prohibition stimulated a bonanza in the production and sale of illegal alcohol by organized crime, causing an intense wave of violence. In 1934, Congress passed the National Firearms Act directed at limiting access to machine guns and short-barreled shotguns and rifles. In 1938, Congress passed the Federal Firearms Act requiring a Federal Firearms License for anyone selling firearms. The law also required firearms dealers to record the names and addresses of all customers.

During the 1960s crime increased at an unprecedented rate. Exacerbating this new wave of violence, several public figures were killed or wounded by assassins using firearms from 1963 to 1972: President John Kennedy in 1963, civil rights activists Malcolm X and Martin Luther King in 1965 and 1968, Senator Robert Kennedy in 1968, and Alabama Governor George Wallace in 1972—all killed (save Wallace who was permanently paralyzed) by an assassin's bullet.

Through the 1960s, debate swirled over the reasons for escalating crime rates and gun violence. Many sociologists and criminologists blamed the rapid increase in crime on continuing high rates of poverty in the United States. By the close of the 1960s, the apparent failure of President Johnson's "Great Society" programs to slow the increase in the crime rate led to demands for a renewed emphasis on law enforcement.

During the 1968 campaign the Republican Party and candidate Richard Nixon made crime a major issue. Besides blaming the crime years on bad Democratic policies, the 1968 Republican Party platform supported the "enactment of legislation to control indiscriminate availability of firearms," while protecting the Second Amendment right of citizens "to collect, own and use firearms for legitimate purposes."

Four years later, with Nixon running for reelection on a "law and order" platform against liberal Democrat George McGovern, Democrats called for "laws to control the improper use of handguns." Specifically, the Democratic platform called for a ban on illegal "Saturday Night Specials." Republicans reiterated their 1968 platform pledge to protect gun ownership.

In 1976 the major parties continued to move in opposite directions on the gun control issue. Democrats called for federal and state action to curtail the availability of handguns. Republicans again defended the right of citizens to "keep and bear arms" and specifically opposed federal registration of firearms. After two bizarre assassination attempts against incumbent president and candidate Gerald Ford, the Republican gun control position seemed inconsistent. Despite the attempts, Republicans viewed gun control as a **wedge issue** vital to winning an electoral majority of southern, western, midwestern, and border states. Through the 1976 campaign, Democratic nominee Jimmy Carter called for the registration of handguns and an outright ban on the sale of cheap handguns. However, gun control did not become a top priority of his administration after his election.

As expected, differences remained between the parties in the 1980 election. Again, the Republican platform reaffirmed its strong opposition to federal registration of firearms. Although the Democratic platform affirmed the right of sportsmen to possess guns, Democrats continued to call for stricter federal regulation of firearms. With Ronald Reagan's electoral victory in November, a Republican administration friendly to gun ownership once again resided in the White House.

Shortly after Reagan's inauguration in 1981, a crazed handgun-wielding assassin seriously wounded him and press secretary James Brady. In the aftermath of the shooting, gun control groups intensified pressure for the passage of new federal gun control laws. At the same time, the National Rifle Association (NRA) increased lobbying to prevent the enactment of state and federal gun control legislation.

Throughout the 1980s the parties continued their typical positions on gun control, Republicans standing fast in spite of nearly losing Reagan to handgun violence. A slight shift in positions occurred with the 1992 Democratic nomination of Governor Bill Clinton who sought to downplay the party's support for further gun control measures. However, it was Clinton who pushed the 1993 enactment of the Brady Bill—named for the fallen press secretary—requiring all states to install a system of background checks prior to all gun purchases.

Gun control reemerged as a key issue in a number of **battleground states** during the **Campaign of 2000**. While the younger George W. Bush, the Republican nominee, expressed support for current gun control laws and restrictions, Vice President Albert Gore, the Democratic nominee, expressed his support for stronger gun control restrictions. While Gore's position played well in the Northeast and on the West coast, Republicans used the gun control issue effectively in a number of battleground states including West Virginia, Tennessee, Missouri, and Pennsylvania. The NRA ran numerous independent **issue ads** in key states attacking Gore's gun control proposal. In the end, Gore lost the key states of Missouri and West Virginia by small margins, and ultimately the election by just one electoral vote. *See also* Hot Button Issue.

Suggested Readings: Thomas B. Edsall, "Gore, Democrats Face Challenge in Wooing South," *Washington Post*, September 28, 2000, p. A4; John Wildermuth, "Bush, Gore Trade Fire, Candidates Trade Fire over Gun Control: Bush Says Enforce Existing Laws, while Gore Presses for New Restrictions," *San Francisco Chronicle*, October 10, 2000, p. A1.

Handlers

Handlers are political professionals hired to help candidates avoid major gaffes during a campaign. Handlers became a prominent campaign feature in 1968 when Richard Nixon's 1968 staff, determined to avoid the mistakes of the near miss of 1960, carefully scripted Nixon's appearances and limited direct access by reporters. *See also* Campaign Manager.

Suggested Reading: Richard Berke, "The 2000 campaign: the decisive moments, missteps have kept presidential contest tight," *New York Times*, November 5, 2000, Section 1, p. 43.

Hanna, Mark (1837–1904)

During the late nineteenth century, Mark Hanna, an Ohio industrialist, became a major figure in national politics. Hanna developed a close friendship with Congressman William McKinley while lobbying for the continuation of the high protective tariffs advocated by the Republican representative. Hanna's career as a kingmaker began in Ohio, directing William McKinley's successful drive for the Governor's mansion in 1891 and his reelection in 1893. In 1892, Hanna shrewdly advised McKinley to actively stump for President Harrison's reelection, thus drawing attention to McKinley as a national figure.

In 1896, as chairman of the Republican National Committee, Hanna directed McKinley's campaign to win the Republican nomination. After McKinley won at the GOP convention, Hanna directed McKinley's election campaign against Democratic nominee William Jennings Bryan.

In 1897, the governor of Ohio appointed Hanna to the United States Senate

Caricature of Mark Hanna dressed in a suit studded with dollar signs and smoking a cigar. Courtesy of Library of Congress.

to fill a vacancy by the resignation of John Sherman. Ohio voters subsequently elected Hanna to a full term. During his time in the Senate, Hanna continued his strong support for protective tariffs. Upon his death in 1904, Hanna was at the peak of his political influence, and was even rumored as a potential inside challenge to the incumbency of fellow Republican Theodore Roosevelt. *See also* Campaign of 1896; Campaign of 1900.

Suggested Readings: Thomas Beer, *Hanna* (New York: A.A. Knopf, 1929); Francis Russell, *The President Makers: From Mark Hanna to Joseph P. Kennedy* (Boston: Little, Brown, 1976); "William McKinley and Mark Hanna, a Political Partnership," The Ohio State University, http://www.history.ohiostate.edu/projects/McKinley/Hanna/default.htm.

"Happy Days Are Here Again"

"Happy Days Are Here Again" served as the official campaign song of the 1932 presidential campaign of Franklin D. Roosevelt.

With the country suffering under the Great Depression, "Happy Days Are Here Again," a particularly bright melody accompanied by hopeful lyrics, captured Roosevelt's confident optimism and served as an effective remedy to the incumbent President Herbert Hoover's stolid message of patience and perseverance. The song, composed by J. Yellen and M. Ager in 1929, became a popular favorite among Democrats, its chorus remaining the most famous campaign song in American history.

Suggested Reading: Rexford Tugwell, *The Brains Trust* (New York: Viking Press, 1968).

"Happy Warrior"

See Campaign of 1968; Politics of Joy.

Hard Money

Under the 1971 Federal Elections Campaign Act (FECA) and as amended in 1974 and 1976, "hard money" campaign contribution prohibitions on corporations and labor unions and limitations on individuals and political action committees (PACS) were established. The FECA permits candidates for federal office to use hard money contributions for any legal campaign activity. Under law, individuals may contribute up to $1,000 to a candidate running for federal election, $5,000, per year to a PAC or state party committee, and $20,000 per year to a national party committee. Additionally, the FECA places a $25,000 total limit on individual contributions. The FECA permits a multi-candidate PAC to contribute up to $5,000 to a candidate for federal office and up to $15,000 to a party committee.

Other than setting contribution limits, the FECA Amendments of 1974 included the Presidential Election Campaign Fund Act, which established a fund to pay for the presidential campaigns of major party candidates. If a presidential campaign accepted federal funding of their campaign, the law prohibited the campaign from making any additional campaign expenditures. The first public funding of a presidential campaign occurred in 1976 in the wake of the Watergate scandal.

Supporters of campaign finance reform applauded the passage of the FECA of 1971 and the 1974 amendments. Within a few years, critics of the FECA contribution limits and the presidential public funding expenditure restrictions began to argue that the reforms had the unintended impact of reducing the role of political parties, making it difficult for political parties to conduct traditional **party-building activities** and **get-out-the-vote** efforts. Responding to criticism, the Federal Election Commission (FEC) in 1979 issued regulations permitting political parties to accept **soft money** contributions for these efforts.

Both major parties have since taken full advantage of soft money loopholes to raise millions of dollars to fund party-building and get-out-the-vote activities. In 1980 the parties collected an estimated $19 million in soft money. In 2000 the parties raised a half billion dollars in soft money.

Although political parties have used new soft money dollars to significantly expand party-building and get-out-the-vote efforts, both parties devoted ample funding from soft money contributions to pay for **issue ads** during the 1990s. In contrast to hard money campaign ads, these soft money issue ads do not advocate the election of a specific presidential candidate. Instead issue ads deal with major issues stressed by the candidates.

By 2000, both parties openly used the soft-money loophole to legally get around federal contribution and expenditure limitations. In the aftermath of the **Campaign of 2000**, Arizona senator John McCain and Wisconsin senator Russell Feingold continued the crusade for a prohibition on soft money contributions. In April 2001, the Senate passed the McCain-Feingold campaign finance reform, banning soft money contributions to political parties. To gain the support of a majority of senators, McCain and Feingold agreed to raise the individual contribution limit from $1,000 to $2,000 and to raise the amount individuals may give to all candidates and parties from $20,000 to $37,500. Through the remainder of 2001, the House failed to take a vote on McCain-Feingold, but in March 2002 the House joined the Senate in finally passing the new legislation. President Bush then signed into law the most sweeping campaign finance reform in decades. *See also* Get-Out-the-Vote Efforts; Issue Ads; Party-building Activities; Soft Money.

Suggested Readings: Helen Dewar, "Campaign Reform Wins Final Approval; Senate Votes 60-40, Bush Says He Will Sign 'Flawed' Bill," *Washington Post*, March 31, 2002, p. A01; "Supporting Federal Candidates: A Guide For Citizens, Contribution Limits," Federal Election Commission, http://www.fec.gov/pages/citn0021.htm.

Harding, Warren G.

See Campaign of 1920; Character Issue.

"Harding and Prosperity"

To support the 1920 candidacy of Warren G. Harding, the Republicans employed the slogan "Harding and Prosperity," claiming that the incumbent Democratic administration had failed to secure American affluence. The country had experienced an economic slump in the aftermath of World War I. Throughout the **Campaign of 1920**, Harding, a former newspaper editor and U.S. Senator, promised the American people a **return to normalcy** and economic prosperity. *See also* "America First"; Campaign of 1920.

Suggested Readings: Wesley Marvin Bagby, *The Road to Normalcy; The presidential campaign of 1920* (Baltimore: Johns Hopkins Press, 1962); "The Presidential Election of 1920," American Memory, Library of Congress, http://memory.loc.gov/ammem/nfhtml/nfexpe.html.

Harrison, Benjamin

See Campaign of 1888; Campaign of 1892.

Harrison, William Henry

See Campaign of 1836; Campaign of 1840.

"Have Another Cup of Coffee?"

Charged with reneging on his 1904 promise not to seek a third term, 1912 Bull Moose candidate Theodore Roosevelt responded by asking, "When a man says at breakfast in the morning, No thank you, I will not take any more coffee,' it does not mean that he will not take any more coffee tomorrow morning, or next week, or next month or next year." The cynicism of such a statement was irresistible to vaudeville comedians of the day, who would often stimulate cascading laughter by asking an audience one simple question, "Have another cup of coffee?" *See also* Campaign of 1912.

Suggested Readings: Francis Broderick, *Progressivism At Risk: Electing a President in 1912* (New York: Greenwood Press, 1989); Frank K. Kelly, *The Fight For the White House: The Story of 1912* (New York: Crowell, 1964).

"He Kept Us Out of War"

"He Kept Us Out of War" served as one of the most effective slogans in campaign history. National concern over possible involvement in World War I dominated the **Campaign of 1916**, leading incumbent President Woodrow Wilson to pledge that he would continue to keep the United States out of war if reelected president. Since August 1914, Wilson had steadfastly refused to entangle the United States in the catastrophic war in Europe by maintaining a strict national policy of neutrality.

On the surface, few differences appeared to exist between the Republican and Democratic parties on the issue of war in Europe. Both major party platforms called for the United States to maintain its neutrality in the conflict. Despite this fact, Republicans and their candidate Charles Evan Hughes attacked Wilson's foreign policy, accusing him of making "shifty expedients" and "phrase making." By attacking Wilson, Republicans sought to raise doubts about his commitment to neutrality. Equally significant, Republicans openly criticized the government's military preparedness by attacking the administration for failing to develop a coherent policy for national defense.

Wilson recognized that Republican attacks could cost large numbers of votes vital to reelection. To counter these allegations, Wilson's campaign made effective use of slogans designed to reassure the public that Wilson remained determined to avoid sending Americans to a foreign war.

Cartoon showing President Woodrow Wilson researching national defense. © National Archives.

From a political perspective, the slogan "He Kept Us Out of War" proved the most effective. The slogan emphasized the fact that the United States had not suffered the terrible losses in men and wealth experienced by European powers bogged down in brutal trench warfare on the Western front.

The slogan also focused attention on the fact that the nation had profited economically by staying out of the war. The war had led to an increased European demand for American food and nonmilitary products.

In a particularly tight electoral vote contest, Wilson received 277 and Hughes 254 electoral votes. Ohio, which usually backed Republican candidates, proved to be the pivotal state in the election. Four years earlier, the renegade campaign of Teddy Roosevelt permitted Wilson to carry the Buckeye State. Many political observers expected Ohio to return to the Republican fold in 1916. Instead, Wilson won the popular vote in Ohio and the election largely because of his promise to keep the nation out of war. *See also* Campaign of 1912.

Suggested Reading: S.D. Lovell, *The Presidential Campaign of 1916* (Carbondale: Southern Illinois University Press, 1954).

Health Care Reform Issue

Health care insurance is a relatively new issue in American political history. Most attention to public health prior to the twentieth century involved concerns over public sanitation and the adulteration of food. In 1908, the Democratic Party became the first major political organization in the United States to devote a platform plank to public health, but it involved the safety and hygiene of factories and tenements, and did not address health insurance for the treatment of illness. By and large the question of providing health care to the needy was left to private philanthropic enterprises, or was addressed by government at the most local level. A national health policy was not even a faint notion until well into the twentieth century.

During the Progressive Era, groups outside the political parties prompted most attention to health care as a public service beyond public hygiene. Progressive labor groups, along with the American Medical Association, were the first to advocate rudimentary public health care provisions as early as the first two decades of the century. But these efforts were met with resistance within the established parties. Progressive Republicans like Teddy Roosevelt admitted to the need for some kind of health insurance accessible to all, but preferred to leave such efforts to private groups. Private insurance companies and more conservative labor groups such as the American Federation of Labor were not amenable to the idea of public health insurance. During World War I, anti-German sentiment spilled over into the health care debate, provoking politicians to denounce any kind of public health care administration as Germanic statism incompatible with American values. This argument was recycled and reinvigorated during the Red Scare of the early to mid-1920s. The ethos of the rugged individual militated against the more "European" and "collectivist" notion of state directed support for health services. Such attitudes remained high even into the Depression, causing Franklin Roose-

President Lyndon B. Johnson signs the Medicare bill on July 30, 1965. © Lyndon B. Johnson Library/National Archives.

velt to abandon hopes of included health care insurance within the 1935 legislation that created Social Security.

Harry Truman was the first president to openly endorse a compulsory national health insurance program, but he met with intense resistance owing to the cold war mentalities that regarded any government-sponsored health care as "socialized medicine." It was not until 1965, at the peak of President Johnson's sweeping social and political reforms, that legislation creating federally sponsored health care—the Medicare and Medicaid programs—was finally enacted. The quality and extent of federal health care remained an ongoing issue throughout the 1970s and 1980s, usually pitting liberal politicians such as Senator Edward Kennedy of Massachusetts against moderates and conservatives of both parties who objected to the specter of "socialized medicine." Health care received prolonged attention during the early to mid-1990s with the ascent of President Bill Clinton and his wife, First Lady Hillary Clinton. Attaching great import to the issue, the Clinton administration experienced its first political failure in the defeat of a proposed comprehensive universal health care program. This contributed to a loss of Democratic credibility, manifested in the 1994 Congressional elections that led to the first Republican majority in Congress since the Eisenhower administration. Nonetheless, by 1996 the aftershocks of the health care debate had subsided, the president's reelection campaign remained unaffected by the failure to successfully institute the sweeping proposals of the early 1990s. *See also* Campaign of 1964; Campaign of 1992; Campaign of 2000.

Suggested Reading: Jacob S. Hacker, *The Road to Nowhere: The Genesis of President Clinton's Plan for Health Security* (Princeton, NJ: Princeton University Press, 1997).

Herblock (1909–2001)

In 1946 a new political cartoonist, Herbert Block joined the staff of the *Washington Post* working under the pen name of Herblock. Unabashedly liberal, Herblock gained a reputation as one of the foremost national political cartoonists by chronicling the political fortunes and misfortunes of major political figures until his death in 2000 at the age of 81. *See also* Political Cartoons.

Suggested Reading: Herbert Block, *Herblock: A Cartoonist's Life* (New York: Times Books, 1998).

Hired Gun

See Political Consultants.

Honest Abe

By the time of his 1860 run for president, Illinois politician Abraham Lincoln had acquired a well-deserved reputation for honesty that distinguished him from his contemporaries. During the campaign of 1860, Lincoln's supporters effectively employed the phrase, "Honest Abe," to emphasize his strong character. Today, Lincoln's honesty remains a feature of the American political mythos. *See also* Campaign of 1860.

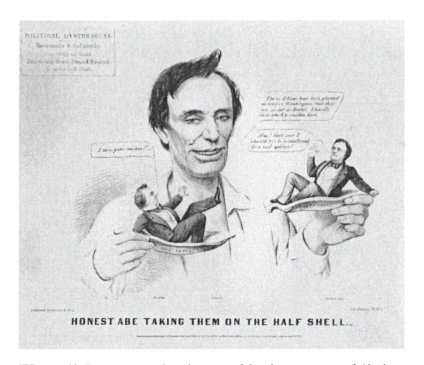

"Honest Abe" was a campaign slogan used by the supporters of Abraham Lincoln, the 1860 Republican presidential nominee. In this cartoon, Lincoln is shown as preparing to swallow his Democratic opponents, Stephen Douglas and John C. Breckinridge. Courtesy of Library of Congress.

Suggested Reading: Harry V. Jaffa, *A New Birth of Freedom: Abraham Lincoln and the Coming of the Civil War* (Lanham, MD: Rowman & Littlefied, 2000).

Hoopla

A word of uncertain origin, hoopla describes a hyperbolic and at times melodramatic flood of rhetoric, images, and symbols, or a series of staged events that are sometimes similar to religious revivals. Hoopla resembles commercial advertising in its uncompromising use of garish style, exaggerated imagery, and simplified text designed to promote a candidate or party with little or no reference to substantive political and social issues. Characterized by a tendency to "accentuate the positive," hoopla is generally employed as a means to produce or sustain campaign momentum among the party faithful and true believers. More rallying point than position statement, more pep turbocharger than serious consideration of issues, hoopla at its most effective stirs into action those who are already committed to a candidate or party, and at the very least provides a spirited reaffirmation of a voter's loyalties.

The "log cabin and hard cider" imagery that defined the campaign of William Henry Harrison in 1840 serves as one of the earliest examples of presidential campaign hoopla on a national scale. Other campaigns that are particularly notable for the intensity and effectiveness of hoopla are, among others, William Jennings

A prime example of hoopla is this depiction of 1884 Democratic presidential candidate Grover Cleveland parading down Main Street in Buffalo, New York, on October 2. Courtesy of Library of Congress.

Bryan's "Cross of Gold" rhetoric of 1896, Teddy Roosevelt's "Bull Moose" run in 1912, John F. Kennedy's image-dependent campaign of 1960, Ronald Reagan's "Morning in America" imagery in 1984 and Ross Perot's outsider theater in 1992.

Appealing to emotion rather than intellect, hoopla is usually harmless boosting of a candidate's image or a party's platform. However, given the tendency toward hyperbole characteristic of hoopla, misleading or dishonest claims often accompany the more credible images and assertions found in such campaigns. At times, the hoopla generated by a campaign can be based on utter falsehood. Harrison's cynical claim to log cabin origins serves as an example of hoopla that is based on sheer fabrication and prevarication. Regardless of the truth of its claims, hoopla generally serves to animate the electorate, and can be effective in dominating a campaign in ways that obscure the depth and complexity of the real issues that press on the polity. At best, hoopla is harmless boosterism, but at its worst it resorts to manipulation and mendacity intentionally designed to forestall or obfuscate debate.

Suggested Readings: Roger A. Fisher, *Tippecanoe and Trinkets Too: The Material Culture of American Presidential Campaigns, 1828–1984* (Urbana: University of Illinois Press, 1988); Keith E. Melder, *Hail to the Candidate: Presidential Campaigns from Banners to Broadcasts* (Washington, DC: Smithsonian Institution Press, 1992); Irwin Silber, *Songs America Voted By; With the Words and Music that Won and Lost Elections and Influenced the Democratic Process* (Harrisburg, PA: Stackpole Books, 1971).

Hoover, Herbert

See Campaign of 1928; Campaign of 1932.

Horse-Race Campaign Coverage

From the very beginning of the republic, presidential campaigns could not reasonably expect impartial coverage in the press. To the contrary, the majority of major newspapers established informal political alliances throughout the latter eighteenth and nineteenth centuries. Prior to the Civil War, newspapers depended on government printing contracts to stay afloat. But after the Civil War newspapers freed themselves from this dependence through advertising revenue.

Equally important, a number of new political magazines were first published right after the Civil War. *Judge, Puck*, and *Harper's Weekly* provided political cartoonists, such as **Thomas Nast**, the opportunity to publish biting political depictions of the major political figures of the era.

More professional journalism emerged in the twentieth century. Gradually, newspapers separated the coverage of news, including presidential campaigns, from their editorial sections. Over time a new generation of political reporters assumed front line positions in the coverage of presidential campaigns. In the early 1930s, radio joined newspapers as a major source of political news. The CBS and NBC radio networks became a major source of political news, and after World War II, television added another dimension to news media.

Through the 1960s and 1970s, the nature of presidential campaign coverage changed from a heavy focus on the issues to a preoccupation with more entertaining coverage, not unlike a sporting event. Resembling the coverage of a college or NFL football game, presidential campaign coverage increasingly focused on campaign strategy and the standing of candidates in the latest poll. Racehorse coverage reached a peak with the 1988 campaign between Vice President George Bush and Massachusetts Democratic governor Michael Dukakis.

After the Democratic National Convention in Atlanta, Dukakis held a commanding lead in public opinion polls. In direct response, the Bush campaign launched an aggressive series of ads attacking the Dukakis record in Massachusetts. By the end of September, Bush had regained the lead in the public opinion polls, going on to victory on Election Day in November.

In the aftermath of the 1988 election, print and electronic news operations faced severe criticism for their horse-race style of campaign coverage. Despite some efforts in the media to supplement horse-race coverage with in-depth analysis of key campaign issues, in the 1990s horse-race coverage continued to dominate media coverage. During the final weeks of the **Campaign of 2000** results of numerous national and state polls were released measuring the relative standing of the two major candidates.

Media critics continue to maintain that horse-race coverage inhibits clear and comprehensive understanding of key issues within the American public. *See also* Media Event.

Suggested Readings: Howard Kurtz, "On TV, Covering 'the Issues' from A to Zzzzzz," *Washington Post*, July 3, 2000, p. C1; Thomas B. Rosenstiel, "Fascination with Tactics Dominates Political Coverage," *Los Angeles Times*, November 4, 1988, Part I, p. 12.

Horse-Race Poll

See Tracking Poll.

Horton, William

See Willie Horton Ad.

Hot Button Issue

See Wedge Issue.

"A House Divided Against Itself Cannot Stand"

Slavery and possible secession were the main issues of the **Campaign of 1860**. Throughout the campaign, supporters of the four sectional candidates, Abraham Lincoln, Stephen Douglas, John Bell, and John Breckinridge, used numerous slogans to attempt to mobilize their supporters. Lincoln in particular could mine his record of oratorical eloquence for aphoristic phrases that could serve as an effective slogan. One such phrase came from his famous "House Divided" speech, originally delivered two years earlier in June of 1858 while accepting the Republican nomination for U.S. Senate from Illinois.

Although Lincoln lost the Senate race to Douglas, the debates catapulted Lincoln into the front-runner position for his party's presidential nomination in 1860 as well as making him a significant spokesman on the issue of slavery.

Lincoln borrowed the "house divided" line from the Gospel according to St. Matthew, 12:25. Lincoln averred that

> A House divided against itself cannot stand. I believe this government cannot endure permanently half slave and half free. I do not expect the Union to be dissolved—I do not expect the house to fall—but I do expect it will cease to be divided. It will become all one thing, or all the other. Either the opponents of slavery will arrest the further spread of it, and place it where the public mind shall rest in the belief that it is in the course of ultimate extinction; or advocates will push it forward till it shall become alike lawful in all the States, old as well as new, North as well as South.

See also Campaign of 1860.

Suggested Reading: "A House Divided Against Itself Cannot Stand," The National Center for Public Policy Research, http://www.project21.org/HouseDivided.html.

Hughes, Charles Evan

See Campaign of 1916.

Hughes, Karen (1957–)

On January 4, 2001, President-elect George Bush named Karen Hughes to the position of counselor to the president. Hughes joined Karl Rove, Bush's senior advisor and chief of staff Andrew Card as part of Bush's so-called *troika* of presidential advisors.

Hughes grew up in a military family, the daughter of Major General Harold R. Parfitt. After graduating from high school in Texas, Hughes attended Southern Methodist University and graduated with a degree in journalism. Upon graduation, Hughes was employed as a reporter for KXAS-TV in Fort Worth, Texas. In 1984 Hughes resigned from reporting to become press secretary for the Reagan-Bush reelection campaign.

In 1992, Hughes moved to Austin, Texas, to take the position as executive director of the Texas Republican Party. Hughes then joined the younger George Bush's 1994 campaign for governor of Texas, serving as press secretary. Throughout the 2000 Republican primary and general election campaign, Hughes served as the chief spokesperson for the Bush campaign.

After the campaign, Hughes became one of President Bush's top policy advisors.

During the spring of 2002, Hughes resigned her White House position to move back to Texas that July. In announcing her resignation, Hughes indicated that her desire to spend more time with her family motivated her decision. *See also* Campaign of 2000.

Suggested Readings: Gerald Baum and Elizabeth Mehren, "She Has the President's Ear, As a Loyalist and Alter Ego, Profile: Karen Hughes Is Part of Bush's Innermost Circle, Turning His Thoughts into Real-World Ideas," *Los Angeles Times*, April 1, 2000, p. A1; Dana Milbank, "Bush Names Rove Political Strategist; Choice Completes Troika Of White House," *Washington Post*, January 5, 2001, p. A1.

Humphrey, Hubert H.

See Campaign of 1968; Civil Rights Issue.

"I Like Ike"

"I Like Ike" served as both a campaign slogan and song for General Dwight D. Eisenhower's presidential run in 1952 and later for his reelection in 1956. As a legendary war hero and former supreme commander of allied forces in World War II as well as NATO's first commander, Eisenhower seemed aloof and inaccessible to political critics. "I Like Ike" was an effective phrase promoting a more affable, personable, and less intimidating Eisenhower.

The Eisenhower campaign commissioned legendary composer Irving Berlin to compose music and lyrics for a campaign song to be titled, "I Like Ike." The

In November 1952, President-elect Dwight D. Eisenhower speaks at the White House after meeting with outgoing President Harry Truman. © Abbie Rowe, National Park Service/Harry S. Truman Library.

campaign subsequently used the slogan in short television spot ads. For the first time, political parties made extensive use of television to reach American voters, purchasing thirty-minute blocks of time for campaign broadcasts and spot ads that ran between twenty seconds and five minutes. The Eisenhower spot ad played off of the "I Like Ike" slogan and persona, and ended with the voice of Dwight Eisenhower stating, "Now is the time for all good Americans to come to the aid of their country."

The Eisenhower campaign made effective use of the "I Like Ike" slogan to humanize Eisenhower. "I Like Ike" effectively spoke to middle America in the 1950s and has remained one of the more famous campaign slogans in political history. *See also* Campaign of 1952.

Suggested Reading: Darrell West, *Air Wars: Television Advertising in Election Campaigns, 1952–1992* (Washington, DC: Congressional Quarterly, 1993).

Image-makers

See Media Consultant; Political Consultants.

Immigration Issue

Through the late nineteenth century, the United States encouraged immigration. From the early seventeenth to mid-nineteenth century, Protestants represented the largest percentage of immigrants to North America. However, the early nineteenth century saw an increasing number of Catholic immigrants from Italy, Ireland, and Poland. Many Irish-Catholic immigrants initially went to work building Eastern canals and railroads. Later, they became a major part of the workforce for the growing number of coal mines. In an effort to escape starvation from the Irish Potato Famine of the late 1840s through the early 1850s, more then one million Irish immigrants came to the United States, settling in cities from Boston to New Orleans.

By the mid-1850s the growing number of Irish-Catholic immigrants provoked nativism among more xenophobic and Anti-Catholic Americans, leading to the establishment of the American Party, popularly known as the Know-Nothings. The Know-Nothings proposed tighter restrictions on European immigration. In 1856 the Know-Nothings held their first and only national convention in Philadelphia. The convention nominated former Whig president Millard Fillmore (1850–1853) for President and Andrew Johnson Donelson for vice president. Fillmore only received Maryland's eight electoral votes, after which the more critical issue of slavery overwhelmed the Know-Nothing movement. Many northern members of the Know-Nothings subsequently joined the Republican Party.

Following the Civil War a number of states passed laws restricting immigration. However, in 1875, the Supreme Court found unconstitutional state immigration laws on the grounds that only the federal government had the authority to regulate immigration. By the early 1880s, growing concern with Chinese immigration in the West led to increased pressure on Congress to enact new laws restricting immigration. In 1880, the national conventions of the Republican, Democratic, and Greenback parties all called for restrictions on Chinese immigration. In response, Congress passed the Chinese Exclusion Act of 1882. In 1884, the Republican and Democratic national conventions called for full enforcement of the Chinese Exclusion Act. Between 1885 and 1887, Congress enacted a series of laws further prohibiting certain laborers from immigrating to the United States.

In 1891, Congress established an Immigration Service within the Treasury Department to screen immigrants. Despite the enactment of restrictive immigration laws, immigration accelerated during the period from 1880 through 1914 and with the beginning of World War I, a large percentage from southern European countries such as Italy.

In response to the high volume of immigration after World War I, Congress passed the Immigration Acts of 1921 and 1924 establishing a quota system.

From the mid-1920s through the 1970s differences in immigration policy did not play a major role in presidential campaigns. However, the 1980s would bring increased tensions over national immigration policy spurred by a growing number of undocumented aliens, mostly from Latin America. In 1986, Congress passed the Immigration Reform and Control Act. The law put into place new sanctions against employers who hired undocumented, or illegal, aliens.

The law did allow certain illegal aliens to obtain legal residence status. Despite the 1986 Immigration Act, the 1988 Republican National Convention included a platform plank that recognized the contributions made by immigrants to the United States, while reaffirming the right of the country to control its borders.

Then in 1992 party platforms adopted different positions on immigration reform. The Democratic platform emphasized the contributions made by immigrants to American society and did not call for additional immigration restrictions or tougher measures to identify and deport illegal immigrants. In contrast, the Republican platform did call for strengthening border patrol activities to stop illegal immigration.

In 1996, the Republican National Convention approved a platform plank stating that illegal aliens should not receive public benefits other than emergency aid. Opposing this, the Democratic platform criticized the Republican Party for attempting to deprive immigrant children of their access to education. Instead, Democrats supported increasing civil and criminal sanctions against employers who hire illegal immigrants.

In 2000, the Republican National Convention nominated Texas governor George Bush. In a critical change in the GOP platform, Republicans again applauded the role of immigrants in building the United States and dropped proposals for new legislation depriving illegal immigrants of social services such as public education. This served to help Bush tailor his message to the large bloc of Hispanic voters.

Since the September 11, 2001 terrorist attacks on the World Trade Center and the Pentagon, the national focus has shifted from undocumented workers to the prevention of terrorist infiltration. *See also* Campaign of 1856; Campaign of 1876; Campaign of 1880; Campaign of 1884.

Suggested Readings: Mark Z. Barabak, "Campaign 2000; Bush Softens Sharp Edges of Republican Platform; Politics: Draft Retains Tough Anti-Abortion Stand, but Harsh Rhetoric of Past Document Gone," *Los Angeles Times*, July 28, 2000, p. A1; Michael C. LeMay and Elliot Robert Barkan, *U.S. Immigration and Naturalization Laws and Issues* (Westport, CT: Greenwood Press, 1999).

Imperialism

Beginning in the early 1880s, politicians and business leaders began to argue that the United States needed to extend its influence beyond the country's continental boundaries to protect American economic and political interests abroad against aggressive European colonization in Africa, Asia, and the South Pacific. Thus during the second half of the nineteenth century, American corporations had acquired substantial business interests in Central America, Cuba, and the Hawaiian Islands. American business also held strong interest in opening markets in the Far East. Finally, a number of missionary organizations believed that the United States had a moral obligation to help spread Christianity throughout the world. These interests coalesced to usher a new "Age of Imperialism" in American politics and foreign policy that spanned the decades from the 1890s to the 1920s.

In 1892, both the Republican and Democratic national conventions expressed strong support for construction of a Nicaragua Canal to boost economic interests and national defense. Both parties responded to a growing chorus of concern that a foreign power might build a canal and thus expand their sphere of influence in the Central American region, challenging the Monroe Doctrine. During the 1880s, a French company failed in an attempt to build a canal through the Isthmus of Panama. In the aftermath of this failure, American interests intensified their efforts to begin an American canal project in Central America.

During the early 1890s, the "imperialism issue" shifted from the canal issue to the Hawaiian Islands. During the early nineteenth century, New England missionaries were actively involved in Hawaii, and by the late nineteenth century a significant number of Americans had immigrated to Hawaii in pursuit of prosperity. Tension developed between settlers and natives, causing business concerns to lobby the federal government on behalf of annexation interests. In January 1893, colonists supporting U.S. annexation seized the main government building in Oahu in an effort to overthrow Queen Liliuokalani. The American minister to Hawaii, John L. Stevens, subsequently dispatched Marines from warships in Honolulu harbor to protect a newly established provisional "government" consisting of colonial leadership. This "government" quickly negotiated a treaty with the Harrison administration for the purpose of annexation. With Harrison's loss to Grover Cleveland in the election of 1892, the treaty was promptly withdrawn from the Senate ratification process. Instead of annexation, Cleveland established a special commission to investigate the overthrow of Queen Liliuokalani and the native Hawaiian government. Late in 1893, Cleveland sent a message to Congress detailing the conspiracy of Minister Stevens and a small group of colonists to overthrow the Hawaiian government and calling for its immediate restoration under Hawaii's queen. Congress refused to intervene and on July 4, 1894, the provisional government declared itself the "Republic of Hawaii."

The Hawaiian controversy continued through the **Campaign of 1896**. The Republican Party platform continued to claim American control of the Hawaiian Islands. Additionally, the Central American canal was again endorsed. But neither the islands nor the canal were a factor in the election of William McKinley. A short time after being sworn in, the Republic of Hawaii again asked the United States to annex the Hawaiian Islands.

Attention was drawn away from Hawaii and toward Cuba when, on February 15, 1898, the United States battleship Maine exploded in Havana harbor killing 266 sailors. Responding to tremendous pressure from the media, especially the efforts of publisher William Randolph Hearst, McKinley asked Congress for a declaration of war against Spain. During the subsequent Spanish-American War, the United States routed the Spanish fleet and defeated Spanish forces in Cuba, Puerto Rico, and the Philippines, ending the war in 1898 with the Treaty of Paris. The treaty left the United States in possession of Cuba, Puerto Rico, and the Philippines.

However, the United States soon found itself facing the problems of a colonial power. The same forces that had revolted against Spanish rule of the Philippines now fought American occupation. Thus, imperialism became a major issue during the **Campaign of 1900**. Against McKinley's expansionist foreign policy, the Democratic Party adopted an anti-imperialism platform arguing that imperialism was inconsistent with the principles of Republican government. In spite of Bryan's initial attempt to revive the free silver debate, imperialism eclipsed the monetary issue that had dominated the previous campaign. But the American public was unconvinced and returned McKinley to the White House along with Rough Rider and war hero Theodore Roosevelt.

Charges of imperialism recur during campaigns that occur during times of international conflict. In the 1960s and 1970s both Democrat Lyndon Johnson and Republican Richard Nixon were accused of imperialist jingoism in Indochina. Ronald Reagan was commonly depicted as an imperialist by the left throughout the 1980s, and both Bushes as well as Bill Clinton have been charged with harboring imperialist and globalist designs from critics from both the extreme right and left. *See also* Campaign of 1888; Campaign of 1896; Campaign of 1900.

Suggested Readings: Robert Beisner, *Twelve Against the Empire: the Anti-Imperialists, 1898–1906* (New York: McGraw-Hill, 1968); H. Wayne Morgan, *America's Road to Empire; the War with Spain and Overseas Expansion* (New York: Wiley, 1965); Ivan Musicant, *Empire by default: the Spanish-American War and the Dawn of the American Century* (New York: H. Holt, 1998).

"In Your Guts, You Know He's Nuts"

During the 1964 campaign, Democratic candidate Lyndon Johnson responded to Republican criticism regarding his defense and foreign policy by portraying Republican nominee Barry Goldwater as a trigger-happy Hawk willing to risk the actual use of thermonuclear weapons, especially with regard to the crisis in Indochina. As stated in the 1964 Democratic platform, "[the] complications and dangers in our restless, constantly changing world require of us consummate understanding and experience. One rash act, one thoughtless decision, one unchecked reaction—and cities could become smoldering ruins and farms parched wasteland."

These extremist allegations put Goldwater on the defensive. In an effort to respond to criticism regarding both his domestic and foreign policy agenda, the Goldwater campaign promoted the slogan, **"In Your Heart, You Know He's Right."** Bill Moyers purportedly coined the Johnson campaign's waggish version of the Goldwater slogan, "In Your Guts, You Know He's Nuts." Alluding to Goldwater's alleged hair-trigger, wags also quipped, "In Your heart, you know he *might!*" Throughout the campaign Democrats continued to press home the theme that Goldwater lacked the restraint needed to manage America's nuclear arsenal. *See also* Campaign of 1964; "Daisy" Campaign Ad.

Suggested Reading: Theodore White, *The Making of the President, 1964* (New York: Atheneum Publishers, 1965).

"In Your Heart, You Know He's Right"

"In Your Heart You Know He's Right" was a slogan used by the 1964 presidential campaign of Republican Barry Goldwater in an attempt to counter attacks by Democrats and moderate Republicans depicting Goldwater as an extremist conservative out of touch with mainstream America.

Goldwater's nomination represented a major shift in the philosophy of the Republican Party. Goldwater criticized the economic, social, and civil rights, and defense policies of the Kennedy and Johnson administrations, preaching libertarian demolition of federal programs at home and military preparedness against the Communist Bloc abroad.

Goldwater forces pushed through an uncompromisingly conservative platform. After receiving the nomination, Goldwater turned aside criticism that the party's conservative platform would drive away moderate voters. Instead, Goldwater insisted on remaining true to conservative principles. To punctuate this point the Goldwater campaign adopted the "In Your Heart, You Knows He's Right" slogan.

Ultimately, the American public rejected Goldwater's species of conservatism, and returned LBJ to the White House in the greatest popular landslide in presidential election history. *See also* Campaign of 1964; "In Your Guts, You Known He's Nuts."

Suggested Reading: Theodore White, *The Making of the President, 1964* (New York: Atheneum Publishers, 1965).

Independent Advocacy Groups

See Independent Presidential Campaign Expenditures.

Independent Presidential Campaign Expenditures

Besides limiting individual campaign contributions to federal candidates, the Federal Election Campaign Act Amendments (FECA) of 1974 included limits on independent political campaign expenditures in support of candidates for federal office. Congress sought to prevent well-funded private interest groups from influencing federal elections.

In the landmark case of *Buckley v. Valeo* (1976), the Supreme Court upheld the constitutionality of campaign contribution limits imposed on individuals. However, the high court held that Congress lacked the authority to limit or prohibit independent political expenditures by private individuals or interest groups. The *Buckley* decision cleared the way for interest groups to increase independent political campaign expenditures. Through the 1970s, 1980s, and 1990s, independent groups gradually increased direct expenditures in presidential campaigns.

The explosion in independent political expenditures drew public and media scrutiny. Critics argued that independently funded campaign ads distorted the political process. First, voters often had a difficult time identifying the sources of the ads. Second, such expenditures indirectly helped presidential campaigns evade contribution limits. The second criticism focused on the fact that interest groups philosophically compatible with a particular presidential candidate often funded campaign ads supporting that candidate.

Prior to the 1988 presidential election, media observers focused little attention on the impact of independent campaign ads on presidential campaigns. The situation changed with the 1988 **Willie Horton ad** funded by an independent organization not directly affiliated with the George Bush presidential campaign. The ad focused on a rape committed by a convicted murderer on prison furlough, attacking Massachusetts governor and Democratic candidate Michael Dukakis for approving the furlough program. Although the Bush campaign denied any involvement in broadcasting the ad, the furlough program became a major issue, providing the Bush campaign with ammunition against Dukakis's alleged soft stance on crime.

Independent groups raised and spent large sums in the **Campaign of 2000**, the balance of which was spent in **battleground states**. For example, the National Rifle Association (NRA) spent millions on ads attacking Democratic candidate Albert Gore for supporting additional gun control measures. On the other hand, Planned Parenthood spent considerable funds supporting Gore for his position on the abortion issue.

Late in March 2002, the younger President Bush signed into law a major overhaul of federal campaign finance laws. The measure included a provision prohibiting independent groups from paying for the broadcast of **issue ads** 30 days before a primary and 60 days before a general election. Critics of the restriction immediately launched legal challenges on the grounds that the provision violates the First Amendment's protection of freedom of speech. *See also* Campaign Finance Reform; Campaign of 1988; Campaign of 1996; Political Reform.

Suggested Reading: "Planned Parenthood Ad Spending at Top of List," *USA Today*, October 16, 2000, p. A17.

Infomercial

In the early days of television presidential candidates purchased 30-minute blocks of broadcast airtime to bring their messages into American homes. Both Republican Dwight Eisenhower and his rival, Democrat Adlai Stevenson, invested money in half-hour programs about their policies as well as the shorter 30-second spot ad. This continued into the early 1960s but tapered considerably throughout the decade. By the 1970s the rising cost of television time, rising voter apathy and the perceived declining attention span of television viewers led presidential campaigns to abandon the practice of purchasing 30-minute blocks of airtime. Instead campaigns relied increasingly upon 30-second spot ads and news sound bites.

When Texas billionaire Ross Perot mounted a third-party challenge to major party nominees George Bush and Bill Clinton he used his own fortune to purchase 30-minute blocks of time in the style of a 1950s campaign. Perot used graphs and charts to dramatize the dangers of annual deficits and the growing national debt. Political commentators quickly came to refer to these appearances as "infomercials."

Long before Perot decided to run for president, the American public had become quite familiar with 30-minute commercials selling everything from exercise equipment to motivational tapes. Even though critics lampooned his infomercials, Perot managed the most successful third-party run since Theodore Roosevelt's 1912 Bull Moose campaign.

Perot returned to the infomercial in his less successful run in 1996. *See also* Presidential Campaign Ads.

Suggested Readings: "Perot Infomercials Win Strong Ratings," *Los Angeles Times*, October 20, 1992, p. A19; J. Max Robins, "Reality TV: Politics Rates," *Variety* 349, October 26, 1992, p. 2; Tom Shales, "Uncanned Ham: Perot's Show," *Washington Post*, October 27, 1992, p. C3.

Internet Campaigning

In the twentieth century presidential campaigns have used television, radio, newspapers, phone banks, and direct mail to reach voters. By the early 1990s, political campaigns slowly began to regard the Internet as a potential campaign tool. By the **Campaign of 2000**, both primary and general election candidates made extensive use of the Internet.

Arizona senator John McCain, Republican candidate in the 2000 presidential primaries, set a new standard for political use of the Internet. During late 1999 and the early months of 2000, the McCain campaign extensively used the Internet to recruit volunteers, notify supporters of campaign events, and raise funds. Through early February 2000, the McCain campaign spent $300,000 on the Internet while raising $3.7 million. After McCain upset the younger George Bush in the New Hampshire primary his campaign was flooded with contributions and new volunteers. Although Bush defeated McCain for the nomination, McCain's use of the Internet demonstrated for the first time its full potential.

Surveys of the political use of the Internet indicate that campaigns frequently use web sites to (1) post biographical information on candidates, (2) distribute issue papers and policy statements, (3) recruit volunteers, (4) raise funds, and (5) use e-mail to communicate with campaign workers, supporters, and the media. Currently, web sites such as www.moveon.org continue to fertilize the growth of internet campaigns. *See also* Campaign of 2000; Campaign Manager.

Suggested Readings: Ron Faucheux, "How Campaigns Are Using the Internet: An Exclusive Nationwide Survey," *Campaigns & Elections*, September 1998, p. 22; John Mintz, "McCain Camp Enjoys a Big Net Advantage," *Washington Post*, February 9, 2000, p. A1.

Iran Hostage Crisis

In January 1979, the Shah of Iran, a long-time friend of American administrations since his installment on the Peacock Throne by the CIA during the Eisenhower administration, fled Iran with his family in fear of a revolutionary situation provoked by militant Islamic fundamentalists. On February 1, 1979, the Ayatollah Ruholla Khomeini, a prominent fundamentalist leader, returned from a prolonged exile in France to assume command of the revolution. In late October 1979, the Carter administration allowed the Shah to enter the United States to receive cancer treatment at Sloan-Kettering Cancer Institute in New York City. On November 1, 1979, massive demonstrations erupted in Iran over the Carter decision. On November 4, 1979, five hundred Iranian students attacked the United States embassy in Tehran and took 61 Americans hostage, holding them for 444 days.

The Iranian hostage crisis could not have come at a worse time for President Jimmy Carter. The combination of high inflation, slow economic growth, rising unemployment, and an energy crisis had seriously eroded public confidence in the Carter White House. With the Iranian crisis Carter's effectiveness was cast in serious doubt, further magnified by a failed rescue mission resulting in the loss of American troops in the Iranian desert. Carter did manage to overcome an intraparty challenge from Massachusetts senator Edward Kennedy for the Democratic nomination, but he could not withstand the challenge of Republican nominee, former California governor Ronald Reagan.

Throughout the 1980 presidential election campaign the Reagan campaign made effective use of the Iranian hostage crisis. *New York Times* columnist William Safire helped the Republican effort by reporting in a paid advertisement that the Ayatollah Khomeini had publicly warned the American people not to elect Ronald Reagan as their president. The Safire ad effectively painted Carter as a weak president who was unable to resolve the hostage crisis. As the unkindest cut of all, the ad was actually purchased by Democrats for Reagan. Reagan defeated the wounded incumbent in a November landslide.

On Inauguration Day, Iran agreed to release the hostages. At 12:30 P.M, one half hour after Ronald Reagan received the oath of office, Iran officially released the hostages. The move seemed to support the idea that President Reagan was viewed as more formidable than his predecessor, causing the release of the Americans. After the inauguration, Republicans accused the Carter campaign of attempting to obtain the release of the hostages prior to the election and Democrats accused the Republicans of secretly trying to delay the release of the hostages until after Election Day. *See also* Campaign of 1980.

Suggested Reading: Gary Sick, *October Surprise: America's Hostages in Iran and the Election of Ronald Reagan* (New York: Times Books, 1992).

Isolationism

From 1895 through 1904, the United States joined a number of European powers in expanding its sphere of influence. With victory of Spain in a war that resulted in the acquisition of American colonies in the Caribbean and Pacific, the United States had become an established international power. By the **Campaign of 1904** growing concern over the impact of expansionism on American democratic values led the Democratic National Convention to include in its platform a strongly worded plank denouncing **imperialism.**

Even though William McKinley easily won reelection by defeating William Jennings Bryan, a growing number of national political figures criticized the government's ambitions abroad. Influential progressives argued that the country faced too many problems at home to afford to squander its wealth and the lives of its young men on dreams of empire. Through the 1908 presidential election, Republicans vigorously defended expansionism by arguing that the country needed to protect important new markets for American business and industry. Democrats continued to declaim against undemocratic and grasping imperial ambitions.

By the opening salvos of World War I in August 1914, the American public had tilted away from expansionism. During the **Campaign of 1916** incumbent President Woodrow Wilson ran for reelection as the proven peace candidate. Wilson rode the campaign slogan **"He Kept Us Out of War"** to victory. Nonetheless, events overtook Wilson, and in 1917 America joined the war against Germany and its allies.

In the war's aftermath, Wilson lobbied hard for membership of the United States in the new League of Nations. While the 1920 Democratic platform supported membership in the League of Nations, the Republican platform expressed strong opposition to the league on grounds that it threatened American sovereignty.

Bitter from high casualties suffered in a seemingly senseless foreign war, wary of events in Russia, and suspicious of foreign entanglements, the American public moved further into isolationism throughout the 1920s and 1930s. World War I had taught Americans the dangers of "entangling alliances"; neutrality and isolation reigned in public sentiment and national policy.

Despite growing concern in the mid-1930s over the emergence of fascism in Germany and Japanese aggression in Asia, both major party platforms of 1936 continued to express strong opposition to foreign alliances or commitments. But by the 1940 conventions, Nazi Germany had conquered all of Western Europe leaving Britain to stand alone against Hitler, while Japan continued its war of aggression in China. Germany and Japan had amassed substantial military might and possessed the will and desire to use it. Even though the U.S. Navy possessed a sizable fleet, America seemed weak compared with Nazi Germany and Imperial Japan. The Republican platform blamed the New Deal policies of the Roosevelt administration for leaving the nation unprepared to defend itself from new threats abroad. And yet, the Republican platform continued to express strong opposition to American participation in foreign wars.

Interestingly, the Democratic platform included a plank pledging that the Roosevelt administration would not involve the United States in a foreign war. Both Republican and Democratic platforms supported materiel support to free nations resisting aggression. But Republican candidate, Wendell Willkie, under pressure from his party's isolationist wing, attacked Roosevelt for his lend-lease arrangement with Britain.

Roosevelt continued to publicly insist on his preference for neutrality. But the issue was decided for Roosevelt by the Japanese attack on American naval forces at Pearl Harbor, ending American isolationism once and for all.

Suggested Readings: Wayne S. Cole, *Roosevelt & the Isolationists, 1932–45* (Lincoln: University of Nebraska Press, 1983); John Milton Cooper, *The Vanity of Power: American Isolationism and the First World War, 1914–1917* (Westport, CT: Greenwood, 1969).

Issue Ads

In 1996 the major parties raised tens of millions of dollars from **soft money** contributions. Regulations issued by the Federal Election Commission (FEC) during the late 1970s permitted political parties to raise unlimited contributions to fund **party-building activities**. Federal Election Campaign Act (FECA) contribution limits did not apply to soft money contributions. Through the 1980s and early 1990s, both parties significantly increased the level of soft money contributions.

Prior to the **Campaign of 1996** legal experts disagreed over the extent to which federal law permitted political parties to use soft money to pay for ads promoting policies supported by a candidate. For many years, independent organizations had paid for ads on various public policy issues. In the 1976 *Buckley v. Valeo* decision, the Supreme Court struck down a provision of the 1974 FECA amendments imposing limits on independent political expenditures supporting or opposing candidates for federal office.

Early in 1995, the Democratic Party undertook a major soft money contribution drive at the request of the Clinton White House. By 1996 the Democratic Party spent some $46 million on ads touting Clinton's record on issues ranging from education to welfare reform. In the aftermath of Clinton's victory over Republican nominee Bob Dole, many political observers credited Clinton's victory to the Democratic Party's multimillion-dollar issue ad campaign.

After the 1996 election, both the FEC and the Department of Justice conducted investigations of both parties in response to allegations of federal election law soft money violations. Both the FEC and the Justice Department declined to take any action as the result of their investigations. Both parties continued the practice of using soft money to pay for issue ads in 2000.

Late in March 2002, Congress, with the younger President Bush's signature, enacted sweeping campaign finance reform legislation—the McCain-Feingold campaign reform bill—prohibiting soft money contributions to political parties.

Overall the legislation sharply restricted soft money contributions to national political parties. Additionally, the law raised the limit on individual **hard money** contributions to candidates for federal office from $1,000 to $2,000 annually. The law also banned unions, corporations, and some independent groups from funding certain types of **issue ads** broadcast within 60 days of an election and 30 days of a primary.

After President Bush signed the new legislation, a number of groups brought suit challenging the constitutionality of the new restrictions on First Amendment grounds. Late in 2003, the Supreme Court upheld key provisions of the law. *See also* Campaign Finance Reform; Campaign of 2000.

Suggested Reading: Helen Dewar, "Campaign Reform Wins Final Approval, Senate Votes 60-40, Bush Says He Will Sign 'Flawed' Bill," *Washington Post*, March 21, 2002, p. A01.

"It's the Economy, Stupid"

"It's the Economy, Stupid" became the unofficial slogan of Arkansas governor Bill Clinton's 1996 presidential campaign. Early in the campaign Clinton's advisors decided to concentrate on **bread-and-butter-issues**. In Clinton's Arkansas headquarters, known as the "War Room," a sign reading "The Economy, Stupid" reminded campaign workers to remain fixed on economic policy and avoid distractions regarding personal conduct. The phrase worked its way into several of Clinton's campaign speeches and television appearances.

The slogan served a dual purpose of providing Clinton with a substantive issue to drive his campaign as well as deflecting repeated indictments of his character stemming from allegations of marital infidelity and draft dodging. Initially many experts and analysts predicted that the character issue would impair Clinton's chances against an incumbent president. But the country faced a lingering recession, and Clinton's calculation was correct: the American public, tired of personal scandal, responded favorably to the "policy wonk" persona of Clinton and his running mate Al Gore, and recognized the importance of economic issues throughout the campaign.

Clinton promised that his economic reform program would create millions of new jobs. He also promised to support a major overhaul of the nation's health care delivery system to provide high-quality health care to millions of uninsured Americans.

Clinton's skill in campaigning on the economic issues, combined with the constant criticism of President Bush's economic policies from third-party candidate Ross Perot, enabled the Democrats to retake the White House for the first time in twelve years. "The Economy, Stupid," or some variation thereof, has since become a familiar phrase in language of campaign politics. *See also* Campaign of 1992.

Suggested Readings: James W. Ceaser and Andrew Busch, *Upside Down and Inside Out: The 1992 Elections and American Politics* (Lanham, MD: Rowman & Littlefield, 1993); Michael Nelson, *The Elections of 1992* (Washington, DC: Congressional Quarterly Press, 1993).

Jackson, Andrew

See Campaign of 1824; Campaign of 1828; Campaign of 1832.

"Jackson and Reform"

In the aftermath of the alleged "corrupt bargain" of 1824, the supporters of Andrew Jackson viewed the **Campaign of 1828** as a crusade against an entrenched political establishment. Jackson's campaign used the slogan, "Jackson and Reform," to emphasize his support for greater democracy in American politics. Jackson was depicted as a champion of the "common man" while incumbent President John Quincy Adams was accused of serving only the wealthy and the cultured elite.

As a consequence of these deep divisions the campaign of 1828 turned into a referendum on democracy versus plutocracy (rule by the wealth). *See also* Campaign of 1824.

Suggested Reading: Robert V. Remini, *The Election of Andrew Jackson* (Philadelphia: Lippincott, 1963).

"Jackson Forever: Go the Whole Hog"

"Jackson Forever: Go the Whole Hog" was a slogan used by the supporters of President Andrew Jackson's 1832 reelection campaign. During an era when the vast majority of Americans worked the land for a living, the hog symbolized financial security.

While the National Republican Party attacked Jackson for attempting to destroy the nation's democratic form of government, Jackson responded with a campaign emphasizing his resolute defense of the common man. The slogan "Jackson Forever, Go the Whole Hog," emphasized Jackson's leadership in securing economic prosperity for the common man. Average Americans, so the slogan implies, had money to purchase a whole hog. During the Van Buren campaign four years later Democrats again made use of the allusion with the slogan "Going the Whole Hog." *See also* Campaign of 1832.

Suggested Reading: Samuel Rhea Gammon, *The Presidential Campaign of 1832* (Baltimore: Johns Hopkins Press, 1922).

"Jefferson, the Friend of the People"

Supporters of Vice President Thomas Jefferson touted their candidate as "Jefferson, the Friend of the People" during the campaign of 1800 in an attempt to portray the Sage of Monticello as a defender of the "Spirit of '76" against the aristocratic Federalists led by President John Adams.

Throughout the campaign, the Republican Press and Jefferson charged Adams with allegedly depriving Americans of their civil liberties in the wake of the successful passage of the Alien and Sedition Acts. The Jeffersonians also attacked the Federalists for ignoring the concerns of average Americans and favoring the interests of a small number of wealthy Americans. Additionally, the Jeffersonian faction was seen as friendly to the principles of the French Revolution, while the Federalists regarded events in France to be little more than anarchic mob violence against an ancient civilization. The lines were drawn by the Republican faction perception between Jefferson and democracy and the Federalists and autocracy. *See also* Campaign of 1800.

Suggested Readings: Gary Holbrook-DeFeo, "The Election of 1800: Alexander Hamilton and the Death of the Federalist Party." *New England Journal of History* 49 (Winter 1993), pp. 26–40; Bernard Weisberger, *America Afire: Jefferson, Adams, and the Revolutionary Election of 1800* (New York: William Morrow, 2000).

Jefferson, Thomas

See Campaign of 1800; Campaign of 1804.

Johnson, Lyndon

See Campaign of 1964.

Jordan, Hamilton (1945–)

Hamilton Jordan served as Jimmy Carter's presidential campaign advisor and White House chief of staff, 1979–1981 and later as campaign advisor to Ross Perot in 1992.

In 1972, Jordan, a close aide and friend of Carter, then governor of Georgia, developed a blueprint for winning the White House. In the wake of Watergate, Democrats made considerable gains in the 1974 off-year congressional elections. Between November 1974 and late 1976, Jordan promoted Carter, positioning him as a Washington outsider and a moderate Democrat.

Jordan devised a strategy whereby Carter entered the little-known Iowa caucus prior to the more famous New Hampshire primary. Busloads of Carter supporters traveled from Georgia to Iowa. Surprisingly Carter won in Iowa, gaining free media coverage of his incipient campaign and boosting his chances in New Hampshire where he would go on to win again. Victory in the Florida primary followed. Jordan's strategy produced the early victories that led to Carter's nomination and eventual election.

Interestingly, Jordan and the Carter campaign greatly underestimated the ability of the Republican Party and incumbent President Gerald Ford to recover from the Watergate scandal. Although the Carter ticket left the convention with a huge lead in the polls, by Election Day his lead had evaporated despite a strong showing in the presidential debates. But Carter won in a close race, and Jordan served as White House chief of staff.

Twelve years later, Texas billionaire, Ross Perot, hired Jordan and Republican political consultant Edward Rollins to manage his independent presidential campaign. However, Perot's partnership with Jordan and Rollins did not last as both men left the unpredictable and idiosyncratic Perot in mid-summer. *See also* Campaign of 1976.

Suggested Readings: Patrick Anderson, *Electing Jimmy Carter: The Campaign of 1976* (Baton Rouge: Louisiana State University Press, 1994); John W. Mashek and Scot Lehigh, "Perot Hires Former Managers for Reagan, Carter; Texan Says New Aides Won't Be 'Handlers'," *Boston Globe*, June 4, 1992, p. 1.

"Keep Cool with Coolidge"

A New Englander with an impeccable reputation, Calvin Coolidge quickly gained the respect of the nation upon his assumption of office following the death of President Warren Harding in 1823, and he was subsequently nominated by the Republican Party to run for president in 1924. Coolidge inherited a corrupt administration hampered by the infamous **Teapot Dome Scandal**. Additionally, a Red Scare and progressive political movements stirred the political waters with suspicion and controversy. Through it all, Coolidge demonstrated a remarkably even temperament, dealing fairly and judiciously with Harding's scandal, remaining unflappable during panic over Bolshevism, and unmoved by the more extreme proposals from progressive activists. Coolidge "kept his cool," thus the voters were advised to "Keep Cool with Coolidge" in 1924. *See also* Campaign of 1924.

Suggested Readings: Burl Noggle, *Teapot Dome: Oil and Politics in the 1920s* (Baton Rouge: Louisiana State University Press, 1962); "Calvin Coolidge: 30th President of the United States," Calvin Coolidge Memorial Foundation, http://www.calvin-coolidge.org.

"Keep the Ball Rolling"

During the wild and woolly campaign of 1840 supporters of Whig nominee, General William Henry Harrison would roll a large ball, at times 10 to 12 feet in diameter and composed of twine, leather, paper, or tin across long distances, even moving from town to town while chanting or singing campaign slogans and songs. It is believed that the phrase "to keep the ball rolling" originates here. *See also* Campaign of 1840.

Suggested Reading: Robert Gray Gunderson, *The Log-Cabin Campaign* (Lexington: University of Kentucky Press, 1957).

Kennedy, John F.

See Campaign of 1960.

Kennedy, Robert

See Campaign of 1968.

King, Larry (1933–)

Famed talk show host Larry King was born in Brooklyn, New York, in 1933. Through 1978, King worked in Miami, Florida, as a disc jockey, talk radio host, and freelance writer. In 1978, the Mutual Radio Network hired King to host a national phone-in talk and interview show. By 1994, some 365 stations carried the King show. In 1983, the Post-Newsweek company hired King to host a 90-minute syndicated talk show. Even though the show failed, Ted Turner, the founder of the Cable News Network (CNN), hired King to host an evening interview/talk show. Over time, *Larry King Live* became a popular forum for celebrities and political figures.

During the **Campaign of 1992**, King played a major role in the candidacy of Texas billionaire Ross Perot. From January of 1992 through the early spring, Perot used King's show to attack the policies of both the Democratic and Republican parties. Perot also used King's show to build a groundswell for an independent candidacy.

In the aftermath of the 1992 presidential campaign, King's show became a mandatory stop for potential presidential candidates. Some in the media have criticized King for avoiding tough questions when interviewing politicians. Despite the criticism, King has established himself as an important and popular vehicle for prospective presidential candidates. *See also* Media Event; News Talk Coverage.

Suggested Readings: Larry King and Rabbi Irwin Katsof, *Anything Goes! What I Learned from Pundits, Politicians, and Presidents* (New York: Warner Books, 2000); Howard Kurtz, "A Debate by Any Other Name . . . Bush, Clinton Try to Regain Spotlight in Back-to-Back CNN Appearance," *Washington Post*, June 5, 1992, A12.

King, Rufus

See Campaign of 1816.

"Korea, Communism, Corruption"

"Korea, Communism, Corruption" was a slogan used by Republicans during the **Campaign of 1952** and designed to place the blame on President Truman and the Democrats for the continued stalemate in the Korean War, the global spread of communism, and alleged corruption within the current administration.

From the outset, the Eisenhower campaign blamed Truman for the Korean quagmire, a move that carried credibility given Ike's record of military command. Additionally, Truman's policy of containment in dealing with communism was viewed by critics as potentially dangerous, bordering on appeasement. In particular, the Republican platform blamed the Truman administration for the communist takeover of China and for allowing communists and "fellow travelers" to serve in high government positions.

Weary of office, Truman elected not to run in 1952, the Democrats turning to

Adlai Stevenson as their new champion. Hence the Truman record, for good or ill, was a less-effective target for Republican broadsides. Thus the real impact of the "Korea, Communism and Corruption" slogan remains somewhat in doubt. As a national hero, General Eisenhower was already immensely popular across party lines, and enjoyed a natural advantage with or without sloganeering. **"I Like Ike"** remains a more memorable slogan owing to Eisenhower's popularity with the general public.

In response, Stevenson avoided directly attacking Eisenhower. Instead, Democrats reminded voters that it was their party that led the nation out of the Great Depression and through World War II, and that Republicans would always remain cozy with big business and indifferent to the concerns of America's workers.

Suggested Reading: Andrew J. Dunar, *The Truman Scandals and the Politics of Morality* (Columbia: University of Missouri Press, 1984).

Landon, Alfred F.

See Campaign of 1936.

Larry King Live

See King, Larry.

"Laughing at Agnew" Campaign Ad

The **Campaign of 1968** was one of the most tumultuous in American history, marked by a controversial war, assassination of beloved public figures, student unrest, race riots, and brutality at the Democratic Convention in Chicago that summer.

In the midst of this social turmoil, Maryland governor Spiro Agnew, a comparatively obscure Republican conservative, was tapped by Richard Nixon to serve as his running mate against the Democratic ticket led by current vice president Hubert Humphrey with Maine senator Edmund Muskie serving in the second spot. Agnew gleefully assumed the role of "hatchet man," attacking Democrats for leading the nation into moral dissolution at home and weakness abroad. Agnew was shrill in his complaint, leaving Nixon the luxury of remaining above the fray, and drawing campaign flack from the Democrats to himself.

The Humphrey campaign took the bait, comparing the more distinguished Muskie to the comic Agnew. A television spot, now known as the "Laughing at Agnew" ad, broadcast the name of "Agnew" in bold letters across the top of the screen. Below viewers read the remainder of the caption, "for Vice President?" while uncontrolled laughter cascaded throughout.

With the recent assassinations that stained the 1960s in blood, Humphrey's handlers argued that the man who "was a heartbeat away" from the presidency needed to be a statesman, not a clownish hatchet man. The ad implied that a vote for Nixon was a vote for Agnew, sheer folly in violent times that had recently seen a president fall to assassination.

Suggested Reading: Theodore White, *The Making of the President, 1968* (New York: Atheneum Publishers, 1968).

Law and Order Issue

From the ratification of the Constitution through the early twentieth century, presidential campaigns rarely focused on law and order issues. Law enforcement was considered a state and local issue. The situation changed with the 1919 ratification of the Eighteenth Amendment that gave Congress the authority to regulate the consumption of alcohol, and pursuant to that end the subsequent passage of the Volstead Act. To enforce the Volstead Act, Congress established within the Department of the Treasury a new Bureau of Prohibition.

Between 1920 and the repeal of prohibition in 1933, the nation experienced a major crime wave caused largely by violations of the Volstead Act. The Bureau of Prohibition and the Federal Bureau of Investigation (FBI) along with state and local police agencies were overwhelmed by the scope and violence of the crime wave.

Along with the rise in gangster violence in the 1920s and 1930s, the nation suffered an increased number of lynching crimes targeting primarily African Americans throughout the South. The Ku Klux Klan was experiencing a revival throughout the country, drawing the efforts of the FBI in an attempt to quell the Klan movement. Repeal of the Eighteenth Amendment solved the rum-running problem, but it was the FBI that effectively shut down the Klan.

Stunned by the frequency of political assassinations during the 1960s, the American public became painfully aware of a new kind of seemingly random violence darkening American culture. Additionally, the 1960s were also rocked by increased urban violence. Crime was on the rise in urban areas, and riots rocked America's cities, one of the worst occurring in the Watts section of Los Angeles during the summer of 1965. In the aftermath of the Watts riot, Congress poured hundreds of millions of dollars into urban areas to combat poverty, create jobs, and build new housing. Then in March 1968, the assassination of civil rights leader Martin Luther King Jr. triggered riots in a number of cities, fueling concern over the state of America's cities.

Urban rioting was only one aspect of the violent 1960s. As the antiwar movement intensified, physical violence between the police and protestors became more common. The smell of tear gas was becoming a familiar odor in some cities and college campuses.

For the first time in American history, law and order became a major presidential campaign issue in the summer of 1968. Republicans accused Democrats of being "soft on crime." **"This Time Vote Like Your Whole World Depended On It"** became one of the favorite slogans of the Republican campaign of Richard Nixon. The Nixon campaign also blamed the rising crime rate on Supreme Court decisions, claiming that the decisions protected criminals while rendering law-abiding citizens defenseless.

In April 1972, President Richard Nixon congratulates Washington, D.C. police officers for their help in achieving a decline in the crime rate for the nation's capital. © Nixon Presidential Materials Staff/National Archives.

After Nixon's 1968 victory over Humphrey, law and order became a recurring **hot button** or **wedge issue** in presidential campaigns. In 1972 and 1976 candidates battled over gun control and the death penalty. Republican Party platforms strongly opposed new restrictions on the rights of Americans to own handguns used for self-defense. In contrast, Democratic platforms supported new restrictions on the sale and possession of handguns. Equally important, the Republican Party strongly supported restoring the right of the states to impose the death penalty while liberal elements of the Democratic Party strongly opposed the death penalty.

Through the 1980s, the Republican Party continued to use law and order as a wedge issue to attract suburban and working-class voters. The 1980 Republican platform endorsed the use of the death penalty to deter criminal activity and the 1984 platform promised sentencing reform to force serious offenders to serve lengthier sentences. Democratic platforms proposed new restrictions on the production and sale of handguns as a solution to some violent crimes.

In 1988, as they did twenty years earlier, Republicans made particularly effective use of the law and order issue. Facing a post-convention bump in the polls favoring Democratic candidate Michael Dukakis, the Republican campaign of the elder Bush launched **negative** or **attack ads** depicting Dukakis as easy on criminals. The ads implicitly blamed Dukakis for a rape committed by convicted murderer **Willie Horton** while on prison furlough. The Horton ad attempted to reinforce the perception that the Democrats were thoughtless bleeding hearts on the issue of crime. Although the Horton ad flirted with racist imagery, the ads were effective. Law and order played a significant role in the defeat of Dukakis.

In 1992 "New Democrat" Bill Clinton moved the Democratic Party to the center by assuming a more conservative posture on a number of law and order positions. Clinton especially expressed his support for the death penalty and proposed devoting federal funds for the deployment of thousands of new police officers on city streets. Clinton's tactical decision on crime helped promote his definition of a New Democrat, and worked in his favor against his opponents in 1992.

Owing to a significant drop in the crime rate nationwide, issues related to law and order did not influence the campaigns of 1996 and 2000.

See also Campaign of 1968; Campaign of 1980; Campaign of 1992.

Suggested Readings: Douglas Jehl, "Bush Attacks Hollywood's 'Sick' Anti-Police Themes," *Los Angeles Times*, June 30, 1991, p. A1; David E. Rovella, "Bush and Gore Seeking More Law and Order, Though Crime Is Way Down, Willie Horton Looms Large," *National Law Journal*, October 2, 2000, p. A1.

"Leadership for the 60s"

Facing Vice President Richard Nixon in the summer of 1960, the campaign of the youthful Democratic nominee, John F. Kennedy, anticipated an indictment of his alleged lack of experience, particularly when compared to the record of an incumbent vice president. As a result, the Kennedy campaign needed to convince voters that despite Kennedy's young age he could lead the nation during a time of continuing Cold War tensions with the Soviet Union and Communist China. The Kennedy-Johnson ticket faced Republican presidential nominee, Vice President Richard Nixon and Henry Cabot Lodge, the Republican's vice presidential nominee who sought to turn the campaign into a referendum on the international experience of the Republican and Democratic tickets.

To counter the expected Republican strategy, the Kennedy campaign emphasized Kennedy's experience as a PT boat commander in the South Pacific during World War II. After a Japanese destroyer rammed and sunk PT-109, a wounded Kennedy heroically led the survivors to safety and eventual rescue. The Kennedy campaign believed that Kennedy's reputation as a war hero would help to persuade voters that Kennedy had the maturity and experience to take on the responsibilities of the Oval Office. The Kennedy campaign also argued that a new decade needed new and vibrant leadership, and would benefit from his youthful "vigor." The slogan "Leadership for the 60s" provided the Kennedy campaign a simple and succinct way of positioning Kennedy as a member of a new generation prepared to take on the challenges of a new decade. *See also* Campaign of 1960.

Suggested Reading: Theodore White, *The Making of the President, 1960* (New York: Atheneum Publishers, 1961).

"Learn to Say President Willkie"

"Learn to Say President Willkie" served as a humorous slogan used by the 1940 presidential election campaign of Wendell Willkie to downplay his underdog status while facing the unprecedented attempt of incumbent President Franklin Roosevelt to run for a third term. The nation was facing crisis abroad, and Roosevelt projected the aura of seasoned leadership in the face of the menace of fascism and imperialism.

Willkie had become the favorite of Republicans for attacking Roosevelt's New Deal policies as well as for defecting from the Democratic Party. As president of Commonwealth and Southern Corporation, the largest electric utility holding company, Willkie had vigorously opposed efforts by the Tennessee Valley Authority (TVA) to transform itself from a federal agency primarily responsible for flood control to a major producer of electric power. In numerous appearances, Willkie argued the TVA and similar programs threatened to move the nation toward socialism and communism.

Instead of viewing his campaign as a hopeless undertaking, Willkie made hundreds of speeches, visited 34 states, and traveled over 30,000 miles to carry his crusade against the New Deal to the American people. Other than attacking the New Deal, Willkie and his fellow Republicans argued that if the American people elected Roosevelt to a third term, a dictatorship would follow. The Willkie campaign hoped the third-term issue would hit a responsive chord. Willkie also accused Roosevelt of attempting to get the country involved in another foreign war. A strong isolationist sentiment common at the time gave Willkie some hope.

Toward the end of the campaign, a number of well-respected political observers believed that Willkie had a chance to win, but Roosevelt beat back Willkie's challenge. Despite Willkie's loss, his campaign gained the respect of the American people. After the United States entered World War II, Willkie worked to unite the nation in the war effort and traveled to a number of countries at the request of his friend, President Roosevelt. *See also* Campaign of 1940.

Suggested Readings: Warren Moscow, *Roosevelt and Willkie* (Englewood Cliffs, NJ: Prentice-Hall, 1968); Herbert S. Parmet and Marie B. Hecht, *Never Again: A President Runs For a Third Term* (New York: Macmillan, 1968).

"Let the People Rule"

A populist slogan crafted by William Jennings Bryan, the 1908 Democratic presidential nominee, "Let the People Rule" was an effort to depict the Republican Party as the party of large and powerful corporations while Democrats were defenders of America's workers. The slogan implied that powerful special interests made national policy leaving average Americans without an effective voice.

Much like the platform adopted by the Democratic Party in 1896, the 1908 platform condemned Republicans for accepting large campaign contributions from major corporations and generally favoring the interests of the wealthy. Besides attacking abuses associated with Republican rule, the Democratic platform called for more vigorous enforcement of antitrust laws, increased powers for the Interstate Commerce Commission, the adoption of a personal income tax, a ban on corporate campaign contributions and restrictions on the power of the courts to issue injunctions against labor unrest. The platform asked, "Shall the people rule?" claiming "[this is] the overshadowing issue which manifests itself in all the questions now under discussion." During the 1908 campaign, Bryan supporters modified the platform question "Shall the people rule?" into the campaign slogan, "Let the People Rule."

Despite Democratic criticism that the Republican Party favored wealth, progressive Republicans led by outgoing President Theodore Roosevelt had established a strong record of opposing large trusts and pursuing social reform policies. Roosevelt used his strong progressive record in his efforts on behalf of Republican nominee William Howard Taft, causing problems for the Bryan campaign by stealing away some of the Democrat's populist thunder. Consequently the majority of progressive voters trusted Taft to continue Roosevelt's policies. *See also* Campaign of 1908.

Suggested Reading: John Milton Cooper, *Pivotal Decades, the United States, 1900–1920* (New York: Norton, 1990).

"Let's Get America Moving Again"

"Let's Get America Moving Again" appeared as a slogan of the 1960 presidential campaign of John F. Kennedy, the Democratic presidential nominee, implying that the country was stagnating under older Republican leadership.

A sluggish economy had significantly slowed the creation of new jobs. After Sputnik, many Americans believed that the Soviet Union had surpassed the United States in the area of science and technology. Although President Eisenhower and Vice President Richard Nixon, the Republican nominee, denied serious economic problems and assured the public that American science was sound, the slogan "Let's Get America Moving Again" successfully emphasized Kennedy as the youthful, forward-looking candidate of change right for the coming new decade. *See also* Campaign of 1960.

Suggested Reading: Theodore White, *The Making of the President, 1960* (New York: Atheneum Publishers, 1961).

"Liberty, Equality and Fraternity, Universal Amnesty and Impartial Suffrage"

In the 1872 contest between incumbent President Grant and Horace Greeley, the "Liberty, Equality and Fraternity, Universal Amnesty and Impartial Suffrage" slogan highlighted Greeley's controversial position on amnesty for and the restoration of citizenship rights to former Confederate loyalists.

Greeley, running on behalf of both Democrats and the Liberal Republican faction that had recently split from the main party, placed the amnesty issue as a priority during his campaign. "Impartial suffrage" was also promised to those former rebels currently denied voting rights. This was a particularly incendiary issue in the South as many white Southerners bristled at federal protection of voting rights for the freed slaves while prominent white leaders were deprived of their votes. Combining their agenda with the famous motto of the French Revolution—"Liberty, Equality, Fraternity," the Greeley campaign attempted to depict their efforts as defiantly democratic in the contest against the corrupt Grant administration friendly to the carpetbaggers.

Greeley proved to be an easy target for Republican counterattacks. Grant won the election, and Congress granted amnesty to former Confederates without Greeley. *See also* Campaign of 1872; "Greeley & Brown—Amnesty."

Suggested Readings: William Harlan Hale, *Horace Greeley: Voice of the People* (New York: Harper, 1950); Erik Lunde, *Horace Greeley* (Boston: Twayne, 1981).

"Life Begins in '40"

After eight years of Democratic government in the 1930s, the Republican Party believed it had a legitimate opportunity to take back the White House. For followers of youthful candidate Wendell Willkie, a strident critic of the New Deal, life would begin again in 1940 after eight years of the Democrats and their allegedly quasi-socialistic programs. *See also* Campaign of 1940; "Learn to Say President Willkie."

Suggested Readings: Warren Moscow, *Roosevelt and Willkie* (Englewood Cliffs, NJ: Prentice-Hall, 1968); Herbert S. Parmet and Marie B. Hecht, *Never Again: A President Runs for a Third Term* (New York: Macmillan, 1968).

Lincoln, Abraham

See Campaign of 1860; Campaign of 1864.

Literature Drop

Modern presidential campaigns spend millions of dollars identifying voters most likely to vote for their candidates. Besides using phone banks to get these supporters to the polls, campaigns often rely on local party workers and volunteers to deliver campaign literature directly to the homes of prospective voters. Literature drops are considered a major component of so-called **ground wars**. *See also* Get-Out-the-Vote Programs.

Suggested Reading: Thomas Oliphant, "Street by Street in a Few Key States," *Boston Globe*, October 29, 2000, p. E-7.

Locofoco

Beginning in the early to mid-1830s the Democratic Party was split into conservative and radical wings, the former supportive of banks, corporate interests, and tied to Tammany Hall, the latter virulently anti-bank, against paper currency, critical of monopolies, and generally regarded as egalitarian. During the New York state party convention at Tammany Hall in 1835, angry conservatives stalked out after a particularly violent disagreement over candidates, extinguishing the gaslights that illuminated the hall as they departed. The "Equal Righters" or radicals that remained in the hall struck their locofoco matches to shed the light needed to cast their votes. Reporters from the *Enquirer* and *New York Courier*, referring to the event, described the Equal Righters as "Locofocos," the name, initially a pejorative to describe the radicals, would evolve to denote any radical, progressive, or anti-establishment faction within an established party. *See also* Campaign of 1836.

Suggested Reading: Paul F. Boller Jr., *Presidential Campaigns* (New York: Oxford University Press, 1996).

"Log Cabin and Hard Cider"

William Henry Harrison's presidential **Campaign of 1840** produced two of America's more famous political slogans, the alliterative **"Tippecanoe and Tyler Too"** and "Log Cabin and Hard Cider," the latter attempting to project images of Harrison's presumed humble origins. Whig leaders knew that the political career of Andrew Jackson, built on a combination of heroism in war and populist appeal, had set a new standard for "common man" campaigns. To this end, Whigs depicted their own General Harrison as war hero and man of the people. This included implying that Harrison had lived in a log cabin and enjoyed drinking hard cider.

In fact, Harrison was from a wealthy Virginia family and had lived only briefly in a log cabin while newly married. He actually resided in a large mansion on a plantation supported by slaves. But the log cabin image stuck, and was widely effective in contrasting Harrison to the seemingly blue-blooded Martin Van Buren. Additionally, a Democratic newspaper allegedly suggested that if the country gave Harrison a barrel of hard cider he would happily live out his days in a log cabin in front of a fire. Instead of taking offense at the remark, a Harrison supporter used the slur to create the "log cabin and hard cider" slogan, further building Harrison's image as a man of the people.

Through the remainder of the campaign, Harrison supporters used the "log cabin and hard cider" slogan to build grassroots support for the Harrison/Tyler ticket. The Whig Party made effective use of log-cabin songbooks, newspapers, and **paraphernalia** to emphasize Harrison's affinity with the common man.

To the dismay of Van Buren and the Democrats, the voters were taken in by the **hoopla** and ignored the issues as well as Van Buren's considerable qualifications. The Democratic Platform included substantive issues of great import, but the "log cabin and hard cider" hoopla overshadowed any attempt to address policy, and helped to sweep Harrison and Tyler into office.

Equally important, the success of Harrison's "Log Cabin and Hard Cider" campaign represented a major turning point in presidential campaigns. The need to appeal to a growing number of voters would force presidential campaigns to devote much more time and energy using hoopla, sloganeering, and boosterism to mobilize supporters and sell candidates to the undecided. For this reason many political historians believe that the **Campaign of 1840** constituted a revolution in American presidential politics.

Suggested Reading: Robert Gray Gunderson, *The Log-Cabin Campaign* (Westport, CT: Greenwood Press, 1977).

"Ma, Ma, Where's My Pa?"

One of the dirtiest campaigns in political memory, the campaign of 1884 generated the mean-spirited attack on Grover Cleveland that produced the mocking slogan, "Ma, Ma Where's My Pa?"

Appearing in September 1884 in *The Judge*, this cartoon attacks Democratic candidate Grover Cleveland for fathering a child out of wedlock. Courtesy of Library of Congress.

The 1884 campaign promised to be a close race. Democrats had regained much of their support throughout the country, and were especially strong in the South where the Republican Party had been frustrated by the disenfranchisement of loyal African American voters. In desperation, mudslinging rather than issues defined the campaign. The Republican candidate, James Blaine, was particularly vulnerable given a checkered past marked by public scandal. Cleveland's record of public service, however, was untainted, but indiscretions in his private life made him vulnerable to scandal mongering.

Blaine supporters uncovered an allegation that Cleveland had fathered a child out of wedlock. In July 1884, the Buffalo *Evening Telegraph* published a story revealing Cleveland's intimate relationship with a Buffalo widow, Maria Halpin during the 1870s. The relationship allegedly produced a child. Questions about Cleveland's paternity lingered, but Cleveland accepted financial responsibility for the child, born in 1874. After Mrs. Halpin suffered an emotional collapse, Cleveland arranged for the private adoption of the child. At all turns Cleveland diffused the issue by accepting full responsibility for the child and for his own actions. Despite the embarrassment to Cleveland, historians generally agree that the paternity allegation did not do serious damage to Cleveland's campaign. Blaine's own past and his blundering mishandling of an anti-Catholic slur handed Cleveland victory on Election Day.

Throughout the campaign Republican loyalists taunted Cleveland supporters with "Ma Ma, where's my Pa?" After Cleveland won, Cleveland supporters answered the taunt, "Gone to the White House Ha Ha Ha." *See also* Campaign of 1884; Rum, Romanism and Rebellion.

Suggested Reading: Mark Wahlgren Summers, *Rum, Romanism & Rebellion: The Making of a President, 1884* (Chapel Hill: University of North Carolina Press, 2000).

Madison, James

See Campaign of 1808; Campaign of 1812.

"Madly for Adlai"

Adlai Stevenson, Democratic nominee for president in 1952, faced the unenviable task of campaigning against a beloved war hero, General Dwight D. Eisenhower, the GOP nominee. While Republicans averred their preference through the slogan "I Like Ike," Stevenson's supporters attempted to ratchet up the emotion by responding that they were decidedly "Madly for Adlai."

Throughout the campaign, Stevenson attempted to remind Americans of the progress the American people had made under Democratic leadership. But the Democrats realized that they had little chance to defeat Eisenhower unless they could build enthusiasm for the Stevenson candidacy. However Stevenson seemed less appealing to many Americans, especially contrasted against Eisenhower and incumbent Democrat and outgoing President Harry Truman. To many Democrats, Stevenson came across as an intellectual who had little connection to middle America. Stevenson's campaign worked hard to overcome this widely held perception. The use of the slogan "Madly for Adlai" represented an example of this appeal. It was to no avail; Eisenhower defeated Stevenson in two separate contests, 1952 and 1956. *See also* Campaign of 1952.

Suggested Reading: Kenneth W. Thompson, ed., *Lessons From Defeated Presidential Candidates* (Lanham, MD: University Press of America, 1994).

"Man from Appomattox"

"Man from Appomattox" was a slogan used by the followers of Ulysses S. Grant, the 1868 Republican presidential nominee, to remind voters of Grant's service as commander of Union forces during the Civil War. General Robert E. Lee surrendered his Confederate forces to Grant at Appomattox courthouse.

After suffering a prolonged confrontation between Radical Republicans in Congress and President Andrew Johnson over issues involving Reconstruction policy, the Republican Party sought new, moderate, yet noteworthy leadership to replace the immense void left by the 1865 assassination of Abraham Lincoln. Johnson had been impeached, and while his presidency was saved by one vote in the Senate, Johnson was no longer a viable Republican leader. Republicans looked to Grant for new leadership. Radical Republicans concluded that Grant would not interfere with their Reconstruction program, and they successfully lobbied for his nomination. To face the celebrated Grant, Democrats nominated New York governor Horatio Seymour.

To take full advantage of Grant's popularity, the Republican Party used a number of slogans to remind voters of Grant's crucial role in the Union's victory. The "Man From Appomattox" was an example of one of these slogans. By focusing on Grant's Civil War record, the Republican Party also hoped to divert the atten-

Nominated by the Republicans in 1868, General Ulysses S. Grant was called the "Man from Appomattox" to remind voters of his distinguished Civil War service. © National Archives.

tion of voters from the growing controversy over Reconstruction. Northern Republicans, especially the Radicals, were strict in their approach to the defeated South. Conservative Republicans and Democrats sympathized with southern sentiments regarding northern oppression and complaints over the federal government's support of the freed slaves. Grant's campaign was designed to promote the warrior, not the Reconstructionist. The strategy worked, the Man from Appomattox won handily. *See also* Campaign of 1868.

Suggested Readings: Charles H. Coleman, *The Election of 1868: The Democratic Effort to Regain Control* (New York: Octagon, 1971, c. 1933); Brooks D. Simpson, *Let Us Have Peace: Ulysses S. Grant and the Politics of War and Reconstruction, 1861–1868* (Chapel Hill: University of North Carolina Press, 1991).

"Man of Destiny"

A slogan used by supporters of Grover Cleveland, the 1884 Democratic presidential nominee, to help build a bandwagon for his election. With almost religious fervor, Democrats saw Cleveland as the best hope to end government corruption that had become commonplace under Republican administrations since President Grant. That the GOP nominated James G. Blaine, notorious for influence peddling and his role in corrupt railroad deals only helped to amplify Cleveland's destiny as a champion tilting against corruption.

To discredit the "Man of Destiny," Blaine's supporters caused scandal by spreading stories about improprieties in Cleveland's private life. The **bloody shirt** was also trotted out for the waving. But neither tactic worked, Cleveland's close election proved that he was indeed a "Man of Destiny." *See also* Campaign of 1884.

To build support for the election of Grover Cleveland, their 1884 presidential candidate, the Democrats christened him the "man of destiny." Courtesy of Library of Congress.

Suggested Reading: Mark Wahlgren Summers, *Rum, Romanism & Rebellion: The Making of the President, 1884* (Chapel Hill: University of North Carolina Press, 2000).

"Man of the People"

Anticipating populist appeals that would become still more pronounced in the next century, Virginia aristocrat and Renaissance man, Thomas Jefferson, ran his 1804 reelection campaign on the claim that he was a "Man of the People."

Jefferson faced Federalist Charles Cotesworth Pinckney and a disorganized Federalist Party. At the height of his popularity, Jefferson needed little to deflect the challenge. But the "Man of the People" slogan remains noteworthy owing to the contrast between the Jeffersonian Republicans, widely regarded as the more democratic faction, and the Federalists, who were often perceived, not always fairly, as part of the elite. But it was Jefferson who was a true elite, a "natural" aristocrat, but also a successful campaigner who anticipated the rhetoric of the Jacksonians by two decades. *See also* Campaign of 1804.

Suggested Reading: Eugene H. Roseboom, *A History of Presidential Elections* (New York: Macmillan 1964).

"The Man Who Made Us Proud Again"

Facing almost certain impeachment by the House of Representatives and probable conviction by the Senate, President Richard Nixon chose resignation, and Gerald R. Ford became the nation's 38th president. Ford immediately resolved to restore integrity to the tainted White House, thus prompting the use of the slogan, "The Man Who Made Us Proud Again," during the 1976 campaign. But Ford's rep-

President Gerald Ford issues a pardon to his predecessor, Richard M. Nixon, on September 8, 1974. © Gerald R. Ford Library/National Archives.

utation was questioned upon his decision to issue a preemptive "full, free, and absolute pardon" of former president Nixon, triggering a firestorm of criticism. Additionally, Ford's opponent, Democrat Jimmy Carter, emphasized the integrity issue, and with more convincing results owing to his status as a political outsider. Carter thus stole Ford's thunder, building an early lead in the post-convention.

To reduce Carter's lead, the Ford campaign argued that Ford had already restored trust in government in the aftermath of the Watergate scandal through his strong leadership. "The Man Who Made Us Proud Again" slogan reflected this theme. Ford did manage to close Carter's lead, but not sufficiently to secure victory. Jimmy Carter won the battle over political integrity. *See also* Campaign of 1976.

Suggested Readings: Malcolm D. MacDougall, *We Almost Made It* (New York: Crown, 1977); Jules Witcover, *Marathon: The Pursuit of the Presidency, 1972–1976* (New York: Viking Press, 1977).

Manifest Destiny

Westward expansion became a major political issue in the 1840s. Advocates of Manifest Destiny argued that it was the rightful fate of the United States to expand the nation's territory to fill the natural boundaries marking the continent. Besides raising the prospect of military conflict with Mexico to the South and British Canada to the North, expansionist pressure exacerbated the slavery issue. New states meant new debates over slavery.

After Texas broke from Mexico in 1836, it sought annexation to the United States. To the great disappointment of Texas, President Martin Van Buren declined to actively support annexation fearing that admission of Texas as a slave state would reignite the slavery controversy. In 1844, President John Tyler negotiated an annexation treaty with Texas, sending it to the Senate for ratification where it met opposition. The Senate's decision not to ratify sent the issue to the voters, and to the campaign for president in 1844.

As the front-runner for the 1844 Democratic presidential nomination, Van Buren made a strategic decision to oppose the annexation of Texas. The decision turned out to be a major mistake as Democrats strongly supported the annexation of Texas. When the Democratic National Convention met at Baltimore in May 1844, Van Buren no longer had a lock on the presidential nomination. After the convention deadlocked, the party turned to dark horse candidate James K. Polk. Rejecting Van Buren's anti-annexation position, the Democratic platform expressed support for the reoccupation of Oregon and the annexation of Texas.

The Whig Party had earlier nominated Henry Clay as their presidential candidate. And the new Liberty Party nominated James G. Birney, executive secretary of the American Anti-Slavery Society of New York, as their presidential candidate. Polk went on to defeat Clay by a margin of 170 to 105 electoral votes.

The election of Polk significantly strengthened the hands of the supporters of westward expansion. After Polk's election, supporters of expansion made effective use of the "Fifty-four Forty or Fight" slogan. The slogan referred to the efforts to set the Northwest border of the United States at the 54th parallel. Subsequent negotiations with Britain led to the border between Canada and the Oregon territory at the 48th parallel. Of much greater importance, between 1846 and 1848 Polk conducted a war with Mexico. In the aftermath of the war, the United States gained possession of California and vast areas of the Southwest.

Manifest Destiny, imagined as Liberty's march across the continent, entered the lexicon of American political culture. But Van Buren's fears were soon realized. With Texas and the newly conquered territories, the slavery controversy burned steadily until it consumed the entire political landscape, leading ultimately to Civil War. *See also* Imperialism.

Suggested Readings: Robert Walter Johannsen, Sam W. Haynes, and Christopher Morris, *Manifest Destiny and Empire: American Antebellum Expansion* (College Station: Texas A & M University Press, 1997); Anders Stephanson, *Manifest Destiny: American Expansionism and the Empire of Right* (New York: Hill and Wong, 1995).

McClellan, George B.

See Campaign of 1864.

McGovern, George

See Campaign of 1972.

McKinley, William J.

See Campaign of 1896; Campaign of 1900.

Media Advisor

See Media Consultant.

Media Consultant

Television entered the realm of presidential politics during the **Campaign of 1952**, both parties soon realizing that an effective use of the new medium was vital to winning elections. Campaign managers naturally turned to New York's Madison Avenue advertising industry for new ways to deliver their candidate's messages.

From the early 1920s through the early 1950s, radio had already evolved into a major campaign tool. Campaigns frequently purchased half-hour broadcast blocks on the networks. This format was followed in the initial days of television campaigning, but it was soon learned that only the most loyal supporters of a candidate would watch a 30-minute campaign talk. To hold the attention of viewers, campaigns began to supplement 30-minute programs with brief spots of 30 to 60 seconds. Political commentators quickly compared these spot ads to commercials produced by ad agencies, criticizing these ads for the mercenary way in which a candidate was "sold" in the same way advertisers promote toilet tissue or cereal. Despite this criticism the spot ad had become a campaign staple by 1956. As a result, it became necessary to hire media experts to oversee the development of campaign spots and to make decisions regarding a campaign's media budget.

The influence of television on national politics went far beyond the use of television spot ads. By the early 1960s, television had become the most important source of news for the average American. Prior to the television revolution, the vast majority of Americans had relied upon newspapers for in-depth campaign coverage. Candidates and campaign managers soon learned that television news coverage had an immediate effect on public opinions and perceptions. By the decade's end, managing news coverage became a priority of serious campaigns. Burned by his experience with the media during the 1960 contest, Richard Nixon's 1968 campaign limited press access to Nixon to carefully staged campaign events.

The late 1980s and early 1990s saw a further expansion of campaign media operations. In contrast to the 1988 campaign of Michael Dukakis, Bill Clinton's 1992 campaign installed a sophisticated media operation enabling quick response to Republican attacks as well as to effectively spin campaign events to their advantage. *See also* Campaign Manager.

Suggested Readings: Robert W. Friedenberg, *Communication Consultants in Political Campaigns: Ballot Box Warriors* (Westport, CT: Praeger, 1997); Dennis W. Johnson, *No Place For Amateurs: How Political Consultants are Reshaping American Democracy* (New York: Routledge, 2001); Howard Kurtz, "The Refocused Democrat; When Media Adviser Mark McKinnon Met George W. Bush, Something Just Clicked," *Washington Post*, October 13, 1999, p. C1; James A. Thurber, *Campaign Warriors: The Role of Political Consultants in Elections* (Washington, DC: Brookings Institution Press, 2000).

Media Event

In addition to spending tens of millions of dollars on paid televised advertising, campaigns devote considerable time and energy staging media events. With the advent of network nightly news broadcasts during the 1960s, presidential campaigns learned that they could reach millions of potential voters without having to buy expensive spot ads.

In 1968 Republican candidate, Richard Nixon conducted the first presidential campaign to take full advantage of **free media**. The Nixon campaign staged hundreds of carefully planned events to maximize television news coverage. Rarely, did the Nixon campaign permit reporters to question Nixon regarding his stance on controversial issues. This strategy played a significant role in Nixon's political comeback and ushered in a new era of sophisticated media event planning and coverage.

Criticism of carefully staged presidential campaigns reached its peak in response to excessive attention devoted to inflated issues such as the Pledge of Allegiance and the Massachusetts prison furlough program during the **Campaign of 1988**. *See also* Earned Media; Photo Opportunity.

Suggested Readings: Shanto Iyengar, *Is Anyone Responsible? How Television Frames Political Issues* (Chicago: University of Chicago Press, 1991); Matthew D. McCubbins, *Under the Watchful Eye: Managing Presidential Campaigns in the Television Era* (Washington, DC: CQ Press, 1992); Martin Schram, *The Great American Video Game: Presidential Politics in the Television Age* (New York: Morrow, 1987).

"Mess in Washington"

After two decades away from the White House, Republicans entered the 1952 contest enjoying the rare advantage of not facing culpability for problems of mismanagement and the inevitable corruption that accompanies sustained holding of power. Such was the case when Republican candidate Dwight Eisenhower promised to "clean up the mess in Washington" in the wake of recent scandals plaguing the Democratic administration of Harry Truman.

From 1950 through 1952 the Truman administration suffered a series of ethics controversies that focused undesirable media attention upon a number of federal agencies and high officials. Allegations involved influence peddling in several agencies, but it was a Bureau of Internal Revenue scandal that proved to be most damaging to the sitting administration as well as to Adlai Stevenson, the 1952 Democratic nominee.

Early in 1951, reports surfaced that government investigations had uncovered instances of bureau employees demanding large payments from delinquent taxpayers to avoid criminal prosecution. The investigation also uncovered allegations that bureau employees used their positions to dodge their own taxes. The allegations sent shock waves throughout the nation. Despite the fact that the Truman White House moved rapidly to reform the operation of the Bureau of Internal Revenue, the Republican Party made effective use of the scandal throughout the presidential campaign of 1952.

"Cleaning up the mess in Washington" has since become a familiar theme in presidential campaigning, particularly for candidates cultivating the image of the outsider. Jimmy Carter, Ronald Reagan, Bill Clinton, and Ross Perot all stepped into this role. *See also* Campaign of 1952; "Korea, Communism, Corruption."

Suggested Reading: Andrew J. Dunar, *The Truman Scandals and the Politics of Morality* (Columbia: University of Missouri Press, 1984).

"Millions for Defense, But Not One Cent for Tribute"

Responding to the infamous XYZ affair, an alleged attempt by French officials to bribe American diplomats hoping to expedite the negotiations, South Carolina Federalist Charles Pinckney exhorted the current administration of John Adams to hold to virtue, protesting "No, not a sixpence!" Soon this phrase was embellished into the more lyrical, "Millions for defense, but not one cent for tribute!" When Pinckney found himself running for president against incumbent Thomas Jefferson, this slogan was the best he had to offer. *See also* Campaign of 1800.

Suggested Reading: Alexander DeConde, *The Quasi-War: The Politics and Diplomacy of the Undeclared War with France, 1797–1801* (New York: Scribner, 1996).

"Millions for Freedom, Not One Cent for Slavery"

Supporters of Abraham Lincoln's 1860 campaign modified the famous slogan, **"Millions for Defense, But Not One Cent for Tribute,"** adapting it to address the critical issue of the day: "Millions for Freedom, Not One Cent for Slavery."

While Lincoln and the Republicans regarded slavery to be a great evil, they did not argue for its immediate abolition where it existed, hoping for its natural extinction. But this extinction depended on containing slavery by preventing its spread into the new western territories. *See also* Campaign of 1860; "Freedom, Freemen and Fremont."

Suggested Readings: Harry Jaffa, *A New Birth of Freedom: Abraham Lincoln and the Coming Civil War* (Lanham, MD: Rowman & Littlefield, 2000); George Harmon Knoles, *The Crisis of the Union, 1860–1861* (Baton Rouge: Louisiana State University Press, 1965).

Mitchell, John (1913–1988)

John Mitchell was attorney general of the United States from 1969 to 1972 under President Richard Nixon and Chairman of Nixon's Committee to Re-elect the President (CREEP) from 1972 to 1973.

From early 1973 through 1975, John Mitchell became one of the central figures in the Watergate scandal that led to the August 1974 resignation of President Richard Nixon. John Mitchell managed Nixon's 1968 election campaign, then regarded as a model of campaign management skill and professionalism. He then served as attorney general of the United States from 1969 to 1972.

At the beginning of 1972, Mitchell left the Justice Department to become the chairman of Nixon's Committee to Re-elect the President. By the early spring of 1973 sustained requests for a presidential appointment of a special prosecutor to investigate allegations of illegal campaign practices increasingly pressured Nixon, leading to the creation of the Senate Watergate Committee, which began investigative hearings in the summer.

The subsequent investigations that revealed the scope of the Watergate scandal and cover-up ultimately forced Nixon's resignation and led to the prosecution of a number of officials formerly associated with either the White House or CREEP, including John Mitchell. Although Mitchell denied any involvement with the break-in, a federal jury convicted Mitchell of obstruction of justice and perjury. Mitchell subsequently spent time at a federal correctional facility. Released on parole on January 20, 1979, John Mitchell died of a heart attack on November 9, 1988. *See also* Campaign of 1968; Campaign of 1972.

Suggested Reading: *Current Biography*, January 1989: p. 62 (Obituary).

Mudslinging

Mudslinging, also known as a "smear" or "smear tactic" is a personal attack usually impugning the character of the opposition in a political campaign while avoiding a discussion of the substantive issues and policy differences. Mudslinging or smear campaigns are perennial features of American politics, and have been since the **Campaign of 1800**.

Some of the more infamous mudslinging smears involve accusations of adultery

Rachel Jackson, the wife of President Andrew Jackson and the victim of one of the most infamous mudslinging attacks in U.S. history. Courtesy of Library of Congress.

against Thomas Jefferson, murder and bigamy against Andrew Jackson, gambling and consorting with prostitutes against Henry Clay, drunkenness against Franklin Pierce and Ulysses Grant, treasonous allegations against Horace Greeley, and the paternity of a child born out of wedlock against Grover Cleveland.

Mudslinging remains a feature of American politics at all levels, but contrary to contemporary perceptions, smear tactics in politics today pale in comparison to the vicious attacks of the nineteenth century. *See also* Campaign of 1828; Campaign of 1884; Campaign of 1992; Campaign of 1996; Character Issue; Feeding Frenzy.

Suggested Readings: Bruce L. Felknor, *Political Mischief, Smear, Sabotage, and Reform in U.S. Elections* (Westport, CT: Praeger, 1992); Jack Mitchell, *How to Get Elected: An Anecdotal History of Mudslinging, Redbaiting, Vote Stealing and Dirty Tricks in American Politics* (New York: St. Martin's Press, 1992); Shelly Ross, *Fall from Grace: Sex, Scandal, and Corruption in American Politics from 1702 to the Present* (New York: Ballantine Books, 1988).

Mulligan Letters

James G. Blaine, a powerful leader in the Republican Party during the two decades following the Civil War, was embroiled in scandal through much of his political career. Critics alleged that, in 1869, Blaine used his position as speaker of the House of Representatives to obtain a federal land grant for the Little Rock & Fort Smith Railroad. In return, a Boston stockbroker and officer of the railroad allowed Blaine to sell securities of the railroad and to pocket large commissions from the sales. Then, when the value of the securities plunged to nearly zero, an officer of the Union and Pacific Railroad allegedly bought back the securities from Blaine and his friends at a price far above market value.

During the spring of 1876, the alleged transactions came to the surface when a former bookkeeper for the Maine Railroad, James Mulligan, testified to the existence of letters from Blaine detailing the transactions. Most damaging to Blaine, Cleveland supporters came into possession of one note from Blaine to Fisher that included a notation "Burn this letter" at the bottom of the note. After retrieving the letter, Blaine went to the floor of the House and denied all of the allegations.

Blaine's defense of his integrity was effective, rallying to his defense his Republican supporters. Blaine then resigned his seat in the House to accept an appointment to the Senate, and the House committee subsequently dropped the investigation. *See also* Campaign of 1884.

Suggested Reading: Mark Wahlgren Summers, *Rum, Romanism & Rebellion: The Making of a President, 1884* (Chapel Hill: University of North Carolina Press, 2000).

"My Hat Is in the Ring"

After some hesitation because of previous promises not to run for a third term, former President Theodore Roosevelt announced his intention to lead the new Progressive Party rebellion against incumbent President William Howard Taft with typical bravado. "My hat is in the ring!" TR proclaimed in February 1912, "The fight is on and I am stripped to the buff!" "Throwing one's hat in the ring" has since become a clichéd expression for new candidates delighting in their enthusiasm; "stripping to the buff" seems to have faded from popular use. *See also* Campaign of 1912.

Suggested Readings: Francis Broderik, *Progressivism at Risk: Electing a President in 1912* (Westport, CT: Greenwood Press, 1989); Frank K. Kelly, *The Fight for the White House: The Story of 1912* (New York: Crowell, 1964).

Myers, Dee Dee (1961–)

During the summer of 1991, Arkansas governor Bill Clinton announced his intention to run for the Democratic presidential nomination. Rated as a heavy underdog at the beginning of the Democratic primary campaign, Clinton assembled a young and fearless campaign staff. Clinton selected Dee Dee Myers as press secretary for his campaign.

Even at the young age of 29, Myers came to the Clinton campaign with years of experience in various national and state campaigns, including the campaigns of Vice President Walter Mondale in 1984 and Governor Michael Dukakis in 1988.

Margaret Jane Myers was born in Quonset Point, Rhode Island, on September 1, 1961. After graduating from Santa Clara University with a degree in political science Myers volunteered for Mondale's campaign.

Shortly after being named to the position of national press secretary of the Clinton campaign, Myers found herself forced to defend Bill Clinton from charges of marital infidelity and draft dodging. After Clinton's nomination and election, Myers was appointed to the position of White House press secretary, working closely with another campaign aide, White House communications director **George Stephanopoulos.** Under the arrangement, Myers and Stephanopoulos divided responsibility for briefing the press. At the end of 1994, Myers left the White House.

In May 1995, Myers became the co-host of CNBC's Washington, D.C.–based "Equal Time." During April 1995, Myers left the show as a result of a decision to move to Los Angeles, California. She currently works as a contributing editor to *Vanity Fair*. *See also* Campaign of 1992.

Suggested Readings: *Current Biography Yearbook 1994*, pp. 392–394 (New York: H.W. Wilson); Ann Devroy, "Departing Myers Recalls Jubilation, Tribulations; The Price of These Two Years Was High'," *Washington Post*, December 23, 1994, p. A1. Kim Masters, "In the Cage with the Beast; White House Spokeswoman Dee Dee Myers, Whipping the Press into Shape," *Washington Post*, April 1, 1993, p. D1.

Nast, Thomas (1840–1902)

Thomas Nast grew up in New York after immigrating with his family to the United States from Pfalz, Germany. The periods shortly prior to and after the Civil War saw the birth of a number of illustrated newspapers such as *Harper's*

Weekly, *New York Illustrated News*, and *Leslie's Weekly*. At the age of fifteen, Nast went to work for *Leslie's Weekly* as an illustrator. Nast used his artistic talents to illustrate widespread corruption on the part of New York City's Tammany Hall. During the Civil War, Nast covered the Civil War for *Harper's Weekly* and other illustrated newspapers. After the war, Nast resumed coverage of New York City and national politics.

In the years following the Civil War, Nast waged a campaign against New York City's Democratic political machine. Headquartered in Tammany Hall, the machine strengthened its grip on city jobs, franchises, and contracts.

Although Nast focused primarily on city politics, Nast also drew a large number of illustrations related to presidential campaigns. Nast reserved some of his strongest attacks for Horace Greeley, the 1872 nominee of both the Liberal Republicans and the Democrats. Throughout the post–Civil War years, Nast remained a strong supporter of the Republican Party and harsh critic of Democrats. Historians credit Nast with creating the Republican elephant and the Democratic donkey.

Between 1885 and 1900 Nast made a series of poor business decisions that pushed him deep into debt. In 1902, President Theodore Roosevelt appointed Nast as consul general to Ecuador. After developing a fever, Nast died in Guayaquil, Ecuador, in December 1902. *See also* Political Cartoons.

Suggested Readings: Lynda Pflueger, *Thomas Nast: Political Cartoonist* (Berkeley Heights, NJ: Enslow Publishers, 2000); Thomas Nast Home Page, http://www.buffnet.net/~starmist/nast/main.htm.

National Bank Issue

Late in 1790, Secretary of the Treasury Alexander Hamilton proposed the establishment of a Bank of the United States. Hamilton's recommendation touched off a controversy over whether the Constitution gave Congress the authority to charter a national bank. After receiving the support of President George Washington, Hamilton successfully persuaded Congress to establish the bank. The Bank of the United States began to operate in December of 1791. Early in 1811, Congress refused to renew the charter of the Bank of the United States on the same constitutional grounds. But by 1817 financial hardship created by the War of 1812 led Congress to approve the establishment of the Second National Bank. Through the 1820s the bank remained uncontroversial.

The situation changed dramatically with the 1832 election of Andrew Jackson, who was hostile to banks in general. Historians attribute Jackson's hostility to personal experience. Jackson suffered financial difficulties during his youth, and he blamed "rag tag banks" for his bad fortune. Many of Jackson's friends and supporters had also lost deposits when Tennessee banks failed. The bank controversy was exacerbated by deep enmity between Jackson and the bank's president, Nicholas Biddle.

Knowing this, Jackson's opponents in the Senate, led by Kentucky's Henry Clay, urged the bank to seek a renewal of its charter in an effort to force an election year showdown with their rival. With the approach of the 1832 presidential election, Clay saw the National Bank issue as a way to mobilize national support against a second Jackson term. Early in July 1832, Jackson vetoed the charter renewal bill on the same constitutional grounds opponents claimed decades earlier.

Clay received the nomination for the National Republicans that summer, and promptly used Jackson's bank veto to accuse him of monarchical delusions. But the strategy grossly backfired; instead of damaging Jackson's reelection chances, the bank battle helped Jackson position himself as the defender of the common man against powerful special interests. Jackson went on to win reelection in a landslide.

In the aftermath of his 1832 victory, Jackson carried through with his threat, allowing the bank to expire. By early 1935, Jackson succeeded in paying off the remaining national debt without the bank. *See also* Campaign of 1832.

Suggested Readings: Robert V. Remini, *Andrew Jackson and the Bank War: A Study in the Growth of Presidential Power* (New York: Norton, 1967); George Taylor, *Jackson versus Biddle: The Struggle over the Second Bank of the United States* (Boston: Heath, 1949).

Nativism Issue

Up through the 1820s anti-immigration sentiment played a relatively minor role in presidential politics, the anti-Masonry movement of the early 1930s being the first political effort reflecting such sentiment. The anti-Masonry movement grew out of the mysterious disappearance of former Mason, William Morgan of New York in 1826. Prior to his disappearance, Morgan had angered Masons for writing a book critical of the fraternal organization. A political movement erupted against "Masonic conspiracies," leading to the formation of the Anti-Masonic Party in 1831. Meeting in Baltimore of that year, the Anti-Masonic Party became the first party in American history to hold a national nominating convention. Former Mason William Wirt of Maryland was nominated as their candidate for president. The Anti-Masonic Party primarily targeted the Masons, but also held anti-immigration positions and xenophobic sentiments.

The "Know-Nothing" movement initiated a second anti-immigration wave during the 1850s. This new wave of xenophobia targeted Catholic immigrants in particular, rather than Masons. When asked about their membership in the movement, many members elusively responded that they "knew nothing" about such a movement.

In February 1856 a group of Know-Nothings formed the American Party, holding their national convention in Philadelphia. The platform supported a preference for all local, state, and federal government positions for native-born citizens. In addition, the platform advocated requiring individuals to reside within the United States for 21 years before being eligible for citizenship. The American Party nominated former president Millard Fillmore for president in 1856. They particularly targeted Republican candidate John C. Fremont, accusing him of being a crypto-Catholic in spite of his membership in an Episcopalian congregation. Ironically, Fillmore won the electoral votes of Maryland, a state with a Catholic heritage. Know-Nothing's lost steam, attention, and members as the slavery issue further polarized the nation.

In the aftermath of the Civil War and Reconstruction, the Ku Klux Klan, which used terror and violence to hatefully repress African Americans while also holding bitter and bigoted anti-Catholic, anti-Semitic, anti-immigrant, and anti-Northern prejudices, emerged as a particularly militant voice of nativism throughout the South, enjoying considerable power by the election of 1880. Klan repression of the black vote in the South inadvertently helped the first election of Grover Cleveland, no friend of the Klan, in 1884.

Besides the rise of the Ku Klux Klan, the post–Civil War era was marred by prejudice against new immigrants from China. Faced with a shortage of laborers during the 1860s, the Central Pacific Railroad brought thousands of Chinese workers to the West to build their section of the transcontinental railroad. Most of these workers decided to remain in the United States upon completion of the railroad, settling in Northern California, particularly in San Francisco, causing a new wave of xenophobia now targeted against Asians. Both parties included planks in their 1876 platforms calling for restrictions imposed on Chinese immigration. These planks were kept in subsequent platforms of both parties, culminating in the passage by Congress of the Chinese Exclusion Act of 1882 accompanied by Alien Contract labor laws in 1885 and 1887.

Between 1890 and the beginning of World War I, millions of new immigrants arrived in the United States from Europe, particularly from Italy. Following the end of the war, the nation again experienced a surge in immigration that stimulated still another nativist movement. Chinese exclusion was again emphasized in the platforms of both parties in 1920. Additionally, the Republican platform supported the enactment of legislation sharply limiting the number of immigrants entering the United States. The growing nativism movement helped to persuade Congress to pass the Immigration Acts of 1921 and 1924 that established a quota system for future immigrants.

In the late twentieth century, the rising number of illegal immigrants from Latin America produced in some public quarters renewed insistence on tighter immigration policy and enforcement. Republican conservative and failed candidate Pat Buchanan held provocative opinions regarding the nature and composition of recent immigration. Surprisingly, the current presidency of the younger Bush has indicated a more tolerant disposition to illegal immigrants.

Suggested Readings: Tyler G. Anbinder, *Nativism & Slavery: The Northern Know Nothings and the Politics of the 1850s* (Cambridge: Oxford University Press, 1995); Chip Berlet and Matthew Nemiroff Lyons, *Right-Wing Populism in America* (New York: Guilford Press, 2000).

Negative Advertising

See Negative Campaigning.

Negative Campaigning

Throughout the history of American political campaigns partisans have used a wide variety of methods to criticize their opponents, attacking both their positions on issues as well as impugning personal character. But only recently has negative campaigning itself come under attack.

A number of different types of campaign ads or messages fall within the broad definition of negative campaigning. Through the second half of the twentieth century, the flip-flop ad became a staple of presidential campaigns. For example, during the contest of 1964 the campaign of incumbent President Lyndon Johnson made extensive use of an ad that attacked Republican nominee Barry Goldwater for changing his positions on a variety of issues. Prior to receiving the Republican presidential nomination, Goldwater had supported making Social Security contributions voluntary and for pulling the United States out of the United Nations. After receiving the nomination, Goldwater changed his position on these key issues.

In addition to the flip-flop ads, campaigns have made frequent use since the 1950s of ads highlighting policy failure, designed to weaken public confidence in the opposition. The 1988 campaign of Republican George Bush made frequent and effective use of dramatic negative ads attacking alleged policy failures of Massachusetts governor and Democratic candidate Michael Dukakis. The Bush campaign's infamous **Willie Horton ad** along with the **Boston Harbor** spot and the laughable tank ad remain memorable to this day as examples of aggressive negative campaigning.

Critics of negative campaigning argue that the increased use of negative ads has produced a general public disaffection with politics and politicians. On the other hand, defenders of negative campaigning argue that there is nothing inappropriate about a political campaign revealing the questionable record of an opponent or the inconsistent positions taken by a candidate. According to this line of reasoning, negative campaigning provides voters essential information about a candidate's shortcomings.

In the aftermath of the negativism of the 1988 contest, many newspapers, magazines, and television news operations instituted **ad watches** in an effort to provide voters information regarding the accuracy of campaign ads. *See also* Attack Ads, Opposition Research.

Suggested Readings: John Franzen, "Common Sense on Going Negative," *Campaigns & Elections* 16 (September 1995) p. 67; Robert Guskind, "Airborne Attacks," *National Journal* 31 (October 1992) pp. 2477–2482; William G. Mayer, "In Defense of Negative Campaigning," *Political Science Quarterly*, 111 (Fall 1996) pp. 437–450.

Negative Slogans

See Negative Campaigning.

"Never Swap Horses in Mid-Stream"

"Never swap horses" was a popular saying used as a slogan by President Franklin Roosevelt's 1944 reelection campaign. During the first wartime election since the **Campaign of 1864**, Roosevelt echoed a slogan from the first campaign of Abraham Lincoln to emphasize the need for continuity during crisis.

Roosevelt was easily nominated at the Democratic convention. Instead of supporting the renomination of New Deal stalwart Vice President Henry Wallace, Roosevelt asked the convention to nominate Missouri senator Harry S. Truman for vice president. Truman had established himself as an expert on war production and procurement and had conducted a series of investigations into allegations of wartime profiteering.

Because of his fragile health, Roosevelt largely left it up to campaign **surrogates** to press the Democratic message of economic and social progress and effective prosecution of the war. Roosevelt did continue to make heavy use of radio to remain in touch with the public, discussing issues surrounding the war and the economy.

Challenging the Great Man, the Republican Party selected New York governor Thomas E. Dewey. Dewey criticized Roosevelt's fourth-term ambitions, insinuated that the president was an authoritarian, and claimed that he could more efficiently see the war to a quick conclusion. The American public rejected these arguments and reelected Roosevelt for a fourth consecutive term. *See also* Campaign of 1944.

Suggested Reading: Robert A. Divine, *Foreign Policy and U.S. Presidential Elections, 1940–1948* (New York: New Viewpoints, 1974).

"A New Deal"

In late June 1932, Democratic delegates traveled to Chicago to select a presidential nominee to challenge the increasingly unpopular President Herbert Hoover, whose administration was reeling from the deepening effects of the Great Depression. New York governor Franklin Roosevelt arrived at the convention with a clear majority of Democratic delegates. On the fourth ballot, Roosevelt won the required two-thirds majority to take the nomination. Breaking with tradition, Roosevelt flew the next day from Albany, New York, to Chicago to accept the Democratic nomination in person.

Roosevelt's acceptance speech laid out a vision that called for the federal government to assume primary responsibility for helping tens of millions of Americans deal with the misery caused by the Great Depression. Roosevelt promised federal aid to help farmers cope with falling prices for farm products, public works programs to help put Americans back to work, and relief programs for the destitute and indigent. Roosevelt also pledged to support the repeal of prohibition.

The most memorable part of Roosevelt's speech was his pledge to provide a new deal for the American people. Throughout the **Campaign of 1932**, Democrats rallied behind Roosevelt's New Deal pledge even though the candidate was somewhat vague about the exact steps a Roosevelt administration would take to pull the nation out of the Great Depression. Roosevelt won the 1932 presidential election in a landslide that also put the Democratic Party in firm control of Congress. After being sworn into office, Franklin Roosevelt and Congress moved quickly to establish numerous new federal programs directed at pulling the nation out of the Great Depression.

Not unexpectedly, the **Campaign of 1936** saw the Republican Party and the

Republican presidential nominee, Alfred Landon, attack the New Deal for placing the power to manage all parts of the national economy into the hands of federal bureaucrats. Big business contributed heavily to the Republican Party in an effort to unseat Roosevelt. To counter big business, the 1936 Roosevelt campaign depended heavily upon the support of organized labor. Despite the efforts by the Republican Party to convince Americans that the New Deal threatened the nation's democratic institutions, Roosevelt won over 60 percent of the popular vote.

In the **Campaign of 1940**, the Republican Party and its presidential nominee, Wendell Willkie, again based their electoral strategy on attacking Roosevelt and his New Deal policies. Willkie and the Republicans also used Roosevelt's decision to seek an unprecedented third term to claim that the president's reelection would start the United States down the road to a totalitarian form of government. The **"No Third Term,"** issue along with continued attacks on the New Deal, put Roosevelt and his policies on the defensive. In the end, Roosevelt prevailed by touting the successes of the New Deal, maintaining the strong support of organized labor, and emphasizing his administration's efforts to provide for a strong national defense. Much like the campaign of 1936, voters in 1940 decided to stay the course with Roosevelt instead of taking a chance with untested Republican leadership.

Bringing World War II to a successful conclusion became the overriding issue of the **Campaign of 1944** despite continuing efforts by the Republican Party and Republican presidential nominee, Thomas E. Dewey, to turn the election into a referendum on Roosevelt's New Deal policies and programs. Like voters in the two previous presidential elections, a clear majority of voters again opted to cast their lot with Roosevelt instead of changing course in the midst of World War II.

Suggested Readings: Keith Anderson, *The Creation of a Democratic Majority, 1928–1936* (Chicago: University of Chicago Press, 1979); Michael Weber, *New Deal Fat Cats: Business, Labor, and Campaign Finance in the 1936 Presidential Election* (New York: Fordham University Press, 2000).

"A New Deal, A New Day"

In 1932 Democratic candidate Franklin Roosevelt, breaking precedent by accepting his nomination with a personal appearance at the convention, established his vision in an acceptance speech promising aid to farmers, public works programs, relief for the indigent, and repeal of the Eighteenth Amendment among other measures. "I pledge to you," Roosevelt averred, "I pledge myself, to a new deal for the American people. Let us all here assembled constitute ourselves prophets of a new order of competence and courage." From this passage the upbeat phrase "A New Deal" became the campaign's most effective slogan and would go on to define the Roosevelt presidency with succinct accuracy. *See also* Campaign of 1932.

Suggested Readings: Keith Anderson, *The Creation of a Democratic Majority, 1928–1936* (Chicago: University of Chicago Press, 1979); Elliot Rosen, *Hoover, Roosevelt, and the Brains Trust: From Depression to New Deal* (New York: Columbia University Press, 1977).

New Freedom

Woodrow Wilson, the 1912 Democratic nominee, used the "New Freedom" slogan to promise policies designed to guarantee every American the opportunity to share in the nation's economic prosperity.

Prior to the selection of Wilson at the Democratic convention, the delegates approved a progressive platform calling for lower tariffs, a constitutional amendment for the adoption of a personal income tax, limiting a president to a single term, and prohibiting corporate contributions to campaign funds. Wilson articulated his "New Freedom," which called for government intervention to free American business and industry from the anticompetitive practices of monopolies and trusts.

Wilson argued that

> American industry is not free, as once it was free; the man with only a little capital is finding it harder to get into the field, more and more impossible to compete with the big fellow. Why? Because the laws of this country do not prevent the strong from crushing the weak. That is the reason, and because the strong have crushed the weak the strong dominate the industry and the economic life of this country.

Wilson, however, left unclear how he planned to protect American business and industry from the predatory practices of monopolies. But Wilson's New Freedom

President Woodrow Wilson called the progressive platform on which he ran in 1912 the New Freedom. Courtesy of Library of Congress.

served as an effective response to Theodore Roosevelt's New Nationalism, which embraced a similar progressive agenda.

However, it was not slogans or promises that gained Wilson the White House, but rather a deep split within the Republican Party between Roosevelt's Progressives and incumbent President William Howard Taft's conservative wing. *See also* Campaign of 1912; New Nationalism.

Suggested Reading: Arthur Stanley Link, *Wilson: the New Freedom* (Princeton, NJ: Princeton University Press, 1956).

New Frontier

The 1960 campaign of Democrat John F. Kennedy used the "New Frontier" phrase, taken from his nomination acceptance speech, as a slogan to appeal to the frontier spirit of Americans looking for new challenges in the decade ahead. Kennedy emphasized his faith that the American people had the ability and resolve to meet any challenge.

> "Today some would say that those struggles are all over—that all the horizons have been explored—that all the battles have been won—that there is no longer an American frontier," stated Kennedy. "But I trust that no one in this vast assemblage will agree with those sentiments. For the problems are not all solved and the battles are not all won—and we stand today on the edge of a New Frontier—the frontier of the 1960s—a frontier of unknown opportunities and perils—a frontier of unfulfilled hopes and threats," continued Kennedy. "Woodrow Wilson's New Freedom promised our nation a new political and economic framework. Franklin Roosevelt's New Deal promised security and succor to those in need. But the New Frontier of which I speak is not a set of promises—it is a set of challenges. It sums up not what I intend to offer the American people, but what I intend to ask of them. It appeals to their pride, not to their pocketbook—it holds out the promise of more sacrifice instead of more security," explained Kennedy.

By positioning himself as the candidate of change, Kennedy contrasted himself to the staid Eisenhower administration and the Republican candidate, Vice President Richard Nixon, and hoped to attract young voters dissatisfied with the status quo. During a series of televised debates, Kennedy embodied the New Frontier enthusiasm by demonstrating a mastery of the issues and exuding a youthful image that may have been the key to defeating Nixon in one of history's closest elections. *See also* Campaign of 1960.

Suggested Readings: Irving Bernstein, *Promises Kept: John F. Kennedy's New Frontier* (New York: Oxford University Press, 1991); "Address of Senator John F. Kennedy Accepting the Democratic Party Nomination for the Presidency of the United States," John F. Kennedy Library and Museum, http://www.jfklibrary.org/j071560.htm.

New Media

The term new media refers to the evolution of alternative communication technologies that provide additional coverage of presidential campaigns and new ways for campaigns to use **earned media** or **paid media** to reach potential voters. "New media" includes cable and satellite news outlets, talk radio, and Internet operations.

Through the early 1920s, Americans relied on newspapers and political parties for political information. Beginning with the **Campaign of 1924**, radio joined newspapers as both news medium and campaign tool. Fewer and fewer Americans attended large political rallies, needing only radio to follow the progress of a campaign. After World War II, television rapidly became the major source of news and campaign information. By the 1960s network television, consisting of the Columbia Broadcasting System (CBS), the National Broadcasting Company (NBC), and the American Broadcast Company (ABC), became the primary source of news for Americans.

Early in the 1980s, Ted Turner established the first 24-hour cable news network (CNN). CNN attempted to distinguish itself from the traditional media by using the latest technology to broadcast breaking stories. CNN's success helped to spawn other satellite and cable news operations. During the 1990s MSNBC and the Fox News Channel joined CNN as major new media operations.

In addition to providing traditional reporting, the new media operations experimented with innovative formats to attract viewers. Interview and call-in shows such as CNN's *Larry King Live* combined aspects of news and entertainment. Nineteen ninety-two was the breakout year for the newer networks. Candidates Bill Clinton, George Bush, and Ross Perot all made appearances on *Larry King Live* and similar programs with news talk formats. In an effort to target young voters, Bill Clinton appeared on MTV's "Rock the Vote" and answered questions about the type of underwear he wore and whether or not he had smoked pot. Clinton and Perot in particular benefited from the newer networks and the alternative formats for campaign coverage, signaling the end of the traditional Big Three dominance over broadcast news. Finally, the campaigns of 1996 and 2000 saw the internet emerge as an important source of campaign news.

Suggested Readings: Edwin Diamond, Martha McKay, and Robert Silverman, "Pop Goes Politics: New Media, Interactive Formats, and the 1992 Presidential Campaign," *American Behavioral Scientist* 37 (November/December) pp. 257–263; Steve McClellan, "Nets Seek Novel Campaign Strategies: Nightly News Casts Attempt to Generate Interest in Election Coverage," *Broadcasting & Cable*, September 30, 1996, pp. 38–40.

New Nationalism

On August 31, 1910, former president Theodore Roosevelt presented a speech in Osawatomie, Kansas that has come to be known as the "New Nationalism" speech. Coming approximately a year and a half after Roosevelt left the presidency, the speech challenged the conservative policies of Republican President William

Howard Taft. Roosevelt had supported Taft's nomination and election during the 1908 campaign.

Roosevelt devoted the majority of his speech to the defense of the progressive policies of his administration. While Roosevelt did not directly criticize Taft, he stressed the role of the national government in dealing with serious problems affecting the American people. As Roosevelt affirmed,

> The national government belongs to the whole American people, and where the whole American people are interested, that interest can be guarded effectively only by the national government. The betterment which we seek must be accomplished, I believe, mainly through the national government. The American people are right in demanding New Nationalism, without which we cannot hope to deal with new problems. The New Nationalism puts the national need before sectional and personal advantage. It is impatient of the utter confusion that results from local legislatures attempting to treat national issues as local issues. It is still impatient of the impotence, which springs from division of governmental powers, the impotence which makes it possible for local selfishness or for legal cunning, hired by wealthy special interests, to bring national activities to a deadlock. This New Nationalism regards the executive power as the steward of the public welfare. It demands of the judiciary that it shall be interested primarily in human welfare rather than in property, just as it demands that the representative body shall represent all the people rather than any one class or section of the people.

When Roosevelt split from the party to run on the Progressive ticket, the new party adopted the principles of New Nationalism in its platform, calling for: (1) Women's suffrage, (2) strict limitations on campaign contributions, (3) the establishment of a National Health Service, (4) vigorous enforcement of anti-trust laws, (5) the establishment of a social insurance program, and (6) the adoption of a graduated national income tax, among other reforms.

Despite losing the election, Roosevelt's third-party run helped to breathe new life into the progressive movement and forced Democrats to follow suit with their own progressive agenda. From 1913 through 1917, President Wilson successfully pursued progressive policies under the banner of "New Freedom" that resembled those endorsed by Roosevelt in his "New Nationalism" speech. *See also* Campaign of 1912; New Freedom.

Suggested Readings: Francis L. Broderick, *Progressivism at Risk: Electing a President in 1912* (New York: Greenwood Press, 1989); "Theodore Roosevelt: The New Nationalism," Program in Presidential Rhetoric, Texas A&M University, http://www.tamu.edu/comm/pres/speeches/trnew.html.

News Talk Coverage

Prior to the 1992 presidential campaign candidates rarely appeared on entertainment shows. Many campaign managers believed that such appearances were undignified. However the trend began to change as early as the 1968 campaign when Hubert Humphrey appeared on a youth-oriented talk show to discuss his "politics of joy" and, more incongruously, when Richard Nixon appeared on *Laugh In* to be doused by a bucket of water. In 1976 Gerald Ford, an incumbent president, added legitimacy to such events with a brief appearance on NBC's *Saturday Night Live*.

But these events were infrequent and mostly inconsequential. However, with the continuing merger of news and entertainment programming in the 1980s and early 1990s, opportunities to merge issues with entertainment soon emerged and quickly multiplied. The power of this type of hybrid programming became apparent during the winter and spring when Texas billionaire Ross Perot made several appearances on CNN's *Larry King Live*. Perot used the show to measure support for a third-party run for president. Bill Clinton and Vice President George Bush also made several appearances on *Larry King Live*.

By the start of the campaign of 1996, MSNBC and Fox News had joined CNN as major satellite news operations. As major networks such as NBC, ABC, FOX, and CBS cut back their election coverage, cable and satellite news operations increased their coverage. Throughout the 1996 campaign, representatives of the Clinton, Dole, and Perot campaigns made numerous appearances on cable and satellite news shows as well as news talk shows produced by the major networks.

By the time of the **Campaign of 2000**, candidate appearances on entertainment programs such as *The Tonight Show With Jay Leno*, *The David Letterman Show*, *Oprah* and *Regis* as well as *Larry King Live* became standard, and even expected.

Critics of the trend argue that candidates use such opportunities to repeat scripted campaign messages, to tell a few nonoffensive jokes, and to avoid answering the questions of seasoned political reporters. On the other hand, supporters of the trend argue that such appearances provide voters additional opportunities to informally evaluate candidates and their campaign messages. *See also* Campaign Manager.

Suggested Readings: Howard Fineman, "The Talk-Show Primary: How Bush and Gore Are Fighting for Oprah-Regis-Leno Audiences—Women and Young Voters Who Make a Difference. The Art of the Gabfest," *Newsweek*, October 2, 2000, p. 26; Marvin Kalb, "Too Much Talk & Not Enough Action," *Washington Journalism Review* 14, September 1992, pp. 33–35; Tom Rosensteil, *Strange Bedfellows: How Television and the Presidential Candidates Changed American Politics, 1992* (New York: Hyperion, 1993).

Newspapers

See Partisan Newspapers.

"Next Frontier"

The "Next Frontier," a slogan used by the 1988 presidential election campaign of Democrat Michael Dukakis, reflected an effort by the Dukakis campaign to resurrect the image of John Kennedy's 1960 campaign slogan, the "New Frontier."

In his July 21, 1988 acceptance speech, Dukakis made use of the phrase the

"Next Frontier" to establish a number of challenges for a Dukakis administration and the American people, including stopping proliferation of nuclear and chemical arms, bringing peace to Central America and the Middle East, and ending apartheid in South Africa. Other than detailing a number of foreign policy goals, Dukakis also used the "Next Frontier" theme to highlight his commitment to economic reform. "It's time to meet the challenge of the next American frontier — the challenge of building an economic future for America that will create good jobs at good wages for every citizen in this land, no matter who they are or where they come from or what color of their skin," stated Dukakis.

To the dismay of the Dukakis campaign, the "Next Frontier" message failed to catch the imagination of the American people. Republicans ignored policy and rather than turn the campaign into a referendum on the "Next Frontier," the campaign of Vice President George Bush, the GOP nominee, attacked Dukakis's record as governor of Massachusetts, putting the Democrats on the defensive. A series of negative **attack ads** distracted Dukakis and the voting public from the Next Frontier agenda. Furthermore, the Bush campaign effectively cast a pejorative connotation onto the term "liberal," thus using Dukakis's record of liberalism against him. Dukakis failed to respond adequately to the opposition's redefinition of liberalism for the American public. *See also* Boston Harbor Campaign Ad; Campaign of 1988; "Revolving Door" Campaign Ad.

Suggested Readings: E.J. Dionne Jr., "The Democrats in Atlanta; Dukakis Promises Competence and Daring at 'Next Frontier'; Party Ratifies Bentsen Choice," *New York Times,* July 22, 1988, p. A1; Jack Germond and Jules Witcover, *Whose Broad Stripes and Bright Stars?: The Trivial Pursuit of the Presidency, 1988* (New York: Warner Books, 1989); Peter Goldman, Tom Mathews, and the Newsweek Special Election Team, *The Quest for the Presidency, 1988* (New York: Simon & Schuster, 1989).

"Nixon's the One"

One of the simplest yet most effective slogans in recent memory, "Nixon's the One" typified the polish that characterized the candidate's successful 1968 comeback campaign. Nixon's campaign perceived weakness in the disorderly divisions experienced by the Democratic Party, and sought to convey an image of unity, cohesion, stability, and sensible leadership as a contrast to the chaotic opposition. "Nixon's the One" exuded the confidence of a candidate who promoted his abilities to serve as a unifier in tumultuous times.

With some irony, Nixon's critics used his own slogan against him as the Watergate scandal unfolded in 1973. As the investigation drew closer to the White House, Nixon's old political rivals were quick to indicate ultimate culpability with the accusation, "Nixon's the One!" *See also* Campaign of 1968; Now More Than Ever.

Suggested Readings: Lewis S. Gould, *1968: The Election That Changed America* (Chicago: Ivan R. Dee, 1993), Joe McGinniss, *The Selling of the President* (New York: Trident Press, 1969).

President Richard Nixon and his wife Pat in a motorcade during the 1968 presidential campaign. © Nixon Presidential Materials Staff/National Archives.

Nixon, Richard M.

See Campaign of 1960; Campaign of 1968; Campaign of 1972.

"No Sectionalism"

A slogan used by the 1856 campaign of Democrat James Buchanan, "No Sectionalism" promised voters that Buchanan would protect the Union.

Reflecting the continued support of the Democratic Party for the Compromise of 1850, the 1856 Democratic platform stressed that Congress lacked the authority to interfere with slavery in any state, territory, or the District of Columbia. In other words, Congress must leave it up to the residents of each state to determine the status of slavery in their states (a doctrine then known as "popular sovereignty"). Challenged by the controversial new Republican Party that was calling for a ban on the addition of any new slave states, Democrats successfully framed the race as a contest between those wanting to maintain the Union (Democrats) and those desiring its destruction (Republicans and other, smaller antislavery parties).

Although many Northerners agreed with the Republican position on slavery they feared a Republican victory would plunge the country into turmoil and possibly war. As a result, many joined with Southern Democrats to vote for fellow Northerner James Buchanan and his pledge, "No Sectionalism." *See also* Campaign of 1856.

Suggested Reading: Elbert B. Smith, *The Presidency of James Buchanan* (Lawrence: University of Kansas, 1975).

"No Third Term"

Three times in American history, controversy has been stimulated by the third term ambitions of a former president or incumbent. An unwritten two-term limit had been accepted as customary since George Washington established the precedent in 1796. Since that time opponents of three terms used the "No Third Term" slogan when Washington's precedent was threatened.

Early in 1880, Stalwart Republicans who had grown unhappy about the reform policies of Republican president, Rutherford B. Hayes, urged former two-term president Ulysses S. Grant to seek a third term as president. Making effective use of the "No Third Term" slogan, the anti-Grant forces successfully stopped the Grant bandwagon. When balloting began at the June 1880 Chicago Republican Convention, Grant fell far short of the votes needed to win the nomination. On the 48th ballot, anti-Grant forces united to nominate 48-year-old James Garfield.

In 1912, former president Theodore Roosevelt decided to seek a second full term as president at the head of the Progressive Party, popularly known as the Bull Moose Party. Because Roosevelt had assumed the presidency in 1901, after

This political cartoon attacks Ulysses S. Grant's attempt to win a third Republican nomination for president. © National Archives.

Crouching before the ghost of George Washington, Theodore Roosevelt attempts to dodge the no-third-term tradition in this political cartoon. © National Archives.

the assassination of President William McKinley, he had not served two full terms. Yet, he faced strong criticism for violating the principle of only two terms. In the 1904 election, Roosevelt promised that he would not seek reelection at the end of his term. Roosevelt went on to lose to Woodrow Wilson, the Democratic nominee.

Twenty-eight years later, incumbent President Franklin Roosevelt faced a decision whether to seek a third term. Through the first half of 1940, Roosevelt struggled over the decision to run again, fully aware of the power of the precedent. After concluding that no other Democratic candidate could both preserve the New Deal and handle the inevitability of another world war, Roosevelt accepted a "draft" at the July 1940 Democratic National Convention.

Throughout the **Campaign of 1940**, Republican candidate Wendell Willkie decried Roosevelt for breaking precedent. "No Third Term" became a Republican slogan, and Republican newspapers warned their readers that the election of Roosevelt to a third term threatened to lead the country into dictatorship. But the "no third term" argument was not well-received, forcing Republicans to turn to isolationism and criticism of Roosevelt's military preparedness and New Deal programs. Roosevelt ran on his record, and handily deflected the lively Republican charge. *See also* Campaign of 1880; Campaign of 1912; Campaign of 1940.

Suggested Readings: Steve Neal, *Dark Horse: A Biography of Wendell Willkie* (Garden City, NY: Doubleday, 1984); Herbert S. Parmet and Marie B. Hecht, *Never Again: A President Runs for a Third Term* (New York: Macmillan, 1968).

Nofziger, Lyn (1924–)

Beginning in early 1960, Lyn Nofziger served as a political consultant to a series of Republican candidates. Nofziger quickly developed a reputation as a tough and skilled political operative. In 1966, film actor and Republican activist Ronald Reagan announced his intention to seek the governorship of the state of California. Nofziger signed on as Reagan's press secretary. After Reagan's surprising victory, Nofziger accepted the position as communications director for Governor Reagan. In 1968, Nofziger turned his attention to helping Republican Richard Nixon win the presidency. From 1969 through 1974, Nofziger served as an aide in the Nixon White House.

Following Nixon's resignation in 1974, Nofziger returned to California. Within a short time Nofziger began to work for a number of organizations supporting Ronald Reagan for president in 1976. Although Reagan failed to win the 1976 nomination, Nofziger joined other California associates of the ex-governor on a successful Reagan campaign against incumbent President Jimmy Carter in 1980.

Nofziger joined Reagan's White House staff as special assistant to the president for political affairs. In his position, Nofziger served as the White House liaison with the Republican National Committee and coordinated nationwide political efforts to build public support for Reagan's agenda. In 1982 Nofziger left the White House to establish a Washington, D.C., public relations firm.

Early in January 1987, Nofziger became the subject of an influence peddling investigation related to the failure of Wedtech, a Bronx defense contractor. The investigation led to Nofziger's conviction for illegally lobbying federal officials on behalf of Wedtech, but the Federal Appeals Court overturned the conviction.

Nofziger remained in Washington and has since continued his work as a public relations and political consultant. *See also* Campaign of 1980.

Suggested Readings: George Lardner Jr., "Nofziger's Convictions Overturned; By 2-1, Conflict Law Is Ruled Ambiguous," *Washington Post*, June 28, 1989, A1; Myra MacPherson, "Ronald Reagan's Coast Artillery," *Washington Post*, June 5, 1980, D6; Howell Raines, "Nofziger Thrives on Tough Reputation," *New York Times*, June 25, 1981, p. 12.

Non-Voters

See Shrinking Electorate.

"Now More Than Ever"

A slogan used by President Richard Nixon's 1972 reelection campaign, "Now More Than Ever" highlighted the serious problems still facing the United States and emphasized Nixon's qualifications as a proven statesman and stable leader.

Nixon faced Democratic candidate George McGovern, senator from South Dakota. Strongly backed by the Vietnam antiwar movement, McGovern promised to unilaterally withdraw American troops from Vietnam if elected. McGovern also called for the shift of funds from national defense to various domestic programs. The Nixon campaign characterized McGovern's plans as reckless and much too liberal for the majority of the American people. Additionally, the Nixon campaign argued that McGovern's position on unilateral withdrawal hampered negotiations with North Vietnam to end the war.

McGovern's perceived extremism and naïveté were contrasted against the image of Nixon, the global statesman, who had completed unprecedented trips to Communist China and to the Soviet Union, resulting in the successful negotiation of a new nuclear arms control agreement. Moreover a gradual reduction in American forces in Vietnam under Nixon's policy of "Vietnamization" helped to deflate the antiwar movement. Faced with choosing between McGovern, a "loopy leftist" and Nixon, a "World Statesman," the voters were admonished that the only good choice was Nixon, "Now More than Ever."

But unknown by the American people at that time, President Nixon's paranoid campaign operatives were neck-deep in dirty tricks, illegal activities, and the elaborate cover-up that concealed the criminal ugliness behind the smooth professionalism of the Nixon effort. Early in 1973, the Watergate scandal unfolded and the cover-up unraveled, leading to Nixon's resignation in August 1974. *See also* Campaign of 1972.

Suggested Reading: Theodore White, *The Making of the President*, 1972 (New York: Atheneum Publishers, 1973).

Nullification Issue

Nullification refers to the principle that instills the states with the right to "nullify" any act of Congress that undermines the sovereignty of that particular state or that is deemed by that state to be contrary to the Constitution. The doctrine traces its conceptual roots to the Virginia and Kentucky resolutions of 1798–1799, but it was not until the 1830s and the controversies surrounding protective tariffs that nullification developed as a focus of divisive conceptual debate commanding the allegiance of regional and ideological partisans.

For years the **tariff issue** had divided Northerners and Southerners. High tariffs had eliminated the federal debt and permitted northern manufacturers to flourish, but at the cost of the imposition by Great Britain, a principal consumer of cotton and tobacco (both southern cash crops) of retaliatory tariffs on United States exports. These tariffs reduced the market for southern commodities, while simultaneously forcing Southerners to purchase higher-priced manufactured goods from Northern merchants who enjoyed reduced competition from Britain as a result of the protective tariff.

In response to the growing crisis, the South Carolina legislature passed in late 1832 a law nullifying the federal tariff within the boundaries of South Carolina.

Despite the southern roots of the current president, Andrew Jackson, he took a firm stand on the side of Union supremacy and argued that states cannot claim a nullification power. Jackson made it clear that he would use force, if necessary, to enforce the tariff laws in South Carolina. Civil War loomed until Henry Clay and newly appointed senator from South Carolina, John C. Calhoun, negotiated the compromise of 1833, which led Congress to agree to lower tariffs over the next ten years and South Carolina to repeal its nullification measure.

The nullification crisis foreshadowed the controversy over slavery that would dominate presidential politics through the 1840s and 1850s. Many Southerners believed that without the authority to nullify federal edicts, Northern agitators would ultimately pressure Congress and the federal government to eliminate slavery. *See also* Campaign of 1856; Campaign of 1860; Secession Issue.

Suggested Reading: Charles Grier Sellers, *Andrew Jackson, Nullification and the State-rights Tradition* (Chicago: Rand McNally 1963).

Off Message

The phrase "off message" refers to the failure of a presidential campaign to put forward a clear message to voters. Through the use of polls and **focus groups**, modern presidential campaigns develop a message most likely to appeal to the largest possible cross-section of voters. Campaigns then make use of **paid media**, **earned media**, and other campaign activities to deliver that message to potential voters. When a campaign finds its candidate behind in the polls it faces the choice of staying "on message" or introducing a new message in an effort to jump-start a faltering campaign.

The **Campaign of 1992** saw the "on message" strategy work particularly well for the primary and general election campaign of Arkansas governor Bill Clinton. The Clinton campaign used the slogan "It's the Economy, Stupid," to remind campaign workers to stay focused on the economy as the key issue. Despite the fact that Clinton faced allegations of marital infidelity, draft dodging, and other improprieties the Clinton campaign did not stray from its economic message. Clinton went on to defeat incumbent President George Bush, the Republican nominee, and Ross Perot, an influential third-party candidate.

In contrast, during the 2000 presidential election campaign, the campaigns of Vice President Albert Gore and Texas governor George W. Bush faced criticism from political **pundits** for jumping from message to message. Bush went from being a **"compassionate conservative"** to a "tax cut" conservative. Al Gore went from a Clinton "New Democrat" to a traditional anti–big-business progressive. *See also* Campaign of 1992; Campaign of 2000.

Suggested Readings: Ken Herman and Jena Health, "Campaign 2000: Bush Will Use Local Media to Get Message Across; Convinced That the National Press Corps Wishes Him No Good, Texas Tries New Strategy," *Atlanta Journal and Constitution*, September 17, 2000, p. 14A; Robert D. Novack, "Dole's Missing Message Helps Clinton Hold Lead," *Chicago Sun-Times*, July 7, 1996, p. 24.

"Old Fuss and Feathers"

"Old Fuss and Feathers" was a pejorative nickname attached to General Winfield Scott, the hero of the Mexican American War and the Whig Party's 1852 presidential candidate. During the war, American troops gave Scott the nickname "Old

Fuss and Feathers." Something of a dandy, Scott was known to dress in ostentatious military regalia, drawing the nickname from his own troops. Despite his military valor and capabilities, the nickname haunted him into his political career, Democrats taking particular delight in ridiculing Scott as a vain fop.

Whigs countered the criticism of Scott with their own smear, unfairly charging Democratic candidate Franklin Pierce, another veteran of the war, with cowardice in the face of battle. Pierce was also accused of drunkenness. *See also* Campaign of 1852; "First In War, First In Peace."

Suggested Readings: John Eisenhower, *Agent of Destiny: The Life and Times of General Winfield Scott* (New York: Free Press, 1997); Charles Elliott, *Winfield Scott, The Soldier and the Man* (New York: Macmillan, 1937); Ava C. Goldberg, *Men Who Lost the Presidency* (Brentwood, TN: J.M. Press, 1992).

"Old Hickory"

Throughout much of his life as a general and presidential candidate, supporters of Andrew Jackson fondly referred to him as "Old Hickory." According to legend, in 1813, Jackson's troops bestowed the name "Hickory" on Jackson after Jackson's superiors refused to provide the funds necessary to bring home Jackson's Tennessee militia. Suspicious of the reasons behind the order, finding his troops stranded but resolved not to allow his regiment to simply disband to promote a superior's ulterior motives, Jackson borrowed money to purchase food for his troops and undertook a grueling march back to Tennessee. As tough as hickory was Jackson's resolve.

Through the 1828 election campaign, supporters of Jackson used the popular nickname "Old Hickory" to rally public support for the Jackson candidacy. Jackson supporters tied hickory poles on "houses, wagons, and steamboats." Hickory clubs organized "rallies, barbecues, songfests, and other kinds of entertainment." Along with the anger associated with the 1824 election, the "Old Hickory" nickname proved remarkably effective in helping to make Jackson a popular folk hero who would stand up for the "common man" if elected president. *See also* Campaign of 1824; Campaign of 1928; Campaign of 1932.

Suggested Readings: Burke Davis, *Old Hickory: A Life of Andrew Jackson* (New York: Dial Press, 1977); Fred L. Israel, *Student's Atlas of American Presidential Elections: 1789–1996* (Washington, DC: Congressional Quarterly, Inc., 1997), p. 26.

On Message

See Off Message.

Opposition Research

Opposition research is a term that refers to the process of researching the personal background, previous statements, prior policy positions, and ideological consistency of political opponents. Many campaign scholars now associate opposition research with **negative campaigning**. Long before the creation of political consulting firms specializing in opposition research, presidential campaigns routinely studied the backgrounds of their opponents. Modern opposition research takes advantage of sophisticated information-gathering tools to collect and analyze increasingly more abundant and detailed information. Digitized archives permit researchers to use personal computers to comb through public records and newspaper archives for information regarding a candidate. If the candidate had served in some type of legislative body, researchers carefully review the candidate's voting record for controversial stands and flip-flops that involve unexplained reversals on the issues.

Critics argue that opposition research deters good candidates from running for public office and has provided campaigns with more ammunition to conduct negative attacks. Advocates argue that opposition research provides a vital public service through the dissemination of detailed information about the candidates. Experts argue that for opposition research to have a major impact on a campaign, the operation must produce accurate information, otherwise voters and journalists alike will disregard critical information.

During the **Campaign of 1988**, for example, opposition research discovered that Democratic candidate Michael Dukakis had opposed a state law that would require recitation of the Pledge of Allegiance by students in public schools. Additionally, research uncovered the controversial prison furlough program supported by the Dukakis administration in Massachusetts, leading to the infamous **Willie Horton ad**.

Suggested Readings: John Bovee, "How To Do Opposition Research on the Internet," *Campaigns & Elections* 19 (September 1998), pp. 48–51; Adam Nagourney, "Researching the Enemy: An Old Political Tool Resurfaces in a New Election," *New York Times*, April 3, 1996, p. A14; John F. Persinos, "Gotcha!" *Campaigns & Elections* 15 (August 1994), pp. 20–26.

Paid Media

The term "paid media" refers to the expenditure of either **hard money** or **soft money** to purchase campaign ads or **issue ads** to assist a presidential campaign in attempts to reach potential voters and journalists. Paid media includes television and radio spot ads broadcast over the air as well as transmitted over cable. It also covers the purchase of longer blocks of radio or television time for **infomercials** or to broadcast coverage of staged "town meetings." Paid media now includes the purchase of Internet banners or pop-ups. In addition to various types of electronic media outlets, paid media also covers the purchase of campaign ads published in newspapers, magazines, and other specialized publications.

Prior to the **Campaign of 1924**, paid media in presidential campaigns consisted primarily of purchasing ads or political announcements in newspapers and other print publications. Up through 1924, however, campaigns depended much more heavily on the distribution of campaign banners, posters, handbills, buttons, and pamphlets to mobilize supporters and communicate with new voters. The campaign of 1924 saw the first widespread use of radio by presidential candidates.

Radio provided campaigns with an effective way to reach millions of potential voters in their homes but it did drive up the cost of waging a presidential campaign.

Franklin Roosevelt made particularly effective use of radio in the presidential campaigns of 1932, 1936, 1940, and 1944. Largely because of his successful use of radio during the 1932 campaign Roosevelt instituted the **fireside chat** early in the following year as an effective means to explain his New Deal policies and programs, and later to discuss the war.

Although the first television broadcasts took place during the late 1930s, not until the **Campaign of 1952** did presidential campaigns begin to produce and pay for the broadcast of large numbers of TV ads. Initially, presidential campaigns attempted to use television the same way they had used radio by purchasing half-hour blocks of time. Campaigns soon learned that many potential voters would not sit through a half-hour talk from a presidential candidate. Taking a page out of the advertising handbook, campaigns experimented with 30-second to one-minute spot ads. The 30-second ad became a fixture of the modern presidential campaign.

The **Campaign of 1964** saw a major shift in paid media. The Johnson campaign used a large number of **negative** or **attack ads** to characterize Arizona senator Barry Goldwater, the Republican presidential nominee, as too unstable to trust with control over the nation's nuclear arsenal. Besides the famous **Daisy ad**, the Johnson campaign ran other spot ads to warn voters of the dangers associated with a Goldwater presidency.

After the campaign of 1964 presidential campaigns became increasingly reliant on spot ads. The escalating cost of paying for television campaign ads, however, forced campaigns to raise increasingly larger amounts of money to pay for costly ads. In 1971, partly in an effort to slow escalating advertisement costs, Congress passed the Federal Election Campaign Act (FECA). Amendments to the FECA law passed in 1974 and 1976, established campaign contributions for federal elections including presidential campaigns. Congress also enacted a system for the public funding of presidential elections. The law provided for the funding of presidential campaigns with federal tax dollars. If a campaign accepted public funds, however, the law prohibited the campaign from spending any more money.

The **Campaign of 1976** was the first presidential campaign paid for with federal funds. From 1976 to 1979, the Republican and Democratic parties lobbied the Federal Election Commission (FEC) to permit the parties to raise unlimited contributions for **party-building activities**. In 1979, the FEC issued a rule that permitted labor unions, corporations, and individuals to make unlimited contributions for party-building activities. FEC regulations, however, prohibited the use of soft money to pay for ads advocating or opposing a specific candidate for federal office.

Even so, both parties used millions of dollars of **soft money** contributions to pay for **issue ads** during the 1996 campaign. To avoid violating FEC regulations, the ads did not expressly mention any specific candidate. The ads, however, took clearly partisan positions on key issues or highlighted the achievements of President Bill Clinton, the Democratic nominee, and Bob Dole, the Republican nominee. During the winter and spring of 1996, the Democratic National Committee spent some $40 million on issue ads favorable to President Bill Clinton. Late in

March 2002, Congress passed legislation prohibiting national parties from raising soft money and banned special interest groups from running issue ads 30 days prior to a primary and 60 days prior to a federal general election. *See also* Targeting.

Suggested Readings: Bruce Mentzer, "A Political Media Buying Strategy for Using Cable," *Campaigns & Elections*, June 2000, pp. 82–83; Bruce Mentzer, "Banner Ads: The New Entry in Paid Political Media Plans," *Campaigns & Elections* 21, July 2000, p. 69; Steven E. Schier, "Why Campaigns Are Now Like Target Practice," *Washington Post*, October 24, 1999, p. B2.

Pamphlet

One of the more popular and effective media for political persuasion in American political history, the pamphlet became a medium of political rhetoric long before the American Revolution. Bound as small books ranging in length from a half dozen pages to 50 or more, the pamphlet was loosely stitched rather than bound as a regular book, and was intended for inexpensive, wide, and rapid dissemination.

Pamphlets remained a fixture of American political rhetoric throughout the nineteenth century, and even circulating with less frequency into the first two decades of the twentieth century. While minor parties continued to print circulars and manifestos in pamphlet form well into the twentieth century, the pamphlet became less common as a method of distributing information about candidates and issues in the major parties. Currently, major candidates prefer authorized biography, autobiography, and video to promote their image, background, and principle, the pamphlet being more commonly the device of choice at the political fringe.

Suggested Reading: Joel H. Silby, ed., *The American Party Battle: Election Campaign Pamphlets, 1828–1876* (Cambridge, MA: Harvard University Press, 1999).

Paraphernalia, Campaign

Presidential campaign paraphernalia has been a feature of American political culture since the mid-1820s. Before that, paraphernalia appeared as post-election commemorative memorabilia celebrating the achievements of the winner, but with the expansion of suffrage to a wider population base in the 1820s and 1830s and the attendant development of a more organized party apparatus, campaign products began to appear prior to the election as visual cues intended to promote a party or candidate. As electoral politics became more responsive to popular interest, paraphernalia multiplied and diversified. Political ephemera (pamphlets, broadsides, posters, handbills, sheet music), "metalets" (metal badges), ribbons, toys, and various novelties and curios all appeared fairly early in the development of major party politics in the antebellum republic.

By the 1840s, paraphernalia had become a prominent and fixed media in the tactics of campaign persuasion. The "log cabin and hard cider" myth spun around

Whig candidate General William Henry Harrison was a natural for the production of sundry campaign promotions and materials. E.C. Booze, a Philadelphia distiller, manufactured one of the more amusing and singular examples of paraphernalia in American political history. Booze packaged his whiskey in bottles blown into the shape of log cabins, labeled "Old Cabin Whiskey," and distributed the product on behalf of the Whigs and General Harrison. Thus was born a new industry driven by campaign **hoopla** and the entrepreneurial spirit. Campaign paraphernalia became a part of American political culture throughout the twentieth century, encompassing a wide variety of items from straw hats, neckties, and pennants to snuff boxes, "soap babies," toy coins, "dinner pail" lanterns, and metallic busts; the variety of paraphernalia limited only by the boundaries of entrepreneurial imagination. With the advent of television and its ever-increasing influence, tangible paraphernalia diminished as a presence in proportion to the sophistication of commercial imagery. Bumper stickers, tee shirts, and political buttons continue to proliferate during a campaign season, but some of the more novel forms of paraphernalia have become less common.

The most popular item of campaign memorabilia is the ubiquitous campaign button. The first buttons appeared in the late 1890s, and enjoyed a stylistic golden age into the early decades of the twentieth century. Campaign buttons remain to this day the most common form of paraphernalia, having generated a subculture for antique collectibles and Americana. *See also* Banners, Political; Broadside.

Suggested Readings: Roger A. Fisher, *Tippecanoe and Trinkets too: The Material Culture of American Presidential Campaigns, 1828–1984* (Urbana: University of Illinois Press, 1988); Theodore L. Hake, *Encyclopedia of Political Buttons* (New York: Dafran House, 1974); Keith Melder, *Hail to the Candidate: Presidential Campaigns from Banners to Broadcasts* (Washington, DC: Smithsonian Institution Press, 1992); Edward Segal, "History . . . Right on the Button; Presidential Merchandise and the Very Image of Campaigns Past," *Washington Post*, July 19, 1992, Outlook, 5.

Parker, Alton B.

See Campaign of 1904.

Partisan Newspapers

From the late eighteenth century through the Civil War, major political parties relied heavily on newspapers to support their presidential nominees. During this period, the vast majority of newspapers made little effort to separate political reporting from editorial content. By the 1850s, newspapers solicited printing contracts from political parties as a way to increase revenue. The printing of campaign literature constituted a major part of these printing contracts. Newspapers also understood that elected officials had the ability to direct lucrative government printing contracts to friendly newspapers.

Between the Civil War and the beginning of the twentieth century, modernized printing permitted the mass marketing of low-cost goods to the exploding American population fed by immigration. Newspaper circulation and ad revenue exploded. Major urban newspapers gradually adopted policies separating news coverage from editorial opinion. By the turn of the century, fact-based political reporting became the rule rather than the exception. From 1900 to 1920, a new generation of "muckraker" journalists focused their efforts on uncovering abuses of the public trust by government officials.

Through the first half of the twentieth century, major newspapers continued to use their editorial power to influence the political process. Powerful newspaper owners, such as William Randolph Hearst, still had the ability to make or break a prospective presidential candidate. And newspaper endorsements continued to carry considerable weight with voters. The inability to win endorsement, however, no longer meant the demise of a presidential candidacy. By 1924, radio gave political parties a new way to reach millions of potential voters in their homes.

Despite being opposed by a high number of large and small newspapers, Franklin Roosevelt won the presidential elections of 1932, 1936, 1940 and 1944. Roosevelt made heavy use of radio to blunt criticism found on the editorial pages of major newspapers. Through his years as president, tens of millions of Americans listened to Roosevelt's radio **fireside chats**.

The emergence of television after World War II further eroded the power of major newspapers in presidential campaigns. From the 1950s through the end of the century, newspaper readership dropped as increasingly larger percentages of the American public relied primarily on television and radio for news. *See also* Earned Media; Free Media; Paid Media.

Suggested Readings: Richard L. Kaplan, *Politics and the American Press: The Rise of Objectivity, 1865–1920* (Cambridge, UK, New York: Cambridge University Press, 2002); Jeffrey Pasley, *"The Tyranny of Printers": Newspapers Politics in the Early American Republic* (Charlottesville: University Press of Virginia, 2001); Mark Wahlgren Summers, *The Press Gang: Newspapers & Politics, 1865–1878* (Chapel Hill: University of North Carolina Press, 1994).

Partisan Press

See Partisan Newspapers.

Party-Building Activities

"Party-building activities" are programs established by political parties to recruit new members or muster current party members during elections. Traditional party-building activities include voter registration drives, candidate recruitment programs, and **get-out-the-vote (GOTV)** operations.

Until the passage of the Federal Election Campaign Act of 1971 (FECA) national political parties had considerable discretion to solicit funds for get-out-the-vote operations and other party-building activities. When the FECA established strict hard money contribution limits, it also closed a number of loopholes that permitted unions, corporations, and individuals to fund party-building activities.

In 1979, the Federal Election Commission (FEC) issued regulations permitting unions, corporations, and individuals to make unlimited contributions to national party committees to fund party-building activities. Through the 1970s, the Democratic and Republican parties had complained that hard money restrictions had made it impossible to fund key programs necessary to conduct traditional party-building activities.

Through the 1980s, the influx of **soft money** contributions permitted the major parties to increase their funding of voter registration and GOTV programs. By the mid-1990s, both parties began to make use of soft money contributions to fund more traditional campaign activities. Early in 1995, the Clinton White House and the Democratic National Committee (DNC) embarked on an ambitious campaign to raise tens of millions of dollars in soft money to pay for the broadcast of **issue ads** touting the achievements of the incumbent Clinton presidency, the 1996 Democratic nominee. Republicans also used soft money contributions to fund issue ads favorable to Bob Dole, their 1996 nominee.

After the 1996 campaign, both the FEC and the Department of Justice conducted lengthy investigations into allegations that the major parties violated federal law by abusing "soft money." Both the FEC and the Justice Department declined legal action regarding the soft money controversy. The **Campaign of 2000** saw both the Democratic and Republican national committees raise record amounts of soft money to fund GOTV programs and broadcast issue ads.

In late March 2002, the younger President Bush signed into law the Bipartisan Campaign Finance Reform Act of 2002. The law prohibited national party campaign committees from raising and spending unlimited amounts of soft money. The law also prohibited independent groups from paying for the broadcast of issue ads one month before a primary election and two months before a general election. However, the law did not prohibit soft money contributions at the state level for party-building activities.

Suggested Readings: Charles Babcock, "$100,000 Donations Plentiful Despite Post-Watergate Restrictions," *Washington Post*, September 22, 1988, p. A27; Howard Kurtz, "Issue Spot Touts Gore's Medicare Plan; Organization Unnamed in 'Party-Building' Ad," *Washington Post*, June 8, 2000, p. A4; Robert Suro, "Clinton Campaign Directed 'Soft Money,' Panetta Says; Outlays Were for Overall 'Democratic Strategy'," *Washington Post*, March 10, 1997, p. A04.

"Patriotism, Protection and Prosperity"

"Patriotism, Protection and Prosperity" was a slogan used by the 1896 campaign of Republican presidential nominee, William McKinley, highlighting the continued Republican support for high protective tariffs as a way to ensure and further stimulate the nation's economic prosperity. McKinley faced populist William Jennings Bryan, the Democratic presidential nominee, who strongly supported taking the nation off the gold standard as a way to revive the economy. At the 1896 Democratic convention, William Jennings Bryan easily won the 1896 nomination after he brought the convention to its feet with the now famous **"Cross of Gold"** speech. McKinley and Bryan thus turned the 1896 campaign into a referendum on national monetary policy.

Accelerated industrialization characterized the American economy in the latter third of the nineteenth century. This transformation did not benefit Midwestern farmers and Western mining interests. Falling farm prices and high railroad rates created severe financial problems for farmers. The overproduction of silver seriously depressed prices, putting thousands of miners out of work. During the late 1870s and early 1880s, the Greenback Party championed the issuance of paper money as legal tender. Other populists supported increasing the money supply by minting large quantities of silver coins. By the mid-1890s, a growing populist wing of the Democratic Party joined the growing **free silver** movement.

In the end voters rejected Bryan and free silver, persuaded by McKinley's pledge of "Patriotism, Protection and Prosperity." *See also* Campaign of 1896; Mark Hanna.

Suggested Readings: Paul W. Glad, *McKinley, Bryan, and the People* (Philadelphia: Lippincott, 1964); Stanley Llewellyn Jones, *The Presidential Election of 1896* (Madison: University of Wisconsin Press, 1964).

"Peace, Prosperity and the Public Trust"

Gerald Ford, incumbent president and the Republican nominee in 1976, used the theme of "Peace, Prosperity and the Public Trust" to convince the American people that he deserved a full term as president. Ford became president after the August 1974 resignation of President Richard M. Nixon.

Ford entered the 1976 campaign with the economy slowly recovering from the recession of 1975. On the whole, Ford's presidency showed signs of promise, yet many Americans still opposed Ford's decision to preemptively pardon Nixon. By Labor Day, Ford found himself far behind Democratic candidate Jimmy Carter in the polls.

By focusing on the recovering economy and his reputation as an honest politician helping to repair the nation in the Watergate's aftermath, Ford was able to close the gap, but not enough as Jimmy Carter narrowly won in November. *See also* Campaign of 1976.

Suggested Readings: Malcolm D. McDougall, *We Almost Made It* (New York: Crown Publishers, 1977); Jules Witcover: *Marathon: The Pursuit of the Presidency, 1972–1976* (New York: Viking Press, 1977).

"Peace without Surrender"

Through much of the 1950s, Republicans had accused Democrats of being "soft on communism." This carried over into the 1960 presidential campaign of Vice President Richard Nixon. Nixon attempted to persuade voters that he had the experience needed in a dangerous world anxiously struggling through the Cold War. The Nixon campaign used the "Peace without Surrender" slogan to reinforce their candidate's credentials while implying that the Democratic nominee, Massachusetts senator John Kennedy, lacked substantial experience. The Kennedy campaign countered with the allegation that the Republican administration had, in neglecting defense spending, allowed the Soviet Union to create a "missile gap" to the detriment of American power. Kennedy's status as a decorated war hero also emphasized his leadership potential. *See also* Campaign of 1960.

Suggested Reading: Theodore White, *The Making of the President, 1960* (New York: Atheneum Publishers, 1961).

Photo Opportunity

A phrase used to describe efforts by a presidential campaign to obtain either **free media** or **earned media** coverage of campaign events. In the course of a campaign, candidates make hundreds of appearances designed to maximize national and local media coverage. For understandable reasons, television transformed politics by giving campaigns the ability to reach many more voters than the standard campaign event covered by a newspaper's political reporter and staff photographer.

Although television permitted presidential campaigns to reach far more voters than a **campaign rally** or newspaper ad, the high cost of television spot ads forced campaigns to seek as much free media coverage as possible. By the **Campaign of 1960** the staging of campaign events to attract the maximum positive media coverage became commonplace.

Richard Nixon's 1968 and 1972 campaigns perfected the use of photo opportunities. During each campaign Nixon made numerous campaign appearances but rarely answered questions from the media. Ronald Reagan's successful 1980 and 1984 presidential campaigns relied heavily on the same strategy.

Efforts to force presidential campaigns to abandon photo-opportunity campaigns have met with only limited success. The **Campaign of 1992** led to the modification of the format established by the Commission on Presidential Debates. At least one debate would be held in which audience members would ques-

In a typical photo opportunity generated by modern presidential campaigns, President Ronald Reagan (left) and Vice President George Bush appear together at the 1984 Republican National Convention. © Ronald Reagan Library/National Archives.

tion candidates. Presidential candidates also began appearing with more frequency on forums such as *Larry King Live*.

Additionally, cable and satellite news operations such as C-SPAN, Fox News, and C-NBC eagerly broadcasted carefully long segments of scripted campaign events during the **Campaign of 2000**. *See also* Media Event.

Suggested Readings: Debra Gersh Hernadez, "Improving Election Reporting," *Editor & Publisher*, October 5, 1996, pp. 16–21; Renee Loth, "ABC Says It Will 'Drop Sound Bite' Coverage; New Format Will Emphasize Issues and Candidate Strategies, Network Asserts," *Boston Globe*, September 11, 1992, p. 13; Thomas B. Rosenstiel, "Media Watch/ Focus on Campaign Coverage; Press Offers a Preview of Its Focus for Fall; Media: Despite Vows of More Substantive Political Coverage, Reports Rely on Atmosphere over Issues," *Los Angeles Times*, July 25, 1992, p. A16; Martin Schram, *The Great American Video Game: Presidential Politics in the Television Age* (New York: Morrow, 1987).

Pierce, Franklin

See Campaign of 1852.

Pinckney, Charles Cotesworth

See Campaign of 1804; Campaign of 1808.

"The Plumed Knight"

A perennial candidate for the Republican nomination, James G. Blaine, the Speaker of the House from Maine who had been tarnished by the **Mulligan Letters** scandal, received the appellation of "the Plumed Knight," during his failed attempt to secure the nomination in 1876. During the 1876 Republican Convention, Robert Ingersoll crafted what has remained one of the great nominating speeches in political convention history.

Referring to Blaine's patriotism as well as his struggles in Congress over scandal, Ingersoll proclaimed, "Like an armed warrior, like a plumed knight, James G. Blaine marched down the halls of the American Congress and threw his shining lance full and fair against the brazen forehead of every traitor to his country and every maligner of his fair reputation." Ingersoll's speech was so effective that Blaine almost stole the nomination from the eventual candidate, Rutherford B. Hayes. Even though Blaine failed in 1876, the nickname remained throughout the remainder of his public life.

Blaine subsequently resigned his seat in the House and received an appointment to the Senate. In 1880, the Plumed Knight again sought the Republican nomination along with former President Ulysses S. Grant and Senator John Sherman. When the convention deadlocked, Blaine threw his support behind James A. Garfield. After his 1880 election, Garfield nominated Blaine for secretary of state, leading him to resign from the Senate to accept the position.

Blaine's tenure as secretary of state proved short. After the assassination of President Garfield, Chester Arthur assumed the presidency. Late in 1881, Blaine

James G. Blaine, the 1884 Republican nominee, became known as the "plumed knight" during his unsuccessful bid for the nomination in 1876. Courtesy of Library of Congress.

resigned as secretary of state and retired to write his memoirs. In 1884, Blaine came out of retirement to again contest for the Republican presidential nomination. This time Blaine was successful, and he soon found himself in the grip of an ugly smear campaign against Democrat Grover Cleveland.

During the campaign, Blaine came to regret his Plumed Knight image. Throughout the campaign, *Harper's Weekly* political cartoonist, **Thomas Nast**, lampooned Blaine with an unflattering Plumed Knight caricature.

From 1889 to 1892, Blaine served as secretary of state in the Republican administration of Benjamin Harrison. Blaine died in Washington, D.C. on January 27, 1893. *See also* Campaign of 1884.

Suggested Readings: David Saville Muzzey, *James G. Blaine: A Political Idol of Other Days* (New York: Dodd, Mead & Company, 1935); Mark Wahlgren. Summers, *Rum, Romanism & Rebellion: The Making of a President, 1884* (Chapel Hill: University of North Carolina Press, 2000).

Pocket-book Issue

"Pocket-book issue" was a term used after World War II to describe economic issues that influence voter behavior. During the **Campaign of 1932**, Franklin Roosevelt successfully turned the election into a referendum on Republican economic policies and the presidency of Herbert Hoover. Since Roosevelt, pocket-book issues have remained a dominant focus in presidential politics. *See also* Bread-and-Butter Issues.

Suggested Readings: Michael Romaro, "Seniors Rebelling against Drug Costs: Higher Prescription Bills Becoming Hot Political Issue for America's Older Citizens," *Denver Rocky Mountain News*, August 25, 2000, p. 5A; Paul Taylor, "Pitching Bread-and-Butter Issues; Convention Aims to Deliver Message of Nonideological Competence," *Washington Post*, July 18, 1988, p. A1.

Political Cartoons

From the Civil War to the present, political caricature has played an important role in presidential campaigns.

Prior to the Civil War, political parties made effective use of political prints or **broadsides** to promote candidates. The broadsides typically included artistic renderings of candidates along with a brief discussion of issues. After the Civil War, a new form of political satire emerged with the establishment of a number of illustrated weekly newspapers such as *Harper's Weekly*, *Judge*, and *Puck*. In an effort to increase circulation, these illustrated newspapers hired illustrators who drew highly critical and sometimes amusing caricatures of major figures, including candidates for president. From the Civil War through the end of the century, illustrators such as Bernard Gillam, Victor Gillam, Joseph Keppler, Joseph Keppler Jr., and **Thomas Nast** drew numerous political cartoons and caricatures.

With the tremendous increase in the circulation of newspapers during the late nineteenth and early twentieth centuries, newspapers gradually put on staff their own editorial cartoonists. In the twentieth century, cartoonists have delighted in exaggerating presidents and presidential candidates, and in so doing, features such as Richard Nixon's five-o-clock shadow, Jimmy Carter's toothy grin and the younger Bush's ears have become familiar sights in the world of political cartoon imagery. *See also* Herblock.

Suggested Readings: Herbert Block, Herblock: *A Cartoonist's Life* (New York: Times Books, 1998); Roger A. Fisher, *Them Damned Pictures: Explorations in American Political Cartoon Art* (North Haven, CT: Archon, 1996); Steven Hess and Sandy Northrop, *Drawn & Quartered: The History of American Political Cartoons* (Montgomery, AL: Elliott & Clark, 1996); Jim Zwick, ed., "Political Cartoons and Cartoonists," BoondocksNet.com, http://www.boondocksnet.com/gallery/pc_intro.html.

Political Consultants

From the 1830s through World War II, major political parties relied on party loyalists at the local, state, and federal level to manage presidential campaigns. After World War II, presidential campaigns began to look outside of their parties for expert assistance particularly in the use of new technology and information-gathering methods.

During the 1950s, presidential campaigns faced the problem of how to make use of the new medium of television to reach voters. Presidential campaigns turned to the advertising industry for experts to craft spot ads. Through the campaigns of 1952, 1956, and 1960 advertising consultants refined the spot ad.

A major shift in the direction of presidential campaign advertising occurred in 1964. At the direction of the Johnson campaign, the Doyle Dane Bernbach ad agency developed a series of hard-hitting spots that depicted Republican presidential nominee, Barry Goldwater, as a danger to world peace and domestic security.

Campaigns also significantly increased the size of polling operations during the 1960s. Although polling had proven unreliable during the late 1940s and 1950s, methodological improvements and, later, computer technology created more certainty in polling data. Presidential campaigns had no choice but to devote more resources to expanded polling operations. This often meant hiring public opinion and polling consultants.

Televised presidential debates also emerged in the 1960s and 1970s. Many presidential historians attribute Richard Nixon's close loss to John Kennedy to his poor showing in the 1960 presidential debates. When presidential debates resumed during the **Campaign of 1976**, both President Gerald Ford (Republican) and challenger Jimmy Carter (Democrat) made use of debate and media consultants to prepare for the debate events.

Additionally during the period following World War II the policy consultant became a more common feature of a campaign. Recruited heavily from colleges, universities, and think tanks, policy consultants (both paid and unpaid) provide campaigns with the technical experience to develop proposals regarding a wide range of economic, social, and international issues. *See also* Campaign Manager.

Suggested Readings: Eleanor Clift and Tom Brazaitis, *War Without Bloodshed: The Art of Politics* (New York: Scribner, 1996); Dennis W. Johnson, *No Place for Amateurs: How Political Consultants are Reshaping American Democracy* (New York: Routledge, 2001); Larry Sabato, *The Rise of Political Consultants: New Ways of Winning Elections* (New York: Basic Books, 1981); James A. Thurber and Candice J. Nelson, *Campaign Warriors: The Role of Political Consultants in Elections* (Washington, DC: Brookings Institution Press, 2000).

Political Prints

See Political Cartoons.

Politics of Joy

"Here we are the way politics ought to be in America; the politics of happiness, the politics of purpose and the politics of joy." With these words, Vice President

Hubert Humphrey, shown here accepting the 1968 Democratic nomination, was known as the "Happy Warrior." © AP/ Wide World Photos.

Hubert Humphrey, the "Happy Warrior," defined his vision of politics and expressed his understanding of the liberal aspirations of the Great Society. These words seemed incongruous then, in 1968 during the most divisive and turbulent political climate since 1860, but in retrospect they typify the "Summer of Love" ethos shared by the youth culture, affirmed by the Beatles song, "All You Need Is Love." While "politics of joy" did not move the culture in the same way, and Humphrey was unable to shake his image as the Establishment pro-war candidate, the slogan accurately taps into the spirit of the times as well as aptly representing the progressive optimism of the Happy Warrior.

Suggested Readings: Lewis Chester, Godfrey Hodgson, and Bruce Page, *An American Melodrama: The Presidential Campaign of 1968* (New York: Viking Press, 1969); Theodore White, *The Making of the President, 1968* (New York: Atheneum Publishers, 1969).

Politics of Personal Destruction

A phrase coined by Bill Clinton and used during the mid and late 1990s, the "politics of personal destruction" describes the use of character attacks aimed at weakening public confidence in public figures and political opponents.

In the aftermath of the 1970s Watergate scandal, journalists intensified their scrutiny of the public and private lives of public officials. During the same period political campaigns increased **opposition research** programs directed at gathering negative information on the public record of political candidates.

Throughout his two terms in office, President Clinton frequently used the phrase to deflect criticism of his personal behavior. *See also* Campaign of 1996; Negative Campaigning; Opposition Research.

Suggested Readings: Ruth Marcus, "Clinton Angrily Denounces Republicans; Party Is 'Committed to Politics of Personal Destruction,' President Says," *Washington Post*, March 15, 1994, A1; Robert North Roberts and Marion T. Doss, *From Watergate to Whitewater: The Public Integrity War* (Westport, CT: Praeger, 1997).

Polk, James K

See Campaign of 1844.

"Polk, Dallas, Texas, Oregon and the Tariff of '42"

"Polk, Dallas, Texas, Oregon and the Tariff of '42" was a slogan used by the 1844 presidential campaign of Democratic nominee, James K. Polk to highlight his support for the annexation of Texas, the Oregon territory, and lower tariffs adopted as part of the 1842 tariff law.

After the Democratic convention deadlocked Polk had become the first "dark horse" presidential candidate. As a strong supporter of the doctrine of **Manifest Destiny**, Polk advocated annexing Texas and confronting Great Britain over the northern boundary between the Oregon territory and Canada.

The Whig Party, in contrast, took a much more cautious position on expansion.

Whig nominee Henry Clay believed that the annexation of Texas would lead to war with Mexico. Most importantly, it would tear open the smoldering embers of the slavery issue by threatening a disruption of the fragile balance between free and slave states. Forcing the Oregon boundary issue might also lead to armed conflict between the United States and Great Britain. *See also* Campaign of 1844; War and Peace Issue.

Suggested Readings: Martha Morrell, *"Young Hickory," The Life and Times of President James K. Polk* (New York: E.P. Dutton, 1949); Anders Stephanson, *Manifest Destiny: American Expansionism and the Empire of Right* (New York: Hill and Wang, 1995).

"Polk and Texas, Clay and No Texas"

See "Polk, Dallas, Texas, Oregon and the Tariff of '42."

Poll-Driven Campaign

As public polling methods have grown more sophisticated, political campaigns have found it easier to sample populations for indicators of popular issues and positions more conducive to drawing favorable attention to a given candidate. Hence, campaign positions and messages owe much to an intelligent reading of the polls. Polls, to an extent, drive the issues in modern democracy.

Critics of poll-driven campaigns argue that in the effort to assemble an electoral majority, campaigns often ignore substantively difficult issues and focus on less important **wedge issues**. In the **Campaign of 2000** both major candidates expressed their support for prescription drug coverage for Medicare recipients. Public opinion polls showed strong support for prescription drug coverage. However, both campaigns failed to adequately explain how they would pay for their multi-billion-dollar programs, a substantively difficult question. *See also* Campaign Manager; Horse-Race Campaign Coverage; Targeting.

Suggested Reading: Josh Getlin, "Regarding Media; For Whom the Polls Toll—the Candidate Who's Trailing," *Los Angeles Times*, September 18, 2000, p. E1.

Poll-Driven Campaign Coverage

See Horse-Race Campaign Coverage.

Pollster

Prior to World War II, presidential campaigns made relatively minor use of polls to attempt to measure public support for presidential candidates or to evaluate public support or opposition to various policy proposals or positions of a presidential candidate. After World War II, successful use of market research by the advertising industry to test potential consumer products led directly to the beginning of the era of political polling. Through the 1950s, the use of presidential preference surveys by presidential campaigns became much more widespread. By the **Campaign of 1960**, presidential campaigns routinely hired **political consultants** with polling expertise to help campaigns tailor messages to appeal to various voting blocs. Through the 1960s, professional pollsters increased their presence in Republican and Democratic campaigns. Pollsters played an increasing role in helping presidential campaigns craft messages directed at key voting blocs.

Through the 1970s and 1980s, the importance of campaign polling operations increased. Pollsters assumed much more important roles within presidential campaigns in crafting the messages of the candidates. Critics of this trend argued that pollsters exercised too much influence over the issues stressed by presidential campaigns. Despite the criticisms, through the 1990s presidential campaigns continued to rely more and more heavily on pollsters to provide campaigns with information.

In addition to the extensive use of pollsters and polls by presidential campaigns, print and electronic news operations made extensive use of polls as part of their coverage of presidential campaigns. Much like the criticism of the use of polls by presidential campaigns, some critics argue that media outlets spend too much time on reporting the result of presidential preference polls instead of discussing important policy differences among presidential candidates. Despite the criticism of so-called **horse-race coverage**, print and electronic news operations. *See also* Political Consultants; Push Polling.

Suggested Readings: Richard Moran and Mario A. Brossard, "Who to Watch in '96: The Political Pros Pick Voting Blocs That Could Make the Difference in November," *Washington Post*, July 14, 1996, C1; William Schneider, "Here's One High-Stakes Game," *National Journal*, May 3, 1997, p. 902.

Posters

Posters appeared as a colorful form of graphic arts in the nineteenth century. In American politics, posters have become a fixture of the media landscape. Unlike broadsides, which are more diverse in their content, posters are almost always graphic and pictorial, usually centered on a photograph, lithograph, cartoon, or slogan; the poster is designed to draw attention to its message from a distance. A poster can in some cases contain information announcing an event or disclosing a venue, but it is usually intended to promote a candidate or cause, for both the affirmation of the party faithful as well as to impress the noncommitted. Famous slogans (e.g., "I Like Ike," "Johnson: Now More Than Ever," "Nixon's the One"), the candidate's unaccompanied name (e.g., "Kefauver," "Mondale '84," "Jesse Jackson"), a clever phrase, symbol, or initials evoking the candidate's name (e.g., AuH2O for Barry Goldwater, "LBJ," or "HHH") or the names of the top and bottom of a party ticket (e.g., Kennedy-Johnson, Reagan-Bush, Dukakis-Bentsen '88), are the most prominent or sole text accompanying a photograph or graphic.

Posters and signs are also important visual tools at the national convention ubiquitously displayed throughout the convention hall as the proceedings are broadcast to the television viewing audience looking on from home. As with any genre of popular culture and political ephemera, posters have endured not only as

Campaign poster for the 1900 Republican ticket of William McKinley and Theodore Roosevelt. Courtesy of Library of Congress.

familiar signs of the campaign season, but also as collectible artifacts and memorabilia. One of the more famous photographic images in American political history captures a 1968 poster projecting the image of a youthful candidate, Robert Kennedy, hopefully displayed above the desk of an anonymous campaign worker at headquarters. One's eye is drawn below the poster to the desk, where shattering news is delivered by the jolting headline of a local paper: "RFK Dead." Such are the eternal destinies of the ephemera of passing ages.

Suggested Readings: Roger A. Fisher, *Tippecanoe and Trinkets Too: The Material Culture of American Presidential Campaigns, 1828–1984* (Urbana: University of Illinois Press, 1988); William R. Tripp, *Presidential Campaign Posters* (New York: Drake Publishers, 1976).

Poverty Issue

Major parties have always claimed for their side the surest remedy for poverty, an abiding confidence that has historically been fueled by a combination of perceptions and attitudes, most notably America's seemingly inexhaustible natural abundance, unflappable Yankee ingenuity, unique good fortune, and ingrained "Protestant work ethic." American culture has thus always held fast, even in the bleakest of times, to the notion that anyone can secure an easy and affluent life.

As America entered the world stage as an industrial giant in the latter nineteenth and early twentieth centuries, politicians and public officials became increasingly concerned with addressing the realities of an economically disadvantaged class in spite of the achievement of unprecedented material wealth. With the economic boom of the 1920s, the possibility of eliminating poverty seemed within reach. Global depression in the 1930s destroyed such illusions, but spirited commitment of government service to the poor and vulnerable found a new voice in the presidency of Franklin Roosevelt. Numbering among his famous "four freedoms" the freedom from want, Roosevelt affirmed the basic American principle that poverty not only can, but should by right, be eradicated from society. Roosevelt further developed an "economic bill of rights" attaching the notion of right to prosperity, and in so doing, advancing the idea of an entitlement to a life without poverty for all citizens. These attitudes continued through the administrations of Truman, Kennedy, and especially Lyndon Johnson. LBJ's "war on poverty" defined his domestic economic policy, and continued to influence American public policy well into the 1970s.

Discontent with entitlement programs during the 1980s drew sharp lines between the Reagan administration, advocating a *laissez-faire* economic policy emphasizing the "trickle down" effect of capital investment and consumer spending in the hopes of raising the living standard for all, and those critics of trickle down who lamented the lack of compassion in leaving the fate of the poor to the caprice of the market. Nonetheless, even though Reaganomics never achieved complete implementation, the electoral success of Reagan and his successor, the elder Bush (who had previously criticized trickle down theories as "voodoo economics"), forced Democrats to modify their approach to meliorist programs.

President Clinton typified the New Democrat through his attempt to develop a "third way" that attempted to incorporate, with mixed results, a greater sensitivity to unfettered, dynamic markets without completely abandoning social programs supportive of the poor. Clinton's failed health care reforms along with alterations in the welfare system are representative of this shift in attitudes among Democrats.

The poor remain. Poverty, homelessness, and urban blight continue to direct much of the debate in presidential campaigning and policy formation. From the "full dinner pail" of McKinley through Johnson's noble war on poverty to the "compassionate conservatism" of the younger Bush, the desire of major candidates to address the fate of the poor has established itself as a feature of presidential campaigns in perpetuity. *See also* Campaign of 1932; Campaign of 1936; Campaign of 1964; Great Society Speech.

Suggested Reading: C. Emory Burton, *The Poverty Debate: Politics and the Poor in America* (Westport, CT: Greenwood Press, 1992).

Presidential Campaign Ads

The 1952 presidential campaign marked the beginning of the use of television ads to support the election of presidential candidates. Both Republican presidential nominee, Dwight David Eisenhower, and Democratic presidential nominee, Adlai Stevenson, made use of the new medium of television to reach voters in their homes. From the **Campaign of 1924** through the **Campaign of 1948**, presidential campaigns had made extensive use of radio to deliver campaign messages to millions of voters in their own homes. However, campaign staffers soon realized that viewers would not watch half-hour talks from a candidate sitting behind a desk or in a comfortable chair. Taking a page out of a television advertising handbook, the thirty or sixty second spot ad soon became the norm for presidential campaign ads. Not unexpectedly, critics attacked the ads for attempting to sell presidential candidates like companies attempted to sell soap or laundry detergent. Despite the criticism, the presidential campaigns of 1956 and 1960 saw continued use of spot ads to highlight the position of a candidate on the issues, to provide voters with biographical information, or to provide testimonials from well-known public figures on behalf of a presidential candidate. Ads which had the camera focus on the face of the presidential candidate who gave a carefully crafted speech became a fixture of campaign ads.

The **Campaign of 1964** marked the beginning of a new era in presidential campaign ads. President Lyndon Johnson's campaign used a series of critical ads to raise doubts in the minds of voters as to whether the country should trust Arizona senator Barry Goldwater, the Republican presidential nominee, with the authority to use nuclear weapons to defend the United States. Coming two years after the Cuban missile crisis, the broadcast of the so-called **"Daisy" Campaign Ad** touched off a firestorm of criticism for implying that the election of Barry Goldwater would move the country closer to nuclear war. Despite the criticism of the Daisy ad and other ads used by the Johnson campaign, the ads proved remarkably successful in putting Goldwater on the defensive and ultimately contributing to Johnson's 1964 landslide victory. In the aftermath of the campaign of 1964, the **negative** or **attack ad** joined **talking head, testimonial**, and person-on-the-street ads as a standard type of presidential campaign ad.

The proven effectiveness of presidential campaign ads led directly to the need for presidential campaigns and the Democratic and Republican parties to significantly increase fund-raising in an effort to pay for the national broadcasting of campaign ads. Between 1971 and 1976, Congress enacted a series of campaign finance reform laws directed at restricting the size of so-called **hard money** contributions to candidates for federal office including presidential campaigns. Congress also enacted legislation providing for the public funding of presidential campaigns. The **Campaign of 1976** saw President Gerald Ford, the Republican presidential nominee, and Jimmy Carter, the Democratic presidential nominee, agree to accept public funds to pay the cost of their campaigns.

The **Campaign of 1980** and the **Campaign of 1984** saw Ronald Reagan make masterful use of campaign ads and television to reassure the American public about the country's future. Although critics of Reagan's 1984 Morning in America ads argued that they failed to address serious problems facing the nation, the ad campaign helped to propel President Ronald Reagan to a landslide victory over former Vice President Walter Mondale, the Democratic presidential nominee. Four years later, the 1988 presidential campaign of Vice President George Bush, the Republican presidential nominee, unleashed a series of attack ads to help the Bush campaign erase an early lead in presidential preference polls by Massachusetts governor Michael Dukakis, the Democratic presidential nominee. After the election, print and electronic news operations faced intense criticism for not pointing out major misstatements and falsehoods in 1988 presidential campaign ads.

The 1992, 1996 and 2000 presidential campaigns saw the spread of cable and satellite stations and a new focus on the **targeting** of voters in key **battleground states** significantly reduce the importance of national presidential campaign ads. Instead of producing and broadcasting ads directed at all voters, campaigns began to tailor ads in an attempt to influence so-called **swing voters**. The same period saw a flood of **soft money** in the coffers of the national Democratic and Republican parties, resulting in both parties' use of unregulated soft money contributions to pay for **issue ads**. During the spring of 2002, Congress passed and President Bush signed into law the McCain-Feingold campaign finance reform bill, which prohibited national parties from raising or spending soft money among other provisions. Critics promised to challenge the soft money ban in the Supreme Court.

Through the 2000 presidential campaign, campaign ads continued to constitute the largest single expenditure for presidential campaigns. *See also* Paid Media; Targeting.

Suggested Readings: Kathleen Hall Jamieson, *Packaging the Presidency: A History and Criticism of Presidential Campaign Advertising* (New York: Oxford University Press, 1996) Darrell W. West, *Air Wars: Television Advertising in Election Campaigns, 1952–2000* (Washington, DC: Congressional Quarterly, 2001).

Presidential Campaign Songs

From the late eighteenth century through the end of the nineteenth century, campaign songs played a central role in presidential campaigns. Even after the beginning of the twentieth century, campaign songs continued to draw attention to candidates. At election rallies, parades, and other campaign events, the partisans routinely sang praises to their candidate accompanied by popular tunes. Wide Awakes, for example, sang of Lincoln in the **Campaign of 1860**, "Oh ain't I glad I joined the Republicans, joined the Republicans, joined the Republicans."

One type of campaign song routinely praised the character and lifetime accomplishments of the candidate. In addition to songs praising the accomplishments of candidates, campaigns have used songs attacking the character and accomplishments of opposing candidates, a tactic particularly common in the nineteenth century. One pro-Lincoln song had fun at the expense of Stephen Douglas, "There was a little man and his name was Stevy Doug, . . . His legs were short, but his speeches were long, and nothing but himself could he see; his principles were weak, but his spirits they were strong, for a thirsty little soul was he."

During the campaign of 1872, Democrats sang about "Grant the Drunkard," to the tune of a popular song, "Captain Jinks of the Horse Marines," to wit, "I am Captain Grant of the Black Marines, the stupidest man that ever was seen." In the **Campaign of 1876** supporters of Democrat Samuel Tilden proudly sang the verses of "Hold The Fort For Tilden," many of which impugned the corrupt administration of the outgoing Grant. "See the rings, the combinations, Whisky, railroad, land; wicked schemes for 'peculations, rife on every hand," went one verse. "See the shameful defalcations in our savings banks, Robbing poor men, widows, orphans, by their thieving pranks," went another verse.

In sharp contrast to the hard-hitting campaign songs of the second half of the nineteenth century, early twentieth century campaign songs adopted a much more upbeat tone. During the **Campaign of 1904**, supporters of Teddy Roosevelt sang tunes such as "We Want Teddy For Four More Years," and "You're All Right, Teddy." During the **Campaign of 1908**, supporters of Republican presidential nominee, William Howard Taft sang the popular tune "Get On the Raft With Taft."

Most campaign songs quickly fade from memory, but there are exceptions. The most famous campaign song, **"Happy Days Are Here Again,"** conveying in melody and lyric the ebullience of Franklin Roosevelt's personality, to this day is easily recognized and identified with the themes and issues of the campaigns of the 1930s. In 1992 the Clinton/Gore campaign sounded a familiar chord with their baby boomer base through effective use of Fleetwood Mac's **"Don't Stop Thinking About Tomorrow."**

Suggested Reading: Irwin Silber, *Songs America Voted By* (Harrisburg, PA: Stackpole Books, 1971).

Presidential Debates

The **Campaign of 1960** introduced presidential politics to the world of television by broadcasting the debates between Massachusetts senator John F. Kennedy (Democrat), and Vice President Richard Nixon (Republican). On September 26, 1960, the first of four televised debates was held in Chicago, Illinois, at the studios of WBBM-TV. CBS News reporter Howard K. Smith moderated the debate, which was watched by some 66 million viewers. Historians credit the debate for giving Kennedy the edge necessary to defeat Nixon. Kennedy appeared as a healthy man at ease, comfortable in his own skin, charming, knowledgeable, and confident. Exhausted by a massive campaign tour and weakened by illness, Nixon was

The presidential debates of 1960 between Republican Richard Nixon (left) and Democrat John F. Kennedy. This debate occurred in New York City on October 21. © AP/Wide World Photos.

The presidential debates of 2000 between Democrat Al Gore (left) and Republican George W. Bush. This debate
occurred in Boston on October 3. © AP/
Wide World Photos.

pale, pasty, and shifty in appearance. Kennedy also made use of the forum to
deftly deflect stereotyped criticism that as a Roman Catholic he would have to
blindly follow the decrees of the Pope.

The next televised presidential debate occurred during the **Campaign of 1976**.
President Gerald Ford, the Republican nominee, competed against Jimmy Carter,
the Democratic nominee. A debate gaffe by Ford created a public relations crisis
when he claimed that the Soviet Union did not dominate Poland and Romania.
The ensuing post-debate flap cost the Ford campaign valuable time and effort.
Jimmy Carter went on to defeat Ford. The Ford gaffe forced future presidential
campaigns to devote more time to debate preparation.

The **Campaign of 1980** saw only one debate between Republican Ronald Reagan and incumbent President Jimmy Carter, held one week before the election.
The Reagan camp prepared a number of **sound bites** directed at reminding voters
of the economic problems draining the nation. Reagan asked the viewing audience
"Are You Better Off Than You Were Four Years Ago?" a question that reso-
nated with voters and helped to propel Reagan to a landslide victory.

To defray the escalating cost of putting on the debates, the nonprofit Commission on Presidential Debates (CPD) was established in the late 1980s. As a result
of intense debate preparations, the debates of 1988, 1992, 1996 and 2000 contained fewer gaffes and less memorable sound bites. A major format change was
introduced in 1992 when candidates agreed to answer questions presented by
citizens in the audience at the University of Richmond.

Finally, debate stalemates have contributed to increased use of campaign **spin
doctors** to attempt to shape coverage of the debates. *See also* Campaign of 1984;
Campaign of 1988; Campaign of 1992; Campaign of 1996; Campaign of 2000.

Suggested Reading: Alan Schroeder, *Presidential Debates: Forty Years of High-risk TV*
(New York: Columbia University Press, 2000); "Debate History," Commission on Presidential Debates, http://www.debates.org/pages/debhis.html.

Prohibition Issue

The prohibition movement had its origins in a pre–Civil War backlash against immigration. The influx of immigrants led to a much stronger demand for distilled spirits. Thus during the 1850s, the **nativism movement** began to associate immigration with excessive alcohol consumption. After the Civil War, German immigrants brought lager beer to the United States, which soon became the beverage of choice for millions of Americans. Large brewers such as Pabst of Milwaukee and Anheuser Busch of St. Louis led to the mass marketing of beer. By 1890, beer consumption had surpassed that of distilled spirits. Saloons, many of them subsidized by brewers, sprang up on street corners across the United States.

In 1869, supporters for banning the production and sale of alcohol established the Prohibition Party. They viewed the explosion in alcohol consumption as a direct threat to the moral fabric of the country. In 1872, the Prohibition Party nominated a presidential candidate. Other grassroots organizations also began to campaign to regulate alcohol consumption. In 1874, a group based in western New York and eastern Ohio established the Women's Christian Temperance Union. In 1893, the Anti-Saloon League was established in Oberlin, Ohio.

Through the 1880s, the major parties avoided the prohibition issue. Heavily dependent on the urban immigrant vote in northern cities, Democrats had nothing to gain from the prohibition issue. By the early 1890s, Republicans cautiously began to support prohibition. The 1892 Republican platform expressed support for "all wise and legitimate efforts to lessen and prevent the evils of intemperance and promote morality." In 1913, the Anti-Saloon League proposed a constitutional amendment prohibiting the production and sale of alcohol.

After World War I, pressure increased on Congress to draft and send to the states a constitutional amendment banning the production and sale of alcoholic

During Prohibition, Detroit police inspect equipment found in a clandestine underground brewery. © National Archives.

beverages. With strong Republican support Congress subsequently drafted the Eighteenth Amendment, which the states ratified by 1919. Congress then passed the Volstead Prohibition Enforcement Act.

Subsequent efforts to cut off the flow of alcohol failed. Particularly in large cities, organized crime groups met the continued public demand for beer and distilled spirits. "Speak easies," "bathtub gin," and "rum runner" entered the American vocabulary. Yet both parties continued to publicly support prohibition, but Democratic candidates were known as "wets" or in favor of alcohol distribution. In 1920 and again in 1928, Democrats James Cox and Al Smith were accused of being "cocktail candidates," causing damage to their campaign efforts. Smith in particular was damaged by his public support for the repeal of the Eighteenth Amendment.

The Great Depression changed the dynamics of the prohibition issue. The 1932 Democratic platform called for the repeal of the Eighteenth Amendment. Even the Republican platform included weak language supporting prohibition. Following the 1932 election, Franklin Roosevelt and a heavily Democratic Congress and the states quickly drafted and ratified the Twenty-first Amendment repealing prohibition. *See also* Campaign of 1928.

Suggested Readings: "Temperance & Prohibition," The Ohio State University, http://prohibition.history.ohio-state.edu; Women's Christian Temperance Union, http://www.wctu.org.

Prosperity Issue

Alexis de Tocqueville once observed that Americans were keenly focused on securing their material "well-being," acutely perceiving the strong connection drawn between political ideology and economic policy as a typical feature of American political culture. Such concerns were present at the very birth of the republic generating two disparate alternatives to the pursuit of prosperity: Thomas Jefferson, who favored an agrarian republic built on the foundations of the self-reliant farmer, and Alexander Hamilton, who envisioned the creation of an economic colossus driven by commerce and industry. In early presidential politics, the Federalists generally favored Hamilton's policies, whereas the Jeffersonian Republicans generally held the attitudes of their namesake. The Hamiltonians attached their hopes for prosperity on close commercial ties to Britain, whereas the Jeffersonians, influenced by both the French Revolution and the philosophy of the Physiocrats magnified by a lingering antipathy to Britain, sought closer political and commercial ties to France.

During the Age of Jackson, the Democratic Party was by and large the heir to the Jeffersonian vision, adding the inclination to promote *laissez-faire* economic attitudes and favoring small business as an important element of an agrarian republic. The Whigs drew upon the doctrine of Hamilton, advocating a close alliance between government and business intended to develop the infrastructure necessary to stimulate manufacturing and trade.

From the late eighteenth century until the Civil War, the **tariff issue** dominated presidential politics. By the 1820s, southern states came to regard protective tariffs as a plot by New England and Middle Atlantic states to permanently hobble their economies. High tariffs on British manufactured goods meant reciprocal high tariffs imposed on outgoing southern cash crops. Northeastern manufacturers supported tariffs to protect them from cheaper English and European manufactured goods. Prior to the Civil War, Whigs generally supported high tariffs while Democrats opposed them.

The promise of prosperity became a reliable fixture in the election campaign cycle. However the issue of which economic course was best for the country, while ever important, became secondary to the more critical social and moral problems confronting the nation over the problem of slavery. But even the debate over slavery was on some occasions tied to pecuniary attitudes. Some proponents of slavery claimed its superiority as an economic system, while some opponents of slavery pointed to the economic weaknesses of such an antiquated form of labor. Additionally, the Union victory in the Civil War resulted not only in the abolition of slavery, but it also sealed the economic fate of the republic along Hamiltonian lines: industrial, commercial, urban, and international.

Prosperity issues in the post-Reconstruction period were again polarized, the Republican Party inclining toward high finance and industry, the Democrats, especially in the South and West, adhering to agrarian and mining interests. The tariff issue was overshadowed by demands for railroad rate regulation and currency reform. The industrial revolution made the national economy less dependent upon farm production, but growing farm production and high rail shipping rates made it nearly impossible for farmers to make a profit. Growing discontent among farmers led to the birth of a number of third parties advocating railroad regulation. Additionally, new labor movements focused on the economic plight of working families, the industrial revolution having left millions of Americans at the mercy of powerful corporate trusts. The Greenback Party, Union Labor Party, and Populist Party pressured the other major parties to address farm and labor problems.

A peculiar but intensely important debate over the nature of the best monetary system spun out of these differences in the 1890s, with Republicans and Conservative Democrats hitching prosperity's star to the gold standard, while Democrats advocated the policy of "bimetallism" allowing for the free coinage of silver to augment the circulation of gold. The Republican nominee, William McKinley, promised voters a **"Full Dinner Pail"** if they rejected Bryan's **free silver** solution. McKinley and the gold standard prevailed. An enormous gold strike in Alaska in the late 1890s accompanied by rising affluence permanently put the coinage issue to rest.

By 1904, a Progressive tide had inundated the country. President Theodore Roosevelt undertook a crusade to break the power of trusts and monopolies once and for all. Democrat Woodrow Wilson pledged to continue progressive policies in his successful 1912 campaign. But in the wake of World War I, American voters turned their back on the progressive movement by electing a sequence of pro-business presidents: Harding, Coolidge, and Hoover.

As the Roaring Twenties gave way to the global Great Depression, the best path to prosperity was acutely debated throughout the 1930s, polarized by the New Deal programs of Franklin Roosevelt, and framed between the Democratic promotion of state intervention to support and strengthen the economy. Republicans

In 1933, as confidence in the banking system declined during the Great Depression, people mill about outside a bank. © Franklin D. Roosevelt Library/ National Archives.

became the party of "rugged individualism," insisting that prosperity depended on minimal government activity and individual initiative. These attitudes defined the centers of both parties through the 1960s during the debate over Lyndon Johnson's Great Society and the war on poverty, and into the early 1970s with the nomination of progressive Democrat George McGovern in 1972.

The severe economic dislocations of the 1970s paved the way for Republican nominee Ronald Reagan's 1980 victory over incumbent President Jimmy Carter. Reagan's, **"Are You Better Off Than You Were Four Years Ago?"** has come to symbolize the **Campaign of 1980** while stimulating a shift in public attitudes regarding government entitlements as guarantors of prosperity. Activist approaches such as the New Deal, Truman's Fair Deal, and the Great Society were widely regarded as having fallen short, and even the Democratic Party moved closer to a less interventionist position, typified by the "third way" economic policies of the Clinton administration in the 1990s.

Clinton purposefully and skillfully emphasized prosperity. His use of the slogan **"It's the Economy, Stupid,"** typifies the successful policy strategy that drove the incumbent President George Bush from office. Four years later, the booming national economy made it exceptionally difficult for Senator Bob Dole, the Republican nominee, to dislodge Clinton on the character issue. Clinton won reelection. Interestingly, Vice President Albert Gore proved unsuccessful in taking credit for eight years of strong economic growth during the **Campaign of 2000**.

While the major parties contain many elements and various opinions regarding the best policies promoting affluence, it is still accurate to say that Democrats are more inclined to "prime the economic pump," Clinton's third way notwithstanding, whereas Republicans remain more firmly devoted to the *laissez-faire* capitalist vision of Hoover and Reagan. *See also* Campaign of 1896; Campaign of 1920; Campaign of 1932; Campaign of 1992; Campaign of 1996.

Suggested Reading: Dan Baltz and Richard Moran, "Gore Has Yet to Make Sale on Economy; Bush Tax Cut Not Seen As Threat, Survey Says," *Washington Post*, October 27, 2000, A01.

Protectionism Issue

See Tariff Issue.

Public Journalism Movement

The Public Journalism Movement is an attempt at improving news coverage within all media, print and electronic, by giving readers, viewers, and listeners a greater role in shaping news coverage.

The movement grew out of a backlash to the coverage of the **Campaign of 1988**. Instead of discussing major issues such as health care reform, the exploding national deficit, and the continuing flood of illegal drugs into the country, coverage focused on the barrage of **attack ads** launched by the Bush and Dukakis campaigns. Many critics attributed exceptionally low voter participation to the tone of election coverage.

In the wake of 1988, public journalism advocates argued that all journalists are obligated to solicit the opinions of their readers, listeners, and viewers regarding media focus during a campaign. Beginning in the early 1990s a number of local newspapers and television stations started public journalism election projects that frequently involved the use of public forums that provide citizens with opportunities to directly question candidates.

News operations made use of a number of public journalism tools in an effort to improve election coverage during the 1992 campaign. **Ad watches** were used to evaluate the truthfulness of campaign spot ads. Presidential candidates frequently appeared on radio and television call-in shows such as *Larry King Live*. The media also expanded in-depth reports of issues such as health care reform and free trade.

Although mainstream news operations adopted some public journalism tools, they did not abandon **horse-race** and **poll-driven** presidential campaign coverage.

Suggested Reading: Anthony J. Eksterowicz and Robert North Roberts, *Public Journalism and Political Knowledge* (Boulder, CO: Rowman & Littlefield, 2000).

"Public Office Is a Public Trust"

In the midst of one of the more defamatory campaigns in the history of democracy, "A Public Office is a Public Trust," became a key slogan of the 1884 campaign of Democratic candidate Grover Cleveland.

Reporter William Hudson coined the phrase as a way to summarize a theme frequently sounded by Cleveland in his public appearances. Cleveland habitually described government officials as "public servants" who held office as "trustees" for the people. In an 1882 letter accepting his party's nomination to run as governor of New York, Cleveland had averred, "Public officers are the servants and agents of the people, to execute the laws which the people have made."

Summarizing this ongoing theme in Cleveland's public letters and speeches, Hudson penned the slogan "Public Office is a Public Trust," much to Cleveland's approval. The Cleveland campaign used the slogan to highlight a long series of allegations of unethical conduct by James G. Blaine, the Republican nominee. With few substantive issues dividing Blaine and Cleveland, the campaign deteriorated into a mudslinging contest. Democrats renewed allegations of Blaine's involvement in the **Mulligan Letters** scandal that had cost him the 1876 nomination.

Additionally, Democrats criticized the Arthur administration for the "Starr Route" scandal for failing to prevent the awarding of fraudulent postal contracts. Even though Arthur had aggressively pursued those involved in the scandals, the scandal helped Democrats to argue that the nation needed new leadership.

Republicans countered with attempts to inculpate Cleveland's personal life by drawing attention to his paternity of a child born out of wedlock. True to his campaign motto, he restored public trust by unabashedly assuming full responsibility for his actions. *See also* Campaign of 1884.

Suggested Readings: Robert North Roberts, *Ethics in Government: An Encyclopedia of Investigations, Scandals, Reforms, and Legislation* (Westport, CT: Greenwood Press, 2001); Mark Wahlgren Summers, *Rum, Romanism & Rebellion: The Making of a President* (Chapel Hill: University of North Carolina Press, 2000).

Pundit

A pundit is a term used to describe an individual who provides political commentary and predictions in print and electronic media outlets. Prior to the 1980s, major newspapers, weekly news magazines, and weekly network news talk shows such as Face the Nation provided the major outlets for political commentary. The establishment of the **Cable News Network (CNN)** and **C-SPAN** during the 1980s provided expanded opportunities for political commentary. The increasing popularity of talk radio, equally important, also increased the demand for individuals with political expertise to comment on political affairs. During the 1990s, the establishment of the Fox News Channel, MSNBC, and other all news cable and satellite channels further increased the demand and opportunities for so-called political pundits.

In addition to former campaign officials and elected officials, the 1990s saw a significant increase in the number of print and electronic journalists who would appear on various news talk programs to express their opinions on the political issues of the day. Critics of pundits argue that many pundits have hidden political agendas and that they attempt to use their notoriety to influence potential voters. Critics also argue that the focus on opinions reduces the time devoted to objective reporting of key campaign issues and events. Defenders of the news talk format argue that the format helps to engage viewers and listeners who otherwise might not pay attention to ongoing debates over various public policy issues.

Suggested Reading: Eric Alterman, *Sound and Fury: The Making of the Punditocracy* (Ithaca, NY: Cornell University Press, 1999); Howard Kurtz, "Political Pundits Foresee A Landslide for Clinton; Prediction Could Become Self-Fulfilling," *Washington Post*, September 30, 1992, A15.

Push Polling

Push polling involves the use of telemarketing firms calling on behalf of a presidential campaign but claiming objectivity in conducting an independent survey. During such a call, negative information of an opposing candidate is then shared.

Campaigns sponsor push polls to distribute negative campaign messages to key voters. Referring to the call as a poll increases the perceived credibility of any negative information distributed to potential voters.

During the 2000 Republican presidential primary battle between Texas Governor George Bush and Arizona senator John McCain, push polling exploded into a major campaign issue. McCain alleged that the Bush campaign paid for a push poll that called McCain a cheat and liar as the South Carolina primary intensified. Although the Bush campaign denied having authorized the push poll, the ensuing controversy focused national attention upon the growing use of push polls to discredit opponents. *See also* Dirty Tricks; Negative Campaigning.

Suggested Readings: Glen Bolger and Bill McInturff, " 'Push polling' stinks," *Campaign & Elections* 17 (August 1996), p. 70; Adam Clymer, "Phony Polls That Sling Mud Raise Questions Over Ethics," *New York Times*, May 20, 1996, p. A2; Karl G. Feld, "What Are Push Polls, Anyway?" *Campaigns & Elections* 21 (May 2000), p. 62.

Race Relations Issue

Race relations have influenced American politics and society since the founding of the North American colonies in the seventeenth century, and continue to be a moral and political concern in the dynamics of electoral politics in the twenty-first century. Race has been used as both a carrot and a stick; with most major candidates today eager to promise new forms of equality and harmony beneficial to all races on the one hand (the carrot), and the occasional instance of race bashing and scare tactics (the stick), sometimes overt, other times subtle, employed by more ruthless candidates in elections of the past.

An early example of the latter can be seen in the politics of Reconstruction, with mostly Southern Democrats using the race card to evoke fears of a carpetbag South dominated by greedy Republicans and their new political lackeys, the recently freed slaves. Throughout the nineteenth and into the early twentieth century, African American voters identified with the GOP, the party of Lincoln, while Democrats opposed efforts to incorporate the black population fully into the democratic process. This situation remained until the realignment of the 1930s, which produced the Roosevelt Coalition, uniting black voters with the Democratic Party. While the Republican Party still sustains a small and loyal conservative African

In 1963, President John F. Kennedy addresses the nation on civil rights and the integration of the University of Alabama. © John F. Kennedy Library/National Archives.

American contingent, it is the Democratic Party that has firmly established itself as the party of choice for African Americans.

Hispanic voters have also historically been associated with the Democratic Party, but not universally. In California and much of the Southwest, as well as the urban Northeast the Hispanic/Latino vote has been predominantly supportive of Democrats. However in the Sunbelt states of Florida and Texas, Spanish-speaking voters have inclined toward the GOP in increasing numbers. As the Hispanic population expands, surpassing African Americans as the nation's largest racial minority, the electoral muscle and divided loyalties of the Hispanic vote will become increasingly critical to the outcome of general elections, and increasingly desired by major candidates.

Other racial minorities, such as Asian Americans, Arab Americans, and Native Americans, have historically attracted far less electoral attention than the two larger minority groups. However, as the United States continues to diversify into an increasingly heterogeneous society, these groups should continue to grow in political clout and social influence.

While race has become less volatile as an issue since the **civil rights** victories of the 1960s, racial division, suspicion, and bigotry continues to corrupt the undercurrent of political culture. Campaigns in the late twentieth century, in spite of a more general enlightenment regarding race compared to the previous century, could through implication or inference cynically play the race card. The "Welfare Queen" imagery spun by the Reagan campaign led many to draw a racially charged inference singling out impoverished, urban African Americans, and the **Willie Horton** television advertisements produced by the elder Bush campaign were perceived as thinly veiled race baiting. Recently, and perhaps as an attempt to correct the impolitic racial tactics of the 1980s, the Republican Party has attempted to overhaul their homogenous reputation by projecting a more diverse image. The

2000 GOP national convention was noticeably conscious of diversity, with politicians of various races and ethnic backgrounds brought on stage to tout the raised consciousness of the party of Lincoln. But such attempts have not produced any major shifts in racial loyalty, at least not at this time.

Race has been and remains a sensitive subject in American political culture, and has both inspired politicians toward nobility and compassion and degraded their sense of fairness and equanimity. Either way, race will be an even more influential variable in the electoral politics of multiplicity promised in the century ahead. *See also* Affirmative Action; Campaign of 1948; Campaign of 1964; Campaign of 1968; Campaign of 1988.

Suggested Readings: Jeremy D. Mayer, *Running on Race: Racial Politics in Presidential Campaigns 1960–2000* (New York: Random House, 2002), Russell L. Riley, *The Presidency and the Politics of Racial Inequality: Nation Keeping from 1831 to 1965* (New York: Columbia University Press, 1999).

Radio and Presidential Campaigns

Beginning with the **Campaign of 1924**, radio became an important tool for reaching potential voters. Radio provided candidates with the ability to remain in one place and reach millions of Americans in their homes. Poor preparation and the absence of radio personalities in the young media initially limited the effectiveness of radio in presidential campaigns.

The situation changed with the **Campaign of 1932**. Prior to winning the 1932

President Calvin Coolidge, the 1924 Republican candidate, places his right hand on a piece of radio equipment used on automobiles during the campaign. Courtesy of Library of Congress.

Democratic nomination, Franklin D. Roosevelt had made extensive use of radio as governor of New York. With this experience, Roosevelt easily used radio in his contest against Republican President Herbert Hoover. Using a warm and confident tone, Roosevelt reassured the public that a Roosevelt administration would lead the nation out of the darkness of the Great Depression.

After his 1932 victory, Roosevelt used radio "**fireside chats**" to reassure the public and to lobby for his New Deal programs. Radio played a key role in Roosevelt's 1936, 1940, and 1944 election victories. Taking a page from Roosevelt's political manual, President Harry Truman made numerous radio broadcasts as he conducted his nationwide "**whistle-stop**" tour. The strategy helped Truman pull off one of the greatest election upsets in political history.

During the **Campaign of 1952**, television spot ads began to replace radio as the primary broadcast tool for reaching voters. By the end of the 1960s, presidential campaigns had significantly reduced the use of radio. And yet in the 1980s and 1990s radio again emerged as a major force in presidential politics. First, **talk radio** gradually built a large audience seeking opportunities to directly question candidates. The popularity of talk radio pressured campaigns into making their candidates more accessible to the public. During the **Campaign of 1992**, Democratic candidate Bill Clinton made frequent use of the **town meeting** format to win the nomination and the presidency.

Campaigns also increased radio time to **target** voters in **battleground states** during the campaigns of the 1990s and the tight race of 2000. Both major parties spent millions on radio advertising in **get-out-the-vote operations**. In comparison to the high cost of television spot ads, radio offered presidential candidates an economical alternative to television and **direct mail**. *See also* Campaign of 1924; Campaign of 1932.

Suggested Readings: John Mintz, "Gore Team Assails Bush's Record in Texas," *Washington Post*, October 14, 2000, A10; Gil Troy, *See How They Ran: The Changing Role of the Presidential Candidate* (Cambridge: Harvard University Press, 1996).

Rail-Splitter

To publicize Abraham Lincoln's humble origins and common-man work ethic, Republicans referred to Lincoln's youthful employment as a rail-splitter. Through the **Campaign of 1860**, periodicals published numerous illustrations of Lincoln splitting logs. These illustrations effectively portrayed a man of the people laboring just like the rest of us. Such imagery remains effective today, and politicians are eager to show themselves as men able to work with their hands. Jimmy Carter's carpentry, Ronald Reagan's firewood splitting, and the younger Bush's weed cutting serve as recent examples. Michael Dukakis's skill with a snowblower was a less effective image.

Suggested Readings: Gary L. Bunker, *From Rail-splitter to Icon: Lincoln's Image in Illustrated Periodicals, 1860–1865* (Kent, OH: Kent State University Press, 2001); Wayne C. Williams, *A Rail Splitter for President* (Denver: University of Denver Press, 1951).

Rally, Campaign

Political rallies are a natural outgrowth of campaigns, and a traditional feature of democracy. In the United States, the earliest political rallies can be traced to the American Revolution, involving public protests against the actions of Crown and Parliament. In presidential politics, the rally emerged as a common event during the expansion of suffrage and the growth of nationally organized party politics associated with the Age of Jackson (mid-1820s–1840s). Rallies in the 1830s and 1840s would often involve thousands of partisans, marching, rolling balls, carrying hickory poles (see **"Old Hickory"**), and engaging in a variety of theatrical and orchestrated activities. At times a rally could run for hours, resemble religious revivals, and even move from town to town, advancing the name of a candidate and the cause of a party. From the French word *rallier*, to join or to ally, a well-orchestrated political rally is an effective and often exciting method for stirring loyal supporters into action and for the publicizing of a party's views of a candidate's image to the undecided.

The remainder of the nineteenth century saw presidential campaign rallies grow more and more grandiose. During the **Campaign of 1860**, tens of thousands of marchers participated in candlelight parades organized by **Wide-Awake clubs** to support the election of Abraham Lincoln, the Republican presidential nominee. By 1900, the growing popularity of **whistle-stop** campaigns led to rallies being coordinated with brief stops by a candidate's train. The **Campaign of 1900** saw President Theodore Roosevelt make hundreds of whistle-stops where he gave fiery speeches designed to energize his supporters.

In the twentieth century, rallies became more sophisticated and structured.

President Harry S. Truman speaks at a Democratic rally in Bolivar, Missouri, during the 1948 campaign. © Missouri Resources Division/ Harry S. Truman Library.

Carefully planned and directed, what would appear to be partisan spontaneity was often staged for the consumption of onlookers or for the encouragement of the faithful. At the level of presidential campaigning, political rallies are particularly crafted and directed by campaign managers and planners. Formulaic in nature, the rally of contemporary politics no longer contains the more spontaneous, uncontrolled characteristics of the hickory pole rallies of the 1830s, or the convivial "hard cider" campaign of 1840. Rallies are carefully staged, designed to attract media coverage, the candidate is "handled" and protected by a scripted set of movements and reactions, and the crowds are generally preselected to ensure partisan enthusiasm. While this imposes an unfortunate artificiality on political events, designed and predetermined movements of presidential candidates are conducive to a candidate's personal security given the potential for violence in modern society. A mad assassin killed candidate Robert Kennedy as he was leaving a campaign rally after the 1968 California primary. It was also at a campaign rally that Governor George Wallace, a 1972 candidate for the Democratic nomination, received a crippling wound from an assassination attempt. Two failed assassins fired upon President Gerald Ford during public appearances. An assassin wounded President Reagan while he was leaving a nonpolitical event in 1981. Since the rash of assassinations and attempted assassinations from 1963 through 1981, the public appearance of presidents and presidential candidates at all public events have required a high degree of security and safe orchestration with the consequence of noticeably diluting the spirit of spontaneity.

With the continuing emphasis on television, the live rally has lost much of its force as a compelling campaign event. A secure rally can only reach crowds of a few hundred to a few thousand, and are often dominated by loyalists and thus lend an air of "preaching to the choir." Modern television commercials can reach millions of undecided voters, and do so in a more controlled and rhetorically sophisticated manner. The campaign rally is not dead, but it has, at least at the presidential level, lost much of its glamour and persuasive power in the wake of the ubiquitous presence of television. *See also* Advance Person; Earned Media; Free Media; Photo Opportunity.

Richard Nixon speaks at a Republican rally during the 1968 campaign. © Nixon Presidential Materials Staff/ National Archives.

Suggested Readings: Dan Balz, "Bush, Perot Lash Clinton; Democrat Upbeat as Race Draws to Close on Negative Note," *Washington Post*, November 2, 1992, A1; Alison Mitchell, "The 2000 Campaign: The Strategy: Bush Recruits Governors and Women for Final Stretch," *New York Times*, October 16, 2000, A24; Howell Raines, "Reagan Attacks President on Economy And Defense," *New York Times*, November 4, 1980, B5.

"Read My Lips, No New Taxes"

Reassuring conservative Republicans that he planned to continue the fiscal policies of President Ronald Reagan, Vice President George Bush, the 1988 Republican nominee, unequivocally affirmed that he would curtly tell anyone seeking his approval for any tax increase to "Read My Lips, No New Taxes." While Bush maintained that he would never raise taxes, he argued that his Democratic opponent, Michael Dukakis, would if given the chance.

Interestingly, the tax issue did not become the central issue of the 1988 campaign. Instead, the Bush campaign succeeded in focusing attention on alleged and sundry failures of Dukakis while serving Massachusetts as governor. Bush went on to easily defeat Dukakis, but his antitax pledge would boomerang on his administration.

Late in 1991, Bush agreed to raise taxes as part of a budget deal to control the exploding federal deficit. A year earlier Bush led a coalition to expel Iraqi invaders from Kuwait during the Persian Gulf War. The military victory abroad triggered a recession at home, forcing the president to, against his own inclinations, assent to a tax increase. Conservative Republicans viewed Bush's action as a betrayal of his convention pledge. Bush countered by claiming that the agreement forced Congress to control unnecessary spending.

Because the budget deal failed to immediately kick-start the sluggish economy, President Bush entered the 1992 campaign facing criticism from conservative Republicans as well as the expected complaints of Democrats. Conservative commentator Pat Buchanan, a former aide to President Richard Nixon, challenged Bush for the Republican nomination by blasting the president on tax increases and new free trade agreements that Buchanan charged were undermining American workers. At some political cost Bush eventually deflected Buchanan's charge only to find himself under constant attack from Democratic nominee Bill Clinton and the new Reform Party candidate, H. Ross Perot, the flamboyant billionaire populist.

Even though Bush publicly admitted to a mistake in signing legislation increasing taxes, his violation of his "Read My Lips, No New Taxes" pledge bruised his credibility and made it difficult to mobilize the conservative Republican base. Bill Clinton's pity reminder, **"It's the Economy, Stupid,"** soon became the most effective slogan of the 1992 campaign, which ended in Bush's defeat to the young governor from Arkansas. *See also* Campaign of 1988.

Suggested Readings: Michael Nelson, *The Elections of 1988* (Washington, DC: CQ Press, 1989); George F. Will, *The New Season: A Spectator's Guide to the 1988 Election* (New York: Simon and Schuster, 1987).

Reagan, Ronald

See Campaign of 1980; Campaign of 1984.

Reality Check

In the aftermath of the **Campaign of 1988**, news operations faced criticism for allowing presidential campaigns to dictate campaign coverage. Instead of focusing on critical issues such as the staggering budget deficit, media coverage focused on controversies over the Pledge of Allegiance, the Massachusetts prison furlough program, and pollution in **Boston Harbor**.

From the beginning of 1989 through the start of the **Campaign of 1992**, media outlets instituted numerous reforms directed at improving the quality of reporting. Instead of simply covering **photo opportunities** and reporting the latest **sound bite**, the number of in-depth reports analyzing important issues increased across all media. Several newspapers, weekly news magazines, and electronic and cable news operations also introduced **ad watches** to monitor and analyze the accuracy of spot ads. The phrase "Reality Check" soon became another name for "Ad Watch."

Through the 1990s, news operations in general made ad watches and reality checks a fixture of presidential campaign coverage. The adoption of ad watches or reality checks, however, did not force campaigns to abandon negative ads. Scholars continue to debate how much attention prospective voters pay to ad watches or reality checks.

Suggested Reading: David Von Drehle, "Reality Check on Decidedly Positive Day," *Washington Post*, August 1, 2000, p. A01.

"Rebuild with Roosevelt"

"Rebuild with Roosevelt" was one of a number of slogans used by Democrat Franklin Roosevelt's 1932 campaign promising Americans a plan to lead the nation out of the Great Depression.

Mired in the worst economic catastrophe in American history, the Democratic Party nominated Roosevelt, then governor of New York, as their candidate against incumbent President Herbert Hoover. In his acceptance speech Roosevelt famously pledged to offer the American people a **"New Deal."**

Roosevelt's simple promise resounded with the growing ranks of the unemployed. Farms, banks, and industries were teetering on the edge of financial collapse. Millions of Americans who were struggling to survive sought aid, comfort, and leadership from the federal government. Roosevelt's optimism and firm confidence persuaded the electorate that the nation could "Rebuild With Roosevelt." *See also* Campaign of 1932.

Suggested Reading: Roy Victor Peel and Thomas C. Donnelly, *The 1932 Campaign: An Analysis* (New York: Farrar & Rinehart, 1935).

Reign of Terror

At the urging of President John Adams, Congress in 1798 passed the Alien and Sedition Acts in an effort to stifle criticism of his administration. The Sedition Act proscribed "any false, scandalous and malicious writing," penalizing violations with fines and even imprisonment. Republican newspapers critical of the government were closed, their editors arrested.

Supporters of Vice President Thomas Jefferson, Adams's challenger for the 1800 election, made the Alien and Sedition Acts into a powerful issue. Adams was characterized as a despot, who imposed a "Reign of Terror" on the public by abridging First Amendment guarantees of a free press. Jefferson went on to narrowly defeat Adams in an election that was thrown into the House of Representatives. *See also* Campaign of 1800.

Suggested Reading: Bernard A. Weisberger, *America Afire: Jefferson, Adams, and the Revolutionary Election of 1800* (New York: William Morrow, 2000).

"Return Integrity to the White House"

"Return Integrity to the White House" was a slogan used by the 1976 campaign of Democratic nominee Jimmy Carter.

Incumbent President Gerald Ford, Carter's opponent, had assumed office as a result of President Richard Nixon's resignation over the Watergate scandal in August of 1974. Carter, a former governor of Georgia, entered the 1976 presidential contest a virtual unknown, but soon won numerous primary victories by positioning himself as a Washington outsider and a new species of Democrat, fiscally conservative and socially progressive, eager to restore dignity to public service. Carter promised, "never to lie to the American people."

After Nixon's resignation, President Ford had positioned himself as a moderate Republican to attempt to unify the country. Ford also ran as an integrity candidate, an image he felt he had earned due to his ethical conduct in office in the aftermath of the Watergate crisis. However, Ford had angered many Americans by his preemptive pardon of Nixon, raising suspicions about his judgment and motives.

Carter enjoyed an early lead over Ford in polls taken in the summer of 1976, but in late September, *Playboy* magazine published an interview with Carter. Besides being strongly criticized for agreeing to an interview with a "girlie magazine," Carter failed to anticipate the intensity of public reaction to confession that he had "lust[ed] in his heart" and that "had looked on a lot of women with lust." Ignorant of the candidate's scriptural literalness, the media accused Carter, a devout Baptist Christian, of hypocrisy and feigned piety.

Through the remainder of the 1976 contest, the Ford campaign claimed that Carter lacked the leadership skills and the experience to serve effectively as president. Carter responded by continuing to stress his promise to restore trust in government and to "return integrity to the White House."*See also* Campaign of 1976.

Suggested Reading: Patrick Anderson, *Electing Jimmy Carter* (Baton Rouge: Louisiana State University Press, 1994).

A Return to Normalcy

See Back to Normalcy; Campaign of 1920.

"Revolving Door" Campaign Ad

The "revolving door" was a television ad used by the 1988 campaign of Vice President George Bush attacking Massachusetts governor Michael Dukakis for a prison furlough program marked by the commission of crimes by several inmates while actually on furlough.

The Massachusetts prison furlough program first became an issue during the New York Democratic primary. A week before the April 1988 primary, Senator Albert Gore, Democrat from Tennessee and challenger for the nomination, criticized Dukakis for granting "weekend passes for convicted criminals." Dukakis responded that Massachusetts had already ended the program.

But once Dukakis secured the Democratic nomination, Republicans took advantage of Gore's earlier accusation, accusing Dukakis of casually issuing "[furloughs to] murderers from jail." In late August, the National Security Political Action Committee, an independent organization based in Washington, D.C., ran an independent ad on cable systems showing a photograph of convict **Willie Horton** who had engaged in a crime spree, which included an incident of rape, while on furlough. The Bush campaign denied any involvement with the ad, but throughout the final two months of the 1988 contest the Bush campaign used the "revolving door" imagery to impugn Dukakis's approach to crime and punishment. The Bush ad did not mention Willie Horton.

Because Horton was an African American, the Dukakis campaign accused Bush of using the "revolving door" ad to polarize the nation along racial lines. Naturally, the Bush campaign denied the accusation and insisted that the issue was about Dukakis's inability to correctly deal with crime. *See also* Campaign of 1988; Negative Campaigning.

Suggested Reading: Sidney Blumenthal, "Willie Horton & the Making of an Election Issue; How the Furlough Factor Became a Stratagem of the Bush Forces," *Washington Post*, October 28, 1988, p. D1.

Road to the White House

See C-SPAN.

Robo-calls

"Robo-calls," or automatic computerized telephone calls, are a part of sophisticated **Get-out-the-vote (GOTV) operations** now typical of presidential campaigns in high-tech efforts that utilize numerous tools to reach **targeted** voters. Long before campaigns began to make use of advanced telemarketing equipment, get-out-the vote operations commonly made use of personally operated phone banks to spur supporters to the polls. With computers, campaigns now have the ability to inexpensively contact millions of voters in a short time.

Robo-calls play a prerecorded message from the candidate or a famous supporter of his campaign. During the final days of the 2000 presidential campaign, for example, New Mexico Democrats received a recorded message from outgoing First Lady Hillary Rodham Clinton claiming that Republicans wanted Democrats to stay home on Election Day. The message continued, "but we can't let them get away with it."

Telemarketing technology permits a campaign to use different prerecorded messages to target select groups in key **battleground states**. Campaigns often lack sufficient volunteers to personally contact the high volume of targeted voters; robo-calls supply the needed support.

Critics of robo-calls argue that campaigns often use the technology to distribute negative information about their opponent. *See also* Push Polling.

Suggested Readings: Eric Bailey, "Campaign 2000: Foot Soldiers Fight to Boost Turnout; Election: With Bush and Gore Deadlocked in Polls, Who Captures the White House May Be Decided by Volunteers and Activists Ferreting out More Voters Block by Block," *Los Angeles Times*, October 29, 2000, p. A1; Jeff Leeds, "Parties Bankroll Get-out-the-Vote Efforts; Strategy: The GOP Plans an Unprecedented $100-Million Campaign, While the Democrats Will Enlist Help from Unions and Other Groups," *Los Angeles Times*, August 9, 2000, p. A12.

Rollins, Edward (1943–)

Edward Rollins entered the national political scene when he joined President Ronald Reagan's White House staff as assistant to **Lyn Nofziger**, White House political director. When Nofziger left the White House in 1982, Rollins replaced him as the new political director.

In 1988, Rollins accepted a position as the director of the Republican Congressional Committee, eventually angering the Bush White House by advising Republican House candidates to distance themselves from Bush's 1990 budget deal that included tax increases. With two years remaining on his contract, Rollins left the Republican Congressional Committee under pressure.

Rollins again demonstrated his strong independent streak by managing the independent presidential bid of Texas billionaire Ross Perot in the **Campaign of 1992**. However Rollins soon fell out with Perot, quitting the campaign. Rollins then accepted a 1993 offer to manage Republican Christine Todd Whitman's run for the governorship of New Jersey. After Whitman's victory, Rollins impoliticly boasted that he had paid $500,000 in "walking around money" to suppress black voter turnout to help Whitman's election chances. Facing controversy, Rollins subsequently apologized.

After the controversy surrounding the New Jersey campaign subsided, Rollins resumed his activities as a political consultant and commentator. *See also* Campaign of 1984; Political Consultant.

Suggested Readings: Andrew Rosenthal, "The 1992 Campaign: Advisors—Edward J. Rollins; The Team Perot Picked to Head His Campaign," *New York Times*, June 4, 1992, p. A18; Michael Weisskopf, "Rumors of His Death . . . A Year After He Was Counted Out, Rollins Is Back in the Political Fight," *Washington Post*, October 10, 1994, p. A1.

Roorback

The Democratic Party nominated James K. Polk of Tennessee to face Whig presidential candidate Henry Clay of Kentucky in 1844. In the midst of the campaign, the Ithaca (NY) *Chronicle* published an account of an 1836 trip through the South by an author named Roorback. Roorback alleged that he had observed a number of slaves branded with the initials J.K.P. Polk supporters quickly uncovered the story as a complete fabrication. The author Roorback did not exist. Such fabrications have since been tagged as "Roorbacks." *See also* Campaign of 1844; Dirty Tricks.

Suggested Reading: Hans Sperber and Travis Trittschuh, *American Political Terms: An Historical Dictionary* (Detroit: Wayne University Press, 1962).

Roosevelt, Franklin D.

See Campaign of 1920; Campaign of 1932; Campaign of 1936; Campaign of 1940; Campaign of 1944.

Roosevelt, Theodore

See Campaign of 1900; Campaign of 1904; Campaign of 1908; Campaign of 1912.

Rove, Karl (1950–)

Karl Rove served as key political strategist during the 2000 presidential campaign of Texas governor and Republican nominee George W. Bush. Prior to joining the Bush campaign, Rove had worked for thirty years as a Republican campaign strategist and political consultant.

Born in Colorado on Christmas Day, 1950, Rove fell in love with politics while attending high school in Holladay, Utah. During the late 1970s, Rove moved to Texas, continuing his career as a Republican political strategist. In 1978 Rove played a key role in the Texas gubernatorial campaign of William P. Clement. Clement became the first Republican governor elected in Texas since the end of Reconstruction.

During the 1980s, Rove formed a friendship with the Bush family that began with the elder George Bush's 1980 bid for the Republican nomination. During the early 1990s, Rove helped to prepare the younger Bush for a 1994 run for Texas governor. Under Rove's direction Bush defeated incumbent Governor Ann Richards.

When the younger Bush decided to make a run for the 2000 Republican presidential nomination, Rove helped to fashion the doctrine of "compassionate conservatism," emphasizing the softer side of conservative ideology. After the dust cleared from the Florida recount controversy, President-Elect Bush named Rove as his senior advisor for strategic and political decisions. Specifically, Bush placed Rove in charge of the White House Office of Political Affairs, the Office of Public Liaison and the Office of Strategic Initiatives. *See also* Campaign of 2000.

Suggested Readings: Dan Baltz, "Team Bush; The Governor's 'Iron Triangle' Points to Washington," *Washington Post*, July 23, 1999, p. C1; Dana Milbank, "Bush Names Rove Political Strategist; Choice Completes Troika of White House Advisers," *Washington Post*, January 5, 2001, p. A1; James C. Moore and Wayne Slater, *Bush's Brain: How Karl Rove Made George W. Bush Presidential* (New York: John Wiley & Sons, 2003).

"Rum, Romanism and Rebellion"

"Rum, Romanism and Rebellion" was a triple accusation originally coined in 1876 without notice by Republican James A. Garfield impugning Democrats of loose morals regarding the use of liquor, undesirable affiliations with the Vatican, and treasonous sympathy to the cause of the recently defeated Confederacy. It became a point of controversy when Reverend Samuel D. Burchard, a prominent New York Presbyterian minister, revived the phrase in an address at a pro-Republican rally on behalf of candidate James G. Blaine in New York City scarcely a week before Election Day. In comments directed toward Blaine, Burchard stated "We are Republicans and don't propose to leave our party and identify ourselves with the party whose antecedents have been rum, Romanism, and rebellion. We are loyal to our flag. We are loyal to you." Frank Mack, the local Associated Press (AP) reporter had been assigned to cover the event. Mack's stenographer recorded Burchard's speech verbatim. The incident would have gone unnoticed had it not been for Blaine's attendance at the event and his subsequent failure to quickly disassociate himself from the bigoted slur. Democratic supporters of Cleveland were quick to use the phrase to mobilize the immigrant population of New York, who were largely Irish-Catholic, against the GOP candidate. Burchard's comments, and Blaine's silence, quickly became a front-page story from coast to coast.

With the base of the Republican Party in the small towns of the Northeast, East, Midwest, and West and the base of the Democratic Party in the rural South and immigrant rich cities of the North and Midwest, both parties understood the outcome of the race would hinge on key **battleground states** such as Indiana, Ohio, and New York. With its 36 electoral votes New York, which was evenly divided between Republican upstate New York and Democratic New York City, was needed for victory.

Historians continue to argue that the controversy led to Cleveland's 5,000 vote victory in New York, delivering the election and the White House to the Democrats for the first time since 1856. But many scholars argue that New York's Tammany machine played a more important role in turning out Democrats than the backlash against the "Rum, Romanism and Rebellion" comment. *See also* Campaign of 1884.

Suggested Reading: Mark Wahlgren Summers, *Rum, Romanism & Rebellion: The Making of a President, 1884* (Chapel Hill: University of North Carolina Press, 2000).

Rumpsey-Dumpsey

Countering the heroic claims of General William Henry Harrison in the campaign of 1840, Democratic Vice President Colonel Richard M. Johnson, also at Tippecanoe, claimed to have been responsible for actually bringing down the great warrior Tecumseh. The chant, "Rumpsey-Dumpsey, Colonel Johnson killed Tecumseh" broadcast the claim, but was countered mockingly by incredulous Whigs responding, "Rumpsey Dumpsey, who killed Tecumseh?" *See also* Campaign of 1840.

Suggested Reading: Robert Gray Gunderson, *The Log-Cabin Campaign* (Lexington: University of Kentucky Press, 1957).

"Safety, Solvency, Sobriety"

"Safety, Solvency, Sobriety" was a slogan used by the 1928 presidential campaign of Republican candidate Herbert Hoover to highlight Hoover's promise to maintain conservative policies of his two predecessors. Hoover promised to continue the economic policies of the Harding and Coolidge administrations that had brought the nation seven years of economic prosperity. Hoover also pledged his full support for the "Noble Experiment" or prohibition.

Hoover faced four-time New York governor Alfred E. Smith. Although very popular in New York State, Smith, a Roman Catholic, did not fit the profile of a national candidate. The Republican Party took full advantage of anti-Catholicism in rural and small town America as leverage against Smith. More importantly, the fact that many Americans continued to unfairly associate Smith with New York's corrupt Tammany Hall machine worked in Hoover's favor. Finally, Smith made the political mistake of endorsing the repeal of prohibition. Although many urban residents strongly favored repeal, prohibition still held firm support throughout rural America.

Republican operatives and surrogates, against Hoover's intentions, conducted one of the dirtiest campaigns in history. They spread the rumor that the Pope would move to the United States if Smith were elected. They also spread the rumor that Smith was a drunkard. The personal attacks on Smith distracted voters from gathering economic storm clouds. *See also* Campaign of 1928.

Suggested Readings: Allan J. Lichtman, *Prejudice and the Old Politics: The Presidential Election of 1928* (Chapel Hill: University of North Carolina Press, 1979); Robert A. Slayton, *Empire Statesman: The Rise and Redemption of Al Smith* (New York: Free Press, 2001).

School Prayer Issue

Prayer in school, an issue revolving around the "no establishment clause" of the First Amendment, has remained an ongoing political debate in the United States since the 1830s when Irish-Catholic immigrants objected to compulsory reading of the Protestant King James Bible and the recitation of Protestant prayer in public schools. Catholic protests provoked an anti-Catholic backlash that led to the expulsion of Catholic children from the classroom, and even to violence between Irish-Catholics and Protestants. The issue appeared again at the height of the Cold War, when in the 1950s public sentiment was receptive to emphasizing the difference between the godly democracy of America and the godless communism of the Soviet Bloc. However, the Supreme Court, beginning with two landmark cases in 1962 and 1963, enforced a strict reading of the First Amendment ruling that the inclusion of mandatory, recited prayer in public school is unconstitutional, and federal law is clear on its prohibition of public, sectarian, organized prayer in schools receiving federal funding. In 1985, the court ruled that even a one-minute period of silent, voluntary meditation was unconstitutional. The debate is largely drawn along partisan lines, with Republicans, led by the conservative wing, critical of government prohibitions against religious expression, even claiming that such prohibitions undermine moral education. Democrats, for the most part, are steadfast in their adherence to the Jeffersonian principle of the "wall of separation between church and state," and argue that prayer in school is necessarily in violation of the no establishment clause.

Republican hopeful Barry Goldwater raised the issue in response to the Supreme Court ruling while gearing up for a campaign run in 1964. Prior to his death, incumbent President John F. Kennedy reflected support for the "wall of separation" principle recently advocated by the Court in ruling on the question of compulsory school prayer. "We have in this case," Kennedy observed, "a very easy remedy, and that is to pray ourselves. And I would think that it would be a welcome reminder to every American family that we can pray a good deal more at home, we can attend our churches with a good deal more fidelity, and we can make the true meaning of prayer much more important in the lives of our children."

For the most part, presidential candidates have historically demurred on questions of religious faith while on the campaign stump, but in recent decades, beginning with the "born again" confession of 1976 Democratic candidate Jimmy Carter, a devout Baptist, political candidates at all levels have made religious profession a *de rigueur* feature of modern campaigning. As such, candidates are more receptive, at least in principle, to the idea of allowing some type of prayer or religious expression in the public schools. While few presidential candidates support efforts to amend the Constitution to restore prayer in school, all candidates have averred the belief that some kind of religious expression is not a violation of the "no establishment" doctrine, and that current restrictions are too rigid in the application of the "wall of separation" principle.

Although the school prayer issue did not have a major impact on the presidential elections of 1980 and 1984, critics of Ronald Reagan argued that a Reagan White House would attempt to appoint conservative members to the Supreme Court who would have fewer concerns about maintaining the separation of church and state. Through the 1980s, the Republican Party and many Republican candidates used **wedge issues** such as the school prayer issue to attract swing voters concerned about a perceived moral decline in American society.

Taking advantage of this growing apprehension, in the **Campaign of 1988,**

Vice President George Bush made effective use of a number of social issues to define Massachusetts governor Michael Dukakis as a liberal opposed to reforms directed at protecting the moral fiber of the nation. The strategy helped Bush to overcome an early Dukakis lead in presidential preference polls. However, the strategy did not work in 1992 when President Bush sought reelection against challengers Bill Clinton, the Democratic presidential nominee, and independent Reform Party candidate Ross Perot. In the end, voters proved much more concerned about the stagnant economy than social issues.

In the **Campaign of 2000**, both Vice President Gore and Governor Bush supported the qualified allowance of voluntary prayer in school. The Supreme Court, however, remains adamant in its position regarding prayer in school, and has consistently ruled unconstitutional any type of religious observance or the recitation of prayer in the classroom or at school events.

Suggested Readings: Douglas Jehl, "Bush Stakes Claim to Moral High Ground; Politics: He Tells Knights of Columbus Convention of His Rigid Opposition to Abortion Rights and His Fight for a School Prayer," *Los Angeles Times*, August 6, 1992, p. A5; Bill Peterson, "Bush Slings Toughest Words at Dukakis in Texas; Republican Rebuts Charges on Drugs, Calls Democrat Foe of Guns, Pledge, School Prayer," *Washington Post*, August 27,1988, p. A10.

Scott, Winfield

See Campaign of 1852.

Secession Issue

Nothing less than the future of the Union was at stake during the campaign of 1860. Fearful that a Republican victory would lead to the eventual end of slavery, Southern Democrats broke with Northern Democrats and nominated secessionist John C. Breckinridge. Northern Democrats nominated Illinois senator Stephen A. Douglas who stood by the provisions of the Compromise of 1850 and supported the doctrine of "popular sovereignty"; leaving it to the citizens of each state to determine the status of slavery within their own boundaries. Southerners who opposed secession formed the Constitutional Union Party and nominated John Bell. The Republican Party turned to Abraham Lincoln.

In a repudiation of the Missouri Compromise, the Republican platform declared opposition to the spread of slavery to any additional territories or states. The fact that the Republican platform did not demand the immediate abolition of southern slavery was not enough to allay abolitionist fears in the slave states. Confronted by the waxing threat of secession, the eventual President-Elect Lincoln maintained that the federal government had the right to use force to stop the secession movement. On December 20, 1860, South Carolina seceded from the Union, stimulating the eventual secession of eleven southern states. *See also* Campaign of 1860.

Suggested Readings: William Freehling, *The Road to Disunion* (New York: Oxford University Press, 1990); Maury Klein, *Days of Defiance: Sumter, Secession and the Coming of the*

Civil War (New York: Knopf, 1997); Robert L. Paquette, *Slavery, Secession, and Southern History* (Charlottesville: University Press of Virginia, 2000).

Sectionalism Issue

See Secession Issue.

Seymour, Horatio

See Campaign of 1868.

"Shall America Elect a Cocktail President?"

Alcohol consumption became a divisive moral issue in the late nineteenth and early twentieth centuries leading to the passage of the Eighteenth Amendment prohibiting the production, distribution, and consumption of alcohol at the national level. Some politicians were critical of such an effort and openly opposed the principle of prohibition. James Cox had done so during the campaign of 1920, leading his opponents to invent the anti-slogan, "Cox and Cocktails." (Cox's opponent, Warren Harding, was not averse to illicitly imbibing in a spot of whiskey, even with the Volstead Act in force.) "Shall America Elect a Cocktail President?" sounded the same theme in 1928 as Republicans attempted to associate Democratic candidate Al Smith, an anti-prohibitionist, with intemperance.

Largely as the result of few major policy differences between the platform planks of the major parties, Republicans resorted to attacks on Smith's character. Although the Democratic platform had promised an "honest effort to enforce the Eighteenth Amendment," Smith had publicly announced his public support for "fundamental changes in the present provisions for national Prohibition." Smith's position was popular in the ethnically diverse cities of the Eastern seaboard and Midwest.

Strong support for **prohibition** continued to exist in rural and small town America. Republican operatives stirred up prohibition groups to publicly oppose the election of Al Smith. For instance, the Anti-Saloon League and Women's Christian Temperance Union worked against Smith. Many women voters, now exercising their full right to vote at the federal level under the recently passed Nineteenth Amendment, supported prohibition because of the impact of alcohol on families. Republicans directed a whispering campaign accusing Smith of being a drunkard, causing "Shall America Elect a Cocktail President?" to become one of the most popular slogans during the **Campaign of 1928**. Meanwhile, weightier matters of greater consequence were neglected, voters having been distracted by another minor wedge issue while the early signs of depression signaled their alarm.

Suggested Readings: Allan J. Lichtman, *Prejudice and the Old Politics: The Presidential Election of 1928* (Chapel Hill: University of North Carolina Press, 1979); Robert A. Slayton, *Empire Statesman: The Rise and Redemption of Al Smith* (New York: Free Press, 2001).

"Shall the People Rule?"

See "Let the People Rule."

Shrinking Electorate

"Shrinking electorate" is a term referring to a significant decline in voter participation at the polls in the decades of the 1970s, 1980s, and 1990s. The shrinking electorate has led campaigns to tailor messages to more likely voters. Consequently, both Democratic and Republican candidates have focused their efforts at turning out their base and **targeting** independent **swing** voters.

By the **Campaign of 2000**, both the Democratic and Republican parties had put into place highly sophisticated programs to identify core supporters and undecided voters. The campaigns of both Republican George W. Bush and Democrat Vice President Albert Gore spent tens of millions of dollars from **soft money** contributions on **get-out-the-vote** programs in key **battleground states**, such as Florida and Michigan. *See also* Soccer Mom.

Suggested Readings: Mark Lawrence Kornbluh, *Why America Stopped Voting: The Decline of Participatory Democracy and the Emergence of Modern American Politics* (New York: New York University Press, 2000); Richard Morin and Claudia Deane, "As Turnout Falls Apathy Emerges As Driving Force," *Washington Post*, November 4, 2000, p. A1; Ruy A Teixera, The Disappearing American Voter (Washington, DC: Brookings Institution, 1992).

Silent Majority

During the volatile, protest-pocked **Campaign of 1968**, the Republican ticket of Richard Nixon and Spiro Agnew called upon the support of America's law-abiding "silent majority" to contribute a sober sensibility to the counter-cultural politics of the late 1960s. Nixon and Agnew argued that a "silent majority" of Americans supported policies directed at restoring law and order and the continuation of military commitment to South Vietnam. They also made effective use of the "silent majority" to attack the media for alleged liberal bias.

Given the turmoil and social unrest of the 1960s, the "silent majority" theme was well received by Republican partisans, disaffected conservative Democrats, and moderate Independents. Critics argued that the Nixon campaign used the slogan to polarize the nation instead of seeking a consensus on how to solve the serious problems facing the nation. *See also* Campaign of 1968.

Suggested Reading: Robert A. Levine, "The Silent Majority: Neither Simple Nor Simple-minded," *Public Opinion Quarterly* 35 (Winter 1971–1972) pp. 571–577.

16 to 1

In the 1830s, the United States adopted a bimetallist currency based around both gold and silver. In 1837, Congress enacted legislation determining the value re-

Political cartoon show-
ing William Jennings
Bryan, the 1896 Demo-
cratic candidate, touting
the principle of "bi-
metallism." Courtesy of
Library of Congress.

lationship between gold, the more precious metal, and silver, the less precious and
less frequently mined metal, at a ratio of 16:1. During the Civil War, silver faded
from currency as a result of natural economic sources, and in 1873 silver was
officially demonetized by law, establishing gold as the only legitimate federal currency.

However, soon after silver was demonetized new discoveries in the West increased the supply. Simultaneously, western and southern farmers, weighed by
debt and supportive of increasing the money supply, favored restoring a bimetallist
currency as well as the circulation of paper "greenbacks." Thus, in the late 1870s
and early 1880s, miners, farmers, and other populist interests began lobbying for
a return to the old 16:1 gold/silver currency.

"16 to 1" thus became a political slogan used by the 1896 presidential campaign
of William Jennings Bryan. The 1896 Democratic platform called for "the free
and unlimited coinage of both silver and gold at the present legal ratio of 16 to
1 without waiting for the aid or consent of any other nation." Bryan and **free
silver** supporters believed that by flooding the nation with new coinage, it would
give farmers the opportunity to pay back debts with inflated coinage. Adoption
of a bimetallic standard would also boost the economy of western states by creating a large market for silver.

Free silver and bimetallism lost their allure by 1900, partly because of new
political interests on the part of both politicians and the electorate, and partly due
to the discovery of massive supplies of gold in Alaska and elsewhere easily extracted
for the market. Silver's appeal as a standard of currency was thereafter tarnished.
See also Campaign of 1896; "Cross of Gold" Speech; Mark Hanna; Sound Money.

Suggested Readings: Stanley Llewellyn Jones, *The Presidential Election of 1896* (Madison:
University of Wisconsin Press, 1964); George Frisbe Whicher, *William Jennings Bryan and
the Campaign of 1896* (Boston: Heath, 1953).

"Slavery Is a Moral, Social, and Political Wrong"

Throughout the 1850s, Abraham Lincoln had opposed slavery on moral, political, economic, and logical grounds. Thus, when he was nominated to run for the Republican ticket in 1860, the slogan, "Slavery is a Moral, Social, and Political Wrong" was a natural encapsulation of the Republican viewpoint regarding the most divisive issue in American history.

However, Lincoln and moderate Republicans rejected efforts by the party's abolitionist wing to turn the election into a referendum on slavery. Such an approach would have likely cost Lincoln the votes of many Northerners who opposed the expansion of slavery but believed that the South would secede if faced with an abolitionist government in Washington. This moderate strategy helped Lincoln to win an electoral vote majority but failed to prevent secession. *See also* Campaign of 1860.

Suggested Readings: Harry Jaffa, *A New Birth of Freedom: Abraham Lincoln and the Coming of the Civil War* (Lanham, MD: Rowman & Littlefield, 2000); George Knoles, *The Crisis of the Union, 1860–1861* (Baton Rouge: Louisiana State University Press, 1965).

Slavery Issue

Slavery—the Peculiar Institution, long a festering sore in American society, erupted as the dominant issue in the Campaign of 1844. Before the ratification of the Constitution, a number of northern states had already outlawed slavery within their borders, and slavery appeared to be waning in the South until the invention of the cotton gin at the turn of the century created conditions that would lead to high demand for cheap labor. To justify the existence of slavery in a republic espousing liberty and equality for all, nineteenth century southern apologists began to defend slavery on moral and religious grounds, adding a new dimension to slavery that had not existed in the previous century. Even eighteenth century slave owners such as Thomas Jefferson and George Washington painfully recognized and admitted the moral problems inherent in slavery, and in their own historically unsatisfying way attempted efforts at eliminating slavery within the law and customs of the day. But slavery was now defended in the nineteenth century as ethically and religiously valid by southern pro-slavery writers in response to the moral outrage of the growing abolitionist movement of the 1830s and 1840s. Slavery thus became economically institutionalized, politically sectionalized, and morally polarized.

Through the 1830s and early 1840s, tension increased over the slavery issue. James K. Polk, the 1844 nominee of the Democratic Party, upset the uneasy truce between slave and non-slave states by supporting Texas annexation, which presented the prospect of a divisive battle over whether to permit Texas to enter the Union as a slave state. Angered over the unwillingness of either the Whig or Democratic parties to address the concern of abolitionists, the new Liberty Party nominated James G. Birney, a former slave owner, as their presidential candidate.

Banner for John C. Fremont and William L. Dayton, the candidates of the anti-slavery Republican Party in 1856. © National Archives.

The platform of the Liberty Party called for the outright abolition of slavery in all states. Birney received a surprising 2.3 percent of the popular vote.

The 1848 birth of the Free Soil Party signaled growing unhappiness of northern voters over the moribund Whig Party's failure to block the possibility of the further expansion of slavery. The platform of the Free Soil Party did not call for the immediate abolition of slavery. Instead, it called for a ban on the admission of any new slave states into the Union. In an effort to build the widest base of support for General Zachary Taylor, the Whig Party avoided taking an explicit position on the issue during the **Campaign of 1848**. With its base of support in the South, the Democratic Party platform defended the right of each state to decide for itself the slavery question.

The Compromise of 1850 became the defining issue of the **Campaign of 1852**. The leadership of both the Whig and Democratic parties had supported the compromise. But the anti-slavery wing of the Whig Party bitterly opposed the Fugitive Slave Act of 1850 that required public officials in free states to cooperate in the return of escaped slaves to their southern owners. To offer voters an alternative, the Free Soil Party nominated John P. Hale of New Hampshire as their standard bearer. Democratic presidential nominee, Franklin Pierce, went on to win the election and seal the fate of the Whig Party. In his Inaugural Address, Pierce brazenly asserted the rights of the slave-owners, thus adding further fuel to the incendiary situation.

After the demise of the Whig Party, anti-slavery interests in the North established the Republican Party in 1854. In 1856, Republicans included in their platform a plank that demanded the admission of the Kansas territory as a free state. Democrats continued to endorse the doctrine of "popular sovereignty" allowing residents of any given state to independently determine the slavery question.

Four years later, Republican presidential nominee Abraham Lincoln defeated three other candidates in a sectional battle over the free state/slave state issue. Lincoln, while not advocating immediate abolition, had long opposed slavery throughout his political career. His preference for the immediate containment and gradual extinction of slavery nonetheless alarmed southern slave owners, who represented the leadership of the southern states. Lincoln's election thus directly led to the secession of southern states and the formation of the rebellious Confederate States of America. *See also* Race Relations Issue.

Suggested Readings: Avery Odelle Craven, *Civil War in the Making 1815–1860* (Baton Rouge: Louisiana State University Press, 1959); William Freehling, *The Road to Disunion* (New York: Oxford University Press, 1990).

Smear Tactics

See Mudslinging; Negative Campaigning; Opposition Research.

Smith, Alfred E.

See Campaign of 1928.

Soccer Mom

"Soccer Mom" was a term that became popular during the **Campaign of 1996** to describe suburban women **swing** voters who devote a considerable amount of time and energy to supporting the various activities of their children, such as chauffeuring them to events like soccer games. Because of their willingness to shift back and forth between Republican and Democratic candidates, the Soccer Mom vote has become an important target group.

Focus groups and public opinion polls have found that Soccer Moms are more concerned with the quality of education and the economic security of their families than **wedge issues** such as **abortion** or **affirmative action**.

In 1996, the campaign of Republican candidate Bob Dole failed to close the **gender gap** due to a failed attempt to convince independent suburban women that large tax cuts constituted the answer to the complex problems involved in raising a family.

Suggested Readings: Carey Goldberg, "Politics—Political Battle of the Sexes Is Tougher Than Ever; Suburbs' Soccer Moms, Fleeing the G.O.P., Are Much Sought," *New York Times*, October 6, 1996, Section 1, p. 1; William Safire, "Candidates Court Soccer Moms," *Pittsburgh Post-Gazette*, October 27, 1996, p. E–8.

Social Security Issue

Established during the mid-1930s under the administration of Franklin Roosevelt, social security has since grown to consume more revenue than any other single federal program. The Social Security program annually provides retirement benefits and disability payments to millions of Americans. Through the early 1960s, the Social Security program rarely became an issue in any political contest, becoming an untouchable "sacred cow" immune to debate.

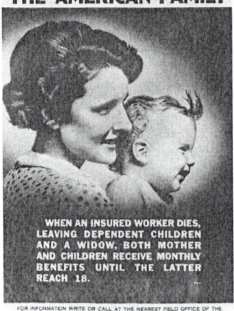

MORE SECURITY FOR THE AMERICAN FAMILY

WHEN AN INSURED WORKER DIES, LEAVING DEPENDENT CHILDREN AND A WIDOW, BOTH MOTHER AND CHILDREN RECEIVE MONTHLY BENEFITS UNTIL THE LATTER REACH 18.

FOR INFORMATION WRITE OR CALL AT THE NEAREST FIELD OFFICE OF THE
SOCIAL SECURITY BOARD

A 1930s poster for the new Social Security Program. © Franklin D. Roosevelt Library/National Archives.

This began to change during the **Campaign of 1964**. President Lyndon Johnson, the Democratic nominee, accused Arizona U.S. senator and Republican nominee Barry Goldwater of seeking to make the program voluntary. Although Goldwater officially expressed his commitment to maintaining the program's status, the Johnson campaign insinuated that a Goldwater administration would destroy Social Security.

By the end of the 1970s, an alarming series of reports indicated that without major changes, the Social Security trust fund would have insufficient funds to pay benefits to members of the "baby boom" as they reached retirement age. In the **Campaign of 1980** President Jimmy Carter accused Ronald Reagan, the Republican challenger, of planning to tamper dangerously with the Social Security system.

Through the campaigns of 1984, 1988, 1992, and 1996, Republican candidates attempted to steer clear of the issue because of the persistent efforts by Democrats to argue that Republicans planned to dismantle Social Security. During the 2000 campaign Texas governor George Bush, the Republican nominee, expressed his support for allowing Social Security participants to voluntarily channel a part of their Social Security contributions in alternative investments. As expected, the campaign of Vice President Albert Gore attacked the proposal. *See also* Campaign of 1980; Campaign of 1996; Campaign of 2000, Third Rail of American Politics.

Suggested Reading: Ben White, "Gore Reaches Out to Union, Candidate Attacks Bush on Texas Record, Social Security Plan," *Washington Post*, July 22, 2000, p. A5.

Soft Money

"Soft Money" refers to those campaign contributions not subject to the **hard money** limits of federal campaign finance laws.

The passage by Congress of the Federal Election Campaign Finance Act (FECA) of 1971 and subsequent amendments in 1974 and 1976 placed sharp limits on the size of individual and political action committee (PAC) contributions to federal political campaigns. Congress also passed legislation in the 1970s permitting the use of federal tax revenues in funding credible presidential campaigns. During the **Campaign of 1976** both President Gerald Ford and challenger Jimmy Carter received funding under this program.

In 1979, the Federal Election Commission (FEC) issued new regulations permitting national political parties to raise unlimited contributions for **party-building activities** such as voter registration and **get-out-the-vote activities**. Soft money contributions would not be subject to hard money limits or presidential campaign public funding provisions, leading to an immediate acceleration of political contributions.

During the **Campaign of 1996** both major parties broadly construed the term "party-building activity" to include the use of soft money to fund televised **issue ads**. Such ads avoid explicitly advocating a candidate while highlighting his or her positions and political record. In the wake of the 1996 campaign critics called for an outright ban on political parties raising soft money for any purpose.

In late March 2002, President George W. Bush signed legislation prohibiting individuals, unions, and corporations from making soft money contributions to national political parties. Equally important, the law limits the right of interest groups to pay for the broadcast of issue ads 60 days before general elections and 30 days before primaries. To reduce the impact on parties, the law also raised the limit on individual donations to candidates from $1,000 to $2,000. Critics argued that the law violated the First Amendment rights of interest groups by restricting their right to broadcast independent ads and that Congress lacked the authority to limit contributions for party-building activities. *See also* Campaign of 2000.

Suggested Reading: "Liberal Split on Shaping of Campaign Finance Rules: Allies Disagree on Regulation of 'Soft Money,' " *Washington Post*, June 5, 2002, p. A21.

"A Solid Man in a Sensitive Job"

Stressing the need for experienced leadership in the White House during difficult times, the campaign of incumbent President Jimmy Carter employed the slogan "A Solid Man in a Sensitive Job" to meet the challenge of Republican nominee Ronald Reagan.

In November of 1979, angry Iranian militants stormed the American embassy in Tehran and took hostage the embassy staff in violation of international law. Additionally, the Soviet Union renewed aggression through an invasion of Afghanistan. In addition to these crises abroad, the country faced serious domestic problems caused by high inflation, high energy prices, and slow economic growth.

The Carter campaign attempted to depict Ronald Reagan as inexperienced and ill prepared to assume the duties of President of the United States. The Carter campaign believed that voters who compared the foreign policy records of Carter and Reagan would vote on their behalf. Learning from history, Carter's managers noted that President Lyndon Johnson's 1964 presidential campaign had successfully depicted Barry Goldwater, a Republican who shared Reagan's political values, as too ideologically extreme and inexperienced to put in charge of the country's nuclear weapons.

On October 28, 1980, Carter and Reagan met in Cleveland, Ohio in the only presidential debate of the **Campaign of 1980**. Carter demonstrated his intellectual mastery of a large number of topics. To the surprise of many political observers, Reagan also appeared well prepared to handle difficult foreign and domestic policy issues. Carter's emphasis on his own solid experience was deflected by Reagan's personal charm and political confidence.

Suggested Readings: Elizabeth Drew, *Portrait of an Election: The 1980 Presidential Campaign* (New York: Simon and Schuster, 1981); Jack Germond and Jules Witcover, *Blue Smoke and Mirrors, How Reagan Won and Why Carter Lost the Election of 1980* (New York: Viking, 1981).

Sound Bite

"Sound bite" is a recently circulated term describing concisely phrased, carefully scripted statements or delivery by a candidate, campaign spokesperson, or **surrogate** designed to attract the immediate television media attention.

Because of the limited dollars available to fund **spot ads**, campaigns depend heavily upon **free media** or **earned media** to transmit messages to the public. Critics of sound bite politics argue that it contributes to a long-term trend in American politics, coeval with the rise of television as the dominant media and avoiding comprehensive and substantive discussion of difficult or controversial public policy issues.

Suggested Readings: Roderick Hart, *Seducing America: How Television Charms the Modern Voter* (New York: Oxford University Press, 1994); Sig Mickelson, *From Whistle Stop to Sound Bite: Four Decades of Politics and Television* (New York: Praeger, 1989); Jeffrey Scheuer, *The Sound Bite Society: Television and the American Mind* (New York: Four Walls Eight Windows, 1999).

Sound Money

"Sound money" was part of the Republican appeal to defuse the populist **free silver movement** of William Jennings Bryan during the **Campaign of 1896**. Under the direction of Ohio industrialist and political mastermind **Mark Hanna**, the Republican Party sought to turn the election into a referendum on continued prosperity under the gold standard while opposing the Democrats' free silver platform.

After raising a record amount of contributions, the McKinley campaign conducted a nationwide education effort arguing that Bryan's bimetallist proposal

William McKinley and Garrett A. Hobart, the members of the Republican ticket in 1896, ran on a sound money platform. Courtesy of Library of Congress.

threatened the nation's economic security. According to the McKinley campaign, only the gold standard protected the value of American currency. To carry this message to every part of the United States, Mark Hanna relied on thousands of campaign **surrogates** to deliver speeches and to distribute literature to prospective voters. *See also* "Cross of Gold" Speech.

Suggested Readings: Paul W. Glad, *McKinley, Bryan, and the People* (Philadelphia: Lippincott, 1964); Stanley Llewellyn Jones, *The Presidential Election of 1896* (Madison: University of Wisconsin Press, 1964).

Spin Doctor

A "spin doctor" is a campaign official responsible for favorably interpreting, or "spinning," campaign events or controversies in a manner that proves beneficial to their candidate or detrimental to opponents. To put a "spin" on a campaign event, statement, or incident has developed into an important rhetorical tool in modern campaigns. Should a candidate fall short of expectations in a debate, for example, a savvy "spin doctor" can diffuse the potential volatility of an impolitic phrase or response, or even turn it to the candidate's advantage. "Spin doctors" also know what to emphasize and how to convey it in post-debate or post-event commentary on behalf of their candidate. *See also* Earned Media; Free Media.

Suggested Reading: Michael Lewis, *Trail Fever: Spin Doctors, Rented Strangers, Thumb Wrestlers, Toe Suckers, Grizzly Bears, and Other Creatures on the Road to the White House* (New York: Knopf, 1997).

Square Deal

In a September 7, 1903, speech at the New York State Fair in Syracuse, President Theodore Roosevelt told a large crowd that "We must treat each man on his worth and merits as a man. We must see that each is given a square deal, because he is entitled to no more and should receive no less." Less than a year later, the Republican Party nominated Roosevelt as their presidential candidate. "Square deal" became the primary slogan of the 1904 Roosevelt campaign.

To Roosevelt, a "square deal" meant that government was obliged to assure fair economic opportunity for individuals and businesses, believing that the president should have executive authority to safeguard the public interest through policies such as the enforcement of antitrust laws. *See also* Campaign of 1904.

Suggested Reading: Eugene H. Roseboom, *A History of Presidential Elections* (New York: Macmillan, 1964).

"The Stakes Are Too High for You to Stay Home"

"The stakes are too high for you to stay home" was the narrated admonition punctuating the controversial **"Daisy" Ad** sponsored by the **Campaign of 1964** of incumbent President Lyndon Johnson depicting Republican Barry Goldwater as an unreliable and unstable choice for an office with its finger on the nuclear trigger. After the ghastly mushroom cloud vaporized the sweet Daisy girl, the voice of Lyndon Johnson warned about the high stakes involved in the November vote. While the provocative ad was pulled, the phrase remained as a slogan for the Johnson campaign.

Suggested Readings: Harold Faber, *The Road to the White House: The Story of the 1964 Election* (New York: McGraw-Hill, 1965); Theodore White, *The Making of the President, 1964* (New York: Atheneum Publishers, 1965).

"Stand Up for America"

Angered by the growing antiwar movement within the Democratic Party and the aggressive enforcement of civil rights laws by the Kennedy and Johnson administrations, Democratic Alabama governor George Wallace broke from the party, offering a third-party alternative reminiscent of the Dixiecrat rebellion of 1948 based on "states rights" and patriotism. "Stand Up for America" became a prominent slogan of this independent bid.

Even though conservative white Southern Democrats still shunned the party of Lincoln, they could express their dissatisfaction with the liberal and moderate wings of their party by defecting to Wallace. Thus, Wallace undermined the Democrat's diverse New Deal coalition, in place since 1932. The split within Democratic ranks led to the loss of their Southern base and aided Republican candidate and eventual winner, Richard Nixon. *See also* Campaign of 1968.

Suggested Reading: Marshall Frady, *Wallace* (New York: World Publishing Co., 1968).

Staying on the Message

"Staying on the message" refers to the need for persistence, focus and consistency during any given presidential contest.

The best example of "staying on the message" in recent campaigns can be seen in Democratic candidate Bill Clinton's steely embrace of the economic issue in 1992. **"It's the Economy, Stupid,"** became the unofficial slogan of the Clinton campaign. The success of Clinton's effort has led scholars to conclude that a successful campaign must select the correct campaign message and avoid any distraction or temptations to stray from that theme. By contrast, many political observers blamed Albert Gore's 2000 loss on his failure to emulate Clinton's 1992 model of focus and persistence. *See also* Stump Speech.

Suggested Readings: Thomas B. Edsall and Dan Balz, "What Does Bush' Do Now? Top Republicans Differ on Staying the Course vs. Reshaping the Message," *Washington Post*, March 10, 2000, p. A4; Bill Sammon, "Gore Campaign Mired in Many Missteps; Scandal, Disarray Overshadow Message," *Washington Times*, June 20, 2000, Part A, p. A1.

Stephanopoulos, George (1961–)

George Stephanopoulos served as a deputy campaign manager and communications director for Bill Clinton's presidential run in 1992. Although **Dee Dee Myers** served as Clinton's press secretary, Stephanopoulos played a key role in developing campaign media strategy. Political historians give Stephanopoulos considerable credit for Clinton's survival in successfully dodging allegations of marital infidelity and draft evasion.

After Clinton's November victory, Stephanopoulos was assigned to serve as White House communications director. Subsequently, Stephanopoulos moved on to become a senior advisor to the president for policy and strategy. He left the White House in 1997 to accept a position with ABC News and to teach as a university professor in New York City.

In June 2002, ABC News named Stephanopoulos anchor of *This Week*. Stephanopoulos is also the author of *All Too Human: A Political Education*, a 1998 publication that includes an unflattering account of President Clinton's behavior. *See also* Campaign of 1992.

Suggested Readings: John F. Harris, "Stephanopoulos Book Tests Loyalty; Yet Another Ex-Clinton Intimate Sells an Unflattering Account of His Presidency," *Washington Post*, March 8, 1999, p. A 03; George Stephanopoulos, *All Too Human: A Political Education* (Thorndike, ME: Thorndike Press, 1999).

Stevenson, Adlai

See Campaign of 1952; Campaign of 1956.

Stump Speech

Stump speeches, a traditional rhetorical tool, are campaign addresses delivered over time to various crowds with little or no change in content. Carefully wrought by speechwriters, stump speeches repeatedly emphasize a candidate's central themes, proposals, principles, beliefs, attributes, and aspirations. **Sound bites** are important components of an effective stump speech. *See also* Staying on the Message.

Suggested Reading: David Lauter, "Dukakis Evokes Quayle Name as Stump Speech Evolves," *Los Angeles Times*, September 20, 1988, Part 1, p. 19.

Suffrage Movement

See Women's Suffrage Movement.

"A Supreme Soldier—A Model President"

"A Supreme Soldier—Model President" was a slogan promoting Democratic nominee Winfield Scott Hancock during the **Campaign of 1880**.

In nominating Hancock, Democratic leaders hoped Hancock's reputation as one of the heroes of Gettysburg would make it more difficult for the Republican Party to wave the **bloody shirt** inciting anti-Democratic sentiment. Republican supporters pounded Hancock as a rebel sympathizer for abandoning the Republican Party and joining the Democrats. But as with every post–Civil War election Republican **surrogates** effectively waved the bloody shirt, mobilizing partisans in the Northeast and Upper Midwest.

Republican candidate and war hero James A. Garfield defeated Hancock by approximately 2,000 votes, but won a more significant Electoral College victory by retaining the Northeast and Midwest for the GOP.

Suggested Reading: Herbert John Clancy, *The Presidential Election of 1880* (Chicago: Loyola University Press, 1958).

Surrogate

Throughout the nineteenth century the majority of presidential candidates considered openly campaigning for votes an undignified activity. Political parties thus relied on party surrogates to deliver their messages to the public. **Front porch campaigns**, typified by Benjamin Harrison in 1888 and William McKinley in 1896, were the preferred style. William Jennings Bryan, McKinley's Democratic opponent, defied tradition by traveling the country personally delivering hundreds of campaign speeches. Theodore Roosevelt followed suit in 1904.

Even with the advent of the **whistle-stop campaign** in the early twentieth century and new campaign technologies such as radio and television in mid-century, presidential campaigns continue to utilize celebrated surrogates to pro-

Julie Nixon Eisenhower campaigns for her father, Richard Nixon, at the 1972 Republican National Convention in Miami. © Nixon Presidential Materials Staff/National Archives.

mote a candidate or issue. More public-oriented first ladies such as Hillary Clinton, and Tipper Gore, have recently performed the surrogate role. *See also* Paid Media; Photo Opportunity.

Suggested Readings: Ann Gerhart, "The Candidate's Lead Drummer, Outgoing, Yet Private, Tipper Gore Keeps the Best for Her Husband," *Washington Post*, July 11, 2000, p. C1; David Hoffman, "GOP Sends Spokesmen to New Hampshire; Reagan Surrogates Stump as the President Presides," *Washington Post*, February 17, 1984, p. A3.

Swing Voters

Swing voters are voting blocs capable of deciding tight races. New York Irish-Catholics delivered victory to Grover Cleveland in 1884. The African-American vote filled this role in 1976 on behalf of Jimmy Carter, while the labor vote, abandoning previous Democratic loyalties, proved decisive for Ronald Reagan's victories in 1980 and 1984. Women voters, especially the "**soccer mom**," influenced outcomes in 1992 and 1996. The Hispanic vote promises to assume this role in the near future, especially in Florida, California, and the Southwest. *See also* Gender Gap; Get-Out-the-Vote; Targeting.

Suggested Reading: David S. Broder and Dan Balz, "Gore Fails to Cash in on Prosperity; Swing Voters Give Vice President Little Economic Credit," *Washington Post*, July 23, 2000, p. A01.

Taft, William H.

See Campaign of 1908; Campaign of 1912.

Talk Radio

See Radio and Presidential Campaigns.

Talking Head Campaign Ad

"Talking heads" is a term originally used in broadcast circles to describe televised images of experts and commentators, viewed from stationary positions without the assistance of elaborate sets or sophisticated camera angles (as if they were disembodied talking heads), analyzing topics at some length revolving around political and social events and issues. In presidential politics, talking head advertisements provide candidates with the opportunity to communicate directly with viewers.

These ads typically focus on issues while attempting to project a positive image for a candidate. During the **Campaign of 1952**, the "Eisenhower Answers America" spot ads provided General Dwight David Eisenhower, the Republican nominee, to present his views on issues ranging from the continuing conflict in Korea, the cost of living, and corruption in Washington. During the **Campaign of 1980**, Ronald Reagan, the Republican presidential nominee, used his decades of work as a movie and television actor to make a series of spot ads where he talked directly to the American people. *See also* Presidential Campaign Ads.

Suggested Readings: William L. Benoit, *Seeing Spots: A Functional Analysis of Presidential Television Advertisements, 1952–1996* (Westport, CT: Praeger, 1999); Robert Kaiser, "Candidates on TV: Reagan Goes Low-Key, Carter Goes Dramatic," *Washington Post*, September 9, 1980, p. A2; Darrell West, *Air Wars: Television Advertising in Election Campaigns, 1952–1996* (Washington, DC: Congressional Quarterly, 1997).

"Tank" Campaign Ad

A particularly effective spot ad used by the 1988 Republican campaign of Vice President George Bush against Democratic challenger Michael Dukakis involved an inadvertently comic image of a helmeted Dukakis blithely riding as a passenger on an M-1 tank. His head barely visible through the turret, Dukakis bobbed along incongruously to the accompaniment of a mocking narration. The ad ended with a tight shot of Dukakis with a silly grin and the words: "Now he wants to be our commander in chief. America can't afford the risk." Such imagery succeeded in raising doubts about the ability of Dukakis to seriously serve as commander in chief. *See also* Campaign of 1988.

Suggested Reading: Joan Vennochi, "The Brains of the Bush Offensive: Strategist Roger Ailes Made the Candidate," *Boston Globe*, October 26, 1988, Living, p. 67.

Targeting

Targeting denotes various campaign activities focusing narrowly on attracting **swing voters**. In the **Campaign of 2000** both of the major parties devoted extensive funds to targeting key blocs of voters in **battleground states**. Democratic strategists targeted single women with college degrees, senior citizens, labor unions, and African Americans. Republicans targeted suburban married mothers, white males opposed to gun control, and religious conservatives.

Critics of targeting argue that narrowing a candidate's focus impairs the development of broad, unifying themes. Supporters of targeting argue that targeting voting blocs is as old as campaigns themselves; modern technology has simply provided better tools to accomplish this objective. *See also* Get-Out-the-Vote; Soccer Mom.

Suggested Readings: Ceci Connolly, "Gore in Big Push for Black Votes: Turnout in Key States Could Deliver White House," *Washington Post*, September 16, 2000, p. A18; Howard Kurtz, "Sunshine State Is Among Markets for Bush's Sunny Pre-Convention Ads," *Washington Post*, July 21, 2000, p. A13; David Von Drehle, "No Stone Is Left Unturned for Turnout: Tight Contest Fires up Faithful in Record Push for Voters," *Washington Post*, November 7, 2000, p. A1.

Tariff Issue

After **slavery**, no political dispute dominated nineteenth century American politics more than questions regarding the rate of tariffs.

Under the Constitution, Congress grants exclusive authority to impose tariffs on all imports into the United States. In the aftermath of the War of 1812, the tariff issue gradually grew into a sectional conflict that seriously complicated the process of building national political coalitions. Throughout the period, strongest opposition to protective tariffs came from the plantation states of the Deep South.

In the candidate-saturated **Campaign of 1824**, four of the five candidates had supported protective tariffs to some degree. Eighteen twenty-eight was also defined by tariffs in addition to the populist backlash to the controversies raised in 1824. Tariffs reemerged as a hot issue in the campaign of 1832. South Carolina had at one point threatened secession over the **Tariff of Abominations**, claiming the right of nullification, a claim that presumes the several states are the primary interpreters of the constitutionality of congressional statutes.

Slavery dominated political debate in the 1840s and 1850s, but tariffs returned as an important issue through the 1870s and 1880s, remaining a major concern during the febrile debates over monetary policy of the 1890s.

While gradually less important, tariffs continued to draw much attention up to the outbreak of World War I. *See also* Campaign of 1828; Campaign of 1896; Campaign of 1912.

Suggested Reading: Eugene H. Roseboom, *A History of Presidential Elections* (New York: Macmillan 1964).

Tariff of Abominations

In 1828, Congress enacted the Morrill Tariff, a protective tariff imposing a 47 percent tax on imported goods. Such a move assisted northern industry and commerce, but was detrimental to southern agrarian interests due to an increase in prices on manufactured goods across the board. Additionally, such measures provoked retaliatory tariffs by British and Continental governments imposed on agricultural goods exported by the American South. Furthermore, revenues raised from such tariffs benefited northern public works projects, such as the building of canals and roads aiding commerce and industry, without similar projects aiding southern economic development. Due to the perception of unfair economic practices, southern opponents of protective tariffs referred to the Tariff of 1828 as the "Tariff of Abomination."

In the **Campaign of 1828**, the Democratic Party, headed by Andrew Jackson adamantly positioned itself against protective tariffs. Whigs, born out of the remnants of Alexander Hamilton's Federalist Party, supported tariffs as a protective measure to buffer fledgling industries from the harsh effects of foreign competition. *See also* Tariff Issue.

Suggested Reading: Robert V. Remini, "Martin Van Buren and the Tariff of Abominations," *The American Historical Review* 63 (July 1958), pp. 903–917.

Taylor, Zachary

See Campaign of 1848.

Teapot Dome Scandal

Elected as vice president in 1920, Calvin Coolidge assumed the presidency in 1923 after the sudden death of President Warren Harding. Forced to clean up a number of serious public corruption scandals involving members of the Harding administration, Coolidge quickly established a reputation as a skilled administrator of impeccable personal honesty.

Teapot Dome, the most famous of the scandals, implicated Secretary of the Interior Albert B. Fall in a scheme involving the leasing of valuable western naval oil fields at Teapot Dome, near Casper, Wyoming, and the Elk Hills of California to oil developers Harry Sinclair and Edward L. Doheny. Coolidge asked Congress to authorize the appointment of well-respected Owen Roberts and former Democratic senator Atlee Pomerene as Justice Department special prosecutors to investigate. Coolidge also proceeded to replace a large number of Harding administration officials implicated in the scandal.

As the 1924 presidential election approached, Democrats believed that Harding's scandals could be used against Coolidge. But voters were not dissuaded from voting for Silent Cal, who won in 1924 despite the corruption of his predecessor.

Suggested Reading: Burl Noggle, *Teapot Dome: Oil and Politics in the 1920s* (Baton Rouge: University of Louisiana Press, 1962).

Television Campaign Spot Ads

Beginning with the **Campaign of 1952**, television transformed the fundamental character of presidential campaigns. Since 1924, campaigns increasingly relied on radio to reach Americans at home. Campaigns typically bought 30-minute blocks of time for candidates to talk directly to the listening public.

With network television's advent in the 1950s, it was quickly learned that few Americans were interested in viewing 30-minute political ads. To the dismay of many political observers, presidential campaigns soon adopted 30-second **spot ads** as a more effective alternative. Despite criticism, spot ads have assumed a permanent place in presidential politics. *See also* Horse-Race Campaign Coverage; Presidential Debates; Testimonial Ads; Town Meeting Campaign Event.

Suggested Readings: Kathleen Hall Jamieson, *Packaging the Presidency: A History and Criticism of Presidential Campaign Advertising* (New York: Oxford University Press, 1996); Alan Schroeder, *Presidential Debates: Forty Years of High-risk TV* (New York: Columbia University Press, 2000).

Temperance Movement

See Prohibition Issue.

Testimonial Campaign Spot Ads

Testimonials are a common type of spot ad involving the endorsement of a celebrity or public figure on behalf of a presidential candidate. Long before the development of television, advertisers used endorsements by public figures to promote a wide range of consumer products. Athletes, actors, musicians, and other public figures frequently endorsed a variety of goods and services.

In the early days of television, testimonials were found to be far more effective than lengthy discussions of the issues by the candidates themselves. Soon celebrities became a feature of presidential politics.

In 1960, the Kennedy campaign made effective use of a testimonial spot ad featuring contemporary singer/actor Harry Belafonte at the height of his popularity. Belafonte effectively highlighted Kennedy's strong support for civil rights as a reason to vote for Kennedy. Distinguished actor Raymond Massey endorsed the Republican candidacy of Senator Barry Goldwater in 1964. Hubert Humphrey's 1968 campaign was represented by veteran actor, E.G. Marshall. And during the **Campaign of 1996**, President Bill Clinton's reelection campaign broadcast a testimonial spot ad by Jim Brady, former President Ronald Reagan's press secretary and a victim of an attempted assassination of Reagan, supporting President's Clinton's crime and gun control legislation.

Suggested Reading: Michael Tackett, "Testimonials Added to Clinton's Ad Arsenal," *Chicago Tribune*, October 23, 1996, p. A1.

"There You Go Again"

On October 28, 1980, Democratic incumbent President Jimmy Carter and Republican challenger Ronald Reagan met in Cleveland, Ohio for their only televised debate. During the debate Carter criticized Reagan for prior statements and controversial positions regarding his alleged opposition to nuclear arms control, doubts about the inviolability of Social Security and Medicare, and open criticism of environmental protection laws.

In the midst of the debate, Reagan disarmingly deflected Carter's relentless criticism with the nonchalant response, "There go again." Reagan then went on to explain that he had supported alternatives and modifications to Medicare and other programs, not their reduction or elimination. It was this rejoinder that captured the lion's share of media attention in the post-debate analysis, not the discussion over the various issues themselves.

Shortly before the debate, preference polls indicated a slight lead for Reagan, which surprisingly expanded to landslide proportions on Election Day. Many commentators have since credited Reagan's debate performance and its probable effect on undecided voters as the decisive factor in his 1980 victory. *See also* Campaign of 1980; Presidential Debates; Sound Bite.

Suggested Readings: William Safire, "There You Go Again," *New York Times*, October 30, 1980, p. A27; Hedrick Smith, "No Clear Winner Apparent; Scene Is Simple and Stark," *New York Times*, October 29, 1980, p. A1; Commission on Presidential Debates, http://www.debates.org.

"They Understand What Peace Demands"

"They Understand What Peace Demands" was a slogan used by Republican presidential candidate and incumbent Vice President Richard Nixon during the 1960 campaign. The slogan sought to emphasize Nixon's reputation as a foreign policy expert capable of dealing with the Soviet Union and Communist China. Ambassador Henry Cabot Lodge, the Republican candidate for vice president, had also established a reputation as a strong anti-Communist.

Nixon was confident that voters would prefer the foreign policy experience of the Nixon/Lodge ticket to the youthful Democratic candidacy of Massachusetts senator John Kennedy. Given recent crises involving the Soviet Union, Cuba, Taiwan, and Eastern Europe, the campaign was able to present credible credentials in this pursuit.

To counter the Republican strategy, the Kennedy campaign highlighted Kennedy's distinguished war record as a PT boat commander in the Pacific. Equally important, during a series of four presidential debates, Kennedy demonstrated a command of a number of complex foreign policy issues. Kennedy took Nixon to task for committing the nation to the defense of the two small islands in the Straits of Taiwan (Quemoy and Matsu) even though the United States had only agreed to the defense of Taiwan. Kennedy also succeeded in convincing the public of the existence of a "missile gap," a charge that ultimately proved spurious.

Nixon's inability to convince the majority of American voters of Kennedy's inexperience constituted a major factor in Kennedy's narrow November victory. *See also* Campaign of 1960.

Suggested Readings: Theodore White, *The Making of the President, 1960* (New York: Atheneum Publishers, 1961); Commission on Presidential Debates, http://www.debates. org.

Third Rail of American Politics

As the high-voltage third rail on a subway track is deadly to touch, certain issues, policies and programs such as Social Security or Medicare are political suicide to any politician who seriously questions their existence or proposes substantively radical reforms. Like a "sacred cow," these and others are revered, immune to deep criticism from any credible candidate for national office. *See also* Social Security Issue.

Suggested Readings: E.J. Dionne Jr., "The Presidential Debate, Bush and Dukakis Quarrel on Pensions, Abortion, Arms and Campaign's Shrill Tone," *New York Times*, October 14, 1988, A1; Alison Mitchell, "The 2000 Campaign: The Texas Governor, Bush Returns Fire over Plan for Social Security Overhaul," *New York Times*, November 1, 2000, A1.

Third Term Issue

See "No Third Term."

"This Time Vote Like Your Whole World Depended on It"

"This Time Vote Like Your Whole World Depended on It" was a slogan used by the 1968 campaign of Republican candidate Richard Nixon dramatizing Nixon's promise to restore order and stability to a nation torn apart by the Vietnam War, urban riots, civil rights conflict and pervasive social turmoil, moral uncertainty, and rapid cultural change.

In the wake of a traumatically tumultuous campaign summer for the Democrats, the Nixon campaign took full advantage of their visible wounds and divisions to blame them and the administration of Lyndon Johnson for the many political and social crises of the mid-1960s. Johnson's vice president, Hubert Humphrey, the Democratic nominee at the violent Chicago convention, was immediately on the defensive. Holding Humphrey against the ropes, Nixon remained demure on Vietnam, moderate on domestic issues, solicitous of the **silent majority**, and statesmanlike in demeanor, leaving the more controversial aspect of the campaign to his running mate, Spiro Agnew.

Although Humphrey succeeded in narrowing Nixon's substantial lead in presidential preference polls, Nixon went on to win a close race in November. *See also* Campaign of 1968.

Suggested Readings: Lewis L. Gould, *1968: the Election that Changed America* (Chicago: Ivan R. Dee, 1993); Joe McGinniss, *The Selling of the President* (New York: Trident Press, 1969); Theodore White, *The Making of the President, 1968* (New York: Atheneum Publishers, 1969).

Tilden, Samuel J.

See Campaign of 1876.

"Tilden and Reform"

To highlight 1876 Democratic candidate Samuel Tilden's strong record for rooting out political corruption as governor of New York, the slogan "Tilden and Reform" encapsulated both Tilden's record as well as drawing attention to the corruption of the previous Republican administration of President Ulysses S. Grant.

From 1869 through 1876 the administration suffered from highly publicized corruption scandals implicating top Grant appointees. The Whiskey Ring scandal indicted General Orville E. Babcock, President Grant's secretary, in a scheme by whiskey distillers to evade federal liquor taxes. Although a federal jury in St. Louis later acquitted Babcock, the Whiskey Ring scandal provided the Democratic Party with additional ammunition to attack the Republicans.

The Republican National Convention broke a convention deadlock by turning to another reform governor, Ohio's Rutherford B. Hayes as their standard-bearer. To distract voters from the recent scandals, Republicans trotted out the **bloody shirt**, once again branding the Democratic Party as the party of rebellious traitors.

Tilden managed a popular majority but fell in the Electoral College by one vote, a vote that eventually went to Hayes and the Republicans but not after a prolonged election dispute that at one point almost precipitated a second civil war. *See also* Campaign of 1876.

Suggested Readings: Paul Leland Haworth, *The Hayes-Tilden Dispute Presidential Election of 1876* (New York: Russell & Russell, 1966); Keith Ian Polakoff, *The Politics of Inertia: The Election of 1876 and the End of Reconstruction* (Baton Rouge: Louisiana State University Press, 1973); "The Presidential Elections 1860–1912," HarpWeek, http://elections. harpweek.com/default.htm.

"Time For Greatness"

A "Time For Greatness" was a slogan used by the 1960 presidential campaign of John F. Kennedy, the Democratic nominee, to position Kennedy as a leader with a history of war heroism in the service of his country. The Kennedy campaign also used the slogan to argue that the country needed Kennedy's leadership to face a variety of international and domestic problems.

Attempting to counter the strong foreign policy experience of Republican nominee Vice President Richard Nixon, Democrats highlighted Kennedy's courage as a PT boat commander in the Pacific theater of operations. After a Japanese destroyer cut Kennedy's PT boat in half, Kennedy helped to get his crew safely to an island and then risked his life in efforts to obtain rescue. *See also* Campaign of 1960.

Suggested Reading: Theodore White, *The Making of the President, 1960* (New York: Atheneum Publishers, 1961).

"Tippecanoe and Tyler Too"

Supporters of Whig Party presidential nominee General William Henry Harrison and running mate John Tyler coined one of the more recognizable political slogans in American history, "Tippecanoe and Tyler Too," during the **Campaign of 1840**.

A reference to Harrison's war heroics, the slogan recalls his exploits and accomplishments in the War of 1812. General Harrison led a small army of 1,000 men in Indiana against native tribes on the frontier under the charismatic leadership of Tecumseh and the Prophet. Tecumseh sought to unite frontier tribes to block further new settlements. Harrison engaged and successfully repelled a vigorous attack near the Tippecanoe River in early November 1811, demoralizing the tribal movement and earning him the nickname of Ole' Tippecanoe.

When the leadership of the Whig Party decided to nominate Harrison for the presidency, they sought to make use of Harrison's distinguished military record to appeal to voters who had previously supported General Andrew Jackson, the hero of the Battle of New Orleans. Following the successful model of Jackson, Harrison supporters distributed thousands of posters depicting Harrison as a national hero during his campaign.

John Tyler of Virginia was plucked to serve as Harrison's running mate, lending an alliterative feature that flowed naturally from the slogan, "Tippecanoe and Tyler Too." Harrison would not live long after his election; President Tyler served the balance of the term that was won in the Campaign of 1840, much to the chagrin of Whigs who saw in Tyler a Democrat in Whig clothing. *See Also* Campaign of 1840; "Log Cabin and Hard Cider."

This untitled woodcut was apparently created for use on broadsides or banners during the Whig campaign of 1840. Courtesy of Library of Congress.

Suggested Readings: Robert Gunderson, *The Log-Cabin Campaign* (Lexington: University of Kentucky Press, 1957); "Tippecanoe Battlefield," Tippecanoe County Historical Association, http:/www.tcha.mus.in.us/battlefield.htm.

Town Meeting Campaign Event

A fixture of modern presidential campaigns, town meeting campaign events provide candidates with an opportunity to directly interact with citizens in a less formal arrangement. Loosely patterned after the New England town meeting, the town meeting format serves as a vehicle to demonstrate a candidate's willingness to communicate directly with the American people.

From 1968 through 1988 presidential campaigns relied increasingly on carefully staged **rallies** and **media events** to reach voters while reducing the risk of gaffes or missteps. All this began to change with the **Campaign of 1992**. Early in his run for the Democratic nomination, Arkansas governor Bill Clinton made frequent use of town meetings to connect with voters. After Clinton secured the nomination, his campaign successfully pushed for a debate using a town meeting format. At an October 15, 1992 University of Richmond debate Clinton, incumbent President George Bush (the elder), and Ross Perot directly answered the questions raised by audience participants. The town meeting format has since become a fixture of presidential primary and general election campaigns.

Supporters of the format argue that it forces candidates to spontaneously answer unrehearsed questions raised by audience members rather than mindlessly following a script with previewed questions and designed answers. Critics assert that the spontaneity is only apparent; well-prepared candidates rarely stray from their carefully scripted answers, and find a way to turn any question into an opportunity to talk about only what they want to talk about. *See also* Media Event; New Media; Presidential Debates; Public Journalism.

Suggested Readings: Tom Baxter, "The Year Voters Tuned In: '92 Campaign Marked by Surge in Interest from TV Talk Shows to Town Hall Meetings, Citizens Took Spotlight," *Atlanta Journal and Constitution*, November 1, 1992, p. G1; Marion R. Just, ed., *Crosstalk: Citizens, Candidates, and the Media in a Presidential Campaign* (Chicago: University of Chicago Press, 1996); Mary Leonard, "Campaign 2000/Formats; Bush, Gore Campaigns Agree to Three-Debate Schedule," *Boston Globe*, September 17, 2000, p. A16; Tom Rosenstiel, *Strange Bedfellows: How Television and the Presidential Candidates Changed American Politics*, 1992 (New York: Hyperion, 1993).

Tracking Poll

Tracking polls attempt to measure daily changes in voter preferences for candidates for elective office including presidential candidates. Prior to the 1990s presidential campaigns conducted the vast majority of tracking polls to measure the effectiveness of various campaign strategies. News operations significantly increased the use of tracking polls as part of their campaign coverage. For instance, tracking polls conducted by MSNBC/Reuters, Zogby International, and the Gallup CNN/

USA were useful references for the media during the exceptionally tight race that marked the **Campaign of 2000.**

Critics argue that the attention paid to tracking polls in the media reduces the amount of time that could be devoted to coverage of the key substantive issues. Critics also argue that the growing preoccupation with tracking polls contributes to **horse-race coverage.** Finally, critics claim that elements of the media greatly overestimate the accuracy of tracking polls. Due to the high expense of contacting high numbers of voters, polls typically contact approximately 600 citizens. Pollsters realize that such a small sample size has a high margin of error.

Suggested Readings: Dan Balz, "Race Still Too Close to Call; Most Polls Show Bush Ahead, but Some Find Gore Gaining Ground," *Washington Post*, November 7, 2000, p. A17; Glen Bolger and Bill McInturff, "Tracking Polls: Avoiding Mistakes," *Campaigns & Elections*, (August 1995), pp. 26–28; Donald P. Green and Alan Gerber, "How to Interpret Tracking Polls," *Campaigns & Elections* 19, August 1998, pp. 23–27.

Truman, Harry S.

See Campaign of 1948.

Trust Busting Issue

During the industrial revolution that spanned the latter half of the nineteenth century, a small number of industrialists acquired unprecedented economic power, wealth and an opulent lifestyle reminiscent of the fabled riches of antiquity. Trust and monopolies dominated the economy, provoking the emergence by the 1870s of grassroots movements demanding government intervention to protect the interests of farmers, small businesses, and workers. These movements argued that monopolistic practices had rained economic ruin on middle America, keeping wages and farm prices artificially low, and devouring the entrepreneurial spirit of small business.

During the **Campaign of 1880** the second Greenback Party broadened its platform to include a plank calling for Congress to regulate interstate commerce to "secure moderate, fair and uniform rates for passenger and freight traffic." The platform also called for an eight-hour day and the abolition of child labor. Despite the fact that Representative James B. Weaver, the nominee of the Greenback Party, received only 300,000 votes, the growth of a farm-labor movement put pressure on the major parties to address the problem of monopoly power.

Concerned over the loss of support from rural Midwestern voters, Republicans promised to support in their 1884 platform the public regulation of railroads. In 1887, Congress established the Interstate Commerce Commission and gave it the authority to set freight and passenger rates. In 1890, Congress passed the Sherman Anti-Trust Act. Neither of these actions seriously weakened the power of the largest monopolies and trusts.

In the early 1890s, the People's Party, popularly known as the Populist Party, increased the pressure on the established parties to continue efforts at controlling the growing power of wealth. The 1892 Populist platform called for the nationalization of the railroads, telegraph, and telephone companies. It also called for a graduated income tax and a significant expansion of federal government power. James B. Weaver, the Populist nominee, received over one million votes.

In 1896, the Populist agenda was partially incorporated into the platform of the Democratic Party, marking a watershed in American political history. With strong populist backing, William Jennings Bryan, "The Great Commoner," won the Democratic nomination. Besides including a **free silver** plank, the Democratic platform called for stricter control of trusts by the federal government as well as for increasing the power of the Interstate Commerce Commission over the nation's railroads. Republicans countered by moving closer to business interests, thus shifting further away from their own progressive roots. William McKinley, their nominee, was supported by big business, his campaign managed by an industrialist turned kingmaker.

Even though McKinley had soundly defeated the populist Bryan four years earlier, growing public anger over the greed of large trusts and corporations forced the Republican Party to include a plank in its 1900 platform calling for legislation to stop price fixing and other monopolistic practices. A vigorous progressive movement appeared among Republicans, led by the magnetic Theodore Roosevelt who became McKinley's reelection running mate in 1904. Unlike McKinley, Roosevelt had established a record for combating trusts and monopolies while serving as governor of New York. Roosevelt assumed the presidency in 1901 upon the assassination of McKinley, and to the alarm of party leaders, Roosevelt aggressively used the Sherman Anti-Trust Act to divide a number of large trusts. Based on his progressive record, Roosevelt easily won reelection in 1904 and secured the temporary dominance of the progressive wing of the Republican Party.

Further left, the Socialist Party proposed a much more radical approach for dealing with the power of trusts and monopolies during the **Campaign of 1908**. Its platform called for nationalization of railroads, steamship lines, telephone companies, and other key industries. Although Socialist candidate Eugene Debs came in a distant third behind the major candidates, the call for public ownership of necessary infrastructure sounded a responsive chord with a portion of the American people.

Progressivism reached its apex in the atypical three-way race of 1912. Two of the three candidates, Roosevelt, now a renegade from the Republican Party, and Democratic nominee Woodrow Wilson, both campaigned on progressive platforms. Wilson took advantage of the Republican split to win 1914, and soon after Congress enacted under his signature the Clayton Anti-Trust Act and the Federal Trade Commission Act. The Clayton Act prohibited any action by a business that "substantially [lessened] competition or [tended] to create a monopoly in any line of commerce." The laws significantly increased the power of the federal government to regulate the predatory trade practices of large corporations.

With the 1920 election of Republican Warren G. Harding, corporate America again enjoyed a friend in the White House. Perhaps more importantly, a corporate-friendly Supreme Court sharply restricted the scope of the major anti-trust laws.

Franklin Roosevelt's 1932 victory ushered in an unprecedented period of government regulation of big business, largely in response to the crisis of the Great Depression. Congress delegated to new federal departments, agencies, bureaus, and boards sweeping authority to regulate large segments of the national economy. Roosevelt's New Deal reforms, along with President Truman's Fair Deal protection of the interests of labor thoroughly reshaped the dynamics of economics in America. By the 1952 election of Republican moderate Dwight Eisenhower, the achievements of Roosevelt and Truman were accepted by both parties as firmly established.

Serious antitrust concerns would not resurface until the energy crisis of the mid-1970s revived the issue during the 1976 campaign. The Democratic platform argued "when competition is inadequate to insure free markets and maximum benefit to American consumers, we support effective restrictions on the right of major companies to own all phases of the oil industry." Republicans maintained that energy independence depends on expanding exploration and production of oil and gas, and supported a more liberal attitude toward private industry.

More recently, antitrust concerns have been raised over issues involving computer technology, but have yet to become an issue of presidential campaign import. *See also* Campaign of 1896; Campaign of 1904; Campaign of 1912; Campaign of 1932; Campaign of 1936; Campaign of 1976.

Suggested Reading: Donald Dewey, *The Antitrust Experiment in America* (New York: Columbia University Press, 1990).

Truth Boxes

See Ad Watches.

Truth Squad

As part of their media operations, modern campaigns routinely establish "truth squads" to expose misstatements by opposing candidates. After the early October 2000 presidential debate between Texas governor George W. Bush and Vice President Albert Gore, campaigns dispatched truth squads to attack the performance of the opposition. For days following the debate, the Bush campaign scolded Gore for falsely claiming to have traveled to Texas in 1998 to observe damage caused by a series of disastrous fires. Gore countered with criticisms of Bush's gubernatorial record.

Critics of truth squads argue that such activities do not improve debate over important issues because they typically draw too much attention to petty campaign missteps and too little attention to major policy differences. Defenders of truth squads argue that they help voters learn more about opposing candidates, ensuring more informed decisions at the polls. *See also* Negative Campaigning; Opposition Research; Spin Doctor.

Suggested Reading: Maria L. LaGanga and Elizabeth Shogren, "Campaign 2000; Bush and Gore Campaigns Tally up the Post-Debate Scores; Politics: Aides Spend the Day Spinning and Clarifying After the Boston Matchup. Texas Visits, Standing Students and Who Has Spent More Is All Fair Game," *Los Angeles Times*, October 5, 2000, A1, p. 22.

"Turn the Rascals Out!"

Indignant over corruption in the administration of Republican President Ulysses S. Grant, liberal Republicans called upon Americans to "turn the rascals out" and vote for their idealist candidate, Horace Greeley. While Greeley was soundly thrashed at the polls, the phrase, often iterated as "Throw the rascals out!" is a sentiment that returns during the occasional period of voter frustration stemming from poorly managed or morally bankrupt government. *See also* Campaign of 1872.

Suggested Reading: William Harlan Hale, *Horace Greeley, Voice of the People* (New York: Harper, 1950).

Twenty-Four-Hour News Cycle

With the relatively recent emergence of cable and Internet news operations, breaking news is now available to the public without interruption, creating a "twenty-four-hour news cycle." Communications scholars trace this media phenomenon to Ted Turner's **Cable News Network** (CNN), established in the early 1980s. By the end of the 1980s, the growth of 24-hour news operations spurred major changes in presidential campaigning.

In addition to trying to get the best possible media coverage for their candidate, the emergence of 24-hour news compelled campaigns to install media monitors to help candidates instantly respond to breaking news. The 1992 campaign of Bill Clinton included in his Little Rock "War Room" means and methods to monitor media coverage of his campaign and to quickly respond to critical stories and reports. Clinton's "War Room" has since become the model for current campaign media operations. *See also* Campaign Manager; Earned Media; Free Media.

Suggested Reading: Patricia Sellers, "The Selling of the President in '88," *Fortune*, December 21, 1987, pp. 113–134.

"Undecideds"

"Undecideds" are voters who remain uncommitted to a presidential candidate late into a campaign. The growth in the percentage of undecideds coincides with increased numbers of voters classifying themselves as Independents. Although many undecideds fail to vote, in close election contests they influence the final outcome. As a result modern campaigns devote considerable resources to win the undecided vote. In the **Campaign of 1996**, President Bill Clinton successfully exploited the **gender gap** by **targeting** suburban politically independent **soccer moms**. Four years later, Texas governor George W. Bush carefully positioned himself as a **"compassionate conservative"** in an effort to attract key swing and undecided voters. *See also* Battleground States.

Suggested Readings: Ron Faucheux, "Hitting the Bull's Eye: Winning Elections by Targeting Voters," *Campaigns & Elections* 20, July 1999, pp. 20–25; Tina Kelley, "Watching, Listening, Hoping for a President: Undecided Voters Weigh Options," *New York*

Times, August 5, 2000, A1; "The Power of the Undecideds," *New York Times,* November 5, 2000, Section 4, p. 14.

Van Buren, Martin

See Campaign of 1836; Campaign of 1848.

"Van Is a Used Up Man"

See Campaign of 1840.

"Vote Grits and Fritz in '76"

During the **Campaign of 1976,** Jimmy Carter's presidential campaign made effective use of the whimsical slogan, "Vote Grits and Fritz in '76." "Grits" humorously referred to Carter's folksy southern heritage with his running mate, Walter F. "Fritz" Mondale contributing the rest.

Carter's homespun version of the southern strategy proved vital to his subsequent victory. Many southern white voters had abandoned the Democratic Party to vote for Republican Richard Nixon in the previous two elections. To win back the South, Carter needed to appeal to the southern vote in general. Successfully emphasizing his rural southern roots and taking pride in his heritage, "Grits" was able to win in the South with the exception of Virginia. Carter's presidency, at least in its first few months, continued to emphasize the theme of the common man. *See also* Campaign of 1976.

Suggested Reading: Patrick Anderson, *Electing Jimmy Carter: The Campaign of 1976* (Baton Rouge: Louisiana State University Press, 1994).

"Vote Yourself a Farm"

While slavery was far and away the dominant issue of the 1860 election, the candidates occasionally proposed unrelated policies. "Vote Yourself a Farm" was a Republican slogan that affirmed Abraham Lincoln's belief in the value of free labor and agrarian virtue, principles that generated his support for the homesteading of land in the West. Lincoln's values regarding the worth of honest work and self-reliance were, for the most part, obscured by the controversy over the plague of slavery. *See also* Campaign of 1860.

Suggested Reading: David Emerson Fite, *The Presidential Campaign of 1860* (Port Washington, NY: Kennikat Press, 1967).

Voting Reform Issue

Voting reform has been an object of the political process since the early years of the republic. The first national voting reforms involved the procedural methods of electing the president.

The Constitution gives the Electoral College full responsibility to select the president of the United States. Federal law, however, leaves it up to each state to decide on the method for selecting electors to the college. Additionally, efforts to open the political process to a wider cross-section of the American public have directly influenced the evolution of presidential election campaigns.

During the 1820s, Andrew Jackson emerged as the first presidential candidate with a populist base. The **Campaign of 1824** pitted Jackson against the political establishment. At that time eighteen states used the popular vote to select presidential electors. However, six states continued to give state legislatures the responsibility for selecting electors. When the Electoral College met to count the electoral votes none of the four candidates—Jackson, John Quincy Adams, George Crawford, and Henry Clay—received a majority of electoral votes, although Jackson did manage to receive a plurality.

Absent an Electoral College majority, the election is decided, under the Constitution, in the House of Representatives. Henry Clay threw his support behind John Quincy Adams, guaranteeing Adams's election. Adams subsequently nominated Clay as secretary of state. The allegedly "corrupt election of 1824" infuriated Jackson's supporters and accelerated the movement to reform the process through the popular and direct election of electors. Four years later, Jackson won the **Campaign of 1828** by a landslide.

By the **Campaign of 1844** a growing rift between slave and free states stimulated the emergence of the abolitionist movement committed to ending slavery. The new Liberty Party nominated James G. Birney of New York, a former slave owner, as their candidate. The platform of the Liberty Party called for the outright abolition of slavery. Four years later, the new Free Soil Party sought to build a broader anti-slavery movement by dropping the demand for the immediate abolition of slavery. Instead, the Free Soil Party sought to prohibit the extension of slavery to any new states or territories. The party nominated former President Martin Van Buren as their standard bearer.

The new Republican Party crusaded against slavery during the **Campaign of 1856**. Resembling the Free Soil Party, the Republican Party called for a ban on slavery in any new state or territory but not the immediate abolition of slavery where it existed. Explorer John C. Freemont received the party's 1856 presidential nomination. Four years later, Republican Abraham Lincoln defeated three other candidates in the 1860 presidential election. The Civil War immediately followed.

The Union victory led to the ratification of the Thirteenth, Fourteenth, and Fifteenth Amendments, which, respectively, abolished slavery, guaranteed citizens of the States' equal protection and due process and prohibited states' from denying African Americans the right to vote. Reconstruction civil rights legislation protected the Fifteenth Amendment rights of the newly freed slaves, but all that effectively ended with the resolution of the disputed election of 1876.

The Democratic nominee, Samuel J. Tilden, won the popular vote but fell one vote short of the majority of electoral votes because of a dispute over the electoral votes of three southern states, most notably Florida. In the end, a Republican-controlled Electoral Commission awarded all of the disputed electoral votes to Rutherford B. Hayes, the Republican nominee. To obtain Democratic backing for Hayes, Congressional Republicans agreed to end Reconstruction funding. Within two decades, the states of the former Confederacy had enacted Jim Crow Laws depriving African Americans of their constitutional rights, ushering in decades of segregation, repression, and terror.

From the 1840s through the 1920 ratification of the Nineteenth Amendment, the **women's suffrage movement** sought to extend voting rights to women. Long before the major parties threw their support behind women's suffrage, the 1880 platform of the Greenback Party endorsed voting rights for women. The 1908 Socialist Party platform included a similar provision, and the 1912 Progressive Party (Bull Moose) platform pledged itself "to the task of securing equal suffrage to men and women alike."

The ratification of the Nineteenth Amendment made the deprivation of voting rights for African Americans even more egregious. From the 1920s through the 1940s, the Civil Rights movement worked hard to end segregation and inequality. The 1944 Republican Party platform called for a constitutional amendment abolishing the poll tax, a method commonly employed to prevent lower-income citizens from voting. The 1948 Democratic platform pledged "the right to full and equal political participation" for all Americans.

Through the 1950s and into the **Campaign of 1960**, both established parties supported the end to the poll tax leading to the 1964 ratification of the Twenty-Fourth Amendment, forever ending this restriction. That year Congress passed the Voting Rights Act of 1965 to give the federal government a direct role in guaranteeing all Americans free access to the polls. *See also* Campaign of 1848; Campaign of 1876.

Suggested Reading: Richard Hofstadter, *The Age of Reform: From Bryan to F.D.R.* (New York: Knopf, 1955).

Wallace, George

See Campaign of 1968.

War and Peace Issue

The **Campaign of 1812** was the first presidential campaign conducted during wartime. Between 1810 and 1812, a bloc of Congressional War Hawks lobbied for a declaration of war against Britain. The ongoing war between France, Britain, and other European powers had contributed to sharp divisions in the United States. The War Hawks, who were mostly from the South and West, saw the European conflict as an opportunity to expand American power against British Canada and Spanish Florida. Needing the support of the War Hawks to obtain the Democratic-Republican nomination, incumbent President James Madison aligned himself with the War Hawks. In June of 1812, a successfully reelected Madison asked Congress to declare war against Britain. Northern high Federalists opposed the war, but the naval victories combined with General Andrew Jackson's unnecessary victory at New Orleans boosted the perception of the war in the public eye, and thus boosted the party that fought it, Madison's.

Rumors of war with Mexico over the proposed annexation of Texas loomed over the **Campaign of 1844**. James K. Polk, the Democratic nominee, was a vocal adherent of the doctrine of **Manifest Destiny**. The Democratic platform included a plank that supported a claim to the entire Oregon territory and endorsed the annexation of Texas at the earliest possible time. Whigs ran under Henry Clay, who opposed war with Mexico, fearing that it would undermine the sectional balance of power.

Polk turned the election into a referendum on Texas. Democrats effectively used the slogans **"Polk, Dallas, Texas, Oregon and the Tariff of '42,"** **"Fifty-four Forty or Fight,"** and similar slogans to propel Polk to a stunning dark-horse upset over the statesmanlike Clay. Texas was annexed, war followed, American might proved superior, and Mexico was deprived of a vast amount of its traditional territory reaching to the Pacific Coast. A treaty with Britain diplomatically settled the ongoing dispute over the Oregon territory.

The future of the Union became the central issue of the **Campaign of 1860**. Demanding an end of the extension of slavery, the young Republican Party nominated Abraham Lincoln of Illinois, long on record as critical of the Peculiar Institution, as their presidential candidate. Pro-slavery southern secessionists warned that the election of Lincoln would result in the dissolution of the Union. Supporters of Northern Democrat Stephen Douglas used the slogan **"Douglas and Johnson: The Union Now and Forever,"** to turn the election into a referendum on preserving the Union rather than a referendum on slavery. John Bell's Southern Constitutional Union Party borrowed from Daniel Webster in proclaiming the principle "Liberty and Union Now and Forever One and Inseparable. No North, No South, No East, No West, Nothing but the Union." John C. Breckinridge represented the pro-slavery, and thus potentially secessionist, South. The result of this election forever transformed American society at all levels: politically, socially, economically, culturally, and morally.

The **Campaign of 1864** found Lincoln's reelection chances threatened by growing Northern disenchantment over the painfully slow progress of the war. The Northern Democratic Party nominated Lincoln's former commander of the Army of the Potomac, General George B. McClellan, as their candidate, their platform attacking Lincoln for allegedly using his war powers to abridge the constitutional rights of citizens.

Faced with prosecuting the war and running for reelection, Republicans relied on slogans such as **"Don't Change Horses in Mid-Stream"** to persuade northern voters to stand with the president. In the end, a variety of military victories beginning with Gettysburg turned the electoral tide in Lincoln's favor. Lincoln won with ease in November.

In response to the 1914 outbreak of World War I, President Woodrow Wilson declared that the United States would apply a strict neutrality policy to prevent the United States from being drawn into the Great War in Europe. On August 19, President Woodrow Wilson delivered to Congress a Declaration of Neutrality.

"The effect of the war upon the United States will depend upon what American citizens say and do. Every man who really loves America will act and speak in the true spirit of neutrality, which is the spirit of impartiality and fairness and friendliness to all concerned," stated Wilson. "The spirit of the nation in this critical matter will be determined largely by what individuals and society and those gathered in public meetings do and say, upon what newspapers and magazines contain, upon what ministers utter in their pulpits, and men proclaim as their opinions upon the street," continued Wilson.

Early in 1916, Germany informed the world that it reserved the right to sink any ship approaching Britain. Then on May 7, 1915, a German U-Boat sank the British steamship Lusitania with the loss of 100 American lives. Even before the sinking of the Lusitania, the United States had made clear to Germany it would not tolerate the sinking of neutral shipping. United States's reaction to the Lusitania's sinking forced Germany to revoke its blockade ultimatum. The Democratic Party and Woodrow Wilson turned the **Campaign of 1916** into a referendum on Wilson's neutrality policy. Peace slogans used by the Wilson campaign included **"He Kept Us Out of War," "War in the East, Peace in the West, Thank God for Woodrow Wilson"** and **"War in Europe, Peace in America."**

Sharp divisions within the Republican Party over the neutrality issue complicated efforts by Charles Evans Hughes to convince voters that he had no intention of getting the United States involved in the conflict. Former Republican president, Theodore Roosevelt, publicly lobbied for the United States to enter the war on the side of Great Britain and the allies. Strong isolationist sentiment in regions beyond the Northeast helped Wilson return for a second term. But by late 1917, the United States was drawn into World War I.

The **Campaign of 1940** again found the United States facing entry into another World War. In Europe, Nazi Germany had defeated Poland and France and threatened an invasion assault on Britain. In the Pacific, Imperial Japan waged a war in China and seemed intent on extending its sphere of influence over all of East Asia and the Pacific Ocean. Given the exigency of the moment, popular President Franklin Roosevelt wrestled with a decision to run for an unprecedented third term, defying the venerable tradition established by George Washington. Roosevelt also faced strong isolationist sentiment reminiscent of 1916.

Roosevelt's decision to seek a third term, not his efforts to help Great Britain fight off Nazi Germany, turned out to be the main issue of the 1940 presidential campaign. Throughout the 1940 campaign, supporters of Wendell Willkie, the Republican nominee, chanted **"No Third Term."** As a result, the Roosevelt campaign devoted most of its energy on rebutting Republican allegations that the election of Roosevelt would start the nation on the road toward dictatorship. Roosevelt also stressed that by providing Britain the tools to combat Nazi Germany it was much less likely that the United States would become embroiled in another war. Roosevelt promoted America as the Arsenal of Democracy, which boosted American industry mitigating some of the economic distress of the lingering Great Depression. Americans backed Roosevelt once again for a third term.

The **Campaign of 1944** constituted the first wartime presidential election since the **Campaign of 1864**. Taking a page out of Lincoln's 1864 campaign, Democrats advised Americans to **"Never Swap Horses in Mid-Stream,"** diffusing the fourth-term issue. Thomas E. Dewey, the Republican candidate, failed to convince the American public that the election of Roosevelt to a fourth term would deliver the country to a homegrown dictator. Dewey also failed to convince voters that his administration would more quickly achieve victory at war.

With the **Campaign of 1952**, the United States was locked in a military stalemate on the Korean Peninsula. An arms race with Stalin's Soviet Union intensified a dangerous world climate. Republican candidate General Dwight Eisenhower proved a credible candidate capable of dealing with crisis abroad. His opponent Adlai Stevenson, a New Deal Democrat, was an able leader who emphasized the domestic legacy of his predecessors. The Stevenson campaign reminded voters that **"You Never Had It So Good"** under Roosevelt's **New Deal**, but the revered war hero overwhelmed his credentials.

Between the 1952 election and the **Campaign of 1960**, persistent and intense Cold War competition with the Soviet Union and Communist China forced presidential campaigns to devote considerable time and energy to national security issues. Republican nominee and Vice President Richard Nixon relied heavily on his experience to persuade voters that he was more qualified to be president than Democratic presidential candidate, Massachusetts senator John F. Kennedy. With slogans such as "Experience Counts," "Peace Without Surrender," and "Keep America Strong," Nixon attempted to overshadow the young Senator's inexperience. The Kennedy campaign countered with a new vision for America. At the same time, the Kennedy campaign attempted to close the experience gap by alleging the existence of a missile gap to the advantage of the Soviets. Kennedy's insistence that if elected president he would close the "missile gap" helped to reassure the public that Kennedy had the strength to deal with foreign threats. Kennedy won, but after the election it became apparent that a "missile gap" never really existed.

Vice President Lyndon Johnson assumed the presidency in November 1963 upon the shocking assassination of President Kennedy. Johnson also was compelled to deal with war and peace, and in depicting Republican candidate Barry Goldwater as an unpredictable War Hawk, LBJ won the November election in the biggest landslide since Franklin Roosevelt. Taking advantage of Goldwater's controversial positions on Vietnam and the feasibility of acceptable thermonuclear warfare, the Johnson campaign characterized Goldwater as an extremist. Johnson became the candidate for peace, an effective stance given the dangers of nuclear warfare. **"The Stakes Are Too High for You to Stay Home,"** became a compelling slogan in Johnson's campaign.

From November of 1964 through 1967, American involvement in the Vietnam War escalated. Against his 1964 campaign pledge, President Johnson deployed hundreds of thousands of troops to the conflict. The antiwar movement strengthened to influence the 1968 election providing momentum to the idealistic campaign of Minnesota senator Eugene McCarthy, ultimately deflating Johnson's reelection hopes by nearly defeating the president in the critical New Hampshire primary. In late March, Johnson withdrew from the race, and shortly thereafter Vice President Hubert Humphrey and Senator Robert Kennedy joined the contest for the Democratic nomination. With his victory in the California primary, Robert Kennedy became the front-runner for the nomination, a fleeting moment of triumph violently obliterated by an assassin's bullet even while partisans celebrated the victory.

With the party in disarray, having lost the incumbent Johnson and the charismatic Kennedy, thousands of antiwar demonstrators descended upon the Democratic summer convention in Chicago. Rioting roiled the streets of Chicago while Humphrey received the nomination.

In 1967, Vietnam War protestors stage a sit-in at the Mall entrance to the Pentagon. © National Archives.

Republicans turned once again to Richard Nixon who claimed to hold a secret plan for ending United States' involvement in the war. In a series of well-crafted ads, Nixon's campaign promised to lead the nation out of the turmoil of the 1960s and into the brighter decade ahead. **"This Time Vote Like Your Whole World Depended On It"** became one of the key slogans for the Nixon campaign.

There has not been another wartime campaign since 1968. However, the campaigns of 1980 and 1984 involved controversies over the lingering Soviet menace and American support for anti-communist interests in Central America. Critics of Ronald Reagan argued that Reagan's military buildup would stimulate a new arms race, raising the risk of nuclear war. Reagan's Strategic Defense Initiative (SDI), or Star Wars, was roundly criticized by the Left as both infeasible and provocative. These concerns were temporarily allayed with the collapse of the Soviet Union in the early 1990s, but new anxieties evoked by emerging "rogue" nations such as Iran, Iraq, North Korea, Libya, Sudan, and Syria compelled the United States to redirect its military focus. Current war policy is driven by the attack against the World Trade Center on September 11, 2001, and the subsequent "war on terrorism" initiated by the younger President Bush. *See also* Campaign of 1860; Campaign of 1864; Campaign of 1916; Campaign of 1940; Campaign of 1944; Campaign of 1964; Campaign of 1968; Campaign of 1972; Campaign of 1980.

Suggested Reading: Frederic Shiver, "The War Election of 1864," *American History Illustrated*, 1968, pp. 5–9, 45–48.

"War in Europe, Peace in America"

"War in Europe, Peace in America" emphasized President Woodrow Wilson's success in sustaining American neutrality while war ripped apart the civilizations of Europe. Wilson's bid for a second term in 1916 was grounded in his ability to preserve "peace in America" while the dogs of war ran wild abroad.

Unfortunately, efforts by Germany to use submarines in the imposition of a naval blockade around the British Isles undermined Wilson's neutrality policy. On February 1, 1917, three months after Wilson's reelection on a peace platform, German revived unrestricted submarine warfare on any ships challenging its naval blockade. The subsequent sinking of American ships coupled with efforts by Germany to enter into a threatening alliance with Mexico led Wilson to ask Congress for a declaration of war on Germany. Congress accommodated Wilson with such a declaration in April of 1917, breaking the "peace in America" that reelected Wilson less than a year earlier. *See also* Campaign of 1916; "He Kept Us Out of War"; "War in the East, Peace in the West, Thank God for Woodrow Wilson."

Suggested Reading: S. D. Lovell, *The Presidential Election of 1916* (Carbondale: Southern Illinois University Press, 1980).

"War in the East, Peace in the West, Thank God for Woodrow Wilson"

"War in the East, Peace in the West, Thank God for Woodrow Wilson" serves as an extended variation of an effective 1916 campaign slogan punctuating Wilson's neutrality policy, favorably received by many Americans, and endorsing the continued efforts of the incumbent in the protection of America's interest in peace. This sentiment played well outside of the Northeast, showing a division in the electorate between the pro-Republican Eastern industrial states who were themselves divided on the issue of war in Europe, and the pro-Democratic regions of the South, West, and urban Midwest, who preferred neutrality. Democrats were successful in garnering support outside the East, however voters in the South and West inexplicably ignored the fact that the Republican platform also contained a strong neutrality plank. *See also* Campaign of 1916; "He Kept Us Out of War"; "War in Europe, Peace In America."

Suggested Reading: S. D. Lovell, *The Presidential Election of 1916* (Carbondale: Southern Illinois University Press, 1980).

War on Poverty Speech

In his first State of the Union address delivered in January of 1964, President Lyndon Johnson urged Congress and the nation to declare a war on poverty. "This administration today, here and now, declares unconditional war on poverty in America," Johnson pledged. "I urge this Congress and all Americans to join with me in that effort." Coming only a few weeks after the November assassination of President John F. Kennedy, the speech affirmed an aggressive legislative agenda for the upcoming election year. Johnson also left little doubt that he intended to seek the Democratic presidential nomination. However, Johnson's proposed "war on poverty" did not become a major issue in the presidential **Campaign of 1964.**

With the Republican nomination of Senator Barry Goldwater, who was regarded on the political fringe by a majority of Americans, the Johnson campaign chose to emphasize Goldwater's extremism and reactionary view of politics both at home and abroad. Warning Americans that a Goldwater presidency might spark a third world war, the war on poverty receded as an issue. With this strategy, and boosted by Johnson's own association with the lost Camelot administration of John Kennedy, the Johnson/Humphrey ticket went on to win an electoral vote and popular vote landslide. Equally important, Johnson's coattails helped to add 37 Democrats to the House of Representatives. Enjoying a solid majority in Congress as well as holding the White House, Democrats were thus able to enact socially and politically progressive legislation in support of Johnson's "Great Society" agenda.

Despite Johnson's great expectations, growing opposition to the Vietnam War significantly reduced public support for the war on poverty, and by the start of the **Campaign of 1968**, LBJ was politically moribund. An astonishingly doubtful performance in the New Hampshire primary augured Johnson's political demise, helping to determine the outcome of his war against poverty in America. *See also* Great Society Speech.

Suggested Reading: "President Lyndon B. Johnson's Annual Message to the Congress on the State of the Union, January 8, 1964," Lyndon Baines Johnson Library and Museum, http://www.lbjlib.utexas.edu/johnson/archives.hom/speeches.hom/64018.asp.

"We Are Going to Win This War and the Peace That Follows"

In 1944 incumbent President Franklin Roosevelt, already into the last year of a singularly historic third term recognized that his decision to seek a fourth term would become the most significant campaign issue. Thus his campaign emphasized Roosevelt's proven ability in leading America toward an inevitable victory through the most destructive war in world history, and confidently claimed that only with Roosevelt can future peace be secured for generations to come. "Win this War With Roosevelt and the Peace that Follows" summarized these hopes.

The Republican ticket of Thomas Dewey and Ohio governor John W. Bricker argued that they would bring the war to a speedier conclusion. Dewey and Bricker also criticized Roosevelt for failing to prepare the nation for war in the first place, even implying that Roosevelt could have prevented the Pearl Harbor attack. Additionally, Dewey charged Roosevelt with poor management and bad judgment in the administration of war resources. As part of this strategy, Republican operatives alleged that Roosevelt had ordered the Navy to assign a destroyer for the single purpose of transporting Roosevelt's Scottish terrier, Fala.

Successfully deflecting Dewey's charges, which included outrageous claims that Roosevelt was leading the country into totalitarian despotism, Roosevelt was again chosen to serve a fourth term, unique in presidential history. However, Roosevelt died in April of 1945, leaving to President Truman the conclusion of the most horrific war in human history. *See also* Campaign of 1944.

Suggested Reading: John E. Vacha, "FDR's Fala: The Dog That Swung an Election," *Timeline* 11, 1994, pp. 36–43.

"We Polked You in '44, We Shall Pierce You in '52"

Vividly reminding their Whig opponents that their dark horse candidate, James K. Polk had "polked" the august Henry Clay in 1844, Democrats promised that Franklin Pierce, another comparatively unknown candidate, would prove equally formidable in 1852 against Whig nominee Winfield Scott, also ridiculed as **"Old Fuss and Feathers."** The combative tenor of the language naturally fit a campaign involving veterans of the Mexican War.

Pierce pierced Scott at the polls, but went on to serve poorly through one term during one of the nation's most dangerous eras. *See also* Campaign of 1852.

Suggested Reading: Lara Gara, *The Presidency of Franklin Pierce* (Lawrence: University Press of Kansas, 1991).

"We Want a Choice, Not an Echo"

"We Want a Choice, Not an Echo" was one of several slogans used by the 1964 presidential campaign of Arizona senator Barry Goldwater, the Republican nominee, rebutting complaints that Goldwater held extremist views. Goldwater had won the GOP nomination as the candidate of the party's conservative wing, defeating New York governor Nelson Rockefeller from the party's liberal side.

Prior to winning the Republican nomination, Goldwater had taken controversial positions on a number of important issues, such as proposing voluntary options for Social Security at home and the possible use of tactical nuclear weapons in Vietnam. In his acceptance speech, Goldwater echoed Cicero, affirming, "Extremism in the defense of liberty is no vice. Moderation in the pursuit of justice is no virtue." The Johnson campaign took full advantage of these provocative policy proposals and statements.

Efforts by Goldwater to deflect the extremist charge were to no avail. Slogans such as **"In Your Heart You Know He's Right,"** and "We Want a Choice, Not an Echo," proved no match for the Johnson campaign's negative onslaught. *See also* Campaign of 1964; "Daisy" Campaign Ad.

Suggested Readings: Harold Faber, *The Road to the White House: The Story of the 1964 Election* (New York: McGraw-Hill, 1965); Rick Perlstein, *Before the Storm: Barry Goldwater and the Unmaking of the American Consensus* (New York: Hill and Wang, 2001); Theodore White, *The Making of the President, 1964* (New York: Atheneum Publishers, 1965).

Wedge Issue

"Wedge issues" are those issues that are used to drive a "wedge" between the parties for the purpose of revealing those differences that are believed to assist swing voters in deciding which candidate to finally choose in the general election. Richard Nixon's 1968 **law and order issue**, the elder Bush's 1988 prison furlough issue and, less successfully, Bob Dole's 1996 character issue all serve as examples of wedge issues.

Since the late 1960s, Republican candidates used a series of wedge issues to attract those voters concerned with a perceived national moral decline. Besides generally blaming the Democrats for moral weakness, Republicans used affirmative action, high crime, the death penalty, immigration reform, gay rights, gun control, and welfare reform as wedge issues to appeal to non-urban whites. On the other hand, the Democratic Party made use of their own wedge issues: abortion rights, the environment, the protection of Social Security benefits, and increased federal support for education.

The **Campaign of 2000** marked a major departure from heavy reliance on wedge issues by Republican candidates. In an effort to attract swing voters in **battleground states**, the campaign of George W. Bush rejected the use of affirmative action and immigration reform as key campaign issues. Instead, the Bush campaign placed education reform and tax cuts at the top of their reform agenda. Democratic nominee Albert Gore emphasized Medicare reform and rising drug costs as his top legislative priority while pledging to resist the privatization of Social Security. *See also* Attack Ads; Negative Campaigning.

Suggested Readings: Thomas B. Edsall, "Bush Abandons 'Southern Strategy'; Campaign Avoids Use of Polarizing Issues Employed by GOP Since Nixon's Time," *Washington Post*, August 6, 2000, p. A19; Thomas B. Edsall, "GOP Honing Wedges for Next Campaign: Party Aims for Partisan Advantages by Making Corruption, Drugs and Crime Divisive Issues," *Washington Post*, February 26, 1989, p. A6.

Wets

A term used during the 1920s and early 1930s to identify individuals supporting the repeal of **prohibition**. In the **Campaign of 1928**, Democratic presidential candidate, Al Smith, publicly announced his support for the repeal of prohibition even though the Democratic platform had pledged to support its continued enforcement. Although large numbers of Americans disliked prohibition, "dry" attitudes in rural America worked against Smith's efforts. Although the Great Depression greatly overshadowed the prohibition issue during the **Campaign of 1932**, Franklin Roosevelt's support for the repeal of the Eighteenth Amendment placed Roosevelt firmly in the camp of the "Wets."

Suggested Readings: Paul A. Carter, "Prohibition and Democracy: The Noble Experiment Reassessed," *Wisconsin Magazine of History* 56 (1973), pp. 189–201; Paul A. Carter, "Temperance, Intemperance, and the American Character: Or, Dr. Jekyll and Mr. Hyde," *Journal of Social History* 14 (1981), pp. 481–484.

"What This Country Needs Is a Good Five-Cent Cigar"

A phrase of indeterminate origins, "what this country needs is a good five-cent cigar" is commonly attributed to Woodrow Wilson's vice president, Thomas Marshal, who offered the quip during a 1917 Senate debate over the current state of the American economy. While Marshal is often credited with coining the phrase, some argue that the quote first appeared during the campaign of 1912, actually originating in the funny papers. Others claim that it is much older, dating back to Mark Twain. Both Calvin Coolidge and Franklin Roosevelt have also been associated with the phrase. Over time the phrase has been used to parody blowhard politicians who declaim bombastically about their intimate knowledge of the needs of the people.

Whip Inflation Now (WIN)

Besides dealing with the aftermath of the Watergate scandal, the young administration of Gerald Ford, President Nixon's successor, faced the dual problems of slowing economic growth and high inflation. In October 1974, the Ford White House launched the Whip Inflation Now (WIN) program directed at lowering inflation and energizing growth. The WIN office distributed thousands of WIN buttons and even commissioned a WIN song. Rejecting the mandatory wage and price controls of the previous administration, the WIN program relied on voluntary wage and price guidelines.

To the surprise of the Ford White House, WIN quickly drew ridicule, turning into a public relations disaster on the eve of the 1974 Congressional midterm elections. Along with President Ford's pardon of former president Richard Nixon, the WIN debacle helped Democrats to gain strength in Congress.

The failure of the WIN program affected the battle for the 1976 Republican nomination and the ensuing general election campaign. Conservative Republicans preferred former California governor Ronald Reagan to Ford. The Reagan challenge forced the Ford White House to abandon the WIN campaign and instead emphasize a proposal to cut taxes across the board. Through his tax cut proposals, Ford sought to put the Democratic Congress in the position of opposing popular tax cuts. Even though Ford lost the election, the strategy was basically sound given that Ford nearly won in spite of the lingering damage inflicted on his party by the recent Nixon scandals. WIN was quickly forgotten by most Americans at the November polls. *See also* Campaign of 1976.

Suggested Reading: James P. Gannon, "Good Reason to Keep Win Button Handy," *Detroit News*, May 7, 1989, A21.

Whistle-Stop Campaign

The **Campaign of 1896** saw Republican presidential nominee, William McKinley, conduct the so-called **front porch campaign** while Democratic presidential nominee, William Jennings Bryan undertook a nationwide whistle-stop campaign by making use of railroad trains to cross the United States in pursuit of the presidency. From the Campaign of 1896 through the **Campaign of 1948** the railroad whistle-stop campaign became a fixture of presidential campaigns. Presidential candidates would board trains and give brief speeches from the back of the last car on the train. After the 1948 campaign, the airplane gradually replaced the train as the preferred method of transportation for presidential campaigns. Presidential campaign historians regard Harry Truman's 1948 use of trains to conduct hundreds of speeches as he traveled back and forth across the country as the most effective of all whistle-stop campaigns. Even today, presidential campaigns frequently make use of trains to target voters in key battleground states.

Suggested Reading: Irwin Ross, *The Loneliest Campaign: The Truman Victory of 1948* (New York: New American Library, 1968).

"Who But Hubert?"

"Who But Hubert?" was an upbeat slogan used by the 1968 presidential campaign of incumbent Vice President Hubert H. Humphrey, the nominee of the Democratic Party, in an effort to reunite the badly divided Democratic Party. Humphrey supporters used the slogan "Who But Hubert?" to argue that Humphrey had the best chance of winning against Republican Richard M. Nixon.

President Lyndon Johnson's decision to withdraw from a reelection bid in the face of the charging insurgent antiwar campaign of Minnesota senator Eugene McCarthy threw the Democratic nomination wide open. Despite the early strength of McCarthy's youthful campaign, Humphrey and New York senator Robert Kennedy soon became the leading contenders for the nomination. An assassin ended Kennedy's life, McCarthy's campaign lost momentum during the violent summer of 1968, and the vice president seemed to moderate Democrats to be the only credible defense against the waxing Nixon campaign.

Facing a deeply divided Democratic Party rocked by the murder of another Kennedy, deep division over Vietnam, and rioting in the streets and parks of Chicago outside its national convention, Humphrey spent the first half of his campaign in a desperate effort to reassemble Johnson's Great Society coalition. The Humphrey campaign used the "Who But Hubert?" slogan to remind voters of Humphrey's crucial leadership in the passage of civil rights legislation, the expansion of Social Security benefits, the establishment of the Medicare program and the commitment of increased federal funds for education and public housing. In other words, no other Democrat was better prepared to carry on the Democratic legacy of social progress.

Not all Democrats agreed with the inevitability of Humphrey. During the infamous nominating convention anti-Humphrey delegates, angry over the Vietnam War, unkindly expressed their disaffection with the chant, "Dump the Hump!" *See also* Campaign of 1968.

Suggested Readings: Lewis L. Gould, *1968: The Election that Changed America* (Chicago: Ivan R. Dee, 1993); Kenneth W. Thompson, ed., *Lessons from Defeated Presidential Candidates* (Lanham, MD: University Press of America, 1994); Theodore White, *The Making of the President, 1968* (New York, Atheneum Publishers, 1969).

"Who Is Polk?"

The Democratic Party was immersed in turmoil at the beginning of the 1844 Democratic convention. Former president, Martin Van Buren, "The Little Magician," seemed assured of the nomination, but he lost support over his public opposition to the annexation of Texas. Although Van Buren won a majority of the delegates on the first ballot, he was far short of the two-thirds required by procedural rules. Lewis Cass of Michigan passed Van Buren in subsequent balloting but he also fell far short of the two-thirds requirement. Faced with a deadlock, Democratic leaders turned to dark horse James K. Polk, an advocate of Texas annexation.

Delighted with the Democrat's nomination of the obscure Polk, Whigs adopted the belittling "Who Is Polk?" slogan. Whigs nominated venerable statesman and national figure Henry Clay, who had long been considered as having the White House in his future. It seemed to Whigs that this election would be no contest.

But to everyone's surprise, Polk's obscurity worked to his advantage. The Democratic Party successfully depicted Polk as a "Young Hickory," drawing a connection to Andrew Jackson, his fellow Tennesseean.

Polk's annexation position found more support than Clay's reputation, leading to a significant victory for the dark horse at the polls in November, and a stunning upset that denied the Great Man of his presumed destiny. *See also* Campaign of 1844; "Polk, Dallas, Texas, Oregon and the Tariff of '42"; "Polk and Texas, Clay and No Texas."

Suggested Readings: John S.D. Eisenhower, "The Election of James K. Polk, 1844," *Tennessee Historical Quarterly* 53 (1994), pp. 74–87; Sam W. Haynes and Oscar Handlin, *James K. Polk and the Expansionist Impulse* (New York: Longman, 1997).

Wide-Awake Clubs

Newspapers first used the term wide-awakes to describe members of the American Party (Know-Nothings) during the early 1850s. The **nativist** movement sought to slow the flood of immigrants into the United States and to hobble the ability of immigrants to become citizens. During the **Campaign of 1856**, the American Party nominated former president Millard Fillmore to run for president. After the 1856 campaign the Know-Nothing movement dissipated largely as the result of a split over the issue of slavery in new states. Following the breakup of the American Party, a number of Know-Nothing supporters joined the fledgling Republican Party.

During the **Campaign of 1860** the term Wide-Awakes was revived to describe political clubs rallying to boost the election of Abraham Lincoln. Wide-Awakes staged campaign rallies and parades through northern towns and cities in support of Lincoln. Wide-Awakes became best known for torchlight parades in which thousands of partisans conducted torchlight nocturnal parades carrying large placards with pictures of large eyes, opened wide and fully awake.

Historians credit Wide-Awake clubs as having played a major role in mobilizing grassroots support for Lincoln's successful election.

Suggested Readings: Hans Sperber and Travis Trittschuh, *American Political Terms: An Historical Dictionary* (Detroit: Wayne State University Press, 1962); Emerson David Fite, *The Presidential Campaign of 1860* (Port Washington, NY: Kennikat Press, 1967, 1911).

Grand procession of Wide-Awakes during the campaign of 1860. Courtesy of Library of Congress.

Willie Horton Ad

Early in the presidential **Campaign of 1988** the National Security Action Committee (NSAC), an independent political action committee, paid for the broadcast of a **spot ad**, titled "Weekend Passes" attacking a prison furlough program in operation during the administration of Massachusetts governor and Democratic presidential nominee Michael Dukakis.

Furloughed on a weekend pass, convicted murderer Willie Horton left Massachusetts, raped a Maryland woman, and stabbed her fiancé. The NSAC ran a spot ad describing the event for 28 days on a number of cable systems. The television spot ignited a firestorm of controversy as it seemed that Republicans were playing the race card, Willie Horton being an African American. Critics of the ad argued that in broadcasting Horton's picture racist imagery was being used to frighten white voters against Dukakis. Although the Bush campaign had already raised the furlough issue, they disavowed any involvement with the ad or the activities of the NSAC. Federal election law prohibits presidential campaigns from coordinating its activities with the activities of independent political groups.

The disavowal of the independent "Weekend Pass" spot ad did not prevent the Bush campaign from criticizing Dukakis for the Massachusetts prison furlough program. The Bush campaign produced their own carefully multiracial **"Revolving Door"** spot ads to sustain the attack. Willie Horton's image was not included. *See also* Attack Ad; Negative Campaigning; Race Relations Issue.

Suggested Readings: Richard L. Berke, Michael Wines, and Stephen Engelberg, "Bush, His Disavowed Backers and a Very Potent Attack Ad," *New York Times*, November 3, 1988,

p. A1; Keith Love, "Media Politics; Both Campaigns Launch Ads on Prison Furlough Issue," *Los Angeles Times*, October 22, 1988, Part 1, p. 20.

Willkie, Wendell

See Campaign of 1940.

Wilson, Woodrow

See Campaign of 1912; Campaign of 1916.

"Win One for the Gipper"

"Win One for the Gipper," a nostalgic reference to a famous line evoking memories of Ronald Reagan's movie career, was an effective slogan used by his supporters in his presidential campaigns.

Ronald Reagan played the role of star Notre Dame football player George Gipp in the 1940 film *Knute Rockne, All American*. Reagan played opposite Pat O'Brien, who played Knute Rockne, Notre Dame's legendary football coach.

The movie dramatized one of the most famous real life events in Notre Dame football history. During 1919 and 1920, George Gipp was Notre Dame's star player. Gipp contracted strep throat and pneumonia before Notre Dame's last game of the 1920 season, which proved fatal to the young athlete. While on his deathbed in the hospital, Gipp is reported to have said to Rockne "Some day, when things are tough, maybe you can ask the boys to go in there and win one for the Gipper."

Eight years later Rockne faced a losing season unless he could turn his team around. Before the start of a crucial game against powerhouse Army, Rockne recounted for his players the conversation that he had with Gipper on the night he died.

Republican presidential nominee Ronald Reagan appears at a 1984 campaign rally in New York holding a jersey that reads "The Gipper." © Ronald Reagan Library/National Archives.

I've got to go Rock, It's all right. I'm not afraid. Some time, Rock, when the team is up against it, when things are wrong and the breaks are beating the boys, tell them to go in there with all they've got and win just one for the Gipper. I don't know where I'll be then, Rock, but I'll know about it, and I'll be happy.

Inspired by the great coach and the memory of Gipp, Notre Dame went on to defeat Army 12 to 6.

In October 1980, in the midst of his campaign against President Jimmy Carter, Reagan returned to his Illinois alma mater, Eureka College. At a campus rally Reagan accepted and wore a red and white football jersey with the line "Win One for the Gipper" sewn into it. Through the remainder of the 1980 campaign, Reagan supporters made frequent use of the "Win One for the Gipper" slogan. *See also* Campaign of 1984.

Suggested Readings: Bill McAllister, "The Gipper Goes Home; Reagan Speaks at Notre Dame," *Washington Post*, March 10, 1988; p. C1; "Win One for the Gipper," Rockne Tribute page, http://home.no.net/birgerro/gippwin.htm.

"Win the War Quicker with Dewey and Bricker"

Implying that a Republican administration could more effectively expedite the conclusion of World War II, Republican nominee Thomas E. Dewey and running mate John W. Bricker endorsed the slogan, "Win the War Quicker with Dewey and Bricker" during the **Campaign of 1944.**

Dewey and Bricker ran an aggressive campaign attacking the "tired old men" of the Roosevelt administration, Roosevelt's **New Deal** programs and policies and his administration of the war. Divisions within the Democratic Party, evinced by Roosevelt's decision to drop his incumbent vice president, New Deal progressive Henry Wallace, in favor of the more moderate and less recognizable Harry Truman, also raised Republican hopes that Roosevelt's New Deal coalition might fragment giving the GOP the opportunity it needed.

With the tide of the war fully turned in favor of the Allies by November, the voters rejected the Republican argument that Roosevelt had not aggressively prosecuted the war.

Suggested Reading: Ava C. Goldberg, *Men Who Lost the Presidency: Profiles of the 29 Men Who Lost Elections to Be President of the United States* (Brentwood, TN: J.M. Press, 1992).

"With Tip and Tyler We'll Bust Van's Biler"

The Whig campaign to unseat incumbent President Martin Van Buren produced some of the more colorful and memorable slogans and phrases in American history. One of the more pugnacious, "With Tip and Tyler We'll Bust Van's Biler," joined "Tippecanoe and Tyler Too" as a slogan boosting the efforts of General William Henry Harrison and his running mate, John Tyler.

Making use of numerous campaign slogans, songs, public meetings, parades, and political ephemera, the Whig Party skillfully transformed Harrison into a man of the people. Popularly known as the **"log cabin and hard cider"** campaign, the Whig Party depicted the Democratic Party as corrupt and unconcerned about the plight of average Americans.

The importance of the **Campaign of 1840** went far beyond the Whig victory. The campaign ushered in the era of **"hoopla"** campaigning in which partisans devote the balance of their time and energy to promoting public image, in some cases without regard to the facts of a candidate's real biography, at the expense of serious debate on public issues. *See also* Campaign of 1840.

Suggested Readings: Robert Gray Gunderson, *The Log-Cabin Campaign* (Lexington: University of Kentucky Press, 1957).

Women's Suffrage Movement

At Seneca Falls, New York, during the summer of 1848, abolitionists and social activists Lucretia Mott and Elizabeth Cady Stanton, among other progressive luminaries, convened the first's women's rights convention, endorsing among other things, the full right of women to the franchise. Thus, historians view the meeting as the formal beginning of the Women's Suffrage Movement in the United States.

The ratification of the three Civil War Amendments protecting the constitutional rights of the freed slaves fueled demands for securing these protections for women as well. Women had been a leading force in the abolition movement, and since Seneca Falls, had begun to work harder on their own behalf as well. In 1869, the new National Women's Suffrage Association selected Elizabeth Cady Stanton as its president. That same year the American Women Suffrage Association selected Henry Ward Beecher as its president. In 1869, the Wyoming Territory granted women the right to vote, followed by Colorado in 1893.

A turning point in the movement occurred in 1872 when New York resident Susan B. Anthony registered to vote in violation of New York State law. Anthony maintained that the Fourteenth Amendment extended to women the right to vote. Subsequently fined $100 for violating state law, Anthony went to jail rather than pay the fine. A year later, the Supreme Court ruled that the Fourteenth Amendment did not grant women the right to vote and that each state had the authority to make its own determination on the issue. In 1878, congressional supporters of women's suffrage responded by proposing a Women's Suffrage Amendment.

In the populist climate that waxed through the remainder of the nineteenth century, the suffragette movement continued to gain strength. As competitive parity was restored between the major parties after two decades of postwar Republican dominance, pressure intensified on Democrats and Republicans alike to support women's suffrage. Both parties saw women voters as a potential pool of new voters. Equally important, the growing strength of third parties added to this pressure. In 1892, the minor Prohibition Party included a plank in its platform stating, "No citizen should be denied the right to vote on account of sex . . ." The 1908 platform of the Socialist Party called for "unrestricted and equal suffrage for men and women." And the 1912 Progressive Party platform pledged the party "to the task of securing equal suffrage to men and women alike." By the **Campaign of 1916** Republicans and Democrats supported the suffrage amendment.

In 1919, Congress sent a Women's Suffrage Amendment to the states for ratification. On August 26, 1920, a sufficient number of states ratified the Nineteenth Amendment to make it the law of the land. *See also* Campaign of 1920; Gender Gap; Soccer Mom; Voting Reform.

Suggested Readings: Sara Hunter, *Woman Suffrage and the New Democracy* (New Haven, CT: Yale University Press, 1996); "US Suffrage Movement Timeline, The Susan B. Anthony Center for Women's Leadership," http://www.rochester.edu/SBA/timeline1.html; "Votes For Women: Selections from the National American Woman Suffrage Association Collection, 1848–1921," Library of Congress, http://lcweb2.loc.gov/ammem/naw/nawshome.html.

"You Never Had It So Good"

During the **Campaign of 1952**, the Democratic Party used the "You Never Had It So Good" slogan as a reminder of the progress made under the New Deal and Fair Deal programs instituted by the Democratic leadership of Franklin Roosevelt and Harry Truman, respectively.

After almost seven years in office, President Harry Truman chose not to run again in 1952. Truman, who had stunned political analysts with his comeback victory over Thomas Dewey in 1948, had lost considerable party support owing to the war in Korea and allegations of corruption within his administration. The Democratic Party selected Illinois governor Adlai E. Stevenson who faced the onerous task of running against Republican candidate and war hero, Dwight D. Eisenhower.

Stevenson faced the difficult task of keeping together Franklin Roosevelt's New Deal coalition in the midst of growing divisions within his party. From the late 1870s through the election of 1948, the "Solid South" had constituted the foundation upon which Democratic presidential candidates had built electoral majorities, and thus attaching themselves to the defense of states' rights. But after World War II growing demands by Democrats for an end to segregation and the protection of the constitutionally grounded voting rights of African Americans spurred disaffected conservative whites toward the Dixiecrat splinter party, initially, and ultimately to the increasingly more conservative Republican Party.

In addition to the growing tensions over civil rights, the spread of communism to China and Eastern Europe gave Republicans another potent issue. The conservative wing of the Republican Party blamed Roosevelt and Truman for the loss of Eastern Europe and Mainland China. Furthermore, the stalemate in Korea troubled millions of Americans, doubting the Democrats' resolve against the communist threat.

While the Eisenhower campaign made use of the slogan **"Korea, Communism, and Corruption,"** the Stevenson campaign countered with "You Never Had It So Good," a slogan emphasizing the economic progress made under Democratic presidents. Throughout the 1952 campaign, Stevenson reminded workers that Democratic administrations had provided Americans with Social Security and unemployment insurance. The Stevenson campaign also reminded voters that Democratic policies had saved family farms by installing a system of commodities price supports. Voters were asked if they really wanted to return control of the White House to Republicans, the party that had led the country into the Great Depression. To the dismay of the Stevenson campaign, these **pocket-book** or **bread-and-butter issues** did not seem to matter in the November election.

From the start of the campaign, Stevenson had little hope of defeating Eisenhower. As one of the most respected Americans of his day, Eisenhower's reputation as a military commander was enough to deflect claims by Stevenson that Eisenhower did not have the leadership abilities requisite to the presidency. Insinuations that an Eisenhower presidency would result in rolling back New Deal and Fair Deal programs were also unpersuasive. The strategy simply did not work and Eisenhower demolished Stevenson in the general election. *See also* Campaign of 1952.

Suggested Reading: Robert F. Burk, *Dwight D. Eisenhower, Hero and Politician* (Boston: Twayne Publishers, 1986).

Appendix
Major Party Platforms:
Selected Planks since 1840

The following table itemizes notable planks in the major party platforms beginning with the campaign of 1840. All parties informally held to unofficial uniform positions prior to 1840, but the more formal platform as a creature of national conventions was not fully in use until the 1840 election. Most platform planks are not included in this table but are selected based on relevance to times, significance to parties, noteworthy timing, and lasting influence on public policy.

Issues	Economic Policies		Social/Political Principles		Civil Rights and Liberties		Foreign Affairs		Other	
Major Party	Dem.	Whigs	Dem.	Whigs	Dem.	Whigs	Dem.	Whigs	Dem.	Whigs
1840	Sternly oppose National Bank, fiscal frugality promised, minimal taxation	No platform, but pro-National Bank	Limited federal power, states rights, adamantly against abolition	No platform, but inclined toward government activism	All free citizens in all sections have equal rights, abolition decried	No platform, Whigs divided on slavery	No position	No platform or stated position	Dedication to the principles of Jefferson and the Declaration of Independence	No platform, "log cabin and hard cider" appeal to the people
1844	Same as 1840, further adding a rejection of government-sponsored internal projects, opposition to distribution to states of revenue from sale of public lands	Well-regulated currency, revenue from tariffs, well-regulated and wise economy, advocates sale of public lands and distribution of revenues to the states	Same as 1840	Reform of executive abuses	Same as 1840	No stated position, Whigs remain divided on slavery	Claim the whole territory of Oregon, advocate annexing Texas	No position	Same as 1840, adding a declaration of faith in the moral rectitude of popular government and rebuking the Federalist creed	Eulogy to public honor, prosperity promised
1848	Same as 1844, promising not to raise more revenue than is required to defray the war	Debt relief, restoration of industry and agriculture promised	Oppose efforts to deprive president of the veto, resist monopoly of power for the few	Reliance on the Constitution, emphasis on the Union, pledge to spirit of Founders	Same as 1840	Same as 1844	Justification of the war against Mexico, support for French democracy	No official position on the war but praise for candidate Taylor's military skill and valor in Mexico	Same as 1844, avowing duty to be the party of the people in the spirit of "liberty, fraternity, equality"	Promise of peace, prosperity and Union

Issues — Major Party	Economic Policies		Social/Political Principles		Civil Rights and Liberties		Foreign Affairs		Other	
	Dem.	Rep.	Dem.	Rep.	Dem.	Rep.	Dem.	Rep.	Dem.	Rep.
1852	Same as 1844 but without reference to the cost of the war against Mexico	Advocate revenue from duties on imports, not taxation, support for government-funded internal projects	Same as 1844, adding a resolve to resist agitation of the slave question in Congress	Power of government restricted to the language of the Constitution, Union promoted	Same as 1840, with the support faithful execution of fugitive slave laws	Acquiescent support for fugitive slave laws and "discountenance" of agitation against said laws	Rejoice at the renewal of friendly relations with Mexico	Affirmation of Washington's warning against entangling alliances	Pledge to uphold the principles of the Virginia and Kentucky Resolutions. States rights repeatedly emphasized	Union should be revered as the palladium of our liberties

Major Parties Re-align from 1854–1860: Republican Party ascends; Whig Party declines and terminates.

Issues — Major Party	Economic Policies		Social/Political Principles		Civil Rights and Liberties		Foreign Affairs		Other	
	Dem.	Rep.	Dem.	Rep.	Dem.	Rep.	Dem.	Rep.	Dem.	Rep.
1856	Continuation of past policies, viz., oppose National Bank, endorse free enterprise, promise of "rigid economy" in conduct of public affairs	Endorse Whig policies favoring government funding of internal improvements, with emphasis on harbors and rivers reaffirmed	Support Kansas-Nebraska Act and endorse the position of "popular sovereignty" on the issue of slavery, States rights affirmed	Oppose the repeal of the Missouri Compromise, Reject the Kansas-Nebraska Act and oppose any provision extending slavery into new territories	Continuation of pledge to defend states rights against efforts of abolitionism	Denounces the "twin relics" of slavery and polygamy, defense of the right of suffrage and elements of the Bill of Rights in the territories	Support for free seas and progressive free trade throughout the world, pledge to hold the Monroe Doctrine as sacred	No position on foreign matters	Support transcontinental railroad	Resolve to admit Kansas as a free state, support transcontinental railroad
1860	Reaffirm planks of the 1856 platform, which is based on previous platforms	Denounce plunder and extravagance in current administration, promise a return to frugality if government, re-affirm support of internal projects	Denounce those State Legislatures that have attempted to impede execution of Fugitive Slave Laws, States Rights again affirmed	Denounce abhorrent schemes for secession, denounce pro-slavery militants in Kansas, regard Constitutional defense of slavery as "heresy"	Reaffirm previous platform planks, support for the Dred Scott ruling	Denounce the principle of unqualified property in persons made law in *Scott v. Sanford*, re-opening of slave trade a "crime against humanity"	Favors just acquisition of Cuba from Spain	No position	Same as 1856	Same as 1856, denounce the Lecompton Constitution in Kansas

From 1862 through the elections of 1864 and 1868, Republicans and pro-Union War Democrats formed a coalition party known as the Union Party, or National Union Republican as they would later be called. By 1872 the Republican Party reverted to its old name, and in the early 1880s was also tagged with an alternative, unofficial name: the Grand Old Party.

Issues	Economic Policies		Social/Political Principles		Civil Rights and Liberties		Foreign Affairs		Other	
Major Party	Dem.	Rep.	Dem.	Rep.	Dem.	Rep.	Dem.	Rep.	Dem.	Rep.
1864	No statement	Recommend frugality with public funds, pledge to quickly pay war debt with just taxation	The war effort against rebel states denounced combined with a demand to cease hostilities	Slavery admitted to be the cause of the war, promise of no compromise with Rebels	Accuses current administration of subverting the rule of law and suspending the rights and liberties of American citizens	Emancipation Proclamation endorsed, Abolition of slavery promised. Full protection of laws to all soldiers, black and white	No statement	Warning against any "European power" to avoid involvement in the insurrection of southern Rebels	Sympathy extended to soldiers and sailors, promise of care and protection of all who served their country at war	Rebel forces must be made to surrender unconditionally, foreign immigration must be encouraged to foster economic growth. Railroad endorsed again
1868	Economy in government, Rapid payment of public debt from tax revenues, mild tariff on foreign imports	Extension of National Debt promise to pay all creditors at home and abroad	Immediate restoration of States rights, amnesty for all former rebels, abolition of Freedman's bureau	Praised efforts at Reconstruction, promise to protect all loyal citizens, debt repudiation denounced	Denounce all methods designed to "secure Negro supremacy," denounce abridged civil liberties	Support of all state constitutions that guarantee equal civil and political rights to all	Protection of the rights of all naturalized citizens against foreign powers	Protection of the rights of all naturalized citizens against repatriating foreign powers	Reduction of standing army and navy, reform of abuses of the executive	Deplore the murder of Abraham Lincoln; regret the ascent of Andrew Johnson to power

1872	Federal taxation consonant with unfettered industry of the people, continued reduction of public debt, denounce attempts to repudiate debt	Reduction of debt by raising duties on imports, denounce attempts to repudiate debt, counsels stronger ties between capital and labor	Reform of Civil Service, advocate local self-government, demand immediate removal of punitive measures against former rebel states	Acknowledges need for impartial suffrage, Oppose reopening of the questions settled by the 13th, 14th, and 15th Amendments	Complete equality and liberty promised to all citizens, affirm 13th, 14th, and 15th Amendments and pledge their support through legislation	Duty of government to honorably cultivate amity with all nations, seek peace while being able to defend right	Seek honorable peace with all nations, jealously guard rights of naturalized citizens against former countries attempting repatriation	Oppose further land grants to railroads, public domain reserved for actual settlers, honor the fallen war dead	Mindful of obligations to loyal women of America, honor the fallen war dead, oppose grants of public land to business, favoring settlers
1876	Denounce present tariff, advocate customs only for revenue, claim land given to railroad has been wasted, and denounce imbecility of Republican fiscal policy	Solemn pledge to discharge all public debt, revenue for debt relief to be raised from duties on imports, oppose further land grants to business	Repeated and extended demand for exhaustive reform of Civil Service which must now be the controlling issue of the upcoming election, oppose sumptuary laws	Affirm that the United States is a nation not a league, permanent pacification of southern section for the protection of the rights of all citizens pledged, promise of reform	Admonish those who seek to create division between races, warn against immigration of Asians into the Pacific coast and the immoral "coolie trade"	Approve the recent advances of women toward equal rights, renewed fidelity to principles of universal liberty and equality; pledge to investigate "Mongolian" immigration	Call to correct omission of needed protections for naturalized citizens from former countries; modify treaty with China to end immigration	Pledge to modify existing treaties to protect all naturalized citizens from foreign attempts at repatriation	Excoriate the rapacity of "carpet bag" tyrannies, deny Republican charges of sectarian division in public schools	Propose new amendment to the Constitution forbidding aid to public schools controlled by sectarian interests, treasonous spirit still present among Democrats

Issues	Economic Policies		Social/Political Principles		Civil Rights and Liberties		Foreign Affairs		Other	
Major Party	Dem.	Rep.	Dem.	Rep.	Dem.	Rep.	Dem.	Rep.	Dem.	Rep.
1880	Pledge to "honest money" in gold, silver and convertible paper, public money for public purposes, Democrats the friend of Labor	Same as 1876	Oppose centralized government; oppose all sumptuary laws, advocate home rule, general and thorough civil service reform	Constitution more than a mere contract but supreme law, warns against dangers of a "solid south"	No more Chinese immigration, complaints against abridgement of voting rights owing to fraud in previous election	Pledge to protect all voters against "terrorism, violence of fraud," promise to enforce all laws uniformly and to honor equal rights	Freedom of commerce on the high seas, amend Burlingame Treaty with China to end Chinese immigration	Promise to increase foreign trade, recognize the demand for restricting Chinese immigration	Denounce the great electoral fraud of 1876–77, eulogize Samuel Tilden and regret the denial of his rightful office, lament his retirement	Charge Democrats with eroding patriotism from greed and lust for office, accuse Democrats of engaging in voter fraud
1884	Same as 1880, tariff reform pledged, all revenues from "war tax" committed to funds for veterans	Urge a fixed international standard for gold and silver, endorse labor reforms, correct tariff inequities	Same as 1880, adding opposition to converting Federal government into tax collecting machine	Complete civil service reforms already begun, preserve public lands for the people, supremacy of nation over states	Same as 1880, added emphasis to anti-immigration, declare belief in "free ballot and a fair count"	Desire that all men be free and equal, denounce servile labor from abroad, pledge "free ballot" honestly counted	Same as 1880, renewed pledge to protect rights of all citizens abroad, regard the purchase of Alaska with contempt	Favor a policy that will avoid "entangling alliances," Particular emphasis on peace and trade in Western Hemisphere	Improvement and maintenance of Mississippi River and other waterways, Samuel Tilden again eulogized	Mourn the death of President Garfield, commend service of President Arthur, promise to suppress Mormon polygamy

Year										
1888	Pledge to eliminate "unnecessary" taxation, support lower tariffs, denounce corporate trusts, support for labor and capital	No compromise on high protective tariffs, oppose corporate trusts, endorse Homestead policy, favor the use of gold and silver	Champion the powers reserved to the "free and indestructible States," endorse administration's civil service reforms	Devotion to Constitution and indissoluble Union reaffirmed, sympathy for the promotion of temperance and morality	No statement	Equal rights for all citizens of every color, commitment to free and honest elections in all states	Desire to ratify treaty with China restricting flow of Chinese immigrants, sympathy for home rule in Ireland	Profess adherence to Monroe Doctrine, condemn Democrats for not protecting fishing rights, support Irish home rule	Support statehood for Western Territories, praise for policies of President Cleveland, denounce Republican resistance to reform	Help facilitate statehood for western territories, condemn political power of Mormon Church, denounce Grover Cleveland
1892	Same as 1888 Protective tariff denounced further, endorse free coinage of both gold and silver	Favor bimetallism with some restrictions determined by Congress, sustain protective tariffs	Warning against Federal control of elections, reaffirm civil service reform, more funds for schools	Same as 1888, indignantly denounce Southern outrages against American citizens	Oppose sumptuary law, abolish child labor, convict labor and sweatshops	Same as 1888, reaffirm devotion to the First Amendment	Same as 1888, condemn Russia for persecution of Jews and Lutherans	Same as 1888, support for Jews in Russia	Continued support of statehood for western territories	Promote construction of canal in Nicaragua, favor earliest possible admission of new states
1896	Money question paramount issue, urge that bimetallism is required in the Constitution and demand 16-1 ratio, renewed rejection of National Bank, all previous economic planks reaffirmed	Adamant pledge to the gold standard, oppose free coinage of silver, denounce the tariff policies of the Democrats and pledge to restore protective tariffs	Maintain rights of states and dual federalism and denounce centralization	Full sympathy with temperance movement and those who seek to promote morality	Rededicate the party to the principles of the First Amendment and other liberties in the Constitution	Same as 1892, sternly condemn barbarous practice of lynching, reassert support for rights and interests of women and endorse equal opportunity, equal work for equal pay, and domestic protection for women	Reaffirmation of Monroe Doctrine, sympathy for Cuba thus expressed	Reassert Monroe Doctrine, belief that U.S. should restore peace in Cuba, denounce Turkey for massacre in Armenia and for abusing American citizens, U.S. should control Hawaii	Same as 1892, declare that no man should be eligible for a third term as president	Same as 1892

Issues	Economic Policies		Social/Political Principles		Civil Rights and Liberties		Foreign Affairs		Other	
Major Party	Dem.	Rep.	Dem.	Rep.	Dem.	Rep.	Dem.	Rep.	Dem.	Rep.
1900	Denounce private monopolies, reaffirm bimetallism and the 16-1 ratio, condemn new tariff laws	Renew firm allegiance to gold standard, condemn monopolies, and renew faith in protective tariffs	Warn that imperialism abroad leads to despotism at home, Constitution must "follow the flag" for the sake of justice	Pledge to protect person and property of every American	Affirm the Declaration of Independence to be the spirit of government, Constitution its form and letter	Condemn state governments that have violated the 15th Amendment	Denounce U.S. postwar actions in Puerto Rico, Cuba, and the Philippines as lawless and exploitative	Commend administration for victory over Spain and wise actions in new colonies; endorse open door policy in China	Favor an amendment to the Constitution providing for direct vote of United States Senators	Same as 1892, endorse the actions of William McKinley, celebrate "new birth of freedom" in new territories won in war
1904	Same as 1900 but bimetallism dropped, tariff issue brought forward, trusts denounced	Same as 1900, reaffirming gold standard and adding a call to expand merchant marine	Re-dedication to fundamental principles of liberty and equality	Same as 1900 only less explicit, or couched in discussing past achievements	Right to labor and property are mentioned as inviolate, lament racial division	Praise for President Roosevelt's defense of equal protection of laws for all citizens of all races and creeds	Same as 1900, inveigh against imperialist actions abroad, promote liberal trade with Canada	Refuse to "palter long with the miseries of Cuba," describe successes in Philippines	Condemn polygamy, deprecate and condemn Republican attempt to foment racial and sectional strife	Mourn the loss of President McKinley, gratitude for the exemplary service of Theodore Roosevelt

1908	Same as 1904, adding right of Congress to exercise complete control over interstate commerce, endorse use of National Banks as security for state banks, urge amendment to authorize federal income tax	Same as 1904, adding the desire to reform labor laws through establishment of an eight hour day in the construction of public works, adopt child labor statute for District of Columbia, promise continued aid to farmers	Express concern over the arbitrary power of the Speaker of the House, condemn patronage in Executive Branch, reaffirm the doctrine of state's rights, strenuously favor direct election of all senators	Republican Party stands for individualism, Democrats accused of socialist tendencies, only Republican Party advocates equality of opportunity	"Equal rights to all, special privileges to none," favor full protection of the rights of resident aliens under treaty, but continue to oppose admission of Asiatic immigrants on racial grounds	Republican Party reaffirms its legacy of friendship for the "American Negro," demand equal justice for all without regard to race, demand enforcement of Civil War Amendments designed to protect rights of "the negro"	Same as 1904, reemphasizing condemnation of imperialism in Philippine Islands; seek closer ties to "sister" nations of Latin America	Same as 1904, adding promise to extend American commerce abroad especially in Latin America	Endorse Republican President Roosevelt's conservationism, favor speedy completion of Panama Canal, extension of land laws to newly acquired territory of Hawaii, favor immediate admission of Arizona and New Mexico	Extensive praise of Theodore Roosevelt, endorse Roosevelt's conservation policies, celebration of the centenary of the birth of Abraham Lincoln, favor immediate admission of New Mexico and Arizona
1912	Same as 1908, with renewed emphasis on low tariffs, oppose establishment of a central bank, high cost of living blamed on Republican policies	Reiterate opposition to privilege and monopoly, reaffirm protective tariff policies, pledge revision of banking system and currency, protect independence of banks, pledge scientific inquiry into high cost of living	States rights reasserted, propose presidential primaries, propose prohibiting corporate campaign contributions, urge adoption of amendment to limit presidency to one term	Reaffirm lofty principles of Abraham Lincoln, dedication to public health, regulation of the labor of women and children, support for worker's compensation laws, encourage quickened interests in public affairs	Focus on the rights of labor and pledge laws that will ensure social and economic justice	Rights of every individual to the free development of his powers compatible with rights of others, protect the rights of the humblest, reaffirm independent judiciary, condemn lynching and other forms of lawlessness	Same as 1908, adding a commendation to those members of Congress who voted to terminate 1832 treaty with Russia in responses to Russian abuses of American citizens	Approve Congressional actions to secure with Russia and other countries a new treaty to recognize expatriation of naturalized American citizens	Pledge the creation of a Department of Labor, reaffirm previous dedication to pure food and public health, denounce the profligacy and oppressive taxation of the Republican Party	Promotion of Republican Party as the party of advanced statesmanship, extended discussion of Republican achievement, renewed declaration of faith in a "government of laws, not of men," Lincoln's example praised

Issues	Economic Policies		Social/Political Principles		Civil Rights and Liberties		Foreign Affairs		Other	
Major Party	Dem.	Rep.	Dem.	Rep.	Dem.	Rep.	Dem.	Rep.	Dem.	Rep.
1916	Economic freedom for businessmen of all ranks encouraged, reaffirm belief in tariffs for revenue purposes only, continued support for labor	Protective tariff again advocated, supports firm and efficient regulation of business, condemn wasteful spending of Democrats, pledge enforcement of all labor laws	Affirm America as a nation of peace but realize necessity of a strong and prepared military, prison reform, aid for public health by combating disease, reaffirm policy of conservation	Republican Party stands for Union, need for an efficient and effective Regular Army, belief in careful husbandry of natural resources	Advocates extension of Federal franchise to women	Advocates extension of Federal franchise to women, but also recognizes the right of each state to settle the issue in its own way	Endorse President Wilson's policies abroad, endorse American neutrality, duty to help secure peace and justice in the world, respect rights of all nations, and endorse military force and territorial occupation against Mexican marauders	Belief in strict and honest neutrality towards belligerent powers, favor establishment of world court, express indignation against Mexican marauders but denounce administration's shameful methods of interference	Promote the unity of America and the patriotism of all Americans, intent to enact laws necessary for the speedy development of Alaska, grant territorial status to Alaska, Hawaii, and Puerto Rico	Appeal to all Americans, native or naturalized, to exhibit fidelity to America in thought and deed, and to foster loyalty, and the spirit of American community
1920	Call to revise tax laws enacted to address war needs to now conform to time of peace, need to reform budget system, support for labor	Pledge for aggressive readjustment of economy to peace time conditions, scolds Wilson impeding efforts slowly in this regard	Removal of illiteracy a Federal concern, urge cooperation with states for the protection of infant children, prohibition of child labor promised	Denounces Wilson's autocratic attachment to war powers, advocates overhaul of Executive Branch	Reaffirm respect for First Amendment but assert intolerance for statements of sympathy with enemies or advocating violent revolution	Excoriate Wilson for despotic abridgement of rights of citizens based on war exigencies, promise to end autocracy and restore rights of the people	Full support for League of Nations, endorse the terms of the armistice. Favor granting independence to the Philippine Islands	Oppose League of Nations, recognize need for some formal agreement among nations, pledge renewed friendship with Mexico	Full support for disabled soldiers promised, favor continued improvement of highways, land reclamation supported	Thorough denunciation of Wilson presidency on grounds that the administration was unprepared to meet the demands of both war and peace

1924	Denounce "cruel and unjust" contraction of currency, call for stable administration of federal reserve system	Pledge progressive tax reduction; promise to justly settle all foreign debt, protective tariff reaffirmed, assert independence of business	Pledge to honest government, vilify Republican corruption and "political depravity," condemn Republican efforts to usurp the powers of the states	Devotion to orderly government affirmed, recent corruption denounced, reminder that most public officials are earnest and conscientious	Democratic party chiefly concerned with human rights, devotion to personal freedoms reaffirmed, pledge enforcement of prohibition	Urge Congress immediately enact federal anti-lynching laws and call for extermination of this hideous crime	Pledge all energy to the abolition of war, call for a national referendum to vote on the League of Nations, demand a strict reduction of arms	Endorse permanent court of international justice, endorse efforts to limit armaments	Pledge to enforce Prohibition law, pledge to suppress narcotic addiction, especially addiction to heroin. Eulogy to the memory of Woodrow Wilson	Eulogy for the late Warren Harding, advocate conscription in time of war, devotion to orderly government
1928	Endorse Federal Reserve System, favor further reduction of federal taxes and tariffs	Same as 1924, adding pledge to stem wasteful spending	Demand the vigorous protection of the rights of the states, oppose expansion of bureaucracy	Reaffirm devotion to the Constitution, belief in the essential unity of American people, for home rule	Human rights must be safeguarded, declare for equality of men and women, and pledge to protect children, need to guarantee free speech in radio communications	Support further protection of the rights of Indian citizens, renewed pledge to fight lynching	Outlaw war, freedom from entangling alliances, non-interference pledged, restore role of Senate in advising the president, especially needed when armed forces are used	Seek multilateral condemnation of war; support the deployment of Marines in Nicaragua in pursuit of free elections	Condemn improper use of excessive spending on campaigns, preserve restrictive immigration, regulation of radio industry necessary to prevent monopolies	Necessary to restrict immigration but also need to respect family ties in immigrant cases, stand for administration of radio, secure to every home free access to radio

Issues	Economic Policies		Social/Political Principles		Civil Rights and Liberties		Foreign Affairs		Other	
Major Party	Dem.	Rep.	Dem.	Rep.	Dem.	Rep.	Dem.	Rep.	Dem.	Rep.
1932	Blame Depression on Republican administration, pledge drastic economic and monetary reforms while reducing government spending through streamlining bureaucracy, support balanced federal budget, pledge restoration of American agriculture, removal of government from all fields of private enterprise except where necessary to develop public works and resources	Recognize the magnitude of the economic crisis, assert that public relief is a local and state responsibility but also see need to coordinate efforts at the national level, need to revise banking laws, support home loan discounts, urge drastic reduction of public spending, renew faith in gold standard, avoid "quack remedies" to address economic distress, revise farm policy	Advocate repeal of the 18th Amendment and pending repeal of prohibition the immediate modification of the Volstead Act, condemn high campaign spending, and condemn paid lobbies of special interests	Retain the 18th Amendment but propose further amendment to allow the states to deal with the problem of enforcement as they see fit, demand reorganization of government bureaus, favor rigid penal laws to assist states in eliminating racketeers, stem kidnapping, continue relentless warfare against illicit narcotics and drug addiction	Simplify legal procedures to ensure attainment of quick and inexpensive justice, renew promise to advance equal rights for all, special privilege to none	Reaffirm faith in First Amendment, reassert the party's historic friendship with African Americans and pledge to advance equal rights for all, pledge protection of the welfare of children, fullest protection of Indian property rights	Same as 1928 dropping the pledge to restore role of the Senate, renewing support for Philippine independence	Seek to establish a "just balance" in the disputes between China and Japan, deny charges of imperialist ambitions in Latin America and pledge return of Marines from Nicaragua after supervision of imminent elections, support for world court, endorse armament restrictions	Ultimate statehood for Puerto Rico	Favor the inclusion of Puerto Rico in all legislative and administrative measures enacted by Congress, committed to development of the St. Lawrence Seaway, criticize House Democrats for selfishness and "pork barrel" politics

1936	Support Social Security Act, public relief programs, constructive occupation for America's youth, and other New Deal programs; endorse government stimulation of private sector; pledge to vigorously enforce anti-trust laws to prevent concentration of economic power	Seek to preserve the system of free enterprise and private competition, abandon New Deal policies that raise production costs, remove restrictions on industry, pledge Social Security for the elderly on "pay as you go" basis, assert the protection of family farms as paramount, return administration of relief to non-political local agencies	Continue to rid country of bandits and kidnappers, pledge protection of family and home, recognize limitations of the states in addressing national problems	Accuse Democrats of using New Deal to dishonor American traditions, violating rights and liberties of American citizens usurping the rights of the states, breeding fear and hesitation in commerce and industry, appealing to class prejudice, and creating dependency upon government	Continue to guard freedom of speech, press, radio, and all First Amendment rights	Pledge to defend First Amendment against all intimidation, oppose legislation which discriminates against women in federal and state employment, pledge to ameliorate living conditions of Indian population, favor equal opportunity for African Americans	Endorse the Good Neighbor Policy of President Roosevelt, promise to continue neutrality in international disputes	Reiterate pledge to refuse membership in the League of Nations and to avoid all entangling alliances, promote and maintain peace abroad by all honorable means, will cooperate with other nations on the limitations of arms	Dedication to a government of liberal American principles, determined to oppose equally the despotism of Communism and the menace of concealed Fascism, pledge to enlarge rural electrification	Claim that "America is in peril" owing to the policies and principles of the Democratic Party, New Deal has granted authority to officials lacking proper experience and competency

Issues	Economic Policies		Social/Political Principles		Civil Rights and Liberties		Foreign Affairs		Other	
Major Party	Dem.	Rep.	Dem.	Rep.	Dem.	Rep.	Dem.	Rep.	Dem.	Rep.
1940	Strengthen democracy by increasing economic efficiency and improving the welfare of the people through extended development of the New Deal	Favor extension of Social Security provisions wherever practical; recognize need for some governmental activity in stimulating parts of the economy but New Deal fails	Strengthen democracy by defensive preparedness against aggression	FDR's policies have fanned the flames of class hatred, Federal Judiciary subjected to Executive Domination, regimentation oppresses Americans	Pledge to fight discrimination against African Americans, pledge the enactment of Indian Claims Commission	Prompt Congress to submit to the states an amendment to the Constitution providing equal rights for women; anti-black mob violence denounced	Resolved to prevent the world war from coming to America and pledge to not send American troops abroad unless attacked, pledge material aid to victims of aggression	Firmly opposed to involving nation in foreign war, G.O.P. stands for Americanism, favor aid to victims of foreign aggression under the rules of international law	Sustain and expand continued electrification, wholehearted support for the leadership of Franklin Roosevelt	Franklin Roosevelt's record fails to secure the goals of the preamble to the Constitution, New Deal is a complete failure
1944	Primary duty to commit all resources to wage war, guarantee full employment and provide prosperity, continue and solidify New Deal reforms, reassert faith in private enterprise, encourage risk capital, promote small business	Restore peacetime industry at earliest possible time, preserve small business and private enterprise in general, reduction of taxes with the onset of peace, reject deficit spending and government spending to restore prosperity	Dedicated to social justice, full benefits and economic assistance for war veterans, commit to enacting additional humanitarian labor, social and farm legislation as time and experience may require, earliest possible release of wartime emergency controls	Pledge devotion to total victory in the war, condemn the injection into American life of appeals to racial or religious prejudice, favor postwar military preparedness, resolve to resist the continued centralization of power wrought by FDR's New Deal	Pledge support for the Four Freedoms both at home and abroad, defend all rights of racial and religious minorities, favor legislation for equal pay for equal work for men and women, extend right of suffrage to residents of District of Columbia	Reiterate equal rights amendment, pledge immediate Congressional inquiry to ascertain prejudice against blacks in the service, recommit to antilynching legislation	To speed victory in war and establish peace, pledge support of the Atlantic Charter, intention to join the other United Nations in formation of permanent international organization, favor the opening of Palestine to unrestricted Jewish immigration	Cooperate with the United Nations to defeat Axis powers, to seek lasting peace and freedom based on justice and security through organized international cooperation while refusing to join World State, free immigration of Jews to Palestine	Favor statehood for Alaska and Hawaii, Earnest and affectionate encomium to Franklin Roosevelt	Propose an amendment to the Constitution to limit the presidency to two terms, propose immediate submission of amendment to abolish the poll tax, imply the "communistic and fascistic techniques" of the New Deal, insinuation that Pearl Harbor could have been prevented

1948	Curb inflation, enact housing legislation which includes slum clearance, pledge balanced budget, favor extension of Social Security, favor national health program, advocate repeal of Taft-Hartley Act	Attack causes of inflation, reduce public debt, reduce taxes, balance the budget, and eliminate government waste	Pledge vigorous enforcement of anti-Communist laws, need to streamline Federal bureaucracy, encourage partnership between government and private sector		Recommend equal rights amendment, continued support for civil rights gains	Same as 1944	Lead the war in the realization of the Four Freedoms, pledge full support of United Nations, endorse Marshall Plan, support state of Israel, advocate control of weapons of mass destruction	Dedicate foreign policy to preservation of a free America, welcome unity in Western Europe, support United Nations, welcome and support the state of Israel, foster friendship with China	Promise to accelerate western land reclamation projects	Amendments for the limitation of presidential tenure, poll tax, and equal rights amendments all restated. Promise land reclamation in Western States
1952	Same as 1948, tax reform emphasized, full employment reiterated, more support for farmers a Fair Deal for workers	Emphasis on small business, reform in taxation and monetary policy, advocate retaining Taft-Hartley and its guarantees	Government assistance in securing a higher standard of living advocated, streamline the federal government pledged	"Man was not born to be ruled but to consent to be governed," Democrats have violated this principle in numerous ways	Commitment to civil rights and eradication of discrimination with emphasis on property rights and higher education	Condemn all bigots as unAmerican, condemn exploitation of racial issues for political gain, reiterate abhorrence of lynching	Ambitious foreign policy including collective security, support for free Germany, friendship with Japan, critique of Soviet imperialism	Blame blundering Democrats for loss of American power and expansion of Soviet sphere, supreme goal to be honorable and just peace	Pledge progressive immigration policies promised, remind America of Republican maladministration that caused Depression	Denounce Democrats as corrupt accusing them of immorality, fraud, bribery, graft influence peddling, and links to gangsters

Issues	Economic Policies		Social/Political Principles		Civil Rights and Liberties		Foreign Affairs		Other	
Major Party	Dem.	Rep.	Dem.	Rep.	Dem.	Rep.	Dem.	Rep.	Dem.	Rep.
1956	Repudiate Republican economic policies, pledge to reduce poverty in America, pledge to balance the budget, eliminate special privilege fostered by G.O.P., Magna Carta for Labor	Support balanced budget, reduced spending, free and creative economy; recommend revising and improving Taft-Hartley, pledge support for American farms	Extensive Federal activism proposed to improve American standard of living in numerous aspects, support Supreme Court rulings but deplore force in their enforcement	State that individual is of extreme importance and denounce centralization of power in government, strong military needed to preserve freedom	Country a government of laws, not men—hence full support of civil rights reiterated	The Bill of Rights affirmed as sacred foundation of liberty, reiterated; accept Supreme Court decisions in education and pledge to desegregate with "all deliberate speed"	Wage peace in the world, support U.N., release American POWs, and meet challenge of Communist power, freedom for captive nations, appeal for Middle East peace	Oppose seating of Communist China at U.N., continue to work with Soviet Union to eliminate possibility of third world war, renewed dedication to U.N. and human liberty	Republican Party full of political amateurs, president responsible for confusion, restore American leadership in atomic power, pledge national policies in water, energy and minerals	Support President's Atoms for Peace program, continue to improve military preparedness with advanced weapons systems of all kinds, extensive management of Western waters
1960	End policy of high interest and tight money, control inflation, support goal of full employment, assistance to depressed areas, promise to raise minimum wage	Private sector mainspring of economic growth, reject loose money policies of and government intervention, pledge tax reform, reduce trade barriers	Pledge to undertake numerous social programs for education, housing, health, child welfare, and a variety of others, develop policies for energy and conservation	Superior national defense a priority, recognize some need for federal assistance in securing high standard of living for all citizens, support for health, education, Social Security	Faith in human dignity, enact laws to protect and promote Constitutional rights, president's duty to protect rights, use legal and political means to secure rights	Racial discrimination denounced as immoral and unjust, full support for Supreme Court decisions to desegregate schools, enforce guarantees of the right to vote	Creation of enduring peace compatible with rights of man, accept challenge of Communist Bloc, improve American image abroad, expand world trade	Inflexible approach to tyranny, collective security against Soviet Bloc, promote the peaceful use of outer space	Democrats the party of Hope, Republicans the party of Memory, establish and enforce a code of ethics for the federal government, predict demise of Communism	Government must stimulate scientific research, pledge to develop more equity between federal and state governments in terms of responsibilities

1964	Seek further tax cuts and tax law reform, balance the budget, full employment remains a priority, extend Fair Labor Standards Act	Protect the free enterprise system, renew faith in limited government, remove restrictive trade practices abroad, tax and budget reform promised	The national purpose must serve the human purpose, extensive support for education emphasized, promise to sustain military supremacy	Democrats undermine their goals for a free society by lavish spending and centralized power, causing moral decline and crass political leadership	Same as 1960, with recognition of recent achievements such as the Civil Rights Act of 1964 led by President Johnson and the Democrats	Faith in the individual affirmed, full support of the Civil Rights Act of 1964, oppose all forms of discrimination	Peace the first concern of all governments, endorse Nuclear Test Ban Treaty, expand the Peace Corps, support Gulf of Tonkin Resolution	Democrats have weakened America's status abroad, victory for freedom pledged, demand removal of Berlin Wall, firm stand against Soviets	Continue to rapidly develop space technology and ensure that the space race is won for freedom and peace	No notable items not otherwise connected to main categories, lengthy diatribe against Democrats, curiously reticent on space program
1968	Modulate between reduced and increased taxation, price stability, support for farms	Same as 1964 need to rebuild inner cities, support family farms	Same as 1964 war on poverty emphasized, need to reduce crime	Must restore peace at home, attack causes of poverty, crime and racism	Same as 1964, promise to protect gains won by the party in 1964, 1965 and 1968 legislation	No explicit position, but express concern over the erosion of moral liberty, reaffirm goal of freedom	Honorably end war in Vietnam, support Paris Peace Talks, end bombing of Hanoi	Condemn President Johnson's campaign pledge to keep "American boys" out of Vietnam	First commitment by major party to combat air, water and industrial pollution	Reach out to American youth, pledge all-out crusade against crime
1972	Renewed pledge to full employment, promise to fight stagflation, progressive tax reform, and replace welfare with new income security program, further increase the minimum wage	Pledge tax reduction, elimination of wasteful programs, discourage relocation of American industry abroad, continue to work towards welfare reform, pledge to retain many federal assistance programs	American society ruled by self-serving elite, restructure society to ensure equitable distribution of wealth and power, pledge to protect citizens from government invasion of privacy	Seek less government but also maintain commitment to aid education, the unemployed, and to guarantee health care, total war on drug abuse, encourage volunteerism	Same as 1968, adding, belief in rights to privacy, to work for a decent income, consumer rights, right to be different, rights of children, ratification of Equal Rights Amendment a renewed priority	Work to ratify Equal Rights Amendment, defend voluntary prayer in school, renew and strengthen promises to protect rights of all racial and ethnic minorities	Promise to end war through immediate withdrawal from Southeast Asia, reduce troop levels abroad, end support for repressive regimes, improve relations with USSR, support for Israel	Endorse Nixon Doctrine, peace in Indochina, reiterate commitment to South Vietnam support efforts at new diplomacy with Russia and China, work toward peace in Middle East	Abolition of the draft, demand reforms in Congress, overhaul campaign funding, eliminate secrecy in Executive branch, lower the age of majority to 18 years, abolish the Electoral College	Move toward an all-voluntary military.

Issues	Economic Policies		Social/Political Principles		Civil Rights and Liberties		Foreign Affairs		Other	
Major Party	Dem.	Rep.	Dem.	Rep.	Dem.	Rep.	Dem.	Rep.	Dem.	Rep.
1976	Same as 1972, with emphasis on defeating inflation and achievement of economic justice throughout society	Same as 1972, oppose full employment legislation deemed "make work," reduce regulatory agencies	Rebuke the abuse of power under the Republican Party; promise a more open and responsive government, reaffirm goals of 1972 platform	Advocate less government, more responsibility to local government, encourage voluntccrism, affirm spirit of initiative and self-reliance	Same as 1972, adding support for *Roe v. Wade* and opposition to a proposed anti-abortion amendment	Alarmed at growing collection of data about private lives and assert right to privacy from such activities, no stand on abortion issue	Promise candor in foreign relations, friendship with Third World, commitment to human rights, détente both political and military	Affirm realistic foreign policy, will pursue détente without unilateral concessions, and condemn Cuban military activity abroad	Seek alternative sources of energy, continued pledge to safeguard and restore natural environment	Devotion to family values, propose a variety of congressional reforms, endorse a number of programs to aid children and the disadvantaged
1980	Commitment to economic fairness, unemployment paramount problem, oppose amendment to balance budget	Extensive tax cuts pledged, demand welfare reform, reject President Carter's call for austerity, encourage enterprise	Reaffirm duty of government to sponsor social programs to improve standard of living, fight substance abuse	Same as 1976 with emphasis on protection of families, local government, and protection of property	Same as 1976, emphasizing "reproductive freedom" and right to privacy	Civil rights for all groups reaffirmed, propose constitutional amendment to protect rights of unborn	Strengthen relations with industrial nations, improve relations with Third World, seek peace in the Middle East	Accuse Carter administration of weak and timid foreign policy, pledge restored strength and firm resolve	Will address domestic violence, commemorate the birth of Martin Luther King, Jr., protect environment	Support for death penalty, emphasize addressing epidemic of drug abuse and high crime
1984	Reduce deficit spending, reduce interest rates, develop flexible economy	Same as 1980, free enterprise a central theme, seek more presidential control over budget	Child care a top priority, invest in infrastructure, restore education, restore environment	Same as 1980, recommend extensive reforms in education and law enforcement	Equality and fairness under law must be matched by justice in the economy and workplace	Same as 1980, support the letter of the Civil Rights Act of 1964, vehement opposition to hiring quotas	Current foreign policy simplistic, oppose Strategic Defense Initiative, promote human rights	Same as 1980, assert moral difference between Western liberalism and Marxist-Leninism	Lengthy criticism of Reagan administration, denounce covert operations in Central America	Sanctity of the family affirmed, oppose any funding linked to research on or support of abortion

Year										
1988	Seek economic justice for all Americans; oppose "Reaganomics," pledge to safeguard Social Security	Same as 1984, praise current administration for reviving American economy, taxpayers "bill of rights"	Reaffirm commitment to extensive programs for the poor, sick, disabled and homeless, celebrate diversity	Support voter registration by mail, seek reform in fair management of elections	Same as 1984, pledge to address the AIDs epidemic, reassert adherence to 10th amendment	Support voluntary prayer in schools, renewed support for right to life of the unborn, reject taxing churches	Same as 1984, stern rebuke of apartheid regime in South Africa	Peace through strength, support for operations in Latin America, resolved to combat terrorism	Impose ban on "cop killer bullets"	Aggressive enforcement of illegal drug laws, tough on crime, pledge to restore supremacy in outer space
1992	Extensive welfare reform: welfare not a way of life, all who work should not be in poverty; sustainable economic growth	Promise to veto Democratic tax increases, cut capital gains taxes, other previous platform planks sustained	Pledge a New Covenant with American people, extensive conversion of military to civilian sector, universal health care	Same as 1988, woman's "right to choose" and support for legal abortion reaffirmed	Reject collectivist government, advance Judeo-Christian values, and fortify self reliance and strong families	Commitment to moral rights of the family, right to choose in education (support for private schooling), defend 2nd amendment	Emphasis on trade accords, international cooperation to solve environmental crises, promote democracy	Continue success in promoting democracy throughout the world, promote free trade, commit resources to high-tech missile defense	Public support for the arts must be free of political manipulation in the spirit of the First Amendment	Enact legislation making knowing transmission of AIDs a crime, promote traditional cultural values now under assault
1996	Continue extensive welfare reform, continue to work for quality health care, tax cuts for working and middle class pledged	Same as 1992, committed to a "flatter, fairer, simpler" tax system	Reinvent government, strengthen childcare and quality of education, and wire all classrooms to Information Superhighway	Reemphasize civil rights record and resolve to fight discrimination of all kinds, oppose divisive "English only" initiatives	Rededicate country to moral leadership and traditional values; promote more efficient and less intrusive government	Same as 1992, adding a proposed Victim's Rights Amendment to the Constitution	Same as 1992, pledge to move beyond cold war mentality emphasizing the new global community as a reality	Same as 1992, missile defense and free trade remain central concerns	Protection of children from the lure of tobacco; Democratic Party must remain the party of inclusion	Denounce the Clinton presidency as offensive and immoral, propose Constitutional Amendment to protect the flag, advocate English only policy

Issues	Economic Policies		Social/Political Principles		Civil Rights and Liberties		Foreign Affairs		Other	
Major Party	Dem.	Rep.	Dem.	Rep.	Dem.	Rep.	Dem.	Rep.	Dem.	Rep.
2000	Create additional voluntary retirement plans to augment Social Security, produce programs to close opportunity gap, extensive investment of resources into education	Save and strengthen Social Security, sweeping tax reforms, reduce federal regulation of small business, employ innovative alternatives to improve education	Work to "bridge the digital divide," increase availability of government technology and Internet, produce an authentic patient's bill of rights	Support faith-based charitable organizations, promise education reform, stand in solidarity with students and faculty who defend conservative ideals on campuses	Endorse a Victim's Rights Amendment, end racial profiling, endorse sensible gun control laws, enforce laws against hate crimes, protect the vulnerable	Promote the dignity and worth of each individual, affirm that rights inhere in individuals and not in groups; protect personal privacy from the intrusive reach of technology	Promote prosperous globalization, continue to defend human rights abroad, dedicate efforts to fight terrorism while protecting American civil liberties	Strong emphasis on free and fair global trade, stem the proliferation of weapons of mass destruction, develop defenses against terrorism, restore credible leadership abroad	Quick and extensive action to protect the Earth's environment, expand Americorp and other community based programs, commission to study lingering effects of slavery	Promote civility in public life, promote leadership that is dignified and honest, require supermajorities in Congress to raise tax levels

Selected Bibliography

Abrahamson, James L. *The Men of Secession and Civil War, 1859–1961*. Wilmington, DE: SR Books, 2000.

Ammon, Harry. *James Monroe: The Quest for National Identity*. New York: McGraw-Hill, 1971.

Anbinder, Tyler. *Nativism and Slavery: The Northern Know Nothings and the Politics of the 1850s*. New York: Oxford University Press, 1992.

Anderson, Donald F. *William Howard Taft: A Conservative's Conception of the Presidency*. Ithaca, NY: Cornell University Press, 1973.

Anderson, Keith. *The Creation of a Democratic Majority, 1928–1936*. Chicago: University of Chicago Press, 1979.

Anderson, Patrick. *Electing Jimmy Carter: The Campaign of 1976*. Baton Rouge: Louisiana State University Press, 1994.

Bagby, Wesley Marvin. *The Road to Normalcy: The Presidential Campaign and Election of 1920*. Baltimore: Johns Hopkins Press, 1962.

Bailey, Thomas. *Presidential Saints and Sinners*. New York: Free Press, 1981.

Beer, Thomas, *Hanna*. New York: A.A. Knopf, 1929.

Bisnow, Mark. *Diary of a Dark Horse: The 1980 Anderson Presidential Campaign*. Carbondale: Southern Illinois University Press, 1983.

Blue, Frederick. *The Free Soilers: Third Party Politics 1848–54*. Urbana: University of Illinois Press, 1973.

Boller, Paul F. *Presidential Campaigns*. New York: Oxford University Press, 1984.

Brady, John. *Bad Boy: The Life & Politics of Lee Atwater*. Reading, MA: Addison Wesley, 1991.

Broadwater, Jeff. *Adlai Stevenson and American Politics: The Odyssey of a Cold War Liberal*. New York: Twayne, 1994.

Broder, David S., and Richard Harwood. *The Pursuit of the Presidency of 1980*. New York: Berkley Books, 1980.

Broderick, Francis L. *Progressivism at Risk: Electing a President in 1912*. Westport, CT: Greenwood Press, 1989.

Brown, Roger Hamilton. *The Republic in Peril: 1812*. New York: Columbia University Press, 1964.

Ceaser, James W., and Andrew Busch. *The Perfect Tie: The True Story of the 2000 Presidential Election*. Lanham, MD: Rowman & Littlefield, 2001.

————. *Upside Down and Inside Out: The 1992 Elections and American Politics*. Lanham, MD: Rowman & Littlefield, 1993.

Cebula, James E. *James M. Cox: Journalist and Politician*. New York: Garland, 1985.

Clancy, Herbert John. *The Presidential Election of 1880*. Chicago: Loyola University Press, 1958.

Coffey, Thomas. *The Long Thirst: Prohibition in America, 1920–1933*. New York: Norton, 1975.

Coleman, Charles H. *The Election of 1868: The Democratic Effort to Regain Control*. New York: Columbia University Press, 1933.

Cramer, Richard. *What It Takes: The Way to the White House*. New York: Random House, 1992.

Crouse, Timothy. *The Boys on the Bus*. New York: Ballantine Books, 1974.

Cunningham, Noble E. *The Presidency of James Monroe*. Lawrence: University Press of Kansas, 1996.

Davis, Burke. *Old Hickory: A Life of Andrew Jackson*. New York: Dial Press, 1977.

Deaver, Michael. *Behind the Scenes*. New York: Morrow, 1987.

Dewey, Donald. *The Antitrust Experiment in America*. New York: Columbia University Press, 1990.

Divine, Robert E. *Foreign Policy and the U.S. Presidential Elections, 1940–1948*. New York: New Viewpoints, 1974.

Donaldson, Gary. *Truman Defeats Dewey*. Lexington: University Press of Kentucky, 1999.

Drew, Elizabeth. *Campaign Journal: The Political Events of 1983–1984*. New York: Macmillan, 1985.

————. *Portrait of an Election: The 1980 Presidential Campaign*. New York: Simon & Schuster, 1981.

————. *Whatever It Takes: The Real Struggle for Political Power in America*. New York: Viking Press, 1997.

Dulce, Benton, and Edward J. Richter. *Religion and the Presidency: A Recurring American Problem*. New York: Macmillan, 1962.

Eisenhower, John S.D. *Agent of Destiny: The Life and Times of General Winfield Scott*. New York: Free Press, 1997.

Evans, Hugh. *The Hidden Campaign: FDR's Health and the 1944 Election*. Armonk, NY: M.E. Sharpe, 2002.

Faber, Harold. *The Road to the White House: The Story of the Election of 1964*. New York: McGraw-Hill, 1965.

Farley, James Aloysisus. *Jim Farley's Story: The Roosevelt Years*. Westport, CT: Greenwood Press, 1984.

Felknor, Bruce L. *Political Mischief, Smear, Sabotage, and Reform in U.S. Elections*. New York: Praeger, 1992.

Fisher, Roger A. *Tippecanoe and Trinkets Too: The Material Culture of American Presidential Campaigns, 1828–1984*. Urbana: University of Illinois Press, 1988.

Fisher, Roger A. *Them Damned Pictures: Explorations in American Political Cartoon Art*. North Haven, CT: Archon, 1996.

Fite, David Emerson. *The Presidential Campaign of 1860*. Port Washington, NY: Kennikat Press, 1967.

Foner, Eric. *Free Soil, Free Labor, Free Men: The Ideology of the Republican Party before the Civil War*. New York: Oxford University Press, 1970.

Freehling, William. *The Road to Disunion*. New York: Oxford University Press, 1990.

Friedenberg, Robert W. *Communication Consultants in Political Campaigns: Ballot Box Warriors.* Westport, CT: Praeger, 1997.

Friedman, Milton, and Anna Jacobson. *A Monetary History of the United States, 1867–1960.* Princeton, NJ: Princeton University Press, 1963.

Gammon, Samuel Rhea. *The Presidential Campaign of 1832.* Baltimore: Johns Hopkins Press, 1922.

Germond, Jack. *Whose Broad Stripes and Bright Stars? The Trivial Pursuit of the Presidency, 1988.* New York: Warner Books, 1989.

Germond, Jack, and Jules Witcover. *Blue Smoke and Mirrors: How Reagan Won and Why Carter Lost the Election of 1980.* New York: Viking, 1981.

———. *Mad as Hell: Revolt at the Ballot Box, 1992.* New York: Warner Books, 1993.

———. *Wake Us When It's Over: Presidential Politics of 1984.* New York: Macmillan, 1985.

Gienapp, William E. *The Origins of the Republican Party 1852–1856.* New York: Oxford University Press, 1987.

Glad, Paul W. *McKinley, Bryan, and the People.* Philadelphia: Lippincott, 1964.

Goldberg, Ava C. *Men Who Lost the Presidency: Profiles of the 29 Men Who Lost Elections to Be President of the United States.* Brentwood, TN: J.M. Press, 1992.

Goldman, Peter, Tony Fuller, and Thomas DeFrank. *The Quest for the Presidency 1984.* Toronto, New York: Bantam Books, 1985.

Goldman, Peter, Tom Mathews, and the Newsweek Special Election Team. *The Quest for the Presidency, 1988.* New York: Simon & Schuster, 1989.

Gould, Louis L. *The Presidency of William McKinley.* Lawrence: Regents Press of Kansas, 1980.

Greene, John Robert. *The Crusade: The Presidential Election of 1952.* Lanham, MD: University Press of America, 1985.

Gunderson, Robert Gray. *The Log-Cabin Campaign.* Lexington: University of Kentucky Press, 1957.

Haynes, Sam W., and Oscar Handlin, eds. *James K. Polk and the Expansionist Impulse.* New York: Longman, 1997.

Hess, Steven, and Sandy Northrop. *Drawn & Quartered: The History of American Political Cartoons.* Washington, DC: Elliott & Clark, 1996.

Hirshon, Stanley. *Farewell to the Bloody Shirt.* Bloomington: Indiana University Press, 1962.

Hoadley, John F. *Origins of American Political Parties, 1789–1803.* Lexington: University Press of Kentucky, 1986.

Hunter, Sara. *Woman Suffrage and the New Democracy.* New Haven, CT: Yale University Press, 1996.

Israel, Fred. *History of American Presidential Elections, 1789–1884.* New York: Chelsea House, 1986.

Iyengar, Shanto. *Is Anyone Responsible? How Television Frames Political Issues.* Chicago: University of Chicago Press, 1991.

Jaffa, Harry. *A New Birth of Freedom: Abraham Lincoln and the Coming Civil War.* Lanham, MD: Rowman & Littlefield, 2000.

Jamieson, Kathleen Hall. *Packaging the Presidency: A History and Criticism of Presidential Campaign Advertising.* New York: Oxford University Press, 1984.

Johannsen, Robert Walter, Sam W. Haynes, and Christopher Morris. *Manifest Destiny and Empire: American Antebellum Expansion.* College Station: Texas A & M University Press, 1997.

Johnson, Dennis W. *No Place for Amateurs: How Political Consultants Are Reshaping American Democracy.* New York: Routledge, 2001.

Jones, Stanley Llewellyn. *The Presidential Election of 1896.* Madison: University of Wisconsin Press, 1964.

Just, Marion R., ed., *Crosstalk: Citizens, Candidates, and the Media in a Presidential Campaign*. Chicago: University of Chicago Press, 1996.

Kaplan, Richard L. *Politics and the American Press: The Rise of Objectivity, 1865–1920*. Cambridge: Cambridge University Press, 2002.

Karabell, Zackery. *The Last Campaign: How Harry Truman Won the 1948 Election*. New York: Knopf, 2000.

Kelly, Frank K. *The Fight for the White House: The Story of 1912*. New York: Crowell, 1961.

Knoles, George Harmon. *The Crisis of the Union, 1860–1861*. Baton Rouge: Louisiana State University Press, 1965.

Kraus, Sidney. *The Great Debates: Carter v. Ford, 1976*. Bloomington: Indiana University Press, 1979.

Leech, Margaret. *In the Days of McKinley*. New York: Harper, 1959.

LeMay, Michael, and Elliot Robert Barkan. *U.S. Immigration and Naturalization Laws and Issues*. Westport, CT: Greenwood Press, 1999.

Levy, Peter B. *Encyclopedia of the Reagan-Bush Years*. Westport, CT: Praeger, 2001.

Lichtman, Alan. *Prejudice and the Old Politics: The Presidential Election of 1928*. Chapel Hill: University of North Carolina Press, 1979.

Link, Arthur Stanley. *Wilson: The New Freedom*. Princeton, NJ: Princeton University Press, 1956.

Lovell, S.D. *The Presidential Election of 1916*. Carbondale: Southern Illinois University Press, 1980.

Matalin, Mary, and James Carville. *All's Fair: Love, War, and Running for President*. New York: Random House, Simon & Schuster, 1994.

Mayer, Jeremy D. *Running on Race: Racial Politics in Presidential Campaigns, 1960–2000*. New York: Random House, 2002.

Mayfield, John. *Rehearsal for Republicanism: Free Soil and the Politics of Antislavery*. Port Washington, NY: Kennikat Press, 1980.

McCubbins, Matthew D. *Under the Watchful Eye: Managing Presidential Campaigns in the Television Era*. Washington, DC: CQ Press, 1992.

McDougall, Malcolm D. *We Almost Made It*. New York: Crown Publishers, 1977.

Melder, Keith. *Hail to the Candidate: Presidential Campaigns from Banners to Broadcasts*. Washington, DC: Smithsonian Institution Press, 1992.

Mitchell, Jack. *How to Get Elected: An Anecdotal History of Mudslinging, Redbaiting, Vote Stealing and Dirty Tricks in American Politics*. New York: St. Martin's Press, 1992.

Moore, Jonathan, ed. *Campaign for President: The Campaign Managers Look at '84*. Dover, MA: Auburn House Publishing, 1986.

Morello, John A. *Selling the President, 1920: Albert D. Lasker, Advertising, and the Election of Warren G. Harding*. Westport, CT: Praeger, 2001.

Morris, Dick. *Behind the Oval Office: Winning the Presidency in the Nineties*. New York: Random House, 1997.

Morris, Edmund. *Theodore Rex*. New York: Random House, 2001.

Morris, Roy. *Fraud of the Century: Rutherford B. Hayes, Samuel Tilden, and the Stolen Election of 1876*. New York: Simon & Schuster, 2003.

Moscow, Warren. *Roosevelt and Willkie*. Englewood Cliffs, NJ: Prentice-Hall, 1968.

Mosher, Frederick C. *Democracy and the Public Service*. New York: Oxford University Press, 1982.

Neal, Steve. *Dark Horse: A Biography of Wendell Willkie*. Garden City, NY: Doubleday, 1984.

Noggle, Burl. *Teapot Dome: Oil and Politics in the 1920s*. Baton Rouge: Louisiana State University Press, 1962.

Oates, Stephen. *The Approaching Fury: Voices of the Storm, 1820–1861*. New York: HarperCollins, 1997.

Parmet, Herbert S., and Marie B. Hecht. *Never Again: a President Runs for a Third Term.* New York: Macmillan, 1968.

Pegram, Thomas R. *Battling Demon Rum: The Struggle for a Dry America, 1800–1933.* Chicago: Ivan R. Dee, 1998.

Perlstein, Rick. *Before the Storm: Barry Goldwater and the Unmaking of the American Consensus.* New York: Hill and Wang, 2001.

Picket, William B. *Eisenhower Decides to Run: Presidential Politics and Cold War Strategy.* Chicago: Ivan R. Dee, 2000.

Polakoff, Keith Ian. *The Politics of Inertia: The Election of 1876 and the End of Reconstruction.* Baton Rouge: Louisiana State University Press, 1973.

Posner, Richard A. *Breaking the Deadlock: The 2000 Election, the Constitution, and the Courts.* Princeton, NJ: Princeton University Press, 2001.

Rawley, James A. *Race & Politics: "Bleeding Kansas" and the Coming of the Civil War.* Philadelphia: Lippincott, 1969.

Remini, Robert V. *Andrew Jackson and the Bank War: A Study in the Growth of Presidential Power.* New York: Norton, 1967.

———. *Andrew Jackson and the Course of American Freedom, 1822–1832.* New York: Harper & Row, 1981.

———. *The Election of Andrew Jackson.* Philadelphia: Lippincott, 1963.

Ritter, Gretchen. *Goldbugs and Greenbacks: The Antimonopoly Tradition and the Politics of Finance in America.* Cambridge: Cambridge University Press, 1997.

Roberts, Robert North. *Ethics in U.S. Government: An Encyclopedia of Investigations, Scandals, Reforms, and Legislation.* Westport, CT: Greenwood Press, 2001.

Rosen, Elliot. *Hoover, Roosevelt, and the Brains Trust: From Depression to the New Deal.* New York: Columbia University Press, 1977.

Roseboom, Eugene H. *Presidential Campaigns.* New York: Oxford University Press, 1984.

Ross, Irwin. *The Loneliest Campaign: The Truman Victory of 1948.* New York: New American Library, 1968.

Ross, Shelly. *Fall from Grace: Sex, Scandal, and Corruption in American Politics from 1702 to the Present.* New York: Ballantine Books, 1988.

Russell, Francis. *The President Makers: From Mark Hanna to Joseph P. Kennedy.* Boston: Little, Brown, 1976.

Sabato, Larry. *Feeding Frenzy: How Attack Journalism Transformed American Politics.* New York: Free Press, 1991.

———. *The Rise of Political Consultants: New Ways of Winning Elections.* New York: Basic Books, 1981.

Schlesinger, Arthur M., Fred Israel, and William P. Hansen, eds. *History of American Presidential Elections, 1789–1968.* Vol. 1. New York: Chelsea House, 1971.

Schram, Martin. *The Great American Video Game: Presidential Politics in the Television Age.* New York: Morrow, 1987.

———. *Running for President, 1976: The Carter Campaign.* New York: Stein and Day, 1977.

Schultz, Jeffrey D. *Presidential Scandals.* Washington, DC: CQ Press, 2000.

Sellers, Charles Grier. *Andrew Jackson, Nullification and the State-Rights Tradition.* Chicago: Rand McNally 1963.

Sharp, James Roger. *American Politics in the Early Republic: The New Nation in Crisis.* New Haven, CT: Yale University Press, 1993.

Sievers, Rodney M. *The Last Puritan? Adlai Stevenson in American Politics.* Port Washington, NY: Associated Faculty Press, 1983.

Silber, Irwin. *Songs America Voted By; with the Words and Music That Won and Lost Elections and Influenced the Democratic Process.* Harrisburg, PA: Stackpole Books, 1971.

Silva, Ruth. *Rum, Religion, and Votes: 1928 Re-examined.* University Park: Penn State University Press, 1962.

Simon, Roger. *Show Time: The American Political Circus and the Race for the White House.* New York: Times Books, 1998.

Simpson, Brooks D. *Let Us Have Peace: Ulysses S. Grant and the Politics of War and Reconstruction 1861–1868.* Chapel Hill: University of North Carolina Press, 1991.

Slayton, Robert. *Empire Statesman: The Rise and Redemption of Al Smith.* New York: Free Press, 2001.

Smith, Elbert B. *The Presidency of James Buchanan.* Lawrence: University of Kansas Press, 1975.

Socolofsky, Edward Homer. *The Presidency of Benjamin Harrison.* Lawrence: University of Kansas Press, 1987.

Sperber, Hans, and Travis Trittschuh. *American Political Terms.* Detroit: Wayne State University Press, 1962.

Stephanson, Anders. *Manifest Destiny: American Expansionism and the Empire of Right.* New York: Hill and Wang, 1995.

Summers, Mark Wahlgren. *The Press Gang: Newspapers & Politics, 1865–1878.* Chapel Hill: University of North Carolina Press, 1994.

———. *Rum, Romanism & Rebellion: The Making of a President, 1884.* Chapel Hill: University of North Carolina Press, 2000.

Thompson, Charles. *The 1956 Presidential Campaign.* Washington, DC: Brookings Institution, 1960.

Thompson, Kenneth W., ed. *Lessons from Defeated Presidential Candidates.* Lanham, MD: University Press of America, 1994.

Thurber, James A., and Candice J. Nelson. *Campaign Warriors: The Role of Political Consultants in Elections.* Washington, DC: Brookings Institution Press, 2000.

Tugwell, Rexford. *The Brains Trust.* New York: Viking Press, 1968.

Van der Linden, Frank. *The Turning Point: Jefferson's Battle for the Presidency.* Washington, DC: R.B. Luce, 1962.

Webber, Michael J. *New Deal Fat Cats: Business, Labor, and Campaign Finance in the 1936 Presidential Election.* New York: Fordham University Press, 2000.

Weed, Clyde P. *The Nemesis of Reform: The Republican Party During the New Deal.* New York: Columbia University Press, 1994.

Weil, Gordon. *The Long Shot: George McGovern Runs for President.* New York: Norton, 1973.

West, Darrell. *Air Wars: Television Advertising in Election Campaigns, 1952–1992.* Washington, DC: Congressional Quarterly, 1993.

Whicher, George Frisbe. *William Jennings Bryan and the Campaign of 1896.* Boston: Heath, 1953.

White, Theodore. *America in Search of Itself: The Making of the President, 1956–1980.* New York: Harper & Row, 1982.

———. *The Making of the President, 1960.* New York: Atheneum Publishers, 1961.

———. *The Making of the President, 1964.* New York: Atheneum Publishers, 1965.

———. *The Making of the President, 1968.* New York: Atheneum Publishers, 1969.

———. *The Making of the President, 1972.* New York: Atheneum Publishers, 1973.

Wilensky, Norman M. *Conservatives in the Progressive Era: The Taft Republicans of 1912.* Gainesville: University of Florida Press, 1965.

Witcover, Jules. *Marathon: The Pursuit of the Presidency, 1972–1976.* New York: Viking Press, 1977.

Index

About the Authors

ROBERT NORTH ROBERTS is Professor of Political Science at James Madison University.

SCOTT JOHN HAMMOND is Associate Professor of Political Science at James Madison University.